# THE PAPERS OF ALEXANDER HAMILTON

Alexander Hamilton, 1796. Pastel by James Sharples.

# THE PAPERS OF

# *Alexander Hamilton*

VOLUME IV: JANUARY 1787–MAY 1788

HAROLD C. SYRETT, EDITOR

JACOB E. COOKE, ASSOCIATE EDITOR

 COLUMBIA UNIVERSITY PRESS

NEW YORK AND LONDON, 1962

Frontispiece: Courtesy the Metropolitan Museum of Art,
bequest of Charles Allen Munn, 1924

# PREFACE

THIS EDITION of Alexander Hamilton's papers contains letters and other documents written by Hamilton, letters to Hamilton, and some documents (commissions, certificates, etc.) that directly concern Hamilton but were written neither by him nor to him. All letters and other documents have been printed in chronological order. Hamilton's legal papers will be published under the editorial direction of Professor Julius Goebel, Jr., of the School of Law, Columbia University.

Many letters and documents have been calendared. Such calendared items include routine letters and documents by Hamilton, routine letters to Hamilton, some of the letters or documents written by Hamilton for someone else, letters or documents which have not been found but which are known to have existed, letters or documents which have been erroneously attributed to Hamilton, and letters to or by Hamilton that deal exclusively with his legal practice.

The notes in these volumes are designed to provide information concerning the nature and location of each document, to identify Hamilton's correspondents and the individuals mentioned in the text, to explain events or ideas referred to in the text, and to point out textual variations or mistakes. Occasional departures from these standards can be attributed to a variety of reasons. In many cases the desired information has been supplied in an earlier note and can be found through the use of the index. Notes were not added when in the opinion of the editors the material in the text was either self-explanatory or common knowledge. The editors, moreover, did not think it desirable or necessary to provide full annotation for Hamilton's legal correspondence. Finally, the editors on some occasions were unable to find the desired information, and on other occasions the editors were remiss.

# GUIDE TO EDITORIAL APPARATUS

## I. SYMBOLS USED TO DESCRIBE MANUSCRIPTS

| | |
|---|---|
| AD | Autograph Document |
| ADS | Autograph Document Signed |
| ADf | Autograph Draft |
| ADfS | Autograph Draft Signed |
| AL | Autograph Letter |
| ALS | Autograph Letter Signed |
| D | Document |
| DS | Document Signed |
| Df | Draft |
| DfS | Draft Signed |
| LS | Letter Signed |
| LC | Letter Book Copy |
| [S] | [S] is used with other symbols (AD[S], ADf[S], AL[S], D[S], Df[S], L[S]) to indicate that the signature on the document has been cropped or clipped. |

## II. MONETARY SYMBOLS AND ABBREVIATIONS

| | |
|---|---|
| bf | Banco florin |
| V | Ecu |
| f | Florin |
| ₶ | Livre Tournois |
| medes | Maravedis (also md and mde) |
| d. | Penny or denier |
| ps | Piece of eight |

| | |
|---|---|
| £ | Pound sterling or livre |
| Ry | Real |
| rs vn | Reals de vellon |
| rdr | Rix daller |
| s | Shilling, sou or sol (also expressed as /) |
| sti | Stiver |

## III. SHORT TITLES AND ABBREVIATIONS

| | |
|---|---|
| *Arch. des Aff. Etr., Corr. Pol., Etats-Unis* | Transcripts or photostats from the French Foreign Office deposited in the Library of Congress. |
| Burgh, *Political Disquisitions* | James Burgh, *Political Disquisitions: or, an Enquiry into Public Errors, Defects, and Abuses* (London, 1774). |
| Burnett, *Letters* | Edmund C. Burnett, ed., *Letters of Members of the Continental Congress* (Washington, 1921–1938). |
| Freeman, *Washington* | Douglas Southall Freeman, *George Washington* (New York, 1948–1954). |
| Gottshalk, *Letters of Lafayette to Washington* | Louis Gottschalk, ed., *The Letters of Lafayette to Washington, 1779–1799* (New York, 1944). |
| *GW* | John C. Fitzpatrick, ed., *The Writings of George Washington* (Washington, 1931–1944). |
| Hamilton, *The Federalist* | John C. Hamilton, ed., *The Federalist: A Commentary on the Constitution of the United States. A Collection of Essays by Alexander Hamilton, Jay, and Madison. Also, The Continentalist and Other Papers by Hamilton* (Philadelphia, 1865). |
| Hamilton, *History* | John C. Hamilton, *Life of Alexander Hamilton, a History of the Republic of the United States of America* (Boston, 1879). |

Hamilton, *Intimate Life*

Allan McLane Hamilton, *The Intimate Life of Alexander Hamilton* (New York, 1910).

Hamilton, *Life*

John C. Hamilton, *The Life of Alexander Hamilton* (New York, 1840).

HCLW

Henry Cabot Lodge, ed., *The Works of Alexander Hamilton* (New York, 1904).

Hopkins

*The Federalist On The New Constitution. By Publius. Written in 1788. To Which is Added, Pacificus, on The Proclamation of Neutrality. Written in 1793. Likewise, The Federal Constitution, With All the Amendments.* Revised and Corrected. In Two Volumes (New York: Printed and Sold by George F. Hopkins, at Washington's Head, 1802).

Hunt, *Writings of Madison*

Gaillard Hunt, ed., *The Writings of James Madison* (New York, 1902).

Hunt and Scott, *Debates*

Gaillard Hunt and James Brown Scott, eds., *The Debates in the Federal Convention of 1787 Which Framed the Constitution of the United States of America. Reported by James Madison* (New York, 1920).

JCC

*Journals of the Continental Congress, 1774–1789* (Washington, 1904–1937).

JCH Transcripts

John C. Hamilton Transcripts. These transcripts are owned by Mr. William H. Swan, Hampton Bays, New York, and have been placed on loan in the Columbia University Libraries.

JCHW

John C. Hamilton, ed., *The Works of Alexander Hamilton* (New York, 1851).

King, *The Life and Correspondence of Rufus King*

Charles R. King, *The Life and Correspondence of Rufus King* (New York, 1894).

*Laws of the State of New York,* I

*Laws of the State of New York Passed at the Sessions of the Legislature Held in the Years 1777, 1778, 1779,*

| | |
|---|---|
| | *1780, 1781, 1782, 1783 and 1784 Inclusive, being the First Seven Sessions* (Albany, 1886). |
| *Laws of the State of New York*, II | Laws of the State of New York Passed at the Sessions of the Legislature Held in the Years *1785, 1786, 1787* and *1788* Inclusive, being the Eighth, Ninth, Tenth, and Eleventh Sessions (Albany, 1886). |
| McLean | *The Federalist: A Collection of Essays, Written in Favour of the New Constitution, As Agreed upon by the Federal Convention, September 17, 1787. In Two Volumes* (New York: Printed and Sold by J. and A. McLean, 1788). |
| Madison, *Letters* | James Madison, *Letters and Other Writings of James Madison* (Philadelphia, 1867). |
| Mitchell, *Hamilton* | Broadus Mitchell, *Alexander Hamilton, Youth to Maturity, 1775–1788* (New York, 1957). |
| New York Assembly *Journal* | *Journal of the Assembly of the State of New York* (Publisher and place vary, 1782–1788). |
| New York Senate *Journal* | *Journal of the Senate of the State of New York* (Publisher and place vary, 1782–1788). |
| *Notes of John Lansing* | Joseph R. Strayer, ed., *The Delegate from New York or Proceedings of the Federal Convention of 1787 from the Notes of John Lansing, Jr.* (Princeton, 1939). |
| Palmer, *Steuben* | John M. Palmer, *General Von Steuben* (New Haven, 1937). |
| PRO: F.O., or PRO: C.O. | Transcripts or photostats from the Public Records Office of Great Britain deposited in the Library of Congress. |
| Sparks, *The Life of Gouverneur Morris* | Jared Sparks, *The Life of Gouverneur Morris* (Boston, 1832). |
| Temple, *Observations upon the United Provinces of the Netherlands* | Sir William Temple, *Observations upon the United Provinces of the Netherlands* (London, 1673). |

Yates, *Secret Proceedings and Debates*          Robert Yates, *Secret Proceedings and Debates of the Convention Assembled at Philadelphia, in the Year 1787, For the Purpose of Forming the Constitution of The United States of America* (Albany, 1821).

Walton, *Records of Vermont*          E. P. Walton, ed., *Records of the Governor and Council of the State of Vermont* (Montpelier, 1875).

## IV. INDECIPHERABLE WORDS

Words or parts of words which could not be deciphered because of the illegibility of the writing or the mutilation of the manuscript have been indicated as follows:

1. ⟨ – – – – – ⟩ indicates illegible words with the number of dashes indicating the estimated number of illegible words.
2. Words or letters in broken brackets indicate a guess as to what the words or letters in question may be. If the source of the words or letters within the broken brackets is known, it has been given in a note.

## V. CROSSED-OUT MATERIAL IN MANUSCRIPTS

Words or sentences crossed out by a writer in a manuscript have been handled in one of the three following ways:

1. They have been ignored, and the document or letter has been printed in its final version.
2. Crossed-out words and insertions for the crossed-out words have been described in the notes.
3. When the significance of a manuscript seems to warrant it, the crossed-out words have been retained, and the document has been printed as it was written.

## VI. TEXTUAL CHANGES AND INSERTIONS

The following changes or insertions have been made in the letters and documents printed in these volumes:

1. Words or letters written above the line of print (for example, 9<sup>th</sup>) have been made even with the line of print (9th).

2. Punctuation and capitalization have been changed in those instances where it seemed necessary to make clear the sense of the writer. A special effort has been made to eliminate the dash, which was such a popular eighteenth-century device.

3. When the place or date, or both, of a letter or document does not appear at the head of that letter or document, it has been inserted in the text in brackets. If either the place or date at the head of a letter or document is incomplete, the necessary additional material has been added in the text in brackets. For all but the best known localities or places, the name of the colony, state, or territory has been added in brackets at the head of a document or letter.

4. In calendared documents, place and date have been uniformly written out in full without the use of brackets. Thus "N. York, Octr. 8, '99" becomes "New York, October 8, 1799." If, however, substantive material is added to the place or date in a calendared document, such material is placed in brackets. Thus "Oxford, Jan. 6" becomes "Oxford [Massachusetts] January 6 [1788]."

5. When a writer made an unintentional slip comparable to a typographical error, one of the four following devices has been used:

   a. It has been allowed to stand as written.

   b. It has been corrected by inserting either one or more letters in brackets.

   c. It has been corrected without indicating the change.

   d. It has been explained in a note.

# 1 7 8 7

## New York Assembly. Remarks on the
## Petition of John Maunsell [1]

[New York, January 16, 1787]

Mr. Hamilton could see no reason why this petition should not be treated as well as others; [2] it was customary to commit, but it did not follow that the prayer must be agreed with, no, if the committee think it improper they will say so; for his own part he did not feel himself alarmed at such an application. The legislative power of granting he should not now give an opinion on, he observed that Mr. Mansell resides in the state and might naturally desire to obtain property, however he was certain no evil could arise from committing it, and it deserved the same attention and respect as many others less important had met with. He therefore hoped both the last motions would be rejected and that the house agree to appoint a committee of three. [3]

*The* [New York] *Daily Advertiser,* January 17, 1787.

1. In the spring of 1787 H was elected to represent the City and County of New York in the state Assembly. The 1787 session of the legislature was scheduled to meet in New York City on January 2, 1787, but because of the lack of a quorum the first legislative session was not held until January 12.

With the exceptions stated below, H's remarks while a member of the legislature, the motions he made, and the reports he submitted have been printed in this edition of H's works.

All of H's remarks or speeches that are recorded in the newspapers of the day are published except for one-sentence statements in which he agreed or disagreed with other speakers. The texts of the speeches are taken principally from *The Daily Advertiser*, which was edited by Francis Childs. According to J. C. Hamilton, Childs's account of the speeches is "very imperfect, and very often in the language the reporter would himself have used" (Hamilton, *History*, III, 183).

The following types of motions made by H have not been printed: motion that a vote be taken or that a bill be recommitted to committee; motion that a bill be read a second or third time; and motion that a certain sum or date be inserted or substituted in an act.

The reports made by H have been included; but when the Assembly *Journal* merely states that H, as chairman of a committee, made a report on a petition and does not give the text of the report, such a report is calendared.

Laws introduced by H have not been printed because the absence of papers of the New York legislature makes it impossible to determine whether H wrote such laws. Whenever there is evidence that he may have drafted an act, the reference to the printed version of it in the *Laws of the State of New York* is given.

2. On January 16, 1787, a petition was read in the Assembly "from John Ma[u]nsel[l], a major general in the service of his Britannic Majesty . . . praying that he, as a British subject might have the right of purchasing and holding land within the territory of this state" (*The Daily Advertiser*, January 17, 1787). Debate arose on whether the petition should be referred to a committee of three members, or to a committee of the whole house, or whether it should be tabled.

3. Consistent with H's suggestion, the petition was referred to a committee composed of William Malcom, James Gordon, and William Harper (New York Assembly *Journal*, 1787, 9).

## New York Assembly. Remarks on the Answer to Governor George Clinton's Message to the Legislature [1]

[New York, January 17, 1787]

Several propositions were now canvassed in a desultory manner, for getting over the motion for amendment; and it was agreed, that the committee should rise and report; they had made some progress, which was agreed to; but first Mr. Hamilton said he would reserve himself on this subject until it came again properly before the house; when he hoped to be enabled to use such argument as would strike with conviction the candid part of this house.

*The* [New York] *Daily Advertiser*, January 18, 1787.

1. On January 13, 1787, Governor George Clinton delivered his annual message to the Senate and Assembly. He discussed briefly his reasons for not complying with a request by the Continental Congress that he convene a special session of the legislature to reconsider its act of the previous spring which granted Congress the revenue from the impost but qualified the grant in a way unsatisfactory to Congress. See "Inhabitants of the City of New York to the Legislature of New York State," January–March, 1786, note 2. Clinton explained his refusal to call a special session by "an anxiety to preserve unimpaired the right of free deliberation on matters not stipulated by the Confederation" (New York Assembly *Journal*, 1787, 6).

On January 16, H reported the draft of a reply to the governor's message, and on the following day the House resolved itself into a committee of the whole to consider the draft. The absence in the reply of any reference to the governor's refusal to call a special session of the legislature produced controversy. H's remarks came at the end of the debate.

## New York Assembly. Motion for Leave to Bring in a Bill for Dividing the Manor of Livingston

[New York, January 18, 1787]

Mr. Hamilton moved for leave to bring in a bill, for dividing the District of the Manor of Livingston.

*Ordered,* That leave be given accordingly.

Mr. Hamilton according to leave brought in the said bill entitled, *An act for dividing the district of the Manor of Livingston,* which was read the first time, and ordered a second reading.[1]

New York Assembly *Journal,* 1787, 14–15.

1. On January 19, 1787, the bill was read a second time and "committed to the Members of this House from the counties of Dutchess and Albany" (New York Assembly *Journal,* 1787, 15). It was passed on March 12, 1787. The act provided for the erection of the town of Clermont, granted township privileges to its inhabitants, and annexed the Manor of Foxhall to the town of Kingston in Ulster County.

Presumably H drafted the act, but the absence of the records of the New York legislature for the period precludes a definite conclusion. The act is printed in *Laws of the State of New York,* II, 455–56.

## New York Assembly. First Speech on the Address of the Legislature to Governor George Clinton's Message [1]

[New York, January 19, 1787]

*Col. Hamilton's Speech in the House of Assembly, delivered on the 19th instant, and which appeared in our paper of the 20th, being*

The [New York] *Daily Advertiser,* January 23, 1787.

1. For the background to H's speech on Governor Clinton's address, see "Remarks on the Answer to Governor George Clinton's Message to the Legislature," January 17, 1787, note 1.

The immediate context of H's speech was a motion by Richard Varick, speaker of the House, that the following words be inserted in the legislature's answer to the governor's message: "We the Representatives of the People of the State of New-York in Assembly, beg leave . . . to express our approbation of your Excellency's conduct in not convening the Legislature at an earlier period, and at the same time" (New York Assembly *Journal,* 1787, 15).

*represented as not doing sufficient justice to his Arguments; we have obtained of him a revision of the same, and with the highest pleasure present it to the Public.*[2]

MR. HAMILTON—This now leads us to examine the important question presented to us by the proposed amendment.[3] For my own part I have seen with regret the progress of this business, and it was my earnest wish to have avoided the present discussion. I saw with regret the first application of Congress to the Governor; because it was easy to perceive that it involved a delicate dilemma: Either the Governor from considerations of inconvenience might refuse to call the Assembly; which would derogate from the respect due to Congress; or he might call them, and by being brought together at an unseasonable period before the time appointed by law for the purpose, they would meet with reluctance, and perhaps with a disposition less favourable than might be wished to the views of Congress themselves. I saw with equal regret the next step of the business. If a conference had been desired with Congress, it might have been had—circumstances might have been explained; reasons might have been assigned satisfactory to them for not calling the legislature, the affair might have been compromised. But instead of this, the Governor thought proper to answer by a flat denial, founded on a constitutional impediment, and the idea of an invasion of the right of free deliberation was brought into view. I earnestly wished the matter to have rested here. I might appeal to gentlemen in this house, and particularly to the honorable Member who is so zealous in support of the amendment,[4] that before the speech appeared I discovered a solicitude that, by passing the subject over in silence, it might not give occasion to the present discussion. It however came before us in a form very different from that which I should

2. On January 19, H made two speeches which were interrupted by remarks of Samuel Jones. The first speech (that printed above) is the revised version printed by *The Daily Advertiser* on January 23, 1787. For the version of H's first speech, as reported on January 20, 1787, see *The Daily Advertiser* for that date. For the second speech, of which no revised version appeared, see "Second Speech on the Address of the Legislature to Governor George Clinton's Message," January 19, 1787.

3. See note 1.

4. Samuel Jones of Queens County who, in a speech preceding H's, had insisted that the governor be commended for refusing to call a special session.

have thought adviseable; for there was no need of an appeal to the legislature. The next step was to appoint a committee to prepare an answer to the speech. It fell to my lot to be a member of that committee.[5] My object still was to avoid the interference of this house in a matter, about which there was a difference of opinion between the United States, and the Governor of this state on constitutional ground. The best way to effect this, was to frame the answer in the most general terms. This has been done; not a word is said *even* about the Revenue System, which occasioned the request of Congress to convene the legislature.[6] The answer is generally, that the house will take into consideration the different acts of Congress, and make such provisions as appear to them compatible with the abilities and constitution of the state. By not touching at all on the topic connected with the origin of the controversy, I thought we might safely be silent without any implication of censure on the Governor. It was neither my wish to condemn, nor to approve. I was only desirous of avoiding an interference in a constitutional question, which belonged entirely to the province of the executive authority of the state, and about which I knew there would be a difference of opinion, even in this house. I submit it to the house, whether this was not a prudent course, and whether it is not to be lamented, that the proposed amendment forces the discussion upon us. Constitutional questions are always delicate, they should never be touched but from necessity.

But, though I shall be readily acquitted of having had any agency in bringing the house into this disagreeable situation, since the question is brought forward, I shall with freedom meet the discussion. This my duty demands from me, and, whoever may be affected by it, I shall proceed under an impression that my constituents expect from me the free exercise of my judgment, and the free declaration of my sentiments on the matters deliberated upon in this house.

The question, by the honorable member on my right,[7] has been wrongly stated. He says it is this; whether a request of Congress to

5. On January 13, Samuel Jones, H, and James Gordon had been appointed a committee to prepare the draft of an address in reply to the governor's message.

6. See "Address of the New York Legislature to Governor George Clinton," January 20, 1787.

7. Samuel Jones.

convene the legislature is *conclusive* upon the governor of the state?
or whether a bare intimation of that honorable body, lays him under
a constitutional necessity of convening the legislature? But this is
not the true question; From the shape in which the business comes
before us, the enquiry truly is, whether a solemn application of the
United States to the executive of this state to convene the legislature, for the purpose of deliberating on a matter, which is considered
by that body, as of essential importance to the union; and which
has been viewed in a similar light by most of the other states individually, is such an extraordinary occasion, as left the governor
under no *constitutional impediment* to a compliance? And it may
be added, whether that application, under all the circumstances was
an attempt to invade the freedom of deliberation in this house?

Here let us ask what does the constitution say upon the subject?
Simply this, that the governor "shall have power to convene the
assembly and senate on extraordinary occasions."

But what is an extraordinary occasion? what circumstances are
to concur, what ingredients combine, to constitute one? what general rule can be imagined by which, to define the precise meaning
of these vague terms and draw the line, between an ordinary and
extraordinary occasion? Will the gentleman on my right (Mr. Jones)
furnish us with such a criterion? Profoundly skilled as he is in law
(at least in the local laws of this state) I fancy it will be difficult for
him to invent one that will suit his present purpose. Let him consult
his law books, they will not relieve his embarrassment. It is easy to
see that the clause allows the greatest latitude to opinion. What one
may think an very extraordinary occasion, another may think a very
ordinary one, according to his bias, his interest, or his intellect.

If there is any rule at all, it is this—the governor shall not call the
legislature with a view to the ordinary details of the state administration. Whatever does not fall within this description, and has
any pretensions to national importance in any view, leaves him at
liberty to exercise the discretion vested in him by the constitution.
There is at least no *constitutional bar* in the way.

The United States are entrusted with the management of the general concerns and interests of the community: They have the power
of war and peace, they have the power of treaty.

Our affairs with respect to foreign nations, are left to their direction. We must entertain very diminutive ideas of the Government of the Union, to conceive that their earnest call on a subject which they deem of great national magnitude, which affects their engagements with two respectable foreign powers, France and the United Netherlands, which relates to the preservation of their faith at home and abroad, is not such an occasion as would justify the executive upon the terms of the constitution in convening the legislature.

If this doctrine is maintained, where will it lead to? what kind of emergency must exist before the constitution will authorise the governor to call the legislature? Is the preservation of our national faith a matter of such trivial moment? Is the fulfilment of the public engagements, domestic and foreign, of no consequence? Must we wait for the fleets of the United Netherlands, or of France, to enforce the observance of them, before the executive will be at liberty to give the legislature an opportunity of deliberating on the means of their just demand?

This is straining the indefinite words of the constitution to a most unreasonable extreme. It would be a tenable position to say, that the call of the United States is alone sufficient to satisfy the idea of an extraordinary occasion. It is easy to conceive, that such a posture of European affairs might exist, as would render it necessary to convene the different legislatures to adopt measures for the public safety, and at the same time inexpedient to disclose the object 'till they were assembled. Will we say, that Congress would be bound to communicate the object of their call to the executive of every state; or that the executive of this state, in complying with their request, would be guilty of a violation of the constitution?

But the present case is not that of a mere general request; it is specifically to deliberate upon an object of acknowledged importance, in one view or another. On one hand it is alledged to be a measure essential to the honor, interest, and perhaps, the existence of the union; on the other, it is said to be on principles subversive of the constitution, and dangerous to the liberty of the subject. It is therefore a matter of delicacy and moment. And the earnest call of the union, to have it considered, cannot fall within the notion of so common, so ordinary an occasion as would *prohibit* the executive from summoning a meeting of the legislature.

The only argument urged to denominate it such, is, that it had been recently determined upon by the legislature. But there is an evident fallacy in this position. The call was addressed to a new and different body, *totally different* in the contemplation of the constitution, and *materially* different in fact, with respect to the members who compose it. A large proportion of the members of the present house were not members of the last. For aught that either Congress or the governor could *officially* know there might have been a total change in the individuals, and therefore a total difference in the sentiments. No inference of course could be fairly drawn from the conduct of the last legislature to that of the present. Indeed, however, it might be wished to prepossess the minds of the members of the former house with a contrary idea, it is plain that there is no necessary connection between what they did, at that time, and what it may be proper for them to do now. The act of the last session proves the conviction of the house then, that the grant of the impost was an eligible measure. Many of the members were led to suppose that it would answer the purpose and might have been accepted by Congress. If the experiment has shewn that they were mistaken in their expectations, and if it should appear to them that Congress could not for good reasons accept it, the same motives, which induced them to the grant already made, would determine them to consent to such alterations, as would accommodate it to the views of Congress and the other States, and make it practicable to carry the system into execution.

It may be observed, that as Congress accompanied their request with an explanation of the object, they by that mode of proceeding, submitted the whole matter to the discretion of the governor to act according to the estimate formed in his own mind of its importance.

It is not denied, that the governor had a discretion upon the occasion. It is not contended, that he was under a constitutional necessity to convene the legislature. The resolution of Congress itself does not imply or intimate this. They do not pretend to require, they only earnestly recommend. The governor might at his peril, refuse, responsible however for any ill consequences that might have attended his refusal. But the thing contended for is, that the call of the United States, under all the circumstances, was sufficient to satisfy the terms of the constitution empowering him to convene the legislature, on extraordinary occasions; and left him at full liberty to comply.

The admission of his discretion does not admit that it was properly exercised, nor does it admit that the footing upon which he placed his refusal was proper.

It does not admit, that the constitution interposed an obstacle in his way, or that the request of Congress implied any thing hostile to the right of free deliberation.

This is the aspect under which the business presents itself to our consideration, as well from the correspondence between Congress and the governor, as from the manner in which it is ushered to us in the speech.[8] A general approbation of his conduct, is an approbation of the principle, by which it is professed to have been actuated.

Are we ready to say, that the constitution would have been violated by a compliance? are we ready to say that the call upon us to *deliberate* is an attempt to infringe the *freedom of deliberation.* If we are not ready to say both, we must reject the amendment.

In particular I think it must strike us all, that there is something singularly forced in intimating, that an application of Congress to the governor of the state to convene a new legislature to consider a very important national subject, has any thing in it dangerous to the freedom of our deliberations. I flatter myself we should all have felt ourselves, as much at liberty to have pursued our sentiments, if we had met upon an extraordinary call, as we now do when met according to our own appointment.

There yet remains an important light, in which the subject merits consideration, I mean as it respects the executive authority of the state itself. By deciding that the application of Congress upon which the debate turns was not such an extraordinary occasion as left the governor at liberty to call the legislature, we may form a precedent of a very dangerous tendency; we may impose a sense on the constitution very different from the true meaning of it—and may fetter the present, or a future executive with very inconvenient restraints. A few more such precedents may tie up the hands of a governor in such a manner, as would either oblige him to act at an extreme peril or to omit acting when public exigencies required it. The mere sense of one governor would be no precedent for his successor, but

8. In his message to the legislature, Clinton said that he had refused to call a special session of the legislature because of "an anxiety to preserve unimpaired the right of free deliberation on matters not stipulated by the Confederation" (New York Assembly *Journal,* 1787, 6).

that sense approved by both houses of the legislature would become a rule of conduct. Suppose a few more precedents of the kind on different combinations of circumstances equally strong, and let us ask ourselves what would be the situation of a governor, whenever he came to deliberate on the propriety of exercising the discretion in this respect vested in him by the constitution? Would he not be apt to act with a degree of caution, or rather timidity, which in certain emergencies might be productive of very pernicious consequences? A mere intimation of the constitution to him not to call the legislature in their recess upon every *triffling affair*, which in its true import would be turned into an injunction not to do it but upon occasions of the *last necessity*.

We see therefore that the question upon which we are pressed to decide is not less delicate, as it respects the constitution of the state itself, than as it respects the union. And that in every possible view it is most prudent to avoid the determination. Let the conduct of the governor stand on its own merits: If he was right our approbation will not make him more right; if he was wrong, it would be improper to give sanction to his error.

Several things have been said in the debate which have no connection with it, but to prevent their making improper impressions, it may not be amiss to take some notice of them. The danger of a power in Congress to compel the convening of the legislature at their pleasure has been strongly insisted upon: It has been urged, that if they possessed it, they might make it an engine to fatigue the legislature into a compliance with their measures. Instances of an abuse of the like power in the crown, under the former government have been cited.[9]

It is a sufficient answer to all this, to say that no such power is contended for. I do not assert that their request *obliged* the governor to convene the legislature, I only maintain, that their request on an important national subject was such an occasion, as left him at liberty to do it without any color for imputing to him a breach

9. Samuel Jones had argued on January 17 that the governor should have refused to comply with the request of Congress to convene the legislature because "Congress might, by reiterated requisitions, perhaps once a month, teaze and worry the Legislature into a compliance with their measures; nor was this exaggerating, for such had been the practice under the former government" (*The Daily Advertiser*, January 18, 1787). In the debate on January 19, he repeated at greater length the same argument.

of the constitution. And that from motives of respect to the union and to avoid any further degradation of its authority, already at too low an ebb, he ought to have complied.

Admitting in the fullest extent that it would be dangerous to allow to Congress the power of requiring the legislature to be convened at pleasure, yet no injury nor inconvenience can result from supposing the call of the United States on a matter by them deemed of importance to be an occasion sufficiently extraordinary to *authorise*, not to *oblige* the governor to comply with it.

I cannot forbear remarking, that it is a common artifice to endeavour to insinuate a resemblance between the king under the former government, and Congress; though no two things can be more unlike each other. Nothing can be more dissimilar [10] than a monarch, permanent, hereditary,[11] the source of honor and emolument; and a republican body composed of a number of individuals appointed annully, liable to be recalled within the year, and subject to a continual rotation, which with few exceptions, is the fountain neither of honor nor emolument. If we will exercise our judgments we shall plainly see that no such resemblance exists, and that all inferences deducted from the comparison must be false.

Upon every occasion, however foreign such observations may be, we hear a loud cry raised about the danger of intrusting power to Congress, we are told it is dangerous to trust power any where; that *power* is liable to *abuse* with a variety of trite maxims of the same kind. General propositions of this nature are easily framed, the truth of which cannot be denied, but they rarely convey any precise idea. To these we might oppose other propositions equally true and equally indefinite. It might be said that too little power is as dangerous as too much, that it leads to anarchy, and from anarchy to despotism. But the question still recurs, what is this *too much or too little?* where is the measure or standard to ascertain the happy mean?

Powers must be granted, or civil Society cannot exist; the possibility of abuse is no argument against the *thing;* this possibility is incident to every species of power however placed or modified. The United States for instance have the power of war and peace: it

10. In original, "dissimular."
11. In original, "heroditary."

cannot be disputed that conjectures might occur in which that power might be turned against the rights of the citizen. But where can we better place it? In short where else can we place it all?

In our State constitutions, we might discover powers, liable to be abused to very dangerous purposes. I shall instance only the council [of] appointment: In that council the governor claims and exercises, the power of nominating to all offices.

This power of nomination, in its operation amounts to a power of appointment, for it can always be so managed as to bring in persons agreeable to him, and exclude all others. Suppose a governor disposed to make this an instrument of personal influence and aggrandizement, suppose him inclined to exclude from office all independent men, and to fill the different departments of the state with persons devoted to himself, what is to hinder him from doing it? who can say how far the influence arising from such a prerogative might be carried?

Perhaps this power, if closely inspected, is a more proper subject of republican jealousy, than any power possessed, or asked by the United States—fluctuating and variable as that body is.

But as my intention is not to instil any unnecessary jealousies, I shall prosecute these observations no further. They are only urged to shew the imperfection of human institutions, and to confirm the principle, that the possibility of a power being abused is no argument against its existence.

Upon the whole, let us venture with caution upon constitutional ground. Let us not court, nor invite discussions of this kind—let us not endeavour, still more to weaken and degrade the federal government, by heaping fresh marks of contempt on its authority. Perhaps the time is not far remote, when we may be inclined to disapprove, what we now seem eager to commend; and may wish we had cherished the union with as much zeal, as we now discover apprehension, of its encroachments.

I hope, Mr. Chairman, the house will not agree to the amendment. In saying this I am influenced by no other motive than a sense of duty. I trust my conduct will be considered in this light. I cannot give my consent to put any thing upon our minutes which it appears to me we may one day have occasion to wish obliterated from them.

# New York Assembly. Second Speech on the Address of the Legislature to Governor George Clinton's Message [1]

[New York, January 19, 1787]

Mr. Hamilton, I am sorry sir that I have to address you a second time, when I have already taken up so much of your attention, but as it is universally allowed to be a question of great importance, I trust I shall be excused for entering into a further discussion. I said in setting out in my former arguments, that the question was improperly stated, that it was put upon a wrong ground, that it was not "that the governor was *obliged* to call the legislature upon the request of Congress"—no, but the question was "whether the words of the constitution *put it out of his power to call them,* now how are we to decide this, the amendment approves his conduct and says he was right, but it does not say why he was right, in not convening you at an earlier period. Therefore this act of ours must be judged by what it is formed upon. This will lead us to inquire in what shape it comes before the house. First, the United States, *upon a new legislature being chosen* and not approving the mode of granting the impost by the last, *requests* of your *governor* as the welfare of the union depended in a great measure upon a more liberal compliance with their requisitions, that he would *convene* them to consider upon that important subject, somewhat earlier than the time affixed by law. He answers them and tells us that *he cannot do it because the constitution is a bar in his way, and the right of free deliberation will be violated by a compliance.* Now we *approve* his *conduct,* and do we not *approve* the *principles* which dictated it.

Surely the question is literally this, whether he was barred from calling the Legislature by the constitution, and whether such a call was an infringement of the right of free deliberation: this is the

---

*The* [New York] *Daily Advertiser,* January 20, 1787.

1. Following H's first speech on January 19, Samuel Jones again defended Governor Clinton's refusal to call a special session of the legislature. He argued that no constitutional question was involved in the legislature's approval of the governor's action and discussed the dangers of countenancing congressional interference in the deliberations of the legislature.

thing we are to decide upon. For is it not a reasonable rule, that the meaning of your act must be determined by the meaning of the act in all its latitude, on which your's is founded. Suppose a person totally indifferent was to read the whole transaction; first, our partial compliance with the requisition of 1783, next the observations of Congress, their request to the Governor, his refusal, and the reasons for the same, and then our vote of approbation. I ask, would he not immediately conclude, that, it was an improper request from Congress, and contrary to the constitution, as well as the right of free deliberation, and that the Governor was precluded by this, from the power of convening us.

Is not this fair reasoning? If this is not the fair and only inference, then I don't know what it is. What shall I say now to the gentlemen who oppose us? Do Sir hear how the one on my right, (Mr. Jones) reasons, he says he was unwilling to have a question of this nature discussed, and says that he would not decide it, these are surely his words, and it must have appeared so to the House; In the next place he says this is not an extraordinary occasion, so the governor was warranted in refusing to comply; and we must determine so; thus we are to decide, and not to decide.

I say therefore Sir, if we give our approbation on this conduct, we do clearly decide that the governor was barr'd, that he lay under a constitutional impediment, which prevented him from complying with a request of Congress. Now this *cannot be made out* to be really the case, notwithstanding the *governor's assertion; nor do the gentlemen pretend to say a word to support such an opinion.*

The gentleman has made use of arguments, which tend to mislead (I do not say intentionally to mislead) but such is their scope. He says if we do not adopt the amendment it will be a reflection on the governor's conduct. Certainly not, here is an answer proposed, which says nothing about it, so that it cannot be said we rejected therefrom our approbation, nor is it a censure that we refuse to say any thing about it, the rejection even now of this amendment, can be construed into nothing more than we are only willing to leave the measure upon its own footing, and wish to be silent on so great a constitutional question, that may force one part or the other of government into embarrassments. It is only saying that this measure is of doubtful import, as is really the case; for I say, the request of

Congress was of such a nature as to make it an extraordinary occasion. He says otherwise; but what necessity is there for us to determine? then do not let us decide the question, but if we must, then I ask what is an extraordinary occasion, if this [is] not one.

But the governor did not think it one; be it so; let him exercise his judgment, yet his thinking it only an ordinary occasion, does not make it so.

It has been said by the gentleman next me (Mr. Jones) that Congress *must always submit the subject* upon which their request to have the legislature called together is grounded, unto the governor, and then he exults over my supposing the contrary.

But Sir, surely it is not necessary to enable him to call them that he should be acquainted with their intentions. It is easy to see, that they may be so circumstanced, and in such situations, as to render it extremely improper to give such intelligence; yet at the same time, be an indispensible necessity for calling the legislature together, and when they were met, it would be time enough to have them assigned when it was improper to do so in the first instance. I therefore contend that it was not *absolutely necessary* to insert their reasons in the request, nor does it follow if a request of Congress should be deemed an extraordinary occasion, that the *governor* is obliged on such an occasion to convene the legislature; no, he may refuse, and yet be wrong in so doing. The constitution says he shall not call but upon extraordinary occasions; but it does not say he shall call on every extraordinary occasion, there might be a thousand circumstances to make it improper, though it should be really, and even in the governor's opinion, an extraordinary occasion.

But let us consider this request in another light. Sir, are we not to respect federal decisions; are we on the contrary to take every opportunity of holding up their resolutions and requests in a contemptible and insignificant light, and tell the world, their calls, their requests are nothing to us, that we are bound by none of their measures; do not let us add to their embarrassment, for it is but a slender tie that at present holds us, you see alas what contempt we are falling into since the peace; you see to what our commerce is exposed to on every side. You see us the laughing stock, the sport of foreign nations, and what may this lead to? I dread Sir, to think. Little will it avail then to say, we could not attend to your wise and earnest requests without inconvenience; little will it avail to say it would have hurt individual interest to have left our farms. These things are trifling when compared to bringing the Councils and powers of the Union into universal contempt, by saying their call was unimportant, and that it did not come under the indefinite meaning of *extraordinary*. See, gentlemen, before you feel what may be your situation hereafter. There is more involved in this measure than what presents itself to your view.

Again, gentlemen, you hear it rung in your ears that from the resemblance between the king, and the Congress of these states, it would be dangerous to come into measures proposed by them and adopted by every state but this. But I say there is no danger; it is impossible; the constitution, the confederation prevents it. Let us hear what kind of reasoning is used, why they have the power of declaring war and peace, and request the power of raising and applying money. This if in a king permanent, hereditary and independent of the people, would be danger, but in an annual body, chosen from ourselves, and liable on the very turn of popular breath to be changed; who are checked by twelve other states, who would not stand by and see the ruin of their associates, as it would involve their own. How can a similitude exist between bodies so different; as different as east from west, or north from south.

I am sorry that these things should be compared, for there is no necessity for sounding this alarm; it is enough the danger of republican governments, that their very nature tends to their destruction, because of their liability to change.

The utmost that the gentleman['s] argument can go to, is to deter us from declaring it to be an extraordinary occasion; but it does not go to prove, that the governor will be obliged to comply with every extraordinary call of that honourable body. I only answer upon his representation of an improper power exercised by Congress, or any other body, that I believe I shall be found equally forward with this gentleman, to effect their correction. But what can Congress do against this country, surely if they tyrannize we have the power to annihilate them. But let us not alarm ourselves with phantoms and bugbears. I shall now recur, to this mere state of the question, which is as I said before, whether a constitutional bar, or whether our right of free deliberation would have been invaded by an acquiescence on the part of the governor, with the requisition of the United States. Now it only remains for the house to determine, will they put such a construction upon it. If we say nothing on the subject, and reject the amendment, we only say that we are willing to let the original answer pass without any alteration and indeed in all cases where we have a doubt, silence is the best mode for us to pursue.[2]

2. Following H's speech the proposed amendment to the legislature's address to the governor was accepted with only nine members dissenting.

## New York Assembly. Address of the New York Legislature to Governor George Clinton [1]

[New York, January 20, 1787]

We the Representatives of the People of the State of New-York in Assembly, beg leave to assure your Excellency, that the several important matters mentioned in your Excellency's Speech, and communicated in the papers that accompany it, shall, in the course of the Session engage our most serious attention.[2]

With dispositions truly fœderal, we shall take into consideration the different acts of the United States, and, with an earnest solicitude for the national honor, credit, and welfare, shall chearfully make such provisions as shall appear to us competent to those great objects, and compatible with the abilities and Constitution of the State.[3]

We learn with peculiar pleasure, that the measures adopted by the Legislature, at the last Session, for settling, otherwise than by a Fœderal Court, the territorial dispute between this State and the Commonwealth of Massachusetts, have been carried into full effect; and that while through the Divine Goodness, we enjoy the blessings of internal peace and order, the sources of external discord and animosity resulting from a controverted boundary, are happily extinguished, the public tranquility in a point of such magnitude secured, and the heavy expence of a judicial investigation avoided. The conduct of our Commissioners in this delicate and important trust, meets with our entire approbation; and we shall freely concur in making adequate provision for the services rendered and expences incurred, either in preparation for trial, or towards the adjustment of the controversy.

We are also happy to observe, that the Commissioners for running the line of jurisdiction between this State and the Commonwealth of Pennsylvania, have made as great a progress as the season would permit. The good understanding which subsisted between them, must have contributed not less to this end, than to the œconomy which appears in their expences, and will no doubt facilitate the final accomplishment of this business.

The arrangement of the Militia under the late law, announced by your Excellency as nearly compleat, is a proof of the attention which has been paid to this interesting object. We doubt not the future conduct of that respectable class of Citizens, will justify the expectations formed from the laudable zeal by which it is thus far distinguished.[4]

We lament, with your Excellency, the fatal ravages to which Wheat, our staple commodity, has of late been exposed, from an insect which has already over-run so large a part of the State; and if any thing in the power of the Legislature can be devised to avert so affecting a calamity, we shall feel ourselves impelled by every motive, to adopt it.

It gives us pleasure to learn that very considerable reductions have lately been made of the debts due from the public to the Citizens of this State; an object which we shall be ready still further to promote by every prudent and equitable measure; convinced of the truth of the sentiment expressed by your Excellency, that a faithful performance of our engagements is essential to the firm establishment of the public credit and prosperity.[5]

*Assembly-Chamber, January 20th, 1787.*

New York Assembly *Journal,* 1787, 15-17.
 1. On January 13, a committee consisting of James Gordon, H, and Samuel Jones, was appointed to prepare an address in reply to the governor's message to the legislature of the same date. On January 16, "Mr. Hamilton, from the Committee appointed to prepare and report a draft of a respectful Address to his Excellency the Governor, in answer to his Speech at the opening of the Session, reported, that the Committee had prepared a draft accordingly; Mr. Hamilton read the draft in his place, and delivered the same in at the table, where it was again read" (New York Assembly *Journal,* 1787, 9).
 The text of the address, except for the first paragraph, is taken from the engrossed address which was read in the Assembly and printed in its *Journal* on January 20. The first paragraph is from the original draft which was probably prepared by H. It is taken from the version of it read in the Assembly on January 19.

The formal title of the address was: "The RESPECTFUL ADDRESS of the *Assembly*, in Answer to his Excellency's Speech, at the opening of the Session."

2. For amendments subsequently made to paragraph one, see "Remarks on the Answer to Governor George Clinton's Message to the Legislature," January 17, 1787, and "Speech [First and Second] on the Address of the Legislature to Governor George Clinton's Message," January 19, 1787.

3. Clinton requested the legislature to comply with the congressional requisition for the services of 1786, with an act augmenting the number of United States troops and a requisition for their support, and with a requisition for arrears due the United States (New York Assembly *Journal*, 1787, 6).

4. "AN ACT to regulate the militia" was passed by the legislature on April 4, 1786. See *Laws of the State of New York*, II, 220–29. Clinton informed the legislature that the arrangements required by the act were almost completed (New York Assembly *Journal*, 1787, 7).

5. Clinton, after informing the legislature that "considerable reductions have lately been made of the debts due from the public, to the citizens of this State," requested appropriations to reduce the debt still further (New York Assembly *Journal*, 1787, 7).

## *New York Assembly. Remarks on an Act for Regulating Elections* [1]

[New York, January 23, 1787]

The house then resolved itself into a committee of the whole, on the election bill, on the paragraph enabling the inspectors to take aside any ignorant person, and to examine him privately touching his ballot. A small debate arose.

Mr. Hamilton, thought it was very apparent, if the clause prevailed in the house, that it would tend to increase rather than prevent an improper influence. For though the inspector takes an oath that his conduct shall be impartial, yet he can easily interpret this oath, so as to correspond with his own wishes. If he is even an honest man, he will think the public good concerned in promoting a candidate to whom he is attached; and under this impression may see no harm in recommending him to the person offering his vote. His suggestion will be generally attended with success, and the consequence will be, that the inspectors will have the disposition of the votes of almost all unlettered persons in favour of the party to which he inclines. Here then is a more concentered influence over the illiterate and uninformed part of the community, than they would have been subject to if left to themselves. Here they will be liable to an influence more dangerous than the one we wish to avoid.

The question then is, whether it is better to leave them to an accidental influence or imposition, or to subject them to a more regular and extensive influence.

The appointment of inspectors will then become more than it is, an object of party; and it will always be in their power to turn the scale of a contested election. On the contrary if the voters are left to themselves the activity of different parties will make the chance equal; and influence and imposition on one side will be ballanced by an equal degree of it on the other. I therefore move that we strike out the clause.[2]

Mr. Hamilton observed, that this was one of those subjects which was more plausible in theory than in practice—that the gentleman's reply did not answer nor could it, the objections he had made—the question is whether it is better to let the illiterate take the chance of imposition from parties equally active; the impositions of the one side being balanced by the exertions of the other, and the result must be the same. The question is whether it is more dangerous to leave it to chance influence, or leave it to party views concentered in one person on whom the certain fate of the election depends. I do not mean to impeach the actions of the inspectors, for at present they can but little bias, but if the clause takes place tho' he swears to do his duty impartially, yet I believe his friendly attention to A. being more than to B. will lead us to conceive that he will little scruple to ask the vote for A. whom he recommends to be as good or a better person than the other; now if this happens sure there are very few ignorant persons, but will be greatly influenced by such inspectors, and on them turns the fate of the election. There is also another reason which should induce us not to adopt the proposed mode, it will occasion a great delay, as some inspectors will have to take down and examine the tickets proposed by the illiterate, while the others will find it difficult to attend the poll. There is therefore the objection of delay as well as influence to avoid which it will be necessary to strike out the clause altogether. I repeat once more it is better to leave them to parties who are equal in their exertions, equally send about tickets and whose chance of influence is wholly equal.[3]

The [New York] Daily Advertiser, January 24, 1787.

1. On January 13, H, Samuel Jones, John Ray, John Livingston, and Caleb Smith were appointed a "Committee to inspect what laws are expired, or

near expiring, and that they, from time to time, report to the House which of them they judge necessary to be revived or continued, and likewise what new laws they shall conceive necessary to be made for the benefit of the State" (New York Assembly *Journal*, 1787, 5). On the same date, Samuel Jones introduced "An Act for Regulating Elections." On January 15, the bill was read a second time and referred to a committee of the whole house. When, on January 23, Peter Vrooman of the committee reported that some progress had been made on the bill and requested "leave to sit again," debate arose on the provision giving inspectors at elections the right to interrogate persons unable to read. This provision appeared in the first law to regulate elections passed under the New York State Constitution. Dated March 27, 1778, the act provided that if an inspector

"shall suspect such person to be unable to read writing and it shall so be found on tryal the elector shall be taken a part and privately asked by one of the inspectors what persons or person be voted for as governor and as lieutenant-governor respectively or either of them, as the case may be, and he having declared the same the said inspector shall destroy the ballot or ticket delivered by such person without inspecting the same and shall immediately make a ballot or ticket to be according to such declaration which he shall never divulge. . . ." (*Laws of the State of New York*, I, 31).

2. At this point H's remarks were replied to by Samuel Jones who argued that the clause to which H objected had been in effect for many years and that "he never heard of any inconvenience or dangerous influence" (*The Daily Advertiser*, January 24, 1787). William Harper, who also wished to retain the clause, suggested that H's objections might be met by preventing the inspectors from recommending the name of any candidate.

3. The Assembly rejected a motion to strike out the clause allowing election inspectors to examine illiterates concerning their ballot. The clause again was debated on January 30. See H's remarks on that date.

# New York Assembly. Motion that a Committee be Appointed to Consider a Letter from the Secretary for Foreign Affairs [1]

[New York, January 23, 1787]

*Resolved,* That it is the opinion of this Committee, that a Committee be appointed to consider and report on the letter from the Secretary of Foreign Affairs to his Excellency the Governor, and the papers accompanying it,[2] together with the act of the Legislature entitled "An act relative to debts due to persons within the enemies lines;" passed the twelfth of July, one thousand seven hundred and eighty-two, and another act of the Legislature, entitled "An act for granting a more effectual relief in cases of certain trespasses;" passed the seventeenth of March, one thousand seven hundred and eighty-three.[3]

New York Assembly *Journal*, 1787, 20.

1. This motion is also printed in *The* [New York] *Daily Advertiser*, January 24, 1787, and is preceded by the following paragraph: "It was moved by Mr. Hamilton, that the house adopt the following resolution."

2. On May 3, 1786, John Jay, Secretary for Foreign Affairs, had written to Governor George Clinton requesting information on the compliance of New York with a congressional resolution of January 14, 1784, which called on the several states to repeal all laws inconsistent with the treaty of peace between the United States and Great Britain. In reply Clinton sent Jay extracts from the journals of the Assembly and Senate of March 30 and 31, 1784. The resolution enclosed by Clinton reads in part as follows:

"*Resolved*, That as on the one Hand, the Rules of Justice do not require, so on the other, the public Tranquillity will not permit, that such Adherents, who have been attainted, should be restored to the Rights of Citizenship.

"And that there can be no Reason, for restoring Property, which has been confiscated or forfeited, the more especially, as no Compensation is offered, on the Part of the said King, and his Adherents, for the Damages sustained by this State and its Citizens, from the Desolation aforesaid.

"*Resolved therefore*, That while this Legislature entertain the highest Sense of national Honor, of the Sanction of Treaties, and of the Deference which is due to the Advice of the United States in Congress Assembled, they find it inconsistent with their Duty to comply with the Recommendation of the said United States, on the subject Matter of the fifth Article of the said Definitive Treaty of Peace." (New York Senate *Journal*, 1784, 75.)

The letters from both Jay and Clinton may be found in the Papers of the Continental Congress, National Archives.

3. The motion was referred to a committee of which H was chairman. This committee reported on March 10 and March 16.

## New York Assembly. Remarks on an Act for Regulating Elections [1]

[New York, January 24, 1787]

A debate arose upon the clause, authorising the inspector or any other person to require the person offering himself to poll, to take an oath of abjuration of ecclesiastical as well as civil obedience.[2]

Mr. Hamilton declared the constitution to be their creed and standard, and ought never to be departed from; but in the present instance it was proper first to examine and inquire how far it applied to the subject under the consideration that there were two different bodies in the state to which this has reference, these were the Roman Catholics already citizens, who were born amongst us and those coming from abroad. Between these two were great distinctions. The foreigner who comes among us and will become a citizen, who wishes a naturalization, may with propriety be asked these terms. It may be necessary he should abjure his former sovereign.

But is the natural subject, the man born amongst us, educated with us, possessing our habits, possessing our manners, with an equal ardent love of his native country, to be required to take the same oath of abjuration—what has he to abjure? he owes no fealty to any other power upon the earth; nor is it so likely his mind should be led astray by bigotry, or the influence of foreign powers, then why give him occasion to be dissatisfied with you, by bringing forward a test which will not add to his fidelity. Moreover the clause in the constitution confines this test to foreigners, and if I am not misinformed, it was not till after much debate and warm contention, that it got admittance, and then only by a small majority in the convention.

It was a question with him whether it was proper to propose this test in the case before them.

But he was decidedly against going so far as to extend it to ecclesiastical matters; why should we wound the tender consciences of any man? and why present oaths to those who are known to be good citizens? why alarm them? why set them upon enquiry which is useless and unnecessary: You give them reason to suppose that you expect too much of them; and they cannot but refuse compliance. The constitution does not require such a criterion to try the fidelity of any citizen: It is solely intended for aliens and foreigners coming from abroad, with manners and habits, different from our own; and what intentions are concealed.

Instead Mr. Chairman, of going so far; I would propose to stop at the word state; and strike out all that followed. Then it would read thus; I do swear, &c. that I renounce and abjure all allegiance and obedience to the King of Great Britain, &c, and to every foreign king, prince, power, potentate, and state. This will bind the person only in civil matters; and is all that we ought, or can require. A man will then not be alarmed in his interpretation; it will not set his mind to enquire if his religious tenets are affected; and much inconvenience would be avoided. Again sir, we should be cautious how we carry the principle of requiring and multiplying tests upon our fellow citizens, so far as to practise it to the exclusion and disfranchisement of any. And as a doubt must arise with every member, on the propriety of extending the use of this abjuration oath. It will be their best mode to decide for the amendment; as in all cases where there is a doubt, it is our duty to oppose the measure.[3]

Mr. Hamilton mentioned again, that so far as the constitution went, it was a rule, and must be adopted; but he questioned the propriety of extending it.[4]

The [New York] *Daily Advertiser*, January 26, 1787.

1. For information on "An Act for Regulating Elections," see "Remarks on an Act for Regulating Elections," January 23, 1787.

The clause of the act discussed on this date is not given in the Assembly *Journal*, nor is it printed in its entirety in *The Daily Advertiser* of January 24. In *The Daily Advertiser* of February 1 the oath of abjuration required by the draft of the bill is given as follows: "I _____ do swear &c. that I abjure and renounce all allegiance and obedience to the King of Great-Britain, &c. and every foreign King, Prince, Potentate and State both in matters ecclesiastical as well as civil." In the act that was passed by the legislature on February 17 nothing was said concerning ecclesiastical obedience; it provided only that inspectors were authorized to require of any person suspected of being disaffected an oath abjuring "all allegiance and subjection to the king of Great Britain, and to all and every other foreign king, prince, potentate, and State whatsoever" (*Laws of the State of New York*, II, 376).

The clause in the original draft of this bill authorizing election officials to require an abjuration of ecclesiastical obedience was doubtless taken from the section of the New York State constitution dealing with naturalization which prescribed that all foreigners who became citizens of New York "take an oath of allegiance to this State, and abjure and renounce all allegiance and subjection to all and every foreign King, Prince, Potentate and State, in all matters ecclesiastical as well as civil" (*The Constitution of the State of New York* [Fishkill, Printed by Samuel Loudon, 1777], 33).

2. Samuel Jones, who spoke before H, defended this clause of the election bill. Jones "went on the ground of the constitution, and no other," for he considered the oath warranted by the constitution and argued that what was required of foreigners at the time of naturalization might also be required of all citizens of the state.

3. William Harper, an assemblyman from Montgomery County, repeated the argument of Samuel Jones that if a foreigner must take the oath before being admitted to citizenship, a native of the state could be required to take the same oath before voting.

4. A vote was taken on the question of amending the clause, and it was agreed to retain the section unamended. Subsequently, however, the requirement for an oath of abjuration of ecclesiastical obedience was deleted. See "Remarks on an Act for Regulating Elections," January 29, 1787.

## New York Assembly. Motion on an Act for Regulating Elections [1]

[New York, January 24, 1787]

A clause in the bill, ordering the judges of election for governor and lieutenant governor, to destroy the whole ballots of every district where there was an excess of even one vote.

This was shewn by Mr. Hamilton to be a very great injustice to the district, as it was in the power of the clerk or any officer, by putting in an additional ballot, to set aside the votes of 500 persons; he therefore moved, that in any case where there was an excess, such excess should be destroyed by lot.[2]

The [New York] *Daily Advertiser*, January 26, 1787.
1. For the background of the debate on "An Act for Regulating Elections," see "Remarks on an Act for Regulating Elections," January 23 and 24, 1787.
2. H's motion was adopted.

## New York Assembly. Remarks on an Act for Regulating Elections [1]

[New York, January 27, 1787]

Mr. Hamilton observed they were going on dangerous ground. The best rule the committee could follow was that held out in the constitution; which it would be safest to adhere to without alteration or addition. If we once depart from this rule, there is no say-

The [New York] *Daily Advertiser*, January 30, 1787.
1. For information on "An Act for Regulating Elections," see "Remarks on an Act for Regulating Elections," January 23 and 24, 1787.
Debate on the proposed act was continued on January 27 when a section on the qualifications of assemblymen was debated. The disputed section read: "And be it further enacted by the authority aforesaid, that no person receiving a pension from, or holding any office or place under the United States of America, shall at any time hereafter have a seat in, or sit or vote as a member of, the Senate or Assembly of this State" (New York Assembly *Journal*, 1787, 26). According to the account of the debate in *The New-York Journal, and Weekly Register* (February 1, 1787), "the foregoing clause gave rise to the discussion of an important question, viz: *Whether the legislature possesses the power of abridging the constitutional rights of the people? Mr. Hamilton, Mr. Jones, and Mr. Malcom,* were the chief speakers on this occasion, and the debates were very lengthy."

ing where it will end. To-day, a majority of the persons sitting here from a particular mode of thinking disqualify one description of men. A future legislature from a particular mode of thinking in another point, disqualify another set of men. One precedent is the pretext of another, 'till we narrow the ground of qualifications to a degree subversive of the spirit of the constitution.

It is impossible to suppose that the Convention who framed the constitution were inattentive to this point. It is a matter of too much importance not to have been well considered, they have fixed the qualification of electors with precision; they have defined those of Senator and Governor; but they have been silent as to the qualifications of Members of Assembly. It may be said that, being silent, they have left the matter to the discretion of the legislature. But is not the language of the framers of the constitution rather this?— we will fix the qualifications of electors—we will take care that persons absolutely indigent shall be excluded—we will provide that the right of voting shall be on a broad and secure basis—and we will trust to the discretion of the electors themselves the choice of those who are to represent them in assembly. Every qualification implies a disqualification: The persons who do not possess the qualification required become ineligible. Is not this to restrain the freedom of choice allowed by the constitution to the body of electors? An improper exercise of this liberty cannot constitutionally be presumed. Why therefore should we circumscribe it within limits unknown to the constitution? why should we abridge the rights of any class of citizens in so important an article?

By the constitution every citizen is eligible to a seat in the Assembly. If we say certain descriptions of persons shall not be so eligible, what is this but to deprive all those who fall within that description of an essential right allowed them by the constitution?

I have observed that if we once break the ground of departing from the simple plan of the constitution it may lead us much farther than we now intend—from the prevalency of a certain system, it is now proposed to exclude all persons from seats who hold offices under Congress—the pretence is to guard against an improper influence. I may think another species of influence more dangerous. I have taken notice upon a former occasion of the decisive agency of the executive in the appointment to all offices. If the persons who derive their official existence from that source sit in this house, it cannot be denied that it might give the executive an undue influence in the legislative deliberations. If in the vicissitude of human events, a majority of a future legislature should view the subject in this light, and if the principle of a right to annex disqualifications unknown to the constitution be admitted in practice, all persons holding offices under the state would then be excluded. I wish here to be clearly understood. I mean only to reason on general principles, without any particular reference whatever. I have hitherto confined my self to the general principle of the clause. There are however particular objections, one just occurs to me—there are officers who have been wounded in the service, and who now have pensions under the United States as the price of their blood; would it be just, would it not be cruel on this account to exclude men from a share in the administration of that government which they have at every hazard contributed to establish?

This instance strikes me: Other members may probably think of other cases equally strong against the exclusion—further reflections may suggest others that do not now occur.

If the committee however should resolve to adopt it; for the sake of consistency, they must carry it one step further—they must say that no member of Congress shall hold a seat. For surely if it be dangerous that the servants of Congress should have a seat in this house, it is more dangerous that the members themselves should be allowed this privilege.

But I would not be understood to advocate this extention of the clause. I am against the whole business. I am for adhering strictly to the present provisions of the constitution, I repeat it if we once break the ground of innovation, we may open a door to mischiefs what we neither know nor think of.[2]

Mr. Hamilton—I still continue Mr. Chairman of the same opinion on this subject. The more I consider the matter, the more forcibly am I struck that it will be dangerous to introduce qualifications un-

2. At this point H's speech was answered by William Harper and Samuel Jones. Harper contended that he had no objection to excluding members of Congress from the legislature. Jones, in a speech which attempted to refute the arguments made by H, stated that the legislature could not impose disqualifications on electors but that it did have the authority to prescribe regulations for those seeking elections to office.

known to the constitution. Is it possible to suppose the framers of the constitution were inattentive to this important subject, or that they did not maturely consider the propriety of annexing qualifications to the elected?

From the silence of the constitution it is inferred that it was intended to leave this point to the discretion of the legislature. I rather infer that the intention of the constitution was to leave the qualifications of their representatives wholly to the electors themselves. The language of the constitution seems to me to be this—Let us take care that the persons to elect are properly qualified, that they are in such a situation in point of property as not to be absolutely indigent and dependent, and let us trust to them the care of choosing proper persons to represent them.

The constitution will not presume that whole districts and counties of electors duly qualified will choose men improper for the trust.

Let us on our part be cautious how we abridge the freedom of choice allowed them by the constitution or the right of being elected, which every citizen may claim under it.

I hold it to be a maxim which ought to be sacred in our form of government, that no man ought to be deprived of any right or privilege which he enjoys under the constitution; but for some offence proved in due course of law.

To declare qualifications or disqualifications by general descriptions, in legislative acts, would be to invade this important principle. It would be to deprive in the gross all those who had not the requisite qualifications, or who were objects of those disqualifications to that right to a share in the administration of the republic which the constitution gives them, and that without any offence to incur a forfeiture.

As to the objection that the electors might even choose a foreigner to represent them within the latitude of the constitution, the answer is that common sense would not tolerate such a construction. The constitution from the fundamental policy of a republican government must be understood to intend citizens. But the gentleman, (Mr. Jones) has not adverted that the same difficulty would attend the case of electors where he admits there is no power in the legislature to make alterations—the expression there is, every *male in-*

*habitant* possessed of certain property shall vote; but there surely could never be a doubt that such male inhabitant must also be a citizen.

But let us pursue the subject a little further; commerce it will be admitted leads to an increase of individual property, property begets influence. Though a legislature composed as we are, will always take care of the rights of the middling and lower classes, suppose the majority of the legislature to consist at a future day, of wealthy men, what would hinder them, if the right of innovating on the constitution be admitted, from declaring that no man not worth ten thousand pounds should be eligible to a seat in either house? and would not this introduce a principle of aristocracy fatal to the genius of our present constitution.

In making this observation I cannot be suspected of wishing to increase the jealousy already sufficiently high of men of property—my situation, prospects and connections forbid the supposition. But I mean to lay honestly before you the dangers to which we expose ourselves by letting in the principle which the clause under consideration rests upon.

I give no opinion on the expediency of the exclusion proposed. I only say, in my opinion, the constitution does not permit it, and I shall be against any qualification or disqualification either of electors or elected, not prescribed by the constitution.

To me it appears that the qualifications of both ought to be fundamental in a republican government; not liable to be varied or added to by the legislature, and that they should for ever remain where the constitution has left them. I see no other safe ground.

It is to be lamented that men to carry some favorite point in which their party or their prejudices are interested, will inconsiderately introduce principles and precedents, which lead to successive innovations destructive of the liberty of the subject and the safety of the government.

For my part, I shall uniformly oppose every innovation not known in the provisions of the constitution. I therefore move that the clause be struck out.[3]

3. After several other members of the Assembly had spoken on the clause, H moved that it be obliterated. His motion was carried.

## New York Assembly. Remarks on an Act for Regulating Elections [1]

[New York, January 29, 1787]

Mr. Hamilton thought the subject was nearly exhausted, from what had been said on a former occasion.

He insisted strongly upon the distinction drawn by the constitution, he thought this clause did not comport with what was there held out. The requisite and constitutional qualifications to be required of electors, was there precisely ascertained, they are to possess certain estates and swear allegiance to the state. The foreigner before he could be admitted to the franchise of a citizen, was required to take this oath of abjuration, and for reasons which do not exist on the part of the person born and educated here, unincumbered with that dangerous fanaticism, which terrified the world some centuries back; but which is now dissipated by the light of philosophy.

These oaths are therefore no longer necessary, for the dangers are now only imaginary and are void of existence, at least with respect to us.

Mr. Hamilton animadverted on the little influence possessed by the Pope in Europe, spoke of the reformation going forward in the German empire, and of the total independence of the French church. He compared bringing forward oaths of this nature to the vigilance of those who would bring engines to extinguish fire which had many days subsided.

He observed that the Roman Catholics were not the only society affected, some of the Dutch reformed churches held a species of ecclesiastical foreign jurisdiction, he alluded to the Clausses of Amsterdam.

He concluded with observing it was unconstitutional in the form it held in the bill.[2]

The [New York] *Daily Advertiser*, February 1, 1787.
    1. On January 29, the debate on the clause of the election bill requiring every person to take an oath abjuring and renouncing "all allegiance and obedience to . . . every foreign King, Prince, Potentate and State both in matters ecclesiastical as well as civil" was renewed. For H's earlier comments on this clause

of the bill, see "Remarks on an Act for Regulating Elections," January 24, 1787.

2. At the conclusion of H's remarks, a motion made earlier by William Malcom that the words "both in matters ecclesiastical as well as civil" be deleted from the clause was put to a vote and carried by a large majority.

## New York Assembly. Remarks on an Act for Regulating Elections [1]

[New York, January 30, 1787]

Mr. Hamilton, the more he thought upon this subject, the more clearly he discovered its mischievous tendency, for nothing was more evident to him than that it put every unlettered person greatly in the power of the inspector—and when we consider the great number of which this class of men consist in some places of one half or one third of the whole district, it is easily perceivable that submitting them to the guidance of the inspector, you put into their power to decide elections.

It was very justly remarked by the gentleman who spoke first (Mr. Malcom) that the unlettered person from his want of knowing personally the candidates will not when taken aside recollect the names even of them, or at least but a few; in this case the inspector not only may, but must suggest the names to him otherwise how can he vote? What then is the consequence? Certainly if he is a man connected with party, he will vote for his friend, for notwithstanding the inspector may be an honest man, and bound by an oath on this occasion, yet, we know how easy it is for people to interpret such oaths to accommodate themselves, especially when they think they are rendering service to their country, they find a thousand ingenious contrivances, a thousand subterfuges to reconcile it to their preferences.

But Mr. Chairman it not only is dangerous but it is totally contrary to the very genius and intention of balloting; which means that a man's vote should be secret and known but to himself—yet you not only permit him but even oblige him to discover his vote. This I submit to the candour of the members, and they cannot but see with me, that this clause is a violation of the right we wish to give ourselves of voting concealed, and it deprives the unlettered person of what his fellow citizen who has it in his power to read, has secured to him. I would wish these persons might be left to themselves, for there would be then less danger than when the influence was regular and concentered.

I hope these reasons will be deemed sufficient to induce the house to reject the clause as repugnant to the genius and liberty of our republic.[2]

*The* [New York] *Daily Advertiser*, January 31, 1787.
1. On January 30 the Assembly again took up the clause of the proposed election bill which authorized election inspectors "to take aside ignorant persons and examine them privately touching the persons for whom they mean to ballot." (See H's remarks on this clause dated January 23, 1787.) H's remarks were preceded by those of Samuel Jones who argued that the question was whether it was preferable "to refer the illiterate to the inspector who is upon oath, or leave him to the chance influence of the people at large" (*The Daily Advertiser*, January 31, 1787).
2. At the conclusion of H's speech, a vote was taken on the retention or deletion of the clause, and it was determined that it should be struck out.

## New York Assembly. Motion for Leave to Bring in a Bill

[New York, February 3, 1787]

Mr. Hamilton moved for leave to bring in a bill to amend the charter of the Corporation for the relief of Widows and Children of Clergymen in communion of the Church of England, in America.[1]

*Ordered,* That leave be given accordingly.

Mr. Hamilton, according to leave, brought in the said bill, entitled *An act to amend the Charter of the Corporation for the relief of the Widows and Children of Clergymen in the communion of the Church of England, in America,* which was read a first time, and ordered a second reading.

New York Assembly *Journal,* 1787, 34.
1. The act introduced by H was passed by the legislature on February 19, 1787. It provided that the name of the corporation be changed; that its by-laws conform to the laws of New York; and that its accounts be subject to the revision of the governor, chancellor, and chief justice of the state (*Laws of the State of New York*, II, 411–12).

## New York Assembly. Remarks on an Act Concerning Wrecks at Sea [1]

[New York, February 3, 1787]

Mr. Hamilton was not satisfied with the punishment of fines and imprisonment to be inflicted on those persons who despoil'd the distressed of their property; persons cast away, were objects of commiseration, and every person who was so callous as to add to their misfortune, deserved more severe punishment.

In England it was made death without benefit of clergy, this he thought too severe, and therefore proposed to soften it, by extending it to corporal punishment, at the discretion of the court, so as not to affect life or limb.

This punishment might be distributed as the case required, but as the law stood at present it was too lenient in its punishment for some aggravated offences.[2]

The [New York] *Daily Advertiser*, February 5, 1787.
1. On the motion of Samuel Jones, the Assembly resolved itself into a committee of the whole to consider "An act concerning wrecks of the Sea, and giving remedy to Merchants who be robbed, or whose goods perish on the Sea" (New York Assembly *Journal*, 1787, 34). H's remarks referred to the section of the act which prescribed punishment for persons who took goods from any stranded ship or vessel.
2. H's suggestion was adopted and incorporated in the act that was passed on February 16. See *Laws of the State of New York*, II, 400–02.

## Horatio Gates to Alexander Hamilton, James Duane, and William Duer

Travellers Rest (Virginia)
5th February 1787

Dear Sirs,

I received The packet you Honoured me with [1] by The Bearer Mr. J. Nourse,[2] and immediately forwarded your Letter with The Books to the State Secretary T. Merriwether Esqr. at Richmond,[3] with a Letter from myself, requesting him to Present it to The Committee, that is appointed to attend The General Meeting in Philadelphia.[4] Previous to my receiving your Letter, I had The Honour to receive a packet from His Excellency General Washington, inclosing his Circular Letter to all the State Meetings of The Union,[5] & herewith, you will receive a Copy of my Answer to His Excellency. The distance I live from Richmond, 200 Miles, ⟨– – – – – – – –⟩ [6] & the Risque of Health at that Severe Season prevented me from going to the State Meeting in November, and I have not yet received the Minutes of what was transacted there. From the President Generals Resignation, I Augur the most unfavourable consequences to The Order, The Honour & Prosperity, of which, I have so much at Heart.   with Great Regards, I am Dear Sirs, Your most Obedient Humble Servant                                                    Horatio Gates

P.S.   The Bearer will return here in Ten days.

Alexander Hamilton
James Duane & William Duer Esqrs.
New York

ALS, New-York Historical Society, New York City.
   1. As president of the Virginia Society of the Cincinnati, Gates received a copy of the circular letter which H, as chairman of a committee of the New York Society, had written to the several state societies on November 1 (Circular Letter to the State Societies of the Cincinnati, November 1, 1787).
   2. Joseph Nourse was the register of the Treasury and a resident of Virginia.
   3. Thomas Meriwether was a major in the First Virginia State Regiment during the American Revolution.
   4. The general meeting of the society was to be held on May 17, 1787.
   5. Washington's letter, announcing the triennial meeting of the society and his refusal to accept the office of president general, was dated October 31, 1786. It is printed in GW, XXIX, 31–33.
   6. At this point approximately eight words were erased either by Gates or by some unknown person at a later date.

## New York Assembly. Remarks on an Act for Regulating Elections [1]

[New York, February 6, 1787]

Mr. Hamilton observed that when the discriminating clauses admitted into the bill by that house, were introduced, he was re-

The [New York] Daily Advertiser, February 8, 1787.
   1. "An Act for Regulating Elections" was returned from the Senate on Febru-

strained by motives of respect for the sense of a respectable part of the house, from giving it any other opposition, than a simple vote. The limited operation, they would have, made him less anxious about their adoption: but he could not reconcile it to his judgment, or feelings, to observe a like silence on the amendment proposed by the senate. Its operation would be very extensive; it would include almost every man in the city, concerned in navigation during the war.

We had in a former debate, travelled largely over the ground of the constitution, as applied to legislative disqualifications; He would not repeat what he had said, but he hoped to be indulged by the house in explaining a sentence in the constitution, which seems not well understood by some gentlemen. In one article of it, it is said no man shall be disfranchised or deprived of any right he enjoys under the constitution, but by the *law of the land,* or the judgment of his peers. Some gentlemen hold that the law of the land will include an act of the legislature. But Lord Coke, that great luminary of the law, in his comment upon a similar clause, in Magna Charta, interprets the law of the land to mean presentment and indictment, and process of outlawry, as contradistinguished from trial by jury. But if there were any doubt upon the constitution, the bill of rights enacted in this very session removes it.[2] It is there declared that, no man shall be disfranchised or deprived of any right, but by *due process of law,* or the judgment of his peers. The words *"due process"* have a precise technical import, and are only applicable to the process and proceedings of the courts of justice; they can never be referred to an act of legislature.

Are we willing then to endure the inconsistency of passing a bill

---

ary 6, 1787. For information on this act, see H's "Remarks on an Act for Regulating Elections," January 23, 24, 27, 29, and 30, 1787. Among the amendments proposed by the Senate was one which altered the section of the act disqualifying certain persons from holding offices of trust. The act, as passed by the Assembly, stated that among those disqualified from holding any office in the state were "persons who shall have acted as captain, lieutenant, or master, of any privateer or privateers, or vessels of war, to cruise against or commit hostilities upon vessels, property or persons of any of the citizens of this State, or any other of the United States" (*Laws of the State of New York,* II, 383). The Senate amendment provided that this section should be changed also to include "owner or owners of such privateers or vessels of war" (New York Assembly *Journal,* 1787, 36).

2. On January 26 the legislature had passed "AN ACT concerning the rights of the citizens of this State" (*Laws of the State of New York,* II, 344-45).

of rights, and committing a direct violation of it in the same session? in short, are we ready to destroy its foundations at the moment they are laid?

Our having done it to a certain degree is to be lamented; but it is no argument for extending it.

He would now make some remarks on the expediency and justice of the clause, distinct from constitutional considerations.

The word privateer is indefinite, it may include letters of marque. The merchants of this city during the war, generally speaking, must abandon their means of livelihood, or be concerned in navigation; if concerned in navigation, they must of necessity have their vessels armed for defence. They would naturally take out letters of marque. If every owner of a letter of marque is disfranchised, the body of your merchants will probably be in this situation. Is it politic, or wise to place them in it? Is it expedient to force by exclusions and discriminations a numerous and powerful class of citizens to be un-friendly to the government?

He knew many individuals who would be comprehended, who are well affected to the prosperity of the country: who are disposed to give every support to the government and who, some of them at least, even during the war, had manifested an attachment to the American cause.

But there is one view in which the subject merits consideration, that must lay hold on all our feelings of justice. By the maritime law, a majority of the owners have a right to dispose of the destina-tion of the vessel. The dissent of the minority is of no avail. It may have happened, and probably has happened in many instances, that vessels have been employed as privateers, or letters of marque, by a majority of the owners, contrary to the sense of the minority. Would it be just to punish the innocent with the guilty; to take away the rights of the minority, for an offence committed by the majority, without their participation, perhaps contrary to their in-clination?

He would mention a further case, not equally strong, but of con-siderable force, to incline the house against the amendment. He had been informed that in one or more instances during the war, some zealous people had set on foot subscriptions for fitting out privateers, perhaps at the instigation of the British government; and had applied to persons suspected of an attachment to us to subscribe; making their compliance a test of their loyalty. Several individuals, well disposed to our cause, to avoid becoming the objects of persecution, had complied; would it not be too rigorous to include them in so heavy a penalty? It may be said they were guilty of a culpable want of firmness. But if there are any of us who are conscious of greater fortitude, such persons should not on that account be too severe on the weaknesses of others. They should thank nature for its bounty to them, and should be indulgent to human frailty. How few are there who would have had strength of mind enough in such circumstances to hazard by a refusal, being marked out as the objects of military resentment?

I hope Mr. Speaker, as well from motives of justice, as a regard to the constitution, we shall stop where we are, and not go any farther into the dangerous practice of disqualifying citizens by general descriptions. I hope we shall reject the amendment. Sir! [3]

Mr. Hamilton explained the intention and meaning of this clause in the constitution. He defined the act of attainder, as being a law, confiscating for treason and misprison of treason, all the property and estate of the attainted traitor, and forfeiting his life unless he appears to take his trial. This was the construction put upon it by the country from which we draw our knowledge of jurisprudence; and he believed an example could not be produced, w[h]ere it had been extended or applied in any other manner, he was positive it could not be exercised to disfranchise a whole party, for this plain reason that it would involve the innocent with the guilty.

This clause therefore in the constitution, was only intended to apply in particular cases w[h]ere an exception to the established mode of common law, became necessary by the persons absenting himself; and did not apply at all into the subject before the house.

He concluded, by observing that precedents of this kind laid the foundation for the subversion of the liberty of the people, and he therefore hoped the amendment would not be agreed to.[4]

3. H's remarks were at this point answered by several members of the Assembly who favored the proposed amendment (*The New-York Journal, and Weekly Register*, February 15, 1787). William Harper, noting the assertion that the proposed amendment was contrary to the New York constitution, read Section 41 of the constitution which prescribed trial by jury and prohibited acts of attainder.

4. The amendment proposed by the Senate was defeated by a vote of 32 to 21.

## From Paul Bascom [1]

*Turks-Island,*[2] *February 8, 1787.* "I wrote you in July last [3] . . . respecting the Business of Mrs. Place's Children, with the Estates of Paul & Stephen Richards at New-York."

ALS, Hamilton Papers, Library of Congress.
    1. Presumably Paul Bascom of Bermuda who had been a searcher of the customs there.
    2. Turks-Island is located in the British West Indies.
    3. Letter not found.

## New York Assembly. Report on a Petition from George Fisher [1]

[New York, February 8, 1787]

Mr. Hamilton, from the Committee to whom was referred the petition of George Fisher, reported, that they have enquired into the circumstances of his case, and are of opinion that it will be proper to grant him relief, either by taking back the land mentioned in his petition, and returning the deposit money, or by setting off to him so much of the land as will amount to the deposit money, in proportion to the whole, and taking back the residue. That a clause be inserted in some proper bill for this purpose, and that in the mean time the Attorney General be directed to suspend all proceedings against the petitioner.

New York Assembly *Journal,* 1787, 39.
    1. George Fisher, who had supplied New York troops during the American Revolution, had purchased extensive tracts of land from the state in 1786. On January 27, 1787, his petition, "praying to be relieved from a purchase of real estate purchased of the State," was read and referred to a committee of which H was chairman. The precise nature of his petition was described in the resolution which was passed by the Assembly consonant with H's report. The resolution ordered the attorney general to ". . . stay all further proceedings upon the bond given by George Fisher to the Commissioners of Forfeitures in the Southern District, for the purchase money of certain lots of ground, forfeited to the People of this State, by the attainder of James De Lancey, Esquire" (New York Assembly *Journal,* 1787, 39.)

## New York Assembly. Remarks on an Act Concerning Murder [1]

[New York, February 8, 1787]

On that part of the bill, which required that women who clandestinely were delivered of children and the same die, or be born dead, that the mother within one month thereafter, should before a magistrate be obliged to produce one witness at least, to prove that the child was not murdered; and in default of concealing the same, to be deemed guilty of murder.

Mr. Hamilton observed, that the clause was neither politic or just, he wished it obliterated from the bill; to shew the propriety of this, he expatiated feelingly on the delicate situation it placed an unfortunate woman in, who might by accident be delivered stillborn; from the concealment of the loss of honor, her punishment might be mitigated; and the misfortune end here. She might reform and be again admitted into virtuous society. The operation of this law compelled her to publish her shame to the world. It was to be expected therefore that she would prefer the danger of punishment from concealment, to the avowal of her guilt. He thought it would involve courts in a delicate dilemma; the law would have no good effect as it would generally be evaded; such circumstances would be viewed leniently.

_The_ [New York] _Daily Advertiser_, February 10, 1787.

1. On February 8, a committee of the whole reported on "AN ACT concerning murder." The section of the bill under dispute is given in the paragraph preceding H's remarks.

2. Following H's remarks, Samuel Jones argued in favor of the clause. H, in turn, replied, according to _The Daily Advertiser_, "in terms of great cogency: The former reasoning in some measure repeated and explained."

H's motion that the clause be "obliterated from the bill" was adopted by the Assembly. "AN ACT concerning murder" was passed on February 14. See _Laws of the State of New York_, II, 391–93.

## New York Assembly. An Act for Raising Certain Yearly Taxes Within This State

[New York, February 9, 1787] [1]

*Introductory Note*

The Assembly of the New York legislature resolved on January 17, 1787, "that a Committee be appointed to consider of and report, ways and means for discharging the debts of the State, and the maintenance of public credit" (New York Assembly *Journal*, 1787, 10). The *Journal*, however, did not give the names of the members appointed to the committee. On February 9, 1787, William Malcom "from the Committee of Ways and Means, . . . reported that it is the opinion of the Committee, that a bill be brought in for raising certain yearly taxes within this State; that the Committee have prepared a draft of a bill for that purpose (*ibid.*, 41). Initially entitled "An Act for Raising Certain Yearly Taxes Within This State," the title of the bill was later changed to "An Act for Raising Monies by Tax."

In the Hamilton Papers, Library of Congress, there are three autograph drafts of this document. Two of them are apparently drafts used in preparation of the third, the draft of "An Act for Raising Certain Yearly Taxes Within This State," which Hamilton submitted to the New York legislature. Arranging them in the order in which Hamilton probably prepared them, they are designated for purposes of identification, First Draft, Second Draft, and Third Draft.

There is also in the Hamilton Papers a fragment which was probably a preliminary outline prepared before the First Draft. The fragment is headed "Objects for taxation" and includes, with certain minor differences, the information contained under the numerals I, II, III, IV, and X in the Second Draft.

The First Draft, although differing in paragraph arrangement, conforms closely to the Second Draft. It is not as complete as the Second Draft and Hamilton left blank spaces which he evidently intended to use for later amplification of statements he had made. The taxes proposed are, with some exceptions, the same in the First and Second Drafts but the estimated amounts to be raised from them are different.

Both the First Draft and the Second Draft conclude with a section on the "mode of collection." It is this subject which, except for the opening paragraphs, is discussed in greater detail in the Third Draft.

The "Act for Raising Certain Yearly Taxes . . . ," or the Third Draft, is incomplete. Page 2 of this MS ends with the sentence: "Upon every room or apartment with a ceiling of stucco work the further sum of twenty shillings." The next page, which is numbered page 7 in an unidentified handwriting, begins "The duty of such surrogate. . . ." The missing pages may have contained the specific taxes enumerated in the Second Draft under numerals III–X.

The Second Draft and the Third Draft are printed below. The First Draft, which is printed in *JCHW*, II, 204–11, has been omitted because, although similar to the Second Draft, it is less complete.

Scholars have assumed that "An Act for Raising Certain Yearly Taxes Within This State," was drafted by Hamilton in 1782. It is printed in *JCHW*, II, 204–11, with no date but among documents for the year 1782. Nathan Schachner (*Hamilton*, 149–50) and Broadus Mitchell (*Hamilton*, 274–75) assume it was written in September, 1782. Although it may have been drafted earlier, the act was introduced in the New York legislature in 1787.

1. For the date given this document, see the "Introductory Note."

The following facts support the contention that the document could have been written in 1782: On July 21, 1782, a joint committee of the New York legislature was appointed to report to the next session of the legislature "a system for establishing such Funds within this State, as may be best calculated to answer the Purposes of this State, and the United States; and for the more effectual Collection of Taxes within this State" (New York Assembly *Journal*, 1782, 117). During August and the first part of September, Hamilton was collecting information on the condition of finances of the state which might have been used in preparation for a report to the committee. The committee met on September 15 and adjourned early in October. Hamilton was in constant attendance and could have submitted his ideas on the proper mode of taxation to be adopted by the state.

It is possible that the recommendations of objects of taxation in the First and Second Drafts were made in 1782 and conceivable, although not likely, that the First Draft may have been written at that time. That a plan similar to the one here printed may have been submitted to the committee of the legislature in 1782 is suggested by a letter Hamilton wrote to Robert Morris on October 5, 1782, describing a plan of taxation adopted by the committee which contained provisions for specific taxation included in Hamilton's First Draft.

There is, therefore, a possibility that the First Draft may have been prepared in 1782 and used by Hamilton in 1787 as the basis for an act for raising taxes. The Second Draft, however, could not have been prepared before 1787, for it refers to the collection of taxes in the counties of Washington, Montgomery, and Columbia, all of which were created after 1782. The names of the counties of Tyron and Charlotte were changed to Montgomery and Washington, respectively, by an act of the legislature in 1784 (*Laws of the State of New York*, I, 613). Columbia County was formed from Albany County in 1786 (*ibid.*, II, 234).

That Hamilton's plan for specific taxation was introduced to the legislature in 1787 is further demonstrated by a partial draft of the proposed act which appeared in *The* [New York] *Daily Advertiser* of March 13 and March 15, 1787. The excerpts from the act printed there are exactly the same as corresponding sections of the act in the Second Draft printed below. The New York Assembly *Journal* also indicates that the act must have been submitted to the legislature in 1787, for a paragraph from the proposed act which was read on March 16 (New York Assembly *Journal*, 1787, 101), precisely corresponds with paragraph two of the Second Draft.

SECOND DRAFT OF AN ACT FOR

RAISING CERTAIN YEARLY TAXES

WITHIN THIS STATE[2]

Plan of Specific Taxation to be substituted to the Present mode by assessment: Together with the supposed product and the appropriation of each tax.

I Land tax of 3 pence per acre upon all meadow land.

2*d.* per acre upon all arable land.

Suppose in the whole state about 40.000 farmers each farm containing upon an average 10 acres of meadow and 40 acres

2. ADf, Hamilton Papers, Library of Congress.

of arable land; The prod⟨uct⟩ of this tax would then stand thus—

$$2000.000 \begin{cases} \text{400.000 acres of meadow land a[t]} \\ 3d. \, ⅌ \text{ acre} \dots\dots\dots\dots\dots\dots\dots\dots\dots\dots\dots £5000 \\ \text{1600.000 acres of arable land at} \\ 2[d] \, ⅌ \text{ do} \dots\dots\dots\dots\dots\dots\dots\dots\dots\dots 13333.6.8 \end{cases}$$

$$\overline{18333.6.8}$$

II House tax (meaning dwelling houses) or so on for habitation.

Upon every log house 2/ for each apartment (exclusive of garrets and cellars).

Upon every other house of three rooms and under 3/ for each apartment exclusive as before.

Upon every other house of four rooms 4/ per apartment exclusive as before.

Upon every other house of five rooms 6/ per apartment exclusive as before.

Upon every other house of 6 rooms and upwards 8/ per room exclusive as before.

For every apartment with a fire place in garret or Cellar 3/
For every tiled Chimney piece 2/
For every Chimney of cut stone 10/

Upon every room of any house of either description (except log houses) painted on the wooden work inside 5/ in addition to the foregoing rates.

Upon every room (except as before) papered inside 10/ in addition to the foregoing rates provided that papered rooms shall not pay as painted.

Upon every marble Chimney piece 20/ in addition to the foregoing rates.

For every Mahogany Stair Case ⟨20⟩/

Upon every stucco roof 40/ in addition to the foregoing rates.

This tax at a moderate computation will produce    4⟨5.000⟩

$$\overline{6333⟨3.6.8⟩}$$

III Salt tax at 6/ per bushell upon importation.

Suppose 40,000 families in the state each family consuming 3 bushels per annum this would amt. to 120.000 bushels at 2/ \dots\dots\dots\dots\dots\dots\dots\dots\dots\dots\dots\dots\dots\dots\dots 12000.

IV Tobacco tax, at 3d. ⅌ lb on importation allowing the same drawback on exportation. Suppose 20.000 consumers of foreign

tobacco at 15 lb each ℔ annum this would make 300.000
at 3d. . . . . . . . . . . . . . . . . . . . . . . . . . . . . . . . . . . . . . . . . . . . . 3750
This calculation is probably *very low*.

V Carriage tax Every coach   £5 per annum
     Every Chariot   4 per annum
     Phaetons & other
     4 Wheeled Carriages  3 per annum
     two Wheeled Carri-
     ages      1. per annum
     Pleasure slays   5/ per annum[3]

Suppose in the state
 20 Coaches . . . . . . . . . . . a[t] 5 £ . . . . . .  100
 60 Chariots . . . . . . . . . . . a[t] 4  . . . . . .  240
 100 Phætons &c. . . . . . . . . a[t] 3  . . . . . .  300
 500 two wheeled Carriages at  1  . . . . . .  500
 4000 pleasure slays . . . . . . . at  5/  . . . . . . 1000
                 —————
                      2140[4]

VII Tavern tax
 For license to keep an Inn or Tavern 40/ ℔ annum
 for license to sell spirituous liquors
 therein          £3 ℔ do.
 for license to sell Wine    £5 ℔ do.
 for license to sell imported Malt
 liquor           £3 ℔ do.
 for license to keep billiard table  £5 ℔ do.
 for license to keep houses for other
 games           2 ℔ do.
 This tax it is apprehended would
 produce                2500
                      —————
                     86223.6.8

3. After each line, in the section on carriage tax, there appeared a number. They were, successively, "3, 2, 30, 10." At the end of the last line the word "Quare?" is written.

4. Following this section of the MS there is a section numbered VI and entitled "Plate tax" which was crossed out either by H or by an unknown person. It reads:

  For every ounce of silver plate    2d
  . . . . . . . . . . . . . . . . . . . . . . . . Gold plate  2/6
  other plated furniture per ounce    ½
  This may be estimated at about . . . . . . . . . . . . . . . 2500

VIII Servant tax

On all male *menial or household* servants of the age of 16 & upward not employed in agriculture 10/ per head; batchelors paying 40/ ℔ head.

This tax will at a moderate computation produce 5000.

IX Lawyers tax (not to be allowed to them in their bills.)

For every seal in the Court of Errors Chancery and in the Supreme Court 2/ in addition to that not paid and taxed.

For every seal in each County and Mayors Court 1/

This may be computed at about 1500

£92723.6.8

X Additional Impost [5]

| | | |
|---|---|---|
| Upon all rum of Jamaica proof ℔ Gallon | | 3d |
| of foreign Manu[facture] Upon all brandies .......... ℔ do. | | 3 |
| Upon all other distilled spirit: liquors ℔ do. | | 2d |
| Upon all spirituous liquors distilled in any of the other states ..................... | | 3d |
| Upon every lb of bohea tea .............. | | 3d |
| Upon Madeira Wine ℔ Gallon .......... | | 2d. |
| Upon all other Wines ℔ do. ............. | | 1d. |
| Upon loaff sugar ℔ lb. ................. | | 1d. |
| Upon snuff ℔ lb. ..................... | | 10d. |
| Upon every coach or Chariot ........... | | £10 |
| Upon every other four wheeled Carriage .. | | £5 |
| Upon every curricle Chaise Kettereen Sulky ................................. | | £2 |
| Upon every gallon of Malt liquor ........ | | 10d. |
| Upon every dozen bottles of ditto ........ | | 2/6 |
| Upon every pound of Cheese ........... | | 2d. |
| Wrought silver plate per ounce ......... | | 1/ |
| Wrought Gold plate ℔ do .............. | | 15/ |
| Gold and silver plated furniture ℔ ounce | | 3d. |

5. The impost was not included in "An Act for Raising Certain Yearly Taxes," but it was provided for by "An Act imposing Duties on Goods and Merchandize, imported into This State," which was passed by the legislature on April 11, 1787. The duties imposed by the act adopted by the legislature were higher than those suggested by H in this draft.

| | |
|---|---|
| Every clock | 20/ |
| Every gold Watch | 20/ |
| Every silver ditto & others | 5/ |
| Hollow Iron Ware ℔ 100 lb | 4/ |
| Scythes or axes ℔ dozen | 12/ |
| Saddles per piece | 8/ |
| Every pr. of womens leather or stuff shoes | 6d. |
| Every pr. of womens silk shoes | 1/ |
| Every pr. of boots | 2/ |
| Every pound of starch or hair powder | 3d. |
| Every gallon of linseed oil | 6 |
| Every pound of dressed or tanned leather | 4d |
| Every pack of playing Cards | 3d |
| barr Iron .......... ad. valorem | 3 ℔ Ct |
| Nails ℔ Cwt | |

Mahogany furniture 5 ℔ Ct ad valorem
Mahogany wood      3 ℔ Ct ad valorem
with a draw back in case of exportation.
Paper hangings      5 ℔ Ct ad valorem

| | |
|---|---|
| This Impost may be computed at | 10000 |
| Total product of Taxes | £ 102723.6.8 |
| Duty on Vendue sales | 5000 [6] |

### Appropriation of the foregoing Taxes

I Land Tax to the support of the Internal Government except
the Chancellor and Judges.

II Lawyers (or seal) tax } to the support of Chancellor and Judges
Carriage Tax

III House Tax to Congress for supplementary fund: when the

6. The First Draft contains the following sections which are not included
in the Second Draft:

Let the bank be incorporated on condition of
lending ⅛ of its Income on landed security
towards forming a loan office.

#### Plan of a Loan Office

The Interest of the 200,000 £ ....... 10,000
The tax on Salt .................... 12,000
The tax on Taverns ............... 2,000
Tobacco Tax

other states shall provide *similar* funds—to be collected in the mean time under the authority of the state and applied in discharge of the annual requisitions.

IV  Salt tax          ⎫  to form together with the Interest
    Tavern tax      ⎬  on the late emission [7] a fund for a
    Tobacco tax    ⎭  *loan office.*

The surplus of these taxes and the other taxes to form an aggregate fund for contingencies.

## Mode of Collection

Land Tax  I°    The Assessors of each town manor precinct and district to meet on the          [8] day of          in each year at
to receive from the owners and possessors of land a statement of the quantity of land in their pos⟨sessi⟩on respectively in the respective towns manors precincts and districts specifying the different kinds thus:

                                                        Acres

            Meadow land _____
            Arable  land _____
            Other land _____

This statement to be made on oath according to the best of the knowlege and belief of the party to be administer⟨ed⟩ by the assessors present or one of them who may examine the party particularly—and to [be] entered in a book to be kept for that purpose in which shall be carried out against each name the amount of his tax; a copy of which book delivered to the several collectors signed by the Assessors present or one of them shall be their warrant to collect.

If any persons do not appear at the time and place the assessors or assessor present to form the best estimate in his power upon his or their own knowlege or the information of others of the quantity and kinds of land in possession of such persons not appearing.

And if the assessors in any case suspect a concealment of arable or meadow land they shall have power to order a sur-

7. H presumably referred to the emission of paper money by the New York legislature in 1786.
8. These and other blank spaces were left in the MS by H.

vey; and in case it shall be found upon such survey that there hath been a concealment to the extent of one acre in twenty of such arabl⟨e or mea⟩dow land the party concealing shall besides paying the additional amount of the tax for the time of such concealment to be added to the succeeding years tax but shall bear the expence of the survey and be liable to a forfieture of 40/ for every acre concealed to be recovered in an action of debt in the name of any assessor provided it shall appear to the jury which shall try the cause that such concealment was with intent to defraud the revenue and not through ignorance or mistake to be collected from the circumstances of the case: The forfieture to be for the benefit of the Assessors, if when they order a survey they shall engage to the surveyor employed that they will themselves bear the expence of the survey in case there shall not be found such concealment as aforesaid. Otherwise to be for the benefit of the state towards defraying the expences of survey, where such concealment is not found: in which case, (unless upon the engagement of the assessor as aforesaid to pay the same) the State shall bear the expence of survey. And in order that it may be known when such engagement is made by the assessors, the surveyor shall take an oath to be annexed to the survey to be taken before any justice of the peace, not being an assessor, declaring that such engagement was made, or that no such engagement was made, as the case may be.

The expence of survey to be paid by the County treasurer upon a certificate of the Assessors directing the same that the same was made by their direction by virtue of this act.

This tax to be paid by the Owner of the Inheritance in possession, the tenant, for life or years or his assignee in possession as the case may be: the possession of tenant at Will to be deemed the possession of his landlord.

And to be collected on the        day of        in each year at which day the collectors according to a previous assignment of the places in which they are respectively to collect to be made by the Assessors (who for that purpose are to provide themselves with a list of the collectors and of their places of abode) shall call for payment at the dwelling house of the possessor of the land if on the premisses or shall call for payment at the premisses if his dwelling house be not there; and in case of non payment shall immediately proceed to distrain for the amount of the tax, to be governed by the same rules as in case of a distress for rent without benefit of a replevin unless the amount of the tax be previously paid, to be restored in case such distress shall be adjudged to have been wrongfully made.

And if no sufficient distress can be found then the amount of the tax to be recovered in an action of debt to be brought by the collector in his own name; with costs of suit.

House tax

II The collectors of each town manor &c. or some one of them to visit every house once a year between the     day of     and the     day of     and to make a list of the rooms and their descriptions (noting the stucco roofs and marble Chimney pieces) liable to the tax—carrying out and calculating each persons tax against his name.

☞ This day should be a different & a distant day from the land tax.

This tax to be paid on the     day of     in each year by the Occupants of houses to be called for and collected in the same manner as the land tax. In case of dispute between Collectors & Owners of houses about the descriptions of the rooms an appeal shall be to the assessors who shall settle the dispute.

III To be collected for the present in the mode now established for collecting duties: This will need revisal hereafter: except that a year should be allowed for payment of Additional duties, after discounting drawbacks.

Salt tax
Tobacco tax
& additional
impost on im-
ported articles

Carriage tax
Plate tax
Servant tax

IV The Collectors when they visit the houses to take a list from the information of the Master or Mistress of the house or in their absence of such other persons as they find in the house of the carriages plate and servants:

And it shall be the duty of the Owners of these articles to furnish such information at the time of such visit on pain of twenty pounds for concealment of each servant or carriage and twenty shillings for concealment of each ounce of plate;

to be recovered by action of debt for the benefit of any informer.

**l tax** V This tax to be paid at the time of sealing the writs to the persons having custody of the seals; who will therefore be chargeable for the tax on every writ sealed; and must account for the same on their respective oaths of office.

In the Mayor and County Courts the proceeds of the tax to be accounted for once a year to the County treasurer.

In the Supreme Court, Court of Admiralty, Court of Chancery and in the Court of errors the proceeds to be accounted for in like manner to the Treasurer of the state.

**vern** VI The treasurer of the state to furnish annually to the County treasurers a sufficient number of licenses of the different kinds signed by him; with which he shall charge the respective County Treasurers in Account. The County treasurers to distribute them among the supervisors charging them in like manner in account; and the supervisors are to deliver them out to Individuals inclining to purchase them on their paying the rates beforementioned. The Supervisors must annually account with the County treasurers for the licenses delivered them, *paying* for all such as they do not return. And the County treasurers must once in each year account with the treasurer of the state, and shall in like manner be chargeable with all such as they do not return unless it should appear that the supervisors having disposed of them were insolvent and unable to pay.

> Quare if it would not be better to confine the transaction immediately between the State treasurer and the Supervisors.

If there are any Charters in the way, let the same rates be collected within the Charter limits to be disposed of according to the Charter 👉

## Rules

I No person to be obliged to serve as supervisor or Assessor more than one year in          years.

II Not more than two assessors to be elected in one ward town Manor precinct or district except the Manors of Rensalaaer and Livingston in which there may be four assessors.

The assessors to be allowed in lieu of all salary and expences 6/ per day and for not more than       days in a year.

Supervisors to be allowed nothing.

If the present collectors are to collect these taxes; let each collector who shall be elected be obliged to give sufficient sureties for his good behaviour diligence and fidel[it]y in the sum of Two thousand pounds.

If the person who has the greatest number of votes cannot do this, the person with the next greatest Number who can find such surety to be deemed duly elected.

The sureties to be approved by two Justices of the peace of the vicinity and to be taken by them in the name of the County Treasurer for the use of the state. The person having the highest number of votes to have ten days after his election to find such surety; and if not found within that time, ten days more to be allowed to the person having the next highest number of votes and so on till there be a person duly qualified.

Each Collector to be allowed 4 per Cent on all the monies by him collected.

Each County treasurer to keep accounts with the Collectors and to be intitled for his trouble to one half per Cent on all the money by him received.

But a better mode would be to offer the collection of taxes for the state to the person who may be willing to undertake it at the lowest rate giving security in the sum of twenty thousand pounds. This person to appoint and pay his own deputies and to be answerable for them.

Or to appoint a person allowing him 5 ℔ Ct on all the monies collected on the same conditions.

### THIRD DRAFT OF AN ACT FOR
### RAISING CERTAIN YEARLY TAXES
### WITHIN THIS STATE[9]

Whereas [10] from the impossibility of finding any determinate rule for ascertaining the comparitive abilities of counties districts and individuals to pay taxes the mode of taxation heretofore in use in this state of quotas and assessments has been found by experience to be productive of great inequalities and inconveniences and has proved inadequate to the exigencies of the state: And Whereas there is reason to believe that the imposition of taxes on specific articles of property will be found upon the whole more equitable as well as more effectual for the purposes of revenue

Be it therefore enacted by the People of the State of New York represented in Senate and Assembly and it is hereby enacted by the authority of the same—that the following taxes and duties shall be and hereby are laid assessed and imposed upon the articles and at the rates hereinafter specified for the service of the present year, that is to say—

Upon every inhabited dwelling house of the description and denomination of a log house at and after the rate of two shillings for each room or apartment thereof with a fire place or stove therein.

Upon every other inhabited dwelling house of two rooms exclusive of garret and cellar at and after the rate of two shillings for each room or apartment thereof with a fire place or stove therein.

Upon every such house of three rooms exclusive as before at and after the rate of three shillings for each room or apartment thereof with a fire place or stove therein.

Upon every such house of four rooms, exclusive as before, at and after the rate of four shillings for each room or apartment thereof with a fire place or stove therein.

Upon every such house of five rooms, exclusive as before, at and after the rate of five shillings for each apartment thereof with a fire place or stove therein.

Upon every such house of six rooms and upwards, exclusive as

9. ADf, Hamilton Papers, Library of Congress.
10. In MS, "whearas."

before, at and after the rate of six shillings for each room or apartment thereof, with a fire place or stove therein.

Upon every room in the garret or cellar of any house of the foregoing descriptions having a fire place or stove and upon every kitchen therein at and after the rate of two shillings for each room or kitchen.

Upon each room or apartment of every such house papered inside the further sum of five shillings.

Upon every Chimney faced with tiles the further sum of two shillings.

Upon every Chimney faced with cut stone other than marble the further sum of two shillings.

Upon every Chimney faced with marble the product of any of the United States of America the further sum of five shillings.

Upon every Chimney faced with marble the product of any foreign country the further sum of twelve shillings.

Upon every Mahogany stair case the further sum of twenty shillings.

Upon every room or apartment with cornishes of stucco work the further sum of ten shillings.

Upon every room or apartment with a ceiling of stucco work the further sum of twenty shillings; [11]
the duty of such surrogate upon information or discovery thereof to prosecute for the penalty aforesaid.

Upon land of the following descriptions

For every acre of meadow arable and pasture land at and after the rate of three pence per acre for the first quality thereof two pence per acre for the second quality thereof and one penny per acre for the third quality thereof to be ascertained as hereinafter mentioned.

For every hundred acres of wood land (barrens, lands subject to a right of commonage and all lands granted since the fourth day of July one thousand seven hundred and seventy six and hereafter to be granted by the Commissioners of the land office excepted) one shilling; which said tax on the said several kinds of land shall be paid

11. Page or pages missing. There are three sets of page numbers on the MS. Two of them are in order and show no missing pages; according to the third, the page which ends at this point is numbered "2," and the next page is numbered "7."

by the actual tenant or holder thereof whether of an estate of inheritance for life for years at sufferance or at will.

Provided always that nothing in this act contained shall be construed to alter change determine or make void any contract covenant or Agreement whatsoever between landlord and tenant or others touching the payment of taxes or assessments any thing herein contained to the contrary notwithstanding. And Provided further that the tax upon any house or tenement which any Ambassador Resident Agent or other public minister of any foreign prince or state now doth or hereafter shall inhabit or occupy shall be paid by the landlord or owner thereof.

And be it further enacted by the authority aforesaid that the tax herein before imposed upon inhabited dwelling houses and building lots shall be collected in manner following to wit: The Assessors of each City town ward manor precinct and district shall in all parts of the state except the City and County of New York in the month of October next and in the said city and county of New York between the tenth day of May and the first day of June next visit and inspect the said houses within their respective Cities towns wards manors precincts and districts and make and enter into books to be by them provided for that purpose at the County charge a list of the names of the several occupiers of the houses liable to the said tax and opposite thereto respectively in separate columns under proper heads the discription of the houses by them respectively occupied, specifying the whole number of rooms or apartments for habitation in each house exclusive of garrets and cellars the number of such rooms with fire places or stoves therein, the number of rooms in garrets or cellars with fire places or stoves, the number of rooms or apartments papered inside the number of chimnies faced with tiles the number of Chimnies faced with cut stone, the number of chimnies faced with marble the product of any of the United States the number of chimnies faced with marble the product of any foreign country the number of mahogany stair cases the number of rooms with cornishes of stucco work the number of rooms with ceilings of stucco work (provided that a room with cornishes and ceiling of such work shall be entered and rated in one column only as a room with a ceiling of such work) the number of square feet of each building lot, and shall carry out in a separate column the amount of the tax to be paid by each person and thereof shall at the time of such visit and inspection give notice to the occupier of each house by leaving a memorandum of such amount in writing with him or her or with one of his or her family or servants or affixing the same upon some public place within such house; and the said amount of the said tax so ascertained shall be payable in the City and County of New York in two equal parts the first moiety thereof on the First tuesday of October next and the second moiety thereof on the first tuesday of April following, and in the Counties of Richmond Columbia Albany and Montgomery in two equal parts the first moiety thereof on the first tuesday in December in each year and the second moiety thereof on the first tuesday of April in each year and in the Counties of Kings Queens Suffolk West Chester Dutchess Orange Ulster and Washington in one payment on the first tuesday of April in each year; and the Collectors of each town ward manor precinct and district shall on the said several days of payment respectively or within twenty days thereafter call at each of the said houses within their respective towns wards manors precincts and districts and demand the payment of the said tax; and in case of refusal of payment or if no proper person can be found of whom such demand may be made shall forthwith proceed, by distress and sale of the goods and chattels found upon the premises to levy the sums respectively due for the said tax, paying the overplus of such sale (if any there be after deducting the tax due and the costs of making such distress and sale) to the owner or owners of the goods distrained; and if such first distress upon sale of the goods distrained shall not prove sufficient to satisfy the said tax then a further distress shall be forthwith made and so on as often as may be necessary to satisfy the full amount of the said tax; and if there should be any rent in arrear upon any such house such distress or distresses to be made as aforesaid shall in no wise be affected thereby; but shall be good and effectual notwithstanding any claim of the landlord or owner for such rent; and if it should happen that no sufficient distress can be found upon the premises than the Collector or Collectors on whose lists respectively the name or names of the person or persons owing the said tax shall be borne shall and may have and are hereby required to bring an action of debt in his or their own [name] or names against the person or persons neglecting or refusing to pay the said tax for the recovery of the sum or sums due with costs of suit. And if any collector shall neglect to distrain within the time and in the manner hereinbefore directed upon the non payment of any part of this tax (except where no distress can be found) such collector shall be himself liable and chargeable with the amount of the tax due from the person or persons in respect to whom such neglect to distrain shall happen: [12] The assessors of each city town ward manor precinct and district after having completed their respective lists of the said occupiers of the said houses and building lots and also of the owners or possessors of the said store houses Grist mills and Saw Mills and the descriptions thereof as aforesaid and also of the said possessors of lands and the quantities and kinds in their possession respectively and also of the persons having such carriages and male servants as aforesaid and of the taxes and duties thereupon shall forthwith deliver to the supervisor of such town ward manor precinct or district exact copies of such lists signed by them respectively: And the said supervisor shall from thence make out other copies for the treasurer of the County and deliver or transmit the same to him and shall also make out proper lists for the collector or collectors of the town ward manor precinct or district for the collection of the said taxes specifying the amount of the tax to be paid by each person and the respective times of payment; which lists signed by such supervisor shall be a sufficient warrant to such collector or collectors. And the collector or collectors of each town ward manor precinct or district shall within ten days after the respective times hereinbefore limited for the collection of the said tax account with and pay to the treasurer of the County the monies by him or them collected and received and also the amount of the monies for which he or they are respectively made liable in case of neglect to distrain as aforesaid; and at every such accounting shall return in writing the names of such persons as may not have fully paid together with the amount and cause of the deficiency in each case; and in every case in respect to the said tax on houses store houses mills and land

12. At this point H wrote the letter "A," a sign which usually indicated an insertion. No insertion has been found.

County
treasur-
ers to
make a
general
return.
in which such cause shall be any other than the want of a sufficient distress or that the same when made was cloined without his or their default such Collector or collectors shall respectively be charged with the deficiency.

And be it further enacted by the authority aforesaid that the Assessors of each City town ward manor precinct & district shall at the time of their yearly visit and inspection of inhabited dwelling houses aforesaid visit and inspect the several store houses grist mills saw mills wharves and lumber yards within such city town ward manor precinct and district and shall ascertain the rent of such store houses if rented and if not rented shall estimate according to the best of their skill and judgment the true amount of what such store houses would and might be rented for; and shall also ascertain the number of grist and saw mills in the possession of each person and the number of runs of stones in such grist mills and the number of saws in such saw mills and the number of feet in front of each wharf; and shall together with the names of the owners or possessors of such store houses grist mills saw mills and lumber yards enter the number and descriptions thereof in the said book to be by them kept as aforesaid under proper heads in distinct columns and the amount of the tax thereupon; whereof a like memorandum in writing shall be delivered or left as is hereinbefore directed in respect to inhabited dwelling houses. And the said tax on the said several articles shall be payable in several Counties at the respective periods hereinbefore limited for the payment of the tax on inhabited dwelling houses and in the same proportions and shall be collected to all intents and purposes within the times and in the manner prescribed for the collection of the said tax last mentioned.

And the Collectors shall have the same powers and shall be chargeable and answerable in the same manner for any default or neglect in respect to the collection of the said tax on the said several articles as in respect to the collection of the said tax on inhabited dwelling houses; and shall account for the proceeds thereof to the respective County treasurers within the same times and in the same manner.

And be it further enacted by the authority aforesaid that the manager or managers director or directors of any play house or theatre shall render an account upon oath once in each calendar month to the treasurer of the County wherein such play houses and theatres shall be of the number of nights whereupon such exhibitions shall be had and shall pay the amount of the tax thereupon to such treasurer upon pain of forfieting one hundred pounds for every neglect or default to be recovered with Costs of suit in an action of debt in the name of the treasurer of the County wherein such play houses or theatres shall be one half to the use of the People and the other half to the use of such treasurer; whose duty it is hereby made to prosecute for the said penalty upon every such default.

And be it further enacted by the authority aforesaid that the said Assessors at their said yearly visit and inspection of inhabited dwelling houses shall inquire of the persons therein inhabiting touching the number of carriages and male servants liable to the duties aforesaid in the possession or service of such persons respectively and shall enter into the said book to be by them provided as aforesaid together with the names of such persons the number of each kind of such carriages and the number of such male servants in the possession or service of such persons respectively, and the amount of the duties thereupon; which shall be payable in the same proportions and at the same periods in the respective counties as the said tax upon inhabited dwelling houses: And it is hereby made the duty of the persons having such carriages and male servants at the time of the said yearly visit and inspection or within ten days thereafter to give to the Assessors who shall visit the houses in which they respectively dwell exact information of the carriages and servants subject to the duties aforesaid in their possession or service respectively on pain of forfieting for every neglect thereof treble the amount of the duty upon the carriages and servants whereof information shall not be given to the recov[er]ed with costs of suit in an action of debt founded upon this statute to be brought in the names of the assessors respectively who shall visit the houses in which such persons respectively shall dwell, one moiety to the use of the people of this state and the other moiety to the use of any person who shall give information thereof or to the use of the assessor in whose name the suit is brought when such neglect shall be discovered by himself; and if any person shall wilfully and with intent to evade the payment of the said duties conceal any carriage or male servant liable thereto such person shall forfeit for every male servant so concealed the sum of five pounds for every coach so concealed the sum of ten pounds for every other four wheeled carriage so concealed the sum of Eight pounds and for every two wheeled carriage so concealed the sum of five pounds to be recovered in like manner and to the like uses as the forfietures last aforesaid. And the said Assessors are hereby required upon discovery by themselves or information by others of such neglect or wilful concealment forthwith to commence and prosecute a suit or suits for the forfietures and penalties aforesaid. And the persons, having such carriages and servants, shall, on the said respective days of payment or within *twenty* days thereafter upon demand of them or at their respective dwelling places by the collectors respectively on whose lists they shall be respectively borne, pay to such collectors the amount of the said duties thereupon, upon pain of forfieting double the said amount for such neglect to be recovered with costs of suit in an action of debt to be brought in the name or names of such collectors respectively, one half thereof to the use of the people of this state and the other half thereof to the use of the collector who shall prosecute for the same.

And be it further enacted by the authority aforesaid that the mode of collecting the duties aforesaid upon licenses to keep inns and taverns and to sell therein the several kinds of liquors herein beforementioned and also to sell strong liquors by retail by others than the keepers of inns or taverns shall be as follows that is to say The Treasurer of the state shall cause such a number of licenses as he shall judge sufficient and in such form as he shall think proper with the necessary blanks therein to be printed at the expence of the state having a separate license for each case that is to say one form of license to keep an inn or tavern and to sell distilled spirituous liquors therein another form of license to sell therein liquors commonly called wines another form of license to sell therein imported malt liquors not distilled and another form of licence to retail strong liquors in other places than in inns or taverns; which said several kinds of licenses shall express that they are to continue in force for one year from the date and shall have an impression of the arms of this state in the margin of each and shall be signed at foot by the treasurer in his own hand writing: And the said treasurer is hereby directed to provide at the expence of the state a proper seal for making such impression to be kept by himself and his successors in office. And the said treasurer shall distribute the said licenses to the treasurers of the several counties in such proportions as he shall think necessary for the supply of each County, and shall debit each County treasurer in account for the number of licenses delivered to him and the amount of the duties thereupon. And the said County treasurers shall dispose of the said licenses to such discreet persons within their respective counties who can procure a certificate from the supervisor and two justices of the town manor precinct or district in which they reside that they are respectively of good moral character, and who will pay for the same on the delivery thereof.[13] And to the end that persons, applying for such licenses may not have too far to travel to procure the same the said County treasurers respectively shall be obliged to employ at their own charge and risk one or more discreet persons at their option in each town manor precinct or district to dispose of the said licenses and to account with them for the proceeds thereof. And each person applying for such licenses before the receipt thereof shall be obliged to enter into a bond to the supervisor of the town manor precinct or district in which he lives with one or more sufficient sureties to be approved by such supervisor in the penal sum of Fifty pounds conditioned for the good behaviour of such person and that he or she will keep an orderly house and will not sell therein any liquors for the sale of which a license is necessary and for which he or she hath not a license. And every keeper of any inn or tavern shall be obliged to fix up in some public place in the bar room or other most public room of such inn or tavern a printed or written paper expressing what kinds of liquors of the descriptions aforesaid he or she hath license to sell, for neglect whereof he or she shall forfeit the sum of ten pounds—to be recovered with costs of suit in the name of any person who will sue

13. The material from the beginning of this paragraph to the words "pay for the same on the delivery thereof" was crossed out. In the margin opposite this paragraph appear the words "provision when to commence"; "good behavior"; and "Mayor."

for the same one moiety to the use of the people of this state and the other moiety to the use of such person. And the several county treasurers aforesaid shall render a yearly account at such periods as the treasurer of the state shall appoint of the disposition of the said licenses to them respectively committed and shall respectively pay to the said treasurer of the state the full amount of the duties for all such licenses to them respectively committed which they do not at such yearly accounting produce to the treasurer of the state undisposed of, deducting thereout six pence in the pound of all the monies by them respectively received on account of the said duties, for their care and trouble and in lieu of all salary and expences thereupon.

Provided always that the said duty shall not begin to take effect until the first Monday of March next.[14] And provided further that in the Cities of New York, Albany & Hudson the said licenses shall be delivered to the respective Mayors of the said Cities to be by them disposed of, according to the direction of this act; and the said Mayors shall respectively be responsible therefore in like manner as the Treasurer of a County.[15] And if any person or persons shall after the period aforesaid keep an inn or tavern without such license as aforesaid for that purpose such person or persons shall forfeit for keeping such inn or tavern the sum of five pounds and if any person or persons shall sell therein any distilled spirituous liquors without such license as aforesaid for that purpose such person or persons shall forfeit for every such sale the sum of ten pounds and if any person or persons shall sell in any Inn or tavern liquors comm⟨only⟩ called wines without such license as aforesaid for that purpose such person or persons shall forfeit for every such sale the sum of ten pounds and if any person or persons shall sell in an inn or tavern imported malt liquors not distilled without such license as aforesaid for that purpose such person or persons shall forfeit for every such sale the sum of ten pounds and if any person or persons shall sell in any other place than in an Inn or Tavern any strong liquors in any quantity less than five gallons without such license as aforesaid for that purpose such person or persons shall forfiet for every such sale the sum of ten pounds; which said several

14. In the margin opposite this sentence H wrote the words "1st of March." Immediately below it he left a space in the MS opposite which the words "Cities of New York Albany" appear in the margin.

15. In the margin opposite this sentence H wrote "when to commence."

forfeitures shall be recoverable with costs of suit in an action or actions of debt one moiety thereof to the use of any person who will sue for the same and the other moiety to the use of the people of this state.

And be it further enacted by the authority aforesaid that the mode of collecting the said duty upon licenses to marry shall be as follows to Wit The Judge of the Court of Probates shall cause one thousand licenses at the least in each year and as many more as he shall find necessary to be printed at the expence of the state in such form as he shall judge proper with blanks therein for the names of the parties; which licenses shall be sealed with the seal of the said Court of Probates and shall be signed by the judge thereof for the time being and shall be by him distributed among the surrogates of the several counties to be by them disposed of to such persons as shall apply for the same paying therefore at the rate aforesaid. And the said Judge shall charge each surrogate in account with the number delivered to him and the amount of the duty thereupon and each surrogate shall account with the said Judge once in each year at such time as he shall prescribe for the licenses delivered to him and shall pay for all such as he shall not at the time of such accounting produce and return to the said Judge undisposed of. And the said Judge shall account for and pay to the treasurer of the state yearly the amount of the monies by him received for the said licenses deducting thereout for his trouble in the management thereof two shillings for each license so disposed of out of which he shall allow and pay to each surrogate six pence for each license by him disposed of and accounted for for his care and trouble therein.

And be it further enacted by the authority aforesaid that the mode of collection of the said tax upon lands shall be as follows to Wit The meadow arable and pasture land within each City town Manor precinct and district shall be distinguished into three classes that of the best quality in the first class to be rated at three pence per acre that of the middling and most common quality into the second class to be rated at two pence per acre and that of the worst quality into the third class to be rated at one pence per acre that is to say all above the middling and most common quality shall be rated in the first class and all below the middling and most common quality shall be rated in the third class. And The Assessors of each City town manor precinct and district shall at the time of the yearly visit and inspection of dwelling houses to be made as aforesaid examine the owners and possessors of lands touching the quantity of lands of the different kinds and qualities that is to say the quantity of meadow arable and pasture land of the several qualities aforesaid and the quantity of wood land except as before excepted in their respective possessions and shall enter in the said book to be by them kept as aforesaid together with the names of such Owners and possessors of lands in separate columns the quantity of the said several kinds of land in the possession of each person that is to say the quantity of meadow arable and pasture land of the first class in one column the quantity of arable meadow & pasture land of the second class in another column the quantity of arable meadow and pasture land of the third class in another column and the quantity of wood land except as before excepted in another column and in another column the amount of the tax thereupon; provided that it shall be at the discretion of such assessors to class the lands of each person according to the best of their information knowlege and judgment and in case any person [16] and in case any owner or possessor of land should be absent at the time of such visit and inspection as aforesaid or should refuse to answer touching the quantity and several kinds of land in his or her possession then and in every such case it shall be lawful for the Assessors respectively and they are hereby required to estimate and enter in the book to be by them kept as aforesaid according to the best of their skill and understanding the quantity and several kinds of land in the possession of each person so being absent or refusing to answer. Provided that when the owner of any farm tract or parcel of land shall not reside within the town manor precinct or district in which such land shall be, his bailiff Agent or overseer having the care and custody of the land shall be examined and received to answer touching the same in his stead. And in case such assessors respectively shall not be satisfied with the account rendered them

16. On the MS H wrote the letter "B," indicating an insertion. The insertion has not been found.

by any possessor or possessors of land but shall see reason to suspect that the same falls short of the quantity of meadow arable and pasture land really in his possession it shall be lawful for such assessors to order a survey of the premises and if it shall be found upon such survey that the real quantity exceeds the quantity alleged in the proportion of one acre in eight the expence of such survey shall be borne and paid by the possessor of the land but if there shall be no excess or if the excess shall fall short of that proportion then the expence of such survey shall be a county charge. And if any possessor of land shall with intent to defraud the public revenue wilfully conceal any part of the land in his possession he shall forfeit and pay for every acre of meadow arable and pasture land so concealed one shilling and for every hundred acres of wood land so concealed four shillings to be recovered with costs of suit in an action or actions of debt founded upon this statute to be brought in the name of any person who will sue for the same, one half to the use of the prosecutor and the other half to the use of the People of this state; which intent to defraud the revenue shall be tried by the jury charged with the cause upon the facts and circumstances of the case. And each [17]

of New York Cities of Albany and Hudson six pence in the pound in the Counties of Richmond Kings Queens Suffolk and West Chester Eight pence in the pound and in the Counties of Orange Ulster Columbia Dutchess Albany Montgomery and Washington nine pence in the pound of all the monies by him collected and received.

And be it further enacted by the authority aforesaid that the Assessors of each town ward manor precinct and district respectively before they enter upon the execution of their respective offices shall take and subscribe an oath to be administered by any justice of the peace of the City or County whereof they are respectively Assessors in the form following I        do swear in the presence of Almighty God that I will faithfully honestly and diligently to the best of my skill and understanding execute the office of Assessor of        without favour or affection prejudice or malice to any person whomsoever; which first blank shall be filled with the name

17. Page or pages missing. In the missing section H probably discussed the responsibilities and remuneration of the collectors.

of such assessor and the last with the name of the place whereof he is assessor [18] and the said Assessors shall be paid for their trouble in the execution of the duties assigned them by this act at the charge of the town manor precinct or district whereof they are respectively assessors according to such allowances as shall be made in that behalf by the respective supervisors to be raised in the same manner as the other contingent expences of the County.

And be it further enacted by the authority aforesaid that the Treasurers of the several counties shall as soon as may be after they have received the returns from the several districts make out a general return distinguished by districts of all the persons in the respective counties liable to the taxes and duties aforesaid specifying in proper and distinct columns the several articles and the descriptions thereof in the possession of each person and the amount of the said taxes and duties thereupon and it is hereby made the duty of the said County treasurers to superintend the Collectors in the execution of their respective offices and to call them to account for all defaults and neglects. And the said County treasurers shall be allowed for their care and trouble in and about the several matters committed to them by this act ten shillings out of every hundred pounds by them respectively received.

And be it further enacted by the authority aforesaid that if any person duly elected an assessor in any City town ward manor precinct or district shall refuse or decline serving in the said capacity of assessor for any other cause than bodily infirmity to be proved to the satisfaction of a jury; such person so refusing or declining to serve shall forfeit Fifty pounds to be recovered with costs of suit in an action of debt founded upon this statute to be brought in the name of the Supervisor of the City town manor precinct or district whereof he shall be so duly elected Assessor one moiety thereof to the use of such supervisor and the other moiety to the use of the People. And each Collector who shall be duly elected &

18. The material beginning with the words "any justice of the peace" and ending with the words "whereof he is assessor" is an insertion to replace crossed out material. Immediately preceding the words "any justice of the peace" the word "or" was written. H then substituted the word "by" but neglected to cross out "or."

who shall refuse or decline serving unless for the cause aforesaid shall forfeit fifty pounds to be recovered and applied in the same manner as the penalty aforesaid on Assessors subject nethertheless to the provisions hereinbefore made for admitting candidates with a smaller number of votes; and provided that the said penalty shall not be incurred until by virtue of the said provisions such collector ought to serve without giving security. Provided also that no person shall be obliged to serve in the offices of Assessor or collector for more than one year in the span of three yrs. And provided lastly that in case any Assessor or Collector shall neglect to execute any of the duties by this act required of him within the time for that purpose limited such Assessor or collector shall be liable to the penalties by this act prescribed or by any other law accruing for such neglect or disobedience; but the powers hereby vested in him shall not cease or be determined thereby but may be executed at any time afterwards.

And be it further enacted by the authority aforesaid that the Treasurer of the State shall do the duties of Treasurer of the City and County of New York and the Mayor Recorder and Alderman or the Majority of them, of whom the Mayor or Recorder always to be one, shall do the duties of and be considered as Supervisors of the City and County of New York.

And be it further enacted by the authority aforesaid that it shall be the duty of the Treasurer of the state and he is hereby required to superintend the assessment and colle⟨ction⟩ of the taxes and duties aforesaid and in order that there may be uniformity in the manner of proceeding the said treasurer shall as soon as may be after the passing of this act prepare a formula or model for the Assessors whereby to regulate the entries to be made in the book to be by them provided as aforesaid according to the directions of this act, and shall transmit a sufficient number of copies of the said formula to the supervisors of the several cities towns manors precincts and districts to be distributed among the assessors, to the end that each assessor may be furnished with one of the said copies for the regulation of his said entries. And the said treasurer shall from time to time give such instructions to the several officers employed in and about the assessment collection and receipt of the said taxes and duties conformably to this [19]

19. Page or pages missing.

Many amendments were made to the bill proposed by H during the course of debate in the Senate and Assembly. The act that was passed on April 11 (*Laws of the State of New York*, II, 505–06), neither imposed specific duties nor incorporated the proposed reforms in the manner of assessment and collection. It merely levied a quota on each county in the state, making the assessors in the respective counties responsible for the determination of taxable property and the rates to be imposed.

For H's remarks on "An Act for Raising Certain Yearly Taxes Within This State," see "Remarks on An Act for Raising Certain Yearly Taxes Within This State," February 17, 20, March 2, 9, 1787.

## New York Assembly. Remarks on an Act for the Relief of Arthur Noble [1]

[New York, February 9, 1787]

The intention of this bill was to enable the commissioners of the land office to convey to Mr. Noble, two townships of ten miles square, at one shilling per acre, for the purpose of settling Irish emigrants.

On considering this bill by paragraphs, some conversation arose in which Gen. Malcom, Col. Hamilton, and Mr. Jones were the principal speakers.

Mr. Hamilton and Mr. Jones were both of opinion that there should be no limitation or stipulation in the bill; [2] it was not within the province of the house to interfere at present, between Mr. Noble and those whom he might induce to come with him from Ireland. Mr. Noble had been naturalized, he could hold lands. The others were foreigners, were not known, and could not therefore make purchases. It might be proper hereafter to make a provision, but was not so now.

Mr. Hamilton observed that Mr. Noble was a gentleman of fortune, whose ambition was to improve a great waste tract of our country, and that he ought to have every encouragement the state could give.

*The* [New York] *Daily Advertiser*, February 12, 1787.

1. "An act for the relief of Arthur Noble, and others" was introduced on

February 6. It provided that the commissioners of the land office should grant to Arthur Noble "a quantity of land equal to one township of ten miles, or two townships of eight miles square, of the waste and unappropriated lands in any part of this State, on such terms and conditions, as to them shall appear most conducive to the interest thereof, on his, the said Arthur Noble's paying into the treasury of this State, at and after the rate of one shilling per acre, in certificates made receivable by law in the treasury, on the sale of unappropriated land" (*Laws of the State of New York*, II, 394-95).

2. William Malcom had argued that the act should stipulate that those to whom land was conveyed by Noble be citizens and freeholders.


## From Israel Beach

*Newark [New Jersey] February 13, 1787.* Requests advice on the payment of certain bonds.

ALS, Hamilton Papers, Library of Congress.


## New York Assembly. Remarks on Report Concerning Citizens of New York who Loaned Money in Hartford during the American Revolution

*New York, February 13, 1787.* Hamilton spoke on the report of a "committee on the petition of those citizens of this state who have loaned their money during the late war, in Hartford, praying this state to take those monies on loan, and put them on the footing of other citizens, who loaned their money at the continental loan-office in this state." Hamilton, according to the newspaper account of his speech, "thought it a subject of some moment, therefore to gain time for examining into its merits, he moved that the report be postponed, which the house agreed to." [1]

*The New-York Journal, and Weekly Register*, February 22, 1787.
   1. The New York Assembly *Journal* contains no reference to this committee report.


## New York Assembly. Report on the Petition of William Edgar [1]

*New York, February 13, 1787.* As chairman of a committee Hamilton on this date issued a report on "the petition of William Edgar, and others, proprietors of lands in the patent commonly called the

Oneida purchase, praying leave to bring in a bill for the partition of the said tract of land." [2]

New York Assembly *Journal*, 1787, 46.

1. For information on William Edgar, see Jeremiah Wadsworth to H, November 11, 1785.

2. The Assembly resolved that the petitioners be given leave to bring in a bill providing for the partition of the lands.


## New York Assembly. Report on the Petition of Margaret Livingston

*New York, February 13, 1787.* On this date Hamilton reported on behalf of a committee of which he was chairman on a petition from Margaret Livingston and others: "Proprietors in part of the Township of New-Stamford, in the County of Ulster, praying leave to present a bill for the partition of the said Township." [1]

New York Assembly *Journal*, 46.

1. The committee report was agreed to by the Assembly which resolved that leave be granted to Margaret Livingston and others to present a bill for the partition of the township.


## New York Assembly. Remarks on the Petition of Catharine Livingston

[New York, February 13, 1787]

The committee on Catharine Livingston's petition, reported, that the state ought to receive their debt from her in loan-office certificates.[1]

Mr. Hamilton did not approve of extending partial relief, many others might be in similar circumstances, and he wished the bill to be brought in on general principles, as by this means, the house would avoid being troubled with repeated particular applications.

*The New-York Journal, and Weekly Register,* February 22, 1787.

1. The New York Assembly *Journal* records neither the receipt of a petition from Catharine Livingston nor a debate on it. *The New-York Journal* may have mistakenly identified the petitioner as Catharine Livingston, for on the same day H, as chairman of a committee, delivered a report on a petition from Margaret Livingston.

## New York Assembly. Remarks on an Act for Settling Intestate Estates, Proving Wills, and Granting Administrations [1]

[New York, February 14, 1787]

Mr. Hamilton said that he did not rise to oppose the motion of the gentleman who last spoke.[2] He should probably vote with him on the question; but he confessed he did not view it in quite so clear a light as that gentleman appeared to do. There appeared to him to be difficulties in the case, which he would candidly lay before the house to assist its judgment. The objection is that a new court is erected, or an old one invested with a new jurisdiction, in which it is not bound to proceed according to the course of the common law. The question is what is meant in the constitution, by this phrase "the common law"? These words have in a legal view two senses, one more *extensive*, the other more *strict*. In their most extensive sense, they comprehend the constitution, of all those courts which were established by immemorial custom, such as the court of chancery, the ecclesiastical court, &c. though these courts proceed according to a peculiar law. In their more strict sense, they are confined to the course of proceedings in the courts of Westminster in England, or in the supreme court in this state. If the words are understood in the first sense, the bill under consideration is not unconstitutional; if in the last, it is unconstitutional. For it gives to an old court a new jurisdiction, in which it is not to proceed according to the course of the common law in *this last sense*. And to give new jurisdictions to old courts, not according to the course of the common law, is in my opinion as much an infringement in substance of this part of the constitution, as to erect new courts with such jurisdictions. To say the reverse, would be to evade the constitution.

But though I view it as a delicate and difficult question; yet I am inclined to think that the more *extensive sense* may be fairly adopted; with this limitation, that such new jurisdictions must proceed according to the course of those courts, having by the common law cognizance of the subject matter. They ought however, never to be extended to *objects*, which at common law, belonged to the jurisdiction of the courts at Westminster, and which in this state are of the peculiar cognizance of the supreme court.

At common law, the ecclesiastical courts, not the courts of Westminster, had cognizance of intestacies and testamentary causes. The bill proposes that the court of Probates shall have cognizance of the same causes, and proceed in the same manner as the ecclesiastical courts, except as to inflicting ecclesiastical penalties.

This distinction I have taken, will I am inclined to think, bear us out in passing the bill under consideration.

But it is certainly a point not without considerable difficulty.[3]

The [New York] *Daily Advertiser*, February 16, 1787.

1. "An act for settling Intestate Estates, proving Wills, and granting Administrations," after amendment by the Senate, was passed by the Assembly on February 2. On February 14, the Assembly received the objections of the Council of Revision to the act. The council objected to the sections of the act which gave the judge of probates authority to hear and determine cases involving legacies or bequests. The council maintained that the Assembly was granting the Court of Probates new powers, a grant contrary to the state constitution. The council argued that facts in a litigation must be submitted to the determination of a jury. It concluded that granting the judge of probates the authority to determine cases without a trial by jury "is depriving the citizens of this State, of a right secured to them, and rendered inviolate by the Constitution, which declares the trial by jury as a firm and unalterable establishment, in all cases where it had been used while this State was a Colony; and is also an indirect infringment of that clause of the constitution, which prohibits the institution of any new courts, but such as shall proceed according to the course of the common law" (New York Assembly *Journal*, 1787, 49).

2. Samuel Jones argued that the Assembly, despite the objections of the Council of Revision, should pass the law.

3. The Assembly, by a vote of more than two-thirds, overrode the objections of the Council of Revision (New York Assembly *Journal*, 1787, 49).

The act was passed under the date of February 20. See *Laws of the State of New York*, II, 419–24.

## New York Assembly. Report on the Petition of Isaac Gouverneur, Junior [1]

[New York, February 14, 1787]

Mr. Hamilton, from the Committee to whom was referred the petition of Isaac Gouverneur, junior, praying a divorce, reported, that it is the opinion of the Committee, that some general provision ought to be made for granting relief in cases of Adultry; that the

Committee have prepared the draft of a bill for that purpose, and have directed him to move for leave to bring in the same.

*Ordered,* That leave be given accordingly.

Mr. Hamilton, according to leave brought in the said bill entitled, *An act directing a mode of Trial, and allowing of Divorces in cases of Adultry;* which was read the first time, and ordered a second reading.

New York Assembly *Journal,* 1787, 48.
   1. On January 22, a petition from Isaac Gouverneur, Jr., son of the prominent New York merchant, praying a divorce was read and referred to a committee of which H was chairman.
   2. The act introduced by H was passed on March 30. See "AN ACT directing a mode of trial, and allowing of divorces in cases of adultery." *Laws of the State of New York,* II, 494–95.

# New York Assembly. Remarks on an Act Granting to Congress Certain Imposts and Duties [1]

[New York, February 15, 1787]

Mr. CHAIRMAN,
   There appears to me to have been some confusion in the manner of voting on the two preceding clauses of this bill; the first, for granting the impost to the United States, having been carried by a

*The* [New York] *Daily Advertiser,* February 26, 1787.
   1. A note printed at the end of this speech reads as follows: "The extreme length of the foregoing speech and an accident which attended the transcribing of the short hand Notes, together with our desire to lay the same before the public, entire and correct, have necessarily delayed the publication of it till this day." *The New-York Journal, and Weekly Register,* February 22, 1787, recorded that "the lengthy speech" made by H was not "even replied to by the other party, notwithstanding he was *one hour* and *twenty minutes* in delivering it."
   Consistent with a congressional resolve of April 18, 1783, calling on the states to grant Congress the authority to collect an impost, William Malcom introduced in the Assembly on February 9, 1787, "An act for granting to the United States in Congress assembled, certain Imposts and Duties upon foreign Goods imported into this State, for the purpose of discharging the Debts contracted by the United States, in the Prosecution of the late War with Great-Britain" (New York Assembly *Journal,* 1787, 41). (For information on New York's earlier response to the congressional resolution of April 18, 1783, see "Remarks on the Answer to Governor George Clinton's Message to the Legislature," January 17, 1787).
   The act introduced by Malcom provided that Congress be allowed specified duties on certain goods imported into New York and a five percent *ad valorem*

majority of one, and the last, for making the officers employed in the collection accountable to them, having been lost by a much larger majority. I was induced to hope, from the success of the first question, that the second would have met with equal success; as I presumed gentlemen who meant to adhere to the act of the last session would have opposed the whole of the present bill as unnecessary; and those who meant to depart from it, would be willing to agree substantially to the system recommended by Congress, as it had been adopted and modified by the other states generally. From the complexion of the votes on the first question, I am obliged to conclude either that I was mistaken in my ideas of the intention of the committee, or that there is some misapprehension in part of the members.

It becomes therefore necessary,—to obviate such misapprehension, if any exists, and to discharge my duty at all events,—to lay the subject fully before the committee, and to detail, at large, my reasons for wishing to see the bill in its present form prevail.

It is a common practice in entering upon the discussion of an important subject, to endeavour to conciliate the good-will of the audience to the speaker, by professions of disinterestedness and zeal for the public good. The example, however frequent, I shall no further imitate than by making one or two general observations. If in the public stations I have filled, I have acquitted myself with zeal, fidelity and disinterestedness; if in the private walk of life my conduct has been unstained by any dishonorable act, if it has been uniformly consistent with the rules of integrity, I have a right to the confidence of those to whom I address myself: They cannot refuse it to me without injustice. I am persuaded they will not refuse it to me.

---

duty on all other goods. Collectors of the tax, according to the act, were to be appointed by the New York State Council of Appointment, but they were to be accountable to and removable by the United States. The United States was granted authority to make such ordinances and regulations as were considered necessary to levy and collect the tax.

On February 15 the Assembly resolved itself into a committee of the whole to consider the act granting the impost. As stated by H in the first paragraph of his speech, the section of the act containing a grant of the impost to Congress was carried by a majority of one, but the clause making the collectors accountable to Congress was lost by a majority of nineteen (New York Assembly *Journal*, 1787, 51-52). H's speech, according to *The Daily Advertiser*, was made in support of the acceptance of the section of the bill giving Congress authority to enact regulations for levying and collecting the tax.

If, on the other hand, my public conduct has been in any instance marked with perfidy, duplicity, or with sinister views of any kind; if any imputations, founded in fact, can be adduced to the prejudice of my private character, I have no claim to the confidence of the committee, nor should I expect it.

Even these observations I should have spared myself, did I not know that, in the rage of party, gross calumnies have been propagated; some I have traced and detected; there may still be others in secret circulation with which I am unacquainted. Against the influence of such arts, I can have no other shield than the general tenor of my past conduct. If *that* will protect me I may safely confide in the candour of the committee; to that standard I chearfully submit.

But indeed of what importance is it who is the speaker? 'tis his *reasons* only that concern the committee; if these are good they owe it to themselves, and to their constituents to allow them their full weight.

The first objection (and that which is supposed to have the greatest force) against the principles of the bill is, that it would be unconstitutional to delegate legislative power to Congress. If this objection be founded in truth, there is at once an end of the enquiry. God forbid that we should violate that constitution which is the charter of our rights. But it is our duty to examine dispassionately whether it really stands in our way; if it does not, let us not erect an ideal barrier to a measure which the public good may require.

The first ground of the objection is deduced from that clause of the constitution which declares "that no power shall be exercised over the people of this state, but such as is granted by or derived from them."

This, it is plain amounts to nothing more than a declaration of that fundamental maxim of republican government, that all power, mediately, or immediately, is derived from the consent of the people, in opposition to those doctrines of despotism which uphold the divine right of kings, or lay the foundations of government in force, conquest, or necessity. It does not at all effect the question how far the legislature may go in granting power to the United States. A power conferred by the representatives of the people, if warranted by the constitution under which they act, is a power derived from the people. This is not only a plain inference of reason, but the terms of the clause itself, seem to have been calculated to let in the principle. The words "derived from" are added to the words "granted by," as if with design to distinguish an indirect derivation of power from an immediate grant of it. This explanation is even necessary to reconcile the constitution to itself, and to give effect to all its parts, as I hope fully to demonstrate in its proper place.

The next clause of the constitution relied upon is, that which declares that "the supreme legislative power *within this state* shall be vested in a senate and assembly. This, it is said, excludes the idea of any other legislative power operating within the state. But the more obvious construction of this clause, and *that* which best consists with the situation and views of the country at this time, with what has been done before and since the formation of our constitution, and with those parts of the constitution itself which acknowledge the federal government, is this— "In the distribution of the different parts of the sovereignty in the *particular* government of this state the legislative authority shall reside in a senate and assembly," or in other words, "the legislative authority of the particular government of the state of New-York shall be vested in a senate and assembly." The framers of the constitution could have had nothing more in view than to delineate the different departments of power in our own state government, and never could have intended to interfere with the formation of such a constitution for the union as the safety of the whole might require.

The justness of this construction will be further elucidated by that part of the constitution which prescribes that "the supreme executive authority *of the state* shall be vested in a governor." If the former clause excludes the grant of legislative power, this must equally exclude the grant of executive power. And the consequence would be, that there would be no federal government at all.

It will be of no avail to say, that there is a difference in the two cases in the mode of expression; that in one the terms of description are "*within the state*," in the other "*of the state*." In grammar, or good sense the difference in the phrases constitutes no substantial difference in the meaning, or if it does, it concludes against the objection; for the words, *within this state*, which are applied to the legislative power, have a certain precision that may be supposed to

intend a distinction between that legislative power which is to operate *within this state* only, and that which is to operate upon this
state in conjunction with the others. But I lay no stress on this observation. In my opinion the legislative power *"within this state,"*
or the legislative power "of this state" amount in substance to
the same thing. And therefore (as has been already observed) if the
constitution prohibits the delegation of legislative power to the
union, it equally prohibits the delegation of executive power—and
the confederacy must then be at an end: for without legislative or
executive power it becomes a nullity.

Unfortunately for the objection, if it proves any thing it proves
too much. It proves that the powers of the union in their present
form are an usurpation on the constitution of this state. This will
appear not only from the reasoning already adduced, but from this
further consideration—that the United States are already possessed
of *legislative* as well as *executive* authority. The objects of executive power are of three kinds, to make treaties with foreign nations,
to make war and peace, to execute and interpret the laws. This description of the executive power will enable us the more readily to
distinguish the legislative; which in general may be defined the power
of prescribing rules for the community.

The United States are authorised to require from the several states
as much money as they judge necessary for the general purposes of
the union, and to limit the time within which it is to be raised:
to call for such a number of troops as they deem requisite for the
common defence in time of war—to establish rules in all cases of
capture by sea or land—to regulate the alloy and value of coin; the
standard of weights and measures, and to make all laws for the government of the army and navy of the union. All these are powers
of the legislative kind, and are declared by the confederation to
be binding upon all the states.

The first is nothing less than a power of taxing the states in gross
though not in detail; and the last is the power of disposing of the
liberty and lives of the citizens of this state, when in arms for the
common defence.

That the powers enumerated are all, or most of them, of a legislative nature, will not be denied by the law members on the other
side of the question. If the constitution forbids the grant of legis-

lative power to the union, all those authorities are illegal and unconstitutional, and ought to be resumed.

If, on the contrary, those authorities were properly granted, then
it follows that the constitution does not forbid the grant of legislative power, and the objection falls to the ground; for there is nothing in the constitution permitting the grant of one kind of legislative
authority, and forbidding that of another. The degree or nature
of the powers of legislation which it might be proper to confer
upon the federal government, would in this case be a mere question
of prudence and expediency—to be determined by general considerations of utility and safety.

The principle of the objection under consideration would not only
subvert the foundation of the union as now established—would not
only render it impossible that any federal government could exist;
but would defeat some of the provisions of the consitution itself.
This last idea deserves particular attention.

The nineteenth clause makes it the duty of the governor "to correspond with the continental Congress." The twentieth provides
"that the judges and chancellor shall hold no other office than delegate to the general Congress;" and the thirtieth directs that "delegates
*to represent* this state in the general Congress of the United States
of America shall be annually appointed."

Now, Sir, I ask, if Congress were to have neither executive nor
legislative authority, to what purpose were they to exist? To what
purpose were delegates to be annually appointed to that body? To
what purpose were these delegates *to represent* this state? Or how
could they be said to represent it at all?

Is not the plain import of this part of the constitution, that they
were *to represent this state* in the general assembly of the United
States, for the purpose of managing the common concerns of the
union? And does not this necessarily imply that they were to be
cloathed with such powers as should be found essential to that object? Does it not amount to a constitutional warrant to the legislature to confer those powers of whatever kind they might be?

To answer these questions in the negative would be to charge
the constitution with the absurdity of proposing to itself an *end*,
and yet prohibiting the means of accomplishing that end.

The words "to represent this state" are of great latitude, and are of themselves sufficient to convey any power necessary to the conduct and direction of its affairs in connection with the other parts of the confederacy.

In the interpretation of laws it is admitted to be a good rule to resort to the co-existing circumstances and collect from thence the intention of the framers of the law. Let us apply this rule to the present case.

In the commencement of the revolution delegates were sent to meet in Congress with large discretionary powers. In short, generally speaking, with full power "to take care of the republic." In the whole of this transaction the idea of an *union* of the colonies was carefully held up. It pervaded all our public acts.

In the declaration of independence we find it continued and confirmed. That declaration, after setting forth its motives and causes, proceeds thus—"We, therefore, the representatives of the United States of America in general Congress assembled, appealing to the Supreme Judge of the world for the rectitude of our intentions, do in the name and by the authority of the good people of these colonies, solemnly publish and declare, that these United Colonies are and of right ought to be free and independent states; that they are absolved from all allegiance to the British crown, and that all political connection between them and the state of Great-Britain is and ought to be totally dissolved; and that as free and independent states they have full power to levy war, conclude peace, contract alliances, establish commerce, and do all other acts and things that [2] independent states may of right do."

Hence we see that the union and independence of these states are blended and incorporated in one and the same act; which, taken together clearly, imports, that the United States had in their origin full power to do all acts and things which independent states may of right do; or, in other words, full power of sovereignty.

Accordingly we find that upon the authority of that act only approved by the several states, they did levy war, contract alliances, and exercise other high powers of sovereignty even to the appointment of a dictator prior to the present confederation.[3]

2. In original, "what."
3. The dictator to whom H alludes cannot be determined. He may have referred to Robert Morris whose powers as Superintendent of Finance were considered by many as dictatorial.

In this situation, and with this plenitude of power, our constitution knows and acknowledges the United States in Congress assembled, and provides for the annual appointment of delegates to represent this state in that body; which in substance amounts to a constitutional recognition of the union with complete sovereignty.

A government may exist without any formal organization or precise definition of its powers. However improper it might have been that the federal government should have continued to exist with such absolute and undefined authority this does not militate against the position that it did possess such authority. It only proves the propriety of a more regular formation to ascertain its limits. This was the object of the present confederation, which is, in fact, an abridgment of the original sovereignty of the union.

It may be said (for it has been said upon other occasions) that, though the constitution did consider the United States in the light I have described, and left the legislature at liberty in the first instance to have organized the federal government in such a manner as they thought proper, yet that liberty ceased with the establishment of the present confederacy. The discretion of the legislature was then determined.

This upon the face of it is a subtilty, uncountenanced by a single principle of government, or a single expression of the constitution. It is saying that a general authority given to the legislature for the permanent preservation and good of the community, has been exhausted and spent by the exercise of a part of that authority. The position is the more destitute of colour; because the confederation, by the express terms of the compact, preserves and continues this power. The last clause of it authorises Congress to propose, and the states to agree to such alterations as might be afterwards found necessary or expedient.

We see therefore that the constitution knows and acknowledges the United States in Congress; that it provides for the annual appointment of delegates *to represent this state* in that body without prescribing the objects or limits of that representation: That at the time our constitution was framed, the union existed with full sovereignty; and that therefore the idea of sovereignty in the union is not incompatible with it. We see further, that the doctrine contained in the objection against granting legislative power, would equally operate against granting executive power; would prove that the powers already vested in the union are illegal and unconstitutional; would render a confederacy of the states in any form impracticable and would defeat all those provisions of our own constitution which relate to the United States. I submit it to the committee, whether a doctrine pregnant with such consequences can be true—whether it is not as opposite to our constitution as to the principles of national safety and prosperity—and whether it would not be lamentable if the zeal of opposition to a particular measure should carry us to the extreme of imposing upon the constitution a sense foreign to it; which might embarrass the national councils upon future occasions, when all might agree in the utility and necessity of a different construction.

If the arguments I have used under this head are not well founded, let gentlemen *come forward and shew their fallacy.* Let the subject have a fair and full examination, and let truth, on whatever side it may be, prevail!

Flattering myself it will appear to the committee that the constitution at least offers us no impediment—I shall proceed to other topics of objection. The next that presents itself is a supposed danger to liberty from granting legislative power to Congress.

But before I enter upon this subject, to remove the aspersions thrown upon that body, I shall give a short history of some material facts relating to the origin and progress of the business. To excite the jealousies of the people, it has been industriously represented as an undue attempt to acquire an increase of power. It has been forgotten or intentionally overlooked, that considering it in the strongest light as a proposal to alter the confederation, it is only exercising a power which the confederation has in direct terms reposed in Congress; who as before observed, are by the 13th article, expressly authorised to propose alterations.

By so far was the measure from originating in improper views of that body, that if I am rightly informed, it did not originate there at all—it was first suggested by a convention of the four Eastern states, and New-York, at Hartford; and I believe was proposed there by the deputies of this state.[4] A gentleman on our bench, uncon-

4. The convention to which H refers was held in Hartford, Connecticut, in November, 1780. It developed from an earlier convention held in Boston in

nected with Congress, who now hears me (I mean judge Hobart) [5] was one of them. It was dictated by a principle which *bitter experience then* taught us, and which in peace or war will always be found true—that adequate supplies to the federal treasury, can never flow from any system which requires the intervention of thirteen deliberatives between the *call* and the *execution*.

Congress agreed to the measure and recommended it. This state complied without hesitation. All parts of the government, senate, assembly, and council of revision concurred—neither the constitution nor the public liberty presented any obstacle—the difficulties from these sources are a recent discovery.

So late as the first session of the legislature after the evacuation of this city, the governor of the state in his speech to both houses, gave a decided countenance to the measure—this he does, though not in express terms, yet by implications not to be misunderstood.

The *leading opponents* of the impost, of the present day, have all of them at other times, either concurred in the measure in its most exceptionable form, and without the qualifications annexed to it by the proposed bill, or have by other instances of conduct contradicted their own hypothesis on the constitution which professedly forms the main prop of their opposition.

The honorable member in my eye, (Mr. Jones,) at the last session brought in a bill for granting to the United States, the power of regulating the trade of the union. This surely includes more ample legislative authority than is comprehended in the mere power of levying a particular duty. It indeed goes to a prodigious extent much farther than on a superficial view can be imagined. Can we believe that the constitutional objection, if well founded would so long have passed undiscovered and unnoticed? or is it fair to impute to Congress criminal motives for proposing a measure which was first recommended to them by five states, or from persisting in that measure after the unequivocal experience they have had of

---

August, 1780, the proceedings of which were sent to New York with a request for its concurrence. The New York legislature appointed commissioners to meet with the representatives of the eastern states in Hartford in November. The convention in Hartford reaffirmed the recommendations previously made in Boston.

5. John Sloss Hobart, a justice of the New York Supreme Court, had represented New York at the Hartford convention.

the total inefficacy of the mode provided in the confederation for supplying the treasury of the union?

I leave the answer to these questions to the good sense and candor of the committee and shall return to the examination of the question, how far the power proposed to be conferred upon Congress, would be dangerous to the liberty of the people. And here I ask,

Whence can this danger arise? The members of Congress are annually chosen by the several legislatures—they are removable at any moment at the pleasure of those legislatures. They come together with different habits, prejudices and interests. They are in fact continually changing. How is it possible for a body so composed to be formidable to the liberties of states, several of which are large empires in themselves?

The subversion of the liberty of these states could not be the business of a day. It would at least require time, premeditation and concert. Can it be supposed that the members of a body so constituted would be unanimous in a scheme of usurpation? If they were not, would it not be discovered and disclosed? If we could even suppose this unanimity among one set of men, can we believe that all the new members who are yearly sent from one state or another would instantly enter into the same views? Would there not be found one honest man to warn his country of the danger?

Suppose the worst—suppose the combination entered into and continued—the execution would at least announce the design; and the means of defence would be easy. Consider the separate power of several of these states, and the situation of all. Consider the extent populousness and resources of Massachusetts, Virginia, Pennsylvania; I might add of New-York, Connecticut, and other states. Where could Congress find means sufficient to subvert the government and liberties of either of these states! or rather where find means sufficient to effect the conquest of all? If an attempt was made upon one, the others from a sense of common danger, would make common cause; and they could immediately unite and provide for their joint defence.

There is one consideration of immense force in this question not sufficiently attended to. It is this, that each state possesses in itself the full powers of government, and can at once in a regular and constitutional way, take measures for the preservation of its rights.

In a single kingdom or state, if the rulers attempt to establish a tyranny, the people can only defend themselves by a tumultary insurrection; they must run to arms without concert or plan; while the usurpers cloathed with the forms of legal authority can employ the forces of the state to suppress them in embryo; and before they can have time or opportunity to give system to their opposition. With us the case is widely different, each state has a government completely organized in itself; and can at once enter into a regular plan of defence, with the forces of the community at its command it can immediately form connections with its neighbours, or even with foreign powers, if necessary.

In a contest of this kind the body of the people will always be on the side of the state governments. This will not only result from their love of liberty and regard to their own safety; but from other strong principles of human nature. The state governments operate upon those immediate familiar personal concerns to which the sensibility of individuals is awake. The distribution of private justice belonging to them; they must always appear to the senses of the people as the immediate guardians of their rights—they will of course have the strongest hold on their attachment, respect and obedience. Another circumstance will contribute to the same end: Far the greatest number of offices and employments are in the gift of the states separately—the weight of official influence will therefore be in favor of the state governments; and with all these advantages they cannot fail to carry the people along with them in every contest with the general government in which they are not palpably in the wrong, and often when they are. What is to be feared from the efforts of Congress to establish a tyranny with the great body of the people under the direction of their state governments combined in opposition to their views? Must not their attempts recoil upon themselves, and terminate in their own ruin and disgrace? or rather would not these considerations, if they were insensible to other motives, forever restrain them from making such attempts.

The causes taken notice of as securing the attachment of the people to their local governments, present us with another important truth—the natural imbecility of federal governments, and the danger that they will never be able to exercise power enough to manage the general affairs of the union. Though the states will have a common interest; yet they will also have a particular interest. For example, as a part of the union, it will be the interest of every state, that the general government should be supplied with the revenues necessary for the national purposes; but it will be the particular interest of each state to pay as little itself and to let its neighbours pay as much as possible. Particular interests have always more influence upon men than general. The several states therefore consulting their immediate advantage may be considered as so many eccentric powers tending in a contrary direction to the government of the union; and as they will generally carry the people along with them, the confederacy will be in continual danger of dissolution.

This, Mr. Chairman is the real rock upon which the happiness of this country is likely to split—this is the point to which our fears and cares should be directed—to guard against this and not to terrify ourselves with imaginary dangers from the spectre of power in Congress will be our true wisdom.

But let us examine a little more closely the measure under consideration. What does the bill before us require us to do? merely to grant certain duties on imposts to the United States for the short period of twenty-five years,—to be applied to the discharge of the principal and interest of the debts contracted for the support of the late war; the collection of which duties, is to be made by officers appointed by the state but accountable to Congress, according to such general regulations as the United States shall establish; subject to these important checks, that no citizen should be carried out of the state for trial; that all prosecutions shall be in our own courts; that no excessive fines or penalties shall be imposed; and that a yearly account of the proceeds and application of the revenue shall be rendered to the legislature, on failure of which, it reserves to itself a right of repealing its grant.

Is it possible for any measure to be better guarded? or is it possible that a grant for such precise objects and with so many checks can be dangerous to the public liberty?

Having now, as I trust, satisfactorily shewn that the constitution offers no obstacle to the measure; and that the liberty of the people cannot be endangered by it; it remains only to consider it in the view of revenue.

The sole question left for discussion, is, whether it be an eligible mode of supplying the federal treasury or not?

The better to answer this question it will be of use to examine how far the mode by quotas and requisitions has been found competent to the public exigencies.

The universal delinquency of the states during the war, shall be passed over with the bare mention of it. The public embarrassments were a plausible apology for that delinquency; and [if] it was hoped the peace would produce greater punctuality the experiment has disappointed that hope to a degree, which confounds the least sanguine. A comparative view of the compliances of the several states, for the five last years will furnish a striking result.

During that period as appears by a statement on our files, New-Hampshire, North-Carolina, South-Carolina and Georgia, have paid nothing. I say nothing because the only actual payment, is the trifling sum of about 7000 dollars, by New-Hampshire. South-Carolina indeed has credits but these are merely by way of discount, on the supplies furnished by her during the war, in consideration of her peculiar sufferings and exertions while the immediate theatre of it.

Connecticut and Delaware, have paid about one third of their requisitions. Massachusetts, Rhode-Island, and Maryland, about one half. Virginia, about three fifths; Pennsylvania, nearly the whole, and New-York, more than her quota.

These proportions are taken on the specie requisitions, the indents have been very partially paid, and in their present state, are of little account.

The payments into the federal treasury have declined rapidly each year. The whole amount for three years past in specie, has not exceeded 1,400,000 dollars, of which New-York has paid 100 per cent, more than her proportion. This sum, little more than 400,000 dollars a year, it will readily be conceived has been exhausted in the support of the civil establishments of the union, and the necessary guards and garrisons at public arsenals, and on the frontiers; without any surplus for paying any part of the debt, foreign or domestic, principal or interest.

Things are continually growing worse, the last year in particular produced less than two hundred thousand dollars, and that from only two or three states. Several of the states have been so long unaccustomed to pay, that they seem no longer concerned even about the appearances of compliance.

Connecticut and Jersey have almost formally declined paying any longer. The ostensible motive is the non-concurrence of this state in the impost system. The real one must be conjectured from the fact.

Pennsylvania, if I understand the scope of some late resolutions, means to discount the interest she pays upon her assumption to her own citizens; in which case, there will be little coming from her to the United States. This seems to be bringing matters to a crisis.

The pecuniary support of the federal government has of late devolved almost entirely upon Pennsylvania and New-York. If Pennsylvania refuses to contine her aid, what will be the situation of New-York? Are we willing to be the Atlas of the union? or are we willing to see it perish?

This seems to be the alternative. Is there not a species of political knight errantry in adhering pertinaciously to a system which throws the whole weight of the confederacy upon this state, or upon one or two more? Is it not our interest on mere calculations of state-policy, to promote a measure which operating under the same regulations in every state, must produce an equal, or nearly equal, effect every where, and oblige all the states to share the common burthen?

If the impost is granted to the United-States, with the power of levying it, it must have a proportional effect in all the states; for the same mode of collection every where, will have nearly the same result every where.

What must be the final issue of the present state of things? Will the few states that now contribute, be willing to contribute much longer? Shall we ourselves be long content with bearing the burthen singly? will not our zeal for a particular system, soon give way to the pressure of so unequal a weight? and if all the states cease to pay, what is to become of the union? It is sometimes asked why do not Congress oblige the states to do their duty; but where are the means? Where are the fleets and armies, where the federal treasury to support those fleets and armies, to enforce the requisitions of the union?

All methods short of coertion, have repeatedly been tried in vain.

Let us now proceed to another most important inquiry. How are we to pay our foreign debt?

This I think is estimated at about 7000,000 of dollars; which will every year increase with the accumulations of interest. It we pay neither principal nor interest, we not only abandon all pretensions to character as a nation; but we endanger the public peace. However, it may be in our power to evade the just demands of our domestic creditors; our foreign creditors must and will be paid.

They have power to enforce their demands, and sooner or later they may be expected to do it. It is not my intention to endeavour to excite the apprehensions of the committee; but I would appeal to their prudence. A discreet attention to the consequences of national measures is no impeachment of our firmness.

The foreign debt, I say, must sooner or later he paid, and the longer provision is delayed, the heavier it must fall at last.

We require about 1,600,000 dollars, to discharge the interest and instalments of the present year; about a million annually upon an average for ten years more, and about 300,000 dollars for another ten years.

The product of the impost, may be computed at about a million of dollars annually. It is an increasing fund—this fund would not only suffice for the discharge of the foreign debt, but important operations might be ingrafted upon it, towards the extinguishment of the domestic debt.

Is it possible to hesitate about the propriety of adopting a resource so easy in itself and so extensive in its effects?

Here I expect I may be told there is no objection to employing this resource; the act of the last session does it. The only dispute is about the mode. We are willing to grant the *money* but not the *power* required from us. Money will pay our debts; power may destroy our liberties. It has been insinuated that nothing but a lust of power would have prevented Congress from accepting the grant in the shape it has already passed the legislature.

This is a severe charge; if true, it ought undoubtedly to prevent our going a step further. But it is easy to show that Congress could not have accepted our grant without removing themselves further from the object, than they now are. To gain one state they must have lost all the others.

The grants of every state are accompanied with a condition, that similar grants be made by the other states. It is not denied that our act is essentially different from theirs. Their acts give the United States the power of collecting the duty—Ours reserves it to the state, and makes it receivable in paper money.

The immediate consequence of accepting our grant would be a relinquishment of the grants of the other states; they must take the matter up anew, and do the work over again, to accommodate it to our standard. In order to anchor one state, would it have been wise to set twelve, or at least eleven others afloat?

It is said that the states which have granted *more* would certainly be willing to grant *less*. They would easily accommodate their acts to that of New-York, as more favorable to their own power and security.

But would Massachusetts and Virginia, which have no paper money of their own, accede to a plan that permitted other states to pay in paper while they paid in *specie?* Would they consent that their citizens should pay *twenty* shillings in the pound, while the citizens of Rhode-Island paid only *four*, the citizens of North-Carolina *ten*, and of other states in different degrees of inequality, in proportion to the relative depreciation of their paper? Is it wise in this state to cherish a plan that gives such an advantage to the citizens of other states over its own?

The paper money of the state of New-York, in most transactions is equal to gold and silver—that of Rhode-Island is depreciated to five for one—that of North-Carolina to two for one—that of South-Carolina may perhaps be worth fifteen shillings in the pound.

If the states pay the duties in paper, is it not evident that for every pound of that duty consumed by the citizen of New-York he would pay 20s. while the citizen of South-Carolina would pay 15s. of North-Carolina, 10s and Rhode-Island, only four!

This consideration alone, is sufficient to condemn the plan of our grant of last session, and to prove incontestably, that the states which are averse to emitting a paper currency, or have it in their power to support one when emitted, would never come into it.

Again, would those states which by their public acts demonstrate a conviction that the powers of the union require augmentation; which are conscious of energy in their own administration—would they be willing to concur in a plan, which left the collection of the duties in the hands of each state, and of course subject to all the inequalities which a more or less vigourous system of collection would produce?

This too is an idea which ought to have great weight with us—we have better habits of government than are to be found in some of the states—and our constitution admits of more energy than the constitution of most of the other states—the duties therefore would be more effectually collected with us than in such states, and this would have a similar effect to the depreciation of the money, in imposing a greater burthen on the citizens of this state.

If any state should incline to evade the payment of the duties, having the collection in its own hands, nothing would be easier than to effect it, and without materially sacrificing appearances.

It is manifest from this view of the subject, that we have the strongest reasons as a state, to depart from our own act: and that it would have been highly injudicious in Congress to have accepted it.

If there even had been a prospect of the concurrence of the other states in the plan, how inadequate would it have been to the public exigencies—fettered with the embarrassments of a depreciating paper.

It is to no purpose to say that the faith of the state was pledged by the act, to make the paper equal to gold and silver—and that the other states would be obliged to do the same; what greater dependance can be had on the faith of the states pledged to this measure, than on the faith they pledged in the confederation, sanctioned by a solemn appeal to heaven. If the obligation of faith in one case, have had so little influence upon their conduct in respect to the requisitions of Congress; what hope can there be that they would have greater influence in respect to the deficiencies of the paper money?

There yet remains an important light in which to consider the subject in the view of revenue. It is a clear point that we cannot carry the duties upon imposts to the same extent by separate arrangements as by a general plan—we must regulate ourselves by what we find done in the neighbouring states: while Pennsylvania has only two and a half per cent. on her importations we cannot greatly exceed her—we must content ourselves with the same or nearly the same rate. To go much beyond it would injure our commerce in a variety of ways, and would defeat itself—while the ports of Connecticut and Jersey are open to the introduction of goods, free from duty and the conveyance from them to us is so easy—while they consider our imposts as an ungenerous advantage taken of them, which it would be laudable to elude, the duties must be light or they would be evaded—the facility of doing it, and the temptation to do it would be both so great that we should collect, perhaps less by an increase of the rates than we do now. Already we experience the effects of this situation. But if the duties were to be levied under a common direction, with the same precautions every where to guard against smuggling, they might be carried without prejudice to trade to a much more considerable height.

As things now are, we must adhere to the present standard of duties, without any material alterations. Suppose this to produce fifty thousand pounds a year. The duties to be granted to Congress ought, in proportion, to produce double that sum. To this it appears by a scheme now before us, that additional duties might be imposed for the use of the state, on certain enumerated articles, to the amount of thirty thousand pounds. This would be an augmentation of our national revenue by indirect taxation to the extent of eighty thousand pounds a year; an immense object in a single state, which alone demonstrates the good policy of the measure.

It is no objection to say that a great part of this fund will be dedicated to the use of the United States. Their exigencies must be supplied in some way or other—the more is done towards it by means of the impost, the less will be to be done in other modes. If we do not employ that resource to the best account, we must find others in direct taxation. And to this are opposed all the habits and prejudices of the community. There is not a farmer in the state who would not pay a shilling in the voluntary consumption of articles on which a duty is paid, rather than a penny imposed immediately on his house and land.

There is but one objection to the measure under consideration that has come to my knowledge, which yet remains to be discussed. I mean the effect it is supposed to have upon our paper currency.

It is said the diversion of this fund would leave the credit of the paper without any effectual support.

Though I should not be disposed to put a consideration, of this kind in competition with the safety of the union; yet I should be extremely cautious about doing any thing that might affect the credit of our currency. The legislature having thought an emission of paper advisable, I consider it my duty as a representative of the people to take care of its credit. But it appears to me that apprehensions on this score are without foundation.

What has hitherto been the principal support of the credit of the paper? Two things—the universal demand for money, and the immediate interest of the merchants to countenance whatever would facilitate the recovery of his debts. The first cause begat a general clamour in the country for a paper emission, and a disposition to uphold its credit. The farmers appeared willing to exchange their produce for it; the merchant on the other hand, had large debts outstanding; they supposed that giving a free circulation to the paper, would enable their customers in the country to pay, and as they perceived, that they would have it in their power to convert the money into produce, they naturally resolved to give it their support.

These causes combined to introduce the money into general circulation, and having once obtained credit, it will now be able to support itself.

The chief difficulty to have been apprehended in respect to the paper, was to overcome the diffidence which the still recent experience of depreciating paper, had instilled into mens minds. This, it was to have been feared, would have shaken its credit at its outset; and if it had once began to sink, it would be no easy matter to prevent its total decline.

The event has however turned out otherwise and the money has been fortunate enough to conciliate the general confidence. This point gained, there need be no apprehensions of its future fate, unless the government should do something to destroy that confidence.

The causes that first gave it credit, still operate, and will in all probability continue to do so. The demand for money has not lessened, and the merchant has still the same inducement to countenance the circulation of the paper.

I shall not deny that the outlet which the payment of duties fur-

nished to the merchant, was an additional motive to the reception
of the paper. Nor is it proposed to take away this motive. There
is now before the house a bill, one object of which is, the establishment of a state impost, on certain enumerated articles, in addition to
that to be granted to the United States. It is computed on very good
grounds that the additional duties would amount to about 30,000 £.
and as they would be payable in paper currency, they would create
a sufficient demand upon the merchant, to leave him in this respect,
substantially the same inducement which he had before. Indeed independent of this, the readiness of the trading people to take the
money, can never be doubted, while it will freely command the
commodities of the country; for this, to them, is the most important
use they can make of it.

But besides the state impost, there must be other taxes; and these
will all contribute to create a demand for the money; which is all we
now mean, when we talk of funds for its support; for there are
none appropriated for the *redemption* of the paper.

Upon the whole the additional duties will be a competent substitute for those now in existence; and the general good will of the
community towards the paper, will be the best security for its credit.

Having now shewn, Mr. Chairman, that there is no constitutional
impediment to the adoption of the bill; that there is no danger to be
apprehended to the public liberty from giving the power in question
to the United States; that in the view of revenue the measure under
consideration is not only expedient, but necessary. Let us turn our
attention to the other side of this important subject. Let us ask ourselves what will be the consequence of rejecting the bill; what will
be the situation of our national affairs if they are left much longer
to float in the chaos in which they are now involved.

Can our national character be preserved without paying our debts.
Can the union subsist without revenue. Have we realized the consequences which would attend its dissolution.

If these states are not united under a federal government, they
will infalliably have wars with each other; and their divisions will
subject them to all the mischiefs of foreign influence and intrigue.
The human passions will never want objects of hospitality. The
western territory is an obvious and fruitful source of contest. Let
us also cast our eye upon the mass of this state, intersected from one

extremity to the other by a large navigable river. In the event of a rupture with them, what is to hinder our metropolis from becoming a prey to our neighbours? Is it even supposeable that they would suffer it to remain the nursery of wealth to a distinct community?

These subjects are delicate, but it is necessary to contemplate them to teach us to form a true estimate of our situation.

Wars with each other would beget standing armies—a source of more real danger to our liberties than all the power that could be conferred upon the representatives of the union. And wars with each other would lead to opposite alliances with foreign powers, and plunge us into all the labyrinths [6] of European politics.

The Romans in their progress to universal dominion, when they conceived the project of subduing the refractory spirit of the Grecian Republics, which composed the famous Achaian league, began by sowing dissensions among them, and instilling jealousies of each other, and of the common head, and finished by making them a province of the Roman empire.

The application is easy; if there are any foreign enemies, if there are any domestic foes to this country, all their arts and artifices will be employed to effect a dissolution of the union. This cannot be better done than by sowing jealousies of the federal head and cultivating in each state an undue attachment to its own power. [7]

6. In original, "laibrynths."
7. Following H's speech the question was put whether or not the committee of the whole agreed to the clause giving Congress power to levy the proposed taxes. It was defeated by a vote of 36 to 21.

# New York Assembly. Motion for Leave to Bring in a Bill Granting Privileges to Columbia College and Erecting a University

[New York, February 16, 1787]

Mr. Hamilton moved for leave to bring in a bill, to render more effectual, the act granting privileges to Columbia College, and erecting a University within this State.

*Ordered*, That leave be given accordingly.

Mr. Hamilton, according to leave, brought in the said bill, entitled, *An act to render more effectual an Act, entitled, An Act for granting certain Privileges to the College, heretofore called King's College, for altering the Name and Charter thereof, and erecting an University within this State;* which was read the first time, and ordered a second reading.[1]

New York Assembly *Journal,* 1787, 53.
  1. On the day following its introduction, the bill proposed by H was read a second time and committed to a committee of the whole house (New York Assembly *Journal,* 1787, 54). No further action was taken on it, presumably because its provisions were similar to a bill passed by the Senate entitled "An Act to Institute an University within This State and for Other Purposes therein Mentioned," which was transmitted to the House on March 20. The Senate bill was concurred in by the Assembly and became law on April 13, 1787 (*Laws of the State of New York,* II, 524-31).

## New York Assembly. Resolution on the Call of a Convention of the States [1]

[New York, February 17, 1787]

*Resolved,* (if the Honorable the Senate concur) that the Delegates of this State, in Congress of the United States of America, be, and they hereby are instructed, to move in Congress for an Act recommending to the States composing the Union, that a Convention of Representatives from the said States repectively, be held, and meet at a time and place to be mentioned in such recommendation, for the purpose of revising the Articles of Confederation and Perpetual Union between the United States of America, and reporting to the United States in Congress assembled, and to the States respectively, such alterations and amendments to the said Articles of Confederation, as the representatives met in such Convention, shall judge proper and necessary, to render them adequate to the preservation and support of the Union.

New York Assembly *Journal,* 1787, 55.
  1. The only evidence that H was the author of this resolution is that it is attributed to him in *JCHW,* II, 340.

## New York Assembly. Remarks on an Act for Raising Certain Yearly Taxes Within This State [1]

[New York, February 17, 1787]

On motion of Mr. Taylor,[2] the house went into a committee of the whole, on the Tax bill. . . .

Mr. Hamilton observed that as the present bill exhibited a new system of taxation, it might be proper to enter into some explanation of its principles. It was agreed on all hands, that the system heretofore in use was full of defects; both in the view of equality among individuals and of revenue to the state.[3] From the legislature to the assessors, all was conjecture and uncertainty. To begin with the legislature, what criterion could any man possibly have by which to estimate the relative abilities of the several counties; for his part, he had thought maturely of the subject, but could find none.[4] The whole must be either a business of *honest guessing*, or interested calculations of county convenience, in which each member would endeavour to transfer the burden from his county to another. The same thing must happen in the sub-divisions among the districts by the supervisors; and in a still more striking manner in the apportionment of the tax to individuals by the assessors. How can they possibly ascertain the comparative abilities of individuals?—appearances more than realities must govern. The merchant or factor who has a large store of goods, for which perhaps he owes more than the amount, will pay much more than a man of less apparent gains, though ten times as much property. This he mentioned by way of example. The same thing happened among other orders of the society. To-day an assessor, my friend, taxes me at ten pounds. To-morrow one less my friend will tax me four times the sum. Infinite differences must happen from the different degrees of judgement men possess, from their different biasses and inclinations—a great inequality results, and all is uncertainty.

Theoretical and practical financiers have agreed in condemning the *arbitrary* in taxation. By the *arbitrary*, is meant the leaving the amount of the tax to be paid by each person, to the discretion of the officers employed in the management of the revenue. It is indeed another word for *assesment*, where all is left to the *discretion* of the assessors.

The English writers have justly boasted the superiority of their system over that of France, and some other countries; because little or nothing is left to the discretion of the officers of the revenue. And the ablest observers among the French, have acknowledged the advantage. The celebrated Mr. Neckar, in a late publication has taken particular notice of this circumstance.[5] The opinion of that statesman, who conducted the finances of France for several years, and during the most critical periods of the late war, with infinite ability and success, is a most respectable authority in a matter of this kind. And his opinions as a philosopher and philanthropist, are equally respectable. These had no small share in his disapprobation of a practice, which puts one citizen so much in the power of another.

He would not say that the practice was contrary to the provisions of our constitution; but it was certainly repugnant to the genius of our government. What is the power of the supervisors and assessors, but a power to tax in detail, while the legislature taxes in gross? Is it proper to transfer so important a trust from the hands of the legislature to the officers of the particular districts?

Equality and certainty are the two great objects to be aimed at in taxation.

The present bill does not pretend to reach absolute equality. This is impossible. No human plan can attain it. The variety of circumstances to be taken into the calculation, are too complicated to be comprised in any scheme that could be devised.

But the principles of the present bill will approach much nearer to equality than the former system; and it will have the great advantage of certainty. It leaves nothing to discretion. Every man can himself estimate what he has to pay, without being dependent on the caprices, the affections, or the enmities of another.

The bill in its present form, is but an imperfect sketch. It is in the power of the committee to make it better. No doubt the combined wisdom of the house will improve it. The land tax in particular, may require great alterations. He had not been able to satisfy himself on this part of the plan. All was of course submitted to the discretion of the committee.

One thing only was clear; that we could not fall upon a worse system than the present. Any change would be for the better; and time and experience would mature and meliorate it.[6]

*The* [New York] *Daily Advertiser*, February 21, 1787.

1. For information on the tax bill, see "An Act for Raising Certain Yearly Taxes Within This State," February 9, 1787.

2. John Tayler, a representative from Albany County.

3. For H's specific objections to the tax system of New York, see his letter to Robert Morris, August 13, 1782.

4. H is referring to the practice of assigning each county a quota of the amount to be raised by state taxes.

5. Jacques Necker, a Swiss banker, was French Minister of Finances, 1777–81. The publication to which H refers was probably Necker's *Compte Rendu au Roi, Par M. Necker, Director Général des Finances. Au Mois de Janvier, 1781* (Paris, de L'Imprimerie Royale, 1781).

6. For additional comments on the tax bill, see H's remarks dated February 20, March 2, 9, 1787.

## New York Assembly. Report on the Petition of Theodosius Fowler [1]

*New York, February 20, 1787.* On this date Hamilton, as chairman of a committee, reported on a petition of Theodosius Fowler and others "praying that the estate of Jonathan Fowler, forfeited to the people of this State (the sale whereof has been stayed for the accomodation of the petitioners) may by law be appropriated to the payment of the debts of the said Jonathan." Hamilton recommended that the petition be granted.[2]

New York Assembly *Journal*, 1787, 59.

1. Fowler was a New York dealer in securities and a land speculator.

2. The legislature concurred in H's recommendation, and "AN ACT for the relief of Theodosius Fowler and others," was passed on April 18 (*Laws of the State of New York*, II, 558).

## New York Assembly. Remarks on an Act for Raising Certain Yearly Taxes Within This State [1]

[New York, February 20, 1787]

On that part of the bill, which enacts that a tax be laid on certain instruments of writing in the courts of justice, and which particularly effects the gentlemen of the law.[2]

Col. Hamilton was of opinion that it was not proper to tax any particular class of men for the benefit of the state at large; but in the present instance it was to answer a very important purpose; [3] it was putting in force that most excellent part of the constitution, which declares the judges should be independent of the legislature; this at present was not the case: He therefore supported the paragraph as it stood: Observing the salaries of the judges should be permanent; that they should neither fear the frowns, nor court the favor of the legislature; he believed it was right that this independence should arise from the tax proposed.[4]

The [New York] *Daily Advertiser,* February 22, 1787.
1. For information on the tax bill, see "An Act for Raising Certain Yearly Taxes Within This State," February 9, 1787.
2. The section of the tax bill to which H is referring is given in the New York Assembly *Journal* as follows:
"Upon every seal affixed to any process or proceeding of the Court for the Trial of Impeachments, and the Correction of Errors, Court of Chancery, Supreme Court, Court of Exchequer, Court of Admiralty, and Court of Probates, in addition to the sums now paid, the further sum of        and the further sum of        upon every seal to any process or proceeding of the Mayors Courts of the cities of New-York, Albany, and Hudson, and the Courts of Common Pleas within the several counties of this State; to be paid in each case, by the Attorney, Solicitor or Proctor, on whose application such process or proceedings shall be had, when any Attorney, Solicitor or Proctor is employed; and when no Attorney, Solicitor or Proctor is employed, then to be paid by the person or persons applying for the same. Provided, that when the same shall be paid by any Attorney, Solicitor or Proctor, he shall have no allowance therefore in his bill of costs, neither shall he charge the same to, or receive the same from the person or persons by whom he is employed, under the penalty of Ten Pounds for every such charge or receipt, to be recovered with costs of suit, in any Court of Record having cognizance thereof, by and for the benefit of any person who will sue for the same, in an action of debt, founded upon this act." (New York Assembly *Journal,* 1787, 58–59.)
3. Before H spoke, Richard Varick had argued that
"He saw no reason why any particular profession or order in society should be partially burthened with taxes. It was not consistent with the principles of equal justice. If gentlemen of the law gained by their practice; that practice was taxed when they were rated according to the wealth they possessed." (*The Daily Advertiser,* February 22, 1787.)
4. The part of the proposed bill printed in the New York Assembly *Journal* and quoted in note 2 does not state the purposes for which the revenues from the suggested tax should be used. Presumably the money was to be used to pay the salaries of the judges of the state.
The Assembly refused on February 20 to strike out this clause. It did not appear, however, in the final version of the act.
Also on this date, according to *The Daily Advertiser,* H made a motion, which was carried, "that part of the bill respecting the impost" be erased. For the section of the bill to which he referred, see "An Act for Raising Certain Yearly Taxes Within This State," February 9, 1787, note 5.

## New York Assembly. Remarks on an Act for Regulating the Fees of Officers and Ministers of the Court [1]

[New York, February 21, 1787]

On the different paragraphs which determined the allowance for certain services—much debate ensued.[2]

Col. Hamilton expressed a hope that the house would not carry matters to an extreme; It would, he thought, be as improper to make the fees of the profession too low as to make them too high. Gentlemen who practised the law, if they were men of ability, would be paid for the services required of them; and if the law did not allow a proper compensation, it would be evaded. Names might be given to things, and charges made; against which there would be no guard. In Pennsylvania and Jersey, attempts had been made to reduce the emoluments of the profession, below the proper standard—this had afforded no relief; on the contrary, the expences of the law and the profits of the practicers had increased since the experiment; the only effect of which had been to transfer the expence from the delinquent debtor to the injured creditor. If the legal fees amount to a reasonable compensation; in most cases the practicer would content himself with them; if they did not, he would consider himself justified in making the best bargain he could—the consequences of this were obvious.

While differences would arise among mankind, and that there would be differences was certain, lawyers would be necessary—and for their services they would be paid. He therefore was of opinion, that in going through the bill, the house should agree reasonable allowances should be made for the services mentioned in the bill, or they would defeat their own object.

The [New York] *Daily Advertiser*, February 24, 1787.
1. "An act for regulating the Fees of the several Officers and Ministers of the Courts of Justice, within this State," which was introduced into the 1787 legislative session, was intended as a revision of an act with the same title which had been passed in 1785. See *Laws of the State of New York*, II, 124-38. Like its predecessor, the bill introduced in 1787 provided maximum fees for officers of the state courts and for counselors, solicitors, and attorneys practicing in the state courts.

The act was passed by the Assembly on March 17 (New York Assembly *Journal*, 1787, 102) and, after several amendments had been made, returned from the Senate on April 3. The Assembly and Senate finally agreed on a compromise measure which was sent to the Council of Revision. On April 21, the last day of the legislative session, the Council returned its veto of the bill to the Assembly. The Council's main objection was that the bill was not to take effect for several months. The Assembly overrode the veto of the Council. The Senate, however, again refused to pass the act, and it did not become law (*ibid.*, 177–78).

2. The paragraphs of the act over which debate arose presumably were those which regulated the fees of counselors and solicitors in chancery and of attorneys in the Supreme Court.

# New York Assembly. Remarks on an Act for the Relief of Persons Holding or Possessing State Agent's Certificates [1]

[New York, February 22, 1787]

Mr. Hamilton was against having the words struck out. The state had received the same advantage from the certificates issued by the deputies of the state agent or his assistant, as of those issued by the state agent only. There was no propriety in making the relief partial. Justice should be alike administered to all.[2]

Mr. Hamilton was of opinion, the state should give all the relief possible, to every class of public claimants; and that there should be no discrimination with respect to possessors of certificates.[3]

*The* [New York] *Daily Advertiser*, February 27, 1787.

1. H is referring to "An act for the relief of persons holding or possessing State agent's certificates." The bill provided "That it shall and may be lawful for the treasurer of this State, to receive on loan until the first day of May next, certificates issued by Udny Hay Esquire, late agent of this State, or any of his assistant agents" (*Laws of the State of New York*, II, 465). On this date John Tayler, an assemblyman from Albany County, made a motion to strike out the words "assistant state agents." It was against this motion that H's remarks were addressed.

2. At this point Tayler spoke in behalf of his motion (described in note 1). Tayler argued "that the state had declared that these certificates were not to be received after the first of September last. That the holders of the certificates who had neglected getting them loaned, finding they were worth little; sold them for a trifle to speculators. He thought that to redeem those certificates would be encouraging them" (*The Daily Advertiser*, February 27, 1787).

3. The Assembly rejected Tayler's motion.

## New York Assembly. Report on the Petition of Joanna Morris

New York, February 24, 1787. As chairman of a committee, Hamilton reported on a petition of Joanna Morris "on behalf of herself and the other Children of Roger Morris, and Mary his wife, setting forth, that the said Roger and Mary have been attainted, and their Estates sold and . . . praying a law to restore to them the remainder of the said estate." Hamilton reported that it was unnecessary for the legislature to interpose as the law was competent to the relief of the petitioners.[1]

New York Assembly *Journal*, 1787, 65–66.
1. The Assembly approved the committee report.

## New York Assembly. Report on a Petition of William Gilbert

New York, February 24, 1787. On this date Hamilton, as chairman of a committee on a petition of "William Gilbert, and others, Collectors of Tax in the City and County of New-York," reported that the request of the petitioners for an allowance of six pence in the pound on the proportion of New York City and County of the state quota for 1787 not be granted.[1]

New York Assembly *Journal*, 1787, 65.
1. The Assembly approved the committee report.

## New York Assembly. Motion for Leave to Bring in a Bill on Bankrupts and Their Estates

[New York, February 26, 1787]

Mr. Hamilton moved for leave to bring in a bill respecting bankrupts and their estates.

*Ordered*, That leave be given accordingly.

Mr. Hamilton, according to leave, brought in the said bill, entitled *An act respecting Bankrupts and their Estates*.[1]

New York Assembly *Journal*, 1787, 67–68.
1. The bill introduced by H was read a first time, and a second reading was ordered. For reasons not given in the *Journal* the bill was not read again.

## *New York Assembly. Resolution on the Appointment of Delegates to the Constitutional Convention* [1]

[New York, February 26, 1787]

*Resolved* (If the Honorable the Senate concur herein) that Five Delegates be appointed on the part of this State, to meet such Delegates as may be appointed on the part of the other States respectively, on the second Monday in May next, at Philadelphia, for the sole and express purpose of revising the Articles of Confederation, and reporting to Congress and to the several Legislatures, such alterations and provisions therein, as shall, when agreed to in Congress, and confirmed by the several States, render the Fœderal Constitution adequate to the exigencies of Government and the preservation of the Union; and that in case of such concurrence, the two Houses of the Legislature will meet, on Thursday next, at such place as the Honorable the Senate shall think proper, for the purpose of electing the said Delegates, by joint ballot.[2]

New York Assembly *Journal*, 1787, 68.
1. The *Journal* of the Assembly does not give the author of this resolution. *The New-York Journal, and Weekly Register*, March 8, 1787, however, states that the resolution was introduced on the motion of H.
Conformable with the recommendation of the commissioners who met at Annapolis in September, 1786 ("Address of the Annapolis Convention," September 14, 1786), the Continental Congress on February 21 proposed that a convention meet in Philadelphia in May for the purpose of "revising the Articles of Confederation . . ." to "render the federal Constitution adequate to the exigencies of the Government." The congressional resolution was transmitted to the Assembly on February 23 by Governor George Clinton.
2. For H's appointment as a delegate, see "Appointment as Delegate to the Constitutional Convention," March 6, 1787.

## New York Assembly. Motion for Leave to Bring in a Bill for the Speedy Trial and Punishment of Grand Larceny

[New York, March 1, 1787]

Mr. Hamilton moved for leave to bring in a bill for the speedy trial and punishment of such persons as shall commit any offence under the degree of Grand Larceny.

*Ordered,* That leave be given accordingly.

Mr. Hamilton according to leave, brought in the said bill, entitled, *An act for the speedy Trial and Punishment of such persons as shall commit any offence, under the degree of Grand Larceny."* [1]

New York Assembly *Journal,* 1787, 72.

1. This bill was passed on March 24, 1787. See *Laws of the State of New York,* II, 485–89.

## New York Assembly. Remarks on an Act for Raising Certain Yearly Taxes Within This State [1]

[New York, March 2, 1787]

Colonel *Hamilton* said, he did not believe it would be of much importance whether the word batchelor was out or not.[2] It was known, however, that there were a great number of rich batchelors, who had no families to maintain, and as the lawyers had been taxed for the support of the judges, the house could, if they thought proper, raise a revenue from the batchelors, to give a bounty on old maids.

*The New-York Journal, and Weekly Register,* March 15, 1787.

1. For background to this document, see "An Act for Raising Certain Yearly Taxes Within This State," February 9, 1787.

2. H's remarks refer to that section of the tax bill which imposed additional taxes on bachelors.

# From Robert R. Livingston

Clermount [New York] 3d March 1787

Dr Sir

I recd. your favor with the Barrons [1] papers in hand, by the post, the letters you mention to have sent by a private hand never reached me.[2] I enclose a letter to the Baron containing my opinion [3] Tho I confess to you that I think that in publishing (as he told me he proposed) he will shew more resentment that prudence.[4] He will provoke replies, he will be called upon to shew what he has lost, the payments to him will be compared wth what other officers have recd. It will be said that Congress have failed in all their engagements from necessity, that there is nothing singular in his situation. In short he will hear many things that will vex & disturb him, and hence exclude him self from all hopes of a further provision, When a more liberal spirit, or a heavier purse may incline Congress to make it. If you think with me you will use your influence with him to drop the Idea of a publication that can do him no good but may injure him.

I recd. your information relative to the Law for dividing the district.[5] I am much obliged by your attention to that object. While I condole with you on the loss of the impost I congratulate you on the lawrels you acquired in fighting *its battles*.[6] I see you are making some progress in the new system of taxation [7] but I could hardly credit my eyes when I saw Jones [8] opposed to the clause for a tax on houses since I am not extreamly deceived I heard him commend to you your Ideas on that subject as a Law of his. Be very Tender on the point of taxation. I am convinced no *direct* tax of any importance can be raised. ⟨The dema⟩nds of the people in this part of the state are ⟨irk⟩some & irritable. The *collectors* are all restrained ⟨& set⟩ upon, not having been able to collect the quota ⟨of⟩ the £50,000 tax.[9] Indeed the imprudent grants of money both in this & Dutches county for the building of court houses & the collection of arrears all within six months have fallen extreamly heavy. You will be astonished when I tell you that my tax in this year upon an estate which has ⟨rare⟩ produced an £40⟨00⟩ per annum is upwards of £600 in certificates & £2⟨80⟩ Specie including arrears of one year & one years arrears when I lived at Philadelphia & was not an inhabitant of the State. I shall endeavour to make myself here useful by affecting some changes in the representation which I have good hopes of accomplishing in Dutches county where I have conversed with most of the leading people at this end of it who agree with me in thinking a change necessary. The county will I think remove five of their old members. I expect that this will produce some attack on me or my salary by those who know I am opposed to them. All I expect from my friends will be that they do not suffer such ⟨exer⟩tions to be made as will be dishonourable to ⟨me.⟩ A liberal or honorable appointment such as would enable me to live as I would wish constantly in New York I can not expect it from the prevailing party.

I am Dr Sir   with esteem & regard   Your Most Obdt hum: Servt.
Robt R. Livingston

Coll Alexander Hamilton

ALS, Hamilton Papers, Library of Congress.
   1. Frederick William Augustus Henry Ferdinand, Baron von Steuben.
   2. Letters not found. H presumably sent Livingston von Steuben's memorial, which the Baron had given to H for presentation to Congress.
   3. H probably had requested Livingston to write to Congress on von Steuben's behalf.
   4. Von Steuben proposed to publish his memorial together with the letters he had received in support of his claim.
   5. See "Motion for Leave to bring in a Bill for Dividing the Manor of Livingston," January 18, 1787, note 1.
   6. See "Remarks on an Act Granting to Congress Certain Imposts and Duties," February 15, 1787.
   7. See "An Act for Raising Certain Yearly Taxes Within This State," February 9, 1787.
   8. Samuel Jones, assemblyman from Queens County, was a leading advocate in the legislature of the program endorsed by Governor George Clinton.
   9. The £50,000 tax to which Livingston referred was levied by the state legislature in April, 1786. The quota of Columbia County, in which Livingston's home was located, was £2,300.

## New York Assembly. Motion for Leave to Bring in a Bill for Vesting the Estate of Richard Maitland in Trustees

[New York, March 5, 1787]

Mr. Hamilton pursuant to concurrent resolutions of both Houses of the Legislature, on the 24th of March last, and the publication thereof in news-papers printed in the city of New-York, moved for leave to bring in a bill to vest the real and personal estate of Richard Maitland, Esq. deceased, in trustees for the payment of his debts, and the maintenance and education of his children.

*Ordered,* That leave be given accordingly.

Mr. Hamilton according to leave brought in the said bill, entitled *An act to vest the estate of Richard Maitland, Esq. deceased, in Trustees, for the payment of his Debts, and other purposes,* which was read the first time, and ordered a second reading.[1]

New York Assembly *Journal,* 1787, 81.
1. The act, passed by the Assembly on April 14, 1787, provided that the estate of Richard Maitland be vested in trustees, that the trustees be empowered to sue to recover the estate, and that the trustees be empowered to receive applications for money (New York Assembly *Journal,* 1787, 162).

## New York Assembly. Remarks on Several Petitions from Columbia County

[New York, March 5, 1787]

On motion of Mr. Sickles,[1] the house went into a committee of the whole on the different petitions[2] from Columbia county, respecting the place of holding courts, &c.

Mr. Bancker[3] in the chair.

After reading several petitions and affidavits, Mr. James Livingston moved that the committee should rise, he did not see, he said, what the committee could do with the petitions.

Mr. Jones[4] thought it was improper for the committee to rise without coming to any determination, he never had heard of such a thing; the motion was out of order. The reasons should be exceeding strong for the house not to decide; he had a resolution in his hand which he moved for, declaring that the house would not grant the prayer of the petitions for removing the court-house and goal of Columbia county from the town of Claverack, to the city of Hudson.

Gen. Malcolm [5] was of opinion that the committee should rise, and that no entry should be made on the minutes.

The question for the committee's rising was then taken and lost.

Before the question on Mr. Jones's motion was called for, Col. Harpur [6] offered to read a bill which he had drawn, he said it contained much information; this was objected to as out of order. Col. Hamilton hoped that nothing would be done which would appear like prejudging the question. He wished that the bill which the hon. member had drawn, might be read for the sake of information, not as a bill, but omitting the enacting clauses.[7]

Col. Hamilton wished that gentlemen would proceed in this business with candor and impartiallity; he saw no reason for postponing the consideration of this subject. The hon. gentleman who had spoke previous to the one who had last sat down, raised objections against complying with the Hudson petition: his principal one was that we ought not to violate the charter of Hudson; this was an objection that vanished in the appearance of an instrument of writing which he held in his hand: This was giving up their authority to appoint the keeper of the public goal, in case Hudson was the county town.

No objections therefore could be made on that head. There is one evident reason why Hudson should be the place for holding the courts, it will do away the inconvenience of having two jurisdictions within a very small circle. There is another objection against the petition, that there is no certainty of a compliance with their offers; certainly the law can be so framed as to compel them to give security for their performance, or say that if the court-house and goal are not built in a given time that they shall lose the advantage. It is easy to force a compliance therein, therefore no difficulty can arise in this respect. He wished some greater light could be thrown on the subject. This however, he knew, that the people of Hudson came into this state with very great property, that they had established the city of Hudson, whose growing importance was not only a valuable acquisition to the state, but that county in particular; and it was bad policy not to give every encouragement to its citizens. This petition he said, he knew had been a great party matter, and circumstances if examined into, might be found differently represented on both sides. The best criterion therefore, for gentlemen to go by, would be to lay aside all consideration of partial county convenience, and to determine whether it would tend more to the public good to place the court-house and goal at Hudson, than at Claverack. His vote should be for Hudson.[8]

Col. Hamilton observed, that until the objection had been raised, that they had not formally moved a deed of conveyance to the supervisors of the county, of the buildings, and the ground on which they stand. He asked what was the state of this business, have they not declared that all their privileges shall be given to the sheriff if it is necessary. Cannot something further be required; can it not be demanded that they comply within one month, or forfeit the privilege; could not also a bond be required of them for the faithful performance; and had not the house power so to frame the law as to bind them to a compliance. The objections, he said, were not well founded. He hoped the house would not agree to the resolution.[9]

*The* [New York] *Daily Advertiser,* March 7, 1787.
1. Thomas Sickles, Albany.
2. The New York Assembly *Journal,* 1787, 81, states:
"The House resolved itself into a Committee of the whole House, on the several petitions from inhabitants of the county of Columbia, praying that the place of holding Courts in the said county may be altered from the town of Claverack, to the city of Hudson; and the several petitions from other inhabitants of the said county, praying that the settings of the courts of Justice may be continued at Claverack."
3. Evert Bancker, Albany.
4. Samuel Jones, Queens County.
5. William Malcom, New York City.
6. William Harper, Montgomery County.
7. At this point Samuel Jones argued in favor of allowing the court to remain in Claverack. William Harper stated "He wished that the committee would rise—The committee, he said, by proceeding in the business would take much trouble on themselves, and find it difficult to get rid of it:—He thought it had best be decided by the house" (*The Daily Advertiser,* March 7, 1787).
8. At this point Jones said:
". . . he could wish that the papers should be read, he was surprised any information like the certificate from the corporation of Hudson, had been so long withheld from the committee (the certificate was then read;—there was also read, a paper from a number of inhabitants of Hudson.) Mr. Jones said he was for encouraging the citizens of Hudson. His objection however he believed was well founded; he believed that fixing the courts at Hudson would create more difficulties than would be removed. A paper had been

produced which gave up the right of appointing the goaler, but would this give the sheriff the exclusive right of the goal, the sheriff must have this right, it must be given to the supervisors of the county. They should do this by a proper conveyance. Until this was done, the sheriff would be in a very improper situation." (*The Daily Advertiser,* March 7, 1787.)

9. The committee resolved "That it is the opinion of this Committee, that it will be improper, at present, for the Legislature to alter the place of holding the Courts in the county of Columbia." The House resolved "That the House do concur with the Committee in the said report" (New York Assembly *Journal,* 1787, 82).

# New York Assembly. Appointment as Delegate to the Constitutional Convention

[New York, March 6, 1787]

*Resolved,* that the Honorable Robert Yates, John Lansing, junior, and Alexander Hamilton, Esquires, be, and they are hereby declared duly nominated and appointed Delegates on the part of this State, to meet such Delegates as may be appointed on the part of the other States respectively, on the second Tuesday in May next, at Philadelphia, for the sole and express purpose of revising the Articles of Confederation, and reporting to Congress, and to the several Legislatures, such alterations and provisions therein, as shall when agreed to in Congress, and confirmed by the several States, render the fœderal Constitution adequate to the exigencies of government, and the preservation of the Union.[1]

New York Assembly *Journal,* 1787, 84.

1. In conformity with the recommendation of the Annapolis Convention and a congressional resolve of February 21, 1787, the legislature of New York appointed delegates to the Constitutional Convention. (See "Resolution on the Appointment of Delegates to the Constitutional Convention," February 26, 1787.) Although the Assembly proposed that five delegates be appointed, the Senate's preference for a delegation of three was accepted (New York Assembly *Journal,* 1787, 68, 71).

# From David Beekman [1]

*St. Croix, March 7, 1787.* Requests Hamilton's opinion on Beekman's liability for a bail bond he signed with Gilbert Woodward.

ALS, Hamilton Papers, Library of Congress.
1. Beekman was a partner in the St. Croix firm of Beekman and Cruger.

# New York Assembly. Remarks on an Amendment to an Act to Empower Justices of the Peace to Try Causes to the Value of Ten Pounds

[New York, March 8, 1787]

Mr. Harpur[1] moved for a clause to be added to the bill, in substance, that no freeholder or citizen shall hereafter be imprisoned for any sum less than ten pounds, but that execution shall issue and remain in force against the debtor, till from time to time by different seizures of his effects, the creditor shall be satisfied and fully paid.[2]

Col. Hamilton confessed that his own judgment was not clearly made up on this subject. It was not however a new one to him, it was a question that had two sides, both of which deserved a serious attention. The clause as it stood, in his opinion was not proper; It might be right to say what shall be done in future contracts. But it would be wrong to meddle with the past. It was very probable if the clause was passed, it would prevent people in poor circumstances from getting assistance from the wealthy, this ought to be considered. Many a poor man who can be favoured with a credit of £10. finds a material advantage in it; if the security is taken away there will be an end to credit. He would wish that every man in distress should meet relief. He was willing to come into any measure that would effect this purpose.[3]

The [New York] *Daily Advertiser*, March 12, 1787.
1. The reference is to William Harper.
2. The Assembly went into a committee of the whole to consider "An act to empower Justices of the Peace, Mayors, Recorders, and Aldermen to try Causes to the value of Ten Pounds, and under, and to repeal the several Acts now in force for that purpose." Harper made a motion that the following clause be inserted in the bill:
"Provided nevertheless, that no execution shall issue against the body of any Freeholder, or inhabitant having a family, in the county where such action is, or shall be commenced, upon any contract hereafter to be made; but the plaintiff shall continue to have execution against the defendants goods, until the debt, damages and costs are satisfied." (New York Assembly *Journal*, 1787, 86.)
The motion occasioned a debate between John Tayler and Samuel Jones. Tayler objected to the clause because "he believed it would encourage many people to defraud their creditors." Jones supported the motion and argued that unless it were adopted "an unfortunate debtor can be hurried away to gaol and kept there for so small a sum as ten pounds, and kept confined while

he might have earned six times that sum if at his liberty." Both Tayler and Jones agreed, however, that if adopted, the clause should be amended to refer only to future contracts (*The Daily Advertiser*, March 12, 1787).

3. Harper's motion was defeated. The act is printed in *Laws of the State of New York*, II, 547–55, under the title "AN ACT for the more speedy recovery of debts to the value of ten pounds."


## New York Assembly. Remarks on an Act for Raising Certain Yearly Taxes Within This State [1]

[New York, March 9, 1787]

Col. Hamilton said that much time had been already spent in the discussion of this bill.[2] He perceived there now was objections, why were they not made before. The bill be believed was perfectly understood by the committee, he wished therefore that a serious question might be taken, if it was to be rejected. he wished it to be done at once, the session was far advanced, and if this system was rejected, some other must be adopted. He wished that gentleman [3] who did not like the bill would offer a better one to the committee. He declared if that part of the bill was rejected, he should move to reject the whole. If this was done, the committee must then go to the old way of quotaing the counties. The committee he was convinced would not agree to reject part of the law affecting the country, and not that part which respects the cities—they could never agree to commit so great an act of injustice.

Col. Hamilton said [4] that he calculated the bill to produce £80,000. but as some articles had been rated lower than he expected, he supposed it would produce, in its present form,[5] about £70,000 per annum.[6]

Col. Hamilton said this subject had been so fully discussed, that he did not think it was proper to follow the gentleman, (Mr. Purdy) in his objections. He was convinced that he was mistaken with respect to any disproportion between the cities and the counties. He asked if the citizens did not pay as much for every thing as any in the country.

He asked on whom [7] did the tax on carriages, on servants, on marble chimney pieces, stucko, and papered rooms, fall; where were the houses that in general would pay for six rooms. Did not the merchant pay a duty on his ships, and many other things of which people in the country pay nothing. In regard to what had been said of the old mode of quotaing; he would only remark one singular instance of its inequality. The last year there was a tax of £10,000. laid on the city of New-York, of which he was assessed to pay £13. The present year a tax of 13,000 he was assessed only £7.[8]

The [New York] *Daily Advertiser*, March 13 and 15, 1787.
  1. For information on the tax bill, see "An Act for Raising Certain Yearly Taxes Within This State," February 9, 1787.
  2. On March 9, a section of the proposed "Act for Raising Certain Yearly Taxes" was read in a committee of the whole. Ebenezer Purdy, a representative from Westchester County, made a motion that the part of the bill imposing a tax on lands and buildings be rejected. H's remarks were made during the debate which followed the introduction of Purdy's motion (*The Daily Advertiser*, March 13, 1787).
  3. Ebenezer Purdy.
  4. These remarks by H were made in answer to a question, asked by Zephaniah Batcheler of Montgomery County, on the amount the tax bill could be expected to produce.
  5. In MS, "farm."
  6. Following these remarks by H, Purdy argued that the proposed mode of taxation was unjust. It would, he said, produce a great inequality between the city and county of New York and the other counties of the state, for it favored the merchants at the expense of the farmers.
  7. In original, "whome."
  8. On this date Samuel Jones made a motion that the Assembly reject the proposed tax system. His motion was carried in the affirmative, and the bill was recommitted (*The Daily Advertiser*, March 15, 1787).

## Lease of College Lots

*New York, March 10, 1787.* On this date Hamilton and six others signed a lease to Frederick Rhinelander for "eleven water lotts adjacent to those he now occupies."[1]

DS, Hamilton Papers, Library of Congress.
  1. In 1787 Columbia College held ninety-one lots of which seventy-eight were leased.

## From Jacob Le Roy and Sons

*New York, March 10, 1787.* Request Hamilton to collect debts owed by several individuals to Broome and Platt, a firm indebted to Le Roy and Sons.

ALS, Hamilton Papers, Library of Congress.

## New York Assembly. Report on a Letter from the Secretary for Foreign Affairs

[New York, March 10, 1787]

Mr. Hamilton from the Committee to whom was referred the letter from the Honorable John Jay, Esquire, Secretary for foreign affairs,[1] reported, that it is the opinion of the said Committee, that so much of the act, entitled, *An act for granting a more effectual relief in cases of certain Trespasses,* as makes all actions to be brought upon the said act transitory, and as declares that no military order shall be pleaded or given in evidence in justification of the defendant, ought to be repealed; and that a bill be brought in for that purpose, that the Committee have prepared a draft of such bill, and have directed him to move for leave to bring in the same.

*Resolved,* That the House do concur with the Committee in the said report, and,

*Ordered,* That leave be given to bring in the said bill.

Mr. Hamilton according to leave brought in the said bill, entitled, *An act to repeal a part of an act, entitled, "an act for granting more effectual relief in cases of certain Trespasses."* which was read the first time and ordered a second reading.[2]

New York Assembly *Journal,* 1787, 91.
 1. For information on the letter from the Secretary for Foreign Affairs and the appointment of the committee which reported on this date, see "Motion that a Committee be Appointed to Consider a Letter from the Secretary for Foreign Affairs," January 23, 1787.
 2. The bill introduced by H was passed on April 4, 1787 (*Laws of the State of New York,* II, 496).

## New York Assembly. Motion for Leave to Bring in a Bill on the Independence of Vermont

[New York, March 14, 1787]

Mr. Hamilton moved for leave to bring in a bill, to authorise the delegates of this State in Congress, to accede to, ratify and confirm, the independence and Sovereignty of the people inhabiting the district of country, commonly called Vermont.[1]

*Ordered,* That leave be given accordingly.

Mr. Hamilton according to leave, brought in the said bill entitled, *An act to authorise the Delegates of [t]his State, in the United States of America, in Congress assembled, to accede to, ratify and confirm, the Independence and Sovereignty of the People inhabiting the District of Territory commonly called Vermont;* which was read the first time, and ordered a second reading.[2]

New York Assembly *Journal,* 1787, 97.
   1. For the early attempts of Vermont to secure recognition of independence, see "Continental Congress. Motion on Vermont," December 5, 1782, and H to George Clinton, July 27, 1783.
   After the Revolution, opposition in New York to the independence of Vermont gradually diminished, but until the introduction of H's bill on this date no formal step was taken to acknowledge it.
   2. For H's "Draft of an Act Acknowledging the Independence of Vermont," see the following document.

# Draft of an Act Acknowledging the Independence of Vermont [1]

[New York, March 14, 1787]

An act to empower and direct the Delegates of this State in Congress to accede to ratify and confirm the Sovereignty and Independence of the People of the Territory commonly called and known by the name of the State of Vermont.

Be it enacted by the People of the State of New York, represented in Senate and Assembly, and it is hereby enacted by the Authority of the same that the Delegates of this State in the Congress of the United States of America or any two of them shall be and hereby are fully authorised empowered and required, wholly, intirely and absolutely, for and in behalf of the people of this state, and in such manner and with such formalities as shall be determined in Congress to accede to recognise ratify approve and confirm the Independence and Sovereignty of the People inhabiting the Territory, commonly called and known by the name of the State of Vermont: Provided always that it be and it hereby is declared to be an indispensable [2] preliminary to such act of accession to and recognition of the Independence and sovereignty of the said people that they explicitly relinquish and renounce all claims and pretensions to any lands

territory or jurisdiction, on the East side of the West bank of Connecticut River and on the West side of a line beginning at a Point
in the North bounds of the state or Commonwealth of Massachusetts
bay at the distance of Twenty Miles on a direct line from Hudsons
River thence running twenty Miles East of Hudson's River, so far
as the said River runs North Easterly in its general course, then
by the West-bounds of the Town ships granted by the late government of New Hampshire to ⟨the river runn⟩ing [3] from South bay
to Lake Champlain thence along said River to Lake Champlain,
thence along the East side of the Lake Champlain to the latitude
of 45 degrees north, excepting only a neck of land between Mis-
siskoy bay and the waters of Lake Champlain Provided also that
such act of accession to and recognition of the independence and
sovereignty of the said People shall be upon this express condition,
that the said People shall thereupon immediately accede to, be received into, and become a member of the Confederacy of the United
States of America to all intents and purposes whatsoever: provided
also that such act of accession to and recognition of the said Independence & sovereignty of the said people shall be upon this further
condition that the rights titles [4] or claims of any person or persons
to lands within the said territory of Vermont by virtue of grants
under the government of the late colony or Province of New York
shall be and remain in as full force as if this act had never passed,
to be asserted prosecuted maintained and determined agreeably to
the mode specified and prescribed in the 9th. of the Articles of Confederation and perpetual union for the determination of controversies
concerning the private right of soil claimed under different grants
of two or more states: And Provided always that nothing in this act
contained, nor any act matter or thing to be done and transacted
by the Delegates of this state in the Congress of the said United
States of America in and concerning the premises, or any part thereof
shall bind or oblige or be construed deemed or taken to bind or
oblige the government Legislature, people, subjects or Inhabitants
of this state, until not less than Eight other of the said United states
of America of which number the State of New Hampshire [5] to be
one, shall accede to recognise ratify approve and confirm the sovereignty and Independence of the said People of the said Territory of
Vermont.

AD, Hamilton Papers, Library of Congress.
1. For H's motion to introduce this bill, see the preceding document.
2. In MS, "indispensible."
3. The bracketed material is taken from a JCH Transcript.
4. In MS, "tittles."
5. In MS, "Hamshire."

# New York Assembly. Remarks on an Act Acknowledging the Independence of Vermont

[New York, March 14, 1787]

Mr. CHILDS,[1]

The public have reason to regret your indisposition, as it deprives them of the satisfaction they would otherwise have received from reading *verbatim*, the judicious speech of that zealous patriot Col. Hamilton, on his bill for recommending to Congress to admit into the union the assumed state of Vermont.[2] As there has and still continues to be much contrariety of opinion on this interesting subject, and as I am anxious that the arguments of this honorable gentleman should not be lost, I here send you a humble representation of the reasoning which he offered with a view to the adoption of the bill. After intimating that he had attempted to introduce this bill as a matter of course yesterday, but in compliance with the opinion of the house, had given previous notice of his intention, he goes on— "This formality having been thought requisite, I presume it will be expected that I should on presenting the bill, accompany it with my reasons for doing so. Perhaps the sentiments, I entertain of the present situation of our national affairs, may induce me to view the object of this bill in a more serious light than many gentlemen, equally solicitous for the public welfare.

I confess I am in the habit of considering the state of this country, as replete with difficulties and surrounded with danger. The anxiety I feel on this head has been my inducement to bring forward the present measure.

*The* [New York] *Daily Advertiser,* March 16, 1787. The same version of H's speech appeared in *The New-York Packet* on March 20.
1. Francis Childs was the publisher of *The Daily Advertiser.*
2. See "Motion for Leave to Bring in a Bill on the Independence of Vermont," and "Draft of an Act Acknowledging the Independence of Vermont," March 14, 1787.

I view with apprehension the present situation of Vermont, over which this state claims jurisdiction, and whose pretensions to independence has never yet been formally recognized either by this state, or the United States. Notwithstanding I believe there is not a member of this house but considers the independence of the district of territory in question as a matter fixed and inevitable, all our efforts to a different point have hitherto proved fruitless, and it is long since we seem to have entirely given up the controversy. Vermont is in fact *independent*, but she is not *confederated*. And I am constrained to add that the means which they employ to secure that independence, are objects of the utmost alarm to the safety of this state, and to the confederation at large. Are they not wisely inviting and encouraging settlers by an exemption from taxes, and availing themselves of the discontents of a neighbouring state, by turning it to the aggrandizement of their own power.

Is it not natural to suppose, that a powerful people both by numbers and situation; unconnected as they now stand, and without any relative importance in the union. Irritated by neglect, or stimulated by revenge, I say, is it not probable under such circumstances they will provide for their own safety, by seeking connections elsewhere? And who that hears [3] me doubts, but that these connections have *already* been formed with the British in Canada. We have the strongest evidence that negotiations have been carried on between that government and the leaders of the people in Vermont. Whatever may be the present temper of that people, it is easy to foresee what it will become under the influence of their leaders. Confederated with a foreign nation, we can be at no loss to anticipate the consequences of such a connection, nor the dangers to this country, from having so powerful a body of people increasing rapidly in numbers and strength, associated with a foreign power, and ready upon any rupture to throw their weight into an opposite scale. In their present situation they bear no part of our public burdens; if they were a part of the confederacy they must of course participate in them. They are useless to us now, and if they continue as they are, they will be formidable to us hereafter. I have observed before that the people there enjoy an exemption from taxes. In these states the taxes must be considerable to fulfill the public engagements; to support

3. In original, "heares."

the government. What a temptation will a comparison of situations in this respect, furnish to the inhabitants of these states bordering on Vermont? It is the policy of the Vermonteers to make proselytes to their government, and the means which they employ for that purpose, are too well calculated to accomplish their designs.

Are they not daily encroaching on our state. In every light 'tis our interest if possible, to put an end to their present situation.

I am aware there is in the minds of some members an objection founded on a supposition, that if we accede to the independence of Vermont, we are bound to make compensation to the citizens who have claims there under the grants of this state. I shall not say what justice may dictate in respect to these citizens. But I shall observe that as far as that obligation is binding upon us, it applies more strongly to the actual state of things, than to that which is intended to be produced by the bill. It is the duty of the state as matters now stand, either to support the claims of its citizens by an exertion of the public force, or to make compensation to those who are sufferers by the neglect. Passively acquiescing in the independence of Vermont, is not less a violation of that protection and security which the public owes to individuals, than formally acceding to it. Indeed by acceding to it we put our citizens in a better situation than that in which they now are. We at least give them a chance for asserting their rights. The bill makes it a condition of the intended acknowledgement of the independence of Vermont, that it should become a part of the confederacy. The claims of individuals may then be submitted to the decision of a federal court, and as far as our citizens have equitable claims, it may be expected they would prevail in such a court.

At any rate we shall not be under a stronger obligation in this respect than we now are; and we may avoid many and extensive mischiefs by acceding to the measure proposed by the bill.

Many more considerations might be urged but I think it unnecessary to enter into them at present. If any gentlemen has arguments to oppose to those I have used, I shall be glad to hear them, and I flatter myself I shall be able to obviate any difficulties that may arise."

Thus I have endeavoured to give you a sketch of the substance of Col. Hamilton's speech yesterday, as exactly as my memory serves me, and unless you can prevail on him to give you a more accurate one, I wish you would insert it to-morrow, for I am one of those who thnk *his* national reflections in general, too valuable not to be extensively promulgated.[4]

March 15.

4. H again defended the Vermont bill on March 28.

## New York Assembly. Report on a Letter from the Secretary for Foreign Affairs

[New York, March 16, 1787]

Mr. Hamilton, from the Committee appointed to consider of and report on the letter from the Secretary of Foreign Affairs, to his Excellency the Governor, and the papers accompanying the same,[1] together with the act of the Legislature, entitled, *An act relative to Debts due to Persons within the Enemies Lines*, reported, that it is the opinion of the Committee, that the said act ought to be amended, and that a bill should be brought in for that purpose: That the said Committee have prepared a draft of such bill, and have directed him to move for leave to bring in the same.

*Resolved*, That the House do concur with the Committee in the said report: And,

*Ordered*, That leave be given to bring in the said bill.

Mr. Hamilton according to leave brought in the said bill, entitled, *An act to amend an act entitled, an act relative to Debts due to persons within the enemies lines, and another act, entitled, an act relative to Debts due to persons within the enemies lines, passed 12th July 1782*, which was read the first time, and order a second reading.[2]

New York Assembly *Journal*, 1787, 102.

1. For information on the letter from the Secretary for Foreign Affairs and the appointment of the committee which reported March 16, 1787, see "Motion that a Committee be Appointed to Consider a Letter from the Secretary for Foreign Affairs," January 23, 1787.

2. The bill introduced by H was passed on April 20, 1787. See *Laws of the State of New York*, II, 562–64.

## From Theodorick Bland [1]

*Richmond, March 20, 1787.* Acknowledges receipt of a circular letter from Hamilton, James Duane, and William Duer [2] concerning proposed alterations in the "Institution" of the Society of the Cincinnati and states that it will be reported to the next meeting of the state society.

ALS, New-York Historical Society, New York City.
1. Bland wrote in his capacity as vice president of the Virginia Society of the Cincinnati.
2. "Circular Letter to the State Societies of the Cincinnati," November 1, 1786.

## New York Assembly. Remarks on an Act for the Relief of Merchants in the City of New York

[New York, March 20, 1787]

Col. Hamilton supposed that it was agreed on all hands, that some relief should be granted—there was, he said two questions before the committee, one, if they would put them on a footing with the other citizens; and the other, if they did not merit something more.[1] If said he, you receive their certificates, and grant them your own, you extend to them only that relief which you have already given to your other citizens, who purchased up the loan-office certificates of other states; but there can be no difference between any one species of our debt; and there can be no substantial difference between taking a certificate of this state, and a certificate of the United States; much has been said about discriminating, but all arguments of discrimination amount to nothing. Whether we by this assumption make our state a creditor state or not, cannot be determined; the present calculation of the public debts is no criterion to go by. He remembered, he said, that when he was in Congress the liquidated debt was some where about 40,000,000, and that it was supposed the unliquidated debt was £40,000,000 more, if this is the case, which he believed it was, the state of New-York would be a debtor state. From the situation of public affairs, it is to be regretted that there is no system existing which can give general relief to public creditors. In the present instance, it is only required that you do that justice to one part of your citizens, which you have already done to another part. If we should make our state a creditor state, by extending this relief to our citizens, can we not obtain redress, if our confederation exists, and God forbid, that it may not;

he was willing he said, to extend the relief, he did not want to confine it to any particular class of the people.[2]

*The* [New York] *Daily Advertiser,* March 22, 1787.
1. The Assembly had resolved itself into a committee of the whole to
consider "An act for the relief of the persons therein mentioned, merchants
in the city of New-York, who previous to the late war were, and still are
indebted to merchants in Great-Britain, and for other purposes therein mentioned." The clause under debate reads, in part, as follows:
"Be it enacted by the People of the State of New-York, represented in
Senate and Assembly, . . . That the Treasurer of the State be, and he is hereby
authorised and required, to receive on loan, in behalf of the People of this
State . . . from the said petitioners, and others in a similar situation, the
amount of the debts which they . . . owe to merchants in Great-Britain . . .
in such public securities as are made receivable in payment for all forfeited
estates, . . . or is such other public securities, as shall be . . . *bona fide* the
property of the person presenting the same, . . . and to issue in lieu thereof
certificates for the principal sums so loaned, payable with interest, at the
rate of six per cent. per annum." (New York Assembly *Journal,* 1787, 138.)
Before H spoke, other members of the Assembly discussed the proposed
clause in the bill for affording relief to New York merchants. See *The Daily
Advertiser,* March 22, 1787.
2. For further information on the bill for the relief of merchants, see
"Remarks on an Amendment to an Act Relative to Debts Due Persons Within
the Enemy's Lines," April 12, 1787.

## Petition to the Corporation of the City of New York in Common Council [1]

*New York, March 21, 1787.* Hamilton was one of eighteen petitioners who, on this date, requested the New York City Common
Council to remove a statute of William Pitt located "in the most
central Part" of Wall and Smith Streets. The statue, the petition
stated, "greatly obstructs the free Passage of Carriages &c., through
both Wall & Smith Streets."

DS, Municipal Archives and Records Center, New York City.
1. This petition was referred to a committee consisting of "the Aldn &
Assistants of the East, Dock, & North Wards." It was not, however, until
February, 1788, that further action was taken. On February 12, 1788, the
petition was read in the New York Senate and on March 7, 1788, a law was
passed giving the City of New York permission to remove the statue (*Laws
of the State of New York,* II, 725). The Council, however, did not carry out the
provisions of the law until July 16, 1788, when the "Aldn & Assists of the Dock
& East Wards" were ordered to remove the remains of the statue (*Minutes of
the Common Council,* I, 285, 386).

## Petition to the Corporation of the City of New York in Common Council

*New York, March 21, 1787.* Hamilton and several other residents of Wall Street on this date petitioned the New York City Common Council to raise "the Pavements of the said Street in the middle thereof, so as to throw the Water on each side of the Street."

DS, Municipal Archives and Records Center, New York City.

## New York Assembly. Remarks on an Act for Repealing Part of the Trespass Act

[New York, March 21, 1787]

On motion of Col. Hamilton, the house went into a committee on the bill for repealing part of the trespass act.

Mr. Hedges [1] in the chair.

Col. Hamilton said that this amendment to the trespass law, was only to repeal that part which was in violation of the public treaty. The courts of justice were at present in a delicate dilemma, obliged either to explain away a positive law of the state or openly violate the national faith by counteracting the very words and spirit of the treaties now in existance. Because the treaty declares a general amnesty, and this state, by this law, declares that no person shall plead any military order for a trespass committed during the war. He said no state was so much interested in the due observance of the treaty, as the state of New-York; the British having possession of its western frontiers. And which they hold under the sanction of our not having complied with our national engagements. He hoped the house would have too much wisdom, not to do away this exception; and indeed he expected the bill would be readily agreed to.[2]

*The* [New York] *Daily Advertiser,* March 23, 1787.
1. David Hedges of Suffolk County.
2. On January 23, 1787, the Assembly appointed a committee, of which H was chairman, to recommend amendments to "An act for granting a more effectual Relief, in cases of certain Trespasses" (New York Assembly *Journal.*

20). Passed on March 17, 1783, and known as the Trespass Act, the measure provided that any person who during the war had left his home because of the British occupation might bring an action of trespass against anyone who had occupied his property. The defendant in such an action was not allowed to plead a military order in justification of his occupation (*Laws of the State of New York,* I, 552).

The bill of 1787 repealed that part of the Trespass Act prohibiting the pleading of a military order. On March 21, 1787, the Assembly approved the bill. It became law on April 4, 1787 (*Laws of the State of New York,* II, 496).

## New York Assembly. Remarks on the Quotas to be Assigned the Several Counties of New York

[New York, March 22, 1787]

Col. Hamilton did not suppose that any arguments would have much influence on the decision of this question.[1] There is no criterion to go by and we fall into the greatest uncertainty—a gentleman has told us plainly, that he has been intriguing, and making the best bargain he could for his county.[2] He would not say that New-York had made any conditions—he hoped that the intrigues might not have the effect which was sought. The county of Albany he said was always rated too low.[3] It was only required to pay £7,000, with 70,000 inhabitants; while Suffolk, with only 14,000 paid £4,500. He asked if the house would permit intrigues to have such an effect. The county of Kings, which numbers only 3000 inhabitants, and contains 18,500 acres of land, is to pay £2400, Richmond county which is equally small, is also over rated; can this be right? New-York had ever been rated too high. One of the gentlemen from New-York had proposed 12,000 [4] from a mere dispair of coming at an equality, but this sum is too high. He asked if it was justice that the city and county of New-York, which was not a tenth part of the value, or population of the state, should bear one fourth of its burthens.[5] He hoped this would be considered, and no partiality exhibited by the legislature.[6]

Col. Hamilton replied, observing that the gentleman (Mr. Taylor) had intimated they had intrigued together on this subject.[7] The intriguing amounted to nothing more he said, than that they had conversed together on the subject. He believed that that gentleman had been the most successful: he had raised much the strongest party. He would only observe, that he had made a most falacious calculation respecting New-York. There is not 1000 houses in New-York that are worth £1500 each.[8] This was far short of the enormous sum mentioned. The county of Albany he knew was worth 2,000,000. He said if it was required, he would make the calculation, and prove that Albany county was worth more than New-York. He believed that every gentleman who would lay his hand on his heart, and vote according to his conscience, would declare, that one fourth part of the taxes, was too great a proportion for New-York. He asked if the citizens of New-York, had not also met with losses? Was not a great part of the city burned? Had not the enemy despoiled their property? And had they not for a long time occupied their city, while they were suffering in exile? Gentlemen, certainly knew this; and it was a subject worthy of their attention.[9]

Mr. Hamilton said he had made a calculation of a tax of £200,000 on the improved lands in this state, and found that 2/6. an acre would be about the proportion of that tax, knowing this, would it be right to make Kings County pay the same proportion of a £50,000 tax as ought to be paid on a tax of 200,000. It was even more than 2s 6d. — £2,400 would make it as 7d per acre.

Mr. Lansing had no objection if New-York would take upon itself, that proportion of which they wished Kings County relieved.

Mr. Hamilton would even consent to this if the house could think that New-York should bear all the burthen of the State.

The [New York] *Daily Advertiser*, March 27, 1787.
1. After the rejection of the proposed "Act for Raising Certain Yearly Taxes Within This State," drafted by H (see draft of the act, February 9, 1787), the Assembly, as it had in previous years, assigned each county a quota of the money to be raised by taxes. On March 22 the question of the quotas to be assigned to the counties of New York and Albany was debated. William Malcom moved that the quota of New York County be £12,000. H spoke after John Lansing, Jr., had seconded Malcom's motion.
2. John Tayler of Albany County had said that "he held a paper in his hand which he supposed would be the proportions of the different counties, as near as he could find out the sentiments of the house. He confessed that taxing in this way, was a system of intrigue, and supposed every county had made the best bargain it could" (*The Daily Advertiser*, March 27, 1787).
3. John Tayler argued that reductions in the quotas of other counties were added to the quota of Albany County.
4. H referred to the proposal of William Malcom.
5. £50,000 was the sum to be raised by the several counties of the state.
6. John Tayler, replying to H's remarks, said that "Perhaps he had expressed himself improperly when he used the word intrigue, but if not, that gentleman knows that he and I have intrigued with each other" (*The Daily Advertiser*, March 27, 1787).

7. See note 6.

8. H replied to Tayler's assertion "that supposing the city and county of New-York to contain 5,000 houses 4,000 of which he would estimate at £1500, this computation, allowing the residue of the houses, the lands and other property to be included, he did not suppose to be very erroneous, by this estimation, 6,000,000 would be amount" of the state assessment which should be assigned New York (*The Daily Advertiser*, March 27, 1787).

9. At the conclusion of H's remarks, the Assembly voted a quota of £13,000 for New York County. The Assembly then debated the amount to be levied on Albany County. H moved that the sum be £5,800, but his motion was defeated and the sum of £5,400 was approved.

## New York Assembly. Report on the Petitions of Samuel Thompson, Josiah Gale, and Lemuel Conckling

*New York, March 24, 1787.* Hamilton, as chairman of a committee on "petitions of Samuel Thompson, Josiah Gale and others, and Lemuel Conckling," recommended that "the said petitions ought to be taken into consideration, when the House shall proceed upon a report of Mr. Attorney general, on the cases of Elijah Hunter and others."

New York Assembly *Journal*, 1787, 118.

## New York Assembly. Remarks on an Act to Institute an University Within This State

[New York, March 24, 1787]

Col. Hamilton hoped the house would not recommit the bill.[1] There was no doubt he said but the legislature possessed the right to give this power. There were frequent examples of the kind in Great Britain, where this power has been granted. No disadvantage he said could arise from it; on the contrary, many would be the benefits. He therefore wished the bill might be finished—as no doubt existed with him, of the power and the propriety of the legislature granting those privileges which were mentioned in the bill.[2]

The [New York] *Daily Advertiser*, March 28, 1787.

1. The bill was "An act to institute an University within this State," which was read a third time. Before a vote was taken on this bill, there was a debate over the provision giving the Regents of the University the power to grant charters of incorporation. John Lansing, Jr., of Albany County objected to

giving the Regents this power, for he argued that it should reside only in the legislature.

2. The bill was recommitted to committee. The act, however, gave the Regents the power to incorporate colleges (*Laws of the State of New York*, II, 526).

# New York Assembly. Remarks on an Act Directing a Mode of Trial and Allowing of Divorces in Cases of Adultery

[New York, March 28, 1787]

The house then went into the consideration of the objections of the council of revision to the *divorce bill*.[1]

The said objections being read.

Col. *Hamilton* moved that, the bill pass into a law, notwithstanding the objections of the council.

He did not he said like the clause which had been introduced by the senate, and on which the objections of the council were founded, but he would remedy that defect, by a bill he would move for leave to bring in, for that purpose. He thought it would be extremely hard, that by reason of one small defect in the law, relief should be denied to many who are real objects of distress.[2]

*The* [New York] *Daily Advertiser*, April 6, 1787.

1. "An act directing, a mode of trial, and allowing of Divorces in cases of Adultery," was passed by the legislature and sent to the Council of Revision on March 12, 1787. On March 20 the council's veto of the bill was submitted to the Assembly; consideration of the veto was postponed until March 28. The Council of Revision objected to the second clause of the bill which prohibited the remarriage of any person convicted of adultery. The Council stated: "It might not, perhaps, be an improper punishment, to confine offenders of this class, to a state of perpetual celibacy and mortification within the walls of a cloyster; but to suffer them to remain in society, without a possibility of remarrying, is, in a degree, to compel them by law, to live in the open violation of the rules of chastity and decency; and will, it is to be apprehended, have a pernicious influence on the public morals" (New York Assembly *Journal*, 1787, 125).

2. The Assembly voted to override the objections of the Council of Revision, and the bill became law on March 30 (*Laws of the State of New York*, II, 494–95).

## New York Assembly. Remarks on an Act
## Acknowledging the Independence of Vermont [1]

[New York, March 28, 1787]

Mr. Chairman,

The counsel for the petitioners has entered into a large field of argument against the present bill. He has endeavoured to shew that it is contrary to the constitution, to the maxims of sound policy and to the rights of property. His observations have not been destitute of weight. They appear to have the more force, as they are to a certain degree founded in truth. But it is the province of the committee to distinguish the just limits of the principles he has advanced; how far they extend, and where they terminate. To aid the committee in this enquiry shall be my endeavour, and following the counsel for the petitioners; through the different heads of his argument, I hope to be able to shew, that neither of the objections he has urged, stands in the way of the measure proposed, and that the constitution permits, policy demands it and justice acquiesces in its adoption.

The first objection is drawn from that great principle of the social compact—that the chief object of government is to protect the rights of individuals by the united strength of the community.[2] The justness of this principle is not to be disputed; but its extent remains

The [New York] Daily Advertiser, April 5, 1787.

1. On March 24 a petition from several persons who owned lands "in the district of territory commonly called Vermont" was received by the legislature. The petitioners asked for a copy of the proposed act for recognizing the independence of Vermont (see H's draft of the act, dated March 14) and asked that they or their counsel be allowed to argue their case before the Assembly. The Assembly resolved that the petitioners be given a copy of the proposed act and that they be granted a hearing on March 28. On March 28 Richard Harison, a prominent New York lawyer, spoke on behalf of the petitioners.

2. Harison had begun his speech by saying that the petitioners for whom he spoke had a right to the protection of the state. "The social compact, to which all the members of society are parties, and by which all of them are bound," he argued, "was first formed to preserve the rights and properties of each, by the united strength of the whole; and this sacred compact must suffer the grossest violation, whenever the rights and properties even of the meanest individual are sacrificed without the most pressing and apparent necessity." Harison's speech is printed in Walton, Records of Vermont, III, 424–30.

to be ascertained. It must be taken with this limitation: The united strength of the community ought to be exerted for the protection of individuals so far as there is a rational prospect of success; so far as is consistent with the safety and well being of the whole. The duty of a nation is always limited by these considerations. It is bound to make efforts and encounter hazards for the protection of its members proportioned to its abilities, warranted by a reasonable expectation of a favorable issue, and compatible with its eventual security. But it is not bound to enter in or prosecute enterprises of a manifest rashness and folly; or which, in the event of success, would be productive of more mischief than good.

This qualification of the principle, can no more be denied than the principle itself. The counsel for the petitioners indeed admits it in substance when he admits that a case of extreme necessity is an exception to the rule; but he adds that this necessity must be apparent and unequivocal.[3]

What constitutes a case of extreme necessity, admits of no precise definition. It is allways a question of fact, to be determined by a consideration of the condition of the parties, and the particular circumstances of the case itself. A case of necessity then exists, when every discerning, unprejudiced man, well acquainted with facts, must be convinced that a measure cannot be *undertaken* or *pursued* with a probability [4] of success. To determine this an experiment is not always necessary: Circumstances may exist so decisive and palpable in their nature, as to render it the extreme of temerity to *begin* as well as to *continue* an experiment. The propriety of doing the one or the other, must equally be decided by a judicious estimater of the national situation.

The tendency of the principle contended for, and the application of it in argument, has been to prove, that the state ought to employ the common strength of the society to protect the rights of its citizens, interested in the district of territory in question, by reducing the revolted inhabitants of that district to an obedience to its laws. The enquiry therefore is—can this be done? Is it in a rational sense practicable? Is the state in a situation to undertake it? Is there a probability that the object will be more attainable at a future day?

3. See the last part of the quotation in note 2.
4. In original, "probabily."

Is there not rather a probability that it will be every day more out of our reach, and that leaving things in their present state, will be attended with serious dangers and incoveniencies? Is it even desireable, if practicable, to reduce the people in question under subjection to this state?

In pursuing this enquiry we ought to bear in mind, that a nation is never to regulate its conduct by remote possibilities or mere contingencies, but by such probability as may reasonably be inferred from the existing state of things, and the usual course of human affairs.

With this caution, no well informed mind can be at a loss in what manner to answer the questions I have proposed. A concise review of the past, and a dispassionate consideration of the present, will enable us to judge with accuracy of the obligations and interests of the state.

The pretensions to independence of the district of territory in question, began shortly after the commencement of the late revolution.[5] We were then engaged in a war for our existence as a people, which required the utmost exertion of our resources to give us a chance of success. To have diverted any part of them from this object to that of subduing the inhabitants of Vermont—to have involved a domestic quarrel which would have compelled that hardy and numerous body of men to throw themselves into the arms of the power, with which we were then contending, instead of joining their efforts to ours in the common cause of American liberty, as they for a long time did, with great advantage to it, would have been a species of phrenzy, for which there could have been no apology, and would have endangered the fate of the revolution more than any one step we could have taken.

This idea is too obvious to need being enlarged upon. The most prejudiced will acquit the state from blame for not trying the effect of force against that people during the continuance of the war. Every moderate measure, every thing short of hostility, or a total sacrifice of those rights, which were the original cause of the revolt, and which are the occasion of the opposition to the present bill, were tried. Conciliating laws were passed, overtures made, negotiations carried on in Congress, but all to no purpose.

5. Vermont's independence was declared in January, 1777.

The peace found the Vermonteers in a state of actual independence, which they had enjoyed for several years—organized under a regular form of government, and increased in strength by a considerable accession of numbers. It found this state the principal seat of the war, exhausted by peculiar exertions and overwhelmed in debt. The embarrassments arising from this situation press us daily. The utmost exertion of wisdom in our public councils, would not be more than equal to extricating us from them. As matters stand, the public debts are unprovided for, and the public credit prostrate.

Are we now then, in a situation to undertake the reduction of Vermont? Or are we likely speedily to be in such a situation? Where are our resources, where our public credit to enable us to carry on an offensive war?

We ought to recollect, that in war, to defend or attack, are very different things—to the first, the mountains, the wildernesses, the militia, sometimes even the poverty of a country will suffice; the latter requires an *army* and a *treasury*.

The population of Vermont will not be rated too high, if stated at nearly one half of that of New-York. Can any reasonable man suppose that New-York, with the load of debt the revolution has left upon it and under a popular government, would be able to carry on with advantage an offensive war against a people half as numerous as itself, in their own territory; a territory defended as much by its natural situation, as by the numbers and hardihood of its inhabitants? Can it be imagined that it would be able finally to reduce such a people to its obedience? The supposition would be chimerical and the attempt madness.

Can we hope a more favorable posture of affairs hereafter? Will not the population and strength of Vermont increase in ratio to our own? There is perhaps no essential difference between their government an[d] ours—the necessity of making provision in one way, or another, for the exigencies of the union, and for the discharge of the debts of the state, must continue to subject our citizens to heavier burthens than are borne by the inhabitants of that country; who have no call for revenue beyond the support of their domestic administration. A country possessing a fertile soil exempt from taxes, cannot fail of having a rapid growth.

The enterprise will of course become more difficult by delay, and procrastination can only serve to render the claims of the state and its citizens, in the opinion of mankind, obsolete, and to give the cement of time to the connection which the people of Vermont have in all appearance already formed with the British government. This last point I shall discuss more fully in another place.

I have confined myself in my reasoning to an examination of what is practicable on the part of this state alone—No assistance is to be expected from our neighbours: Their opinion of the origin of the controversy between this state and the people of Vermont, whether well or ill founded, is not generally in our favor; and it is notorious that the eastern states have uniformly countenanced the independence of that country. This might suggest to us reflections that would confirm the belief of the impracticability of destroying, and the danger of attempting to destroy that independence.

The scheme of coertion would ill suit even the disposition of our own citizens; the habits of thinking, to which the revolution has given birth, are not adapted to the idea of a contest for dominion over a people disinclined to live under our government.

And in reality it is not the interest of the state ever to regain its dominion over them by force. We shall do well to advert to the nature of our government and the extent of the state, according to its acknowledged limits. Are we sure we shall be able to govern what we already possess, or would it be wise to wish to try the strength of our government over a numerous body of people disaffected to it, and compelled to submit to its authority by force? For my part I should regard the re-union of Vermont to this state as one of the greatest evils that could befall it, as a source of continual embarrassment and disquietude.

It is hinted by the counsel for the petitioners that many of the inhabitants of Vermont are desirous of living under our government; and sanguine tempers have long ago predicted that they would shortly grow weary of their independence, throw it off and become reunited with us and New-Hampshire of their own accord. There are clear principles of human nature to which we may resort to falsify this prediction. In popular governments the sentiments of the people generally take their tone from their leaders. The leaders of Vermont cannot desire a reunion with New-York, because this would amount to an abdication of their own power and consequence. The people of Vermont will not desire it; because no people ever desired to pass from a situation in which they were exempted from taxes, and in which they suffered no particular oppression, to one in which they would be subject to burthens comparatively heavy.

I pass now to an examination of the constitutionality of the measure proposed by the bill. It is observed that by the constitution, the counties of Charlotte, Cumberland and Gloucester are constituent parts of the state—that one article of it declares that no power shall be exercised over the people, but such as is derived from, and granted by them, that no express power is given to the legislature to dismember any part of the state; and that this silence of the constitution is a tacit reservation of that power to the people.

To all this I answer, that the sovereignty of the people by our consitution is vested in their representatives in senate and assembly, with the intervention of the council of revision and, that the power of dismembering the state under certain circumstances is a necessary appendage of the sovereignty. The practice of nations and the authority of writers conspire to establish this principle; and the safety of society requires it. There are certain situations of Kingdoms and states in which the sacrifice of a part is essential to the preservation or welfare of the rest.

History furnishes abundant examples of such sacrafices. Nations in making peace frequently cede parts of their territories to each other. Civil commotions have many times produced similar dismemberments. The monarchy of Spain after a destructive and fruitless contest to preserve it was obliged at last to surrender its dominion over the Netherlands. The Crown of Austria was in like manner compelled to abandon its jurisdiction over the Swiss Cantons. And the United-States are a recent and still more signal instance of the exercise of the same right. Neither of these instances has been censured or condemned nor the power of the sovereign to accede to the separation called in question.

The celebrated author quoted by the council for the petitioners [6]

6. H is referring to the following statement by Harison:
"Such are the ideas of the great Vattel, in his first book, chap. 21st. The same masterly writer declares in the second chapter of the same book, that 'if a nation is obliged to preserve itself, it is not less obliged carefully to preserve all its members. The nation (says he) owes this to itself, since the loss of even one of its members weakens it and is injurious to its own preservation. It

is explicit on this article and decides with clearness that the prince or body entrusted with the sovereign authority may in certain emergencies dismember the empire and lop off a limb for the good of the body. This inferrence from the silence of a constitution, is the reverse of that drawn by the council for the petitioners. Doubts have been raised by particular theorists upon this subject; but their theories were too abstract for practice, and are now exploded by the ablest writers on the laws of nations. Indeed those doubts were chiefly applied to the case of a cession or relinquishment of a part of the empire, still in possession of the sovereign; it has been long considered as a clear point, that where a part of an empire is *actually severed* by conquest, or a revolution, the prince or body, vested with the administration of the government, has a right to assent to, and to ratify that separation. This is an obvious and important distinction; from which other inferrences of moment will be drawn in another place. It will be found in Vattel. Book IV Chap 2d §.[7]

Vermont is in fact severed from New-York, and has been so for years. There is no reasonable prospect of recovering it, and the attempt would be attended with certain and serious calamities. The legislature have therefore an undoubted right to relinquish it, and policy dictates that it should be done.

It is of no force to say that this principle would authorise the dismemberment of Long Island, or of any other part of the state; there is no doubt, the same circumstances concurring, the same consequences would result, but not sooner; and it will be the duty of the state to endeavour to prevent a similar extremity.

The next thing, in the order observed by the counsel for the petitioners that presents itself to our discussion, is the policy of the measure.

Against this it is objected that the precedent would be dangerous; that the facility with which the Vermonteers will have accomplished their object, might invite other parts of this state, and the United States to follow the example.

To this I answer, that examples have little to do with the revolutions of empire: wherever such a state of things exist as to make it

---

owes this also to the members in particular in consequence of the very act of association.'" (Walton, *Records of Vermont*, III, 425–26.)

7. Vattel, *The Law of Nations.*

the interest or the inclination of a large body of people to separate from the society with which they have been connected, and at the same time to afford a prospect of success, they will generally yield to the impulse, without much inquiry or solicitude about what has been done by others, or upon other occasions; and when this is not the case, precedents will never create the disposition. Events of this kind are not produced or controled by the ordinary operations of human policy, care or contrivance.

But whatever may be the effect of the example, it is too late to prevent or redress the evil. It sprang up under circumstances which forbade the application of an effectual remedy, and it has now acquired a maturity which would mock all our efforts to counteract it. Vermont is lost to New-York, beyond the possibility of a recovery; and a passive acquiescence in its independence, cannot make it more formidable, as an example, than a direct recognition of it. Success and impunity are the ingredients that are to constitute the force of the example, and these will exist in either case.

On the other hand the policy of the measure results from two important considerations; the one, that by the union of Vermont to the confederacy, it must of course bear a proportion of the public burdens; the other, that it would be detached from the completion of a connection, already in all appearance begun with a foreign power. The incorporation of Vermont into the confederacy is by the bill, made an express condition of the acknowledgement of their independence.

The first advantage was too obvious to be denied; though observations have been made to diminish its importance. Its inland situation has been noted as a circumstance that precluded the expectation of any considerable revenue from it. But the same thing might be said of the interior parts of this and of the other states; and yet we should make a much worse figure than we do, if our resources were to be drawn wholly from our Atlantic settlements. The country of Vermont is fertile and will soon be populous; and the resources which it may be capable of affording at a day not far remote, though not of great magnitude, will by no means be contemptible.

But the principal advantage to be expected from the measure, is the one mentioned last. Here it is asked, where is the evidence of the fact, where the proof of the connection? Would Great Britain,

which has so recently, in a solemn treaty, acknowledged the territory
in question, to be comprehended within the limits of the United
States, derogate from that treaty, and for so insignificant an object
as a connection with a small corner of one of the states, hazard a
rupture with the whole confederacy?

Not expecting a formal call for the evidence of the fact, my memory is not prepared to enter into all the details requisite to its full
elucidation. I well remember, that during the latter periods of the
war, a variety of circumstances produced a connection of its existence every where; in the army, in the legislature, and in Congress.
Among other transactions, that came to my knowlege, I shall mention
one as nearly as my recollection will serve me. Some time in the
year 1781, *Fay*,[8] and *Ira Allen*, two of the most influential individuals
in that country, went into Canada, and we were well informed, had
repeated interviews with General Haldimand.[9] Not long after, a
party of the British under St. Leger, penetrated as far Ticonderoga.

A detachment from that body, fell in by accident with a small
party of Vermonteers, fired upon them, killed one of their number
and took the rest prisoners. Discovering their mistake, they interred
the dead body with the honors of war, and sent the prisoners home
loaded with kindnesses and caresses. From that period a free intercourse subsisted between Canada and Vermont.[10] This is one proof,
and a pretty decisive one to shew that a connection was formed during the war. I doubt not there are others equally strong, within the
recollection of other members of the committee. Since the peace,
this intercourse has been cultivated with reciprocal zeal, and there
are circumstances related (which I shall not repeat as they do not
come to me with sufficient authenticity) that look strongly to a
continuance of the connection.

8. Joseph Fay acted as the emissary of Ethan and Ira Allen in negotiations
with the British.

9. After unsuccessful attempts to secure recognition of Vermont's independence by the Continental Congress, Ethan and Ira Allen became interested
in the possibility of a separate peace and an alliance with Great Britain. General Frederick Haldimand, governor of the province of Quebec, served as the
British representative in subsequent negotiations.

10. In the autumn of 1781 a British scouting party encountered a group
of Vermonters. A skirmish ensued, and one of the Vermonters, Sergeant
Archelaus Tupper, was killed. Colonel Barry St. Leger, the commander of
the British expedition, sent a letter to the governor of Vermont, Thomas

If this connection ever existed, what reason have we to believe that it has been since dissolved? To me, I confess, there appears none. On the contrary, the situation of the parties in my opinion forbid the supposition of its dissolution.

I flatter myself, those who know my manner of thinking, will acquit me from a disposition to sow groundless jealousies of any nation. I consider a conduct of this kind, as undignified and indelicate, in a public character; and if I were not persuaded the suspicions I entertain [11] are well founded, no motive would have induced me to bring them forward.

It is asked, in substance, what object Great Britain can have in cultivating such a connection; this admits of several answers.

Great Britain cannot but perceive that our governments are feeble and distracted; that the union wants energy; the nation concert. That our public debts are unprovided for; our federal treasury empty; our trade languishing. She may flatter herself that this state of things will be productive of discontents among the people; and that these discontents may lead to a voluntary return to her dominion. She may hope to see in this country a counterpart of the restoration of Charles the second. However mistaken they may be, it is not impossible, that speculations of this kind may enter into the head of a British minister.

The government lately established in Canada—the splendid title of viceroy—seem to look beyond the dreary regions of Canada and Nova Scotia.[12]

In this view she would naturally lay hold of Vermont as a link in the chain of events. It would be a positive acquisition of so much, and nothing could better answer the purpose of accelerating the progress of discontent than the example of a country, part of ourselves, comparativly speaking, free from taxes. Nothing could have

---

Chittenden, expressing his regret that British troops had killed a citizen of Vermont.

11. In original, "entertrin."

12. H is probably referring to the changes made by the British in the Canadian governmental system in 1786. Before 1786, the provinces of Canada had been administered by governors. In August, 1786, Sir Guy Carleton, recently raised to the peerage as Lord Dorchester, was named governor-in-chief of all the British North American provinces except Newfoundland. H was mistaken in using the title of viceroy.

a more powerful influence than such an example, upon the inhabitants of the settlements bordering upon that Country. How far and how rapidly it might extend itself is a matter not easy to be calculated.

But laying aside every supposition of this nature, there are motives of immoderate interest which would dispose the British government to cultivate Vermont. A connection with Vermont will hereafter conduce to the security of Canada and to the preservation of the western posts. That Great-Britain means to retain these posts may be inferred from the interest she has in doing it. The ostensible reason for not having delivered them up heretofore is the infractions of the treaty on our part; but though these infractions in some instances cannot be denied, it may fairly be presumed that they are nothing more than the pretext for witholding the posts while the true motive is the prodigious advantage which the monoply [13] of the furr trade affords to the commerce of the English nation.

If Great-Britain has formed the design of finally retaining those posts she must look forward sooner or later to a rupture with this country; for degraded as we are by our mismanagement she can hardly entertain so mean an opinion of us as to expect we shall eventually submit to such a violation of our rights and interests without a struggle. And in such a case Vermont would be no despicable auxiliary.

But would Great Britain hazard a war with the United-States for so inconsiderable an object?

In the first place the object is not inconsiderable; in the next, our situation is not such as to render our resentment formidable. This situation is perhaps better understood by every body else than ourselves; and no nation would forego a present advantage to our detriment, while it knew that a change of government must precede any inconveniencies from our displeasure.

I do not suppose that the British government would in the present state of things commit itself to any avowed engagements with the people of Vermont. It will no doubt take care to be in such a situation as to leave itself at liberty to act according to circumstances; but it will, and I have no doubt does, by the intermediation of its

13. In original, "monolopy."

officers, keep up a secret intercourse with the leaders of that people, to endeavour gradually to mould them to its interest, and to be ready to convert them to its own purposes upon any favourable conjuncture, or future emergency. This policy is so obvious and safe, that it would be presumeable, without any evidence of its existence.

On the part of Vermont, while their fate in the American scale remains suspended, considerations of safety would direct them to such a connection with the British government. They would not choose to lie at our mercy, or to depend on their strength if they could find refuge and support else where.

There is a circumstance too mentioned, with a different view, by the counsel for the petitioners, which would contribute to this connection. I mean the relative situation of Canada and Vermont. It is asked "may not this situation induce Vermont to regret the offer of independence and prompt the people of that country for the sake of commerce, to form still closer connections with a foreign power?" [14] I ask does not this situation, which it is supposed might have so powerful an influence, afford a strong presumption of the existence of such a connection. And is it not our true policy to take away every additional temptation?

I shall readily admit that it is very doubtful whether Vermont will accept the proffered acknowledgment of its independence, upon the condition annexed. I firmly believe, that she does not desire it, and that she would be perplexed by the dilemma to which she would be reduced. But whether she accepts it or not, the offer may be expected to have a good effect. It would at least serve to ascertain facts. Her refusal would be a conclusive evidence of a determined predilection to a foreign connection; and it would shew the United States the absolute necessity of combining their efforts to subvert an independence, so hostile to their safety. If they should find them-

14. Harison's complete statement from which H quoted was as follows:
"But, Sir, if such a connexion actually subsists between Canada and Vermont, can this honorable house be assured that the present bill will dissolve it? May we not rather suppose that their inland situation and proximity to the lakes may prompt them, for the sake of commerce, to form still closer connexions with a foreign power, and will they not possess opportunities of doing mischief much greater than they have at present, when in consequence of this bill they are admitted into the public councils, and become acquainted with all the secrets of the union." (Walton, *Records of Vermont*, III, 426.)

selves unequal to the undertaking, it must operate as a new inducement to the several states to strengthen the union.

In every light therefore the measure on national ground appears
adviseable; but it still remains to inquire what will be our duty in
respect to the citizens of this state, who are owners of land in Vermont. How far shall we violate their rights, and how far are we
bound to make them compensation?

The claim to a compensation is the thing which has been with
most propriety urged, by the counsel for the petitioners. Let us
however, examine its nature and foundation.

But before I enter into this examination, I shall repeat an observation which I made upon a former occasion—whatever obligations
there may be on the part of the state, cannot be encreased by acceding to the measure proposed. If Vermont is not irretrievably lost
to this state, the duty of protection which it owes to individuals
obliges it to employ the common strength to reinstate them in their
rights; if it is irretrievably lost, no rights capable of being rendered
effective will be sacrificed; of course no obligation to making a
recompence will exist.

But the truth is, the present bill, so far from surrendering the
rights of individuals, puts things in the only train in which they will
ever have an opportunity of giving validity. The third clause of
the ninth article of the confederation expressly declares that all controversies about the private right of soil between the citizens of
different states shall be decided by a Federal Court. The counsel
for the Petitioners tells us that *his Clients* doubt the operation of
this clause, but as he gives us no reason for the doubt, I shall only
say that the terms of it appear to me clear and explicit.

I have no doubt that the petitioners would be entitled to a federal
court; and though that court would not decide in such a question
like the tribunals of New-York, but upon general principles of
natural and political right, I should confidently expect that all
equitable claims of our citizens would have their full effect.

It is however further observed on this head, that the expence of
such court would exceed the abilities of individuals, and could only
be compassed by the resources of sovereign states.

If this suggestion should be admitted to be true (though I think
the expence is greatly over rated) yet surely it would be more

reasonable to ask the state for its assistance, in procuring a federal court to obtain justice to the petitioners, than to ask it to undertake a ruinous war for that purpose. The difference in expence would not bear a comparison. Indeed the first would be a trifling object to the state, while the last would exceed its abilities, and perhaps end in its disgrace.

But if the bill even contained no provision for obtaining justice to the petitioners, I should hold that the state would not be under a strict obligation to recompence them for their losses. The distinction I would lay down upon the subject is this; If a government voluntarily bargains away the rights or disposes [15] of the property of its citizens, in their enjoyments, possession, or power, it is bound to make compensation for the thing of which it hath deprived them; but if they are actually dispossessed of those rights or that property by the casualties of war, or a revolution, the state, if the public good requires it, may abandon them to the loss, without being obliged to make reparation. The author quoted by the counsel for the petitioners, has in view the case of a voluntary disposition of the property of citizens in the power of the state; and his doctrine is unquestionably just—but it does not apply to the case of an actual dispossession by any of those events in which nations have no choice. In wars between states, the sovereign is never supposed to be bound to make good the losses which the subject sustains by the captures or ravages of the enemy, tho' they should amount to the destruction of his whole property; and yet nothing can be more agreeable to natural equity, than that those who happen to be the unlucky victims of the war should be indemnified by the community. But in practice such a principle would be found attended with endless difficulties and inconveniences; and therefore the reverse of it has been adopted as a general rule. The individual sufferer, however, might with great colour of justice, say to the government, why did you make peace without stipulating a reparation for the damage done to your citizens? If it was necessary for the public good to sacrifice my interests, I have a right to a public compensation for my losses.

Though this case may upon a superficial view appear dissimilar to the one under consideration; yet the principle upon examination will be found as applicable to the one as to the other. The true

15. In original, "disposses."

reason is that the resources of nations are not adequate to the reparation of such extensive losses as those which are commonly occasioned by wars and revolutions; and it would therefore be contrary to the general good of society to establish it as a rule that there is a strict obligation to repay such losses. It is better that there should be individual sufferings, than to admit a rule which would fetter the operations of government and distress the affairs of the community.

Generousity and policy may in particular instances dictate such compensations, sometimes they have been made by nations, but much oftener omitted. The propriety of doing the one or the other must depend on circumstances in which the ability of the public will always be a primary consideration.

I think, sir, I have by this time gone through all the arguments that have been brought against the bill and I hope satisfactorily refuted them.

I shall say a little in answer to the observations drawn from the examples of Roman magnanimity.[16] Neither the manners nor the genius of Rome are suited to the republic or age we live in. All her maxims and habits were military, her government was constituted for war. Ours is unfit for it, and our situation still less than our constitution, invites us to emulate the conduct of Rome, or to attempt a display of unprofitable heroism.

One more observation will conclude what I have to say—the present situation [of] our national affairs appears to me peculiarly critical. I know not what may be the result of the disordered state of our government. I am therefore the more solicitous to guard against danger from abroad. Gentlemen who view our public affairs in the same light in which they present themselves to my mind, will, I trust, vote with me upon the present occasion. Those on the contrary, who think all is well—who suppose our government is full of energy—our credit high—and trade and finances flourishing—will probably see no room for any anxiety about the matter, and may be disposed to leave Vermont in its present state. If the bill should fail, I hope they will never have occasion to regret the opportunity they have lost.

16. Stating that the Americans should prove themselves as valiant as the Romans, Harison had asked what the Romans would have done "if an inconsiderable part of their citizens had presumed to declare themselves a separate and independent state" (Walton, *Records of Vermont*, III, 427).

As to the petitioners, I shall only say that I have no reason to doubt the purity of the motives with which they are actuated. With many of them I am too well acquainted to permit me to entertain any unfavourable impression of their conduct; but however, their opinion of their own rights or interests may have misled them in estimating the merits of the question before the committee, I trust we shall be cautious how we suffer our judgment of a national question to be biassed or misguided by the speciousness of the arguments, or appearances on which their opposition is supported.[17]

17. On April 11 the Assembly passed the bill recognizing the independence of Vermont. It was rejected by the Senate.

## New York Assembly. Report on the Petition of Margaret Livingston

*New York, March 31, 1787.* On this date Hamilton, as chairman of a committee on the petition of Margaret Livingston, brought in a bill entitled "An act for dividing the township of New Stamford in Ulster county." [1]

New York Assembly *Journal*, 1787, 129.
1. The bill introduced by H was incorporated in "AN ACT for the relief of persons who paid money into the treasury of this State . . . and for other purposes therein mentioned" (*Laws of the State of New York*, II, 580–90).

## From Daniel Coxe [1]

*London, April 4, 1787.* ". . . Interested as I am in a large landed Property in the State of New Yorke; under former Grants of the Crown, and which not having been confiscated, is considered to be secure to me in virtue of the Treaty, I am anxious to be informed, from a Gentleman of your high Professional merit, whether or not, and how far, the Principle of *Alienism*, is adopted seriously by your State, or Law Courts, or intended to be put in Execution on any Event occuring on the Death of any Landholder, being a *British Subject.* . . ."

ALS, Hamilton Papers, Library of Congress.
1. Daniel Coxe was a former Loyalist.

## From Marquis de Lafayette

Paris April the 12th 1787

My dear Hamilton

It is an Age since I Heard from you. Of you I Hear By some of our friends, and in the News Papers. But altho I Have a Right to Complain, I want to let you know the proceedings of our Assembly, which as it is Unusual in France, May Raise Your Curiosity.

Our Constitution is pretty much what it was in England Before it Had Been fairly writen down, and Minutely preserved; so that we Have great claims to freedom, to a National Representation, to the Denial of Taxes, &c., &c. But despotism on one hand, and levity on the other Have Maneuvred us out of allmost Every privilege & they will subsist However more or less in some provinces, and particularly those of Bretagne.

Now that the follies of Courts Had obliged Governemens to saddle us with new taxes and the opposition of our Magistrats did present itself as an obstacle to the Ministers, they Have thought proper to Call an Assembly of Notables, chosen By the King,[1] But taken among the first people in Each order, and to Begin with granting them what is more wished for By the Nation, an Assembly in each province.[2]

The last Assembly of Notables in 1626 Had Been obedient to the Ministers. This one Came at a more enlightened period. It Happened Under a minister, M. de Calonne,[3] who altho He Has parts, is not equal to some of the Members, Men of the first Abilities. We are Backed By the Nation, and altho not Her Representatives, Have Behaved as Her interpreters, and we Have formed a great Majority in favour of popular Measures.

The speeches from the throne, those of M. de Calonne all Have Been printed—the last one Contains Many false Hoods. The first Measure we took was for the Clergy to declare they were Ready to pay in the same proportion with other people, for the ⟨Noblesse⟩ [4] to Make the same declaration and Reject a pecuniary privilege that was offered in lieu of the other that is taken off.

We Have Gratefully Accepted the provincial Elective assemblies,

But Have united on such Alterations as will Envigorate them: M. de Calonne Had made a Mixture of democracy and despotism which did Anhiliate those Checks and graduations that are Necessary Evils where Ever there is a King. But I think the provincial Assemblies as they are proposed By us, May lay a foundation for a good Building.[5]

Several plans for the removal of Internal Custom offices, for the free Exportation of Corn, for the change in the salt tax, for the Anihilation of some duties, and Now for the disposal of the King's domanial possessions all Have Been Examined and Underwent several Alterations. To some we Have only left the titles of the Chapters, But changed them in my opinion much for the Better.

The idea of a General tax in kind was proposed By the Governement,[6] But we said it was not practicable. As to any new imposition, we Have Answered it is impossible to form an opinion Before we know the Returns of the Exportes of the two last years, and the plans of Œconomy that are intended.[7] We Have not, it is true, Any powers from the Nation—But our Opinion is asked, and in a Measure Has Become Necessary—and a Majority of us do not think theyr opinion Can Be given, Untill those preliminaries are fulfilled.

There is a very interesting Contrast Between the King's power at Versailles, and the Opposition of the Assembly which is Held there—and Divided in seven Committees of 20, or 22 each—presided By a prince of the Blood. Hitherto we Have not voted in a General Assembly altho' we Had some to Hear the Minutes. But the opinions of the Committees only are not taken—and in the end, each vote will Be prono[u]nced in the Whole House, Beginning from the last up to the first in Rank. You know that we Have the Clergy, Noblesse, Magistracy, and Tiers etat.

At the last meeting we Had Before the Recess of these Holy ⟨Days⟩ I Had a personal Battle to ⟨–⟩ of some importance—the King's domanial property Has Been a pretence to lavish Monney on princes of the Blood, favourites and Powerfull people of the Country. I Had the day Before Moved for an examination of those Bargains, wherein more than fifty millions Have Been thrown a way. The great people Being afraid of Being found out, and particularly M. de Calonne who is guilty of the most Indecent depredation, thought they must intimidate me and the Bishop of Langres

(M de La Luzerne's Brother) who Had seconded My Motion.[8] They in consequence of it persuaded the king to Have us told By His Brother our president,[9] that Such Motions ought to Be signed— upon which I signed the inclosed paper—and the Bishop said that after the Recess He would Bring in some Accounts Signed by Him of the Bargain of sinecure made by M. de Calonne.

The King was very Angry with me. M. de Calonne, who Had His Confidence, intended signal Revenge. I was preparing to support what I Had said, when we suddenly Heard that M. de Calonne Had Been dismissed. The Keeper of the seals Has also Been sent off. I am glad we got Rid of M. de Calonne and wish His successor, who unfortunately is an old Broken man,[10] may improve the opportunity of this Assembly and let us make useful arrangements.

Adieu, my dear Hamilton, My Best Respects wait on Mrs. Hamilton. Remember me to Gnl Knox, Wadsworth—all our friends, and particularly the good doctor.[11] Most affectionately   Yours

Lafayette

Don't tell the french chargé d'affaires [12] that you Have this paper from me, except that there is nothing in it, for Copies have spread every where.

ALS, Hamilton Papers, Library of Congress.

1. The Assembly of Notables, summoned to give assent to the fiscal and administrative reforms of the Crown, met on February 22 and remained in session until May 25, 1787.

2. Among the many recommendations which Charles-Alexandre de Calonne, the Controller General of Finance, made to the Assembly of Notables was one which provided that in the provinces there should be assemblies charged with the apportionment of the taxes and given a share in the local administration.

3. Calonne, who succeeded Necker as Controller General of Finance in 1783, retained the post until 1787.

4. The word in broken brackets is from *JCHW*, I, 432–35.

5. The Notables objected to some aspects of Calonne's plan to establish provincial assemblies. Arguing that it would be unconstitutional not to distinguish among the three orders, the Notables demanded that provincial assemblies consist of the three orders according to a predetermined proportion.

6. Calonne had recommended the imposition of a land tax which was to be levied upon the annual production of the land at the time of harvest.

7. The Notables, arguing that before authorizing new taxes they must know the amount of the deficit in the royal treasury, asked Calonne for a statement of the receipts and expenses of the government. The accounts of the royal treasury previously had been kept secret.

8. Cesar-Guillaume de La Luzerne was the Bishop of Langres. "M. de la Luzerne" may have been either the Chevalier de La Luzerne, who was French

Minister to the United States during the American Revolution, or the Comte de La Luzerne, who was Minister of the Marine in France.

9. Charles-Philippe, Comte d'Artois, later King Charles X of France, was chairman of the Second Bureau of the Council of Notables.

10. Michel Bouvard de Fourqueux was Calonne's *ad interim* successor.

11. Henry Knox, Jeremiah Wadsworth, and Dr. John Cochran.

12. Louis Otto was the French chargé d'affaires in the United States.

## New York Assembly. Remarks on an Amendment to an Act Relative to Debts Due Persons Within the Enemy's Lines

[New York, April 12, 1787]

Went into a committee on the bill to repeal the citation acts. . . .[1]

Mr. Hamilton advocated the bill with great ability and candor; he mentioned the bad effects of the present laws; the difficulties that the courts of justice threw in the way of them—and the impossibility ever to amend them is such a manner as to have them acted upon. He urged the influence the opinion of our courts ought to have on the legislature. The courts were not interested, and then decision were perfectly impartial. He asked if the southern district of the state, instead of having fared tolerably well, had been ruined, would the legislature have compelled their debtors who were without the lines to have paid additional sums. This he did not believe. And why then, said he, compel the creditors to take a less sum. He mentioned that in several instances, the severity of the law fell on gentlemen who were attached to the American cause, and who had acted meritoriously in the revolution. It was certainly not right to view all the creditors as enemies. Remarking on the ill effects of the legislature interfering in private contracts, and the violation of public faith which it occasioned, he observed, that it would destroy all credit; and be the means of injuring many whom the legislature had intended to benefit.

*The* [New York] *Daily Advertiser,* April 17, 1787.

1. A committee of the whole house reported on a bill entitled "An act to amend an act entitled an act relative to debts due to persons within the enemy's lines, and another act entitled an act to explain and amend the act entitled an act relative to debts due persons within the enemy's lines." The first act relative to debts due persons within the enemy lines, passed on July 12, 1782, stayed prosecutions for debts owed to such persons and discharged New York

citizens from the payment of interest on claims due them (*Laws of the State of New York*, I, 499–501). This act was amended in November, 1784. The clause of the proposed bill which was under debate provided that debts due persons who, during the War, were within the enemy lines should be paid in three annual installments, and that interest should be paid on the sum due from a date unspecified in the act. After H's remarks the Assembly took up the question of the date from which interest should be paid. H made a motion that "the blanks in the said clause should be filled up by inserting the first day of January 1784." His motion was defeated, and the Assembly voted to insert the "first day of May 1786" (New York Assembly *Journal*, 1787, 157).

The bill was passed on April 20 (*Laws of the State of New York*, II, 562–64).

## New York Assembly. Report on the Petition of Henry Ludenton [1]

*New York, April 14, 1787.* In his petition, Ludenton asserted that "certain depreciation certificates" had been stolen from him and, after passing through several hands, used for the purchase of a forfeited estate. Ludenton then asked that these certificates be returned. Hamilton, as chairman of a committee, recommended "as an act of generosity in the State," that the treasurer be instructed to return the certificates.

New York Assembly *Journal*, 1787, 161.

1. Ludenton had been a member of the New York Assembly from Dutchess County in 1780, 1781, and 1786.

## New York Assembly. Motion for Leave to Bring in a Bill on Places at Which the Legislature Shall Meet

[New York, April 16, 1787]

Mr. Hamilton moved for leave to bring in a bill to establish the places at which the ordinary sessions of the Legislature shall be holden.[1]

*Ordered*, That leave be given accordingly.

Mr. Hamilton, according to leave, brought in the said bill, entitled *An act to establish the places at which the ordinary sessions of the Legislature shall be holden*, which was read the first time, and ordered a second reading.

New York Assembly *Journal*, 1787, 164.

1. Each session of the legislature decided the location of the succeeding session. The 1786 and 1787 sessions met in New York City; the 1788 session met in Poughkeepsie. As the bill proposed by H was neither passed nor considered by the legislature, no complete version of it exists. According to J. C. Hamilton (*History*, III, 242) "Hamilton . . . proposed to fix, by law, the sessions of the legislature alternately at Albany and New-York, hoping thus to counterpoise their local influences, and to have it in his power to retain a seat in the assembly. It being known that his professional engagements would not permit him to sojourn at Poughkeepsie, that place was selected for the meeting of the next legislature." The first part of J. C. Hamilton's statement is substantiated by the notice of the motion given in *The* [New York] *Daily Advertiser* of April 19. "This bill," *The Daily Advertiser* reported, "declares that the legislature shall meet alternately at New-York and Albany."

## New York Assembly. Motion that Five Delegates be Appointed to the Constitutional Convention

[New York, April 16, 1787]

Mr. Hamilton made a motion that the House would agree to a resolution in the words following, *viz.*

*Resolved*, (if the Honorable the Senate concur herein) That two Delegates be appointed, in addition to those already appointed to represent this State at the Convention proposed to be holden at Philadelphia, on the second Monday of May next; and that any three of the persons heretofore appointed and of those now to be appointed, shall be sufficient to represent this State at the said Convention; and that this House will be ready on Wednesday next to proceed to the appointment of the said two Delegates, in the manner in which Delegates are appointed to Congress.

The question being put, whether the House would agree to the said resolution, it was carried in the affirmative.[1]

New York Assembly *Journal*, 1787, 165–66.

1. For information on the appointment of New York delegates to the Constitutional Convention, see "Resolution on the Appointment of Delegates to the Constitutional Convention," February 26, 1787, and "Appointment as Delegate to the Constitutional Convention," March 6, 1787.

Despite the Assembly's agreement on February 28 with the Senate's preference for a delegation of three to the Convention, H revived the Assembly's earlier recommendation that five delegates be appointed. H's motion was agreed to by the Assembly, but rejected by the Senate (New York Assembly *Journal*, 1787, 166, 171).

According to *The* [New York] *Daily Advertiser* of April 19, H accompanied his motion with the following remark: "He mentioned the great benefits that would arise from sending, either Mr. Chancellor [Robert R.] Livingston,

Mr. [Egbert] Benson, Mr. [James] Duane, or Mr. [John] Jay, particularly the latter. These were names he threw out for the consideration of the members." For an amplification of these remarks, see "Remarks on a Motion that Five Delegates Be Appointed to the Constitutional Convention," April 16, 1787.

# New York Assembly. Remarks on a Motion that Five Delegates be Appointed to the Constitutional Convention [1]

[New York, April 16, 1787]

I think it proper to apprise the house of the gentlemen on some of whom I wish their choice to fall, and with a view to which I bring forward the present motion.[2] Their abilities and experience in the general affairs of the country cannot but be useful upon such an occasion. I mean Mr. Chancellor [Robert R.] Livingston, Mr. [James] Duane, Mr. [Egbert] Benson, and Mr. [John] Jay. The particular situation of the latter may require an observation or two. His being a servant of Congress might seem an objection to his appointment, but surely this objection if it had any weight would have applied with equal force to the appointment of a member of that body. In the case of Mr. Lansing [3] the two houses appear to have thought there was no force in it; and I am persuaded there can be no reason to apply a different rule to Mr. Jay. His acknowledged abilities, tried integrity and abundant experience in the affairs of this country, foreign and domestic will not permit us to allow any weight to any objection which would imply a want of confidence in a character that has every title to the fullest confidence.

The [New York] *Daily Advertiser*, April 24, 1787.
  1. The *Advertiser* of April 19 reported that, after the introduction of his motion on the appointment of five delegates to the Constitutional Convention, H "mentioned the great benefits that would arise from sending, either Mr. Chancellor Livingston, Mr. Benson, Mr. Duane, or Mr. Jay, particularly the latter. These were names he threw out for the consideration of the members." In the issue of April 24, the paragraph was reprinted with the following comment by the editor: "On a review of our notes we find that there is an idea conveyed in the above short account of the matter which does not correspond with what was said. Mr. Hamilton after several introductory observations went on thus."
  2. For the text of H's motion, see "Motion that Five Delegates be Appointed to the Constitutional Convention," April 16, 1787.
  3. John Lansing, Jr., was one of the delegates appointed by the New York

legislature as a delegate to the Constitutional Convention. He also had been appointed, on January 26, 1787, as a delegate to the Continental Congress.

## New York Assembly. Remarks on the Petition of Robert Henry, Robert McClellan, and Robert Henry, Junior [1]

[New York, April 16, 1787]

Mr. Hamilton expressed great regret that he was obliged to oppose this bill; he knew the gentlemen; he knew their peculiarly unfortunate situation, and felt as much for their distresses as any member of the committee. But his objection to the bill, arose from his aversion to any discriminations; there were others, and he was sorry for it, in equally unfortunate circumstances. But he would oppose the bill from another consideration, it held out a provision entirely ideal; the bill stated that the interest should be paid out of any unappropriated monies in the treasury, but would this ever be the case; he doubted that there ever would be any money in the treasury unappropriated.

*The* [New York] *Daily Advertiser*, April 19, 1787.
    1. The three petitioners were from Albany. John Tayler of Albany County identified the petitioners and described the petition as follows:
    "He informed the committee, that these gentlemen previous to the war, were merchants, respectable and opulent. That their zeal for the common cause had induced them to go into Canada, and make purchases of articles that were much wanted for the service; and for such they received continental paper money. That they had purchased those goods with hard money. He thought much credit was due to their exertions." (*The Daily Advertiser*, April 19, 1787.)

## New York Assembly. Remarks on the Claim of New York City to Fort George

[New York, April 16, 1787]

Mr. Hamilton proposed a resolution, which would set aside the order of the day, and answer the purposes much better, in his opinion; it was to direct the attorney general to enquire into the claim of the corporation to the Fort St. James, and its dependencies, now called fort George;[1] and that the commissioners of the land office have a survey made of the property of the state therein; and that a report be made to the legislature at their next meeting, of the said claim of the corporation, and the best manner of disposing of the same.[2]

The [New York] *Daily Advertiser*, April 19, 1787.

1. Successively called Fort Amsterdam, Fort William Hendrick, Fort James, Fort William, Fort William Henry, Fort Anne, and Fort George, this fort was located in the lower part of Manhattan Island. On March 21 it was suggested in the Common Council of New York City that a bill be introduced into the Assembly for the sale of lands at the fort and the Battery. A committee was appointed to inquire into the rights of the city regarding these lands. On March 28 the Common Council in a petition to the legislature asserted the claim of New York City to the site which the legislature proposed to sell (*Minutes of the Common Council*, I, 285, 287).

2. The text of the resolution made by H is printed in New York Assembly *Journal*, 1787, 165. It was passed by the Assembly on the date of its introduction and concurred in by the Senate on April 18.

The attorney general's report was read in the Assembly on March 12, 1788. He affirmed the claim of the state to Fort George and adjoining lands (New York Assembly *Journal*, 1788, 125–57).

## New York Assembly. Remarks on an Act Repealing Laws Inconsistent With the Treaty of Peace [1]

[New York, April 17, 1787]

Mr. Hamilton in a very animated and powerful speech, expressed great uneasiness that any opposition should be made to this bill, particularly as this state was individually interested therein. He felt greater regret from a conviction in his own mind, on this occasion, that the bill should be objected to, as there was not a single law in existence in this state, in direct contravention of the treaty of peace. He urged the committee to consent to the passing of the bill, from the consideration, that the state of New-York was the only state to gain any thing by a strict adherence to the treaty. There was no other state in the union that had so much to expect from it. The restoration of the western posts, was an object of more than £100,000 per annum. Great Britain, he said, held those posts on the plea that the United States have not fulfilled the treaty. And which we have strong assurances, she will relinquish, on the fulfillment of our engagements with her. But how far Great Britain might be sincere in her declaration, was unknown. Indeed, he doubted it himself. But while he doubted the sincerity of Great Britain, he could not but be of opinion that it was the duty of this state to enact a law for the repeal of all laws which may be against the said treaty, as by doing away all exceptions, she would be reduced to a crisis. She would be obliged to shew to the world, whether she was in earnest or not; and whether she will sacrifice her honor and reputation to her interest. With respect to the bill as it was drafted in conformity to the recommendation of Congress; he viewed it as a wise, and a salutary measure; one calculated to meet the approbation of the different states, and most likely to answer the end proposed. Were it possible to examine an intricate maze of laws, and to determine which of them, or what parts of laws were opposed to the treaty, it still might not have the intended effect, as different parties would have the judging of this matter. What one should say was a law not inconsistent with the peace, another might say was so, and there would be no end, no decision of the business. Even some of the states might view laws in a different manner. The only way to comply with the treaty, was to make a general and unexceptionable repeal. Congress with an eye to this, had proposed a general law, from which the one before them was a copy. He thought it must be obvious to every member of the committee, that as there was no law in direct opposition to the treaty, no difficulty could arise from passing the bill.

Some gentlemen, he observed, were apprehensive that this bill would restore the confiscated estates, &c. This he did not admit. However, if they were so disposed they might add a proviso to prevent it. He had wrote one, which any of the gentlemen might move for if they thought it necessary; in his opinion it was not.

The treaty only provided that no future confiscations should take place; and that Congress should *earnestly recommend* a restoration of property. But there was nothing obligatory in this.

If this state should not come into the measure, would it not be a very good plea for the other states to favor their own citizens, and say why should we do this, when New-York, the most interested of any of the states, refuses to adopt it; and shall we suffer this imputation when, in fact, we have no laws in existence that militate against the treaty. He stated the great disadvantages that our merchants experienced from the western posts being in the hands of the British, and asked if it was good policy to let them remain so.

It had been said that the judges would have too much power;[2] this was misapprehended. He stated the powers of the judges with great clearness and precision. He insisted that their powers would be the same, whether this law was passed or not. For, that as all treaties were known by the constitution as the laws of the land, so must the judges act on the same, any law to the contrary notwithstanding.

Cicero, the great Roman Orator and lawyer, lays it down as a rule, that when two laws clash, that which relates to the most important matters ought to be preferred. If this rule prevails, who can doubt what would be the conduct of the judges, should any laws exist inconsistent with the treaty of peace: But it would be impolitic to leave them to the dilemma, either of infringing the treaty to enforce the particular laws of the state, or to explain away the laws of the state to give effect to the treaty.

He declared that the full operation of the bill, would be no more than merely to declare the treaty the law of the land. And that the judges viewing it as such, shall do away all laws that may appear in direct contravention of it. Treaties were known constitutionally, to be the law of the land, and why be afraid to leave the interpretation of those laws, to the judges; the constitution knows them as the interpreters of the law. He asked if there was any member of the committee that would be willing to see the first treaty of peace ever made by this country violated. This he did not believe, he could not think that any member on that floor harboured such sentiments.

He was in hopes the committee would agree with him in sentiment, and give a proof of their attachment to our national engagements by passing the bill, which would do away every exception of the British Court.[3]

The [New York] Daily Advertiser, April 23, 1787.

1. In HCLW, IV, 291–94, and Hamilton, History, III, 196–99, H's remarks are erroneously assumed to have been made on an act entitled "An act relative to debts due to persons within the enemy's lines," and another act entitled "An act to explain and amend the act entitled an act relative to debts due to persons within the enemy's lines."

On March 21, 1787, the Continental Congress resolved that the states should repeal all acts repugnant to the treaty of peace and recommended that the several states "make such repeal rather by describing than reciting the said acts and for that purpose to pass an Act declaring in general terms that all such acts and parts of acts repugnant to the treaty of peace . . . shall be and thereby are repealed" (*JCC*, XXXII, 125). On April 13, 1787, Samuel Jones introduced in the New York legislature a bill entitled "An act to repeal all the laws of this State, inconsistent with the treaty of peace between the United States of America, and the King of Great-Britain." The bill was read a second time on April 14 and committed to a committee of the whole house (New York Assembly *Journal*, 1787, 160, 162).

On April 17, the committee of the whole house reported that the title of the proposed act should be changed to "An act complying with the act of the United States in Congress assembled, of the twenty-first day of March, one thousand seven hundred and eighty-seven (New York Assembly *Journal*, 1787, 169).

2. The resolution of the Continental Congress had recommended that all laws repugnant to the treaty be repealed and that "the courts of law and equity in all causes and questions cognizable by them respectively and arising from or touching the said treaty shall decide and adjudge according to the true intent and meaning of the same" (*JCC*, XXXII, 125).

3. At the conclusion of his speech, the following exchange took place between H and William Denning, assemblyman from New York City:

"Mr. Denning rose to reply. He had no doubt of the gentleman (Mr. Hamilton's) candour: but he was still of opinion that the laws should be mentioned particularly. He had a proper sense of the importance of the western posts, and was as great an advocate for national and constitutional measures as any man; but what he had heard on the occasion, served to convince him he was right in his first observations.

"Col. Hamilton replied in a few words that it was absolutely necessary to pass the bill, and that no disadvantage would arise from it, as he again declared, we had no laws in existence that would be affected by it.

"Mr. Denning thought otherwise; and said that the opinion of a very great lawyer and civilian had been taken to the contrary.

"Mr. Hamilton doubted if such an opinion had been given; but if it had, could only have been for partial purposes." (*The Daily Advertiser*, April 23, 1787.)

On April 18 the bill was passed by the Assembly and sent to the Senate for concurrence. The Senate did not approve it.

## From Mary Bryant [1]

*New York, April 23, 1787.* Asks Hamilton's assistance in securing a disputed legacy left to her by her husband.

ALS, Hamilton Papers, Library of Congress.
1. Mary Bryant was the widow of Dr. William Bryant of Trenton, New Jersey.

## Declination of Candidacy for Seat in the New York Legislature

[New York, April 23, 1787]

Mr. Hamilton observing his name in several nominations [1] thinks it his duty to inform such of his fellow citizens as might incline to honor him with their choice at the approaching election, that the adjournment of the legislature to meet at Poughkepsie,[2] which happened on Saturday last renders it impracticable for him to serve them as a member of that body for the ensuing year.

The [New York] Daily Advertiser, April 23, 1787.
  1. The election for the legislature was to be held late in April. H presumably had been recommended for a seat in the Assembly.
  2. See "Motion for Leave to Bring in a Bill on Places at Which the Legislature Shall Meet," April 16, 1787.

## From Catherine Bayard [1]

New York, April 24, 1787. "I wish you Could so Much advance the Settlement of My affairs as to Make Me Receive of the Trustees of Bayards Estate a Sum Sufficient to Provide for My Urgent Expences during your Absence and Reimburse you what you so Obliginly have Sent to Me. . . ."

ALS, Hamilton Papers, Library of Congress.
  1. Catherine Bayard was the widow of Samuel Bayard.

## From Augustus Van Cortlandt

Yonkers, New York, April 29, 1787. Requests that Hamilton take legal steps to secure the payment of money owed Van Cortlandt.

ALS, Hamilton Papers, Library of Congress.

## To Samuel Breeze, William Malcom, and Aaron Burr [1]

[New York, April, 1787] "Mrs. Bayard Widow of Mr Samuel Bayard deceased has applied to me to arrange with you some provision for her in persuance of the Will of her husband representing her situation as distressed in the extreme, and assuring me that she is willing to do whatever I shall advise towards a fair adjustment of matters between you and her. . . ."

Copy, Hamilton Papers, Library of Congress.
  1. Breeze, Malcom, and Burr were the executors of Samuel Bayard's estate.

## From John Jay

[New York, May 2, 1787. On May 3, 1787, Hamilton wrote to Jay: "I this morning received your letter of yesterday." *Letter not found.*]

## To John Jay

[New York, May 3, 1787]

My Dear Sir

I this morning received your letter of yesterday.[1] I have seen with pain the progress of the transactions, which have excited irritations between Mr. Livingston and yourself,[2] and as my dispositions to both, in whatever I have had to do with the matter, have been friendly, I should with reluctance do any thing, that might affect either, further than a regard to truth and propriety should make it a duty.

I can however have no scruple about stating what passed between Mr. Livingston and myself, shortly previous to your issuing the execution against him, which indeed was the principal thing, in which I had an agency relating to the subject of your Inquiry.

In consequence of conversations with Mr. Morris [3] and yourself, happening to meet Mr. Livingston near the exchange, I introduced to him the Subject of your Judgment against him as bail to Mr. Littlepage,[4] observing to him that it was a pity the affair could not be concluded in a manner that would satisfy both parties. To this he replied that he had offered certain notes of persons of undoubted sufficiency, indorsed by himself, in satisfaction of the demand, which had been refused by you—that he was now ready to sign or deposit a bond for a greater sum from General Schuyler to Mr. Loudon.[5] I answered, in substance, that I had heared of his offer and your refusal—that I did not think he could complain, because you were not willing either to transfer the debt or to take the trouble of collecting it from others, that as to General Schuyler's bond, the same objection would occur and indeed I could not with delicacy undertake to propose any thing about it—that I was however authorised to say, on your part, that there was no desire of precipitating him in the payment of the money—that what was chiefly wished was to obviate the necessity of any further proceedings on the judgment and to ascertain a period, at which it would be convenient to him to pay—that for this he might name his own time, and his note, or even his assurance would be taken—that in saying this I took it for granted he would not be unreasonable. Mr. Livingston utterly declined putting the matter upon this footing; saying that if you would not accept the offers he had made, you might do as you thought proper upon the judgment.

This is the substance of what passed between us. I shortly after communicated to you my proposal and his refusal, and I in a few days after understood that an execution was issued. I have no objection to your making such use of this letter as you think proper. I remain with sincere esteem and attachment Dr Sir   Yr Obedient Ser                                                           A Hamilton

New York. May 3d. 87.
J Jay Esqr

ALS, Columbia University Libraries.
    1. Letter not found.
    2. When John Jay went to Spain as American Minister he took with him as private secretary his brother-in-law, Henry Brockholst Livingston who, because of his attacks on the Continental Congress and his refusal to cooperate with Jay, produced both problems and embarrassment for Jay. Jay's difficulties were compounded when in October, 1780, Lewis Littlepage of Virginia became a member of his household in Madrid. Littlepage, a youth of twenty years, had been recommended by Thomas Adams, delegate to the Continental Congress; and Jay, reluctantly, agreed to accept responsibility for Littlepage's education. The responsibility soon became a burden, for Littlepage not only intrigued with Brockholst Livingston and William Carmichael, also one of

Jay's secretaries, but openly expressed his contempt for Jay while securing large loans from him.

Littlepage, after he left Jay's household, traveled in Europe. In 1784 he met the King of Poland who offered him a position at his court. Before accepting the post, Littlepage returned to America to settle his affairs and secure, although it was unnecessary, congressional approval of his service to the King of Poland. His application for a letter of recommendation from Congress had to be approved by Jay, then the Secretary for Foreign Affairs, and Littlepage promised to repay the money Jay had loaned him in Spain. Although Jay endorsed his protégé's request, Congress adjourned without having provided the letter.

Jay, having heard that Littlepage was able to repay the money he had borrowed, brought suit through H and Robert Morris for collection of the debt. Littlepage was arrested on December 3, 1785, and was released with Brockholst Livingston signing his bail. Littlepage, after attacking Jay in the pages of *The* [New York] *Daily Advertiser*, sailed for France; and Jay, employing the legal assistance of H, presumably secured a judgment against Livingston.

3. Robert Morris.
4. Lewis Littlepage.
5. Samuel Loudon, publisher of *The New-York Packet*.

## Statement of Expenses Incurred by Alexander Hamilton and Egbert Benson in Attending the Annapolis Convention [1]

[New York, May 8, 1787]

The People of the State of New York
                    To Egbert and Alexander Hamilton Drs.
For our expences in attending the Convention at
Annapolis in September last  .  .  .  .  .  .  .  £113..1.4
including the journey thither and back

New York to Wit. Egbert Benson and Alexander
Hamilton severally make oath and first the said
Egbert Benson saith that of the above mentioned
sum he did disburse Thirty six pounds three shillings
and four pence and the said Alexander Hamilton
saith that he did disburse seventy six pounds and
Eighteen shillings being the residue thereof.

Egbt: Benson
Alexander  Hamilton

Sworn this 8th day of May 1787 before me
Richd. Varick Recorder [2]

DS, in writing of H, Hamilton Papers, Library of Congress.

1. For an account of H's role at the Annapolis Convention, see "Address of the Annapolis Convention," September 14, 1786.

2. At the bottom of the page on which the statement by H and Benson is written there appears the following:

"Auditors Office New York 8 May 1787. I have examined the above account and allow to be due thereon to Egbert Benson & Alexander Hamilton Esqrs: the Sum of one hundred thirteen Pounds one Shilling & four Pence

          Gerard Bancker Esqr, Treasurer   Peter S. Curtenius State Audr."

## From P. I. More [1]

*Charleston, South Carolina, May 12, 1787.* Requests Hamilton to collect a debt owed More by "Mr. John Tayleur formerly Merchant in this Place, now keeping a Jeweller's Shop in Queen Street near the Coffee house in New York."

LS, Hamilton Papers, Library of Congress.

1. More was a Charleston physician.

## Credentials as Delegate to the General Society of the Cincinnati

*Philadelphia, May 18, 1787.* On this date Hamilton filed his credentials and instructions as a delegate from New York to the general meeting of the Society of the Cincinnati held in Philadelphia.

*Proceedings of the General Society of the Cincinnati, 1784–1884* (Philadelphia, 1887), 31.

## Constitutional Convention. Nomination of William Jackson as Secretary of the Constitutional Convention [1]

*Philadelphia, May 25, 1787.* On this date Hamilton nominated Major William Jackson [2] as secretary of the Constitutional Convention. [3]

Gaillard Hunt and James Brown Scott, eds., *The Debates in the Federal Convention of 1787 Which Framed the Constitution of the United States of America. Reported by James Madison* (New York, 1920), 18.

1. Of the many editions of Madison's notes of debates in the Convention the

most reliable are: Hunt, *Writings of Madison*, III, IV; Max Farrand, ed., *The Records of the Federal Convention of 1787* (New Haven, 1911), I, II; *Documentary History of the Constitution of the United States of America* (Washington, 1900), III; and Hunt and Scott, *Debates*. As the edition by Hunt and Scott is as accurate a transcription of Madison's notes as can be made, it has been cited rather than earlier editions of Madison's notes or the MS notes which are in the James Madison Papers, Library of Congress.

There are four detailed accounts of the debates in the Constitutional Convention: the notes of James Madison (described above); John Lansing, Jr. (Joseph R. Strayer, ed., *The Delegate from New York or Proceedings of the Federal Convention of 1787 from the Notes of John Lansing, Jr* [Princeton, 1939], cited hereafter as *Notes of John Lansing*); Robert Yates (*Secret Proceedings and Debates of the Convention Assembled at Philadelphia, in the Year 1787, For the Purpose of Forming the Constitution* [Albany, 1821], cited hereafter as Yates, *Secret Proceedings and Debates*); and Rufus King (Charles R. King, ed., *The Life and Correspondence of Rufus King* [New York, 1894], I, cited hereafter as King, *The Life and Correspondence of Rufus King*).

Since the notes of Madison are indubitably the most complete (for a comparative study of the notes made by Madison and Yates see Arnold A. Rogow, "The Federal Convention: Madison and Yates," *The American Historical Review*, LX [January, 1955], 323–35) and probably the most accurate, they have been used as the source of Hamilton's motions, speeches, and reports. Whenever another account presents a version of H's remarks which differs from that given by Madison, the difference is indicated in notes.

H, Robert Yates, and John Lansing, Jr., were appointed on March 6, 1787, to represent New York State at the Constitutional Convention. See "Appointment as Delegate to the Constitutional Convention," March 6, 1787. H did not arrive on May 14, the day appointed for the convening of the Convention, but reached Philadelphia on May 18. The proceedings of the Convention began on May 25, 1787, the date on which a quorum of delegates was first present.

2. Jackson had served as assistant Secretary at War.

3. On May 25, the first day of the Convention, James Wilson, delegate from Pennsylvania, moved "that a Secretary be appointed, and nominated Mr. Temple Franklin" (Hunt and Scott, *Debates*, 18). H's substitute nomination of William Jackson was accepted by the Convention.

## Constitutional Convention. Appointment to Committee for Establishing Rules for the Constitutional Convention

*Philadelphia, May 25, 1787.* On this date, Hamilton, George Wythe of Virginia, and Charles Pinckney of South Carolina were appointed a committee to prepare "standing rules & orders" for the Constitutional Convention.[1]

Hunt and Scott, *Debates*, 18.

1. The rules were reported on May 28 and 29. See Hunt and Scott, *Debates*, 18, 21.

## From Jacob Sarly

*Delaware Mills near Trenton, May 26, 1787.* "On my arrival at Newyork your Letter [1] was handed me. . . . I will endeavour to fulfill the proposition I made of paying the Remainder due on the Bond I gave, previous to my leaving Newyork for England which will be in the Course of the next Month; for the Ballance which will satisfy one half of the Debt, I will put such Security in your hands as I trust you will approve of. . . ."

ALS, Hamilton Papers, Library of Congress.
    1. Letter not found.


## Constitutional Convention. Motion that Representation in the National Legislature Ought to be Proportioned to the Number of Free Inhabitants

*Philadelphia, May 30, 1787.* The Convention having before it a proposition by Edmund Randolph [1] that "the rights of suffrage in the National Legislature ought to be proportioned to the quotas of contribution, or to the number of free inhabitants, as the one or the other rule may seem best in different cases," Hamilton "moved to alter the resolution so as to read 'that the rights of suffrage in the national Legislature ought to be proportioned to the number of free inhabitants.' " [2]

Hunt and Scott, *Debates*, 29–30.
    1. Edmund Randolph had proposed to the Convention on May 29, 1787, fifteen resolutions, known as the Virginia Plan, which contained his ideas on the proper plan to be adopted for a national government. The Convention on May 30 debated the first of his resolutions.
    2. Consideration of H's resolution, seconded by Richard Dobbs Spaight, delegate from North Carolina, was postponed.

*Constitutional Convention.*
*Notes Taken in the Federal Convention* [1]

[Philadelphia, June 1–26, 1787]

[NOTES FOR JUNE 1, 1787] [2]

[Madison]    1—The way to prevent a majority from having an interest to oppress the minority is to enlarge the sphere.

Madison    2—Elective Monarchies turbulent and unhappy— [3] Men unwilling to admit so decided a superiority of merit in an individual as to accede to his appointment to so preeminent a station.

If several are admitted as there will be many competitors of equal merit they may be all included—contention prevented—& the republican genius consulted.

AD, Hamilton Papers, Library of Congress.
1. This document consists of rough notes made by H of debates in the Constitutional Convention. Not so complete as those taken by Madison, Yates, Lansing, or King, H's notes, unlike other records of the debates in the Convention, include his opinion of the remarks made by other delegates.
H's notes have been printed, as nearly as possible, in chronological order. The order in which they were made cannot be precisely determined, for H's versions of the remarks made by the various delegates do not always correspond with those reported by Madison, Lansing, Yates, or King. Nor is it always possible to determine whether an opinion recorded in his notes was made by one of the delegates or represented his own thoughts, for he sometimes inserted his own ideas into the record he made of remarks by others. The arrangement of H's notes printed here differs in minor particulars from that made by Worthington C. Ford in "Alexander Hamilton's Notes in the Federal Convention of 1787," *The American Historical Review*, X (October, 1904), 97–109, and from the order in which they are arranged in the Hamilton Papers, Library of Congress.
2. On June 1 the Convention debated the seventh resolution of the plan of government proposed by Edmund Randolph of Virginia. The resolution provided for a national executive to be chosen by the national legislature for an unspecified number of years.
3. Madison made no record of his remarks on this date, but Rufus King's version of this statement reads as follows: "If [the Executive Power is] large, we shall have the Evils of Elective Monarchies" (King, *The Life and Correspondence of Rufus King*, I, 588).

Randolph [4]          I   Situation of this Country peculiar.

II—Taught the people an aversion to Monarchy.

III   All their constitutions opposed to it.

IV—Fixed character of the people opposed to it.

V—If proposed it will prevent a fair discussion of the plan.

Voice of  ⎱ —      VI—Why cannot three execute.
America  ⎰

—Great exertions only requisite on particular occasions.

—Legislature may appoint a dictator when necessary.

—Seeds of destruction—Slaves [5] might be easily enlisted.

Safety to liberty ⎱
the great object  ⎰

—May appoint men devoted to them—& even bribe the legislature by offices.

—Chief Magistrate must be free from impeachment.

Wilson [6]            extent—manners—

Confederated republic unites advantages & banishes disadvantages of other kinds of governments.

☞                    —rendering the executive ineligible an infringement of the right of election—

Bedford [7]          —peculiar talents requisite for *executive*, there-

4. Madison's version of Edmund Randolph's remark reads:
"Mr. Randolph strenuously opposed a unity in the Executive magistracy. He regarded it as the fœtus of monarchy. We had he said no motive to be governed by the British Governmt. as our prototype. He did not mean however to throw censure on that Excellent fabric. If we were in a situation to copy it he did not know that he should be opposed to it; but the fixt genius of the people of America required a different form of Government. He could not see why the great requisites for the Executive department, vigor, despatch & responsibility could not be found in three men, as well as in one man. The Executive ought to be independent. It ought therefore in order to support its independence to consist of more than one." (Hunt and Scott, *Debates*, 38.)

5. H substituted "slaves" for the words "former Continental army" which he wrote and crossed out.

6. James Wilson, delegate from Pennsylvania, spoke five times on June 1. None of his remarks as recorded by Madison (Hunt and Scott, *Debates*, 37–41) closely corresponds to the remarks attributed to him by H.

7. Gunning Bedford, delegate from Delaware. James Madison recorded the following version of Bedford's speech:

fore ought to be opportunity of ascertaining his talents—therefore frequent change.

Princ [8]

1  The further men are from the ultimate point of importance the readier they will be [to] concur in a change.

2  Civilization approximates the different species of governments.

3  Vigour is the result of several principles—Activity wisdom—confidence.

4  Extent of limits will occasion the non attendance of remote members & tend to throw the government into the hands of the Country near the seat of government—a reason for strengthening the upper branch & multiplying the Inducements to attendance.

Sent [9]

A free government to be preferred to an absolute monarchy not because of the occasional violations of *liberty* or *property* but because of the tendency of the Free Government to interest the passions of the community in its favour beget public spirit and public confidence.

Re:

When public mind is prepared to adopt the present plan they will outgo our proposition. They will never part with Sovereignty of the state till they are tired of the state governments.

---

"Mr. Bedford was strongly opposed to so long a term as seven years. He begged the committee to consider what the situation of the Country would be, in case the first magistrate should be saddled on it for such a period and it should be found on trial that he did not possess the qualifications ascribed to him, or should lose them after his appointment. An impeachment he said would be no cure for this evil, as an impeachment would reach misfeasance only, not incapacity. He was for a triennial election, and for an ineligibility after a period of nine years." (Hunt and Scott, *Debates*, 40–41.)

8. According to the several recorded versions of debates in the Convention, Bedford did not make the observations which H recorded under the rubric "Princ[iple]." They probably were H's own comments.

9. The notes following the word "Sent[ence]" are probably H's own ideas

[NOTES FOR JUNE 6, 1787]¹⁰

| | |
|---|---|
| Mr. Pinkney. | If Legislatures do not partake in the appointment of [the first branch of the national legislature] they will be more jealous. |
| Pinckney— | Elections by the state legislatures will be better than those by the people.¹¹ |
| Principle— | Danger that the Executive by too frequent communication with the judicial may corrupt it. They may learn to enter into his passions. |
| Note—¹² | At the period which terminates the duration of the Executive there will be always an awful crisis—in the National situation. |
| Note— | The arguments to prove that a negative would not be used would go so far as to prove that the revisionary power would not be exercised. |
| Mr. Mason—¹³ | The purse & sword will be in the hands of the legislature. |

rather than a summary of the remarks of someone else and do not necessarily pertain to the debate of June 1. They appear at the top of the MS page which records the first statement made by Charles Pinckney, delegate from South Carolina, on June 6.

10. On this date the Convention considered a motion by Charles Pinckney "that the first branch of the national Legislature be elected by the State Legislatures, and not by the people" (Hunt and Scott, *Debates*, 62).

11. The remarks by Charles Cotesworth Pinckney were recorded in greater length by Madison (Hunt and Scott, *Debates*, 66). The remarks immediately following were also made by Charles Cotesworth Pinckney.

12. Charles Pinckney's motion (see note 10) was negatived; and the Convention took up a motion by James Wilson "to reconsider the vote excluding the Judiciary from a share in the revision of the laws and to add after 'National Executive' the words 'with a convenient number of the national Judiciary'" (Hunt and Scott, *Debates*, 67). H's comments, recorded under "Principle" and "Note," were apropos of Wilson's motion.

13. According to Madison, George Mason, delegate from Virginia, "was for giving all possible weight to the revisionary institution. The Executive power ought to be well secured agst. Legislative usurpations on it. The purse & the sword ought never to get into the same hands whether Legislative or Executive" (Hunt and Scott, *Debates*, 68).

PRINCIPLES

1—Human mind fond of Compromise—
Maddisons Theory— [14]

Two principles upon which republics
ought to be constructed—

I that they have such extent as to render
combinations on the ground of Interest
difficult—

II By a process of election calculated to
refine the representation of the People—

Answer—There is truth in both these
principles but they do not conclude so
strongly as he supposes.[15]

The Assembly when chosen will meet in
one room if they are drawn from half the
globe—& will be liable to all the passions
of popular assemblies.

If more *minute links* are wanting others
will supply them. Distinctions of Eastern
middle and Southern states will come into
view; between commercial and non commercial states. Imaginary lines will influence
&c. Human mind prone to limit its view by
near & local objects. Paper money is capable
of giving a general impulse. It is easy to
conceive a popular sentiment pervading the
E states.

Observ:  { large districts less liable to be influenced by
factions demagogues than small.[16]

14. H's statement of "Maddisons Theory" is based on Madison's speech of
June 6 in which, in the course of arguing that one branch of the legislature
should be elected by the people, Madison discussed the ideas which he believed should be the basis for a new government (Hunt and Scott, *Debates*,
64–65).

15. This and the two paragraphs which follow are, of course, H's objections
to Madison's theory.

16. This is presumably a rough paraphrase of the following remarks made
by Madison: "The gentleman (Mr. Sharman) had admitted that in a very small
State, faction & oppression wd. prevail. It was to be inferred then that wherever

Note—This is in some degree true but not so generally as may be supposed. Frequently small
portions of the large districts carry elections.
An influential demagogue will give an impulse to the whole. Demagogues are not
always *inconsiderable* persons. Patricians
were frequently demagogues. Characters are
less known & a less active interest taken in
them.

I    One great defect of our Governments are
that they do not present objects sufficiently
interesting to the human mind.

I—A reason for leaving little or nothing to the
state legislatures will be that as their objects
are diminished they will be worse composed.
Proper men will be less inclined to participate in them.

[NOTES FOR JUNE 7, 1787][17]

Dickinson            II—He would have the state legislatures elect
senators, because he would bring into the
general government the sense of the state
Governments &

II—because the more respectable choices would
be made.

Note—Separate states may give stronger organs to
their governments & engage more the good
will of Ind: while Genl Gov

☞            Consider the Principle of Rivalship by excluding the state Legislatures.

---

these prevailed the State was too small. Had they not prevailed in the largest
as well as the smallest tho' less than in the smallest; and were we not thence
admonished to enlarge the sphere as far as the nature of the Govt. would
admit. This was the only defence agst. the inconveniences of democracy consistent with the democratic form of Govt" (Hunt and Scott, *Debates*, 64).

17. On this date John Dickinson, delegate from Delaware, spoke in support
of his motion that members of the second branch of the government be chosen
by the state legislatures. H reported the first of two speeches which Dickinson
made on this date (Hunt and Scott, *Debates*, 70, 72).

*Mason* [18] $\left\{\begin{array}{l}\end{array}\right.$ General government could not know how to make laws for every part—such as respect *agriculture* &c.

particular governments would have *no defensive* power unless let into the constitution as a Constituent part.

[ NOTES FOR JUNE 8, 1787 ] [19]

Pinckey [20]            —For general Negative—

Gerry                   —Is for a negative on paper emissions— [21]
                        New states will arise which cannot be controuled—& may outweigh & controul. [22]

Wilson                  —Foreign influence may infect certain corners of confederacy which ought to be restrained. [23]
                        Union basis of our oppos & Ind [24]

18. According to Madison's account of George Mason's speech, Mason contended that some powers under the proposed new form of government must be left with the states. The states, he concluded, should be made "a constituent part of, the Natl. Establishment" (Hunt and Scott, *Debates*, 74).

19. On this date the Convention debated a motion by Charles Pinckney "that the National Legislature shd. have authority to negative all laws which they shd. judge to be improper" (Hunt and Scott, *Debates*, 75).

20. Charles Pinckney.

21. Elbridge Gerry, delegate from Massachusetts, according to Madison's account, was opposed to giving the national legislature power to negative any state law it should consider improper. He favored "a remonstrance agst. unreasonable acts of the States" and proposed the use of force if the remonstrance was unavailing. Gerry, however, "had no objection to authorize a negative to paper money and similar measures" (Hunt and Scott, *Debates*, 76).

22. Madison reported Gerry as saying that new states would not enter the union if the national legislature were given a negative on state laws (Hunt and Scott, *Debates*, 76).

23. H was probably mistaken in attributing this remark to James Wilson. Madison attributed it to Elbridge Gerry who, he reported, argued that the national legislature should not be given a negative on state laws because new states entering the union "may even be under some foreign influence; are they in such case to participate in the negative on the will of the other States?" (Hunt and Scott, *Debates*, 76).

24. This statement presumably was made by Wilson. The meaning of the laconic statement written by H is that the union of the states was responsible both for their opposition to Great Britain and the establishment of their independence. This meaning conforms to Madison's account of Wilson's remarks (Hunt and Scott, *Debates*, 77).

Bedford— [25]      { Arithmetical calculation of proportional in-
                   { fluence in General Government—

                   { Pensyl. & Delaware may have rivalship in
                   { commerce—& influence of Pens—sacrifice
                   { *delaware.*

                   If there be a negative in GG—yet if a law
                   can pass through all the forms of SC it will
                   require force to abrogate it.[26]

Butler— [27]       Will a man throw afloat his property & con-
                   fide it to a government a thousand miles *dis-
                   tant?*

### [NOTES FOR JUNE 16, 1787] [28]

Mr. Lansing— [29]  NS—proposes to draw representation from
                   the whole body of people, without regard to
                   S Sovereignties.

                   Subs: proposes to preserve the state Sov-
                   ereignties.

                   Powers—  { Different Legislatures had a dif-
                            { ferent object.
                            { Revise the Confederation.
                            { Ind. States cannot be supposed
                            { to be willing to annihilate the
                            { States.
                            { State of New York would not
                            { have agreed to send members on
                            { this ground.

25. Gunning Bedford, delegate from Delaware.
26. Madison gives a different version of this statement. He states that Bedford said, "if a State does not obey the law of the new System, must not force
be resorted to as the only ultimate remedy, in this as in any other system"
(Hunt and Scott, *Debates,* 78).
27. Pierce Butler, delegate from South Carolina. Madison's version of Butler's remarks is as follows: "Mr. BUTLER was vehement agst. the Negative
in the proposed extent, as cutting off all hope of equal justice to the distant
States. The people there would not he was sure give it a hearing" (Hunt and
Scott, *Debates,* 79).
28. On this date the Convention debated the merits and deficiencies of the
two major plans for a new government which had been submitted, the New
Jersey Plan, introduced by William Paterson, and the Virginia Plan, introduced
by Edmund Randolph.
29. John Lansing, Jr., H's fellow delegate from New York.

In vain to devise systems however good which will not be adopted.

If convulsions happen nothing we can do will give them a direction.

Legislatures cannot be expected to make such a sacrifice.

The wisest men in forming a system from theory apt to be mistaken.

The present national government has no precedent or experience to support it.

General opinion that certain additional powers ought to be given to Congress.

Mr. Patterson—    1—plan accords with powers
2—accords with sentiments of the People.

If Confederation radically defective we ought to return to our states and tell them so. Comes not here to sport sentiments of his own but to speak the sense of his Constituents.

States treat as equal.

Present Compact gives one *Vote to* each state.

alterations are to be made by Congress and all the Legislatures.

All parties to a Contract must assent to its dissolution.

States collectively have advantages in which the smaller states do not participate—therefore individual rules do not apply.

Force of government will not depend on proportion of representation—but on

Quantity of power—

Check not necessary in a geral government
of communities—but
in an individual state spirit of faction is to
be checked—

How have Congress hitherto conducted
themselves?

The People approve of Congress but think
they have not powers enough.

Body constituted like Congress from the
*fewness* of their numbers more wisdom and
energy—

than the complicated system of Virginia

Expence enormous—

| | |
|---|---|
| 180 [30]—commons | |
| 90 —Senators | |
| 270 — | |

Wilson—      Points of Di[s]agreement—
V[irginia]                                        NJ

| | | |
|---|---|---|
| 1 | 2 or three branches . . . . . | One branch |
| 2 | Derives authority from People . . | from states— |
| 3 | Proportion of suffrage . . . . | Equality— |
| 4 | Single Executive . . . . . . | Plural— |
| 5 | Majority to govern . . . . . | Minority to govern— |
| 6 | Legislates in all matters of general Concern . . . . . . . | partial objects— |
| 7 | Negative . . . . . . . | None— |
| 8 | Removeable by impeachment . . | on application of majority of Executive |
| 9 | Qualified Negative by Executive . | None |
| 10 | Inf. tribunals . . . . . . | None— |

---

30. William Paterson, according to Madison's record of the Convention
debates, said: "The plan of Mr. R. will also be enormously expensive. Allowing Georgia & Del. two representatives each in the popular branch the aggregate number of that branch will be 180. Add to it half as many for the other
branch and you have 270" (Hunt and Scott, *Debates*, 107).

11 Orig: Jurisdiction in all cases of
Nat: Rev . . . . . . . . None—

12 National Government to be ratified⎤ to be ratified
by People . . . . . . .⎦ by Legislatures—

Empowered to propose every thing
to conclude nothing.

Does not think state governments the idols
of the people.

Thinks a competent national government
will be a favourite of the people.

Complaints from every part of United States
that the purposes of government cannot be
answered.

In constituting a government not merely
necessary to give proper powers—but to
give them to proper hands.

Two reasons against giving additional
powers to Congress.

First it does not stand on the authority of
the people.

Second—It is a single branch.

Inequality—the poison of all governments— [31]
Lord Chesterfield speaks of a Commission to
be obtained for a member of a small province.[32]

Pinkney— [33]

31. Madison's version of this statement by Wilson reads as follows: "He would not repeat the remarks he had formerly made on the principles of Representation. He would only say that an inequality in it, has ever been a poison contaminating every branch of Govt." (Hunt and Scott, *Debates*, 108).

32. Madison's account of Wilson's statement reads: "When Lord Chesterfield had told us that one of the Dutch provinces had been seduced into the views of France, he need not have added, that it was not Holland, but one of the *smallest* of them" (Hunt and Scott, *Debates*, 108–09).

33. Charles Pinckney, whose remarks H failed to record, said, according to Madison, that "the whole comes to this, as he conceived. Give N. Jersey an

Mr. Elseworth— [34]

Mr. Randolp—       Spirit of the People in favour of the Virginian scheme.

We have powers; but if we had not we ought not to scruple.

[NOTES FOR JUNE 19, 1787] [35]

Maddison       Breach of compact in one article releases the whole. [36]

Treaties may still be violated by the states under the Jersey plan.

Appellate jurisdiction not sufficient because second trial cannot be had under it. [37]

Attempt made by one of the greatest monarchs of Europe to equalize the local peculiarities of their separate provinces—in which the Agent fell a victim. [38]

---

equal vote, and she will dismiss her scruples, and concur in the Natl. system. He thought the Convention authorized to go any length in recommending, which they found necessary to remedy the evils which produced this Convention" (Hunt and Scott, *Debates*, 109).

34. Madison reported that Oliver Ellsworth, delegate from Connecticut, "proposed as a more distinctive form of collecting the mind of the Committee on the subject, 'that the Legislative power of the U. S. should remain in Congs.'" (Hunt and Scott, *Debates*, 109).

35. On this date the Convention again took up the plan offered by William Paterson of New Jersey.

36. Madison's version of his own remarks reads as follows: "It had been alledged (by Mr. Patterson), that the Confederation having been formed by unanimous consent, could be dissolved by unanimous Consent only. Does this doctrine result from the nature of compacts? does it arise from any particular stipulation in the articles of Confederation? If we consider the federal union as analogous to the fundamental compact by which individuals compose one Society, and which must in its theoretic origin at least, have been the unanimous act of the component members, it can not be said that no dissolution of the compact can be effected without unanimous consent. A breach of the fundamental principles of the compact by a part of the Society would certainly absolve the other parts from their obligations to it" (Hunt and Scott, *Debates*, 121).

37. Madison, as proof of his contention that the New Jersey Plan would fail to prevent state encroachments on the federal authority, pointed out the provision in the Plan which gave only appellate jurisdiction to the Federal Court. "Of what avail," he questioned, "cd. an appellate tribunal be, after an acquittal?" (Hunt and Scott, *Debates*, 123).

38. This illustration was given by Madison to assure the smaller states that

Mr. Pinckney [39]     is of opinion that the first branch ought to be appointed in such manner as the legislatures shall direct.

Impracticable for general legislature to decide contested elections.

[NOTES FOR JUNE 20, 1787]

Mr. Lansing—     Resolved that the powers of legislation ought to be vested in the United States in Congress.

If our plan be not adopted it will produce those mischiefs which we are sent to obviate.

Principles of system—
—Equality of Representation—
      Dependence of members of Congress on States—

So long as state distinctions exist states prejudices will operate whether election be by *states* or *people*—

If no interest to *oppress* no need of *apportionment*— [40]

Virginia 16—Delaware 1— [41]

Will General Government have leisure to examine state laws?

---

under the proportional representation proposed by the Virginia Plan they would not be under the complete dominance of the larger states. The monarch to whom Madison referred was the King of France (Hunt and Scott, *Debates*, 126).

39. Charles Cotesworth Pinckney's remarks were placed by H with his notes on the debates of June 19. According to Madison's record, these statements were made by Pinckney on June 21.

40. Madison's version of this statement is as follows:

"It had been asserted by his colleague (Col. Hamilton) that there was no coincidence of interests among the large States that ought to excite fears of oppression in the smaller. If it were true that such a uniformity of interests existed among the States, there was equal safety for all of them, whether the representation remained as heretofore, or were proportioned as now proposed." (Hunt and Scott, *Debates*, 133.)

41. This phrase is not in any other account of Lansing's speech.

|                  | Will G Government have the necessary information? |
|------------------|--------------------------------------------------|

Will G Government have the necessary information?

Will states agree to surrender?

Let us meet public opinion & hope the progress of sentiment will make future arrangements.

Would like my system if it could be established.[42]

System [43] without example.

Mr. Mason—

Objection to granting power to Congress arose from their constitution.[44]

*Sword* and *purse* in one body—

Two principles in which *America* are unanimous

   1 attachment to Republican government.
   2 — to two branches of legislature.

Military *force* & *liberty* incompatible.

Will people maintain a standing army?

Will endeavour to preserve state governments & draw lines—trusting to posterity to amend.

Mr. Martin— [45]

General Government originally formed for the preservation of state governments.

Objection to giving power to Congress has originated with the legislatures.

42. Lansing did not, according to Madison, endorse the whole of the system of government proposed by H but said only that he believed "the National Govt. must have the influence arising from the grant of offices and honors. In order to render such a Government effectual he believed such an influence to be necessary. But if the States will not agree to it, it is in vain, worse than in vain to make the proposition" (Hunt and Scott, *Debates*, 133).

43. That is, the system proposed by Edmund Randolph of Virginia.

44. This statement, as recorded by H, is not closely paralleled in Madison's record of debates. According to Yates's account of the debates, Mason stated that the opposition of the people to a unicameral legislature arose from their state constitutions (Yates, *Secret Proceedings and Debates*, 144).

10 of the states interested in an equal voice.[46]

Real motive was an opinion that there ought to be distinct governments & not a general government.

If we should form a general government would break to pieces.

For common safety instituted a General government.

Jealousy of power the motive.

People have delegated all their authority to state governments.

*Coertion* necessary to both systems.

Requisitions necessary upon one system as upon another.

In their *system* made requisitions necessary in the first instance but left Congress in the second instance—to assess themselves.[47]

Judicial tribunals in the different states would become odious.

If we always to make a change shall be always in a state of infancy.

☞      States will not be disposed hereafter to strengthen the general government.

Mr. Sherman— [48]      Confederacy carried us through the war.

Non compliances of States owing to various embarrassment.

Why should state legislatures be unfriendly?

45. Luther Martin, delegate from Maryland.
46. Madison wrote that Martin said, "Nor could the rule of voting have been ground of objection, otherwise ten of the States must always have been ready, to place further confidence in Congs" (Hunt and Scott, *Debates,* 136).
47. This remark by Martin is not found in other versions of the Convention debates. Madison's version, which also mentions requisitions, states only that the Virginia Plan "must depend for the deficiency of its revenues on requisitions & quotas" (Hunt and Scott, *Debates,* 136).
48. Roger Sherman, delegate from Connecticut.

State governments will always have the confidence & government of the people: if they cannot be conciliated no efficacious government can be established.

Sense of all states that one *branch is sufficient.*

If consolidated all treaties will be void.

State governments more fit for local legislation customs habits &c.

[NOTES, PROBABLY FOR JUNE 26, 1787] [49]

I Every government ought to have the means of self preservation
II Combinations of a few large states might subvert
II Could not be abused without a revolt
II Different genius of the states & different composition of the body
  Note. Senate could not desire to promote such a class
III Uniformity in the time of elections.

Objects of a Senate

To afford a double security against Faction in the house of representation

Duration of the Senate necessary to its
  Firmness
  Information
  sense of national character
  Responsibility

49. On June 26 the Convention debated the proposals for forming a Senate. These remarks by H were probably recorded on that date. They do not, however, conform to the record of debates given by any other notes of debates on that date, and they may have constituted H's ideas on the proper organization of the Senate.

## Constitutional Convention. Second of Benjamin Franklin's Motion that Proposed Executive Serve Without Pay

*Philadelphia, June 2, 1787.* On this date Benjamin Franklin moved that the expenses of the proposed Executive should be paid but that he should receive "no salary, stipend fee or reward whatsoever" for his service. "The motion was seconded by Col. HAMILTON with the view he said merely of bringing so respectable a proposition before the Committee, and which was besides enforced by arguments that had a certain degree of weight." [1]

Hunt and Scott, *Debates*, 46.
1. "No debate ensued," on Franklin's motion, "and the proposition was postponed for the consideration of the members. It was treated with great respect, but rather for the author of it, than from any apparent conviction of its expediency or practicability" (Hunt and Scott, *Debates*, 46).

## Constitutional Convention. Second of a Motion by James Wilson and Remarks Thereon

*Philadelphia, June 4, 1787.* James Wilson on this date made a motion, which Hamilton seconded, that a motion by Elbridge Gerry stating "that the National Executive shall have a right to negative any Legislative act which shall not be afterwards passed by        [1] parts of each branch of the national Legislature" be replaced by a provision "so as to give the Executive an absolute negative on the laws. There was no danger they thought of such a power being too much exercised. It was mentioned by Col: HAMILTON that the King of G. B. had not exerted his negative since the Revolution."

Hunt and Scott, *Debates*, 51–52.
1. Space left bank in original.

## Constitutional Convention. Objection of Order

*Philadelphia, June 4, 1787.* To a motion by James Wilson, seconded by James Madison, that "a convenient number of the National Judiciary" act with the executive in vetoing acts of the national legislature, Hamilton made "an objection of order . . . to the introduction of the last amendment at this time." [1]

Hunt and Scott, *Debates*, 56.
1. After H's objection, Wilson and Madison announced that they would make the same motion on the following day.

## Constitutional Convention. Remarks on the Virginia and New Jersey Plans [1]

[Philadelphia, June 15, 1787]

Col. Hamilton cannot say he is in sentiment with either plan— [2] supposes both might again be considered as federal plans, and by this means they will be fairly in committee, and be contrasted so as to make a comparative estimate of the two.

Yates, *Secret Proceedings and Debates*, 121–22.
    1. Robert Yates was the only one of the delegates keeping a record of the debates of the Convention who recorded remarks by H on this date.
    2. On June 15 William Paterson proposed to the Convention a plan of government—the New Jersey Plan—which he wished to have substituted for the Virginia Plan.

## Constitutional Convention Speech on a Plan of Government

[Philadelphia, June 18, 1787]

### Introductory Note

There are five versions of Hamilton's speech of June 18 to the Constitutional Convention. In the first place, there are Hamilton's own notes which he presumably used while he was delivering the speech. In the second place James Madison, Robert Yates, John Lansing, Jr., and Rufus King all made notes on the speech while Hamilton was delivering it. Because the several accounts of the speech are different and because this speech is perhaps the most important address ever made by Hamilton—if its importance can be measured either by its use in subsequent evaluations of Hamilton's political philosophy or by the controversy about it during his lifetime—both Hamilton's notes and the other four versions of the speech have been printed.

The footnotes are numbered consecutively throughout the five documents that appear below. Whenever an explanation is required for any material which, although phrased differently, appears in more than one version of Hamilton's speech, the note has been given for the material in the first version in which that material appears.

ALEXANDER HAMILTON'S NOTES

Introduction

I    Importance of the occasion

II    Solid *plan* without regard to temporary *opinion*.

III If an ineffectual plan be again proposed it will beget despair & no government will grow out of consent

IV There seem to be but three lines of conduct

    I A league offensive and defensive, treaty of commerce, & apportionment of the public debt.

    II An amendment of the present confederation by adding such powers as the public mind seems nearest being matured to grant.

    III The forming a new government to pervade the whole with decisive powers in short with complete sovereignty.

B Last seems to be the prevailing sentiment—

I Its practicability to be examined—

Immense extent unfavourable to representation—

Vast expence—

double setts of officers—

Difficulty of judging of local circumstances—

☞ Distance has a physical effect upon mens minds—

Difficulty of drawing proper characters from home—

Execution of laws feeble at a distance from government—

particularly in the collection of revenue—

SENTIMENT of Obedience

Opinion

I [1] Objections to the present confederation

I Entrusts the great interests of the nation to hands incapable of managing them—

All matters in which foreigners are concerned—

The care of the public peace: DEBTS

Power of treaty without power of execution

Common defence without power to raise troops—have a fleet—raise money

Power to contract debts without the power to pay—

These great interests of the state must be well managed or the public prosperity must be the victim—

LEGISLATES upon communities—

Where the legislatures are to act,

AD, Hamilton Papers, Library of Congress.

   1. The portion of H's notes beginning with "Objections to the present confederation" and ending with "No Sanction" have no counterpart in the versions of the speech made by Madison, Yates, Lansing, and King.

they will deliberate— ⎧ TO ASK MONEY  
                     ⎪ not to collect  
No sanction—         ⎨ & by an unjust  
                     ⎩ measur⟨e⟩  

C    Amendment of CONFEDERATION according to present Ideas

1—Difficult because not agreed upon any thing  
Ex—IMPOST  
    COMMERCE different THEORIES  
To ascertain practicability of this let us examine the principles of civil obedience— [2]  
SUPPORTS OF GOVERNMENT—  
I    INTEREST to Support it  
II   OPINION of Utility & necessity  
III  HABITUAL sense of obligation  
IV   FORCE  
V    INFLUENCE.

I    INTEREST  
C    *Particular* & general *interests*  
     Esprit de Corps—  
     *Vox* populi *vox Dei*  
II   Opinion of Utility & necessity  
1—First will decrease with the growth of the *states*.  
III  *Necessity*  
     This does not apply to Fœderal Government—  
     This may dissolve & yet the order of the community continue—  
     *Anarchy* not a necessary consequence  
IV   HABITUAL SENSE of obligation  
     This results from administration of private justice—  
     DEMAND of service or money odious.  
V    FORCE of two kinds.  
     COERTION of laws COERTION of arms.  
     First does *not exist*—& the last *useless*—  
     Attempt to *use it* a war between the states—

2. At this point H wrote and crossed out the following heading: "I. Maxim Particular Interests General Int. Esprit de Corps."

FOREIGN aid—

DELINQUENCY not confined to one.

VI INFLUENCE

   1 from municipal Jurisdiction

   2 appointment of Officers [3]

   4 Military Jurisdiction

   5 FISCAL Jurisdiction

D   All these [4] now reside in particular states

Their governments are the chief sources of honor and emolument.

## AMBITION     AVARICE

To effect any thing PASSIONS must be turned towa⟨rd⟩ general government?

PRESENT Confederation cannot be amended unless the most important powers be given to Congress constituted as they are—

This would be liable to all objections against any form of general government with the addition of the want of *Checks*—

E   PERPETUAL EFFORT in each member

Influence of Individuals in office employed to excite jealousy & clamour

STATE LEADERS

EXPERIENCE corresponds

Grecian Republics

Demosthenes says [5]

   Athens 73 years

   Lacedaemon 27

   Thebans after battle of Leuctra

---

PHOCIANS consecrated ground

3. At this point H wrote and crossed out "3. Fiscal Jurisdiction."

4. At this point H wrote and crossed out the word "powers."

5. The example from Demosthenes was probably the same used later in essay 18 of *The Federalist*. In describing the weakness of the confederacies of antiquity, Athens was used as an example: "Athens, as we learn from Demosthenes, was the arbiter of Greece 73 years. The Lacedemonians next governed it 29 years; at a subsequent period, after the battle of Leuctra, the Thebans had their turn of domination."

PHILIP [6]

[F]    GERMANIC *Empire*
       charlemagne & his successors
       DIET Recesses—
       ELECTORS now 7 excluding other
G      SWISS CANTONS
       Two diets—
       opposite *alliances*
       BERNE LUCERNE [7]
       To strengthen the Foerderal government powers too great
       must be given to a single branch!
H      Leag[u]e Offensive & Defensive &c
       particular Govs. might exert themselves in &c
       But liable to usual VICISSI[tudes]—
                —INTERNAL PEACE affected—
       PROXIMITY of situation—natural enemies—
       Partial confederacies from unequal extent
       Power inspires ambition—
       Weakness begets jealousy

       _____

       Western territory

       _____

6. Examples of "Phocian" and "Philip" were developed more fully in essay 18 of *The Federalist*. In that essay the following example was given of the lessons to be learned from a study of ancient confederacies:

"As a weak government, when not at war, is ever agitated by internal dissentions; so these never fail to bring on fresh calamities from abroad. The Phocians having ploughed up some consecrated ground belonging to the temple of Apollo, the Amphyctionic Council, according to the superstition of the age, imposed a fine on the sacrilegious offenders. The Phocians, being abetted by Athens and Sparta, refused to submit to the decree. The Thebans, with others of the cities, undertook to maintain the authority of the Amphyctions, and to avenge the violated God. The latter being the weaker party, invited the assistance of Philip of Macedon, who had secretly fostered the contest. Philip gladly seized the opportunity of executing the designs he had long planned against the liberties of Greece."

7. H's remarks on "Two diets" probably can be reconstructed by remarks on the Swiss Cantons in essay 19 of *The Federalist*: "The Protestant and Catholic Cantons have since had their separate diets; where all the most important concerns are adjusted, and which have left the general diet little other business than to take care of the common bailages." His remarks on "opposite *alliances* Berne Lucerne" probably were similar to the following passage from the same number of *The Federalist*: "That separation had another consequence which merits attention. It produced opposite alliances with foreign powers; of Berne at the head of the Protestant association, with the United Provinces; and of Luzerne, as the head of the Catholic association, with France."

Obj: Genius of republics pacific—

---

Answer—Jealousy of commerce as well as jealousy of **power**
begets war—
Sparta Athens Thebes Rome
Carthage Venice Hanseatic League [8]
ENGLAND as many
Popular as Royal Wars
Lewis the 14th—AUSTRIA BOURBON [9]
William & Anne—

---

Wars depend on triffling circumstances every where—
Dutchess of Malboroughs Glov[es] [10]

---

8. The examples given by H were explained in essay 6 of *The Federalist*, written a year later:

"Have there not been as many wars founded upon commercial motives, since that has become the prevailing system of nations, as were before occasioned by the cupidity of territory or dominion?

"Sparta, Athens, Rome, and Carthage, were all Republics; two of them, Athens and Carthage of the commercial kind. Yet were they as often engaged in wars, offensive and defensive, as the neighbouring Monarchies of the same times. Sparta was little better than a well regulated camp; and Rome was never sated of carnage and conquest.

"Carthage, though a commercial Republic, was the aggressor in the very war that ended in her destruction."

9. The references to "Lewis the 14th" and to "AUSTRIA BOURBON," were explained by H when he treated the same subject in essay 6 of *The Federalist*:

"The Provinces of Holland . . . took a leading and conspicuous part in the wars of Europe. They had furious contests with England for the dominion of the sea; and were among the most persevering and most implacable of the opponents of Lewis XIV. . . .

"The cries of the nation [of England] and the importunities of their representatives have, upon various occasions, dragged their monarchs into war, or continued them in it contrary to their inclinations, and, sometimes, contrary to the real interests of the State. In that memorable struggle for superiority, between the rival houses of *Austria* and *Bourbon* which so long kept Europe in a flame, it is well known that the antipathies of the English against the French . . . protracted the war beyond the limits marked out by sound policy, and for a considerable time in opposition to the views of the Court."

10. H is referring to an incident which took place between Sarah Churchill, the Duchess of Marlborough, and Queen Anne of England over a pair of gloves. There are at least two versions of this incident. In one the Duchess refused to surrender a pair of gloves when asked for them by the Queen. In the other, the Duchess, upon being asked by Abigail Hill Masham, a woman of the Bedchamber, for a pair of the Queen's gloves, which the Duchess had inadvertently put on, said: "Ah! have I on anything that has touched the odious hands of that disagreeable woman?" (Mrs. Arthur Colville, *Duchess*

FOREIGN CONQUEST
Dismemberment—POLAND— [11]
FOREIGN INFLUENCE—
Distractions set afloat Vicious humours [12]
STANDING armies by dissensions
DOMESTIC FACTIONS—
Montesquieu
*Monarchy* in Southern States—

---

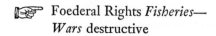 Foedral Rights *Fisheries*—
*Wars* destructive

---

I     Loss of advantages
—Foreign nations would not respect our rights nor grant us
reciprocity—
Would reduce us to a PASSIVE COMMERCE
Fisheries Navigation of the lakes, of the MISSISSIPPI

---

FLEET [13]

The general government must, in this case, not only have a strong soul, but *strong organs* by which that soul is to operate.

Here I shall give my sentiments of the best form of government—not as a thing attainable by us, but as a model which we ought to approach as near as possible.

British constitution best form.

---

*Sarah* [New York, 1904], 214–15). This remark was supposed to have been overheard by Queen Anne and to have been one of the many incidents that led to the rupture between the Duke and Duchess of Marlborough and the Queen. Voltaire states that Queen Anne's desire to complete the break led to the Peace of Utrecht and the end of Marlborough's power in England (Jean François Marie Arouet de Voltaire, *The Age of Louis XIV*, 237–41).

11. H's use of Poland as an example in his argument can be conjectured by the similar use made of it in essay 19 of *The Federalist*. In that essay H discussed the perils of a weak government and described Poland "as a government over local sovereigns. . . . Equally unfit for self-government, and self defence." That nation had, it was stated, "long been at the mercy of its powerful neighbours; who have lately had the mercy to disburden it of one third of its people and territories."

12. At this point H wrote and then crossed out: "Hats Caps."

13. H's MS notes end with the word "Fleet." The remaining notes, published below, are taken from Hamilton, *Life*, II, 486–89.

Aristotle—Cicero—Montesquieu—Neckar.

Society naturally divides itself into two political divisions—the *few* and the *many*, who have distinct interests.

If government in the hands of the *few*, they will tyrannize over the many.

If (in) the hands of the many, they will tyrannize over the few. It ought to be in the hands of both; and they should be separated.

This separation must be permanent.

Representation alone will not do.

Demagogues will generally prevail.

And if separated, they will need a mutual check.

This check is a monarch.

Each principle ought to exist in full force, or it will not answer its end.

The democracy must be derived immediately from the people.

The aristocracy ought to be entirely separated; their power should be permanent, and they should have the *caritas liberorum.*

They should be so circumstanced that they can have no interest in a change—as to have an effectual weight in the constitution.

Their duration should be the earnest of wisdom and stability.

'Tis essential there should be a permanent will in a community.

Vox populi, vox Dei.

Source of government—the unreasonableness of the people—separate interests—debtors and creditors, &c.

There ought to be a principle in government capable of resisting the popular current.

No periodical duration will come up to this.

This will always imply hopes and fears.

Creature and Creator.

Popular assemblies governed by a few individuals.

These individuals seeing their dissolution approach, will sacrifice.

The principle of representation will influence.

The most popular branch will acquire an influence over the other.

The other may check in ordinary cases, in which there is no strong public passion; but it will not in cases where there is—the cases in which such a principle is most necessary.

☞ Suppose duration seven years, and rotation.

One-seventh will have only one year to serve.

One-seventh——two years.

One-seventh——three years.

One-seventh——four years.

A majority will look to a dissolution in four years by instalments.

The monarch must have proportional strength. He ought to be hereditary, and to have so much power, that it will not be his interest to risk much to acquire more.

The advantage of a monarch is this—he is above corruption—he must always intend, in respect to foreign nations, the true interest and glory of the people.

Republics liable to foreign corruption and intrigue—Holland—Athens.

Effect of the British government.

> A vigorous execution of the laws—and a vigorous defence of the people, will result.
>
> Better chance for a good administration.
>
> It is said a republican government does not admit a vigorous execution.

It is therefore bad; for the goodness of a government consists in a vigorous execution.

The principle chiefly intended to be established is this—that there must be a permanent *will*.

Gentlemen say we need to be rescued from the democracy. But what the means proposed?

A democratic assembly is to be checked by a democratic senate, and both these by a democratic chief magistrate.

The end will not be answered—the means will not be equal to the object.

It will, therefore, be feeble and inefficient.

### RECAPITULATION

I. Impossible to secure the union by any modification of fœderal government.

II. League, offensive and defensive, full of certain evils and greater dangers.

III. General government, very difficult, if not impracticable, liable to various objections.

What is to be done?

Answer. Balance inconveniences and dangers, and choose that which seems to have the fewest objections.

Expence admits of this answer. The expense of the state governments will be proportionably diminished.

Interference of officers not so great, because the objects of the general government and the particular ones will not be the same—Finance—Administration of private justice. Energy will not be wanting in essential points, because the administration of private justice will be carried home to men's doors by the particular governments.

And the revenues may be collected from imposts, excises, &c. If necessary to go further, the general government may make use of the particular governments.

The attendance of members near the seat of government may be had in the lower branch.

And the upper branch may be so constructed as to induce the attendance of members from any part.

But this proves that the government must be so constituted as to offer strong motives.

In short, to interest all the *passions* of individuals.

And turn them into that channel.

### JAMES MADISON'S VERSION [14]

MR. HAMILTON, had been hitherto silent on the business before the Convention, partly from respect to others whose superior abilities age & experience rendered him unwilling to bring forward ideas dissimilar to theirs, and partly from his delicate situation with respect to his own State, to whose sentiments as expressed by his Colleagues, he could by no means accede. The crisis however which now marked our affairs, was too serious to permit any scruples whatever to prevail over the duty imposed on every man to contribute his efforts for the public safety & happiness. He was obliged therefore to declare himself unfriendly to both plans. He was particularly opposed to that from N. Jersey, being fully convinced, that no amendment of the Confederation, leaving the States in possession of their Sovereignty could possibly answer the purpose. On the other hand he confessed he was much discouraged by the amazing extent of

14. Hunt and Scott, *Debates*, 111–20.

Country in expecting the desired blessings from any general sovereignty that could be substituted. As to the powers of the Convention,
he thought the doubts started on that subject had arisen from distinctions & reasonings too subtle. A *federal* Govt. he conceived to
mean an association of independent Communities into one. Different
Confederacies have different powers, and exercise them in different
ways. In some instances the powers are exercised over collective
bodies; in others over individuals, as in the German Diet—& among
ourselves in cases of piracy. Great latitude therefore must be given
to the signification of the term. The plan last proposed [15] departs
itself from the *federal* idea, as understood by some, since it is to
operate eventually on individuals. He agreed moreover with the
Honble gentleman from Va. (Mr. R.) that we owed it to our Country, to do on this emergency whatever we should deem essential to
its happiness. The States sent us here to provide for the exigences
of the Union. To rely on & propose any plan not adequate to these
exigences, merely because it was not clearly within our powers,
would be to sacrifice the means to the end. It may be said that the
*States* can not *ratify* a plan not within the purview of the article of
Confederation providing for alterations & amendments. But may
not the States themselves in which no constitutional authority equal
to this purpose exists in the Legislatures, have had in view a reference
to the people at large. In the Senate of N. York, a proviso was moved,
that no act of the Convention should be binding untill it should be
referred to the people & ratified; and the motion was lost by a single
voice only, the reason assigned agst. it being, that it might possibly
be found an inconvenient shackle.

   The great question is what provision shall we make for the happiness of our Country? He would first make a comparative examination of the two plans—prove that there were essential defects in both
—and point out such changes as might render a *national one*, efficacious. The great & essential principles necessary for the support of
Government are 1. an active & constant interest in supporting it.
This principle does not exist in the States in favor of the federal
Govt. They have evidently in a high degree, the esprit de corps.
They constantly pursue internal interests adverse to those of the
whole. They have their particular debts—their particular plans of

15. The New Jersey Plan.

finance &c. All these when opposed to, invariably prevail over the requisitions & plans of Congress. 2. The love of power. Men love power. The same remarks are applicable to this principle. The States have constantly shewn a disposition rather to regain the powers delegated by them than to part with more, or to give effect to what they had parted with. The ambition of their demagogues is known to hate the controul of the Genl. Government. It may be remarked too that the Citizens have not that anxiety to prevent a dissolution of the Genl. Govt. as of the particular Govts. A dissolution of the latter would be fatal; of the former would still leave the purposes of Govt. attainable to a considerable degree. Consider what such a State as Virga. will be in a few years, a few compared with the life of nations. How strongly will it feel its importance & self-sufficiency? 3. An habitual attachment of the people. The whole force of this tie is on the side of the State Govt. Its sovereignty is immediately before the eyes of the people: its protection is immediately enjoyed by them. From its hand distributive justice, and all those acts which familiarize & endear Govt. to a people, are dispensed to them. 4. *Force* by which may be understood a *coertion of laws* or *coertion of arms*. Congs. have not the former except in few cases. In particular States, this coercion is nearly sufficient; tho' he held it in most cases, not entirely so. A certain portion of military force is absolutely necessary in large communities. Masss. is now feeling this necessity & making provision for it. But how can this force be exerted on the States collectively. It is impossible. It amounts to a war between the parties. Foreign powers also will not be idle spectators. They will interpose, the confusion will increase, and a dissolution of the Union will ensue. 5. *influence*. he did not mean corruption, but a dispensation of those regular honors & emoluments, which produce an attachment to the Govt. Almost all the weight of these is on the side of the States; and must continue so as long as the States continue to exist. All the passions then we see, of avarice, ambition, interest, which govern most individuals, and all public bodies, fall into the current of the States, and do not flow in the stream of the Genl. Govt. The former therefore will generally be an overmatch for the Genl. Govt. and render any confederacy, in its very nature precarious. Theory is in this case fully confirmed by experience. The Amphyctionic Council had it would seem ample powers for general

purposes. It had in particular the power of fining and using force
agst. delinquent members. What was the consequence. Their decrees
were mere signals of war. The Phocian war is a striking example
of it. Philip at length taking advantage of their disunion, and in-
sinuating himself into their Councils, made himself master of their
fortunes. The German Confederacy affords another lesson. The
authority of Charlemagne seemed to be as great as could be necessary. The great feudal chiefs however, exercising their local sovereignties, soon felt the spirit & found the means of, encroachments,
which reduced the imperial authority to a nominal sovereignty. The
Diet has succeeded, which tho' aided by a Prince at its head, of great
authority independently of his imperial attributes, is a striking illustration of the weakness of Confederated Governments. Other
examples instruct us in the same truth. The Swiss cantons have scarce
any Union at all, and have been more than once at war with one
another. How then are all these evils to be avoided? only by such
a compleat sovereignty in the general Governmt. as will turn all
the strong principles & passions above mentioned on its side. Does
the scheme of N. Jersey produce this effect? does it afford any
substantial remedy whatever? On the contrary it labors under great
defects, and the defect of some of its provisions will destroy the
efficacy of others. It gives a direct revenue to Congs. but this will
not be sufficient. The balance can only be supplied by requisitions:
which experience proves can not be relied on. If States are to deliberate on the mode, they will also deliberate on the object of the
supplies, and will grant or not grant as they approve or disapprove
of it. The delinquency of one will invite and countenance it in
others. Quotas too must in the nature of things be so unequal as to
produce the same evil. To what standard will you resort? Land is
a fallacious one. Compare Holland with Russia: France or Engd. with
other countries of Europe. Pena. with N. Carola. will the relative
pecuniary abilities in those instances, correspond with the relative
value of land. Take numbers of inhabitants for the rule and make
like comparison of different countries, and you will find it to be
equally unjust. The different degrees of industry and improvement
in different Countries render the first object a precarious measure
of wealth. Much depends too on *situation*. Cont. N. Jersey & N.
Carolina, not being commercial States & contributing to the wealth

of the commercial ones, can never bear quotas assessed by the ordinary rules of proportion. They will & must fail in their duty, their example will be followed, and the Union itself be dissolved. Whence then is the national revenue to be drawn? from Commerce? even from exports which notwithstanding the common opinion are fit objects of moderate taxation, from excise, &c &c. These tho' not equal, are less unequal than quotas. Another destructive ingredient in the plan, is that equality of suffrage which is so much desired by the small States. It is not in human nature that Va. & the large States should consent to it, or if they did that they shd. long abide by it. It shocks too much the ideas of Justice, and every human feeling. Bad principles in a Govt. tho slow are sure in their operation, and will gradually destroy it. A doubt has been raised whether Congs. at present have a right to keep Ships or troops in time of peace. He leans to the negative. Mr. Ps. plan provides no remedy. If the powers proposed were adequate, the organization of Congs. is such that they could never be properly & effectually exercised. The members of Congs. being chosen by the States & subject to recall, represent all the local prejudices. Should the powers be found effectual, they will from time to time be heaped on them, till a tyrannic sway shall be established. The general power whatever be its form if it preserves itself, must swallow up the State powers. Otherwise it will be swallowed up by them. It is agst. all the principles of a good Government to vest the requisite powers in such a body as Congs. Two Sovereignties can not co-exist within the same limits. Giving powers to Congs. must eventuate in a bad Govt. or in no Govt. The plan of N. Jersey therefore will not do. What then is to be done? Here he was embarrassed. The extent of the Country to be governed, discouraged him. The expence of a general Govt. was also formidable; unless there were such a diminution of expence on the side of the State Govts. as the case would admit. If they were extinguished, he was persuaded that great œconomy might be obtained by substituting a general Govt. He did not mean however to shock the public opinion by proposing such a measure. On the other hand he saw no *other* necessity for declining it. They are not necessary for any of the great purposes of commerce, revenue, or agriculture. Subordinate authorities he was aware would be necessary. There must be district tribunals: corporations for local purposes. But cui bono, the vast & expensive apparatus now appertaining to the States. The only difficulty of a serious nature which occurred to him, was that of drawing representatives from the extremes to the center of the Community. What inducements can be offered that will suffice? The moderate wages for the 1st. branch would only be a bait to little demagogues. Three dollars or thereabouts he supposed would be the utmost. The Senate he feared from a similar cause, would be filled by certain undertakers who wish for particular offices under the Govt. This view of the subject almost led him to despair that a Republican Govt. could be established over so great an extent. He was sensible at the same time that it would be unwise to propose one of any other form. In his private opinion he had no scruple in declaring, supported as he was by the opinions of so many of the wise & good, that the British Govt. was the best in the world: and that he doubted much whether any thing short of it would do in America. He hoped Gentlemen of different opinions would bear with him in this, and begged them to recollect the change of opinion on this subject which had taken place and was still going on. It was once thought that the power of Congs. was amply sufficient to secure the end of their institution. The error was now seen by every one. The members most tenacious of republicanism, he observed, were as loud as any in declaiming agst. the vices of democracy. This progress of the public mind led him to anticipate the time, when others as well as himself would join in the praise bestowed by Mr. Neckar on the British Constitution, namely, that it is the only Govt. in the world "which unites public strength with individual security." In every community where industry is encouraged, there will be a division of it into the few & the many. Hence separate interests will arise. There will be debtors & creditors &c. Give all power to the many, they will oppress the few. Give all power to the few, they will oppress the many. Both therefore ought to have power, that each may defend itself agst. the other. To the want of this check we owe our paper money, instalment laws &c. To the proper adjustment of it the British owe the excellence of their Constitution. Their house of Lords is a most noble institution. Having nothing to hope for by a change, and a sufficient interest by means of their property, in being faithful to the national interest, they form a permanent barrier agst. every pernicious innovation, whether attempted on the part of the Crown or of the Commons. No temporary Senate will have the firmness eno' to answer the purpose. The Senate (of Maryland) which seems to be so much appealed to, has not yet been sufficiently tried. Had the people been unanimous & eager, in the late appeal to them on the subject of a paper emission they would have yielded to the torrent. Their acquiescing in such an appeal is a proof of it. Gentlemen differ in their opinions concerning the necessary checks, from the different estimates they form of the human passions. They suppose seven years a sufficient period to give the senate an adequate firmness, from not duly considering the amazing violence & turbulence of the democratic spirit. When a great object of Govt. is pursued, which seizes the popular passions, they spread like wild fire, and become irresistable. He appealed to the gentlemen from the N. England States whether experience had not there verified the remark. As to the Executive, it seemed to be admitted that no good one could be established on Republican principles. Was not this giving up the merits of the question: for can there be a good Govt. without a good Executive. The English model was the only good one on this subject. The Hereditary interest of the King was so interwoven with that of the Nation, and his personal emoluments so great, that he was placed above the danger of being corrupted from abroad—and at the same time was both sufficiently independent and sufficiently controuled, to answer the purpose of the institution at home. one of the weak sides of Republics was their being liable to foreign influence & corruption. Men of little character, acquiring great power become easily the tools of intermedling Neibours. Sweeden was a striking instance. The French & English had each their parties during the late Revolution which was effected by the predominant influence of the former. What is the inference from all these observations? That we ought to go as far in order to attain stability and permanency, as republican principles will admit. Let one branch of the Legislature hold their places for life or at least during good behaviour. Let the Executive also be for life. He appealed to the feelings of the members present whether a term of seven years, would induce the sacrifices of private affairs which an acceptance of public trust would require, so so as to ensure the services of the best Citizens. On this plan we should have in the Senate a permanent will, a

weighty interest, which would answer essential purposes. But is this
a Republican Govt., it will be asked? Yes if all the Magistrates are
appointed, and vacancies are filled, by the people, or a process of
election originating with the people. He was sensible that an Executive constituted as he proposed would have in fact but little of the
power and independence that might be necessary. On the other
plan of appointing him for 7 years, he thought the Executive ought
to have but little power. He would be ambitious, with the means of
making creatures; and as the object of his ambition wd. be to *prolong*
his power, it is probable that in case of a war, he would avail himself
of the emergence, to evade or refuse a degradation from his place.
An Executive for life has not this motive for forgetting his fidelity,
and will therefore be a safer depository of power. It will be objected
probably, that such an Executive will be an *elective Monarch*, and
will give birth to the tumults which characterize that form of Govt.
He wd. reply that *Monarch* is an indefinite term. It marks not either
the degree or duration of power. If this Executive Magistrate wd. be
a monarch for life—the other propd. by the Report from the Comtte
of the whole, wd. be a monarch for seven years. The circumstance
of being elective was also applicable to both. It had been observed
by judicious writers that elective monarchies wd. be the best if they
could be guarded agst. the *tumults* excited by the ambition and
intrigues of competitors. He was not sure that tumults were an
inseparable evil. He rather thought this character of Elective Monarchies had been taken rather from particular cases than from general principles. The election of Roman Emperors was made by the
*Army*. In *Poland* the election is made by great rival *princes* with
independent power, and ample means, of raising commotions. In
the German Empire, the appointment is made by the Electors &
Princes, who have equal motives & means, for exciting cabals &
parties. Might not such a mode of election be devised among ourselves as will defend the community agst. these effects in any
dangerous degree? Having made these observations he would read
to the Committee a sketch of a plan which he shd. prefer to either
of those under consideration. He was aware that it went beyond the
ideas of most members. But will such a plan be adopted out of doors?
In return he would ask will the people adopt the other plan? At
present they will adopt neither. But he sees the Union dissolving or

already dissolved—he sees evils operating in the States which must soon cure the people of their fondness for democracies—he sees that a great progress has been already made & is still going on in the public mind. He thinks therefore that the people will in time be unshackled from their prejudices; and whenever that happens, they will themselves not be satisfied at stopping where the plan of Mr. R. wd. place them, but be ready to go as far at least as he proposes. He did not mean to offer the paper he had sketched as a proposition to the Committee. It was meant only to give a more correct view of his ideas, and to suggest the amendments which he should probably propose to the plan of Mr. R. in the proper stages of its future discussion. He read his sketch in the words following: towit. . . ." [16]

On these several articles he entered into explanatory observations corresponding with the principles of his introductory reasoning.[17]

## ROBERT YATES'S VERSION [18]

*Mr. Hamilton.* To deliver my sentiments on so important a subject, when the first characters in the union have gone before me, inspires me with the greatest diffidence, especially when my own ideas are so materially dissimilar to the plans now before the committee. My situation is disagreeable, but it would be criminal not to come forward on a question of such magnitude. I have well considered the subject, and am convinced that no amendment of the confederation can answer the purpose of a good government, so long as state sovereignties do, in any shape, exist; and I have great doubts whether a national government on the Virginia plan can be made effectual. What is federal? An association of several inde-

16. See "Constitutional Convention. Plan of Government," June 18, 1787.
17. The "explanatory observations" may not have been those remarks which appear in the Yates version of H's speech after, according to Yates, H introduced his "Plan of Government." In the transcript of Madison's notes, made by his secretary John C. Payne and approved by Madison, there is the following explanation of the order of Yates's version of H's speech: "Judge Yates, in his notes, appears to have consolidated the explanatory with the introductory observations of Mr. Hamilton. It was in the former, Mr. Madison observed, that Mr. Hamilton, in speaking of popular governments, however modified, made the remark attributed to him by Judge Yates, that they were *'but pork still with a little change of sauce'* " (Hunt and Scott, *Debates,* 120n).
18. Yates, *Secret Proceedings and Debates,* 129–37.
Because of a typographical error in the printing of the *Secret Proceedings and Debates* the proceedings for June 18 appear under the date of "Monday, June 19th, 1787."

pendent states into one. How or in what manner this association is formed, is not so clearly distinguishable. We find the diet of Germany has in some instances the power of legislation on individuals. We find the United States of America have it in an extensive degree in the cases of piracies.

Let us now review the powers with which we are invested. We are appointed for the *sole* and *express* purpose of revising the confederation, and to *alter* or *amend* it, so as to render it effectual for the purposes of a good government. Those who suppose it must be federal, lay great stress on the terms *sole* and *express,* as if these words intended a confinement to a federal government; when the manifest import is no more than that the institution of a good government must be the *sole* and *express* object of your deliberations. Nor can we suppose an annihilation of our powers by forming a national government, as many of the states have made in their constitutions no provision for any alteration; and thus much I can say for the state I have the honor to represent, that when our credentials were under consideration in the senate, some members were for inserting a restriction in the powers, to prevent an encroachment on the constitution: it was answered by others, and thereupon the resolve carried on the credentials, that it might abridge some of the constitutional powers of the state, and that possibly in the formation of a new union it would be found necessary. This appears reasonable, and therefore leaves us at liberty to form such a national government as we think best adapted for the good of the whole. I have therefore no difficulty as to the extent of our powers, nor do I feel myself restrained in the exercise of my judgment under them. We can only propose and recommend—the power of ratifying or rejecting is still in the states. But on this great question I am still greatly embarrassed. I have before observed my apprehension of the inefficacy of either plan, and I have great doubts whether a more energetic government can pervade this wide and extensive country. I shall now show, that both plans are materially defective.

1. A good government ought to be constant, and ought to contain an active principle.

2. Utility and necessity.

3. An habitual sense of obligation.

4. Force.

5. Influence.

I hold it, that different societies have all different views and interests to pursue, and always prefer local to general concerns. For example: New-York legislature made an external compliance lately to a requisition of congress; but do they not at the same time counteract their compliance by gratifying the local objects of the state so as to defeat their concession? And this will ever be the case. Men always love power, and states will prefer their particular concerns to the general welfare; and as the states become large and important, will they not be less attentive to the general government? What, in process of time will Virginia be? She contains now half a million inhabitants—in twenty-five years she will double the number. Feeling her own weight and importance, must she not become indifferent to the concerns of the union? And where, in such a situation, will be found national attachment to the general government?

By *force*, I mean the *coercion* of law and the coercion of arms. Will this remark apply to the power intended to be vested in the government to be instituted by theire plan? A delinquent must be compelled to obedience by force of arms. How is this to be done? If you are unsuccessful, a dissolution of your government must be the consequence; and in that case the individual legislatures will reassume their powers; nay, will not the interest of the states be thrown into the state governments?

By *influence*, I mean the regular weight and support it will receive from those who will find it their interest to support a government intended to preserve the peace and happiness of the community of the whole. The state governments, by either plan, will exert the means to counteract it. They have their state judges and militia all combined to support their state interests; and these will be influenced to oppose a national government. Either plan is therefore precarious. The national government cannot long exist when opposed by such a weighty rival. The experience of ancient and modern confederacies evince this point, and throw considerable light on the subject. The amphyctionic council of Greece had a right to require of its members troops, money and the force of the country. Were they obeyed in the exercise of those powers? Could they preserve the peace of the greater states and republics? or where were they obeyed? History shows that their decrees were disregarded, and that the stronger states, regardless of their power, gave law to the lesser.

Let us examine the federal institution of Germany. It was instituted upon the laudable principle of securing the independency of the several states of which it was composed, and to protect them against foreign invasion. Has it answered these good intentions? Do we not see that their councils are weak and distracted, and that it cannot prevent the wars and confusions which the respective electors carry on against each other? The Swiss cantons, or the Helvetic union, are equally inefficient.

Such are the lessons which the experience of others affords us, and from whence results the evident conclusion that all federal governments are weak and distracted. To avoid the evils deducible from these observations, we must establish a general and national government, completely sovereign, and annihilate the state distinctions and state operations; and unless we do this, no good purpose can be answered. What does the Jersey plan propose? It surely has not this for its object. By this we grant the regulation of trade and a more effectual collection of the revenue, and some partial duties. These, at five or ten per cent, would only perhaps amount to a fund to discharge the debt of the corporation.

Let us take a review of the variety of important objects, which must necessarily engage the attention of a national government. You have to protect your rights against Canada on the north, Spain on the south, and your western frontier against the savages. You have to adopt necessary plans for the settlement of your frontiers, and to institute the mode in which settlements and good government are to be made.

How is the expense of supporting and regulating these important matters to be defrayed? By requisition on the states, according to the Jersey plan? Will this do it? We have already found it ineffectual. Let one state prove delinquent, and it will encourage others to follow the example; and thus the whole will fail. And what is the standard to quota among the states their respective proportions? Can lands be the standard? How would that apply between Russia and Holland? Compare Pennsylvania with North-Carolina, or Connecticut with New-York. Does not commerce or industry in the one or other make a great disparity between these different countries, and may not the comparative value of the states from these circumstances, make an unequal disproportion when the data is numbers? I therefore conclude that either system would ultimately destroy the confederation, or any other government which is established on such fallacious principles. Perhaps imposts, taxes on specific articles, would produce a more equal system of drawing a revenue.

Another objection against the Jersey plan is, the unequal representation. Can the great States consent to this? If they did it would eventually work its own destruction. How are forces to be raised by the Jersey plan? By quotas? Will the states comply with the requisition? As much as they will with the taxes.

Examine the present confederation, and it is evident they can raise no troops nor equip vessels before war is actually declared. They cannot therefore take any preparatory measure before an enemy is at your door. How unwise and inadequate their powers! and this must ever be the case when you attempt to define powers. Something will always be wanting. Congress, by being annually elected, and subject to recall, will ever come with the prejudices of their states rather than the good of the union. Add therefore additional powers to a body thus organized, and you establish a *sovereignty* of the worst kind, consisting of a single body. Where are the checks? None. They must either prevail over the state governments, or the prevalence of the state governments must end in their dissolution. This is a conclusive objection to the Jersey plan.

Such are the insuperable objections to both plans: and what is to be done on this occasion? I confess I am at a loss. I foresee the difficulty on a consolidated plan of drawing a representation from so extensive a continent to one place. What can be the inducements for gentlemen to come 600 miles to a national legislature? The expense would at least amount to £ 100,000. This however can be no conclusive objection if it eventuates in an extinction of state governments. The burthen of the latter would be saved, and the expense then would not be great. State distinctions would be found unnecessary, and yet I confess, to carry government to the extremities, the state governments reduced to corporations, and with very limited powers, might be necessary, and the expense of the national government become less burthensome.

Yet, I confess, I see great difficulty of drawing forth a good representation. What, for example, will be the inducements for gentlemen of fortune and abilities to leave their houses and business to attend annually and long? It cannot be the wages; for these, I presume, must be small. Will not the power, therefore, be thrown into the hands of the demagogue or middling politician, who, for the sake of a small stipend and the hopes of advancement, will offer himself as a candidate, and the real men of weight and influence, by remaining at home, add strength to the state governments? I am at a loss to know what must be done; I despair that a republican form of government can remove the difficulties. Whatever may be my opinion, I would hold it however unwise to change that form of government. I believe the British government forms the best model the world ever produced, and such has been its progress in the minds of the many, that this truth gradually gains ground. This government has for its object *public strength* and *individual security*. It is said with us to be unattainable. If it was once formed it would maintain itself. All communities divide themselves into the few and the many. The first are the rich and well born, the other the mass of the people. The voice of the people has been said to be the voice of God; and however generally this maxim has been quoted and believed, it is not true in fact. The people are turbulent and changing; they seldom judge or determine right. Give therefore to the first class a distinct, permanent share in the government. They will check the unsteadiness of the second, and as they cannot receive any advantage by a change, they therefore will ever maintain good government. Can a democratic assembly, who annually revolve in the mass of the people, be supposed steadily to pursue the public good? Nothing but a permanent body can check the imprudence of democracy. Their turbulent and uncontrouling disposition requires checks. The senate of New-York, although chosen for four years, we have found to be inefficient. Will, on the Virginia plan, a continuance of seven years do it? It is admitted, that you cannot have a good executive upon a democratic plan. See the excellency of the British executive. He is placed above temptation. He can have no distinct interests from the public welfare. Nothing short of such an executive can be efficient. The weak side of a republican government is the danger of foreign influence. This is unavoidable, unless it is so constructed as to bring forward its first characters in its support. I am therefore for a general government, yet would wish to go the full length of republican principles.

Let one body of the legislature be constituted during good behaviour or life.

Let one executive be appointed who dares execute his powers.

It may be asked is this a republican system? It is strictly so, as long
as they remain elective.

And let me observe, that an executive is less dangerous to the liberties of the people when in office during life, than for seven years.

It may be said, this constitutes an elective monarchy? Pray, what
is a monarchy? May not the governors of the respective states be
considered in that light? But by making the executive subject to
impeachment, the term monarchy cannot apply. These elective
monarchs have produced tumults in Rome, and are equally dangerous to peace in Poland; but this cannot apply to the mode in
which I would propose the election. Let electors be appointed in
each of the states to elect the executive—(*Here Mr. H. produced his
plan, a copy whereof is hereunto annexed,*) [19] to consist of two
branches—and I would give them the unlimited power of passing
*all laws* without exception. The assembly to be elected for three
years by the people in districts—the senate to be elected by the
electors to be chosen for that purpose by the people, and to remain
in office during life. The executive to have the power of negativing
all laws—to make war or peace, with the advice of the senate—to
make treaties with their advice, but to have the sole direction of all
military operations, and to send ambassadors and appoint all military
officers, and to pardon all offenders, treason excepted, unless by
advice of the senate. On his death or removal, the president of the
senate to officiate, with the same powers, until another is elected.
Supreme judicial officers to be appointed by the executive and the
senate. The legislature to appoint courts in each state, so as to make
the state governments unnecessary to it.

All state laws to be absolutely void which contravene the general
laws. An officer to be appointed in each state to have a negative
on all state laws. All the militia and the appointment of officers to
be under the national government.

I confess that this plan and that from Virginia are very remote
from the idea of the people. Perhaps the Jersey plan is nearest their

19. See "Constitutional Convention. Plan of Government," June 18, 1787.

expectation. But the people are gradually ripening in their opinions of government—they begin to be tired of an excess of democracy— and what even is the Virginia plan, but *pork still, with a little change of the sauce.*

## JOHN LANSING'S VERSION[20]

Hamilton—The Situation of the State he represents and the Diffidence he has of his own Judgment induced him to Silence tho his Ideas are dissimilar from both Plans.

No Amendment of Confederation can answer the Exigencies of the States. State Sovereignties ought not to exist. Supposes we have Powers sufficient. Foederal an Association of States differently modified. Diet of Germany has Power to legislate for Individuals. In United States Confederacy legislate for States and in some Instances on Individuals—*Instances Piracies.* The Term *sole* he supposes was to impress an Idea only that we were not to govern ourselves, but to revise Government.

Another Difficulty that the Legislature cannot be supposed to have delegated a Power they did not possess themselves—So far as Respects the State of New York one of the Branches of the Legislature considered it—It was *said they might have Recourse to the People*— this had its Influence and it was carried by one Vote. We ought not to sacrafice the public Good to narrow Scruples. All America, all Europe, the World would condemn us. The only Enquiry ought to be what can we do to save our Country. Five Essentials indispensible in foederal Government.

    1. A constant and active Interest.
    2. Utility and Necessity.
    3. A habitual Sense of Obligation.
    4. Force.
    5. Influence.

Every Set of men who associate acquire an *Esprit de Corps.* This will apply forcibly to States—they will have distinct Views—their own Obligations thwart general Good.

Do we not find a Jealousy subsisting? In the State of New York we had an Instance. The last Requisition was partially paid—the

20. *Notes of John Lansing*, 61–68.

principal Part of their Funds applied to discharge State Obligations —the Individual States hostile to general Interest.

Virginia will in 25 Years contain a Million of Inhabitants—It may then be disposed to give up an Union only burthensome. The Distribution of Justice presents itself to every Eye—this has a powerful Influence and must particular attach Individuals to the State Governments.

Two modes of Coercion—of Laws—of Military.

Individuals are easily controuled—not so Society—You must carry the Force to Individuals—If only State delinquent it would cause a war—If more they would associate and make a common Cause of it.

We must resort to Influence—Dispensations of Honors and Emoluments of Office necessary—these are all in the Hands of the State Governments. If they exist in State Governments their Influence too great. our Situation is peculiar. *It leaves us Room to dream* as we think proper. Groecian Confederacy lost for Want of adequate Powers—German the same. Swiss Cantons—general Diet has lost its Powers. Cannot combine States but by absorbing the *Ambition and Avarice* of all.

Jersey Propositions—Regulating Trade—Revenue not adequate to meet our Debt—where are we to find it? Requisitions—the several States will deliberate on them. Requisitions founded on Quotas must always fail. There is no general Standard for Wealth in Communities—Pennsylvania and North Carolina—Connecticut and New York compared. New York derives great Wealth from Commerce—Connecticut none. Indirect Taxation must be multiplied.

Equality of Suffrage ruinous to the Union.

Doubts have been entertained whether the United States have a Right to build a Ship or raise a Reg(imen)t in Time of Peace— this Doubt might involve almost our Ruin.

The Organization of Congress exceptionable—They are annually appointed and subject to recal.—They will of Consequence represent the Prejudices of the States not general Interests. No Power will be executed if the States think proper to obstruct it. If general Government preserves itself it must extinguish State Governments.

If Congress remains Legislature the Sovereignty must ultimately vest in them.

The Expence of national Government is a Consideration with him —it will probably amount to £100,000 per ann.—this however surmountable. It will not do to propose formal Extinction of State Governments. It would shock public Opinion too much. Some subordinate Jurisdictions—something like limitted Corporations. If general Government properly modified it may extinguish State Governments gradually. Representation is another difficulty. British Government the best. Dispairs of ever uniting the great Objects of Government which have been so successfully attained by the British, public Strength and individual Safety, in any Republican System. He thinks here it would support itself—the Citizens of America may be distinguished into the wealthy well born and well educated—*and the many*. If Government in the hands of the latter they sacrafice the few—are as often in the wrong as right.

You can only protect the few by giving them exclusive Rights—they have Nothing to hope from Change. Monarchy is essential to them. One Branch of Legislature ought to be independent to check popular Frenzy—or Democraties will prevail. Seven Years is no Check—It is no Object for Men of first Importance. Little Daemagogues will fill Assembly. Undertakers your Senate.

In Republics trifling Characters obtrude—they are easily corrupted —the most Important Individuals ought to [be] drawn forth for Government—this can only be effected by establishing upper House for good Behaviour. Congress are Objects of foreign Corruption.

Executive ought to be during good Behaviour. He will part with his Power with Reluctance. You ought to interest him in the Government.

This may be objected to as establishing an elective Monarchy— but he will be liable to Impeachment for mal-conduct. The Election it supposed would cause Tumults. To avoid this the People in each District should chuse Electors—those should elect a few in that State who should meet with Electors from the other States and elect *the Governor*.

Roman Emperor—elective—by Army.

German Emperor—by great Electors.

Polish King—great Barons who have numerous Dependents.

These were tumultous from their Institutions. We may guard against it.

The principal Citizens of every State are tired of Democracy—he then read his Plan and expatiated on it—See [21]

### RUFUS KING'S VERSION [22]

Federal is an association of distinct Govt: into one—these fed. Govt. in some instances legislate on collective bodies, in others on individuals. The Confederation partakes of both—Piracies are cognizable by the Congress—&c.

Our powers have this object—the Freedom & Happiness of our Country—we must go all lengths to accomplish this Object—if the Legislatures have no powers to ratify because thereby they diminish their own Sovereignty, the people may come in on revolution principles—

*We have power,*

Upon the plan of the separation & indipendence of the States, you incourage those Habits, and opinions, that Esprit de Corps which is peculiar to the State and to every individual. These habits prefer their own State to those of the Genl. or fed. Govt. This has been the case, State Debts, State Crs. have always stood before the fedl. Debr or Cr.

Man loves power—State magistrates will desire to increase yr. own powers at the Expence of the Genl. or fed. Govt.

One great Objt. of Govt. is personal protection and the security of Property—if you establish a federal Govt. men will not be interested in the protection or preservation of the Genl. Govt. but they will in the existence of the State Govt. if the latter is dissolved and the former remains their persons & fortune will be safe—Besides the large States will be indisposed to remain connected.

Habits of Obedience
Men will see their fortunes secured, their persons protected, offenders punished by State laws and State magistrates—they will love the Govt. that is thus immediate—

*Force*
The Force of law or the strength of Arms—The former is ineffi-

21. See "Constitutional Convention. Plan of Government," June 18, 1787.
22. AD, New-York Historical Society, New York City.

cient unless the people have the habits of Obedience—in this case you must have Arms—if this doctrine is applied to States—the system is utopian—you could not coerce Virginia.—a fedl. Govt. is impracticable—you must call in foreign powers to aid the Genl. Govt. agt. the individual States—this will desolve the Union and destroy your Freedom.

*Influence*

No govt. will be good without Influence that is unless men of merit or the Pillars of Govt. are rewarded with Offices of Honor & profit—the State Govts. have this influence—the fed. Govt. will be without it—this being true the Genl. Govt. will fail—as long as the States are rivals of the Genl. Govt. so long the Genl. will be subordinate—

How does History illustrate this point

The *amphictions*—had power to levy money men &c on the States—it was peculiarly federal—when a State failed the Amphictions fined—this was the case of the Phocians when Philip interposed—

*Germany*

*their Diets* are as weak as the amphictions, although the Emperor is bound to carry their Decrees into Execution—they put an electorate under the Ban, & the Electorate puts the Diet & the Emperor at Defiance—

Switzerland

Their Diet is divided, their union is destroyed—part are in alliance wt. France and the other part wt. the U Netherlands.

The Result is that all the passions of avarice, pride, ambition &c. shd. depend on the Genl. & not the State Govts.—you must make the national Sovereignty transcendent & entire—
The plan of N. Jersey

It proposes Requisitions on the States for such monies as the Impost does not yield—States will not comply—they have not—you have no Standard to Quota

Numbers or Lands will not be a just Standard—an equal Difficulty arises in the Quotas of men—the States find men only in proportion to their Zeal—this was the Case in the late war—they cannot now obtain an honest adjustment of ye. Expence—for this gave large pecuniary bounties—

The Hic labor the hoc Opus is the Genl. Government

---

The Extent of Territory, the variety of opinions, & numerous considerations, seem to prevent a General Govt: The expence of the Genl. Govt. is important—not less yn. 100,000 £ any.

How will you induce Genl. to come into the Genl Govt.—what will be ye. inducement: you can give them perhaps 3 Dols. pr. Diem. Men of first consequence will not come forward—it will be managed by undertakers & not by the most able hands. I fear Republicanism ⟨will⟩ not answr. and yet we cannot go beyond it—I think the British Govt. is the only proper one for such an extensive Country—This govt. unites the highest public strength with the most perfect individual security—we are not in a Situation to receive it—perhaps if it was established it wd. maintain itself—I am however sensible that it can't be established by consent, and we ought not to think of other means—We may attempt a general and not a federal Govt: let the senate hold ye. office for life or during good behaviour; so of the Executive—This is republican if the people elect and also fill vacancies.

## Constitutional Convention. Plan of Government [1]

[Philadelphia, June 18, 1787]

I The Supreme Legislative Power of the United States of America to be vested in two distinct [2] bodies of men—the one to be called the *Assembly* [3] the other the *senate;* who together shall form the Legislature of the United States, with power
A   to pass all *laws whatsoever*, subject to the *negative* hereafter mentioned.

B   II The Assembly to consist of persons elected *by the People* to serve for three years.

III The Senate to consist of persons elected to serve during
C   *good behaviour*. Their election to be made by *Electors* chosen

for that purpose by the People. In order to this The States
to be divided into election districts. On the death removal or
resignation of any senator his place to be filled out of the district
from which he came.

IV  The Supreme Executive authority of the United States to
D   be vested in a *governor* to be elected to serve *during good*
E   *behaviour*. His [4] election to be made by *Electors* chosen by *elec-*
F   *tors* [5] chosen by the people in the election districts aforesaid [6] or
by electors chosen for that purpose by the respective legislatures
—provided that [if] an election be not made within a limit⟨ed⟩
time the President of the Senate shall ⟨–⟩ be the Governor. The
Governor [7] to have *a negative* upon [8] all laws about to be passed
and to have [9] the execution of all laws passed—to be the Commander in Chief of the land and naval forces and of the Militia
of the United States [10]—to have the [11] direction of war, when
authorised or began [12]—to have with the *advice* and *approbation*
of the Senate the power of making all treaties—to have the [13]
G   appointment of the *heads or chief* officers of the departments of
H   finance war and foreign affairs—to have the *nomination* of all
other officers (ambassadors to foreign nations included) subject
to the approbation or rejection of the Senate—to have the power
I   of pardoning all offences but [14] *treason*, which he shall not pardon without the approbation of the Senate.

V  On the death resignation or removal of the Governor his
authorities to be exercised by the President of the Senate.[15]

K  VI  The Senate to [16] have the sole power of *declaring war*—
the power of advising and approving all treaties—the power
of approving or rejecting all appointments of officers except
the heads or chiefs of the departments of finance war [17] and
foreign affairs.

VII  The Supreme Judicial authority of the United States [18] to
be vested in [19] twelve [20] Judges, to hold their offices [21] during
good behaviour with adequate and permanent salaries. This
Court to have original jurisdiction in all causes [22] of capture

and an appellative jurisdiction (from the Courts of the several states) [23] in all causes [24] in which the revenues of the general government or the citizens of foreign nations are concerned.

L   VIII   The Legislature [25] of the United States to have power to institute Courts in each state for the determination of all causes of capture and of all matters relating to their revenues, or in which the citizens of foreign nations are concerned.[26]

IX   The Governor Senators and all Officers of the United States to be liable to impeachment for mal and corrupt conduct, and upon conviction to be removed from office and disqualified for holding any place of trust or profit.[27] All impeachments to be tried by a Court to consist of the judges of the Supreme Court chief or Senior Judge of the superior Court of law of each state—provided that such judge hold his place during good behaviour and have a permanent salary.[28]

X   All laws of the [29] particular states contrary to the constitution or laws of the United States to be utterly void. And the better to prevent such laws being passed the Governor or President of each state shall *be appointed by the general government*
M   and shall have a *negative* upon the laws about to be passed in the state of which he is governor or President.

XI   No state to have any forces land or naval—and the *Militia*
N   of all the states to be under the sole and *exclusive direction* of the United States *the officers* of which [30] to be appointed and commissioned by them.

ADf, Hamilton Papers, Library of Congress.
    1. H included this "Plan of Government" in his speech to the Convention on June 18, 1787. For the point at which he incorporated the "Plan" in his speech, see "Constitutional Convention. Speech on a Plan of Government," June 18, 1787, notes 16, 19, 21.
    Notes on the "Plan" were made by James Madison (Hunt and Scott, *Debates*, 118-20), Robert Yates (*Secret Proceedings and Debates*, 225-227), and John Lansing, Jr. (*Notes of John Lansing*, 119-22). Except for minor differences in punctuation and occasional abbreviations in Lansing's account, the versions of the "Plan," as recorded by Madison, Yates, and Lansing, are exactly the same. There are, however, minor differences between H's draft of his "Plan" and the versions of it by Madison, Yates, and Lansing. Differences in wording

between H's draft and the other versions are indicated in the following notes. Differences in capitalization and punctuation have not been noted.

For the more complete plan of government which H gave to Madison near the end of the Convention, see "Draft of a Constitution," September 17, 1787.

2. In Madison, "different."

3. In Lansing the word "and" is inserted.

4. In Madison and in Lansing, "the."

5. Madison omits "chosen by electors."

6. At this point H indicated by an asterisk an insertion of the remainder of this sentence which he wrote at the bottom of the page. This insertion appears in no other version of H's "Plan."

7. The other accounts of H's "Plan" omit the words "The Governor" and give instead the following phrases. Madison: "The authorities & functions of the Executive to be as follows"; Yates: "His authorities and functions to be as follows"; Lansing: "The Authorities and Functions to be as follows."

8. In Madison, "on."

9. The words "to have" appear in no other account of the "Plan."

10. The phrase "to be the Commander in Chief of the land and naval forces and of the Militia of the United States" appears in no other version of the "Plan."

11. In Lansing and in Yates the word "entire" is inserted at this point.

12. In Madison and in Yates "begun."

13. In Madison, Yates, and Lansing the word "sole" is added at this point.

14. In Madison, Yates, and Lansing, "except."

15. Madison, Yates, and Lansing add the phrase "till a successor be appointed."

16. In Lansing "to" is omitted.

17. Lansing omits "war."

18. Madison omits "of the United States."

19. At this point H wrote and crossed out the words "not less than six nor more than."

20. In Madison, Yates, and Lansing there is a blank space instead of the number twelve.

21. In Lansing, "office."

22. In Lansing, "cases."

23. The part which H enclosed in parentheses does not appear in Madison, Yates, or Lansing.

24. In Lansing, "cases."

25. In Lansing, "legislatures."

26. Except for the variation noted in note 25 this paragraph is given in Madison, Yates, and Lansing as follows: "The Legislature of the United States to have power to institute Courts in each State for the determination of all matters of general concern."

27. At this point H wrote and crossed out the following words: "The Governor to be impeachable by consent of the national legislature or by the legislative bodies of any        states. The Senators and all officers by either branch of the national legislature or by the legislative bodies of any states."

28. The versions of the last sentence of this section which appear in Madison, Yates, and Lansing are as follows. Madison: "All impeachments to be tried by a Court to consist of the Chief     or Judge of the superior Court of Law of each State, provided such Judge shall hold his place during good behavior, and have a permanent salary." Yates: "All impeachments to be tried by a court to consist of the chief, or senior judge of the superior court of law in each

state; provided, that such judge hold his place during good behaviour, and have a permanent salary." Lansing: "All Impeachments to be tried by Court to consist of the chief or senior Judge of the superior Court of Law of each State—provided that such Judge shall hold his Place during good Behaviour and have a permanent Salary."

At this point H wrote and crossed out the following words: "After removal from office either of the foregoing characters may be prosecuted in the ordinary course of law for any crime committed while in office." Above "the foregoing characters" H wrote and crossed out "The Governor."

29. The word "the" is omitted in Lansing.

30. In Yates's version the word "are" appears at this point.


## Constitutional Convention. Remarks on the Abolition of the States [1]

[Philadelphia, June 19, 1787]

Col. HAMILTON coincided with the proposition as it stood in the Report.[2] He had not been understood yesterday.[3] By an abolition of the States, he meant that no boundary could be drawn between the National & State Legislatures; that the former must therefore have indefinite authority. If it were limited at all, the rivalship of the States would gradually subvert it. Even as Corporations the extent of some of them as Va. Massts. &c. would be formidable. As *States*, he thought they ought to be abolished. But he admitted the necessity of leaving in them, subordinate jurisdictions The examples of Persia & the Roman Empire, cited by (Mr. Wilson) [4] were he thought in favor of his doctrine: the great powers delegated to the Satraps & proconsuls, having frequently produced revolts, and schemes of independence.

Hunt and Scott, *Debates*, 129.

1. The version of H's first remarks on June 19 reported by Robert Yates differed in minor particulars from that given by Madison. It reads:

"I agree to the proposition. I did not intend yesterday a total extinguishment of state governments; but my meaning was, that a national government ought to be able to support itself without the aid or interference of the state governments, and that therefore it was necessary to have full sovereignty. Even with corporate rights the states will be dangerous to the national government, and ought to be extinguished, new modified, or reduced to a smaller scale." (Yates, *Secret Proceedings and Debates,* 141.)

2. The Convention, after rejecting the propositions of William Paterson of New Jersey, took up the Virginia Plan, proposed by Edmund Randolph, as amended and agreed to by a committee of the whole. A copy, in an unidentified handwriting, of the Virginia Plan, thus amended, is in the Hamilton Papers, Library of Congress. H is referring to the first proposition of that plan which

read: "Resolved that it is the opinion of this Committee that a national government ought to be established consisting of a Supreme Legislature, Judiciary, and Executive" (Hunt and Scott, *Debates*, 127).

3. Speaking before H, James Wilson had observed "that by a Natl. Govt. he did not mean one that would swallow up the State Govts. as seemed to be wished by some gentlemen" (Hunt and Scott, *Debates*, 129).

4. In arguing for the retention of state governments under the new form of government, Wilson had said that "All large Governments must be subdivided into lesser jurisdictions. As Examples he mentioned Persia, Rome, and particularly the divisions & subdivisions of England by Alfred" (Hunt and Scott, *Debates*, 129).

## Constitutional Convention. Remarks on the Necessity for a National Government [1]

[Philadelphia, June 19, 1787]

Col. HAMILTON, assented to the doctrine of Mr. Wilson.[2] He denied the doctrine that the States were thrown into a State of Nature. He was not yet prepared to admit the doctrine that the Confederacy, could be dissolved by partial infractions of it. He admitted that the States met now on an equal footing but could see no inference from that against concerting a change of the system in this particular. He took this occasion of observing for the purpose of appeasing the fears of the small States, that two circumstances would render them secure under a National Govt. in which they might lose the equality of rank they now held: one was the local situation of the 3 largest States Virga. Masts. & Pa. They were separated from each other by distance of place, and equally so, by all the peculiarities which distinguish the interests of one State from those of another. No combination therefore could be dreaded. In the second place, as there was a gradation in the States from Va. the largest down to Delaware the smallest, it would always happen that ambitious combinations among a few States might & wd. be counteracted by defensive combinations of greater extent among the rest. No combination has been seen among large Counties merely as such, agst. lesser Counties. The more close the Union of the States, and the more compleat the authority of the whole: the less opportunity will be allowed the stronger States to injure the weaker.

Hunt and Scott, *Debates*, 131.

1. The version of H's second remarks on June 19 reported by Robert Yates

and John Lansing, Jr., differed in minor particulars from that given by Madison. Yates's version reads:

"I agree to Mr. Wilson's remark. Establish a weak government and you must at times overleap the bounds. Rome was obliged to create dictators. Cannot you make propositions to the people because we before confederated on other principles? The people can yield to them, if they will. The three great objects of government, *agriculture, commerce and revenue,* can only be secured by a general government." (Yates, *Secret Proceedings and Debates,* 142.)

Lansing's version reads:

"Hamilton—agrees with Wilson—this is calculated to destroy many Heresies in Politics—How is general Government to affect Interests of smaller States? In Agriculture, Commerce and Revenue—large States are remote from each other—Commercial Interests are not the same—on what Principle can they combine to affect agricultural Interest?" (*Notes of John Lansing,* 70.)

2. The Convention debated a resolution of the Virginia Plan which provided "that a Natl. Govt. ought to be established" (See H's first remarks on June 19). To Luther Martin's argument that "the separation from G. B. placed the 13 States in a state of Nature towards each other; that they would have remained in that state till this time, but for the confederation; that they entered into the confederation on the footing of equality." James Wilson replied that, according to the Declaration of Independence, the states "were independent, not individually, but Unitedly" (Hunt and Scott, *Debates,* 130–31).

## Constitutional Convention. Remarks on the Organization of the House of Representatives [1]

[Philadelphia, June 21, 1787]

Col. HAMILTON considered the motion [2] as intended manifestly to transfer the election from the people to the State Legislatures, which would essentially vitiate the plan. It would increase that State influence which could not be too watchfully guarded agst. All too must admit the possibility, in case the Genl. Govt. shd. maintain itself, that the State Govts. might gradually dwindle into nothing. The system therefore shd. not be engrafted on what might possibly fail.

Hunt and Scott, *Debates,* 142–43.

1. The versions of these remarks recorded by Robert Yates and John Lansing, Jr., were as follows. Yates: "It is essential to the democratic rights of the community, that this branch be directly elected by the people. Let us look forward to probable events. There may be a time when state legislatures may cease, and such an event ought not to embarrass the national government" (Yates, *Secret Proceedings and Debates,* 149). Lansing: "If you permit Legislatures to elect you will have *State Interests* represented" (*Notes of John Lansing,* 76).

2. The motion was made by Charles Cotesworth Pinckney and stated "that the 1st. branch [of the legislature] instead of being elected by the people, shd. be elected in such manner as the Legislature of each State should direct" (Hunt and Scott, *Debates,* 142).

## Constitutional Convention. Remarks in Support of a Three-Year Term for Members of the House of Representatives [1]

[Philadelphia, June 21, 1787]

Col. HAMILTON urged the necessity of 3 years.[2] There ought to be neither too much nor too little dependence, on the popular sentiments. The checks in the other branches of Governt. would be but feeble, and would need every auxiliary principle that could be interwoven. The British House of Commons were elected septennially, yet the democratic spirit of ye. Constitution had not ceased. Frequency of elections tended to make the people listless to them; and to facilitate the success of little cabals. This evil was complained of in all the States. In Virga. it had been lately found necessary to force the attendance & voting of the people by severe regulations.

Hunt and Scott, *Debates*, 145–46.

1. These remarks were recorded by Robert Yates, John Lansing, Jr., and Rufus King.

Yates's version reads:

"There is a medium in every thing. I confess three years is not too long. A representative ought to have full freedom of deliberation, and ought to exert an opinion of his own. I am convinced that the public mind will adopt a solid plan. The government of New-York, although higher toned than that of any other state, still we find great listlessness and indifference in the electors; nor do they in general bring forward the first characters to the legislature. The public mind is perhaps not now ready to receive the best plan of government, but certain circumstances are now progressing which will give a different complexion to it." (Yates, *Secret Proceedings and Debates*, 151.)

Lansing's version reads:

"The Opinion of the People is fluctuating—You must exercise your Judgment, convinced that the Pressure of unavoidable Circumstances will direct the public Mind.

"Listlessness prevails in New York on Acc(oun)t of annual Election—Consequence is that Factions are represented in that Government." (*Notes of John Lansing*, 78).

King's version reads:

"I prefer three years to a longer or shorter Term. The Dependence on Constituents is sufficient, & the independence of the members as little as it ought to be." (King, *The Life and Correspondence of Rufus King*, I, 606).

2. The Convention debated a motion that the lower branch of the proposed legislature be elected for three years.

## Constitutional Convention. Remarks on Wages to Be Paid Members of the National Legislature [1]

[Philadelphia, June 22, 1787]

Mr. HAMILTON apprehended inconveniency from *fixing* the wages.[2] He was strenuous agst. making the National Council dependent on the Legislative rewards of the States. Those who pay are the masters of those who are paid. Payment by the States would be unequal as the distant States would have to pay for the same term of attendance and more days in travelling to & from the seat of the Govt. He expatiated emphatically on the difference between the feelings & views of the *people*—& the *Governments* of the States arising from the personal interest & official inducements which must render the latter unfriendly to the Genl. Govt.

Hunt and Scott, *Debates*, 147–48.
1. Robert Yates's version of H's speech reads:
"I do not think the states ought to pay the members, nor am I for a fixed sum. It is a general remark, that he who pays is the master. If each state pays its own members, the burthen would be disproportionate, according to the distance of the states from the seat of government. If a national government can exist, members will make it a desirable object to attend, without accepting any stipend —and it ought to be so organized as to be efficient." (Yates, *Secret Proceedings and Debates*, 152.)
2. The Constitutional Convention debated the section of the third resolution of the Virginia Plan which provided that members of the national legislature should "receive fixed stipends to be paid out of the Nationl. Treasury" (Hunt and Scott, *Debates*, 146). Oliver Ellsworth of Connecticut objected to the resolution and argued that the state legislatures should pay the salaries of congressmen. In the debate which ensued, Nathaniel Gorham and Roger Sherman supported Ellsworth's motion, while Edmund Randolph, James Wilson, and James Madison opposed it. H's remarks followed those of Madison.

## Constitutional Convention. Remarks in Opposition to the Payment of Members of the National Legislature by the States [1]

[Philadelphia, June 22, 1787]

Mr. HAMILTON renewed his opposition to it.[2] He pressed the distinction between State Govts. & the people. The former wd. be the rivals of the Genl. Govt. The State legislatures ought not therefore to be the paymasters of the latter.

Hunt and Scott, *Debates,* 148.

1. Robert Yates's version of H's second speech of June 22 reads:

"It has been often asserted, that the interests of the general and of the state legislatures are precisely the same. This cannot be true. The views of the governed are often materially different from those who govern. The science of policy is the knowledge of human nature. A state government will ever be the rival power of the general government. It is therefore highly improper that the state legislatures should be the paymasters of the members of the national government. All political bodies love power, and it will often be improperly attained." (Yates, *Secret Proceedings and Debates,* 153.)

2. Following H's first remarks on this date ("Constitutional Convention. Remarks on Wages to be Paid Members of the National Legislature," June 22, 1787), James Wilson made a motion that the salaries of the members of the first branch of the proposed national legislature *"be ascertained by the National Legislature."* After the Convention defeated Wilson's motion, a motion made earlier by Oliver Ellsworth providing that the members of the lower house of the legislature be paid by the states was discussed. It was to this motion by Ellsworth that H "renewed his opposition" (Hunt and Scott, *Debates,* 148).

## Constitutional Convention. Remarks on the Ineligibility of Members of the House of Representatives for Other Offices [1]

[Philadelphia, June 22, 1787]

Mr. Hamilton. In all general questions which become the subjects of discussion, there are always some truths mixed with falsehoods. I confess there is danger where men are capable of holding two offices.[2] Take mankind in general, they are vicious—their passions may be operated upon. We have been taught to reprobate the danger of influence in the British government, without duly reflecting how far it was necessary to support a good government. We have taken up many ideas upon trust, and at last, pleased with our own opinions, establish them as undoubted truths. Hume's opinion of the British constitution confirms the remark, that there is always a body of firm patriots, who often shake a corrupt administration. Take mankind as they are, and what are they governed by? Their passions. There may be in every government a few choice spirits, who may act from more worthy motives. One great error is that we suppose mankind more honest than they are. Our prevailing passions are ambition and interest; and it will ever be the duty of a wise government to avail itself of those passions, in order to make them subservient to the public good—for these ever induce us to action. Perhaps a few men in a state, may, from patriotic motives, or to display their talents, or to reap the advantage of public applause, step forward; but if we adopt the clause we destroy the motive. I am therefore against all exclusions and refinements, except only in this case; that when a member takes his seat, he should vacate every other office. It is difficult to put any exclusive regulation into effect. We must in some degree, submit to the inconvenience.

Yates, *Secret Proceedings and Debates*, 156–57.
    1. Robert Yates's version of H's third speech on June 22 has been printed, for it is more detailed than that given by Madison.
    Madison's account of H's remarks reads:
    "There are inconveniences on both sides. We must take man as we find him, and if we expect him to serve the public must interest his passions in doing so. A reliance on pure patriotism had been the source of many of our errors. He thought the remark of Mr. Ghorum a just one. It was impossible to say what wd. be effect in G.B. of such a reform as had been urged. It was known that one of the ablest politicians (Mr. Hume) had pronounced all that influence on the side of the crown, which went under the name of corruption, an essential part of the weight which maintained the equilibrium of the Constitution." (Hunt and Scott, *Debates*, 150.)
    2. Among the motions relating to the organization of the lower branch of the legislature debated by the Convention on June 22 was a motion by Nathaniel Gorham, delegate from Massachusetts, proposing a change in the section of the Virginia Plan which provided that members of the first branch of the legislature be ineligible for other offices, not only during their term in the legislature but for one year after. Among the members of the Convention who spoke on Gorham's motion was George Mason of Virginia who declared that he "was for shutting the door at all events agst. corruption. He enlarged on the venality and abuses in this particular in G. Britain: and alluded to the multiplicity of foreign Embassies by Congs. The disqualification he regarded as a corner stone in the fabric" (Hunt and Scott, *Debates*, 150). H's remarks followed those by Mason.

## Constitutional Convention. Remarks on the Ineligibility of Members of the House of Representatives for Other Offices [1]

[Philadelphia, June 23, 1787]

Mr. HAMILTON.[2] Evasions cd. not be prevented—as by proxies —by friends holding for a year, & them opening the way &c.

Hunt and Scott, *Debates*, 155.
    1. Robert Yates's version of H's speech reads: "The clause may be evaded many ways. Offices may be held by proxy—they may be procured by friends, &c" (Yates, *Secret Proceedings and Debates*, 161).

2. Near the close of debate on June 22, the Convention again took up a proposal that members of the lower branch of the legislature be declared ineligible for office for a year after the expiration of the term for which they had been elected, a proposal on which H had spoken on June 22. See "Constitutional Convention. Remarks on the Ineligibility of Members of the First Branch of the Legislature for Other Offices," of that date.

Before H spoke, George Mason argued that he thought the proposal "essential to guard agst. evasions by resignations, and stipulations for office to be fulfilled at the expiration of the legislative term" (Hunt and Scott, *Debates*, 155).

## Constitutional Convention. Remarks on the Term of Office for Members of the Second Branch of the Legislature [1]

[Philadelphia, June 26, 1787]

Mr. HAMILTON. He did not mean to enter particularly into the subject.[2] He concurred with Mr. Madison[3] in thinking we were now to decide for ever the fate of Republican Government; and that if we did not give to that form due stability and wisdom, it would be disgraced & lost among ourselves, disgracèd & lost to mankind for ever. He acknowledged himself not to think favorably of Republican Government; but addressed his remarks to those who did think favorably of it, in order to prevail on them to tone their Government as high as possible. He professed himself to be as zealous an advocate for liberty as any man whatever, and trusted he should be as willing a martyr to it though he differed as to the form in which it was most eligible. He concurred also in the general observations of (Mr. Madison) on the subject, which might be supported by others if it were necessary. It was certainly true: that nothing like an equality of property existed: that an inequality would exist as long as liberty existed, and that it would unavoidably result from that very liberty itself. This inequality of property constituted the great & fundamental distinction in Society. When the Tribunitial power had levelled the boundary between the *patricians* & *plebians*, what followed? The distinction between rich & poor was substituted. He meant not however to enlarge on the subject. He rose principally to remark that (Mr. Sherman) seemed not to recollect that one branch of the proposed Govt. was so formed, as to render it particularly the guardians of the poorer orders of Citizens;[4] nor to have adverted to the true causes of the stability which had been exemplified in Cont.[5] Under the British system as well as the federal, many of the great powers appertaining to Govt. particularly all those relating to foreign Nations were not in the hands of the Govt. there. Their internal affairs also were extremely simple, owing to sundry causes many of which were peculiar to that Country. Of late the Governt. had entirely given way to the people, and had in fact suspended many of its ordinary functions in order to prevent those turbulent scenes which had appeared elsewhere. He asks Mr. S. whether the State at this time, dare impose & collect a tax on ye. people? To these causes & not to the frequency of elections, the effect, as far as it existed ought to be chiefly ascribed.

Hunt and Scott, *Debates*, 169.

1. Versions of this speech were reported by Robert Yates and John Lansing, Jr.

Yates's version reads:

"This question has already been considered in several points of view. We are now forming a republican government. Real liberty is neither found in despotism or the extremes of democracy, but in moderate governments.

"Those who mean to form a solid republican government, ought to proceed to the confines of another government. As long as offices are open to all men, and no constitutional rank is established, it is pure republicanism. But if we incline too much to democracy, we shall soon shoot into a monarchy. The difference of property is already great amongst us. Commerce and industry will still increase the disparity. Your government must meet this state of things, or combinations will in process of time, undermine your system. What was the tribunitial power of Rome? It was instituted by the plebeans as a guard against the patricians. But was this a sufficient check? No—The only distinction which remained at Rome was, at last, between the rich and poor. The gentleman from Connecticut forgets that the democratic body is already secure in a representation. As to Connecticut, what were the little objects of their government before the revolution? Colonial concerns merely. They ought now to act on a more extended scale, and dare they do this? Dare they collect the taxes and requisitions of congress? Such a government may do well, if they do not tax, and this is precisely their situation." (Yates, *Secret Proceedings and Debates*, 170–71.)

Lansing's version reads:

"Hamilton—We are now considering the Cause of Democracy—he is attached to a free Government and would chearfully *become a Martyr to it*—The occasional Violence of Democracy and the uniform Tyranny of a Despot are productive of the same Consequences.—to prevent them he is for tuning the Government high—In the ordinary Progress of Things we must look to a Period as not very remote when Distinctions arising from Property will be greater— You must devise a Repository of the Rights of the wealthy—At Rome after the Institution of the tribunitian Power greater Distinctions arose from the unequal Distribution of Riches and *Rich* and *Poor* were more oppressive Distinctions than *patrician* and *plebian*. Under the Colonial Government of Connecticut its Objects were contracted—but we have taken a new Station—Its Powers ought to be enlarged in Proportion to the Magnitude of the Objects it is intended to embrace. He will therefore go beyond any of the Ideas advocated by either Party. Is for nine Years." (*Notes of John Lansing*, 84-85.)

2. The Convention debated the term of office to be prescribed for members of the second branch of the proposed legislature.

3. Madison's remarks occurred earlier in the debate on June 26.

4. Roger Sherman, whose remarks preceded those made by H, argued that as government was instituted for the governed "it ought . . . to be so constituted as not to be dangerous to their liberties. The more permanency it has the worse if it be a bad Govt. Frequent elections are necessary to preserve the good behavior of rulers" (Hunt and Scott, *Debates*, 168).

5. Sherman had said that in Connecticut frequency of elections had promoted stability in government (Hunt and Scott, *Debates*, 169).

## Constitutional Convention. Remarks on Equality of Representation of the States in the Congress [1]

[Philadelphia, June 29, 1787]

Mr. HAMILTON [2] observed the individuals forming political Societies modify their rights differently, with regard to suffrage. Examples of it are found in all the States. In all of them some individuals are deprived of the right altogether, not having the requisite qualifications of property. In some of the States the right of suffrage is allowed in some cases and refused in others. To vote for a member in one branch, a certain quantum of property, to vote for a member in another branch of the Legislature, a higher quantum of property is required. In like manner States may modify their right of suffrage differently, the larger exercising a larger, the smaller a smaller share of it. But as States are a collection of individual men which ought we to respect most, the rights of the people composing them, or of the artificial beings resulting from the composition. Nothing could be more preposterous or absurd than to sacrifice the former to the latter. It has been sd. that if the smaller States renounce their *equality*, they renounce at the same time their *liberty*. The truth is it is a contest for power, not for liberty. Will the men composing the small States be less free than those composing the larger. The State of Delaware having 40,000 souls will *lose power*, if she has ⅒ only of the votes allowed to Pa. having 400,000: but will the people of Del: *be less free*, if each citizen has an equal vote with each citizen of Pa. He admitted that common residence within the same

State would produce a certain degree of attachment; and that this principle might have a certain influence in public affairs. He thought however that this might by some precautions be in a great measure excluded: and that no material inconvenience could result from it, as there could not be any ground for combination among the States whose influence was most dreaded. The only considerable distinction of interests, lay between the carrying & non-carrying States, which divide instead of uniting the largest States. No considerable inconvenience had been found from the division of the State of N. York into different districts of different sizes.

Some of the consequences of a dissolution of the Union, and the establishment of partial confederacies, had been pointed out. He would add another of a most serious nature. Alliances will immediately be formed with different rival & hostile nations of Europes, who will foment disturbances among ourselves, and make us parties to all their own quarrels. Foreign Nations having American dominions are & must be jealous of us. Their representatives betray the utmost anxiety for our fate, & for the result of this meeting, which must have an essential influence on it. It had been said that respectability in the eyes of foreign Nations was not the object at which we aimed; that the proper object of republican Government was domestic tranquility & happiness. This was an ideal distinction. No Governmt. could give us tranquility & happiness at home, which did not possess sufficient stability and strength to make us respectable abroad. This was the critical moment for forming such a Government. We should run every risk in trusting to future amendments. As yet we retain the habits of union. We are weak & sensible of our weakness. Henceforward the motives will become feebler, and the difficulties greater. It is a miracle that we were now here exercising our tranquil & free deliberations on the subject. It would be madness to trust to future miracles. A thousand causes must obstruct a reproduction of them.[3]

Hunt and Scott, *Debates*, 186–87.
   1. The remarks attributed to H by Robert Yates are as follows:
"The course of my experience in human affairs might perhaps restrain me from saying much on this subject. I shall, however, give birth to some of the observations I have made during the course of this debate. The gentleman from Maryland [Luther Martin] has been at great pains to establish positions which are not denied. Many of them, as drawn from the best writers on government,

are become almost self-evident principles. But I doubt the propriety of his application of those principles in the present discussion. He deduces from them the necessity that states entering into a confederacy must retain the equality of votes—this position cannot be correct—Facts plainly contradict it. The parliament of Great Britain asserted a supremacy over the whole empire, and the celebrated Judge Blackstone labors for the legality of it, although many parts were not represented. This parliamentary power we opposed as contrary to our colonial rights. With that exception, throughout that whole empire, it is submitted to. May not the smaller and greater states so modify their respective rights as to establish the general interest of the whole, without adhering to the right of equality? Strict representation is not observed in any of the state governments. The senate of New-York are chosen by persons of certain qualifications, to the exclusion of others. The question, after all is, is it our interest in modifying this general government to sacrifice individual rights to the preservation of the rights of an *artificial* being, called states? There can be no truer principle than this—that every individual of the community at large has an equal right to the protection of government. If therefore three states contain a majority of the inhabitants of America, ought they to be governed by a minority? Would the inhabitants of the great states ever submit to this? If the smaller states maintain this principle, through a love of power, will not the larger, from the same motives, be equally tenacious to preserve their power? They are to surrender their rights—for what? for the preservation of an artificial being. We propose a free government—Can it be so if partial distinctions are maintained? I agree with the gentleman from Delaware [George Read], that if the state governments are to act in the general government, it affords the strongest reason for exclusion. In the state of New-York, five counties form a majority of representatives, and yet the government is in no danger, because the laws have a general operation. The small states exaggerate their danger, and on this ground contend for an undue proportion of power. But their danger is increased, if the larger states will not submit to it. Where will they form new alliances for their support? Will they do this with foreign powers? Foreigners are jealous of our encreasing greatness, and would rejoice in our distractions. Those who have had opportunities of conversing with foreigners respecting sovereigns in Europe, have discovered in them an anxiety for the preservation of our democratic governments, probably for no other reason, but to keep us weak. Unless your government is respectable, foreigners will invade your rights; and to maintain tranquillity, it must be respectable—even to observe neutrality, you must have a strong government. I confess our present situation is critical. We have just finished a war which has established our independency, and loaded us with a heavy debt. We have still every motive to unite for our common defence. Our people are disposed to have a good government, but this disposition may not always prevail. It is difficult to amend confederations—it has been attempted in vain, and it is perhaps a miracle that we are now met. We must therefore improve the opportunity, and render the present system as perfect as possible. Their good sense, and above all, the necessity of their affairs, will induce the people to adopt it." (Yates, *Secret Proceedings and Debates*, 185–87.)

John Lansing, Jr., made the following record of H's remarks:

"Hamilton— In the Course of his Experience he has found it difficult to convince Persons who have been in certain Habits of thinking. Some desultory Remarks may not be improper. We can modify Representation as we think proper.

"The Question simply is, what is general Interest. Larger States may submit to an Inequality of Representation to their Prejudice for a short Time—but it cannot be durable. This is a Contest for Power—the People of all States have an Inequality of Representation.

"So long as State Governments prevail State Influence will be perpetuated.

"There may be a Distinction of Interests but it arises merely from the carrying and noncarrying States.

"Those Persons who have had frequent Opportunities of conversing with the Representatives of European Sovereignties know they are very anxious to perpetuate our Democracies. This is easily accounted for—Our weakness will make us more manageable. Unless your Government is respectable abroad your Tranquility cannot be preserved.

"This is a critical Moment of American Liberty—We are still too weak to exist without Union. It is a Miracle that we have met—they seldom occur.

"We must devise a System on the Spot— It ought to be strong and nervous, *hoping* that the good Sense and principally *the Necessity of our Affairs* will reconcile the People to it." (*Notes of John Lansing*, 92–94.)

Rufus King's version of H's remarks reads:

"Men are naturally equal, and societies or States, when fully independent, are also equal. It is as reasonable, and may be as expedient, that States should form Leagues or compacts, and lessen or part with their national Equality, as that men should form the social compact and, in doing so, lessen or surrender the natural Equality of men. This is done in every society; and the grant to the society affects Persons and Property; age, minority & Estates are all affected.

"A Man may not become an Elector or Elected, unless of a given age & having a certain Estate. Let the People be represented according to numbers, the People will be free: every Office will be equally open to all and the majority of the People are to make the Laws. Yet it is said that the States will be destroyed & the People will be Slaves—this is not so. The People are free, at the expense of an artificial & ideal Equality of the States." (King, *The Life and Correspondence of Rufus King,* I, 610–11.)

2. On June 27, the Convention took up the resolutions of the Virginia Plan dealing with representation in the two houses of the legislature. The plan proposed that representation in both houses be in proportion to population. The debate was continued on June 28 and 29.

3. H left the Constitutional Convention on June 29. Although he did not again take part in the debates until August 13, he probably returned soon after August 6. In his first speech of June 23, 1788, to the New York Ratifying Convention he stated: "Some private business calling me to New-York, I left the Convention for a few days: On my return, I found a plan, reported by the committee of details; and soon after, a motion was made to increase the number of representatives." On August 6 the Committee of Detail reported a plan of a constitution. It was not until September 8, however, that a motion was made to increase the number of representatives. It was probably this plan and motion to which H referred in his speech of June 23, 1788, before the New York Ratifying Convention.

## To George Washington

[New York, July 3, 1787]

Dr. Sir.

In my passage through the Jerseys and since my arrival here I have taken particular pains to discover the public sentiment and I am more and more convinced that this is the critical opportunity for establishing the prosperity of this country on a solid foundation. I have conversed with men of information not only of this City but from different parts of the state; and they agree that there has been an astonishing revolution for the better in the minds of the people. The prevailing apprehension among thinking men is that the Convention, from a fear of shocking the popular opinion, will not go far enough. They seem to be convinced that a strong well mounted government will better suit the popular palate than one of a different complexion. Men in office are indeed taking all possible pains to give an unfavourable impression of the Convention; but the current seems to be running strongly the other way.

A plain but sensible man, in a conversation I had with him yesterday, expressed himself nearly in this manner. The people begin to be convinced that their "excellent form of government" as they have been used to call it, will not answer their purpose; and that they must substitute something not very remote from that which they have lately quitted.

These appearances though they will not warrant a conclusion that the people are yet ripe for such a plan as I advocate, yet serve to prove that there is no reason to despair of their adopting one equally energetic, if the Convention should think proper to propose it. They serve to prove that we ought not to allow too much weight to objections drawn from the supposed repugnancy of the people to an efficient constitution. I confess I am more and more inclined to believe that former habits of thinking are regaining their influence with more rapidity than is generally imagined.

Not having compared ideas with you, Sir, I cannot judge how far our sentiments agree; but as I persuade myself the genuineness of my representations will receive credit with you, my anxiety for the event of the deliberations of the Convention induces me to make this communication of what appears to be the tendency of the public mind. I own to you Sir that I am seriously and deeply distressed at the aspect of the Councils which prevailed when I left Philadelphia. I fear that we shall let slip the golden opportunity of rescuing the American empire from disunion anarchy and misery. No motley or feeble measure can answer the end or will finally receive the public support. Decision is true wisdom and will be not less reputable to the Convention than salutary to the community.

I shall of necessity remain here ten or twelve days; if I have reason to believe that my attendance at Philadelphia will not be mere waste of time, I shall after that period rejoin the Convention.[1]

I remain with sincere esteem Dr Sir   Yr. Obed serv   A Hamilton

July 3d. 87
General Washington

ALS, George Washington Papers, Library of Congress.
1. For the date of H's return to the Convention, see "Constitutional Convention. Remarks on Equality of Representation of the States in the Congress," June 29, 1787, note 3.

## From George Washington

Philadelphia 10th. July 87.

Dear Sir,

I thank you for your communication of the 3d. When I refer you to the State of the Councils which prevailed at the period you left this City—and add, that they are now, if possible, in a worse train than ever; you willfind that little ground on which the hope of a good establishment can be formed. In a word, I *almost* dispair of seeing a favourable issue to the proceedings of the Convention, and do therefore repent having had any agency in the business.

The Men who oppose a strong & energetic government are, in my opinion, narrow minded politicians, or are under the influence of local views. The apprehension expressed by them that the *people* will not accede to the form proposed is the *ostensible*, not the *real* cause of the opposition—but admitting that the present sentiment is as they prognosticate, the question ought nevertheless to be, is it or is it not, the best form? If the former, recommend it, and it will assuredly obtain mauger opposition.

I am sorry you went away. I wish you were back. The crisis is equally important and alarming, and no opposition under such circumstances should discourage exertions till the signature is fixed. I will not, at this time trouble you with more than my best wishes and sincere regards.

I am Dear Sir   Yr Obedt Servt                     Go: Washington

Alexr. Hamilton Esqr

ALS, Hamilton Papers, Library of Congress; LC, George Washington Papers, Library of Congress.

## To Nathaniel Mitchell [1]

[New York, July 20, 1787]

Dear Sir

Agreeably to what passed between us I have had an interview with Mr. Auldjo,[2] and I flatter myself, if there is (as I doubt not there will be) as much moderation on the part of Major Peirce [3] as there appears to be on that of Mr. Auldjo, that the affair between them [4] may yet be amicably terminated.

But Mr. Auldjo observes, I confess in my opinion with propriety, that he ought to know with some precision the matters which have given offence to Major Pearce before he can enter into explanations, which he declares himself to be ready to do with coolness and candour, the moment he shall be enabled to do it by a specification of the subjects of complaint.

If a personal interview is for any reason disagreeable to Major Pearce I entreat you, my dear Sir to obtain from him and to communicate to me by letter the substance of what has occasioned his dissatisfaction, with so much particularity only, as will put it in the power of Mr. Auldjo to give an explicit answer. Major Pearce will, I hope, have no scruples about this, for as the door of explanation has been opened by Mr. Auldjo, there is no punctilio which stands in his way; and I trust he will feel the force of a sentiment, which prudence and humanity equally dictate, that extremities ought then only to ensue, when, after a fair experiment, accommodation has been found impracticable. An attention to this principle interests the characters of both the Gentlemen concerned and with them our own; and, from every other consideration, as well as that of personal friend ship to the parties, I sincerely wish to give it its full operation. I am convinced you are not less anxious to effect this than myself and I trust our joint endeavours will not prove unsuccessful.

I cannot hewever conclude without making one remark. Though Mr. Auldjo has expressed and still entertains a desire of explanation it would ill become him to solicit it. Whatever therefore in my expressions may seem to urge such an explanation with the earnestness

of entreaty must be ascribed to my own feelings and to that inclination which every man of sensibility must feel—not to see extremities take place if it be in his power to prevent them or until they
become an absolutely necessary sacrifice to the prejudices of public
opinion.

I remain with sincere regard   Dr Sir   Your Obed ser

Alex Hamilton

New York July 20. 1787
The Honble Mr. Mitchell

ALS, Mr. Hall Park McCullough, North Bennington, Vermont; ADfS, Hamilton Papers, Library of Congress. The draft, which is unaddressed, is printed
without an addressee in *JCHW*, I, 437-39, and *HCLW*, IX, 419-20.

1. Nathaniel Mitchell of Delaware was a member of the Continental Congress
from 1786 to 1788.

2. John Auldjo, a partner in an English mercantile house, was at this time
handling his firm's affairs in the United States.

3. Major William Pierce served during the Revolution as aide-de-camp to
Major General Nathanael Greene. After his retirement from the Army in 1783,
he was the head of a mercantile house in Savannah, Georgia. In 1786, Pierce was
elected a member of the Continental Congress and, in 1787, appointed a member
of the Georgia delegation to the Constitutional Convention.

4. Having challenged Auldjo to a duel, Pierce requested Mitchell to be his
second. Auldjo asked H to be his second. The circumstances of the controversy
are described in the following letter from Pierce to Mitchell:

"New York July 19th 1787.

"My dear Sir

"Having received an insult from Mr. Jno. Auldjo, I have to request that you
will be my Friend, and bear to him the enclosed challenge.

"Mr. Auldjo, is a partner of the House of Strachan McKenzie & Co of London, with whom I have had considerable mercantile dealings. Some difficulties
having arisen, in which I was involved with an old concern, I, in order to remove any uneasiness on the part of Mr. Auldjo made an assignment of a parcel
of Accounts & Bonds to him. The Books in which the Accounts lay not being
fully adjusted, and stated, he made a loud complaint of the irregularity of
things, and called forth the attention of every Person in Savannah to my private
affairs, as if they, or any other set of People had any business with them. In consequence of this report, my Enemies triumphed, and my Friends grew cool.

"On Mr. Auldjo's arrival in Philadelphia, he waited on me, and behaved in a
manner that would have called forth my resentment then, but some public as
well as private circumstances restrained me. In a conversation which passed
between us he was not only indelicate in his langage as it applied to me, but
insulting in his reflections on my State and the People in it. I preserved my
temper, and heard him with marks of civility and decency. I had been accustomed to respect the Man and could have wished always to have been on the
best terms with him, but on this occasion he forfeited every thing.

"Notwithstanding all this, I agreed to make any farther collateral security
in my power for the balance of the debt due by Wm. Pierce & Co. to his House
in London, and did actually made over to him a great deal of real, and some
personal property. European debts I hold sacred, and as far as I am able I will

prove that I think so. You sir can witness for me, that in my public capacity, I have always indulged this idea, that all foreign transactions ought to be supported even at the expence of every other consideration.

"Besides the injuries I have already mentioned, I have a great many more which I will give you in detail, and which warrant my highest resentment against Mr. Auldjo.

"Having taken up this matter, under full conviction that I am right, I am determined amidst every difficulty, to have compleat redress. In support of my feelings and honor on the present occasion, I hold no sacrifice too great.

"I am my dear sir   Your affectionate Friend   Wm. Pierce

"I remitted the House of Strachan McKenzie & Co. a considerable quantity of Rice & Indigo in two or three shipments. I sent them a remittance in Indigo by the way of Amsterdam. I sent a large ship laden with live Oak for Amsterdam, and had her ensured in London for £2000 sterling. She was lost and the insurance ought to have been paid. Mr. Auldjo will acknowledge, and did acknowledge that few of his Debtors had made such payments as I had done.

"The honble Mr. Mitchell" (ALS, Mr. Hall Park McCullough, North Bennington, Vermont.)

## To William Pierce [1]

[New York, July 20–26, 1787] [2]

Dr. Sir

As the inclosed contains details relating to your private affairs it is judged most delicate to put it under cover to you. Permit me to use the privilege of a friend to say that ⟨whatever⟩ appeared to you offensive in the conduct of Mr. Auldjo seems to have been a verry natural result of disappointments on his side, to which your disappointments gave birth, influenced too, perhaps, in some degree by incidents which may have been misrepresented or misunderstood. His explanations speak a language, which I sincerely think may put an end to your controversy. I as sincerely hope this may be the case. I speak with the more freedom, because in a difference between men I esteem, a difference evidently foreign from any real enmity between them, I can never consent to take up the character of a second in a duel 'till I have in vain tried that of a mediator. Be content with *enough* for *more* ought not to be expected.

I remain with sincere attachment   Your friend & servant

Alex Hamilton

ADfS, Hamilton Papers, Library of Congress.
    1. For background to this letter, see H to Nathaniel Mitchell, July 20, 1787.
    2. In *HCLW*, IX, 420–21, this letter is dated "1787." It must have been written between July 20, the date on which H wrote to Mitchell, and July 26, the date of H's letter to John Auldjo.

## To The Daily Advertiser [1]

[New York, July 21, 1787]

It is currently reported and believed, that his Excellency Governor CLINTON has, in public company, without reserve, reprobated the appointment of the Convention, and predicted a mischievous issue of that measure. His observations are said to be to this effect:— That the present confederation is, in itself, equal to the purposes of the union: That the appointment of a Convention is calculated to impress the people with an idea of evils which do not exist: That if either nothing should be proposed by the Convention, or if what they should propose should not be agreed to, the one or the other would tend to beget despair in the public mind; and that, in all probability, the result of their deliberations, whatever it might be, would only serve to throw the community into confusion.

Upon this conduct of his Excellency, if he is not misrepresented, the following reflections will naturally occur to every considerate and impartial man:

*First.* That from the almost universal concurrence of the states in the measure of appointing a Convention, and from the powers given to their Deputies, "to devise and propose such alterations in the Federal Constitution as are necessary to *render it adequate* to the purposes of government, and to the exigencies of the union," it appears clearly to be the general sense of America, that the present confederation *is not* "equal to the purposes of the union," but requires material alterations.

*Secondly.* That the concurrence of the legislatures of twelve out of the thirteen states, which compose the union (actuated as they are by a diversity of prejudices and supposed interests) in a measure of so extraordinary a complexion, the direct object of which is the abridgement of their own power, in favor of a general government,

*The* [New York] *Daily Advertiser*, July 21, 1787.

1. H's authorship of this unsigned attack on George Clinton is beyond question. On September 15, 1787, H wrote in reply to a defense of Clinton which had been published in *The New-York Journal, and Weekly Register* of September 6: "Mr. Hamilton . . . has been attacked by name, as the Writer of a publication printed in Mr. Childs's paper of the 21st of July last. In fixing that publication upon him, there is certainly no mistake" (see H to The Daily Advertiser, September 15, 1787).

is of itself a strong presumptive proof that there exist real evils; and that these evils are of so extensive and cogent a nature, as to have been capable of giving an impulse from one extremity of the United States to the other.

*Thirdly.* That some of these evils are so obvious, that they do not seem to admit of doubt or equivocation; of this description are,

1. The *defective* and *disproportionate* contributions of the several states to the common treasury, and, in consequence of this, the total want of means in the United States to pay their debts, foreign or domestic, or to support those establishments which are necessary to the public tranquillity.

2. The general stagnation of commerce, occasioned no doubt, in a great degree, by the exclusions, and restraints with which foreign nations fetter our trade with them; while they enjoy in our ports unlimited freedom, and while our government is incapable of making those defensive regulations, which would be likely to produce a greater reciprocity of privileges.

3d. The degradation of our national character and consequence, to such an extreme of insignificance, that foreign powers in plain terms, refuse to treat with us, alledging, and alledging truly, that we have no government to ensure the performance of the stipulations on our part.

*Fourthly.* That these and many other facts and circumstances, prove to a demonstration, that the general government is fundamentally defective; that the very existence of the union is in imminent danger, and that there is great reason to dread, that without some speedy and radical alterations, these states may shortly become thirteen distinct and unconnected communities, exposed, without a common head, to all the hazard of foreign invasion, and intrigue, of hostility with each other, and of internal faction and insurrection.

*Fifthly.* That at this very instant the union is so far nominal, that it is not only destitute of the necessary powers to administer the common concerns of the nation, but is scarcely able to keep up the appearances of existence; sunk to so low an ebb that it can with difficulty engage the attendance of a sufficient number of members in Congress, even to *deliberate* upon any matter of importance.

*Sixthly.* That this state of our affairs called for the collective wisdom of the union to provide an effectual remedy; that there were only two ways of uniting its councils to that end, one through the medium of Congress, and the other through the medium of a body specially appointed for the purpose; that several reasons conspired to render the latter mode preferable. Congress, occupied in the ordinary administration of the government could not give so steady and undivided an attention to the national reform as the crisis demanded: The parties, which will always grow up in an established body, would render them less likely to agree in a proper plan. Any plan they should agree upon, would have greater prejudices to encounter in its progress through the states; for the mind is naturally prone to suspect the aims of men who propose the encrease of a power, of which they themselves have the present possession; and, in several of the states, industrious and wicked pains have been taken by the parties unfriendly to the measures of the union, to discredit and debase the authority and influence of Congress. In addition to these considerations, the states would have it in their power, in a special Convention, to avail themselves of the weight and abilities of men, who could not have been induced to accept an appointment to Congress; and whose aid, in a work of such magnitude, was on many accounts desirable. The late illustrious Commander in Chief stands foremost in this number.

*Seventhly.* That though it is too justly to be apprehended that local views, state prejudices, and personal interests, will frustrate the hope of any effectual plan from any body of men whatever, appointed by so many separate states, yet the object was worthy of an experiment, and that experiment could not be made with so much advantage in any way, as in that which has been fallen upon for the purpose.

*Eighthly.* That however justifiable it might be in the governor to oppose the appointment of a convention, if the measure were still under deliberation; and if he sincerely believed it to be a pernicious one, yet the general voice of America having decided in its favor, it is *unwarrantable* and *culpable in any man*, in so serious a posture of our national affairs, to endeavour to prepossess the public mind against the hitherto undetermined and unknown measures of a body to whose councils America has, in a great measure, entrusted its future fate, and to whom the people in general look up, under the blessing of heaven, for their political salvation.

*Ninthly.* That such conduct in a man high in office, argues greater attachment to his *own power* than to the *public good,* and furnishes strong reason to suspect a dangerous predetermination to oppose whatever may tend to diminish the *former,* however it may promote the *latter.*

If there be any man among us, who acts so unworthy a part, it becomes a free and enlightened people to observe him with a jealous eye, and when he sounds the alarm of danger from another quarter, to examine whether they have not more to apprehend from *himself.*

## To Thomas Mullett [1]

[*New York*] *July 23, 1787.* "The want of Some original papers which Mr. Brailsford [2] was to have Sent me, puts it out of my power to proceed to a trial of his Cause with Wooldridge. . . . Mr. Wooldridge [3] is willing, if I will let him out on Common bail, to give me a Bond in any Sum . . . that he will not go out of this State . . . and that *he* will not give any impedment or delay to the attachments now pending. I have no doubt that it is Mr. Brailsford's interest to accept of this Arrangement; but . . . I have thought proper to Communicate the Matter to you to take your instructions as Attorney in fact to him."

LS, Hamilton Papers, Library of Congress.
    1. Mullett is listed in *The New York Directory for 1789* as a merchant at 32 Broadway.
    2. Samuel Brailsford.
    3. Thomas Wooldridge.

## From Thomas Mullett

*New York, July 23, 1787.* Advises Hamilton to accept the settlement which has been arranged in a cause pending between Samuel Brailsford and Thomas Wooldridge.

ALS, Hamilton Papers, Library of Congress.

## *To John Auldjo* [1]

[New York, July 26, 1787]

Sir,

I have delivered the paper you committed to me as it stood altered to Major Peirce from whose conduct I am to conclude the affair between you is at an end.[2] He informs me that he is shortly to set out on a jaunt up the North River.

As you intimate a wish to have my sentiments in writing on the transaction I shall with pleasure declare that the steps you have taken in consequence of Mr. Pearces challenge have been altogether in conformity to my opinion of what would be prudent proper and honorable on your part. They seem to have satisfied Mr. Pearces scruples arising from what he apprehended, in some particulars, to have been your conduct to him and I presume we are to hear nothing farther of the matter.

I remain with great esteem   Sir Your obedient & humble servant

Alex Hamilton

New York   July 26 1787

ALS, Hamilton Papers, Library of Congress.

1. For background to this letter, see H to Nathaniel Mitchell, July 20, 1787, and H to William Pierce, July 20–26, 1787.

2. The denouement of the controversy between Pierce and Auldjo was described in the following statement by Mitchell, Pierce's second:

"I do certify the following to be a true statement of what passed between Majr. Pierce & Mr. Aldjo from ye. 19th. to the 25th. July 1787—

"In the Morning of the 19th. of July 1787—I received a letter from the Honble William Pierce Esqr by which my attention was called to an affair between him and a Mr Aldjo. I was solicited as a friend to be the bearer of a challenge which the letter contained, the cause for which was stated in general Terms. I immediately waited on Majr. Pierce and after having a conference with him and being satisfied as to the propriety of the measure I waited on Mr Aldjo, who read the challenge but said he could not subscribe to the terms proposed by Majr. Pierce. He said he had business that then demanded his attention, and which in justice to his convictions must adjust before he could return a reply to Majr. Pierce—but that he should hear from him in due season; on the same day Majr. Pierce received a letter from Mr. Aldjo who said he was not a little surprized at the letter which I delivered him—that his then situation rendered a hasty acceptance of his challenge improper—& a consciousness of his own fallability disposed him to leave the door open to such explanation as was calculated to discover and accommodate any just cause of offence, and that he had prevailed on Colo. Hamilton to wait on him, but if he had determined otherwise, then Colo. Hamilton would settle what might be necessary for his Honor. Major Pierce assigned the letter & business to me. I met with Colo. Hamilton at the City Hall about three OClock and talked the business over. He mentioned to me the propriety of our interposing first as Mediators and endeavouring to effect a reconciliation in which I most heartily concurred, and the mode proposed was a meeting of the parties, which I suggested to Major Pierce who conceived an interview improper after what had passed; this I reported to Colo. Hamilton at our next meeting. Colo. Hamilton then wrote to Major Pierce desiring of him a full & explicit statement of the offence given by Mr. Aldjo—which Major Pierce gave him. Mr. Aldjo then made such Reply as was thought sufficiently satisfactory by Colo. Hamilton, & myself.                                          Nathl Mitchell

"N York, Septr. 10th. 1787." (ADS, Mr. Hall Park McCullough, North Bennington, Vermont.)

## *To* ————

*New York, August 6, 1787.* Introduces "a son of Mr. Israel, who is going to Philadelphia to endeavour to effect the settlement of his fathers demand upon the Administrator of Barnard Levi."

ALS, Charles Roberts Autograph Collection of the Haverford College Library, Haverford, Pennsylvania.

## *Constitutional Convention. Motion on Citizenship Requirement for Membership in the House of Representatives* [1]

[Philadelphia, August 13, 1787]

Col. HAMILTON was in general agst. embarrassing the Govt. with minute restrictions.[2] There was on one side the possible danger that had been suggested [3] On the other side, the advantage of encouraging foreigners was obvious & admitted. Persons in Europe of moderate fortunes will be fond of coming here where they will be on a level with the first Citizens. He moved that the section be so altered as to require merely citizenship & inhabitancy.[4] The right of determining the rule of naturalization will then leave a discretion to the Legislature on this subject which will answer every purpose.

Hunt and Scott, *Debates,* 384.

1. Both Robert Yates and John Lansing, Jr., left the Convention early in July. As a consequence, James Madison's notes constitute the only source of H's remarks in the Constitutional Convention after July.

The exact date of H's return to the Convention cannot be determined, but it was between August 6, the date of the preceding letter (H to _____, August

6, 1787), and August 13, the date on which he again spoke in the Convention.

On July 26, the Convention appointed a Committee of Detail to prepare and report a detailed constitution conformable to the resolution previously adopted by the Convention. The committee reported on August 6, and its report was debated from that date until the last day of August.

2. H's remarks were made in the course of a debate on the qualifications to be imposed on members of the House of Representatives. James Wilson and Edmund Randolph had proposed that four years of citizenship be imposed for membership in the House of Representatives. Elbridge Gerry then suggested that "the eligibility might be confined to Natives," and Hugh Williamson of North Carolina "moved to insert 9 years." H's remarks followed Williamson's motion (Hunt and Scott, *Debates*, 384).

3. H presumably referred to Gerry's remark that if membership in the House of Representatives were not confined to natives "Foreign powers will intermeddle in our affairs, and spare no expence to influence them. Persons having foreign attachments will be sent among us & insinuated into our councils, in order to be made instruments for their purposes" (Hunt and Scott, *Debates*, 384).

4. After a brief debate, H's motion was defeated.

## To Rufus King

[New York, August 20, 1787]

Dr Sir

Since my arrival here,[1] I have written to my colleagues,[2] informing them, that if either of them would come down I would accompany him to Philadelphia. So much for the sake of propriety and public opinion.

In the mean time if any material alteration should happen to be made in the plan now before the Convention, I will be obliged to you for a communication of it. I will also be obliged to you to let me know when your *conclusion* is at hand; for I would choose to be present at that time.

I remain with sincere regard   Yr. Obed Servt        A Hamilton

Aug. 20. 87

ALS, New-York Historical Society, New York City.

1. H presumably had returned to Philadelphia between August 6 and August 13, 1787. See "Constitutional Convention. Remarks on Equality of Representation of the States in the Congress," June 29, 1787, note 3. He must have returned to New York soon after August 13.

2. Letter not found. Robert Yates and John Lansing, Jr., left the Constitutional Convention on July 10. Since they objected to the formation of the general government which the Convention seemed certain to propose, they did not plan to return. (See Yates and Lansing to George Clinton, no date, Yates, *Secret Proceedings and Debates*, 280–83.)

## *To Jeremiah Wadsworth*

[New York, August 20, 1787]

My Dear Sir

The inclosed [1] is said to be the Copy of a letter circulating in your state. The history of its appearance among us is that it was sent by one *Whitmore* [2] of Stratford, formerly in the Pay Master Generals Office to a James Reynold [3] of this City.

I am at a loss clearly to understand its object—and have some suspicion that it has been fabricated to excite jealousy against the Convention with a view to an opposition to their recommendations. At all events I wish if possible to trace its source and send it to you for that purpose. Whitmore must of course say where he got it and by pursuing the information we may at last come at the author. Let me know the political connections of this man and the complexion of the people most active in the circulation of the letter. Be so good as to attend to this inquiry somewhat particularly, as I have different reasons of some moment ⟨for⟩ setting it on foot.

I remain &c                                                          A H

Augt. 20—87

Copy, Hamilton Papers, Library of Congress.
   1. The enclosure was probably a copy of a letter which appeared in *The Fairfield* [Connecticut] *Gazette or The Independent Intelligencer* on July 25, 1787. The letter purported to be an "Extract of a Letter from Philadelphia, dated June 19" to someone in Portsmouth, New Hampshire. "I am happy to inform you," the anonymous writer stated, "that by our latest accounts from England, the scheme for a mission, which originated in Connecticut, and which is so agreeable to the people of America, and so manifestly for their interest, meets with a favorable reception from the British Court." The scheme to which the writer referred was to invite the second son of George III, Frederick, Duke of York, who was the secular Bishop of Osnaburgh, a town in the Prussian province of Hanover, to become king of the United States. The writer in *The Gazette* argued that the members of the Constitutional Convention "have the subject in their deliberation, and are harmonious in their opinions; the means only of accomplishing so great an event, appears principally to occupy their counsels." An account of the plan to establish a monarchy was also published by two Philadelphia papers—*The Pennsylvania Gazette*, August 15, 1787, and *The Pennsylvania Journal*, August 22, 1787.
   2. Presumably Hezekiah Wetmore who, during the American Revolution, was deputy paymaster general. Information on Wetmore is contained in Wadsworth's reply to H's letter, dated August 26, 1787.
   3. James Reynolds was the husband of the woman with whom H later had a much publicized affair.

## From Jeremiah Wadsworth

Hartford August 26 1787

My Dear Sir

I recd your favor this day with the inclosed Copy of a letter said to be circulating in this State.[1] Some time since a Paragraph in the New Haven Paper hinted at such a letter, & appeared to be written to scare the antifederal Party or alarm them—and I believed it was well intended as it seemed to be meant to prepare them to comply with the doings of the convention, least worse befell them—but the close of this letter appears to be calculated for other purposes. Wetmore[2] has always associated with Men who wished well to America & a good Government. He is half Brother to the Spirited federal Writer in our papers who Signs him self Cato,[3] and if he has really written or circulated the letter in question I am quite at a loss to know his intentions. I have communicated this matter to Col Humphry[4] in confidence who is on his way to New Haven (where Wetmore lives tho formerly of Stratford) he will enquire carefully into ye matter & write you. He has lived in the same house with Wetmore & can easily fathom him—Wetmore is naturally sanguine has some tallents & I believe is enterprizing—but ⟨fickle⟩. Who the Active people in this business are I have Yet to learn as it certainly has not circulated hereabout. But from Humphry you may expect to know all that is true in Wetmores neighborhood. I have always been Humphrys friend—but a nearer acquaintance with him Convince me he is a Man of great integrity and several talents as would wear well in any employment of consequence. If he comes to New York I wish you to be more Acquainted with him.

I am dear Sir   Your very Hum set                    Jere Wadsworth

ALS, Hamilton Papers, Library of Congress.

1. See H to Wadsworth, August 20, 1787.

2. Hezekiah Wetmore. See H to Wadsworth, August 20, 1787.

3. William P. Beers, Wetmore's half-brother by his mother's marriage after his father's death to Samuel Beers of Stratford, Connectictut. The "Cato" articles appeared in *The New-Haven Gazette, and the Connecticut Magazine* on November 30, 1786; January 25, February 8, March 9 and 15, 1787.

4. David Humphreys, aide-de-camp to General Washington during the Revolution and post-war diplomat, was at this time residing in Connecticut where, in 1786, he had been elected a member of the Assembly.

## To Rufus King

[New York, August 28, 1787]

Dear Sir,

I wrote to you some days since, that to request you to inform me when there was a prospect of your finishing as I intended to be with you, for certain reasons, before the conclusion. It is whispered here that some late changes in your scheme have taken place which give it a higher tone.[1] Is this the case?

I leave town today, to attend a circuit in a neighbouring County, from which I shall return the last of the week, and shall be glad to find a line from you explanatory of the period of the probable termination of your business.

New York Aug 28.

AL[S], New-York Historical Society, New York City.
   1. H is referring to the various proposals to grant additional powers to the legislature and the judiciary, and to strengthen the executive. See James Madison's record in Hunt and Scott, *Debates*, 384–465.

## From Baron von Steuben

[New York, August–September 1787] [1]

Mon Cher Ami. L'amour pour la justice, autant que L'Amitié dont Vous m'avez honoré depuis dix ans Vous a induit d'acquiescer à ma Sollicitation & de Vous charger de ma demande Envers les E: U: [2] Vous Ayant Exposé les titres sur lesquelles ma pretention est fondé, Votre Opinion joint a Ceux de Mr: Douane, Chancellier Livingston et Mr: jay, etoit Unanime,[3] que la stipulation fait entre les E:U: et moi, avant mon Entré dans le service, Attesté et Certifier par les Memes personnes que le Congres avoit chargé de traiter avec moi, Avoit toute la Validité d'un Contract Entre un Souverain et un individu. Vous etiez d'Accord que ce contract etoit remplie de mon côté, dans toute son Etendue, et qu'il ne L'etoit qu'en partie du côté des E:U:

Vous Avez pris la peine Monsieur d'Exposer la justice de mes demandes dans un jour, que mes plus Ardens Antagoniste seront obligé de Ceder à la Verité. Ainsi tout mes desirs, tout mes Esperences, se bornent a la reconnoissance de ce Contract. Si le Congres ne peut ou ne Veut pas remplir ses Engagemens, il n'y Vat que de ma fortune, & dans le Catalogues des personnes rendue Malheureux, par un Gouvernement plus Malheureux Encore, je ne ferai qu'un individue de plus. Mais si le Congrès denie le Contract, allors il y Vat de mon honneur, et si J'ai le Courage de braver la pauvrete a laquelle L'injustice ma reduit, je n'aurez jamais la lacheté, de me Voir Accusé d'Escrocquerie & de fauseté. Dans ce Cas je suis determiner de publie, tout les transactions & la Mauvaise fois avec laquelle, le Congres a rencontre mes proposition Generuse & comme il a recompenser mes services.

Je doit a mon honneur la poursuite de cette Affaire, je le doit encore pour ma justification, envers les honnettes Gens, quil m'ont Avancé la somme neccessaire pour Venir de L'Europe servir les E. U. et dont il etoit hors de mon pouvoir de payer ni Capital ni interet. Les payement chetives & periodique que J'ai touché depuis la paix, ne servoit qu'a me faire Vivotter, dans une dependence, aussi humiliante, que le plus Cruëll tirant, ne feroit Essuyer a son Esclave. Cet a ce payement periodique que J'attribue le Comble de mes Malheur, parcequ'il ma barrer toutes les Moyens pour faire un Etablissement sollide soit en Europe ou meme dans ce païs cy. Mais pourquoi Vous Ennuyerai je d'un recit de mes Malheur, dont Vous Connoissez trop bien tout les detailles. Il S'agit de portez L'Afaire a une decision definitive, il S'agit de mettre ma derniere application devant le Congrès. L'Esperence que nos Affaires publique prendrons une tournure plus Avantageuse nous a fait suspendre, cette demarche finale depuis dix huit mois.[4] Ce retard m'a approche a ma derniere resource, et tout changement pour le Mieux dans les Affaires Publique, S'emble S'eloigner a mesure que je m'approche de ma derniere Ruine.

Comme il ne S'agit point d'un payement, Mais d'une Reconnoissence de la justice de mes pretentions je Vous demande S'il Vaut la peine de suspendre plus longtems la presentation du Memoire en question Cependant je me repose entierement sur Vos lumieres: faites ceque Vous juges apropos, Mais Epargnez moi L'a demarche humiliante, de sollicité; même d'exposer mon Affaire, personnellement a cette Classe des Gens, que je croie insensible aux sentimens de L'honneur & de delicatesse.

je Viendroi Vous Voir pour Vous Epargnez la peine de m'ecrire. bon soir                                                            .                    steuben [5]

ALS, Hamilton Papers, Library of Congress.

1. This letter is undated. Because von Steuben states in the first sentence that he had known H for ten years, the letter must have been written in 1787 or 1788, as the two men could not have been acquainted before 1777 and probably did not meet until 1778. A more precise date can be ascribed on the basis of von Steuben's statement in the third paragraph that "the hope that our public affairs will take a more advantageous turn has made us hold up this final step for the last 18 months." Von Steuben had not petitioned Congress in 1786, but he renewed his application in 1787 by sending a memorial which was read in Congress on October 6 (see JCC, XXXIII, 617, note 1). H must have agreed before this date, probably in August or September to aid the Baron again. He solicited the aid of Washington for von Steuben, for example, on October 30, 1787.

2. Beginning in December, 1782 (see H's report as chairman of a committee of the Continental Congress on von Steuben's claim, dated December 30, 1782), von Steuben repeatedly petitioned Congress for compensation for his services in the Continental Army during the American Revolution.

3. Von Steuben contended that Congress was bound by contract to idemnify him for his sacrifices during the American Revolution. To buttress his contention the Baron "applied to men eminent in the law, to wit, the Chancellor Livingston, Messrs. Jay, Hamilton and Duane; he communicated to them the facts and proofs, asking their opinion, if the stipulation ought to have the validity of a contract in form; their concurrent determination decided the question in the affirmative" (from an undated, printed pamphlet in the Papers of the Continental Congress, National Archives).

4. See note 1.

5. Von Steuben enclosed a statement of money owed him by the United States. It is in the Hamilton Papers, Library of Congress.


# From David Humphreys [1]

New Haven [Connecticut] Septr. 1st. 1787

My dear Sir

Our friend Col Wadsworth has communicated to me a letter in which you made enquiries respecting a political letter that has lately circulated in this State.[2] I arrived in this Town yesterday & have since conversed with several intelligent persons on the subject. It appears to have been printed in a Fairfield Paper as long ago as the 25th of July.[3] I have not been able to trace it to its source. Mr Wetmore [4] informs me that when he first saw this letter it was in the hands of one Jared Mansfield,[5] who, I believe, has formerly been reputed a Loyalist. Indeed it seems to have been recieved & circulated with avidity by that Class of People, whether it was fabricated by them or not. I think, however, there is little doubt that it was manufactured in this State. I demanded of Mr Wetmore what he thought were the wishes & objects of the writer of that letter; he said he believed it might be written principally for the amusement of the author & perhaps with some view to learn whether the People were not absolutely indifferent to all government & dead to all political sentiment.

Before I saw the letter in question, a Paragraph had been published by Mr. Meigs,[6] giving an account of it & attempting to excite the apprehension of the Antifederalists, with an idea, that the most disastrous consequences are to be expected, unless we shall accept the Proceedings of the Convention. Some think this was the real design of that fictitious performance; but others, with more reason, that it was intended to feel the public pulse & to discover whether the public mind would be startled with propositions of Royalty. The quondam Tories have undoubtedly conceived hopes of a future union with G. Britain, from the inefficacy of our Government & the tumults which prevailed in Massachusetts during the last winter. I saw a letter written, at that period, by a Clergyman of considerable reputation in Nova Scotia to a Person of eminence in this State; stating the impossibility of our being happy under our present Constitution & proposing (now we could think & argue calmly on all the consequences) that the efforts of the moderate, the virtuous & the brave should be exerted to effect a reunion with the parent State. He mentioned among other things, how instrumental the Cincinnati might be & how much it would redound to their emolument. It seems by a conversation I have had here, that the ultimate practicability of introducing the Bishop of Osnaburgh is not a novel idea among those who were formerly termed Loyalists.[7] Ever since the peace it has been occasionally talked of & wished for. Yesterday, where I dined, half jest, half earnest, he was given as the first Toast.

I leave you now, my dear friend, to reflect how ripe we are for the most mad & ruinous projects that can be suggested, especially when, in addition to this view, we take into consideration how thoroughly the patriotic part of the Community, the friends of an efficient Government are discouraged with the present System &

irritated at the popular Demagogues who are determined to keep themselves in office at the risque of every thing. Thence apprehensions are formed, that tho' the measures proposed by the Convention, may not be equal to the wishes of the most enlightened & virtuous; yet that they will be too high-toned to be adopted by our popular Assemblies. Should that happen our political Ship will be left afloat on a Sea of Chance, without a Rudder as well as without a Pilot.

I am happy to see you have (some of you) had the honest boldness to attack in a public Paper, the Antifederal Dogmas of a great Personage in your State.[8] Go on & prosper. Were the men of talents & honesty, throughout the Continent, properly combined into one Phalanx, I am confident they would be competent to hew their way thro' all opposition. Were there no little jealousies, bickerings, & unworthy sinister views to divert them from their object, they might by perseverance establish a Government calculated to promote the happiness of Mankind & to make the Revolution a blessing instead of a curse.

I think it probable that I shall soon go to the Southward, in the mean time, I beg you to be persuaded that I am, with sentiments of sincerest friendship & esteem, My dear Hamilton,

Your most obedient & Most humble Servant      D. Humphreys

Col. Hamilton.

ALS, Hamilton Papers, Library of Congress.
    1. Humphreys, wartime aide to Washington, and diplomat, was at this time residing in Connecticut.
    In *JCHW*, I, this letter is misdated September 16, 1787.
    2. See H to Jeremiah Wadsworth, August 20, 1787, and Wadsworth to H, August 26, 1787.
    3. For the newspaper annd letter referred to, see H to Wadsworth, August 20, 1787, note 1.
    4. Hezekiah Wetmore. For a discussion of Wetmore, see Wadsworth to H, August 26, 1787.
    5. Mansfield at this time was rector of the Hopkins Grammar School in New Haven, Connecticut. He later acquired fame as a mathematician, and in 1803 became surveyor general of the United States.
    6. Josiah Meigs who published *The New-Haven Gazette and the Connecticut Magazine*.
    7. In his letter of August 20, 1787, to Wadsworth, H had enclosed a letter which, he said, was circulating in New York and which suggested that the second son of George III, Frederick, Duke of York, the secular Bishop of Osnaburgh, a town in the Prussian province of Hanover, be made monarch of the United States.
    8. H's attack on George Clinton was published in *The* [New York] *Daily Advertiser* of July 21, 1787.

## Constitutional Convention. Remarks on the Election of the President [1]

[Philadelphia, September 6, 1787]

Mr. HAMILTON said that he had been restrained from entering into the discussions by his dislike of the Scheme of Govt. in General; but as he meant to support the plan to be recommended, as better than nothing, he wished in this place to offer a few remarks.[2] He liked the new modification, on the whole, better than that in the printed Report.[3] In this the President was a Monster elected for seven years, and ineligible afterwards; having great powers, in appointments to office, & continually tempted by this constitutional disqualification to abuse them in order to subvert the Government. Although he should be made re-eligible, still if appointed by the Legislature, he would be tempted to make use of corrupt influence to be continued in office. It seemed peculiarly desireable therefore that some other mode of election should be devised. Considering the different views of different States, & the different districts Northern Middle & Southern, he concurred with those who thought that the votes would not be concentered, and that the appointment would consequently in the present mode devolve on the Senate. The nomination to offices will give great weight to the President. Here then is a mutual connection & influence, that will perpetuate the President, and aggrandize both him & the Senate. What is to be the remedy? He saw none better than to let the highest number of ballots, whether a majority or not, appoint the President. What was the objection to this? Merely that too small a number might appoint. But as the plan stands, the Senate may take the candidate having the smallest number of votes, and make him President.

Hunt and Scott, *Debates*, 520–21.

1. H probably had returned to the Convention between September 1 and September 6, 1787.

2. On the last day of August the unfinished parts of the Constitution were referred to a Committee of Eleven consisting of one member from each state. On September 4, the committee reported its recommendations. Among them was a plan for the election of the executive which, with minor changes, became a part of the Constitution.

3. The printed report was the report of the Committee of Detail which had been appointed on July 26 to prepare and report a constitution conformable to the resolutions adopted by Congress. The new modification was the plan pro-

posed by the Committee of Eleven. In the report of the Committee of Detail the President was to be elected by ballot by the national legislature and to hold office for seven years. In the report of the Committee of Eleven of September 4, he was to be chosen by electors in such manner as the legislature in each state should direct. If the electors gave no candidate a majority of votes, the choice was to devolve on the Senate.

## Constitutional Convention. Remarks in Favor of a Motion Increasing the Number in the House of Representatives

[Philadelphia, September 8, 1787]

Col: HAMILTON expressed himself with great earnestness and anxiety in favor of the motion.[1] He avowed himself a friend to a vigorous Government, but would declare at the same time, that he held it essential that the popular branch of it should be on a broad foundation. He was seriously of opinion that the House of Representatives was on so narrow a scale as to be really dangerous, and to warrant a jealousy in the people for their liberties. He remarked that the connection between the President & Senate would tend to perpetuate him, by corrupt influence. It was the more necessary on this account that a numerous representation in the other branch of the Legislature should be established.[2]

Hunt and Scott, *Debates,* 538.
1. Near the end of the session of September 8, Hugh Williamson, delegate from North Carolina, made a motion that "the clause relating to the number of the House of Representatives shd. be reconsidered for the purpose of increasing the number" (Hunt and Scott, *Debates,* 538). The clause to which he referred provided that, until the first census should be taken, the House of Representatives should consist of sixty-five members apportioned according to population among the several states.
2. Williamson's motion, supported by H, was negatived by the Convention.

## Constitutional Convention. Remarks on Amending the Constitution

[Philadelphia, September 10, 1787]

Mr. HAMILTON 2ded. the motion, but he said with a different view from Mr. Gerry.[1] He did not object to the consequence stated by Mr. Gerry. There was no greater evil in subjecting the people of the U.S. to the major voice than the people of a particular State. It had been wished by many and was much to have been desired that an easier mode for introducing amendments had been provided by the articles of Confederation It was equally desireable now that an easy mode should be established for supplying defects which will probably appear in the New System The mode proposed was not adequate. The State Legislatures will not apply for alterations but with a view to increase their own powers. The National Legislature will be the first to perceive and will be the most sensible to the necessity of amendments, and ought also to be empowered, whenever two thirds of each branch should concur to call a Convention. There could be no danger in giving this power, as the people would finally decide in the case.

Hunt and Scott, *Debates*, 539.

1. Elbridge Gerry's motion recommended a change in the proposed article relating to the amendment of the Constitution. The proposed article stated that "On the application of the Legislatures of two thirds of the States in the Union, for an amendment of this Constitution, the Legislature of the U.S. shall call a Convention for that purpose." In support of his motion Gerry said that the Constitution was "to be paramount to the State Constitutions. It follows, hence, from this article that two thirds of the States may obtain a Convention, a majority of which can bind the Union to innovations that may subvert the State-Constitutions altogether. He asked whether this was a situation proper to be run into" (Hunt and Scott, *Debates*, 538–39).

## Constitutional Convention. Second to James Madison's Motion on Amending the Constitution

*Philadelphia, September 10, 1787.* On this date, Hamilton seconded the following motion made by James Madison: "The Legislature of the U.S. whenever two thirds of both Houses shall deem necessary, or on the application of two thirds of the Legislatures of the several States, shall propose amendments to this Constitution, which shall be valid to all intents and purposes as part thereof, when the same shall have been ratified by three fourths at least of the Legislatures of the several States, or by Conventions in three fourths thereof, as one or the other mode of ratification may be proposed by the Legislature of the U S."

Hunt and Scott, *Debates*, 540.

## Constitutional Convention. Remarks on the Manner of Ratifying the Constitution

[Philadelphia, September 10, 1787]

Mr. HAMILTON concurred with Mr. Gerry as to the indecorum of not requiring the approbation of Congress.[1] He considered this as a necessary ingredient in the transaction. He thought it wrong also to allow nine States as provided by art XXI. to institute a new Government on the ruins of the existing one.[2] He wd. propose as a better modification of the two articles (XXI & XXII) that the plan should be sent to Congress in order that the same if approved by them, may be communicated to the State Legislatures, to the end that they may refer it to State Conventions; each Legislature declaring that if the Convention of the State should think the plan ought to take effect among nine ratifying States, the same shd. take effect accordingly.

Hunt and Scott, *Debates*, 541.

1. Before H spoke, Elbridge Gerry moved to reconsider those articles of the proposed Constitution dealing with the manner in which it was to be ratified. Article XXII of the plan of government reported by the Committee on Detail on August 6 provided that "This Constitution shall be laid before the United States in Congress assembled, for their approbation; and it is the opinion of this Convention, that it should be afterwards submitted to a Convention chosen, under the recommendation of its legislature, in order to receive the ratification of such Convention." In debate on this article on August 31, it was agreed to strike out the words "for their approbation" (Hunt and Scott, *Debates*, 346, 499). Gerry wished to restore the phrase which had been deleted on August 31.

2. Article XXI provided that the ratification of nine states should be sufficient to institute the new government (Hunt and Scott, *Debates*, 346).

## Constitutional Convention. Remarks on the Ratification of the Constitution

[Philadelphia, September 10, 1787]

Mr. HAMILTON. No Convention convinced of the necessity of the plan will refuse to give it effect on the adoption by nine States.[1] He thought this mode less exceptionable than the one proposed in the article, and would attain the same end.

Hunt and Scott, *Debates*, 541.

1. Nathaniel Gorham had made the following objection to H's earlier remarks of the same day (see "Constitutional Convention. Remarks on the Manner of Ratifying the Constitution," September 10, 1787): "Some States will say that nine States shall be sufficient to establish the plan, others will require unanimity for the purpose. And the different and conditional ratifications will defeat the plan altogether" (Hunt and Scott, *Debates*, 541).

# Constitutional Convention. Motion on the Ratification of the Constitution

[Philadelphia, September 10, 1787]

Mr. HAMILTON then moved to postpone art XXI[1] in order to take up the following, containing the ideas he had above expressed,[2] viz

Resolved that the foregoing plan of a Constitution be transmitted to the U.S. in Congress assembled, in order that if the same shall be agreed to by them, it may be communicated to the Legislatures of the several States, to the end that they may provide for its final ratification by referring the same to the Consideration of a Convention of Deputies in each State to be chosen by the people thereof, and that it be recommended to the said Legislatures in their respective acts for organizing such convention to declare, that if the said Convention shall approve of the said Constitution, such approbation shall be binding and conclusive upon the State, and further that if the said Convention should be of opinion that the same upon the assent of any nine States thereto, ought to take effect between the States so assenting, such opinion shall thereupon be also binding upon such State, and the said Constitution shall take effect between the States assenting thereto."[3]

Hunt and Scott, *Debates*, 542.

1. Article XXI provided the Constitution should go into effect when ratified by nine states.

2. See "Constitutional Convention. Remarks on the Manner of Ratifying the Constitution," September 10, 1787, and "Constitutional Convention. Remarks on the Ratification of the Constitution," September 10, 1787.

3. H's motion to postpone the vote on Article XXI was defeated. Article XXI was then agreed to unanimously.

## Constitutional Convention. Withdrawal of a Motion

[Philadelphia, September 10, 1787]

Col: HAMILTON withdrew the remainder of the motion to postpone art XXII,[1] observing that his purpose was defeated by the vote just given.[2]

Hunt and Scott, *Debates*, 543.

1. In "Constitutional Convention. Motion on the Ratification of the Constitution," September 10, 1787, H had moved to postpone consideration of Article XXI of the proposed Constitution in order to take up his substitute for it. By withdrawing "the remainder of the motion to postpone art XXII," H presumably meant that his motion would have superseded both articles and that its rejection obviated any specific motion on Article XXII.

2. The Convention had defeated H's proposal to postpone Article XXI.

## Constitutional Convention. Remarks on the Number of Votes Required in Congress to Override a Presidential Veto

[Philadelphia, September 12, 1787]

Mr. HAMILTON added his testimony to the fact that ⅔ in N. York had been ineffectual either where a popular object, or a legislative faction operated; of which he mentioned some instances.[1]

Hunt and Scott, *Debates*, 555.

1. A committee of style had furnished the members of the Convention a digest of the plan they had prepared. Hugh Williamson then "moved to reconsider the clause requiring three fourths of each House to overrule the negative of the President, in order to strike out ¾ and insert ⅔." Gouverneur Morris, in opposing Williamson's motion, mentioned, among examples, that "the example of N. York shews that ⅔ is not sufficient to answer the purpose" (Hunt and Scott, *Debates*, 554–55). H's remarks followed those by Gouverneur Morris.

## To The Daily Advertiser [1]

[New York, September 15, 1787]

Mr. Hamilton, in his absence from New York on public duty (with how much propriety and temper his fellow citizens must

ADf, Hamilton Papers, Library of Congress.

1. This letter was printed in *The* [New York] *Daily Advertiser* on September 15, 1787. In *JCHW*, II, 422–26, Hamilton, *History*, III, 363–66, and *HCLW*, I,

decide) has been attacked by name, as the Writer of a publication printed in Mr. Childs' paper of the 21st of July last.[2] In fixing that publication upon him, there is certainly no mistake; nor did he ever mean to be concealed. He left his name with the Printer, to be disclosed to any person who should apply for it on the part of the Governor; with instructions to make that circumstance known, which was accordingly done. The fairness of this conduct speaks for itself. The Citizens of the state have too much good sense to be deceived into an opinion, that it could have been dictated by a wanton disposition to calumniate a meritorious character. They must and will consider it as an honorable and open attempt to unmask, what appeared to the Writer, the pernicious intrigues of a man high in office, to preserve power and emolument to himself, at the expence of the Union, the Peace and the Happiness of America.

To say, that it would have been derogatory to the first Magistrate of the state to enter the lists in a news paper with an "anonymous scribbler"[3] is a miserable subterfuge. Though Mr. Hamilton, to avoid the appearance of ostentation, did not put his name to the piece; yet, having left it with the Printers to be communicated to the party concerned, there is no pretence to consider it in the light of an anonymous publication. If the matter alleged had been false, the Governor had his choice of two modes of vindicating himself

---

424–29, it is dated "1787." H sent the draft as an enclosure to his letter of October 15, 1787, to George Washington.

2. See H's letter to *The Daily Advertiser* of July 21, 1787.

On September 6, 1787, H's attack on Clinton was answered in *The New-York Journal* by "A Republican" who, because he did not think it proper for the governor "to enter the list in a newspaper with an anonymous scribler," undertook to "unmask the motives" which prompted the attack on Clinton. "A Republican," however, did not directly name H as the anonymous author of the July 21 article (*The New-York Journal*, September 6, 1787). Instead he concluded the article with "a few lines from the works of the celebrated Churchill" leaving "the application to the reader":

"Smit with the love of honor, or the pence,
O'er-run with wit, and destitute of sense,
Legions of factious authors throng at once;
Fool beckons fool, and dunce awakens dunce.
To Hamilton's the ready lies repair;
Ne'er was lie made which was not welcome there.
Thence, on maturer judgment's anvil wrought,
The polish'd falsehoods into public brought;
Quick circulating slanders mirth afford,
And reputation bleeds in ev'ry word."

3. This quotation and those which follow were made by "A Republican" in *The New-York Journal*, September 6, 1787. See note 2.

from the aspersion; one, by giving a simple and direct denial to it in the public prints; the other, by having a personal explanation on the subject with the Writer. Neither of these modes could have wounded his dignity. The first is practiced in most governments where public opinion is respected. A short paragraph to the following effect would have answered the purpose—"The Printer of this Paper is authorised to assure the public, that His Excellency the Governor never made use of the expressions attributed to him, in a publication contained in Mr. Childs paper of the 21st July, nor of any others of similar import." This would have thrown it upon Mr. Hamilton to bring forward to public view the sources of his information and the proofs of his charge. And this he has too much regard for his reputation not to have been prepared to do. This he is still ready to do, whenever such a denial shall appear.

The Governor, if he had had any objection to this mode of proceeding, might have had recourse to the other,—that of a personal explanation with the Writer. Mr. Hamilton would have conceived himself bound, by the principles of candour and honor, to declare on what grounds he had proceeded, and, if he could have been satisfied they were erroneous, to retract the imputations founded upon them. Would it have impaired the dignity of the first Magistrate of a republic to have had such an explanation with any *reputable* Citizen? Would it have impaired his dignity to have had such an explanation with a Citizen, who is at this moment acting in an important and delicate trust, by the appointment of the legislature of the State?

Mr. Hamilton freely submits to the judgment of his fellow citizens, whether there was any thing in the manner of his animadversions, that preclude⟨d⟩ such an explanation. They were strong and pointed; but he flatters himself they were free from indecorum. He states the charge as matter of Report, and mak⟨es⟩ his observations hypothetically, even seeming to admi⟨t⟩ a possibility of misrepresentation. As he was not himself present at the conversation; but spoke from the information of those who were, he could not with propriety have expressed himself in more positive terms. As he was speaking of an officer of the first rank in the state, he was disposed to use as much moderation in the manner of exhibiting his misconduct, as was consistent with that explicitness and energy, which were necessary to place it in its proper light.

These remarks, while they explain Mr. Hamilton's motives, will serve to refute the ca⟨vil –⟩ respecting his doubt of the truth of the fact alleged by him. He now declares, that from the nature of his information he had no doubt of the kind and that since the publication he has understood from different partisans of the Governor, that he did not deny the expressions attributed to him to be in substan⟨ce⟩ true, with some minute and unessential distinctions.

It is insinuated, that the circulation of the fact is calculated to produce the evil pretended to be guarde⟨d⟩ against, by diffusing throu⟨gh⟩ the community a knowlege of the Governors sentiments. This remark admits of an obvious answer. If his Excellency was predetermined to oppose the measures of the Convention, as his conduct indicates, he would take care himself to propagate his sentiments, in the manner in which it could be done with the most effect. This appears to have been his practice. It was therefore proper that the antidote should go along with the poison; and that the community should be apprised, that he was capable of forming such a predetermination, before, it can be presumed, he had any knowlege of the measures themselves, on which to found his judgment.

A cry is attempted to be raised against the publication of Mr. Hamilton, as if it were an invasion of the right of the first Magistrate of the State to deliver his sentiments on a matter of public concern. The fallacy of this artifice will easily be detected. The Governor has an undoubted right to give his sentiments freely on every public measure. Under proper circumstances, it will be always his duty to do it. But every *right* may be abused by a *wrong exercise* of it. Even the constitutional powers vested in him may be so employed, as to subject him justly not only to censure, but to impeachment. The only question then is, whether he has in the present instance used his right properly, or improperly—whether it became him, by *anticipation*, to endeavour to prejudice the community against the "unknown and undetermined" measures of a body, to which the general voice of the union had delegated the important trust of concerting and proposing a plan for reforming the national constitution? Let every man answer this question to himself.

The apologists for the Governor, in the intemperate ardor of their zeal for his character, seem to forget another *right*, very precious to the citizens of a free country, *that* of examining the conduct of their rulers. *These* have an undoubted right, within the limits of the constitution, to speak and to act their sentiments; but the citizen has an equal right to discuss the propriety of those sentiments, or of the manner of advancing, or supporting them. To attempt to abrige this last right, by rendering the exercise of it odious, is to attempt to abrige a privilege, the most essential of any to the security of the people. The laws, which afford sufficient protection to the Magistrate, will punish the excess of this privilege; within the bounds ⟨they allow, it is the bulwark of public liberty.

But, observations of either kind might mutually have been spared. There is no danger that the rights of a man, at the head of the Government (possessing all the influence to be derived from long continuance in office, the disposition of lucrative places, and *consummate talents* for popularity) can be injured by the voice of a private individual. There is as little danger, that the spirit of the people of this State will ever tolerate attempts to seduce, to awe, or to clamor them out of the privilege of bringing the conduct of men in power to the bar of public examination.

To all the declamation and invective, with which the Republican winds up his performance, and labors to mislead the public attention from its *true object,* a short answer will be given. It is the stale trick of the party to traduce every⟩ [4] *independent man,* opposed to their views, the better to preserve to themselves that power and consequence, to which they have no other title than their arts of deceiving the people.

Mr. Hamilton can however defy all their malevolent ingenuity to produce a single instance of his conduct public, or private, inconsistent with the strictest rules of integrity and honor—a single instance, that may even denominate him selfish, or interested—a single instance in which he has either *"forfieted"* the confidence of the people or failed in obtaining any proof of their favour for which he has been a candidate.[5] It would be ingratitude in him not to ac-

4. As a part of the MS is missing, the section in broken brackets is taken from *The Daily Advertiser* of September 15, 1787.

5. This paragraph by H was prompted by the following accusation of "A Republican":

". . . a certain lordly faction exists in this state, composed of men, possessed of an insatiable thirst for dominion, and who, having forfeited the confidence of their fellow-citizens, and being defeated in their hopes of rising into power, have, for sometime past, employed themselves with unremitted industry, to embarrass every public measure." (*The New-York Journal,* September 6, 1787.)

knowlege that the marks of their confidence have greatly exceeded his deserts.

## Constitutional Convention. Remarks on Signing the Constitution [1]

[Philadelphia, September 17, 1787]

Mr. HAMILTON expressed his anxiety that every member should sign. A few characters of consequence, by opposing or even refusing to sign the Constitution, might do infinite mischief by kindling the latent sparks which lurk under an enthusiasm in favor of the Convention which may soon subside. No man's ideas were more remote from the plan than his were known to be; but is it possible to deliberate between anarchy and Convulsion on one side, and the chance of good to be expected from the plan on the other.

Hunt and Scott, *Debates*, 580.

1. On September 17, 1787, the final day of the Constitutional Convention, the engrossed Constitution was read. Before it was signed, several members addressed the Convention urging that all delegates sign it.

## Draft of a Constitution [1]

[Philadelphia, September 17, 1787] [2]

§ 6   ~~A senator when impeached shall continue to exercise his office~~

~~until conviction~~

1. ADF, MS Division, New York Public Library. In the Hamilton Papers, Library of Congress, and in the JCH Transcripts there are two facsimiles of a copy of this document. The facsimiles at first glance appear to be in H's writing. A close examination, however, reveals minor variations of the kind a copyist might make while attempting an exact duplicate of a draft. A plausible reason for the existence of the facsimiles has not been found. Another copy of the "Draft of a Constitution," in an unidentified handwriting, is also in the Hamilton Papers, Library of Congress. A copy that James Madison made is in the James Madison Papers, Library of Congress.

This document has been printed exactly as it was written. H's deletions have been retained and his insertions, unless otherwise indicated, have been printed just as he made them; also a number of blank spaces left in the MS for later insertions. Material in broken brackets is taken from the facsimile in the Hamilton Papers, Library of Congress.

2. The precise date on which H finished his "Draft of a Constitution" cannot be determined. It must have been completed near the end of the Convention,

of America

The People of the United States∧do ordain and establish this con-

stitution for the government of themselves and their Posterity.

## ARTICLE I

§ 1   The Legislative power shall be vested in two distinct bodies of

men one to be called the Assembly the other the Senate, subject to

the negative hereinafter mentioned.

§ 2   The executive power, with the qualifications hereinafter speci-

fied, shall be vested in a President of the United States.

§ 3   The Supreme Judicial authority, except in the cases other wise

provided for in this constitution, shall be vested in a court to be

called the SUPREME COURT to consist of not less than six nor more

than twelve judges.

## ARTICLE II

§ 1   The Assembly shall consist of persons to be called representa-

tives, who shall be chosen, except in the first instance, by the free

male citizens and inhabitants of the several states comprehended in

the Union; all of whom of the age of twenty one years and upwards

shall be intitled to an equal vote.

§ 2   But this first Assembly shall be chosen in the mann⟨er⟩ pre-

scribed in the last article and shall consist of one hundred members

---

for the statements of both Madison and H agree that he presented it to Madison
a few days before or after the final day of the Convention. September 17 has
been selected as the date on which H handed it to Madison and that date has
been ascribed to the document. J. C. Hamilton (Hamilton, *History*, III, 284–302,
and Hamilton, *Life*, II, 490–507), eager to prove the inaccuracy of James Madison's record of H's remarks in the Convention, gives a confusing account of the
times at which the "Plan of Government" (see enclosure to "Constitutional
Convention. Speech on a Plan of Government," June 18, 1787) and the
"Draft" were composed. He evidently assumed that H read the more detailed
version of his proposed constitution, the "Draft," on June 18. Lodge (*HCLW*, I,
347) correctly stated that the "Plan" was introduced on June 18 and that the
"Draft of a Constitution," representing H's elaboration of the "Plan," was
handed to Madison near the end of the Convention.

of whom New Hampshire shall have five Massachusettes thirteen Rhode Island two Connecticut seven New York nine New Jersey six Pensylvania twelve Delaware two Maryland Eight Virginia six-

teen North Carolina Eight South Carolina ~~seven~~ <sup>Eight</sup> Georgia ~~five~~ four.

§ 3 The Legislature shall provide for the further elections of representatives, apportioning them in each state, from time to time, as nearly as may be to the number of persons described in the 4 § of the 7 article, so as that the whole number of representatives shall never be less than One hundred nor m⟨ore⟩ than        hundred. There shall be a census taken for this purpose within three years after the first meeting of the legislature and within every successive period of ten years. The term for which representatives shall be elected shall be determined by the Legislature but shall not exceed

There shall be a general election at least once ⟨in three years⟩ three years.ₐ ⟨and the⟩ time of service ofₐ <sup>all</sup> the members in each

Assemblyₐ ⟨except in filling vacancies⟩ ~~shall begin~~ ⟨shall begin⟩ on the same day

and shallₐ <sup>always</sup> end on the same day.

§ 4 ~~Fifty one~~ Forty members shall make a house sufficient to proceed to business; but this number may be increased by the Legislature, yet so as never to exceed a majority of the whole number of representatives.[3]

§ 5 The Assembly shall choose its President and other officers shall judge of the qualifications & elections of its own members, ~~shall~~ punish them for improper conduct in their capacity of Repres: not

3. This paragraph is inserted in the margin.

extending to life or limb [4] and shall exclusively possess the power of impeachment except in the case of the President of the United States; but no impeachment of a member of the senate shall be by less than two thirds of the representatives present.

⟨Qu⟩aere? { § 6 ~~Member~~ Representatives may act ⟨by proxy⟩ but no representative present shall be proxy ⟨for more⟩ than one who is absent.

vote

§ 7 Bills for raising revenue, and ∧appropriating monies for ∧ ~~carrying on war and~~ paying the salaries of the officers of government, shall originate in the Assembly; but may be altered and amended by the Senate.

bills for   the support of fleets and armies and for

§ 8 The acceptance of an office under the United States ~~shall~~ by a representative shall vacate his seat in the Assembly.

### ARTICLE III

§ 1 The Senate shall consist of persons to be chosen, except in the first instance, by electors elected for that purpose by the ~~pers~~ citizens and inhabitants of the several states comprehended in the Union who shall ~~hold~~ ∧have in their own right or in the right of their wives an estate in land for not less than life, or a term of years, whereof at the time of giving their votes there shall be at least fourteen years unexpired.

§ 2 But the first senate shall be chosen in the manner prescribed in the last article and shall consist of forty members to be called

4. The material beginning with the words "shall judge" and ending with the words "life or limb" is inserted in the margin.

Senators of whom New Hampshire shall have        Massachu-

settes      Rhode Island      Connecticut      New York

     New Jersey      Pensylvania      Delaware

Maryland      Virginia      North Carolina      South

Carolina      Georgia

§ 3  The Legislature shall provide for the future elections of Sena-

tors; for which purpose the states respectively, which have more

than one senator, shall be divided into convenient districts to which

           A

           ~~Each~~ state having but one senator shall be itself a district

the Senators shall be apportioned. On the death resignation or re-

moval from office of a Senator his place shall be supplied by a new

election in the district from which he came. Upon each election

there shall be not less than six nor more than twelve electors chosen

in a district.

§ 4  The number of Senators shall never be less than forty, nor

shall any state, if the same shall not hereafter be divided, ever have

less than the number allotted to it in the second section of this

                            whole

article; but the legislature may ⟨incr⟩ease the ∧number of Senators,

in the same proportion to the whole number of representatives as

forty is to one hundred, and such increase, beyond the present num-

ber, shall be apportioned to the respective states in a ratio to the

respective numbers of their representatives.

                                       boundaries

§ 5  If states shall be divided or if a new arrangement of the ~~limits~~∧

of two or more states shall take place, the Legislature shall apportion

the number of Senators, (in elections succeeding such division or new arrangement) to which the constituent parts were intitled according to the change of situation having regard to the number of persons described in the 4th § of the 7th. article.

§ 6 The Senators shall hold their places, during good behaviour,
removeable only by conviction on impeach$_\wedge$for some crime or mis- $^{ment}$
demeanor. They shall continue to exercise their offices when im-
peached until a conviction shall take place. Sixteen Senators$_\wedge$shall $^{attending\ in\ person}$
be sufficient to make a house; but the legislature may increase this $^{to\ transact\ business}$
number yet so as never to exceed a majority of the whole number
of Senators. The ~~absent~~ Senators may vote by proxy but no senator$_\wedge$ $^{who\ is\ present}$
shall be proxy for more than two who are absent.[5]

§ 7 The Senate shall choose its President and other officers; ~~and~~ shall judge of the qualifications and elections of its members and shall punish them for improper conduct in their capacity of senators; but such punishment shall not extend to life or limb; nor to expulsion. In the absence of their President they may choose a temporary president. The President shall only have a casting vote when the house is equally divided.

§ 8 The Senate shall exclusively possess the power of declaring
~~and granting pardons for treason~~
war$_\wedge$ No treaty shall be made without their advice and consent;
~~nor~~ shall also be necessary to the appointment of all officers, except $^{which}$
such for which a different provision$_\wedge$~~shall be~~ made, in this con- $^{is}$
stitution.

5. The material beginning "shall be sufficient" through the rest of this paragraph is inserted in the margin.

ARTICLE IV

§ 1   The President of the United States of America shall‸be elected
(except in the first instance)

in manner following—

The judges of the Supreme Court shall within sixty days after

a vacancy shall happen, cause public notice to be given in each state

of such vacancy appointing therein three several days for the

‸purposes following to wit—a day for commencing the election of
several

electors for the purposes hereinafter ~~described~~ specified‸~~with~~ which
to be called the first electors

day shall be not less than forty *xxx* nor more than sixty days *xx*

after the ~~time~~‸of the publication of the notice in each state—another
day

day‸not less than ~~thirty~~ nor more than ninety days from the day
r the meeting of the electors    forty

for commencing their election—another day for the meeting of

electors, to be chosen by the first electors, for the purpose hereinafter

specified, and to be called the second electors, which day shall be

not less than forty *xx* ~~days~~ nor more than sixty days after the day

for the meeting of the first electors.

§ 2   After notice of a vacancy shall have been given there shall be

chosen in each state a number of persons, as the first electors in the

preceding section mentioned, equal to the whole number of the

representatives and senators of such state in the legislature of the

United States; which electors shall be chosen by the citizens of such

state having an estate of inheritance or for three lives in land, or

a clear personal estate of the value of ~~five hundred~~ one thousand

spanish milled dollars of the present standard.

in their respective states
§ 3 These first electors shall meet∧at the time appointed, at one place, and shall proceed to vote by ballot for a President who shall not be one of their own number, unless the legislature upon experi-
two
ment should hereafter ⟨di⟩rect otherwise.[6] They shall cause ~~a~~ lists to be made of the name or names of the person or persons voted for,
or the major part of them each
which they∧shall sign and certify. They shall ~~also~~ then proceed∧to
the
nominate ~~individually and~~ openly in the presence of ~~each~~ others two persons as for second electors and out of the persons who shall have the four highest numbers of nominations they shall afterwards by ballot by plurality of votes choose two who shall be the second electors, to each of whom shall be delivered one of the lists beforementioned. These second electors shall not be any of the persons
signed and certified in like manner
voted for as President.[7] A copy of the same list∧shall be transmitted by the first electors to the seat of the government of the United States under a sealed cover directed to the President of the Assembly, which after the meeting of the second electors shall be opened for the Inspection of the two houses of the legislature.

precisely on day (and not on another day)
§ 4 These second electors shall meet∧~~at~~ the ~~time~~ appointed∧at one place.[8] The Chief Justice of the Supreme Court, or if there be no chief Justice, the judge senior in office in such Court, or if there be no one judge senior in office, some other judge of that court by

6. The material beginning "who shall no" through "otherwise" is inserted in the margin. The insertion is preceded by the letter "A."
7. This sentence is inserted in the margin.
8. There is an indecipherable, crossed-out insertion in the margin.

the choice of the rest of the Judges or of a majority of them, shall

attend at the same place and shall preside at the meeting but shall

have no vote. Two thirds of the whole number of the electors shall

constitute a
be sufficient ~~to execute their~~ meeting for the execution of their

trust. At this meeting the lists delivered to the respective electors

shall be produced and inspected, and if there be any person who has

a majority of the whole number of the votes given by the first

electors, he shall be the President of the United States; but if there

be no such person, the second electors so met shall proceed to vote,

one      ~~a President out of~~
by ballot, for such of the *persons*, named in the lists, *who* shall have

the three highest numbers of the votes of the first electors; and if

on the day of this meeting
upon the first or any succeeding ballot, ~~thereof~~ either of those per-

sons shall ~~a~~ have a ~~majority~~ number of votes equal to a majority

of the whole number of second electors chosen, he shall be the

President. But if no such choice be made on the day appointed for

the meeting either by reason of the non attendance of the second

electors or their not agreeing or any other matter the person having

the greatest number of votes of the first electors shall be the President.

§ 5   If it should happen that the Chief Justice or some other judge

of the Supreme Court should not attend in due time, the second

electors shall proceed to the execution of their trust without him.

§ 6   If the judges should neglect to cause the notice required by

the first section of this article to be given within the time therein

limited, they may nevertheless cause it to be afterwards given; but

their neglect, if wilful, is hereby declared to be an offence for which they may be impeached and if convicted<sub>∧</sub><sup>they</sup> shall be punished as in other cases of<sub>∧</sub><sup>conviction on</sup> impeachment.

§ 7   The Legislature shall by permanent laws provide such further regulations as may be necessary for the more orderly election of the President ei not contravening the provisions herein contained.

§ 8   The President before he shall enter upon the execution of his office shall take an oath or affirmation faithfully to execute his office, <sup>the same</sup> and to the utmost of his judgment and power to protect the rights of the people and preserve the constitution inviolate, unless altered in the mode specified in the. This oath or affirmation shall be administered by the President of the Senate for the time being in the presence of both houses of the legislature.

§ 9.   The two houses of the Legislature <sup>Senate and the Assembly</sup> shall always assemble, <sup>convene in session</sup> on the day appointed for the meeting of the second electors and shall continue sitting till a the President be sworn into off take the oath or affirmation of office. He shall hold his office during good behaviour removeable only by conviction by <sup>upon</sup> an impeachment for some crime or misdemeanor.[9]

§ 10   If the President depart out of the United States without the consent of the Senate and Assembly he shall thereby abdicate his office.

§ 10   The President at the beginning of every meeting of the Legis-

9. The words "office" through "misdemeanor" are inserted in the margin. They are preceded by the letter "A."

lature as soon as they shall be ready to proceed to business shall convene them together at the place where the Senate shall sit and shall communicate to them all such matters as may be necessary for their information or as may require their consideration. He may by message during the session communicate all other matters which may appear to him proper. He may, whenever in his opinion the public business shall require it convene the Senate and Assembly or either of them and may prorogue them for a time not exceeding forty days at one prorogation; and if they should disagree about their adjournmt. he may adjourn them to such time as he shall think

proper.[10] He shall have a right to negative all bills‸or acts of the two
                                                      resolutions

of the Legislature
houses‸about to be passed into laws. He shall take care that the laws be faithfully executed. He shall be the commander in Chief of the

army and navy of the United States and of the Militia ~~of~~ the several
                                                      within

states and shall have the direction of war when commenced; but he shall not take the actual command in the field of an army, without the consent of the Senate and Assembly. All treaties conventions and agreements with foreign nations shall be made by him, by and with the advice and consent of the Senate. He shall have the appointment of the principal or chief officer of each of the departments of war naval affairs finan⟨ce⟩ and foreign affairs; and shall have the nomination, and, by and with the ~~advice~~ consent of the Senate, the appointment of all other officers to be appointed under the authority

10. This sentence is inserted in the margin.

except such for whom different provision is made by this constitution and [11]
of the United States; provided that this shall not be construed to

prevented the legislature from appointing, by name, in their laws,

persons to special and particular trusts created in such laws, nor

shall be construed to prevent principals in offices merely ministerial,

from constituting deputies. In the recess of the Senate he may fill

vacancies in offices by appointments to continue in force until the

and
end of the next session of the Senate He shall commission all

officers. He shall have power to pardon all offences except treason

ni    and Assembly
for which he may grant a reprieves until the opion of the Senate

can be had, and with their concurrence may pardon the same.[12]

§ 12 11 He shall receive a fixed compensation for his services to

be paid to him at stated times and not to be increased nor diminished

during his continuance in office.

§ 12 If he depart out out of the United States without the consent

of the Senate and Assembly, He shall thereby abdicate his office.

§ 13 He may be impeached for any crime or misdemeanor by the

two houses of the legislature, two thirds of each house concurring,

and if convicted shall be removed from office. He may be afterwards

tried and punished in the ordinary course of law. His impeachment

shall operate as a suspension from office until the determination

thereof.[13]

§ 14 The President of the Senate shall be vice President of the

---

11. The words "constitution and" are inserted in the margin.

12. Beginning with the words "to pardon," the rest of this paragraph is inserted in the margin.

13. Beginning with the words "as a," the rest of this sentence is inserted in the margin.

United States. On the death, resignation<sub>∧</sub>removal from office<sub>∧</sub> or, <sup>impeachment</sup> absence from the United States, of the President thereof, The Vice President shall exercise all the powers by this constitution vested in the President until another shall be appointed or until he shall return within the United States if his absence was with the consent of the Senate and Assembly.

ARTICLE V

§ 1  There shall be a Chief Justice of the Supreme Court who together with the other judges thereof shall hold their offices during good behaviour removeable only by conviction on impeachment for some crime or misdemeanor. Each judge shall have a competent salary to be paid to him at stated times and ~~to~~ not to be diminished during his continuance in office.

The Supreme Court shall have original jurisdiction in all causes, in which the United States shall be a party, ~~except touching a claim and~~ in all controversies between the United States and a particular state or [14] between two or more states, except, ~~in either case,~~ such as relate <sup>to</sup> a claim of territory between the United States and one or more states, ~~or between two or more states~~ which shall be determined in the mode prescribed in the VI Article, in all cases affecting foreign ministers consuls and Agents; and an appellate jurisdiction ~~in all~~ both as to law and fact in all cases which shall concern the citizens of foreign nations and in all questions between the citizens of different states ~~su~~ and in all others in which the fundamental rights of

14. The words "between the United States and a particular State or" are inserted in the margin.

this constitution are involved, subject to such exceptions ⟨as⟩ are

herein contained and to such regulations∧as the Legislature shall

~~and restrictions~~

provide.

The judges of all Courts which may be constituted by the Legis-

lature shall∧hold their places during good behaviour removeable

*also*

only∧~~on~~ conviction on impeachment for some crime or ~~offence;~~

*by* . misdemeanor

and shall have competent salaries to be paid at stated times and not

to be diminished during their continuance in office; but nothing

herein contained shall be construed to prevent the legislature from

abolishing such [15] ~~the~~ Courts themselves.

All crimes, except upon impeachment shall be tried by a jury of

twelve men and if they ~~ha~~ shall have been committed within any

state, shall be tried within such state and all civil causes arising under

this constitution of the like kind with those which have been hereto-

fore triable by jury in the respective states [16] ~~except those between~~

~~the United States and one or more states or between different states~~

shall∧be tried by jury ~~in the~~ unless in special cases the Legislature

*in like manner*

shall think proper to make different provision to which provision

the concurrence of two thirds of both houses shall be necessary.

§ Impeachments of the President∧of the *U S*∧the Governors and

*and V. Pres:* *members of the Senate*

Presidents of the several States the principal or chief officers of the

departments enumerated in the 10 § of the 4th article ambassadors

15. The word "such" is inserted in the margin.
16. The part of this sentence beginning with the words "of the like kind" and ending with the word "states" was inserted in the margin.

and other like public ministers, the judges of the Supreme Court, generals and admirals of the navy shall be tried by a Court to consist of the Judges of the Supreme Court and the Chief Justice or first or senior judge of the superior court of law in each state of whom twelve shall constitute a Court. A majority of the Judges present may convict. All other persons shall be tried on impeachment, ~~by~~ the by a court to consist of the judges of Supreme Court ~~provided that it shall require the assent of six judges~~ and six senators drawn by lot; a majority of whom may ~~to~~ convict.

Impeachments shall clearly specify the particular offence for which the party accused is to be tried and judgment on conviction upon the trial thereof shall be either, of removal from office singly or removal from office and disqualification for holding any future office or place of trust, but no judgment on impeachment shall prevent prosecution and punishment in the ordinary course of law, provided that no judge concerned in such conviction shall sit, as Judge on the second trial. The Legislature may ~~except~~ remove the disabilities incurred by ~~an~~ conviction on impeachment.

ARTICLE VI

Trial of Territorial claims [17] All Controversies about the right of territory between the United States and, ~~one or more~~ particular states shall be ~~constituted in~~ determined by a Court to be constituted in manner following.[18] The state or states claiming in opposition to the United

17. The words "Trial of Territorial claims" were inserted in the margin.
18. In the margin opposite this sentence H wrote and crossed out "general idea takes in the plan in the Confederation."

States as parties shall nominate a number of persons, equal to double
the number of the Judges of the Supreme Court for the time being,
of whom none shall be citizens<sub>∧</sub>of the states which are parties nor
~~actual~~ inhabitants thereof when nominated and of whom not more
than two shall have their actual residence is one state. Out of the
persons so nominated the senate shall elect one half who together
with the Judges of the Supreme Court ~~and majority~~ of the whole
number ~~present shall decide the Controversy~~ may hear and determine the controversy, ⟨-⟩ [19] by plurality of voices. The states
concerned may at their option claim ~~claim~~ a decision by the Supreme
Court only. All the members of the Court hereby instituted shall
prior to the hearing of the cause take an oath impartially and according to the best of their judgments and consciences to hear and
determine the controversy.[20]

by birth ~~by treaty~~

shall form the Court. Two thirds

### ARTICLE VII

§ 1 The legislature of the United States shall have power to pass
all laws which they shall judge necessary to the common defence
and safety and to the general welfare of the Union: But no bill
resolution or act of the Senate and Assembly shall have the force
of a law until it shall have received the assent of the President or of
the vice president when exercising the powers of the President; ~~for~~
~~which purpose~~ and if such assent shall not have been given within
ten days after such bill ~~shall~~ resolution or other act shall have been

---

19. H at this point wrote and crossed out a word which is indecipherable.
20. Following this paragraph on the MS there is a section on the compensation of the legislature. Opposite this section H wrote "Section the 8 of Article
7." It has been, accordingly, transposed.

presented for that purpose the same shall not be a law. No bill resolution or other act not assented to shall be revived in the same session of the legislature. The mode of [21] signifying such assent shall be by signing the bill act or resolution and returning it to the house through (-) [22] which it last passed of the legislature.

§ 2   The enacting stile of all laws shall be "Be it enacted by the People of the United States of America."

§ 3   No bill of attainder shall be passed, nor any ex post facto law; nor shall any title of nobility by granted by the United States or by either of them; nor shall any person holding an office or place of trust under the United States without the permission of the legislature accept any present, emolument, office, or title from a foreign prince or state. Nor shall any religious sect or denomination, or religious test for any office or place, be ever established by law.[23]

§ 4   Taxes on lands houses and other real estate and capitation taxes shall be proportioned in each state by the whole number of free persons (except indians not taxed) and by three fifths of all other persons.[24]

§ 5   The two houses of the Legislature may by joint ballot appoint a Treasurer of the United States. Neither house (in the session of both houses) without the consent of the other shall adjourn for more than three days at a time. The place of meeting shall always be at the seat of government which

21. At this point, which is at the bottom of a page of the MS, H wrote: "Vide A above."
22. This word is indecipherable.
23. Beginning with the word "religious," the rest of this sentence is inserted in the margin.
24. This paragraph is inserted in the margin.

shall be fixed by law. The Senators and representatives in attending<sub>∧</sub>
going to and coming from
the session of their respective houses shall be privileged from arrest
except for crimes and breaches of the peace.[25]

§ 6    The laws of the United States and the treaties which have been
made under the articles of confederation and<sub>∧</sub>shall be made under
which
this constitution shall be the supreme law of the land and shall be so
construed by the Courts of the several states. ~~Any thing to the contrary notwithstanding.~~

§ 7    The Legislature shall convene at least once in each year ~~s~~ which
unless otherwise provided for by law shall be the first monday in
December.[26]

§ 8    The<sub>∧</sub>two houses of the Legislature shall receive a reasonable
members of the
compensation for their services to be paid out of the treasury of the
United States and ascertained by law. ~~The first D~~ The law for making
such provision shall ~~except in the first instance~~ be passed with the
concurrence of the first assembly and shall extend to succeeding
assemblies; and no succeeding assembly shall concur in an alteration
of such provision so as to increase its own compensation; but there
shall<sub>∧</sub>always a law in existence for making such provision.
be

ARTICLE VIII THE GOVER

§ 1    The Governor or President of each state shall be appointed
under the authority of the United States and shall have a right to
negative all laws about to be passed in the state of which he shall

25. This paragraph is inserted in the margin.
26. The words "Vide 8 Page 14" are inserted at the bottom of this paragraph.
See note 18.

be Governor or President subject to such qualifications and regulations as the Legislature of the United States shall prescribe. He shall
in other respects have the same powers only which the constitution
of the state does or shall allow to t its governor or President except
as to the appointment of Officers of the Militia.

§ 2  Each governor or President of a state shall hold his office until
a successor be actually appointed, unless he die or resign or be removed from office by conviction on impeachment. There shall be no
appointment of such governor or President in the recess of the
Senate.

The Governors and Presidents of the several states at the time of
the ratification of this constitution shall continue in office in the
same manner and with the same powers as if they had been appointed
pursuant to the first section of this article.

The officers of the Militia in the several states may be appointed

⟨-⟩ 27
under the authority of the U: S; The Legislature ~~thereof~~ may authorise the Governors or Presidents of states to make such appointments with such restrictions as they shall think proper.

ARTICLE THE IX

§ 1  No person shall be eligible to the office of President of the
United States unless he be now a citizen of one of the states or hereafter be born a ~~free~~ citizen of the United States.

§ 2  No person shall be eligible as a senator or Representative unless
at the time of his election he be a citizen and inhabitant of the state

27. Above the word "thereof" H wrote and then crossed out a word which
is indecipherable.

in which he is chosen; provided that he shall not be deemed to be disqualified by a temporary absence from the state.

§ 3 No person intitled by this constitution to elect or to be elected President of the United States, or a senator or representative in the legislature thereof shall be disqualified but by the conviction of some offence for which the law shall have previously ordained the punishment of disqualification. But the Legislature may by law ~~powers~~ provide that persons holding offices under the United States or either

to a place
of them shall not be eligible in the Assembly or Senate and shall be during their continuance in office suspended from sitting in the senate.[28]

§ 4 No person having an office or place of trust under the United States shall without permission of the Legislature accept any present emolument office or title from any foreign prince or state.

§ 5 The Citizens of each state shall be intitled to the rights privileges and immunities of citizens in every other state; and full faith and credit shall be given in each state to the public acts, records, and judicial proceedings of another.

§ 6 Fugitives from justice from one state who shall be found in another shall be delivered up⟨on⟩ the application of the state from which they fled.

§ 7 No new state shall be erected within the limits of another or by the junction of two or more states without the concurrent consent of the legislatures of the United States and of the states con-

28. Beginning with the words "may by law," the rest of this paragraph is inserted in the margin.

cerned. The Legislature of the United States may admit new states into the Union.

§ 8 The United States are hereby declared to be bound to guarantee to each state a republican form of government and to protect each state as well against domestic violence as foreign invasion.

§ 9 All treaties contracts and engagements of the United States of America under the articles of Confederation and perpetual Union shall have equal validity under this constitution.

§ 10 No state shall enter into a treaty alliance contract with another not or with a foreign power without the consent of the United States.[29]

§ 11 The members of the Legislature of the United States and of each state and all officers executive and judicial of the one and of the other shall take an office or affirmation to support the constitution of the United States.

§ 12 This constitution may received such alterations and amendments as may be proposed by the Legislature of the United States with the concurrence of two thirds of the members of both houses and ratified by the legislatures of, or by conventions of deputies chosen by the people in, two thirds of the states composing the Union.

ARTICLE X

§ This constitution shall be submitted to the consideration of Conventions in the several states w- the members whereof shall be

29. This paragraph is inserted in the margin, followed by the deleted words "§11. The two houses of the."

chosen ~~of~~ by the People of such states respectively under the direction of ~~the state~~ their respective legislatures. Each Convention which shall ratify the same shall appoint the first ~~members of Assemb~~ representatives and senators from such state according to the rule prescribed in the § of the Article. The representatives so appointed shall continue in office for one year only. ~~When~~ Each convention so ratifying shall give notice thereof to the Congress of the United States ~~to~~ transmitting at the same time a list of the representatives and senators chosen. When the constitution shall have been duly ratified Congress shall give notice of a day and place for the mee⟨ting⟩ of the Senators and representatives from the severall states; and when these or a majority of them shall have assembled according to such notice they shall by join ballot by plurality of votes elect ~~choose~~ a President of the United States; and the Constitution thus organized shall be carried into effect.[30]

30. The following list appears on a page following the last page of H's "Draft of a Constitution":

~~proxy~~                          ~~Qualifications of persons to be elected~~
~~Inferior tribunals~~             ~~prevent two Quorums~~
courts their own clerks           ~~Electors not to elect out of their own body~~
~~quorum of senate & Assembly~~    ~~No religious establishment~~
~~Court of Impeachment~~           ~~Treasurer~~
                                  ~~Oath of State officers~~

## Constitution of the United States [1]

*Philadelphia, September 17, 1787.* Not only was Hamilton one of the signers of this document but the names of the states listed before the names of the signers are also in Hamilton's writing.

1. D, on display at the National Archives.

## Conjectures about the New Constitution [1]

[September 17–30, 1787] [2]

The new constitution has in favour of its success these circumstances—a very great weight of influence of the persons who framed it, particularly in the universal popularity of General Washington—the good will of the commercial interest throughout the states which will give all its efforts to the establishment of a government capable of regulating protecting and extending the commerce of the Union—the good will of most men of property in the several states who wish a government of the union able to protect them against domestic violence and the depredations which the democratic spirit is apt to make on property; and who are besides anxious for the respectability of the nation—the hopes of the Creditors of the United States that a general government possessing the means of doing it will pay the debt of the Union—a strong belief in the people at large of the insufficiency of the present confederation to preserve the existence of the Union and of the necessity of the union to their safety and prosperity; of course a strong desire of a change and a predisposition to receive well the propositions of the Convention.

Against its success is to be put the dissent of two or three important men in the Convention; who will think their characters pleged to defeat the plan—the influence of many *inconsiderable* men in possession of considerable offices under the state governments who will fear a diminution of their consequence, power and emolument by the establishment of the general government and who can hope for nothing there—the influence of some *considerable* men in office possessed of talents and popularity who partly from the same motives and partly from a desire of *playing a part* in a convulsion for their own aggrandisement will oppose the quiet adoption of the new government—(some considerable men out of office, from motives of ⟨am⟩bition may be disposed to act the same part)—add ⟨to⟩ these causes the disinclination of the people to taxes, and of course to a strong government—the opposition of all men much in debt who will not wish to see a government established one object of which is to restrain the means of cheating Creditors—the democratical jealousy of the people which may be alarmed at the appearance of institutions that may seem calculated to place the power of the community in few hands and to raise a few individuals to stations of great preeminence—and the influence of some foreign powers who from different motives will not wish to see an energetic government established throughout the states.

In this view of the subject it is difficult to form any judgment whether the plan will be adopted or rejected. It must be essentially [a] matter of conjecture. The present appearances and all other circumstances considered the probability seems to be on the side of its adoption.

But the causes operating against its adoption are powerful and there will be nothing astonishing in the Contrary.

If it do not finally obtain, it is probable the discussion of the question will beget such struggles animosities and heats in the community that this circumstance conspiring with the *real necessity* of an essential change in our present situation will produce civil war. Should this happen, whatever parties prevail it is probable governments very different from the present in their principles will be established. A dismemberment of the Union and monarchies in different portions of it may be expected. It may however happen that no civil war will take place; but several republican confederacies be established between different combinations of the particular states.

A reunion with Great Britain, from universal disgust at a state of commotion, is not impossible, though not much to be feared. The most plausible shape of such a business would be the establishment of a son of the present monarch in the supreme government of this country with a family compact.

If the government be adopted, it is probable general Washington will be the President of the United States. This will insure a wise choice of men to administer the government and a good administration. A good administration will conciliate the confidence and affection of the people and perhaps enable the government to acquire more consistency than the proposed constitution seems to promise for so great a Country. It may then triumph altogether over the state governments and reduce them to an intire subordination, dividing the larger states into smaller districts. The *organs* of the general government may also acquire additional strength.

If this should not be the case, in the course of a few years, it is probable that the contests about the boundaries of power between the particular governments and the general government and the *momentum* of the larger states in such contests will produce a dissolution of the Union. This after all seems to be the most likely result.

But it is almost arrogance in so complicated a subject, depending so intirely on the incalculable fluctuations of the human passions, to attempt even a conjecture about the event.

It will be Eight or Nine months before any certain judgment can be formed respecting the adoption of the Plan.

ADf, Hamilton Papers, Library of Congress.
1. The purpose for which this essay was written cannot be determined. The MS is endorsed in H's writing "Conjectures about the New Constitution." It has not been found in the newspapers and is not incorporated in any extant letter which H wrote about the new Constitution. It may have been an article which he intended to send to the newspapers but which he may have put aside after beginning work on *The Federalist* papers.
2. It is not possible to determine the date of H's "Conjectures about the New Constitution." J. C. Hamilton (Hamilton, *History*, III, 356) states that "observations of Hamilton, written just as the general convention adjourned, give his impressions at that time." It probably was written during the last two weeks of September.

## To William Neilson [1]

[*New York*] *September 21, 1787.* "You will recollect the cause of *Hayton* against *van Kleeck* put into my hands by you. . . . I hope it will not be inconvenient to you [to] take care of my Costs."

ALS, Historical Society of Pennsylvania, Philadelphia.
1. Neilson was an alderman and merchant of New York City.

## From Ezekiel Forman

*Philadelphia, September 24, 1787.* ". . . I wish to know if the process against Mr. Livingston was served and return made to the . . . July Term and if any thing more is wanted for the effectual prosecution of that suit. Please to look over the papers I left, and judge, if the accts. stated by the sheriff, and the writing thereon be not sufficient to empower me to carry on a suit. . . ."

ALS, Hamilton Papers, Library of Congress.

## *From Samuel Brailsford* [1]

*Charleston, South Carolina, September 25, 1787.* "Mr Mullett [2] lately transmited me Copy of your Letter to him of the 22d July,[3] together with his answer, which I approve, tho' he was mistaken in saying that the terms on which Wooldridge [4] has been liberated, were all that I required; as there was another matter of great importance that I wished to accomplish previous to that event, & on which I have ℔ this conveyance wrote Mr Mullett fully, & requested of him to endeavour to obtain it, & if W. should in consequence of his being at large refuse to comply with what he repeatedly proposed to me at the different interviews I had with him in Gaol, & which Mr. M. will explain to you, I must beg Sir, that you will give him your assistance. . . . Mr Mullett . . . informed me that you had mentioned to him your having wrote me several times. . . ." [5]

ALS, Hamilton Papers, Library of Congress.
1. Brailsford, a member of a prominent Charleston merchant family and a former partner of John Chapman, had employed H to represent him.
2. Thomas Mullett.
3. Brailsford was mistaken about the date. See H to Mullett, Mullett to H, July 23, 1787.
4. Thomas Woolridge.
5. Letters not found.

## *[Ceasar No. 1]* [1]

[New York, September 28, 1787]

The [New York] *Daily Advertiser*, October 1, 1787.
1. The only evidence for the assumption that H wrote the "Caesar" letters in reply to the letters of "Cato," presumably written by George Clinton, is a letter printed by Paul Leicester Ford (*Essays on the Constitution of the United States* [Brooklyn, New York, 1892], 245). Ford states that this letter is in the George Clinton Papers, New York State Library, Albany. A careful search of these papers has not produced this letter. The letter, according to Ford, is in the writing of John Lamb. It reads as follows:

October 18, 1787.
Dear Sir:
Since my last the chief of the state party has declared his opposition to the government proposed, both in private conversation and in print. That you may judge of the *reason* and *fairness* of his views, I send you the two essays, with a reply by Caesar. On further consideration it was concluded to abandon this personal form, and to take up the principles of the whole subject. These will be

sent you as published, and might with advantage be republished in your gazettes.

A. HAMILTON

The authenticity of this letter cannot, in the absence of further evidence, be established. Since there is convincing evidence that H did not write the "Caesar" letters, they have not been printed. (The second "Caesar" letter is dated October 15, 1787.) For a full discussion on the authorship of the "Caesar" letters, see Jacob E. Cooke, "Alexander Hamilton's Authorship of the 'Caesar' Letters," *The William and Mary Quarterly*, XVII (January, 1960), 78–85.

## From Angelica Church [1]

[London, October 2, 1787]

You had every right my dear brother to believe that I was very inattentive not to have answered your letter; [2] but I could not relinquish the hopes that you would be tempted to ask the reason of my Silence, which would be a certain means of obtaining the second letter when perhaps had I answered the first, I should have lost all the fine things contained in the Latter. Indeed my dear, Sir if my path was strewed with as many roses, as you have filled your letter with compliments, I should not now lament my absence from *America:* but even Hope is weary of doing any thing for so assiduous a votary as myself. I have so often prayed at her shrine that I am now no longer heard. Church's head is full of Politicks, he is so desirous of making once in the British house of Commons,[3] and where I should be happy to see him if he possessed your Eloquence. All the graces you have been pleased to adorn me with, fade before the generous and benevolent action of My Sister in taking the orphan Antle under her protection.[4]

I do not write by this packet to either of my sisters, nor to my father. It is too Meloncholy an employment to day, as church is not here to be my consolation: he is gone to New Market. You will please to say to them for me every thing you think that the most tender and affectionate attachment can dictate. Adieu, my dear brother! be persuaded that these sentiments are not weakened when assiged to you and that I am very sincerely your friend.

*AC*

Town Place [5] Oct: 2, 1787

Is Kitty Livingston [6] Married?

ALS, Hamilton Papers, Library of Congress.

1. Angelica Schuyler Church, H's sister-in-law, had lived in England since 1782.

2. Letter not found.

3. At the next parliamentary election, which was held in 1790, John B. Church was elected to the House of Commons from Wendover Borough.

4. J. C. Hamilton states that

"Colonel [Edward] Antil of the Canadian Corps, a friend of General [Moses] Hazen, retired penniless from the service—his military claims, a sole dependence, being unsatisfied. Hoping to derive subsistence from the culture of a small clearing in the forest, he retired to the wilds of Hazenburgh. His hopes were baffled, and in his distress he applied to Hamilton for relief. His calamities were soon after embittered by the loss of his wife, leaving infant children. With one of these Antil visited New York, to solicit the aid of the Cincinnati, and there sank under the weight of his sorrows. Hamilton immediately took the little orphan home, who was nurtured with his own children and became the wife of a prosperous merchant [Arthur Tappan]." (Hamilton, *History*, III, 361.)

5. "Town Place" presumably referred to the Church's town house, the "Albany," on Sackville Street, Piccadilly, London.

6. Catharine Livingston, daughter of William Livingston, governor of New Jersey.

# To George Washington

[October 11–15, 1787][1]

D Sir,

You probably saw some time since some animadversions on certain expressions of Governor Clinton respecting the Convention. You may have seen a piece signed a Republican, attempting to bring the fact into question and endeavouring to controvert the conclusions drawn from it, if true. My answer you will find in the inclosed.[2] I trouble you with it merely from that anxiety which is natural to every man to have his veracity at least stand in a fair light. The matter seems to be given up by the Governor and the fact with the inferences from it stand against him in full force, and operate as they ought to do.

It is however, of some importance to the party to diminish whatever credit or influence I may possess; and to effect this they stick at nothing. Among many contemptible artifices practiced by them, they have had recourse to an insinuation that I *palmed* myself upon you and that you *dismissed* me from your family.[3] This I confess hurts my feelings, and if it obtains credit, will require a contradiction.

You Sir will undoubtedly recollect the manner in which I came into your family and went out of it; and know how destitute of foundation such insinuations are. My confidence in your justice will not permit me to doubt your readiness to put the matter in its true light in your answer to this letter. It cannot be my wish to give any complexion to the affair which might excite the least scruple in you; but I confess it would mortify me to be under the imputation either of having obtruded myself into the family of a General or of having been turned out of it.

The New Constitution is as popular in this City as it is possible for any thing to be—and the prospect thus far is favourable to it throughout the state. But there is no saying what turn things may take when the full flood of official influence is let loose against it. This is to be expected, for though the Governor has not publicly declared himself his particular connections and confidential friends are loud against it.

I remain with perfect esteem   Yr. Excellency's obed ser

A Hamilton

Mrs Hamilton joins in respectful compliments to Mrs. Washington

General Washington

ADfS, Hamilton Papers, Library of Congress; LS, George Washington Papers, Library of Congress.

1. This letter is undated. If it is assumed that from three to seven days were required for a letter to go from New York to Mount Vernon, H must have written this letter between October 11 and October 15. Washington replied on October 18 that H's letter "came to my hand by the last Post."

2. The "animadversions on certain expressions of Governor Clinton" was written by H and published in The [New York] Daily Advertiser, July 21, 1787 (see H to The Daily Advertiser, July 21, 1787). The "piece signed a Republican," which was written in defence of Clinton, was published in The New-York Journal, September 6, 1787. H's answer, a copy of which he enclosed to Washington, had been published in The Daily Advertiser of September 15, 1787 (see H to The Daily Advertiser, September 15, 1787).

3. The accusation to which H is referring was made by "Inspector" in The New-York Journal, September 20, 1787. It reads as follows:

"I have also known an upstart attorney, palm himself upon a great and good man, for a youth of extraordinary genius, and under the shadow of such a patronage, make himself at once known and respected; but being sifted and bolted to the brann, he was at length found to be a superficial, self-conceited coxcomb, and was of course turned off, and disregarded by his patron."

## *From Marquis de Lafayette*

Paris October the 15th 1787

My dear Hamilton

While you Have Been Attending your Most Important Convention, debates were also Going on in france Respecting the Constitutional Rights, and Matters of that kind. Great Reforms are taking place at Court. The Parliaments are Remonstrating,[1] and our provincial Assemblies Begin to pop out.[2] Amidst Many things that were not Much to the purpose, some Good principles Have Been laid out, and altho our Affairs have a proper Arrangement, the Nation will not in the last Be the looser. The prime Minister is a Man of Candour, Honesty, and Abilities.[3] But Now the Rumour of War has us a Going. Not that france is Wishing for it, and great Britain ought to be Satisfied With an Advantageous treaty of Commerce, and the profit of Hers, and Prussia's treachery in Holland.[4] But while I consider the Madness of the Turks,[5] the Movements of the Imperial Courts,[6] the folly of His prussian Majesty, the late Catastrophe in Holland, and the Cry of England for war,[7] I Hardly think that the peacefull dispositions of this Ministry, and they say [of] Mr Pitt, will Be able to Extinguish a fire that is Catching at Every Comit of Europe.

It would Be Consistent with My Inclination and *self* views that America Be engaged in an Active Cooperation. But as I Do not think it Consistent with Her interest, I have taken the liberty to Express My ideas in an official letter to Mr jay to whom I refer you. It seems to me that a friendly, Helping Neutrality would Be Useful to france, profitable to the United States, and perfectly safe on the footing of the treaties. Should America Be forced to War, I wish it would Be But for the last Campaign, time enough to Occupy Canada and Newfoundland. But I see no inconvenience in privateering with french letters of Marque.

Inclosed is the journal of a preliminary Assembly in Auvergne. I am returning there as soon as we Have done some Arrangements Respecting American Commerce which will put it on as Good footing in this Kingdom as it is for the Moment possible—the Ministry are Most favourably disposed.

I Hope You will be satisfied with Count de Moustier,[8] and the Countess de Brehan [9] His Sister in law. I Beg leave to introduce Both to You and Mrs Hamilton to whom I offer My Most affectionate Respects. Remember me to the Rest of the family and all friends. My Best Compliments wait on genl Schuyller and the doctor.[10] Adieu, My good friend, the post is going to Brest. I have only time to tell you that I am for Ever

Your Most affectionate friend                              Lafayette

There goes a young gentleman in the frigate Named Mr dupont—a son to a man of much merit, who is emploied By Administration in our Commercial Arrangements.[11] I Recommend Him to your Acquaintance and patronage.

Tell Colonel Lee [12] that I depend on you to introduce the passengers to Him and that I shall write fully to Him By the November packet that sails in a fortnight—pray don't forget it.

The journals they say will go By post. I shall send them By the packet.

ALS, Hamilton Papers, Library of Congress.
   1. In February, 1787, the King of France had summoned the Assembly of Notables to approve proposed administrative and fiscal reforms. The Assembly refused to cooperate, and it was dismissed on May 25, 1787. Etienne Charles de Loménie de Brienne, Archbishop of Toulouse and Controller-General of Finances, attempted to have various fiscal measures approved by the Parlement of Paris, a measure which was made necessary by the ancient practice of having all royal declarations inscribed on the register of the appropriate parlement. The Parlement of Paris, however, refused to register some of the tax measures proposed by the King, and in August it was exiled to Troyes. Remonstrances followed against the proposed measures of the King, not only from the exiled Parlement of Paris, but from the parlements of Rennes, Rouen, Bordeaux, Pau, Toulouse, Grenoble, and Besançon. The Parlement of Paris was recalled on September 24, but continued its resistance when Brienne proposed new loans.
   2. Lafayette presumably is referring to the organization of provincial assemblies, the formation of which had been provided for by an edict of June, 1787.
   3. Brienne became Prime Minister on August 28, 1787.
   4. In 1787, William V, the Stadholder, called in Prussian troops to restore his authority in the Netherlands. The Prussian army, with the English fleet standing guard to safeguard the victory, routed the rebels and restored the House of Orange. "The rumor of war" to which Lafayette is referring did not materialize, for on October 23, 1787, France renounced all intentions of giving aid to the Dutch.
   5. In August, 1787, the Turks, after the rejection of their ultimatum for the restitution of the Crimea and the end of Russian control in Georgia, had declared war on Russia.
   6. In the early summer of 1787, Catherine, Empress of Russia, and Joseph II, Emperor of the Holy Roman Empire, had concluded a tour of the Balkans.

7. See note 4.

8. Eléanor François Elie, Marquis de Moustier, recently had been appointed French Minister to the United States.

9. The Marquise de Bréhan accompanied Moustier to the United States.

10. Philip Schuyler and Dr. John Cochran.

11. Victor Marie du Pont, son of the famous physiocrat Pierre Samuel du Pont de Nemours, came to the United States as an attaché to the French legation.

12. Henry Lee.

## [Ceasar No. II] [1]

[New York, October 15, 1787]

The [New York] Daily Advertiser, October 15, 1787.

1. For a discussion of the arguments for and against H's authorship of the "Caesar" letters, see "Caesar No. I," September 28, 1787. The second "Caesar" letter was written in reply to "Cato II" which was published in The New-York Journal, and Daily Patriotic Register, October 11, 1787.

## From George Washington

Mount Vernon Octr. 18th. 1787.

Dear Sir;

Your favor without date came to my hand by the last Post.[1] It is with unfeigned concern I perceive that a political dispute has arisen between Governor Clinton and yourself.[2] For both of you I have the highest esteem and regard. But as you say it is insinuated by some of your political adversaries, and may obtain credit, "that you *palmed* yourself upon me, and was *dismissed* from my family;" and call upon me to do you justice by a recital of the fact. I do therefore, explicitly declare, that both charges are entirely unfounded. With respect to the first, I have no cause to believe that you took a single step to accomplish, or had the most distant ⟨idea⟩ [3] of receiving, an appointment in my ⟨fam⟩ily 'till you were envited thereto. And ⟨with⟩ respect to the second, that your quitting ⟨it was⟩ altogether the effect of your own ⟨choice⟩.

When the situation of this country ⟨calls⟩ loudly for unanimity & vigor, it is to be lamented that Gentlemen of talents and character should disagree in their sentiments for promoting the public weal; but unfortunately, this ever has been, and more than probable, ever will be the case, in the affairs of man.

Having scarcely been from home since my return from Philadelphia, I can give but little information with respect to the *general*
reception of the New Constitution in *this* State. In Alexandria however, and some of the adjacent Counties, it has been embraced with
an enthusiastic warmth of which I had no conception. I expect notwithstanding, violent opposition will be given to it by *some* characters of weight & influence, in the State.

Mrs. Washington unites with me in best wishes for Mrs. Hamilton
and yourself.

I am—Dear Sir   Yr. most obedt. & affecte. Hble. servt.

Go: Washington

Alexr. Hamilton Esqr.

ALS, Hamilton Papers, Library of Congress, LC, George Washington Papers,
Library of Congress.
    1. See H to Washington, October 11–15, 1787.
    2. For the newspaper controversy between H and Governor George Clinton,
see H to Washington, October 11–15, 1787.
    3. The words in broken brackets are taken from Washington's letter book.

## From Gaspard Joseph Amand Ducher [1]

Wilmington, 26. 8bre. 1787
Caroline du Nord

Monsieur

je suis arrivé ici apres bien des fatigues et des dangers; je me Repose et j'en ai grand Besoin.

Rappelles vous, je vous prie, que vous m'aves promis *Deux* pièces
Relatives à *La nouvelle constitution;* je les attends avec Le plus grand
empressement et je vous scaurai gré de me faire passer tous les *pam-
phlets* qui seront imprimés sur ce sujet.

mes Respects je vous prie à Madame hamilton.

jai l'honneur d'etre avec un Respectueux attachement   Monsieur
Votre tres humble et tres obeissant Serviteur                    Ducher

ALS, Hamilton Papers, Library of Congress.
    1. Ducher had come to America from France in 1784. In a letter to George
Washington of September 14, 1784, Lafayette had written that Ducher "came
with a good sum of monney which he intended to settle with in America—But
the greatest part, having been lost in a shipwrek he still more stands in need of
advice and patronage" (Gottschalk, *The Letters of Lafayette to Washington,*

285). Ducher was later appointed to the French consular service in the United States and in 1787 was stationed at Wilmington, North Carolina.

## Baron von Steuben to George Washington

[October 26, 1787]

Sir

I have lately made a fresh application to Congress for a final settlement of my affairs on the ground of a contract made with that honorable body previous to my joining the American army.[1] The particulars and the evidence of that contract are stated in a printed pamphlet[2] a copy of which Mr. Hamilton informs me he has transmitted to your Excellency. I have been just informed that Congress intend making some inquiry of Your Excellency respecting a matter which they suppose will throw light upon the subject.[3] I am glad of this reference, because though I doubt that it will be in your power to elucidate the question of the contract, I have entire confidence in your justice and favourable sentiments towards me as to any collateral point which may arise in the inquiry.

The truth is my situation is peculiarly grievous. The manner in which the compensations, I have received from the public have been dealt out to me, has been such as to prevent their having been of any use to me beyond a momentary supply. I trust I shall not be necessitated to abandon a country to which I am attached by the strongest ties to return to Europe destitute of resources with no consolation for my services but the right of complaining of the unkindness of those to whom they were rendered. Surely it cannot redound to the Credit of America to drive me to so painful an extremity. I am persuaded Your Excellencys feelings will not approve of my experiencing so ill-deserved a lot.

I have the honor to be   With the most perfect respect and esteem Yr. Excellencys   Most Obed & hum servant

Df, in writing of H, Historical Society of Pennsylvania, Philadelphia.
  1. For an explanation of Baron von Steuben's claims against the United States, see H to Washington, October 30, 1787. The Baron's claim again had been taken up by Congress on October 6, 1787.
  2. This undated, printed pamphlet is in the Papers of the Continental Congress, National Archives. See von Steuben to H, August–September, 1787.
  3. The "enquiry" is explained in Washington to H, November 10, 1787. Washington wrote:

"Application has been made to me by Mr. Secretary [Charles] Thompson (by order of Congress) for a copy of ye report, of a Committee, which was appointed to confer with the Baron de Steuben, on his first arrival in this Country; forwarded to me by Mr. President [Henry] Laurens."

The committee of Congress had been appointed in February, 1778, to confer with the Baron on the conditions under which he would serve in the Army. Von Steuben had given the committee his terms and had assumed that they had been accepted (Palmer, *Steuben*, 123–25). Laurens, President of the Continental Congress, on February 19, 1778, sent Washington a copy of the report of the committee which had been appointed to confer with the Baron. Laurens's letter is in Burnett, *Letters*, III, 91; the committee report which he enclosed is in the Papers of the Continental Congress, National Archives.

# The Federalist

## [New York, October 27, 1787–May 28, 1788]

### Introductory Note

*The Federalist* essays have been printed more frequently than any other work of Hamilton. They have, nevertheless, been reprinted in these volumes because no edition of his writings which omitted his most important contribution to political thought could be considered definitive. The essays written by John Jay and James Madison, however, have not been included. They are available in many editions, and they do not, after all, properly belong in the writings of Alexander Hamilton.

*The Federalist*, addressed to the "People of the State of New-York," was occasioned by the objections of many New Yorkers to the Constitution which had been proposed on September 17, 1787, by the Philadelphia Convention. During the last week in September and the first weeks of October, 1787, the pages of New York newspapers were filled with articles denouncing the Constitution.[1] The proposed government also had its defenders, but their articles were characterized by somewhat indignant attacks on those who dared oppose the Constitution rather than by reasoned explanations of the advantages of its provisions.[2]

The decision to publish a series of essays defending the Constitution and explaining in detail its provisions was made by Alexander Hamilton. Both the reasons for his decision and the date on which he conceived the project are conjecturable. Having gone to Albany early in October to attend the fall session of the Supreme Court, he was not in New York City during the early weeks of the controversy over the Constitution.[3] He must, nevertheless, have concluded

---

1. The most important of these was by "Cato," presumably George Clinton. The first "Cato" letter was published in *The New-York Journal, and Weekly Register* on September 27, 1787.

2. See, for example, the two articles by "Caesar" (September 28 and October 15, 1787), which erroneously have been attributed to H.

3. An anonymous newspaper article, signed "Aristides" and published in *The [New York] Daily Advertiser* on October 6, stated that H's absence from the city prevented him from defending himself against newspaper attacks. An entry in H's Cash Book dated November 4 (see "Cash Book," March 1, 1782–1791) indicates that he attended the October session of the Supreme Court in Albany.

that if it were to be adopted, convincing proof of its merits would have to be placed before the citizens of New York. His decision to write the essays may have been made before he left Albany, for according to tradition he wrote the first number of *The Federalist* in the cabin of his sloop on the return trip to New York.[4]

At some time before the appearance of the first essay, written under the pseudonym "Publius," Hamilton sought and found collaborators, for the first essay, published in *The* [New York] *Independent Journal: or, the General Advertiser* on October 27, 1787, was followed in four days by an essay by John Jay. Neither Hamilton nor Jay left a record of any plans they might have made, but the third collaborator, James Madison, later wrote that "the undertaking was proposed by Alexander Hamilton to James Madison with a request to join him and Mr. Jay in carrying it into effect. William Duer was also included in the original plan; and wrote two or more papers, which though intelligent and sprightly, were not continued, nor did they make a part of the printed collection."[5] Hamilton also sought the assistance of Gouverneur Morris, who in 1815 remembered that he had been "warmly pressed by Hamilton to assist in writing the Federalist."[6]

In reprinting the text of *The Federalist* the original manuscripts have been approximated as nearly as possible. As the first printing of each essay, despite typographical errors, was presumably closest to the original, the text published in this edition is that which was first printed. The texts of those essays among the first seventy-seven which were written by Hamilton or are of doubtful authorship are taken from the newspapers in which they first appeared; the texts of essays 78–85 are taken from the first edition of *The Federalist*, edited by John and Archibald McLean.[7]

With the exception of the last eight numbers, all the issues of *The Federalist* were first printed in the newspapers of New York City. The first essay was published on October 27, 1787, in *The Independent Journal: or, the General Advertiser*, edited by John McLean and Company. Subsequent essays appeared in *The Independent Journal* and in three other New York newspapers: *The New-York Packet*, edited by Samuel and John Loudon; *The Daily Advertiser*, edited by Francis Childs; and *The New-York Journal, and Daily Patriotic Register*, edited by Thomas Greenleaf.[8]

---

4. The story was first related in Hamilton, *History* III, 369, and has been repeated in most works on *The Federalist*.

5. A memorandum by Madison entitled "The Federalist," quoted in J. C. Hamilton, ed., *The Federalist: a Commentary on the Constitution of the United States. A Collection of Essays by Alexander Hamilton, Jay, and Madison. Also, The Continentalist and Other Papers by Hamilton* (Philadelphia, 1865), I, lxxxv.

The essays by William Duer, signed "Philo-Publius," are published at the end of the second volume of J. C. Hamilton's edition of *The Federalist*.

6. Morris to W. H. Wells, February 24, 1815, in Sparks, *The Life of Gouverneur Morris*, III, 339.

7. Drafts of only two essays, 5 and 64, both of which were written by John Jay, have been found. The draft of essay 5 is in the John Jay Papers, Columbia University Libraries. The draft of essay 64 is in the New-York Historical Society, New York City. The draft of essay 3 is now owned by Mr. Ruddy Ruggles of Chicago.

8. Most writers have stated that all the essays first appeared in *The Independent Journal: or, the General Advertiser* or *The New-York Packet*. Others (J. C. Hamilton and Henry B. Dawson, for example) were aware that they

The first seven essays, published between October 27 and November 17, 1787, appeared on Saturdays and Wednesdays in *The Independent Journal*, a semi-weekly paper, and a day or two later in both *The New-York Packet* and *The Daily Advertiser*. At the conclusion of essay 7 the following announcement appeared in *The Independent Journal*: "*In order that the whole subject of these Papers may be as soon as possible laid before the Public, it is proposed to publish them four times a week, on Tuesday in the New-York Packet and on Thursday in the Daily Advertiser.*" The intention thus was to publish on Tuesday in *The New-York Packet*, on Wednesday in *The Independent Journal*, on Thursday in *The Daily Advertiser*, and on Saturday in *The Independent Journal*.

The announced plan was not consistently followed. On Thursday, November 22, *The Daily Advertiser*, according to the proposed schedule, published essay 10, but after its publication no other essay appeared first in that newspaper. To continue the proposed plan of publication—a plan which occasionally was altered by publishing three instead of four essays a week—the third "Publius" essay of the next week appeared on Friday in *The New-York Packet*. After November 30 the essays appeared in the following manner: Tuesday, *The New-York Packet*, Wednesday, *The Independent Journal*, Friday, *The New-York Packet*, and Saturday, *The Independent Journal*. The third essay of the week appeared either on Friday in the *Packet* or on Saturday in *The Independent Journal*. This pattern of publication was followed through the publication of essay 76 (or essay 77, in the numbering used in this edition of Hamilton's works) on April 2, 1788. The remaining essays were first printed in the second volume of McLean's edition of May 28, 1788, and beginning on June 14 were reprinted, at intervals of several days, first in *The Independent Journal* and then in *The New-York Packet*.

The first edition, printed by J. and A. McLean[9] and corrected by Hamilton, is the source from which most editions of *The Federalist* have been taken. On January 1, 1788, McLean, having observed "the avidity" with which the "Publius" essays had been "sought after by politicians and persons of every description," announced plans for the publication of "The FEDERALIST, A Collection of Essays, written in favour of the New Constitution, *By a Citizen of New-York*, Corrected by the Author, with Additions and Alterations."[10] The promised volume, including the first thirty-six essays, was published on March

appeared first in different newspapers, but they did not determine accurately the newspaper in which each essay first appeared.

*The Independent Journal* and *The New-York Packet* carried the entire series of essays, while *The Daily Advertiser* ceased to print them after essay 51. *The New-York Journal* carried only essays 23 through 39. At no time, however, did an essay appear in *The New-York Journal* without appearing in at least one of the three other papers at the same time. On January 1, 1788, Thomas Greenleaf, editor of the *Journal* and supporter of George Clinton, printed a letter signed "45 Subscribers" which complained about Greenleaf's publication of "Publius," which was already appearing in three newspapers. Shortly after this, on January 30, 1788, Greenleaf discontinued publication of the essays with number 39 (numbered by him 37).

9. The full title is *The Federalist: A Collection of Essays, Written in Favour of the New Constitution, As Agreed Upon by the Federal Convention, September 17, 1787. In Two Volumes* (New York: Printed and Sold by J. and A. McLean, No. 41, Hanover-Square. MDCCLXXXVIII). This is referred to hereafter as the "McLean edition."

10. *The Independent Journal: or, the General Advertiser* January 1, 1788.

22, 1788. Hamilton was not altogether pleased with the volume, for he stated in the preface [11] that it contained "violations of method and repetitions of ideas which cannot but displease a critical reader." Despite such imperfections, he hoped that the essays would "promote the cause of truth, and lead to a right judgment of the true interests of the community." Interested readers were promised a second volume of essays as soon as the editor could prepare them for publication.

"*This Day is published,*" *The Independent Journal* advertised on May 28, 1788, "The FEDERALIST, VOLUME SECOND." This volume contained the remaining essays, including the final eight which had not yet appeared in the newspapers. As in the first volume, there were editorial revisions which probably were made by Hamilton. The final eight essays, which first appeared in this volume were reprinted in *The Independent Journal* and in *The New-York Packet* between June 14, 1788, and August 16, 1788.

In addition to the McLean edition, during Hamilton's lifetime there were two French editions [12] and two American editions of *The Federalist*. The second American edition, printed by John Tiebout in 1799, was not a new printing but a reissue of the remaining copies of the McLean edition with new title pages. The third American edition, published in 1802, not only was a new printing; it also contained revisions presumably approved by Hamilton. It is this, the Hopkins edition, which must be taken as Hamilton's final version of *The Federalist.*[13]

George F. Hopkins announced his plan for a new edition of *The Federalist* in the January 13, 1802, issue of *The New-York Evening Post.* "Proposals, By G. F. Hopkins, 118 Pearl Street," read the advertisement in the *Post,* "For Publishing by Subscription, in Two handsome Octavo Volumes, THE FEDERALIST, ON THE CONSTITUTION, BY PUBLIUS Written in 1788. TO WHICH IS ADDED, PACIFICUS, ON THE PROCLAMATION OF NEUTRALITY. Written in 1793. The whole Revised and Corrected. *With new passages and notes.*" Hopkins proposed not only to issue a revised text but to give the author of each essay; by naming Hamilton, Madison, and Jay as the authors of *The Federalist,* he publicly broke the poorly kept secrecy surrounding its authorship. Almost a year passed before Hopkins, on December 8, 1802,

11. There is no question that H was the author of the preface and that he corrected the essays. Not only was this stated by McLean's advertisement, but Madison, writing years later, said that the essays "were edited as soon as possible in two small vols. the preface to the 1st. vol. drawn up by Mr. H., bearing date N. York Mar. 1788" (Hunt, *Writings of Madison,* VIII, 411).

12. The first French edition, published in two volumes in 1792, listed the authors as "MM. Hamilton, Madisson et Gay, Citoyens de l'Etat de New-York." The second edition, published in 1795 and also in two volumes, named "MM. Hamilton, Madisson et Jay" as the authors. For a description of these editions, see *The Fœderalist: A Collection of Essays, Written in Favor of the New Constitution, as Agreed upon by the Fœderal Convention, September 17, 1787. Reprinted from the Original Text.* With an Historical Introduction and Notes by Henry B. Dawson. In Two Volumes (Morrisania, New York, 1864), I, lxiv–lxvi.

13. *The FEDERALIST, On the New Constitution. By Publius. Written in 1788. To Which is Added, PACIFICUS, On the Proclamation of Neutrality. Written in 1793. Likewise, The Federal Constitution, With All the Amendments. Revised and Corrected. In Two Volumes* (New York: Printed and Sold by George F. Hopkins, At Washington's Head, 1802). Cited hereafter as the "Hopkins edition."

offered to the public "in a dress which it is believed will meet with general approbation" the new edition.

Although it is certain that Hamilton did not himself revise the text published in the Hopkins edition, available evidence indicates that he approved the alterations which were made. In 1847 J. C. Hamilton wrote to Hopkins requesting information on the extent to which Hamilton had made or approved the revisions. Hopkins replied that the changes had been made by a "respectable professional gentleman" who, after completing his work, had "put the volumes into the hands of your father, who examined the numerous corrections, most of which he sanctioned, and the work was put to press." The editor, who was not named by Hopkins, was identified by J. C. Hamilton as John Wells, an eminent New York lawyer. The Hopkins edition, Hamilton's son emphatically stated, was "*revised and corrected* by John Wells . . . and *supervised* by Hamilton."[14] Henry B. Dawson in his 1864 edition of *The Federalist* contested J. C. Hamilton's conclusion and argued that the changes were made by William Coleman, editor of *The New-York Evening Post,* and that they were made without Hamilton's authorization or approval. According to Dawson, Hopkins declared on two different occasions in later years—once to James A. Hamilton and once to John W. Francis—that Hamilton refused to have any changes made in the essays.[15] Although it is impossible to resolve the contradictory statements on Hamilton's participation in the revisions included in the 1802 edition of *The Federalist,* J. C. Hamilton presents the more convincing evidence. He, after all, quoted a statement by Hopkins, while Dawson related only a conversation.

The McLean and Hopkins editions thus constitute Hamilton's revision of the text of *The Federalist.* Hamilton made some minor changes in essays written by Jay and Madison—changes which in the McLean edition they presumably authorized. Jay never revised the essays he wrote, and it was not until 1818 that Madison authorized the publication of an edition which included his own corrections of his essays. This edition was published by Jacob Gideon,[16] a printer in Washington, D.C.

It is, then, from the newspapers of the day, the McLean edition of 1788, and the Hopkins edition of 1802 that a definitive text of Hamilton's contribution to *The Federalist* must be reconstructed. In the present edition, as stated above, the texts of essays 1–77 have been taken from the newspapers in which they first appeared; the texts of essays 78–85 are from volume two of the McLean edition. All changes which Hamilton later made or approved in the texts of the essays he wrote have been indicated in notes. Thus in essays 1–77 all changes made in the McLean and Hopkins editions in Hamilton's essays are given. In essays 78–85 all the changes which appeared in the Hopkins edition are noted. The edition in which a revision was made is indicated by a short title, either by the name "McLean" or "Hopkins." To this rule there are, however, three exceptions: 1. When an obvious typographical error appears in the text taken from

---

14. J. C. Hamilton, *The Federalist,* I, xci, xcii.

15. Henry B. Dawson, *The Fœderalist,* I, lxx–lxxi.

16. *The Federalist, on The New Constitution, written in the year 1788, By Mr. Hamilton, Mr. Madison, and Mr. Jay with An Appendix, containing The Letters of Pacificus and Helvidius, on the Proclamation of Neutrality of 1793; Also the Original Articles of Confederation, and The Constitution of the United States, with the Amendments Made Thereto. A New Edition. The Numbers Written by Mr. Madison corrected by Himself* (City of Washington: Printed and Published by Jacob Gideon, Jun., 1818). Cited hereafter as the "Gideon edition."

the newspaper, it has been corrected without annotation. 2. When in McLean there is a correction of a printer's error which, if left unchanged, would make the text meaningless or inaccurate, that correction has been incorporated in the text; the word or words in the newspaper for which changes have been substituted are then indicated in the notes. 3. Obvious printer's errors in punctuation have been corrected; a period at the end of a question, for example, has been changed to a question mark. When a dash is used at the end of a sentence, a period has been substituted.

Because of changes made in the McLean edition, the numbering of certain essays presents an editorial problem. When McLean, with Hamilton's assistance, published the first edition of *The Federalist*, it was decided that the essay published in the newspaper as 35 should follow essay 28, presumably because the subject matter of 35 was a continuation of the subject treated in 28. It also was concluded, probably because of its unusual length, that the essay which appeared in the newspapers as essay 31 should be divided and published as two essays. When these changes were made, the original numbering of essays 29–36 was changed in the following way:

| Newspaper Number | Number in the McLean Edition |
|:---:|:---:|
| 29 | 30 |
| 30 | 31 |
| 31 | 32 and 33 |
| 32 | 34 |
| 33 | 35 |
| 34 | 36 |
| 35 | 29 |

Essays 36–78 in the McLean edition thus were one number higher than the number given the corresponding essay in the newspaper.

Because McLean changed the numbers of some of the essays, later editors have questioned whether there were 84 or 85 essays. This is understandable, for there were only 84 essays printed in the newspapers, the essays 32 and 33 by McLean having appeared in the press as a single essay. The last essay printed in *The Independent Journal* accordingly was numbered 84. The last eight essays published in *The New-York Packet*, on the other hand, were given the numbers used in the second volume of McLean's edition. The last number of *The Federalist* printed by *The New-York Packet* in April had been numbered "76"; the following essay, published in June, was numbered "78." By omitting the number "77," the editor of *The New-York Packet*, like McLean, numbered the last of the essays "85."

Later editions of *The Federalist*, except for that published by Henry B. Dawson, have followed the numbering of the McLean edition. Since no possible purpose would be served and some confusion might result by restoring the newspaper numbering, the essays in the present edition have been given the numbers used by McLean in 1788, and the newspaper number has been placed in brackets.

Almost a century and a half of controversy has centered on the authorship of certain numbers of *The Federalist*. Similar to most other eighteenth-century newspaper contributors, the authors of *The Federalist* chose to write anonymously. When *The Federalist* essays appeared in the press, many New Yorkers probably suspected that Hamilton, if not the sole author of the "Publius" essays, was the major contributor. Friends of Hamilton and Madison, and perhaps those of Jay, certainly knew that this was a joint enterprise and who the authors were.[17] The number of essays written by each author, if only because the ques-

---

17. Three days after the publication of the first essay, Hamilton sent George Washington a copy of it. Hamilton wrote that the essay was "the first of a

tion probably never arose, aroused no curiosity. *The Federalist*, after all, was written for the immediate purpose of persuading the citizens of New York that it was to their interest to adopt the Constitution; certainly not the authors, and probably few readers, realized that the essays which in the winter of 1788 appeared so frequently in the New York press under the signature of "Publius" would become a classic interpretation of the Constitution of the United States. In 1802, George F. Hopkins proposed to publish a new edition of *The Federalist* in which the authors would be identified; but because of Hamilton's "decided disapprobation"[18] no identification of the authors was made in that edition. It was not until three years after Hamilton's death that *The Port Folio*, a Philadelphia weekly, published a list of the authors of the essays, thus opening a controversy which still remains unsettled.[19]

The evidence on the authorship of several of the essays is contradictory because both Hamilton and Madison made, or allegedly made, several lists in which they claimed authorship of the same essays. It is neither necessary nor instructive to discuss the minor discrepancies found in the claims by the two men in their respective lists.[20] The whole problem is simplified by keeping in

series of papers to be written in its [the Constitution's] defense." Washington, of course, knew that H was the author, for H customarily sent to Washington anonymous newspaper articles which he wrote. On December 2, 1787, Madison wrote to Edmund Randolph:

"The enclosed paper contains two numbers of the Federalist. This paper was begun about three weeks ago, and proposes to go through the subject. I have not been able to collect all the numbers, since my return to Philad, or I would have sent them to you. I have been the less anxious, as I understand the printer means to make a pamphlet of them, when I can give them to you in a more convenient form. You will probably discover marks of different pens. I am not at liberty to give you any other key, than, that I am in myself for a few numbers; and that one, besides myself was a member of the Convention." (Hunt, *Writings of Madison*, V, 60–61.)

18. The first edition of *The Federalist* which attributed specific essays to individual authors appeared as the second and third volumes of a three-volume edition of H's writings published in 1810 (*The Federalist, on the new constitution; written in 1788, by Mr. Hamilton, Mr. Jay, and Mr. Madison . . . A new edition, with the names and portraits of the several writers.* In Two Volumes [New York, published by Williams & Whiting, 1810]).

19. The letter in *The Port Folio* of November 14, 1807, reads as follows:

"Mr. OLDSCHOOL,

"The Executors of the last will of General HAMILTON have deposited in the Publick Library of New-York a copy of 'The Federalist,' which belonged to the General in his lifetime, in which he has designated, in his own hand-writing, the parts of that celebrated work written by himself, as well as those contributed by Mr. JAY and Mr. MADISON. As it may not be uninteresting to many of your readers, I shall subjoin a copy of the General's *memorandum* for publication in 'The Port Folio.' M.

"Nos. 2, 3, 4, 5, 54 Mr. JAY. Nos. 10, 14, 37, to 48 inclusive, Mr. MADISON. Nos. 18, 19, 20, Mr. HAMILTON and Mr. MADDISON jointly—all the rest by Mr. HAMILTON."

20. There are several lists other than those subsequently discussed in the text. On the flyleaf of volume 1 of his copy of *The Federalist*, Thomas Jefferson wrote the following: "No. 2. 3. 4. 5. 64 by Mr. Jay. No. 10. 14. 17. 18. 19. 21. 37. 38. 39. 40. 41. 42. 43. 44. 45. 46. 47. 48. 49. 50. 51. 52. 53. 54. 55. 56. 57. 58. 62. 63. by Mr. Madison. The rest of the work by Alexander Hamilton." Jefferson's copy of *The Federalist*, now in the Rare Book Room of the Library of Congress, came to him indirectly from H's wife, Elizabeth. It bears the inscription: "For Mrs.

mind that of the eighty-five essays the authorship of only fifteen is disputed. Despite contrary claims in several of the least credible lists published during the first two decades of the nineteenth century, it has long been accepted that Hamilton wrote essays 1, 6–9, 11–13, 15–17, 21–36, 59–61, and 65–85; that Madison was the author of essays 10, 14, 37–48; and that Jay contributed essays 2–5 and 64.[21] The authorship of only essays 18–20, 49–58, and 62–63 is therefore debatable.

The number of disputed essays can be reduced by examining the reliability of the several Madison and Hamilton lists. There are four reputed Madison lists: 1. An article, signed "Corrector," which appeared in the *National Intelligencer* on March 20, 1817, and which, according to the anonymous author, was copied from "a penciled memorandum in the hand of Madison."[22] 2. A statement of authorship, supposedly endorsed by Madison, made by Richard Rush, a member of Madison's cabinet, in his copy of *The Federalist*.[23] 3. An article in the *City of Washington Gazette*, December 15, 1817, claiming to set forth a list "fur-

---

Church from her *Sister*. Elizabeth Hamilton." The words, "For Mrs. Church from her *Sister*," are in the handwriting of Elizabeth Hamilton. Angelica Schuyler Church, despite her admiration for her brother-in-law, had long been a friend of Jefferson and must have sent her copy of *The Federalist* to him. It is not known from whom Jefferson got his information on the authorship of the essays, but presumably it was from Madison. It will be noted that there is only one minor difference between Jefferson's attribution of the essays and that made by Madison: Jefferson attributed essay 17 to Madison. A facsimile is printed in E. Millicent Sowerby, *Catalog of the Library of Thomas Jefferson* (Washington, D.C., 1953), III, 228.

On the title page of George Washington's copy of *The Federalist* there is an assignment of authorship which reads as follows: "Jay author—1, 2, 3, 4, 5, and 54. Madison—10, 14, 37–48 exclusive of last. 18, 19, 20, productive of Jay, AH and Madison. All rest by Gen'l Hamilton." This memorandum is in an unidentified handwriting. Except for two differences it conforms to the Benson list. Without more information on the source of the list, its reliability is highly suspect (Washington's copy of *The Federalist* is in the National Archives).

Henry Cabot Lodge in his edition of *The Federalist* (*HCLW*, XI, xxvii), placed in evidence lists of authors which he found in copies of *The Federalist* owned by Fisher Ames and George Cabot. Both correspond to the Benson list.

21. Jay's authorship of these essays is incontestable. H supposedly stated in the Benson list that he wrote 64 and that Jay was the author of 54. The draft of 64, in the writing of Jay, is in the New-York Historical Society, New York City. Both H and Madison agreed that Jay wrote 2, 3, 4, and 5. That Jay contributed only five essays was due to an attack of rheumatism which lasted through the winter of 1787. It was not due, as his earlier biographers stated, to an injury which he received in the "Doctors' Riot" in New York. The riot did not occur until April, 1788, by which time most of the "Publius" essays had been written (Frank Monaghan, *John Jay* [New York, 1935], 290).

22. "I take upon me to state from indubitable authority," Corrector wrote "that Mr. Madison wrote Nos. 10, 14, 18, 19, 20, 37, 38, 39, 40, 41, 42, 43, 44, 45, 46, 47, 48, 49, 50, 51, 52, 53, 54, 55, 56, 57, 58, 62, 63, and 64. Mr. Jay wrote Nos. 2, 3, 4, and 5; and Mr. Hamilton the residue" ([Washington] *National Intelligencer*, March 20, 1817).

23. Benjamin Rush, the oldest son of Richard, sent Henry B. Dawson the following description of the notes in the edition of *The Federalist* owned by his father: "On a fly-leaf of the second volume there is the following memorandum in my father's handwriting. I copy it exactly as it appears: 'The initials, J.M.

nished by Madison himself." [24] 4. The edition of *The Federalist* published by Jacob Gideon in 1818, which based its attribution of authorship on Madison's own "copy of the work which that gentleman had preserved for himself." [25] There is no evidence that Madison approved the first three lists; the fourth, the Gideon edition, was not only based on Madison's copy, but it was endorsed by him as correct.

Hamilton's claims to authorship are more complicated. Despite statements by his partisans, there are only three Hamilton lists that merit the serious attention of the historian who applies any known tests for evaluating historical evidence. They are the so-called "Benson list," the list allegedly preserved by Hamilton in his own copy of *The Federalist*, and the "Kent list."

The Benson list, according to a story first related by William Coleman in March, 1817, was left by Hamilton, shortly before his death, between the pages of a book in the library of his long-time friend, Judge Egbert Benson. Arriving at Benson's office, Hamilton was told by Robert Benson, Jr., Egbert's nephew and clerk, that the Judge and Rufus King had gone to Massachusetts for a few days. As Hamilton conversed with the law clerk, he idly handled one of the volumes on the shelves in the office. After Hamilton's death which occurred two days later, Benson remembered the incident and, looking in the book Hamilton had picked up, he found a scrap of paper, unsigned but in Hamilton's hand, listing the essays he had written. [26] Judge Benson, according to the traditional account, pasted it on the inside cover of his copy of *The Federalist* but somewhat later, fearing that he might lose such a valuable document, deposited it in the New York Society Library. The memorandum was presumably stolen in 1818. [27]

The existence of the Benson list was corroborated by two witnesses, Robert Benson and William Coleman. Coleman, editor of *The New-York Evening Post*, is the less credible authority; he may have seen the Benson list, but it is significant that he never definitely stated that he did. The most emphatic statement that he made, elicited by the demands for proof made by an an-

---

J.J. and A.H. throughout the work, are in Mr. Madison's hand, and designate the author of each number. By these it will be seen, that although the printed designations are generally correct, they are not always so'" (Benjamin Rush to Dawson, August 29, 1863, New-York Historical Society, New York City).

Madison's attribution of authorship, according to Benjamin Rush, was exactly the same as that which the Virginian authorized in the Gideon edition.

24. The anonymous author of the article in the *City of Washington Gazette* stated that Madison wrote essays 10, 14, 17, 18, 19, 21, 37–58, 62–63, that Jay was the author of essays 2, 3, 4, 5, and 64, and that H wrote the rest.

25. Gideon, p. 3. In this edition, essays 10, 14, 18–20, 37–58, 62–63 are assigned to Madison; 2, 3, 4, 5, and 64 to Jay; and the remainder to H. Madison's copy of *The Federalist*, with corrections in his handwriting, is in the Rare Book Room of the Library of Congress.

26. The memorandum by H, as printed by William Coleman, reads as follows: "Nos. 2. 3. 4. 5. 54, Mr. Jay; Nos. 10, 14, 37 to 48 inclusive, Mr. Madison; Nos. 18, 19, 20, Mr. Hamilton and Mr. Madison jointly; all the rest by Mr. Hamilton" (*The New-York Evening Post*, March 25, 1817).

27. According to Coleman the memorandum was deposited by Egbert Benson in "the city library," as the New York Society Library was then sometimes known. The remainder of the story related in this paragraph is taken from J. C. Hamilton's account of a "*Copy* of a statement in my possession made for me by Egbert Benson, Esq., a nephew of Judge Benson." It is quoted in Hamilton, *The Federalist*, I, xcvi–xcvii.

tagonist in a newspaper controversy over the authorship of *The Federalist,* was as follows:

"I, therefore, for the entire satisfaction of the public, now state, that the memorandum referred to is in General Hamilton's own hand writing, was left by him with his friend judge BENSON, the week before his death, and was, by the latter, deposited in the city library, where it now is, and may be seen, pasted in one of the volumes of *The Federalist.*" [28]

The statement of Robert Benson, the law clerk to whom Hamilton spoke on the day before his encounter with Burr, is more convincing, but it was made many years after the event, and it is far from being conclusive. "I was then a student in the office," Benson recalled "and well known to the General" who called and enquired for Judge Benson.

"I replied that he had left the city with Mr. King. The General in his usual manner then went to the book case and took down a book which he opened and soon replaced, and left the office. Some time after the General's death, a memorandum in his handwriting was found in a volume of Pliny's letters, *I think,* which, *I believe,* was the book he took down, and which memorandum was afterwards wafered by the Judge in the inside cover of the first volume of the Federalist, and where it remained for several years. He subsequently removed it, and, *as I understand,* gave it to some public library. . . . The marks of the wafers still remain in the volume, and above them in Judge Benson's handwriting is, *what is presumed, and I believe to be,* a copy of the General's memorandum above referred to." [29]

The Benson list is suspect, then, because the claim for its authenticity is based on the evidence of two men neither of whom stated that he actually *saw* it. If there had not already been too much fruitless speculation on Hamilton's thoughts and intentions, it would be interesting to explain why Hamilton chose such a roundabout method to make certain that future generations would recognize his contribution to such a celebrated book. Perhaps he knew that Robert Benson would search all the volumes in his uncle's office on the suspicion that Hamilton, however uncharacteristically, had concealed a note on some important subject; or perhaps he thought that Benson frequently read Pliny's *Letters* and thus could be sure the note would be found. One can speculate endlessly on the motives for Hamilton's extraordinary behavior, but the significant fact is that the Benson list is inadequate as historical evidence.

Evidence of the existence of Hamilton's own copy of *The Federalist* in which he supposedly listed the essays he wrote comes from a notice which appeared on November 14, 1807, in *The Port Folio.* "The Executors of the last will of General Hamilton," the Philadelphia weekly announced, "have deposited in the Publick Library of New-York a copy of '*The Federalist,*' which belonged to the General in his lifetime, in which he has designated in his own handwriting, the parts of that celebrated work written by himself, as well as those contributed by Mr. JAY and Mr. MADISON." No one has seen Hamilton's

---

28. *The New-York Evening Post,* January 23, 1818.
The volume from which the memorandum was stolen may have been at one time in the New York Society Library; however, it is no longer there. That library has no McLean edition of *The Federalist* that bears any marks which indicate that a piece of paper once had been pasted on the inside cover.

29. Hamilton, *The Federalist,* I, xcvi–xcvii. The italics have been inserted. J. C. Hamilton did not get this statement from Robert Benson. It was, as has been stated, from the "*Copy* of a statement in my possession made for me by Egbert Benson, Esq., a nephew of Judge Benson" (*ibid.,* xcvii).

copy in the last 150 years; whether it existed or what happened to it, if it did exist, cannot now be known.[30]

While the numbers claimed by Hamilton in the Benson list and in his own copy of *The Federalist* are the same, the list by Chancellor James Kent disagrees in several particulars from the other two. The Kent list, in the Chancellor's own writing, was found on the inside cover of his copy of *The Federalist*, now in the Columbia University Libraries. Because of differences in the ink and pen he used, Kent's statement may be divided into three parts, each of which was written at a different time. In the following copy of Kent's notes the three parts are indicated by Roman numerals:

    I. "I am assured that Numbers 2. 3. 4. 5. & 54 [number '6' was later written over the number '5'] were written by *John Jay*. Numbers 10, 14. 37 to 48 [the number '9' was later written over the number '8'] both inclusive & 53 by *James Madison Jun*. Numbers 18. 19. 20. by Messrs *Madison & Hamilton* jointly—all the rest by Mr. *Hamilton*.

    II. "(Mr. Hamilton told me that Mr. *Madison* wrote No. 68 [the number '4' was later written over the number '6'] & 69 [the number '4' was later written over the number '6'] or from pa. 101 to 112 of Vol 2d)

    III. "NB. I showed the above *Mem*. to General Hamilton in my office in Albany & he said it was correct saving the correction above made—See Hall's Law Journal Vol 6 p 461."

The numbers which were written over the numbers Kent first wrote are not in Kent's writing. However familiar one is with the handwriting of another, it is difficult to determine if a single numeral is in his writing. But despite the impossibility of positive identification, a close comparison of numerals made by Hamilton with the numerals which were added to the Kent list strongly indicates that the changes are in the writing of Hamilton. The Kent list thus becomes the only evidence in Hamilton's writing which now exists.

Certain reasonable deductions can be made from the evidence presented by Kent's notes. The ink clearly reveals that the three notes were made at different times. The information in part I of the notes was obtained from someone other than Hamilton, for otherwise Kent would not have written in part II "that Mr. Hamilton told me." The information in part II must have been given to Kent in a conversation, for it is evident that Kent was not sure that he remembered what Hamilton had said or that Hamilton could remember, without reference to a copy of *The Federalist*, which essays he had written.

---

30. For the attribution of authorship which H made in his copy of *The Federalist*, see note 20.

H's copy is now in neither the New York Society Library, the New-York Historical Society, nor the New York Public Library, and those libraries have no record of ever having owned it. G. W. Cole, ed., *A Catalogue of Books Relating to the Discovery and Early History of North and South America, The E. D. Church Library* (New York, 1907), V, Number 1230, lists an item purporting to be H's copy of *The Federalist* with notes in his writing. According to the librarian of the Huntington Library, San Marino, California, which acquired the Church library, the notes were not in the writing of H. The book, which is no longer in the Huntington Library, was sold to an unknown purchaser.

J. C. Hamilton, probably unintentionally, contradicts the statement that the names of the authors in his father's copy of *The Federalist* were in H's handwriting. He stated that his father dictated to *him* the authors of the essays which *he* then copied into H's copy (*The Federalist*, I, xcvi-xcvii).

Part III—because it refers to Hamilton as "general" (a rank which he attained in 1798), and because the conversation alluded to took place in Albany—must have been made between 1800, the year in which Hamilton resumed his law practice after completing his duties as inspector general of the Army, and his death in 1804. The third section of Kent's memorandum also indicates that Hamilton corrected and approved the Kent list. It constitutes, therefore, the most reliable evidence available on Hamilton's claims of authorship. It should be noted, however, that Kent later doubted the accuracy of Hamilton's memory, for on the page opposite his memorandum he pasted a copy of the article from the City of Washington Gazette, which stated that Madison had written essays 10, 14, 17, 18, 19, 21, 37-58, 62-63, and that Jay was the author of essays 2, 3, 4, 5, 64. Underneath this clipping Kent wrote:

"I have no doubt Mr. Jay wrote No 64 on the Treaty Power—He made a Speech on that Subject in the NY Convention, & I am told he says he wrote it. I suspect therefore from internal Ev. the above to be the correct List, & not the one on the opposite page." [31]

A comparison of the Kent list (for those essays claimed by Hamilton) with the Gideon edition (for those essays claimed by Madison) makes it clear that there is room for doubt only over the authorship of essays 18, 19, 20, 50, 51, 52, 54-58, and 62-63. About three of these—18, 19, and 20—there should be no dispute, for there is a statement by Madison which Hamilton's claim does not really controvert. On the margin of his copy of The Federalist opposite number 18 Madison wrote:

"The subject matter of this and the two following numbers happened to be taken up by both Mr. H and Mr. M. What had been prepared by Mr. H who had entered more briefly into the subject, was left with Mr. M on its appearing that the latter was engaged in it, with larger materials, and with a view to a more precise delineation; and from the pen of the latter, the several papers went to the Press."

The problem of determining the authorship of these three essays is merely one of deciding on the comparative contributions of the two men. Although there are several sentences which are very similar to remarks Hamilton recorded in the outline for his speech of June 18, 1787, on the Constitution, most of the material was undoubtedly supplied by Madison who without doubt wrote these essays. Essay 20, for example, is virtually a copy of notes which Madison had

---

31. Not too much reliance should be placed on Kent's endorsement of the Madison list in the City of Washington Gazette. According to that list, Madison wrote not only all the disputed essays but also essay 17. As Madison's most ardent defenders assign this essay to H, it seems that Kent's statement indicated nothing more than his suspicion that H may have made errors in his assignment of authors of the essays.

While Kent's statement shows that he doubted the accuracy of the attribution of essays made by H, it raises several questions that cannot satisfactorily be answered. The clipping from the City of Washington Gazette was dated December 15, 1817, and the notes on the opposite page of the flyleaf, as stated in the text, could not have been written later than 1804. How, then, could Kent have written that he doubted that Jay wrote essay 64 when the essay was attributed to Jay on a page which was in front of Kent as he wrote? The only possible answer is that Kent, when writing in 1817 or later, failed to look carefully at the changes which had been made in his earlier memorandum and had his uncorrected list in mind. Whatever the explanation for his later statement, it is at least certain that he did not change the earlier list after he saw the article in the City of Washington Gazette.

taken in preparation for the Constitutional Convention.[32] On the other hand, Hamilton, however slight his contribution, did contribute to these essays. The authorship of 50, 51, 52, 54, 55, 56, 57, 58, 62, and 63 is more difficult to determine,[33] but Madison's claim as represented by the Gideon edition appears more convincing than Hamilton's claim as represented by the Kent list.

Internal evidence has proved to be of little assistance in determining the authorship of *The Federalist*. The ablest studies in this field are those by Edward G. Bourne [34] and J. C. Hamilton.[35] Bourne attributes all disputed essays to Madison; J. C. Hamilton asserts that they were written by his father. Bourne and J. C. Hamilton attempt to prove their respective cases by printing excerpts from the disputed essays parallel to similar, and sometimes identical, passages from other writings by each man. Bourne presents very convincing evidence for Madison's authorship of numbers 49, 51, 53, 62, 63, and a fair case for Madison having written numbers 50 and 52; his case for 54, 55, 56, 57, and 58 is particularly weak as he offers no evidence from Madison's other writings and

---

32. "Notes of Ancient and Modern Confederacies, preparatory to the federal Convention of 1787" (Madison, *Letters*, I, 293–315).

33. A favorite argument of those who support Madison's claim to essays 49–58 of *The Federalist* is that since those essays constitute a unit, one man must have written all of them. The essays deal with: 1. the necessity of the departments of government having checks on each other, and 2. the House of Representatives. Madison's defenders, in their desire to prove his authorship, forget that essays 59, 60, and 61, essays which they attribute to H, also deal with the House of Representatives. There are, furthermore, several obvious breaks in continuity among the essays from 48 to 58, at which a change of authors could have taken place. Essay 51, for example, ends the discussion of the necessity that "these departments shall be so far connected and blended as to give to each a constitutional control over the others," and essay 52 begins the discussion of the House of Representatives. A change could also have occurred after essay 54 or essay 57. This is not to say that changes in authorship *did* occur; it is to indicate that the "unit" argument will not stand up under scrutiny.

34. "The Authorship of the Federalist," *The American Historical Review*, II (April, 1897), 443–60.

35. The fact that only Bourne and J. C. Hamilton are cited does not mean that other studies of the authorship of *The Federalist* have been ignored or overlooked. It means rather that other authors, while sometimes introducing new arguments, have relied heavily on the research of Bourne and J. C. Hamilton. To cite all those who have agreed with Bourne or Hamilton would be redundant; to summarize all the arguments of the numerous students of *The Federalist*—based for the most part on Bourne and Hamilton's original research—is a task best left to the historiographer of that work.

There have been, of course, other able studies of the authorship of the disputed essays. Among the defenders of H's claim, Henry Cabot Lodge ("The Authorship of the Federalist," *HCLW*, XI, xv–xlv) and Paul L. Ford ("The Authorship of The Federalist," *The American Historical Review*, II [July, 1897], 675–82) have been the most able advocates. The most convincing exponent of Madison's claim since Bourne is Douglass Adair ("The Authorship of the Disputed Federalist Papers," *The William and Mary Quarterly*, 3rd. ser., Vol. I, Numbers 2 and 3 [April and July, 1944], 97–122, 235–64). In two essays which brilliantly summarize the century-old controversy over the authorship of the disputed essays, Adair amplifies the research of Bourne and attempts to assign the disputed essays on the basis of the political philosophy which they reveal.

relies on the argument that, as essays 48–58 are a group, the author who wrote the earlier essays must also have written the later ones in the group. J. C. Hamilton, on the other hand, produces some evidence that Hamilton wrote essays 55–58, and he offers contrived and unconvincing arguments in support of Hamilton's authorship of the remaining disputed essays. The significant point, however, is that each man was able to find evidence that his candidate wrote all the disputed essays. The contradictory conclusions of these two men—one of whom studied intensively the previous writings of Madison and the other whose life-long study of his father gave him a knowledge of Hamilton's writings which never has been excelled—point up the difficulties of deciding this dispute on the basis of internal evidence.

The problems posed by internal evidence are made even more difficult by the fact that both Hamilton and Madison defended the Constitution with similar arguments and by the fact that they both had a remarkably similar prose style. To attempt to find in any of the disputed essays words which either man used and which the other never employed is futile, if only because the enormous amount which each wrote allows the assiduous searcher to discover almost any word in the earlier or subsequent writings of both.[36] The search for parallel statements in the disputed essays and in earlier writings is also an unrewarding enterprise. Madison doubtless did not approve of the ideas expressed in Hamilton's famous speech on June 18, 1787, to the Convention; but before 1787 both men agreed on the weaknesses of the Confederation and the necessity of a stronger central government.[37] The similarity of their thinking is particularly apparent to one who examines their collaboration when they were both members of the Continental Congress in 1783. Their later political differences prove little about what they wrote in 1787–88.

If one were to rely on internal evidence, it would be impossible to assign all the disputed essays to either Hamilton or Madison. While such evidence indicates that Madison surely wrote numbers 49–54 and probably 62–63, it also sug-

---

36. See, for example, S. A. Bailey, "Notes on Authorship of Disputed Numbers of the Federalist," *Case and Comments*, XXII (1915), 674–75. Bailey credits Madison with sole authorship of the disputed essays on the basis of the use of the word "while" by H and "whilst" by Madison. Although the evidence for Bailey's conclusion is convincing—and there is far more evidence than he produces—his argument is destroyed by H's occasional use of "whilst." In essay 51, for example, H, who himself edited the essays for publication by McLean, substituted "whilst" for "and." In essay 81, certainly written by H, the word "whilst" is used. Edward G. Bourne (see note 35), to give another example, offers as evidence for Madison's authorship of essay 56 his use of the word "monitory," which, according to Bourne, was "almost a favorite word with Madison." Yet in essay 26, H, in revising the essays for publication in the McLean edition, changed "cautionary" to "monitory." Similarly, to assign authorship on the basis of differences in the spelling of certain words in different essays—for example, "color" or "colour," "federal" or "fœderal"—would be hazardous. The editors of the various newspapers in which the essays appeared obviously changed the spelling of certain words to conform to their individual preferences.

37. Similarity between a statement in one of the disputed essays and an earlier remark in the writings of either Madison or H is perhaps valid evidence. It does not seem relevant, however, to attempt to prove authorship by reference to the later writings of either of the men. As both presumably read *all* the essays, they might later have borrowed a statement from a number of *The Federalist* written by the other without being aware of its source.

gests that Hamilton wrote 55–58. In this edition of Hamilton's writings, however, greater weight is given to the claims made by the disputants than to internal evidence. Madison's claims were maturely considered and emphatically stated; Hamilton, on the other hand, showed little interest in the question, and he died before it had become a matter of acrimonious controversy. But the fact remains that Hamilton's claims have never been unequivocally refuted, and the possibility remains that he could have written essays 50–52, 54–58, 62–63. As a consequence, these essays have been printed in this edition of Hamilton's writings. Madison's adherents may, however, derive some consolation from the fact that in the notes to each of these essays it is stated that Madison's claims to authorship are superior to those of Hamilton.

## The Federalist No. 1 [1]

[New York, October 27, 1787]

*To the People of the State of New York.*

AFTER an unequivocal [2] experience of the inefficacy [3] of the subsisting [4] Fœderal Government, you are called upon [5] to deliberate on [6] a new Constitution for the United States of America. The subject speaks its own importance; comprehending in its consequences, nothing less than the existence of the UNION, the safety and welfare of the parts of which it is composed, the fate of an empire, in many respects, the most interesting the world. It has been frequently remarked, that it seems to have been reserved to the people of this country, [7] by their conduct and example, to decide [8] the important question, whether societies of men are really capable or not, of establishing good government from ref[l]ection and choice, or whether they are forever destined to depend, for their political constitutions, on accident and force. If there be any truth in the remark, the crisis, at which we are arrived, may with propriety be regarded as the æra in which [9] that decision is to be made; and a

*The* [New York] *Independent Journal: or, the General Advertiser,* October 27, 1787. This essay appeared on October 30 in both *The New-York Packet* and *The* [New York] *Daily Advertiser.*

1. For the background to this document, see "The Federalist. Introductory Note," October 27, 1787–May 28, 1788.
2. "full" is substituted for "an unequivocal" in Hopkins.
3. "insufficiency" substituted for "inefficacy" in Hopkins.
4. "existing" substituted for "subsisting" in Hopkins.
5. "invited" substituted for "called upon" in Hopkins.
6. "upon" substituted for "on" in Hopkins.
7. "to decide" is inserted here in Hopkins.
8. "to decide" is omitted in Hopkins.
9. "period when" is substituted for "æra in which" in Hopkins.

wrong election of the part we shall act, may, in this view, deserve to be considered as the general misfortune of mankind.

This idea will add [10] the inducements of philanthropy to those of patriotism to [11] heighten the sollicitude, which all considerate and good men must feel for the event. Happy will it be if our choice should be directed [12] by a judicous estimate of our true interests, unperplexed and unbiassed by considerations not connected with the public good.[13] But this is a thing more ardently to be wished,[14] than seriously to be expected. The plan offered to our deliberations, affects too many particular interests, innovates upon too many local institutions, not to involve in its discussion a variety of objects foreign [15] to its merits, and of views, passions and prejudices little favourable to the discovery of truth.

Among the most formidable of the obstacles which the new Constitution will have to encounter, may readily be distinguished the obvious interest of a certain class of men in every State to resist all changes which may hazard a diminution of the power, emolument and consequence of the offices they hold under the State-establishments—and the perverted ambition of another class of men, who will either hope to aggrandise themselves by the confusions of their country, or will flatter themselves with fairer prospects of elevation from the subdivision of the empire into several partial confederacies, than from its union under one government.

It is not, however, my design to dwell upon observations of this nature. I am well [16] aware that it would be disingenuous to resolve indiscriminately the opposition of any set of men [17] (merely because their situations might subject them to suspicion) into interested or ambitious views: [18] Candour will oblige us to admit, that even such men may be actuated by upright intentions; and it cannot be

10. "by adding" is substituted for "will add" in Hopkins.
11. "will" is substituted for "to" in Hopkins.
12. In the newspaper "decided"; "directed" was substituted in McLean and Hopkins.
13. "uninfluenced by considerations foreign to the public good" is substituted for "unperplexed" through "good" in Hopkins.
14. "for" is inserted at this point in Hopkins.
15. "extraneous" is substituted for "foreign" in Hopkins.
16. "well" omitted in Hopkins.
17. "into interested or ambitious views" inserted here in Hopkins.
18. "into" through "views" omitted in Hopkins.

doubted, that much of the opposition which has made its appearance,[19] or may hereafter make its appearance, will spring from sources, blameless at least, if not respectable, the honest errors of minds led astray by preconceived jealousies and fears. So numerous indeed and so powerful are the causes, which serve to give a false bias to the judgment, that we upon many occasions, see wise and good men on the wrong as well as on the right side of questions, of the first magnitude to society. This circumstance, if duly attended to, would [20] furnish a lesson of moderation of those, who are ever so much [21] persuaded of their being in the right, in any controversy.[22] And a further reason for caution, in this respect, might be drawn from the reflection, that we are not always sure, that those who advocate the truth are influenced [23] by purer principles than their antagonists. Ambition, avarice, personal animosity, party opposition, and many other motives, not more laudable than these, are apt to operate as well upon those who support as upon those who oppose the right side of a question. Were there not even these inducements to moderation, nothing could be more illjudged than that intolerant spirit, which has, at all times, characterised political parties. For, in politics as in religion, it is equally absurd to aim at making proselytes by fire and sword. Heresies in either can rarely be cured by persecution.

And yet however just these sentiments will be allowed to be,[24] we have already sufficient indications, that it will happen in this as in all former cases of great national discussion. A torrent of angry and malignant passions will be let loose. To judge from the conduct of the opposite parties, we shall be led to conclude, that they will mutually hope to evince the justness of their opinions, and to increase the number of their converts by the loudness of their declamations, and by the bitterness of their invectives. An enlightened zeal for the energy and efficiency of government will be stigmatised,

19. "already shown itself" substituted for "made its appearance" in Hopkins.
20. "always" inserted at this point in Hopkins.
21. "thoroughly" substituted for "much" in McLean.
22. "who are engaged in any controversy, however well persuaded of being in the right" substituted for the words "who" through "controversy" in Hopkins.
23. "actuated" substituted for "influenced" in Hopkins.
24. "And yet, just as these sentiments must appear to candid men," substituted for "And" through "to be" in Hopkins.

as the off-spring of a temper fond of despotic [25] power and hostile
to the principles of liberty. An overscrupulous jealousy of danger
to the rights of the people, which is more commonly the fault of
the head than of the heart, will be represented as mere pretence and
artifice; the [26] bait for popularity at the expence of public good. It
will be forgotten, on the one hand, that jealousy is the usual con-
comitant of violent love, and that the noble enthusiasm of liberty
is too apt to be infected with a spirit of narrow and illiberal distrust.
On the other hand, it will be equally forgotten, that the vigour of
government is essential to the security of liberty; that, in the contemplation of a sound and well informed judgment, their interest
can never be separated; and that a dangerous ambition more often
lurks behind the specious mask of zeal for the rights of the people,
than under the forbidding appearance of zeal for the firmness and
efficiency of government. History will teach us, that the former has
been found a much more certain road to the introduction of despotism, than the latter, and that of those men who have overturned
the liberties of republics the greatest number have begun their car-
reer, by paying an obsequious court to the people, commencing
Demagogues and ending Tyrants.

In the course of the preceeding observations I have had an eye,
my Fellow Citizens, to putting [27] you upon your guard against all
attempts, from whatever quarter, to influence your decision in a
matter of the utmost moment to your welfare by any impressions
other than those which may result from the evidence of truth. You
will, no doubt, at the same time, have collected from the general
scope of them that they proceed from a source not unfriendly to
the new Constitution. Yes, my Countrymen, I own to you, that,
after having given it an attentive consideration, I am clearly of
opinion, it is your interest to adopt it. I am convinced, that this
is the safest course for your liberty, your dignity, and your happiness. I effect not reserves, which I do not feel. I will not amuse
you with an appearance of deliberation, when I have decided. I
frankly acknowledge to you my convictions, and I will freely lay

25. This word omitted in Hopkins.
26. "stale" inserted here in McLean and Hopkins.
27. "it has been my aim, fellow citizens to put" substituted for "I" through
"putting" in Hopkins.

before you the reasons on which they are founded. The consciousness of good intentions disdains ambiguity. I shall not however multiply professions on this head. My motives must remain in the depository of my own breast: My arguments will be open to all, and
may be judged of by all. They shall at least be offered in a spirit,
which will not disgrace the cause of truth.

I propose in a series of papers to discuss the following interesting
particulars—*The utility of the UNION to your political prosperity
—The insufficiency of the present Confederation to preserve that
Union—The necessity of a government at least equally energetic
with the one proposed to the attainment of this object—The conformity of the proposed constitution to the true principles of republican government—Its analogy to your own state constitution*—and
lastly, *The additional security, which its adoption will afford to the
preservation of that species of government, to liberty and to property.*

In the progress of this discussion I shall endeavour to give a satisfactory answer to all the objections which shall have made their appearance that may seem to have any claim to your [28] attention.

It may perhaps be thought superfluous to offer arguments to prove
the utility of the UNION, a point, no doubt, deeply engraved on
the hearts of the great body of the people in every state, and one,
which it may be imagined has no adversaries. But the fact is, that
we already hear it whispered in the private circles of those who oppose the new constitution, that the Thirteen States are of too great
extent for any general system, and that we must of necessity resort
to separate confederacies of distinct portions of the whole.* This
doctrine will, in all probability, be gradually propagated, till it has
votaries enough to countenance an open avowal of it.[29] For nothing
can be more evident, to those who are able to take an enlarged view
of the subject than the alternative of an adoption of the new [30] Constitution, or a dismemberment of the Union. It will [31] therefore be

* *The same idea, tracing the arguments to their consequences, is held out in
several of the late publications against the New Constitution.*

28. This word omitted in Hopkins.
29. "its open avowal" substituted for "an" through "it" in Hopkins.
30. "new" omitted in Hopkins.
31. "may" substituted for "will" in Hopkins.

of use to begin by examining [32] the advantages of that Union, the certain evils and the probable dangers, to which every State will be exposed from its dissolution. This shall accordingly constitute the subject of my next address.[33]

PUBLIUS.

32. "essential to examine particularly" substituted for "of use" through "examining" in Hopkins.

33. "be done" substituted for "constitute" through "address" in Hopkins.

## To George Washington

[New York, October 30, 1787]

I am much obliged to Your Excellency for the explicit manner in which you contradict the insinuations mentioned in my last letter.[1] The only use I shall make of your answer will be to put it into the hands of a few friends.

The constitution proposed has in this state warm friends and warm enemies. The first impressions every where are in its favour; but the artillery of its opponents makes some impression. The event cannot yet be foreseen. The inclosed is the first number of a series of papers to be written in its defence.[2]

I send you also at the request of the Baron De Steuben a printed pamphlet containing the grounds of an application lately made to Congress.[3] He tells me there is some reference to you, the object of which he does not himself seem clearly to understand—But imagines it may be in your power to be of service to him.[4]

There are public considerations that induce me to be somewhat anxious for his success. He is fortified with materials which in Europe could not fail to establish the belief of the contract he alleges. The documents of service he possesses are of a nature to convey an exalted idea of them. The compensations he has received though considerable, if compared with those which have been received by American officers, will according to European ideas be very scanty in application to a *stranger* who is acknowleged to have rendered essential services. Our reputation abroad is not at present too high— To dismiss an old soldier empty and hungry, to seek the bounty of those on whose justice he has no claims & to complain of unkind returns and violated engagements will certainly not lend to raise it. I confess too there is something in my feelings which would incline me in this case to go farther than might be strictly necessary rather than drive a man at the Baron's time of life, who has been a faithful servant, to extremities. And this is unavoidable if he does not succeed in his present attempt.

What he asks would, all calculations made, terminate in this— an allowance of his Five hundred and Eighty guineas a year. He only wishes a recognition of the contract. He knows that until affairs mend no money can be produced. I do not know how far it may be in your power to do him any good; but I shall be mistaken, if the considerations I have mentioned do not appear to Your Excellency to have some weight

I remain with the great respect and esteem    Yr. Excellys Obed
serv                                            A Hamilton

October 30. 1787
His Excellency General Washington

ALS, George Washington Papers, Library of Congress.
    1. See H to Washington, October 11–15, 1787, and Washington to H, October 18, 1787.
    2. The enclosure was the first *Federalist* essay which had been printed in *The* [New York] *Independent Journal: or, the General Advertiser* on October 27, 1787. See Washington to H, November 10, 1787.
    3. The undated, printed pamphlet setting forth von Steuben's claim is in the Papers of the Continental Congress, National Archives. For an account of von Steuben's claims against the United States, see "Continental Congress. Report on the Claim of Baron von Steuben," December 30, 1782, and H to John Jay, December 7, 1784.
    Von Steuben continued, through the seventeen-eighties, to press his claims upon Congress. On April 14, 1787, he wrote his wartime aide, Benjamin Walker, that "My memorial is signed. Hamilton has promised to present it at the proper time. I have decided to trust myself entirely to his discretion" (Palmer, *Steuben*, 346). On October 6, 1787, von Steuben's memorial was considered in Congress and referred to a committee. H, in support of von Steuben's claim, urged distinguished men familiar with the Baron's services in the Revolutionary Army to write Congress on his behalf (*ibid.*, 353).
    4. See the letter to Washington dated October 26, 1787, which H wrote for von Steuben.

## To James Madison

[New York, October, 1787–March 4, 1788] [1]

If Mr. Madison should be disengaged this Evening Mr. Hamilton would be obliged by an opportunity of conversing with him at his lodgings for half an hour. If engaged this Evening he will thank him to say whether tomorrow Evening will suit.

Wednesday

AL, James Madison Papers, Library of Congress.

1. H's note is undated. It probably was written between October, 1787, and March 4, 1788, a period during which Madison was in New York and the only period when the two men were in frequent contact.

## From George Washington

Mount Vernon Novr. 10th. 1787

Dear Sir;

I thank you for the Pamphlet, and for the Gazette contained in your letter of the 30th. Ulto.[1] For the remaining numbers of Publius, I shall acknowledge myself obliged as I am persuaded the subject will be well handled by the Author.

The new Constitution has, as the public prints will have informed you, been handed to the people of this state by an unanimous vote of the Assembly; but it is not to be inferred from hence that its opponents are silenced; on the contrary, there are many, and some powerful ones—some of whom, it is said by overshooting the mark, have lessened their weight: be this as it may, their assiduity stands unrivalled, whilst the friends to the Constitution content themselves with barely avowing their approbation of it. Thus stands the matter with us, at present; yet, my opinion is, that the major voice is favourable.

Application has been made to me by Mr. Secretary Thompson (by order of Congress) for a copy of ye report, of a Committee, which was appointed to confer with the Baron de Steuben, on his first arrival in this Country [2]—forwarded to me by Mr. President Laurens.[3] This I have accordingly sent. It throws no other light on the subject than such as are to be derived from the disinterested conduct of the Baron. No terms are made by him "nor will he accept of any thing but with general approbation." [4] I have however, in my letter enclosing this report to the Secretary, taken occasion to express an unequivocal wish, that Congress would reward the Baron for his Services, sacrifices and merits, to his entire satisfaction.[5] It is the only way in which I could bring my Sentiments before that honble body, as it has been an established principle with me, to ask nothing from it.

With very great esteem & regard  I am—Dear Sir  Yr Most Obedt. Servt                                    Go: Washington

Alexr. Hamilton Esqr.

ALS, Hamilton Papers, Library of Congress: LC, George Washington Papers, Library of Congress.

1. In his letter of October 30, 1787, H enclosed a pamphlet setting forth the claims of Baron von Steuben for compensation by the United States and a newspaper containing the first *Federalist* essay.

2. The Continental Congress had again taken up the question of von Steuben's claim in October, 1787. For an explanation of the request made to Washington by Charles Thomson, secretary of Congress, see von Steuben to Washington, October 26, 1787, note 3.

3. From November 1, 1777, to December 9, 1778, Henry Laurens was president of the Continental Congress.

4. The quotation is from the report of a committee of the Continental Congress, which was appointed in February, 1778, to confer with Baron von Steuben. It was the report of this committee which Thomson had asked Washington to forward to him. The report is in the Papers of the Continental Congress, National Archives.

5. Washington's letter to Thomson is printed in *GW*, XXIX, 307.


## *The Federalist No. 6* [1]

[New York, November 14, 1787]

*To the People of the State of New-York.*

THE three last numbers of this Paper [2] have been dedicated to an enumeration of the dangers to which we should be exposed, in a state of disunion, from the arms and arts of foreign nations. I shall now proceed to delineate dangers of a different, and, perhaps, still more alarming kind, those which will in all probability flow from dissentions between the States themselves, and from domestic factions and convulsions. These have been already in some instances slightly anticipated, but they deserve a more particular and more full investigation.

*The* [New York] *Independent Journal; or, the General Advertiser,* November 14, 1787. This essay appeared on November 15, 1787, in *The* [New York] *Daily Advertiser* and on November 16, 1787, in *The New-York Packet.*

1. For the background to this document, see "The Federalist. Introductory Note," October 27, 1787–May 28, 1788.

2. "work" substituted for "Paper" in Hopkins.

A man must be far gone in Utopian speculations who can seriously doubt, that[3] if these States should either be wholly disunited, or only united in partial confederacies,[4] the subdivisions into which they might be thrown would have frequent and violent contests with each other. To presume a want of motives for such contests, as an argument against their existence, would be to forget that men are ambitious, vindictive and rapacious. To look for a continuation of harmony between a number of independent unconnected sovereignties, situated in the same neighbourhood, would be to disregard the uniform course of human events, and to set at defiance the accumulated experience of ages.

The causes of hostility among nations are innumerable. There are some which have a general and almost constant operation upon the collective bodies of society: Of this description are the love of power or the desire of preeminence and dominion—the jealousy of power, or the desire of equality and safety. There are others which have a more circumscribed, though an equally operative influence, within their spheres: Such are the rivalships and competitions of commerce between commercial nations. And there are others, not less numerous than either of the former, which take their origin intirely in private passions; in the attachments, enmities, interests, hopes and fears of leading individuals in the communities of which they are members. Men of this class, whether the favourites of a king or of a people, have in too many instances abused the confidence they possessed; and assuming the pretext of some public motive, have not scrupled to sacrifice the national tranquility to personal advantage, or personal gratification.

The celebrated Pericles, in compliance with the resentments of a prostitute, (A) at the expence of much of the blood and treasure of his countrymen, attacked, vanquished and destroyed, the city of

(A) *ASPASIA*, vide *PLUTARCH'S* life of Pericles.[5]

3. "A man" through "that" omitted in Hopkins.
4. "a man must be far gone in Utopian speculations, who can seriously doubt that" inserted here in Hopkins.
5. The edition of Plutarch used by H probably was *Plutarch's Lives in six volumes: Translated from the Greek. With Notes, Explanatory and Critical, from Dacier and others. To which is prefix'd the Life of Plutarch, Written by Dryden* (London, Printed for J. and R. Tonson in the Strand, 1758). The article on "Pericles," is in Volume II, page 34.

the *Samnians*. The same man, stimulated by private pique against the *Megarensians*, (B) another nation of Greece, or to avoid a prosecution with which he was threatened as an accomplice in a supposed theft of the statuary *Phidias*, (C) or to get rid of the accusations prepared to be brought against him for dissipating the funds of the State in the purchase of popularity, (D) or from a combination of all these causes, was the primitive author of that famous and fatal war, distinguished in the Grecian annals by the name of the *Pelopponesian* war; which, after various vicissitudes, intermissions and renewals, terminated in the ruin of the Athenian commonwealth.

The ambitious Cardinal,[9] who was Prime Minister to Henry VIIIth. permitting his vanity to aspire to the Tripple-Crown, (E) entertained hopes of succeeding in the acquisition of that splendid prize by the influence of the Emperor Charles Vth. To secure the favour and interest of this enterprising and powerful Monarch, he precipitated England into a war with France,[11] contrary to the plainest dictates of Policy, and at the hazard of the safety and independence, as well of the Kingdom over which he presided by his councils, as of Europe in general—For if there ever was a Sovereign who bid fair to realise the project of universal monarchy it was the Emperor Charles Vth, of whose intrigues Wolsey was at once the instrument and the dupe.

The influence which the bigottry of one female, (F) the petu-

---

(B) – – – – – – Idem.[6]
(C) – – – Idem. Phidias was supposed to have stolen some public gold with the connivance of Pericles for the embelishment of the statue of Minerva.[7]
(D) Idem.[8]
(E) Worn by the Popes.[10]
(F) Madame De Maintenon [12]

6. *Ibid.*, 40–42. This note is omitted in Hopkins.
7. *Ibid.*, 42. This note is omitted in Hopkins.
8. *Ibid.*, 43–44. This note is omitted in Hopkins.
9. Thomas Wolsey (c. 1475–1530), the English Cardinal and statesman.
10. This note is omitted in Hopkins.
11. H is referring to the alliance which Wolsey concluded with Charles V in 1521 against France. Among other things, Wolsey promised that England would invade France the following summer with 40,000 men.

12. Madame de Maintenon was secretly married to Louis XIV of France in 1684. "The bigottry" to which H is referring was probably Madame de Maintenon's successful attempt to persuade Louis XIV to persecute the Huguenots.

lancies of another, (G) and the cabals of a third, (H) had in the co[n]temporary policy, ferments and pacifications of a considerable part of Europe are topics that have been too often descanted upon not to be generally known.

To multiply examples of the agency of personal considerations in the production of great national events, either foreign or domestic, according to their direction would be an unnecessary waste of time. Those who have but a superficial acquaintance with the sources from which they are to be drawn will themselves recollect a variety of instances; and those who have a tolerable knowledge of human nature will not stand in need of such lights, to form their opinion either of the reality or extent of that agency. Perhaps however a reference, tending to illustrate the general principle, may with propriety be made to a case which has lately happened among ourselves. If SHAYS had not been a *desperate debtor* it is much to be doubted whether Massachusetts would have been plunged into a civil war.[15]

But notwithstanding the concurring testimony of experience, in this particular, there are still to be found visionary, or designing men, who stand ready to advocate the paradox of perpetual peace between the States, though dismembered and alienated from each other. The genius of republics (say they) is pacific; the spirit of commerce has a tendency to soften the manners of men and to

(G) Dutchess of Marlborough.[13]
(H) Madame De Pompadoure.[14]

13. The Duchess of Marlborough, wife of the great soldier John Churchill, the first Duke of Marlborough, was confidante and adviser to Queen Anne who acceded to the throne of England in March, 1702. The imperious manners of the Duchess, as well as her political activities, alienated the Queen, and the two friends became bitter foes. The dismissal of the Duchess from her various offices came in 1710 and was shortly followed by the fall of the Duke.

14. Madame de Pompadour acquired a preponderant influence in the French government during twenty years (1745–1765) as the mistress of Louis XV. Because Louis XV took no interest in choosing his ministers, they were appointed or chosen through court intrigues and cabals in which Madame de Pompadour played a prominent role.

15. Shays' Rebellion of 1786 and early 1787 in central and western Massachusetts expressed the discontent which was widespread throughout New England during the economic depression following the Revolution. Led by Daniel Shays, a Revolutionary War veteran and officeholder of Pelham, Massachusetts, the insurgents resorted to armed efforts to intimidate and close the courts to prevent action against debtors. By February, 1787, state troops, under the leadership of Major General Benjamin Lincoln, had suppressed the rebellion.

extinguish those inflammable humours which have so often kindled into wars. Commercial republics, like ours, will never be disposed to waste themselves in ruinous contentions with each other. They will be governed by mutual interest, and will cultivate a spirit of mutual amity and concord.

Is it not [16] (we may ask these projectors in politics) [17] the true interest of all nations to cultivate the same benevolent and philosophic spirit? If this be their true interest, have they in fact pursued it? Has it not, on the contrary, invariably been found, that momentary passions and immediate interests have a more active and imperious controul over human conduct than general or remote considerations of policy, utility or justice? Have republics in practice been less addicted to war than monarchies? Are not the former administered by *men* as well as the latter? Are there not aversions, predilections, rivalships and desires of unjust acquisition that affect nations as well as kings? Are not popular assemblies frequently subject to the impulses of rage, resentment, jealousy, avarice, and of other irregular and violent propensities? Is it not well known that their determinations are often governed by a few individuals, in whom they place confidence, and [18] are of course liable to be tinctured by the passions and views of those individuals? Has commerce hitherto done any thing more than change the objects of war? Is not the love of wealth as domineering and enterprising a passion as that of power or glory? Have there not been as many wars founded upon commercial motives, since that has become the prevailing system of nations, as were before occasioned b[y] the cupidity of territory or dominion? Has not the spirit of commerce in many instances administered new incentives to the appetite both for the one and for the other? —Let experience the least fallible guide of human opinions be appealed to for an answer to these inquiries.

Sparta, Athens, Rome and Carthage were all Republics; two of them, Athens and Carthage, of the commercial kind. Yet were they as often engaged in wars, offensive and defensive, as the neighbouring Monarchies of the same times. Sparta was little better than a well

16. "Is it not" omitted in Hopkins.
17. "whether it is not" inserted at this point in Hopkins.
18. "that they" inserted at this point in Hopkins.

regulated camp; and Rome was never sated of carnage and conquest.

Carthage, though a commercial Republic, was the aggressor in the very war that ended in her destruction. Hannibal had carried her arms into the heart of Italy and to the gates of Rome, before Scipio, in turn, gave him an overthrow in the territories of Carthage and made a conquest of the Commonwealth.

Venice in latter times figured more than once in wars of ambition; 'till becoming an object of terror to the other Italian States, Pope Julius the Second found means to accomplish that formidable league, (I) which gave a deadly blow to the power and pride of this haughty Republic.

The Provinces of Holland, 'till they were overwhelmed in debts and taxes, took a leading and conspicuous part in the wars of Europe. They had furious contests with England for the dominion of the sea; and were among the most persevering and most implacable of the opponents of Lewis XIV.

In the government of Britain the representatives of the people compose one branch of the national legislature. Commerce has been for ages the predominant pursuit of that country.[19] Few nations, nevertheless,[20] have been more frequently engaged in war; and the wars, in which that kingdom has been engaged, have in numerous instances proceeded from the people.

There have been, if I may so express it, almost as many popular as royal wars. The cries of the nation and the importunities of their representatives have, upon various occasions, dragged their monarchs into war, or continued them in it contrary to their inclinations, and, sometimes, contrary to the real interests of the State. In that memorable struggle for superiority, between the rival Houses of *Austria* and *Bourbon* which so long kept Europe in a flame, it is well known that the antipathies of the English against the French, seconding the ambition, or rather the avarice of a favourite leader, (K), protracted the war[21] beyond the limits marked out by sound policy

(I) The LEAGUE OF CAMBRAY, comprehending the Emperor, the King of France, the King of Arragon, and most of the Italian Princes and States.
(K) The Duke of Marlborough.

19. "yet" inserted at this point in Hopkins.
20. "nevertheless" omitted in Hopkins.
21. The reference is to the War of the Spanish Succession, 1701–1714. The Duke of Marlborough, commander-in-chief of the united armies of England and

and for a considerable time in opposition to the views of the Court.

The wars of these two last mentioned nations have in a great measure grown out of commercial considerations—The desire of supplanting and the fear of being supplanted either in particular branches of traffic or in the general advantages of trade and navigation [and sometimes even the more culpable desire of sharing in the commerce of other nations, without their consent.

The last war but two between Britain and Spain sprang from the attempts of the English merchants, to prosecute an illicit trade with the Spanish main.[22] These unjustifiable practices on their part produced severities on the part of the Spaniards, towards the subjects of Great Britain, which were not more justifiable; because they exceeded the bounds of a just retaliation, and were chargeable with inhumanity and cruelty. Many of the English who were taken on the Spanish coasts were sent to dig in the mines of Potosi; and by the usual progress of a spirit of resentment, the innocent were after a while confounded with the guilty in indiscriminate punishment. The complaints of the merchants kindled a violent flame throughout the nation, which soon after broke out in the house of commons, and was communicated from that body to the ministry. Letters of reprisal were granted and a war ended, which in its consequences overthrew all the alliances that but twenty years before had been formed, with sanguine expectations of the most beneficial fruits.] [23]

From this summary of what has taken place in other countries, whose situations have borne the nearest resemblance to our own, what reason can we have to confide in those reveries, which would

---

Holland, refused in 1709 to accept the plea of the King of France for peace, despite the opposition of the Tory party in England to the continuance of the French war.

22. H is referring to the war between England and Spain which began in 1739. By a contract auxiliary to the Treaty of Utrecht in 1713, England was given a monopoly of supplying slaves to Spanish America and was allowed to send one ship a year to trade at Porto Bello on the Isthmus of Panama. The English anchored only the one ship but resupplied it from other ships anchored nearby and thus sent a steady stream of supplies into Spanish America. Individual Englishmen, maintaining no pretense of legality, merely tried to avoid the Spanish coast guard.

23. The material in brackets did not appear in the newspaper. It is found in McLean and Hopkins.

H's reference to the overthrow of "all the alliances that but twenty years before had been formed" is to the breakup of the continental balance of power established by the Treaty of Utrecht in 1713.

seduce us into an [24] expectation of peace and cordiality between the members of the present confederacy, in a state of separation? Have we not already seen enough of the fallacy and extravagance of those idle theories which have amused us with promises of an exemption from the imperfections,[25] weaknesses and [26] evils incident to society in every shape? Is it not time to awake from the deceitful dream of a golden age, and to adopt as a practical maxim for the direction of our political conduct, that we, as well as the other inhabitants of the globe, are yet remote from the happy empire of perfect wisdom and perfect virtue?

Let the point of extreme depression to which our national dignity and credit have sunk—let the inconveniences felt every where from a lax and ill administration of government—let the revolt of a part of the State of North-Carolina— [27] the late menacing disturbances

24. "the" substituted for "an" in Hopkins.
25. "the" inserted at this point in McLean and Hopkins.
26. "the" inserted at this point in McLean and Hopkins.
27. "The revolt of a part of the State of North-Carolina" refers to the establishment in 1784 of a separate state, Franklin, by the inhabitants of four western counties of North Carolina. The opposition of North Carolina and internal dissensions within the infant state led at the end of 1787 to the submission of the inhabitants of Franklin to the authority of North Carolina.
28. "The late menacing disturbances in Pennsylvania" had occurred in 1787 in the Wyoming Valley, an area in which contention and violence were not new. The disturbances to which H is referring are best described in a message, dated October 27, 1787, from the president and the Supreme Executive Council of Pennsylvania to the General Assembly:
"GENTLEMEN,
"SINCE the last session there has been a renewal of the disturbances at *Wyoming;* some restless spirits there having imagined a project of withdrawing the inhabitants of that part of this state, and some part of the state of *New-York,* from their allegiance, and of forming them into a new state, to be carried into effect by an armed force, in defiance of the laws of the two states. Having intelligence of this, we caused one of the principal conspirators to be apprehended, and secured in the gaol of this city—and another who resided in the state of New York, at our request, has been taken up by the authority of that government. The papers found on this occasion fully discover the designs of these turbulent people, and some of their letters are herewith laid before you. . . . To protect the civil officers of our new county of *Luzerne* in the exercise of their respective functions, we have ordered a body of militia to hold themselves in readiness to march thither, which will be done, unless some future circumstances, and informations from those parts, may make it appear unnecessary."
(*Minutes of the General Assembly of the Commonwealth of Pennsylvania* [Philadelphia, 1787], 8.)
Four days later, on October 31, 1787, the Assembly "*Resolved,* As in the opinion of this House a permanent force of enlisted troops may be necessary to secure the peace of the county of *Luzerne,* that the Supreme Executive Council be authorized and requested to obtain permission of Congress to raise any

in Pennsylvania [28] and the actual insurrections and rebellions in Massachusettes declare—! [29]

So far is the general sense of mankind from corresponding with the tenets of those, who endeavour to lull asleep our apprehensions of discord and hostility between the States, in the event of disunion, that it has from long observation of the progress of society become a sort of axiom in politics, that vicinity, or nearness of situation, constitutes nations natural enemies. An intelligent writer expresses himself on this subject to this effect—"NEIGHBOURING NATIONS (says he) are naturally ENEMIES of each other, unless their common weakness forces them to league in a CONFEDERATE REPUBLIC, and their constitution prevents the differences that neighbourhood occasions, extinguishing that secret jealousy, which disposes all States to aggrandise themselves at the expence of their neighbours." (L) This passage, at the same time points out the EVIL and suggests the REMEDY.

PUBLIUS.

(L) Vide Principes des Negotiations par L'Abbe de Mably.[30]

---

number of troops for the aforesaid purpose, not exceeding five hundred men" (*ibid.*, 14).

29. See note 15.

30. The quotation is from Gabriel Bonnot de Mably, *Des Principes des Négociations, pour servir d'introduction au Droit Public d l'Europe, fondé sur les Traités* (Amsterdam, 1757). It is more easily found in *Collection Complète Des Œuvres de L'Abbé de Mably* (Paris, 1794-1795), V, 93.

The passage of which this is a translation reads:

"Des états voisins sont naturellement ennemis les uns des autres, à moins que leur foiblesse commune ne les force, à se liguer pour former une république fédérative, et que leur constitution, semblable ou équivalente à celle des Suisses, ne prévienne les différends qu'occasionne le voisinage, et n'étouffe cette jalousie secrète qui porte tous les états a s'accroître au préjudice de leurs voisins."

## To Pierre Van Cortlandt [1]

[*New York, November 15, 1787.* The catalogue description of this letter reads as follows: "Hamilton's letter relates to a mortgage held by Col. Trumbull the title to which is in question, and asks Mr. Van Cortlandt to search the title." *Letter not found*].

ALS, sold at Parke-Bernet Galleries, February 11, 1941, Lot 137.

1. In 1777 Van Cortlandt became the first lieutenant governor of New York, a position he held until 1795.

## From John Witherspoon [1]

Princeton [New Jersey] Nov 16. 1787

Sir

I have just received your Letter [2] inclosing Baron Steubens Printed Paper [3] In answer please to knew that Nothing passed between me & the Committee that can be constructed as the least Contradiction to which I certified formerly. They asked now [4] whether there was an actual or explicit Contract with Baron Steuben verbally though not written I answerd that there was not any proper formal Contract between him & the Committee this could be as the Committee had no Such Powers & that it did not appear that the Baron himself alledged that there was. He made his proposals & I remember mentioned his having sacrificed good Appointments in Europe but I cannot recollect the Amount nor did it Seem of any Importance as he referred himself to the Success of the War & the Justice & Generosity of Congress in the Circumstances in which they should find themselves at the End of it. The Committee you perceive by other Testimonies repeated the whole of this to Congress so that the Facts are as well established as They can be. The Barons Claim is a Claim of Equity & Generosity on Congress the Grounds of which can be as clearly laid before Congress now as formerly.

I should have been glad to have knew whether the Paper No 15 immediately preceeding my Certificate [5] is an exact Copy of that to which the Certificate was adjected because there is a reference on the Certificate to a preceeding representation At any Rate it can differ very little.

I have the honour   Sir   Your most obedt humble Servant

Jno Witherspoon

Honble Alexr Hamilton Esqr

ALS, RG 46, First Congress, 1789–1791, Reports of Select Committees, Claim of Baron de Steuben, National Archives; copy, Papers of the Continental Congress, National Archives.

1. Dr. John Witherspoon, president of the College of New Jersey (Princeton), was a member of the committee of the Continental Congress which was appointed in February, 1778, to confer with Baron von Steuben on the terms of

his acceptance of a commission in the Continental Army. Von Steuben later maintained that Congress had promised him compensation at the war's end. His claim was repeatedly presented to Congress, and on October 6, 1787, Congress again considered it. H on behalf of von Steuben sent to prominent men, whose influence might be useful in securing the success of the claim, a pamphlet (Papers of the Continental Congress, National Archives) exhibiting von Steuben's service in the Patriot cause. See H to George Washington, October 30, 1787, and Washington to H, November 10, 1787.

2. Letter not found.

3. The reference is to the pamphlet described in note 1.

4. The copy, in the Papers of the Continental Congress, reads "me."

5. Witherspoon is referring to his statement, dated November 1, 1785, in the von Steuben pamphlet, which described the part he had played as chairman of the committee which had conferred with von Steuben. Number 15 was an account of the meeting of that committee with von Steuben in February, 1778.


## The Federalist No. 7 [1]

[New York, November 17, 1787]

*To the People of the State of New-York.*

It is sometimes asked, with an air of seeming triumph, what inducements could the States have,[2] if disunited, to make war upon each other? It would be a full answer to this question to say—precisely the same inducements, which have, at different times, deluged in blood all the nations in the world. But unfortunately for us, the question admits of a more particular answer. There are causes of difference within our immediate contemplation, of the tendency of which, even under the restraints of a Fœderal Constitution, we have had sufficient experience, to enable us to form a judgment of what might be expected, if those restraints were removed.

Territorial disputes have at all times been found one of the most fertile sources of hostility among nations. Perhaps the greatest proportion of the wars that have desolated the earth have sprung from this origin. This cause would exit, among us, in full force. We have a vast tract of unsettled territory within the boundaries of the United States. There still are discordant and undecided claims between several of them; and the dissolution of the Union would lay

*The [New York] Independent Journal: or, the General Advertiser,* November 17, 1787. This essay appeared on November 19, 1787, in *The [New York] Daily Advertiser,* and on November 20, 1787, in *The New-York Packet.*

1. For the background to this document, see "The Federalist. Introductory Note," October 27, 1787–May 28, 1788.

2. "the States could have" substituted for "could the States have" in Hopkins.

a foundation for similar claims between them all. It is well known, that they have heretofore had serious and animated discussions concerning the right to the lands which were ungranted at the time of the revolution, and which usually went under the name of crownlands. The States within the limits of whose colonial governments they were comprised have claimed them as their property; the others have contended that the rights of the crown in this article devolved upon the Union; especially as to all that part of the Western territory which either by actual possession or through the submission of the Indian proprietors was subjected [3] to the jurisdiction of the King of Great Britain, till it was relinquished in [4] the treaty of peace. This, it has been said, was at all events an acquisition to the confederacy by compact with a foreign power. It has been the prudent policy of Congress to appease this controversy, by prevailing upon the States to make cessions to the United States for the benefit of the whole. This has been so far accomplished, as under a continuation of the Union, to afford a decided prospect of an amicable termination of the dispute. A dismemberment of the confederacy however would revive this dispute, and would create others on the same subject. At present, a large part of the vacant Western territory is by cession at least, if not by any anterior right, the common property of the Union. If that were at an end, the States which made the cession [5] on a principle of Fœderal compromise, would be apt, when the motive of the grant had ceased, to reclaim the lands as a reversion. The other States would no doubt insist on a proportion, by right of representation. Their argument would be that a grant, once made, could not be revoked, and that the justice of their participating in territory acquired, or secured by the joint efforts of the confederacy remained undiminished—If contrary to probability it should be admitted by all the States, that each had a right to a share of this common stock, there would still be a difficulty to be surmounted, as to a proper rule of apportionment. Different principles would be set up by different States for this purpose; and as they would affect the opposite interests of the parties, they might not easily be susceptible of a pacific adjustment.

3. "subject" substituted for "subjected" in Hopkins.
4. "by" substituted for "in" in Hopkins.
5. "have made cessions" substituted for "made the cession" in McLean and Hopkins.

In the wide field of Western territory, therefore, we perceive an ample theatre for hostile pretensions, without any umpire or common judge to interpose between the contending parties. To reason from the past to the future we shall have good ground to apprehend, that the sword would sometimes be appealed to as the arbiter of their differences. The circumstances of the dispute between Connecticut and Pennsylvania, respecting the land [6] at Wyoming admonish us, not to be sanguine in expecting an easy accommodation of such differences.[7] The articles of confederation obliged the parties to submit the matter to the decision of a Fœderal Court. The submission was made, and the Court decided in favour of Pennsylvania. But Connecticut gave strong indications of dissatisfaction with that determination; nor did she appear to be intirely resigned to it, till by negotiation and management something like an equivalent was found for the loss she supposed herself to have sustained.[8] Nothing here said is intended to convey the slightest censure on the conduct of that State. She no doubt sincerely believed herself to have been injured by the decision; and States like individuals acquiese with great reluctance in determinations to their disadvantage.

Those, who had an opportunity of seeing the inside of the trans-

6. "lands" in Hopkins and McLean.

7. The Wyoming controversy concerned lands on the upper waters of the Susquehanna, the ownership of which was contested by Connecticut settlers and Pennsylvania land claimants. This dispute, which began before the Revolution, was referred, as H states, to a court established under the auspices of the Continental Congress. On December 30, 1782, the Court of Commissioners handed down the so-called "Trenton Decree," which stated that "the State of Connecticut has no right to the lands in controversy" and that "the jurisdiction and preemption of all the territory lying within the charter boundary of Pensylvania, and now claimed by the State of Connecticut, do of right belong to the State of Pensylvania" (*JCC*, XXIV, 31–32). To settle the question of jurisdiction, however, was not to solve the problem of ownership of land, and Connecticut and Pennsylvania land claimants continued their controversy over the disputed area.

8. The equivalent which Connecticut secured was the Western Reserve. In 1786, Connecticut granted to Congress all its lands to the Mississippi, beginning 120 miles westward of the western boundary of Pennsylvania. The lands ceded were within the region already granted to the United States by Virginia. Had the cession meant only that Connecticut ceded lands to Congress which Virginia had already ceded, no difficulty would have arisen. But Connecticut retained a tract of land in the ceded territory known as the Western Reserve. Congress's acceptance of Connecticut's demand for reserved land in the cession was generally understood to be a bribe to that state for its acquiescence in the decree awarding the Wyoming Valley to Pennsylvania.

actions, which attended the progress of the controversy between
this State and the district of Vermont,[9] can vouch the opposition we
experienced, as well from States not interested as from those which
were interested in the claim; and can attest the danger, to which
the peace of the Confederacy might have been exposed, had this
State attempted to assert its rights by force. Two motives pre-
ponderated in that opposition—one a jealousy entertained of our
future power—and the other,[10] the interest of certain individuals of
influence in the neighbouring States, who had obtained grants of
lands under the actual government of that district. Even the States
which brought forward claims, in contradiction to ours, seemed
more solicitous to dismember this State, than to establish their own
pretentions. These were New-Hampshire, Massachussets and Connecticut. New-Jersey and Rhode-Island upon all occasions discovered
a warm zeal for the independence of Vermont; and Maryland, 'till
alarmed by the appearance of a connection between Canada and
that place, entered deeply into the same views. These being small
States, saw with an unfriendly eye the perspective of our growing
greatness. In a review of these transactions we may trace some of
the causes, which would be likely to embroil the States with each
other, if it should be their unpropitious destiny to become disunited.

The competitions of commerce would be another fruitful source
of contention. The States less favourably circumstanced would be
desirous of escaping from the disadvantages of local situation, and
of sharing in the advantages of their more fortunate neighbours.
Each State, or separate confederacy, would pursue a system of commercial polity peculiar to itself. This would occasion distinctions,
preferences and exclusions, which would beget discontent. The
habits of intercourse, on the basis of equal privileges, to which we
have been accustomed from the earliest settlement of the country,
would give a keener edge to those causes of discontent, than they

9. Vermont was formed from lands claimed by New York, New Hampshire,
and Massachusetts. For several years before the Revolution, settlers in the New
Hampshire Grants had objected to policies of the New York officials and
Assembly. In January, 1777, independence was proclaimed, and in July of the
same year a convention adopted a constitution for the new state. Vermont then
requested permission to join the Union. This permission was withheld, largely
because of the opposition of New York, until after the adoption of the Constitution.

10. "another" substituted for "and the other" in Hopkins.

would naturally have, independent of this circumstance. *We should be ready to denominate injuries those things which were in reality the justifiable acts of independent sovereignties consulting a distinct interest.* The spirit of enterprise, which characterises the commercial part of America, has left no occasion of displaying itself unimproved. It is not at all probable that this unbridled spirit would pay much respect to those regulations of trade, by which particular States might endeavour to secure exclusive benefits to their own citizens. The infractions of these regulations on one side, the efforts to prevent and repel them on the other, would naturally lead to outrages, and these to reprisals and wars.

The opportunities, which some States would have of rendering others tributary to them, by commercial regulations, would be impatiently submitted to by the tributary States. The relative situation of New-York, Connecticut and New Jersey, would afford an example of this kind. New-York, from the necessities of revenue, must lay duties on her importations. A great part of these duties must be paid by the inhabitants of the two other States in the capacity of consumers of what we import. New York would neither be willing nor able to forego this advantage. Her citizens would not consent that a duty paid by them should be remitted in favour of the citizens of her neighbours; nor would it be practicable, if there were not this impediment in the way, to distinguish the customers in our own markets. Would Connecticut and New-Jersey long submit to be taxed by New-York for her exclusive benefit? Should we be long permitted to remain in the quiet and undisturbed enjoyment of a metropolis, from the possession of which we derived an advantage so odious to our neighbours, and, in their opinion, so oppressive? Should we be able to preserve it against the incumbent weight of Connecticut on the one side, and the co-operating pressure of New-Jersey on the other? These are questions that temerity alone will answer in the affirmative.

The public debt of the Union would be a further cause of collision between the separate States or confederacies. The apportionment, in the first instance, and the progressive extinguishment, afterwards, would be alike productive of ill humour and animosity. How would it be possible to agree upon a rule of apportionment satisfactory to all? There is scarcely any, that can be proposed, which is entirely free from real objections. These, as usual, would be exaggerated by the adverse interests [11] of the parties. There are even dissimilar views among the States, as to the general principle of discharging the public debt. Some of them, either less impressed with the importance of national credit, or because their citizens have little, if any, immediate interest in the question, feel an indifference, if not a repugnance to the payment of the domestic debt, at any rate. These would be inclined to magnify the difficulties of a distribution. Others of them, a numerous body of whose citizens are creditors to the public, beyond the proportion of the State in the total amount of the national debt, would be strenuous for some equitable and effectual provision. The procrastinations of the former would excite the resentments of the latter. The settlement of a rule would in the mean time be postponed, by real differences of opinion and affected delays. The citizens of the States interested, would clamour, foreign powers would urge, for the satisfaction of their just demands; and the peace of the States would be hazarded [12] to the double contingency of external invasion and internal contention.

Suppose [13] the difficulties of agreeing upon a rule surmounted, and the apportionment made. Still there is great room to suppose, that the rule agreed upon would, upon [14] experiment, be found to bear harder upon some States than upon others. Those which were sufferers by it would naturally seek for a mitigation of the burthen. The others would as naturally be disinclined to a revision, which was likely to end in an increase of their own incumbrances. Their refusal would be too plausible a pretext to the complaining States to withhold their contributions,[15] not to be embraced with avidity; and the non compliance of these States with their engagements would be a ground of bitter dissention and altercation. If even the rule adopted should in practice justify the equality of its principle, still delinquencies in payment, on the part of some of the States, would result from a diversity of other causes—the real deficiency of resources—

11. "interest" in Hopkins.
12. "exposed" substituted for "hazarded" in Hopkins.
13. "But" inserted before the word "Suppose" in Hopkins.
14. "in the" substituted for "upon" in Hopkins.
15. "afford to the complaining states a pretext for withholding their contributions, too plausible" substituted for "be too" through "contributions" in Hopkins.

the mismanagement of their finances, accidental disorders in the administration of the government—and in addition to the rest the reluctance with which men commonly part with money for purposes, that have outlived the exigencies which produced them, and interfere with the supply of immediate wants. Delinquencies from whatever causes would be productive of complaints, recriminations and quarrels. There is perhaps nothing more likely to disturb the tranquillity of nations, than their being bound to mutual contributions for any common object, which does not yield an equal and coincident benefit. For it is an observation as true, as it is trite, that there is nothing men differ so readily about as the payment of money.

Laws in violation of private contracts as they amount to aggressions on the rights of those States, whose citizens are injured by them, may be considered as another probable source of hostility. We are not authorised to expect, that a more liberal or more equitable spirit would preside over the legislations of the individuals States hereafter, if unrestrained by any additional checks, than we have heretofore seen, in too many instances, disgracing their several codes. We have observed the disposition to retaliation excited in Connecticut, in consequence of the enormities perpetrated by the legislature of Rhode-Island; [16] and we may reasonably infer, that in similar cases, under other circumstances, a war not of *parchment* but of the sword would chastise such atrocious breaches of moral obligation and social justice.

The probability of incompatible alliances between the different States, or confederacies, and different foreign nations, and the effects of this situation upon the peace of the whole, have been sufficiently unfolded in some preceding papers.[17] From the view they have exhibited, of this part of the subject, this conclusion is to be drawn, that America, if not connected at all, or only by the feeble tie of a simple league offensive and defensive, would by the operation of such opposite and jarring alliances be gradually entangled in all the

16. The paper money and stay laws of Rhode Island to which creditors not only in that state but in other states objected were especially resented in Connecticut where a law was passed forbidding Connecticut courts to try cases of Rhode Island creditors against Connecticut debtors. When this retaliatory measure failed, Connecticut in 1787 sent to Congress a protest against the Rhode Island laws as violations of the Articles of Confederation.

17. This is a reference to essay 5 of *The Federalist*.

pernicious labyrinths of European politics and wars; and by the destructive contentions of the parts, into which she was divided, would be likely to become a prey to the artifices and machinations of powers equally the enemies of them all. *Divide et impera* \* must be the motto of every nation, that either hates, or fears us.[19]

PUBLIUS

\* *Divide and command.*[18]

18. This note omitted in Hopkins.
19. In the newspaper the following note was added: "*In order that the whole subject of these Papers may be as soon as possible laid before the Public, it is proposed to publish them four times a week, on Tuesday in the* New-York Packet *and on Thursday in the* Daily Advertiser." The way in which this plan was carried out is discussed in "The Federalist. Introductory Note," October 27, 1787–May 28, 1788.

## *The Federalist No. 8* [1]

[New York, November 20, 1787]

*To the People of the State of New-York.*

ASSUMING it therefore as an established truth that [2] the several States, in case of disunion,[3] or such combinations of them as might happen to be formed out of the wreck of the general confederacy, would be subject to those vicissitudes of peace and war, of friendship and enmity with each other, which have fallen to the lot of all neighbouring nations not united under one government, let us enter into a concise detail of some of the consequences, that would attend such a situation.

War between the States, in the first periods of their separate existence, would be accompanied with much greater distresses than it commonly is in those countries, where regular military establishments have long obtained. The disciplined armies always kept on foot on the continent of Europe, though they bear a malignant

*The New-York Packet,* November 20, 1787. This essay appeared on November 21 in both *The* [New York] *Independent Journal: or, the General Advertiser* and *The* [New York] *Daily Advertiser.*
1. For the background to this document, see "The Federalist. Introductory Note," October 27, 1787–May 28, 1788.
2. "in case of disunion" inserted here in Hopkins.
3. "in case of disunion" omitted in Hopkins.

aspect to liberty and œconomy, have notwithstanding been productive of the [4] signal advantage, of rendering sudden conquests impracticable, and of preventing that rapid desolation, which used to mark the progress of war, prior to their introduction. The art of fortification has contributed to the same ends. The nations of Europe are incircled with chains of fortified places, which mutually obstruct invasion. Campaigns are wasted in reducing two or three frontier garrisons, to gain admittance into an enemy's country. Similar impediments occur at every step, to exhaust the strength and delay the progress of an invader. Formerly an invading army would penetrate into the heart of a neighbouring country, almost as soon as intelligence of its approach could be received; but now a comparatively small force of disciplined troops, acting on the defensive with the aid of posts, is able to impede and finally to frustrate the enterprises of one much more considerable. The history of war, in that quarter of the globe, is no longer a history of nations subdued and empires overturned, but of towns taken and retaken, of battles that decide nothing, of retreats more beneficial than victories, of much effort and little acquisition.

In this country the scene would be altogether reversed. The jealousy of military establishments, would postpone them as long as possible. The want of fortifications leaving the frontiers of one State open to another, would facilitate inroads. The populous States would with little difficulty overrun their less populous neighbours. Conquests would be as easy to be made, as difficult to be retained. War therefore would be desultory and predatory. PLUNDER and devastations ever march in the train of irregulars. The calamities of individuals would make the principal figure in the events, which would characterise our military exploits.

This picture is not too highly wrought, though I confess, it would not long remain a just one. Safety from external danger is the most powerful director of national conduct. Even the ardent love of liberty will, after a time, give way to its dictates. The violent destruction of life and property incident to war—the continual effort and alarm attendant on a state of continual danger, will compel nations the most attached to liberty, to resort for repose and security, to institutions, which have a tendency to destroy their civil and politi-

4. In the newspaper, "this." The change was made in McLean and Hopkins.

cal rights. To be more safe they, at length, become willing to run the risk of being less free.

The institutions [5] alluded to are STANDING ARMIES, and the correspondent appendages of military establishments. Standing armies it is said are not provided against in the new constitution; and it is therefore [6] inferred, that they may [7] exist under it.* Their existence however from the very terms of the proposition, is, at most,[10] problematical & uncertain. But standing armies, it may be replied, must inevitably result from a dissolution of the confederacy. Frequent war and constant apprehension, which require a state of as constant preparation, will infallibly produce them. The weaker States or confederacies, would first have recourse to them, to put themselves upon an equality with their more potent neighbours. They would endeavour to supply the inferiority of population and resources, by a more regular and effective system of defence, by disciplined troops and by fortifications. They would, at the same time, be necessitated [11] to strengthen the executive arm of government; in doing which, their constitutions would acquire a progressive direction towards monarchy. It is of the nature of war to increase the executive at the expence of the legislative authority.

The expedients which have been mentioned, would soon give the States or confederacies that made use of them, a superiority over their neighbours. Small States, or States of less natural strength, under vigorous governments, and with the assistance of disciplined armies, have often triumphed over larger [12] States, or States of greater natural strength, which have been destitute of these advantages.

---

* This objection will be fully examined in its proper place,[8] and it will be shown that the only rational [9] precaution which could have been taken on this subject has been taken; and a much better one than is to be found in any constitution that has been heretofore framed in America, most of which contain no guard at all on this subject.

5. "chiefly" inserted here in McLean and Hopkins.
6. "thence" substituted for "therefore" in McLean and Hopkins.
7. "would" substituted for "may" in McLean and Hopkins.
8. The objection that the proposed constitution included no proscription of standing armies in time of peace was discussed in essays 24-29.
9. In the newspaper, "natural." The substitution was made in McLean and Hopkins.
10. "This inference, from the very form of the proposition, is, at best," substituted for "Their" through "at most" in McLean and Hopkins.
11. "obliged" substituted for "necessitated" in Hopkins.
12. "large" substituted for "larger" in McLean and Hopkins.

Neither the pride, nor the safety of the more important States, or confederacies, would permit them long to submit to this mortifying and adventitious inferiority.[13] They would quickly resort to means similar to those by which it had been effected, to reinstate themselves in their lost pre-eminence. Thus we should in a little time see established in every part of this country, the same engines of despotism, which have been the scourge of the old world. This at least would be the natural course of things, and our reasonings will be the more [14] likely to be just, in proportion as they are accommodated to this standard.

These are not vague inferrences drawn [15] from supposed or [16] speculative defects in a constitution, the whole power of which is lodged in the hands of the people, or their representatives and delegates, but [17] they are solid conclusions drawn from the natural and necessary progress of human affairs.

It may perhaps be asked, by way of objection to this,[18] why did not standing armies spring up out of the contentions which so often distracted the ancient republics of Greece? Different answers equally satisfactory may be given to this question. The industrious habits of the people of the present day, absorbed in the pursuits of gain, and devoted to the improvements of agriculture and commerce are incompatible with the condition of a nation of soldiers, which was the true condition of the people of those republics. The means of revenue, which have been so greatly multiplied by the encrease of gold and silver, and of the arts of industry, and the science of finance, which is the offspring of modern times, concurring with the habits of nations, have produced an intire revolution in the system of war, and have rendered disciplined armies, distinct from the body of the citizens, the inseparable companion of frequent hostility.

There is a wide difference also, between military establishments in a country, seldom exposed by its situation to internal invasions,[19] and in one which is often subject to them, and always apprehensive

13. "superiority" substituted for "inferiority" in Hopkins.
14. "the more" omitted in Hopkins.
15. "deduced" substituted for "drawn" in Hopkins.
16. "supposed or" omitted in Hopkins.
17. "but" omitted in Hopkins.
18. "to this" omitted in Hopkins.
19. "which, by its situation, is seldom exposed to invasions," substituted for "seldom" through "invasions" in Hopkins.

of them. The rulers of the former can have no good pretext, if they are even so inclined, to keep on foot armies so numerous as must of necessity be maintained in the latter. These armies being, in the first case, rarely, if at all, called into activity for interior defence, the people are in no danger of being broken to military subordination. The laws are not accustomed to relaxations, in favor of military exigencies—the civil state remains in full vigor, neither corrupted nor confounded with the principles or propensities of the other state. The smallness of the army renders the natural strength of the community an overmatch for it; [20] and the citizens, not habituated to look up to the military power for protection,[21] or to submit to its oppressions, neither love nor fear the soldiery: They view them with a spirit of jealous acquiescence in a necessary evil, and stand ready to resist a power which they suppose may be exerted to the prejudice of their rights. The army under such circumstances,[22] may usefully aid the magistrate to suppress a small faction, or an occasional mob, or insurrection; but it will be unable to enforce encroachments [23] against the united efforts of the great body of the people.

In a country, in the predicament last described, the contrary of all this happens. The perpetual menacings of danger oblige the government to be always prepared to repel it—its armies must be numerous enough for instant defence.[24] The continual necessity for their [25] services enhances the importance of the soldier, and proportionably degrades the condition of the citizen. The military state becomes elevated above the civil. The inhabitants of territories, often the theatre of war, are unavoidably subjected to frequent infringements on their rights, which serve to weaken their sense of those rights; and by degrees, the people are brought to consider the soldiery not only as their protectors, but as their superiors. The transi-

20. "forbids competition with the natural strength of the community," substituted for "renders" through "for it," in Hopkins.

21. In the newspaper, "perfection." The change was made in both McLean and Hopkins.

22. "though it" inserted at this point in Hopkins.

23. "will be utterly incompetent to the purpose of enforcing encroachments" substituted for "but it will be unable to enforce encroachments" in Hopkins.

24. "But in a country, where the perpetual menacings of danger oblige the government to be always prepared to repel it, her armies must be numerous enough for instant defence" substituted for the first two sentences of this paragraph in Hopkins.

25. "his" substituted for "their" in Hopkins.

tion from this disposition to that of considering them as masters, is neither remote, nor difficult: But it is very difficult to prevail upon a people under such impressions, to make a bold, or effectual resistance, to usurpations, supported by the military power.

The kingdom of Great Britain falls within the first description. An insular situation, and a powerful marine, guarding it in a great measure against the possibility of foreign invasion, supercede the necessity of a numerous army within the kingdom. A sufficient force to make head against a sudden descent, till the militia could have time to rally and embody, is all that has been deemed requisite. No motive of national policy has demanded, nor would public opinion have tolerated a larger numbers of troops upon its domestic establishment. There has been, for a long time past, little room for the operation of the other causes, which have been enumerated as the consequences of internal war.[26] This peculiar felicity of situation[27] has, in a great degree, contributed to preserve the liberty, which that country to this day enjoys, in spite of the prevalent venality and corruption. If, on the contrary,[28] Britain had been situated on the continent, and had been compelled, as she would have been, by that situation, to make her military establishments at home coextensive with those of the other great powers of Europe, she, like them, would in all probability, be at this day[29] a victim to the absolute power of a single man. 'Tis[30] possible, though not easy, that[31] the people of that island may[32] be enslaved from other causes, but it cannot be by the powers[33] of an army so inconsiderable as that which has been usually kept up in that[34] kingdom.

If we are wise enough to preserve the Union, we may for ages

26. This sentence is omitted in Hopkins.
27. At this point Hopkins adds the following footnote: "The recent prodigious aggrandizement of France has, probably, altered the situation of Great-Britain in this respect: it will be happy if the alteration has no tendency inauspicious to British liberty." The editor of the Hopkins editon referred, of course, to the territorial acquisitions of France during the years of the French Revolution. This is one of the two interpolations in the Hopkins edition which related statements in *The Federalist* to events after 1787–1788. For the other, see essay 77, note 3.
28. "on the contrary" omitted in Hopkins.
29. "at this day be" substituted for "be at this day" in Hopkins.
30. "It is" substituted for " 'tis" in Hopkins.
31. "for" substituted for "that" in Hopkins.
32. "to" substituted for "may" in Hopkins.
33. "prowess" substituted for "powers" in Hopkins.
34. "within the" substituted for "in that" in Hopkins.

enjoy an advantage similar to that of an insulated situation. Europe is at a great distance from us. Her colonies in our vicinity, will be likely to continue too much disproportioned in strength, to be able to give us any dangerous annoyance. Extensive military establishments cannot, in this position, be necessary to our security. But if we should be disunited, and the integral parts should either remain separated, or which is most probable, should be thrown together into two or three confederacies, we should be in a short course of time, in the predicament of the continental powers of Europe—our liberties would be a prey to the means of defending ourselves against the ambition and jealousy of each other.

This is an idea not superficial nor futile, but solid and weighty. It deserves the most serious and mature consideration of every prudent and honest man of whatever party. If such men will make a firm and solemn pause, and meditate dispassionately on the importance of this interesting idea,[35] if they will contemplate it, in all its attitudes, and trace it to all its consequences, they will not hesitate to part with trivial objections to a constitution, the rejection of which would in all probability put a final period to the Union. The airy phantoms that[36] flit before the distempered imaginations of some of its adversaries, would[37] quickly give place to the more substantial forms[38] of dangers real, certain, and[39] formidable.

PUBLIUS.

35. "its vast importance;" substituted for "the importance of this interesting idea," in Hopkins.
36. "now" inserted in Hopkins here.
37. "then" inserted in Hopkins.
38. "prospects" substituted for "forms" in McLean and Hopkins.
39. "extremely" inserted here in Hopkins.

## To Benjamin Rush [1]

[New York] November 21st [1787]

Dear Sir:

I send you herewith a Series of political papers under the denomination of the Federalist published in favor of the new Constitution. They do good here and it is imagined some of the last numbers might have a good effect upon some of your Quaker Members of Convention. They are going on and appear evidently to be written by different hands and to aim at a full examination of the subject. Perhaps even if they are not wanted with you, it might be well to give them a passage through your papers to your more Southern neighbors.

Upon the whole I think we have a good majority thus far in this State in favor of the Constitution.

I remain with Sincere esteem   Yr obt servt   Alex Hamilton

Bancroft Transcripts, MS Division, New York Public Library.
1. Rush, the renowned physician, had been elected to the Pennsylvania Ratifying Convention, in which he and James Wilson led the movement for adoption of the Constitution.

## *The Federalist No. 9* [1]

[New York, November 21, 1787]

*To the People of the State of New-York.*

A Firm Union will be of the utmost moment to the peace and liberty of the States as a barrier against domestic faction and insurrection. It is impossible to read the history of the petty Republics of Greece and Italy, without feeling sensations of horror and disgust at the distractions with which they were continually agitated, and at the rapid succession of revolutions, by which they were kept in a state of perpetual vibration,[2] between the extremes of tyranny and anarchy. If they exhibit occasional calms, these only serve as short-lived contrasts to the furious storms that are to succeed. If now and then intervals of felicity open themselves to view, we behold them with a mixture of regret arising from the reflection that the pleasing scenes before us are soon to be overwhelmed by the tempestuous waves of sedition and party-rage. If momentary rays of glory break forth from the gloom, while they dazzle us with a transient and fleeting brilliancy, they at the same time admonish us to lament that the vices of government should pervert the direction

The [New York] *Independent Journal: or, the General Advertiser*, November 21, 1787. This essay appeared on the same date in The [New York] *Daily Advertiser*, and on November 23 in *The New-York Packet*.
1. For the background to this document, see "The Federalist. Introductory Note," October 27, 1787–May 28, 1788.
2. "perpetually vibrating" substituted for "in a state of perpetual vibration" in Hopkins.

and tarnish the lustre of those bright talents and exalted indowments, for which the favoured soils, that produced them, have been so justly celebrated.

From the disorders that disfigure the annals of those republics, the advocates of despotism have drawn arguments, not only against the forms of republican government, but against the very principles of civil liberty. They have decried all free government, as inconsistent with the order of society, and have indulged themselves in malicious exultation over its friends and partizans. Happily for mankind, stupendous fabrics reared on the basis of liberty, which have flourished for ages, have in a few glorious instances refuted their gloomy sophisms. And, I trust, America will be the broad and solid foundation of other edifices not less magnificent, which will be equally permanent monuments of their errors.[3]

But it is not to be denied that the portraits, they have sketched of republican government, were too just copies of the originals from which they were taken. If it had been found impracticable, to have devised models of a more perfect structure, the enlightened friends to [4] liberty would have been obliged to abandon the cause of that species of government as indefensible. The science of politics, however, like most other sciences has received great improvement. The efficacy of various principles is now well understood, which were either not known at all, or imperfectly known to the ancients. The regular distribution of power into distinct departments—the introduction of legislative [5] ballances and checks—the institution of courts composed of judges, holding their offices during good behaviour—the representation of the people in the legislature by deputies of their own election—these are either wholly new discoveries or have made their principal progress towards perfection in modern times. They are means, and powerful means, by which the excellencies of republican government may be retained and its imperfections lessened or avoided. To this catalogue of circumstances, that tend to the amelioration of popular systems of civil government, I shall venture, however novel it may appear to some, to add one more on a principle, which has been made the foundation of an objection to the

3. "error" substituted for "errors" in Hopkins.
4. "of" substituted for "to" in Hopkins.
5. In the newspaper, "legislature." The change was made in McLean and Hopkins.

New Constitution, I mean the ENLARGEMENT of the ORBIT within which such systems are to revolve either in respect to the dimensions of a single State, or to the consolidation of several smaller States into one great confederacy. The latter is that which immediately concerns the object under consideration. It will however be of use to examine the principle in its application to a single State which shall be attended to in another place.[6]

The utility of a confederacy, as well to suppress faction and to guard the internal tranquillity of States, as to increase their external force and security, is in reality not a new idea. It has been practiced upon in different countries and ages, and has received the sanction of the most applauded[7] writers, on the subjects of politics. The opponents of the PLAN proposed have with great assiduity cited and circulated the observations of Montesquieu on the necessity of a contracted territory for a republican government.[8] But they seem not to have been apprised of the sentiments of that great man expressed in another part of his work, nor to have adverted to the consequences of the principle to which they subscribe, with such ready acquiescence.

When Montesquieu recommends a small extent for republics, the standards he had in view were of dimensions, far short of the limits of almost every one of these States. Neither Virginia, Massachusetts, Pennsylvania, New-York, North-Carolina, nor Georgia, can by any means be compared with the models, from which he reasoned and to which the terms of his description apply. If we therefore take[9] his ideas on this point, as the criterion of truth, we shall be driven

6. See essays 10 and 14.
7. "approved" substituted for "applauded" in Hopkins.
8. H is doubtless referring to the "observations of Montesquieu" quoted in the third letter of "Cato," published in *The New-York Journal, and Daily Patriotic Register* on October 25, 1787. "Cato," probably Governor George Clinton of New York, quoted Montesquieu as follows:

It is natural says Montesquieu *to a republic to have only a small territory, otherwise it cannot long subsist; in a large one, there are men of large fortunes, and consequently of less moderation; there are too great deposits to intrust in the hands of a single subject, an ambitious person soon becomes sensible that he may be happy, great, and glorious by oppressing his fellow citizens, and that he might raise himself to grandeur, on the ruins of his country. In large republics, the public good is sacrificed to a thousand views; in a small one the interest of the public is easily perceived, better understood, and more within the reach of every citizen; abuses have a less extent, and of course are less protected."

The "Cato" letters are published in Ford, *Essays on the Constitution*, 247-78.
9. "receive" substituted for "take" in Hopkins.

to the alternative, either of taking refuge at once in the arms of monarchy, or of splitting ourselves into an infinity of little jealous, clashing, tumultuous commonwealths, the wretched nurseries of unceasing discord and the miserable objects of universal pity or contempt. Some of the writers, who have come forward on the other side of the question, seem to have been aware of the dilemma; and have even been bold enough to hint at the division of the larger States, as a desirable thing. Such an infatuated policy, such a desperate expedient, might, by the multiplication of petty offices, answer the views of men, who possess not qualifications to extend their influence beyond the narrow circles of personal intrigue, but it could never promote the greatness or happiness of the people of America.

Referring the examination of the principle itself to another place,[10] as has been already mentioned, it will be sufficient to remark here, that in the sense of the author who has [11] been most emphatically quoted upon the occasion, it would only dictate a reduction of the SIZE of the more considerable MEMBERS of the Union; but would not militate against their being all comprehended in one Confederate Government. And this is the true question, in the discussion of which we are at present interested.

So far are the suggestions of Montesquieu from standing in opposition to a general Union of the States, that he explicitly treats of a CONFEDERATE REPUBLIC as the expedient for extending the sphere of popular government and reconciling the advantages of monarchy with those of republicanism.

"It is very probable (says he) * that mankind would have been obliged, at length, to live constantly under the government of a SINGLE PERSON, had they not contrived a kind of constitution, that has all the internal advantages of a republican, together with the external force of a monarchical government. I mean a CONFEDERATE REPUBLIC.

"This form of Government is a Convention, by which several

---

* *Spirit of Laws, Vol. I. Book IX. Chap. I.*[12]

10. See essays 10 and 14.

11. In the newspaper, "had"; the substitution was made in McLean and Hopkins.

12. The first edition of the Baron de Montesquieu's *L'Esprit des Lois* appeared in 1748. An English translation appeared soon thereafter. The references that have been supplied are to *The Spirit of Laws. Trans. by Mr. Nugent* (3rd ed., 2 Vols., London, Printed for J. Nourse and P. Vaillant in the Strand, 1758).

smaller *States* agree to become members of a larger *one*, which they intend to form. It is a kind of assemblage of societies, that constitute a new one, capable of encreasing by means of new associations, till they arrive to such a degree of power as to be able to provide for the security of the united body.

"A republic of this kind, able to withstand an external force, may support itself without any internal corruption. The form of this society prevents all manner of inconveniencies.

"If a single member should attempt to usurp the supreme authority, he could not be supposed to have an equal authority and credit, in all the confederate states. Were he to have too great influence over one, this would alarm the rest. Were he to subdue a part, that which would still remain free might oppose him with forces, independent of those which he had usurped, and overpower him before he could be settled in his usurpation.

"Should a popular insurrection happen, in one of the confederate States, the others are able to quell it. Should abuses creep into one part, they are reformed by those that remain sound. The State may be destroyed on one side, and not on the other; the confederacy may be dissolved, and the confederates preserve their sovereignty.

"As this government is composed of small republics it enjoys the internal happiness of each, and with respect to its external situation it is possessed, by means of the association of all the advantages of large monarchies."

I have thought it proper to quote at length these interesting passages, because they contain a luminous abrigement of the principal arguments in favour of the Union, and must effectually remove the false impressions, which a misapplication of other parts of the work was calculated to produce.[13] They have at the same time an intimate connection with the more immediate design of this Paper; which is to illustrate the tendency of the Union to repress domestic faction and insurrection.

A distinction, more subtle than accurate has been raised between *a confederacy* and a *consolidation* of the States. The essential characteristic of the first is said to be, the restriction of its authority to the members in their collective capacities, without reaching to the

13. In the newspaper, "produce." The substitution was made in McLean and Hopkins.

individuals of whom they are composed. It is contended that the national council ought to have no concern with any object of internal administration. An exact equality of suffrage between the members has also been insisted upon as a leading feature of a Confederate Government. These positions are in the main arbitrary; they are supported neither by principle nor precedent. It has indeed happened that governments of this kind have generally operated in the manner, which the distinction, taken notice of, supposes to be inherent in their nature—but there have been in most of them extensive exceptions to the practice, which serve to prove as far as example will go, that there is no absolute rule on the subject. And it will be clearly shewn, in the course of this investigation, that as far as the principle contended for has prevailed, it has been the cause of incurable disorder and imbecility in the government.

The definition of a *Confederate Republic* seems simply to be, an "assemblage of societies" or an association of two or more States into one State. The extent, modifications and objects of the Fœderal authority are mere matters of discretion. So long as the separate organisation of the members be not abolished, so long as it exists by a constitutional necessity for local purposes, though it should be in perfect subordination to the general authority of the Union, it would still be, in fact and in theory, an association of States, or a confederacy. The proposed Constitution, so far from implying an abolition of the State Governments, makes them constituent parts of the national sovereignty by allowing them a direct representation in the Senate, and leaves in their possession certain exclusive and very important portions of [14] sovereign power. This fully corresponds, in every rational import of the terms, with the idea of a Fœderal Government.

In the Lycian confederacy, which consisted of twenty three CITIES, or republics, the largest were intitled to *three* votes in the COMMON COUNCIL, those of the middle class to *two* and the smallest to *one*. The COMMON COUNCIL had the appointment of all the judges and magistrates of the respective CITIES. This was certainly the most delicate species of interference in their internal administration; for if there be any thing, that seems exclusively appropriated to the local jurisdictions, it is the appointment of their

14. "the" inserted at this point in Hopkins.

own officers. Yet Montesquieu, speaking of this association, says "Were I to give a model of an excellent confederate republic, it would be that of Lycia." [15] Thus we perceive that the distinctions insisted upon were not within the contemplation of this enlightened civilian,[16] and we shall be led to conclude that they are the novel refinements of an erroneous theory.

PUBLIUS.

15. The quotation is from Montesquieu, *The Spirit of Laws*, Book IX, Ch. 3.
16. "writer" substituted for "civilian" in Hopkins.

## The Federalist No. 11 [1]

[New York, November 24, 1787]

*To the People of the State of New-York.*

The importance of the Union, in a commercial light, is one of those points, about which there is least room to entertain a difference of opinion, and which has in fact commanded the most general assent of men, who have any acquaintance with the subject. This applies as well to our intercourse with foreign countries, as with each other.

There are appearances to authorise a supposition, that the adventurous spirit, which distinguishes the commercial character of America, has already excited uneasy sensations in several of the maritime powers of Europe. They seem to be apprehensive of our too great interference in that carrying trade, which is the support of their navigation and the foundation of their naval strength. Those of them, which have colonies in America, look forward,[2] to what this country is capable of becoming, with painful solicitude.[3] They foresee the dangers, that may threaten their American dominions from the neighbourhood of States, which have all the dispositions, and would possess all the means, requisite to the creation of a powerful

*The* [New York] *Independent Journal: or, the General Advertiser,* November 24, 1787. This essay appeared in *The New-York Packet* on November 27. It was begun in *The* [New York] *Daily Advertiser* on November 27 and concluded on November 28.
 1. For background to this document, see "The Federalist. Introductory Note," October 27, 1787–May 28, 1788.
 2. "with painful solicitude" inserted at this point in Hopkins.
 3. "with painful solicitude" omitted at this point in Hopkins.

marine. Impressions of this kind will naturally indicate the policy of fostering divisions among us, and of depriving us as far as possible of an ACTIVE COMMERCE in our own bottoms. This would answer [4] the threefold purpose of preventing our interference in their navigation, of monopolising the profits of our trade, and of clipping the wings, by which we might soar to a dangerous greatness. Did not prudence forbid the detail, it would not be difficult to trace by facts the workings of this policy to the cabinets of Ministers.

If we continue united, we may [5] counteract a policy so unfriendly to our prosperity in a variety of ways.[6] By prohibitory regulations, extending at the same time throughout the States, we may oblige foreign countries to bid against each other, for the privileges of our markets. This assertion will not appear chimerical to those who are able to appreciate the importance [7] of the markets of three millions of people—increasing in rapid progression, for the most part exclusively addicted to agriculture, and likely from local circumstances to remain so [8]—to any manufacturing nation; [9] and the immense difference there would be to the trade and navigation of such a nation, between a direct communication in its own ships, and an indirect conveyance of its products and returns, to and from America, in the ships of another country. Suppose, for instance, we had a government in America, capable of excluding Great-Britain (with whom we have at present no treaty of commerce) from all our ports, what would be the probable operation of this step upon her politics? Would it not enable us to negotiate with the fairest prospect of success for commercial privileges of the most valuable and extensive kind in the dominions of that kingdom? When these questions have been asked, upon other occasions, they have received a plausible but not a solid or satisfactory answer. It has been said, that prohibitions on our part would produce no change in the system of Britain; because she could prosecute her trade with us, through the medium of the Dutch, who would be her immediate customers and paymasters for those articles which were wanted for the supply

4. "then" inserted at this point in Hopkins.
5. "in a variety of ways" inserted at this point in Hopkins.
6. "in a variety of ways" omitted in Hopkins.
7. "to any manufacturing nation" inserted at this point in McLean and Hopkins.
8. "in this disposition" substituted for "so" in McLean and Hopkins.
9. "to any manufacturing nation" omitted in McLean and Hopkins.

of our markets. But would not her navigation be materially injured, by the loss of the important advantage of being her own carrier in that trade? Would not the principal part of its profits be intercepted by the Dutch, as a compensation for their agency and risk? Would not the mere circumstance of freight occasion a considerable deduction? Would not so circuitous an intercourse facilitate the competitions of other nations, by enhancing the price of British commodities in our markets, and by transferring to other hands the management of this interesting branch of the British commerce?

A mature consideration of the objects, suggested by these questions, will justify a belief, that the real disadvantages to [10] Britain, from such a state of things, conspiring with the prepossessions of a great part of the nation in favour of the American trade, and with the importunities of the West-India islands, would produce a relaxation in her present system, and would let us into the enjoyment of privileges in the markets of those islands and elsewhere, from which our trade would derive the most substantial benefits. Such a point gained from the British government, and which could not be expected without an equivalent in exemptions and immunities in our markets, would be likely to have a correspondent effect on the conduct of other nations, who would not be inclined to see themselves, altogether supplanted in our trade.

A further resource for influencing the conduct of European nations towards us, in this respect would arise from the establishment of a fœderal navy. There can be no doubt, that the continuance of the Union, under an efficient government, would put it in our power, at a period not very distant, to create a navy, which, if it could not vie with those of the great maritime powers, would at least be of respectable weight, if thrown into the scale of either of two contending parties. This would be more particularly [11] the case in relation to operations in the West-Indies. A few ships of the line sent opportunely to the reinforcement of either side, would often be sufficient to decide the fate of a campaign, on the event of which interests of the greatest magnitude were suspended. Our position is in this respect a very commanding one. And if to this considera-

10. "Great" inserted at this point in McLean and Hopkins.
11. In the newspaper, "peculiarly"; the substitution was made in McLean and Hopkins.

tion we add that of the usefulness of supplies from this country, in the prosecution of military operations in the West-Indies, it will readily be perceived, that a situation so favourable would enable us to bargain with great advantage for commercial privileges. A price would be set not only upon our friendship, but upon our neutrality. By a steady adherance to the Union we may hope ere long to become the Arbiter of Europe in America; and to be able to incline the ballance of European competitions in this part of the world as our interest may dictate.

But in the reverse of this elegible situation we shall discover, that the rivalships of the parts would make them checks upon each other, and would frustrate all the tempting advantages, which nature has kindly placed within our reach. In a state so insignificant, our commerce would be a prey to the wanton intermeddlings of all nations at war with each other; who, having nothing to fear from us, would with little scruple or remorse supply their wants by depredations on our property, as often as it fell in their way. The rights of neutrality will only be respected, when they are defended by an adequate power. A nation, despicable by its weakness, forfeits even the privilege of being neutral.

Under a vigorous national government, the natural strength and resources of the country, directed to a common interest, would baffle all the combinations of European jealousy to restrain our growth. This situation would even take away the motive to such combinations, by inducing an impracticability of success. An active commerce, an extensive navigation, and [12] a flourishing marine would then be the inevitable offspring of moral and physical necessity. We might defy the little arts of little politicians to controul, or vary, the irresistible and unchangeable course of nature.

But in a state of disunion these combinations might exist, and might operate with success. It would be in the power of the maritime nations, availing themselves of our universal impotence, to prescribe the conditions of our political existence; and as they have a common interest in being our carriers, and still more in preventing our being theirs,[13] they would in all probability combine to embarrass our navigation in such a manner, as would in effect destroy

12. "and" omitted in McLean and Hopkins.
13. "us from becoming theirs" substituted for "our being theirs" in Hopkins.

it, and confine us to a PASSIVE COMMERCE. We should thus be compelled to content ourselves with the first price of our commodities, and to see the profits of our trade snatched from us to enrich our enemies and persecutors. That unequalled spirit of enterprise, which signalises the genius of the American Merchants and Navigators, and which is in itself an inexhaustible mine of national wealth, would be stifled and lost; and poverty and disgrace would overspread a country, which with wisdom might make herself the admiration and envy of the world.

There are rights of great moment to the trade of America, which are rights of the Union. I allude to the fisheries, to the navigation of the Western [14] lakes and to that of the Mississippi. [15] The dissolution of the confederacy would give room for delicate questions, concerning the future existence of these rights; which the interest of more powerful partners would hardly fail to solve to our disadvantage. The disposition of Spain with regard to the Mississippi needs no comment. France and Britain are concerned with us in the fisheries; and view them as of the utmost moment to their navigation. They, of course, would hardly reamin long indifferent to that decided mastery of which experience has shewn us to be possessed in this valuable branch of traffic; and by which we are able to undersell those nations in their own markets. What more natural, than that they should be disposed to exclude, from the lists, such dangerous competitors?

This branch of trade ought not to be considered as a partial benefit. All the navigating States may in different degrees advantageously participate in it and under circumstances of a greater extension of mercantile capital [16] would not be unlikely to do it. As a nursery of seamen it now is, or when time shall have more nearly assimilated the principles of navigation in the several States, will become an universal resource. To the establishment of a navy it must be indispensible.

To this great national object of a NAVY, Union will contribute in various ways. Every institution will grow and flourish in proportion to the quantity and extent of the means concentered towards

14. "Western" omitted in McLean and Hopkins.
15. For information on these "rights," see Jay's discussion in essay 4.
16. "capacity" substituted for "capital" in Hopkins.

its formation and support. A navy of the United States, as it would embrace the resources of all, is an object far less remote than a navy of any single State, or partial confederacy, which would only embrace the resources of a part. It happens indeed that different portions of confederated America possess each some peculiar advantage for this essential establishment. The more Southern States furnish in greater abundance certain kinds of naval stores—tar, pitch and turpentine. Their wood for the construction of ships is also of a more solid and lasting texture. The difference in the duration of the ships of which the navy might be composed, if chiefly constructed of Southern wood would be of signal importance either in the view of naval strength or of national œconomy. Some of the Southern and of the middle States yield a greater plenty of iron and of better quality. Seamen must chiefly be drawn from the Northern hive. The necessity of naval protection to external or maritime commerce, does not require a particular elucidation, no more than the conduciveness of that species of commerce to the prosperity of a navy.[17] They, by a kind of reaction, mutually beneficial, promote each other.

An unrestrained intercourse between the States themselves will advance the trade of each, by an interchange of their respective productions, not only for the supply of reciprocal wants at home,[18] but for exportation to foreign markets. The veins of commerce in every part will be replenished, and will acquire additional motion and vigour from a free circulation of the commodities of every part. Commercial enterprise will have much greater scope, from the diversity in the productions of different States. When the staple of one fails, from a bad harvest or unproductive crop, it can call to its aid the staple of another. The variety not less than the value of products for exportation, contributes to the activity of foreign commerce. It can be conducted upon much better terms, with a large number of materials of a given value, than with a small number of materials of the same value; arising from the competitions of trade and from the fluctuations of markets. Particular articles may be in

17. "The necessity of naval protection to external or maritime commerce, and the conduciveness of that species of commerce, to the prosperity of a navy, are points too manifest to require a particular elucidation" substituted for this sentence in McLean and Hopkins.
18. "at home" omitted in Hopkins.

great demand, at certain periods, and unsaleable at others; but if there be a variety of articles it can scarcely happen that they should all be at one time in the latter predicament; and on this account the operations [19] of the merchant would be less liable to any considerable obstruction, or stagnation. The speculative trader will at once perceive the force of these observations; and will acknowledge that the aggregate ballance of the commerce of the United States would bid fair to be much more favorable, than that of the thirteen States, without union, or with partial unions.

It may perhaps be replied to this, that whether the States are united, or disunited, there would still be an intimate intercourse between them which would answer the same ends: But this intercourse would be fettered, interrupted and narrowed by a multiplicity of causes; which in the course of these Papers have been amply detailed. An unity of commercial, as well as political interests, can only result from an unity of government.

There are other points of view, in which this subject might be placed, of a striking and animating kind. But they would lead us too far into the regions of futurity, and would involve topics not proper for a Newspaper discussion. I shall briefly observe, that our situation invites, and our interests prompt [20] us, to aim at an ascendant in the system of American affairs. The world may politically, as well as geographically, be divided into four parts, each having a distinct set of interests. Unhappily for the other three, Europe by her arms and by her negociations, by force and by fraud, has, in different degrees, extended her dominion over them all. Africa, Asia, and America have successively felt her domination. The superiority, she has long maintained, has tempted her to plume herself as the Mistress of the World, and to consider the rest of mankind as created for her benefit. Men admired as profound philosophers have, in direct terms, attributed to her inhabitants a physical superiority; and have gravely [21] asserted that all animals, and with them the human species, degenerate in America—that even dogs cease

19. "operation" substituted for "operations" in Hopkins.
20. In the newspaper this reads: "prompts to"; in McLean it reads "prompts"; the change made by Hopkins has been printed here.
21. In the newspaper, "greatly"; the substitution was made in McLean and Hopkins.

to bark after having breathed a while in our atmosphere.* Facts have too long supported these arrogant pretensions of the European: It belongs to us to vindicate the honor of the human race, and to teach that assuming brother moderation. Union will enable us to do it. Disunion will add another victim to his triumphs. Let Americans disdain to be the instruments of European greatness! Let the thirteen States, bound together in a strict and indissoluble union, concur in erecting one great American system, superior to the controul of all trans-atlantic force or influence, and able to dictate the terms of the connection between the old and the new world!

PUBLIUS.

* *Recherches philosophiques sur les Americains.*[22]

22. Cornelis Pauw, *Recherches Philosophiques Sur les Américains, ou Mémoires intéressants pour servir à l'Histoire de l'espece Humaine. Par M. de P. . . .* (3 Vols., Berlin, 1770).
The reference is to two passages in Volume I which read as follows:
"Le climat de L'Amérique etoit au moment de la découverte, très-contraire à la plûpart des animaux quadrupèdes, qui s'y sont trouvés plus petits d'un sixième que leurs analogues de l'ancien continent.
"Ce Climat étoit sur-tout pernicieux aux hommes abrutis, énervés & viciés dans toutes les parties de leur organisme d'une façon étonnante. (p. 4)
"Les Moutons de l'Europe souffrent aussi une forte altération à la Barbade; & on sait que les Chiens amenés de nos Pays, perdent la voix, & cessent d'aboier dans la plûpart des contrees du Nouveau Continent." (p. 13)

## From David Forman

*November 27, 1787.* Asks for a statement of the amount due Forman from a judgment secured against Robert Cox.

ALS, Hamilton Papers, Library of Congress.

## The Federalist No. 12 [1]

[New York, November 27, 1787]

*To the People of the State of New-York.*

THE effects of union upon the commercial prosperity of the

*The New-York Packet,* November 27, 1787. This essay appeared on November 28 in *The* [New York] *Independent Journal: or, the General Advertiser,* and on November 29 in *The* [New York] *Daily Advertiser.*
1. For background to this document, see "The Federalist. Introductory Note," October 27, 1787–May 28, 1788.

States have been sufficiently delineated. Its tendency to promote the interests of revenue will be the subject of our present enquiry.

The prosperity of [2] commerce is now perceived and acknowledged, by all enlightened statesmen, to be the most useful as well as the most productive source of national wealth; and has accordingly become a primary object of their political cares. By multiplying the means of gratification, by promoting the introduction and circulation of the precious metals, those darling objects of human avarice and enterprise, it serves to vivify and invigorate [3] the channels of industry, and to make them flow with greater activity and copiousness. The assiduous merchant, the laborious husbandman, the active mechanic, and the industrious manufacturer, all orders of men look forward with eager expectation and growing alacrity to this pleasing reward of their toils. The often-agitated question, between agriculture and commerce, has from indubitable experience received a decision, which has silenced the rivalships, that once subsisted between them, and has proved to the [4] satisfaction of their friends, that their interests are intimately blended and interwoven. It has been found, in various countries, that in proportion as commerce has flourished, land has risen in value. And how could it have happened otherwise? Could that which procures a free vent for the products of the earth—which furnishes new incitements to the cultivators of land—which is the most powerful instrument in encreasing the quantity of money in a state—could that, in fine, which is the faithful handmaid of labor and industry in every shape, fail to augment the value of that article, which is the prolific parent of far the greatest part of the objects upon which they are exerted? It is astonishing, that so simple a truth should ever have had an adversary; and it is one [5] among a multitude of proofs, how apt a spirit of ill-informed jealousy, or of too great abstraction and refinement is to lead men astray from the plainest paths of reason and conviction.

The ability of a country to pay taxes must always be proportioned, in a great degree, to the quantity of money in circulation, and to the celerity with which it circulates. Commerce, contributing to both these objects, must of necessity render the payment of taxes easier,

2. "A prosperous" substituted for "The prosperity of" in Hopkins.
3. "all" inserted at this point in McLean and Hopkins.
4. "entire" inserted at this point in McLean and Hopkins.
5. "one" omitted in the newspaper; it was inserted in McLean and Hopkins.

and facilitate the requisite supplies to the treasury. The hereditary dominions of the Emperor of Germany, contain a great extent of fertile, cultivated and populous territory, a large proportion of which is situated in mild and luxuriant climates. In some parts of this territory are to be found the best gold and silver mines in Europe. And yet, from the want of the fostering influence of commerce, that monarch can boast but slender revenues. He has several times been compelled to owe obligations to the pecuniary succours of other nations, for the preservation of his essential interests; and is unable, upon the strength of his own resources, to sustain a long or continued war.

But it is not in this aspect of the subject alone, that union will be seen to conduce to the purposes of revenue. There are other points of view, in which its influence will appear more immediate and decisive. It is evident from the state of the country, from the habits of the people, from the experience we have had on the point itself, that it is impracticable to raise any very considerable sums by direct taxation. Tax laws have in vain been multiplied—new methods to enforce the collection have in vain been tried—the public expectation has been uniformly disappointed, and the treasuries of the States have remained empty. The popular system of administration, inherent in the nature of popular government, coinciding with the real scarcity of money, incident to a languid and mutilated state of trade, has hitherto defeated every experiment for extensive collections, and has at length taught the different Legislatures the folly of attempting them.

No person, acquainted with what happens in other countries, will be surprised at this circumstance. In so opulent a nation as that of Britain, where direct taxes from superior wealth, must be much more tolerable, and from the vigor of the government, much more practicable, than in America, far the greatest part of the national revenue is derived from taxes of the indirect kind; from imposts and from excises. Duties on imported articles form a large branch of this latter description.

In America it is evident, that we must a long time depend, for the means of revenue, chiefly on such duties. In most parts of it, excises must be confined within a narrow compass. The genius of the people will ill [6] brook the inquisitive and peremptory spirit of excise laws. The pockets of the farmers, on the other hand, will reluctantly yield but scanty supplies in the unwelcome shape of impositions on their houses and lands. And personal property is too precarious and invisible a fund to be laid hold of in any other way, than by the imperceptible agency of taxes on consumption.

If these remarks have any foundation, that state of things, which will best enable us to improve and extend so valuable a resource, must be [7] best adapted to our political welfare. And it cannot admit of a serious doubt, that this state of things must rest on the basis of a general union. As far as this would be conducive to the interests of commerce, so far it must tend to the extention of the revenue to be drawn from that source. As far as it would contribute to rendering [8] regulations for the collection of the duties more simple and efficacious, so far it must serve to answer the purposes of making the same rate of duties more productive, and of putting it in [9] the power of the government to increase the rate, without prejudice to trade.

The relative situation of these States, the number of rivers, with which they are intersected, and of bays that wash their shores, the facility of communication in every direction, the affinity of language, and manners, the familiar habits of intercourse; all these are circumstances, that would conspire to render an illicit trade between them, a matter of little difficulty, and would insure frequent evasions of the commercial regulations of each other. The seperate States, or confederacies would be necessitated [10] by mutual jealousy to avoid the temptations to that kind of trade, by the lowness of their duties. The temper of our governments, for a long time to come, would not permit those rigorous precautions, by which the European nations guard the avenues into their respective countries, as well by land as by water; and which even there are found insufficient obstacles to the adventurous stratagems of avarice.

In France there is an army of patrols (as they are called) con-

6. "illy" substituted for "ill" in Hopkins.
7. "the" inserted at this point in McLean and Hopkins.
8. "render" substituted for "rendering" in Hopkins.
9. "into" substituted for "in" in McLean and Hopkins.
10. "driven" substituted for "necessitated" in Hopkins.

stantly employed to secure her [11] fiscal regulations against the inroads of the dealers in contraband trade.[12] Mr. *Neckar* [13] computes the number of these patrols at upwards of twenty thousand. This shews [14] the immense difficulty in preventing that species of traffic, where there is an inland communication, and places [15] in a strong light the disadvantages with which the collection of duties in this country would be incumbered, if by disunion the States should be placed in a situation, with respect to each other, resembling that of France with respect to her neighbours. The arbitrary and vexatious powers with which the patrols are necessarily armed would be intolerable in a free country.

If on the contrary, there be but one government pervading all the States, there will be as to the principal part of our commerce but ONE SIDE to guard, the ATLANTIC COAST. Vessels arriving directly from foreign countries, laden with valuable cargoes, would rarely choose to hazard [16] themselves to the complicated and critical perils, which would attend attempts to unlade prior to their coming into port. They would have to dread both the dangers of the coast, and of detection as well after as before their arrival at the places of their final destination. An ordinary degree of vigilance would be competent to the prevention of any material infractions upon the rights of the revenue. A few armed vessels, judiciously stationed [17] at the entrances of our ports,[18] might at a [19] small expence be made useful centinels of the laws. And the government having the same interests to provide against violations every where, the co-operation of its measures in each State would have a powerful tendency to render them effectual. Here also we should preserve by union an advantage which nature holds out to us, and which

11. In the newspaper, "their"; the substitution was made in both McLean and Hopkins.

12. "trade" omitted in McLean and Hopkins.

13. H took his information from *A Treatise on the Administration of the Finances of France. In Three Volumes. By Mr. Necker . . . Translated from the genuine French Edition, 1784, By Thomas Mortimer, . . . And Dedicated, by Permission to the Marquis of Lansdown* (London, 1785), I, 199.

14. "proves" substituted for "shews" in McLean and Hopkins.

15. "shows" substituted for "places" in McLean and Hopkins.

16. "expose" substituted for "hazard" in Hopkins.

17. "and employed" inserted at this point in Hopkins.

18. "at the entrances of our ports" omitted in Hopkins.

19. "a" omitted in McLean and Hopkins.

would be relinquished by seperation. The United States lie at a great distance from Europe, and at a considerable distance from all other places with which they would have extensive connections of foreign trade. The passage from them to us, in a few hours, or in a single night, as between the coasts of France and Britain, and of other neighbouring nations, would be impracticable. This is a prodigious security against a direct contraband with foreign countries; but a circuitous contraband to one State, through the medium of another, would be both easy and safe. The diference between a direct importation from abroad and an indirect importation, through the channel of a neighbouring [20] State, in small parcels, according to time and opportunity, with the additional facilities of inland communication, must be palpable to every man of discernment.

It is therefore, evident, that one national government would be able, at much less expence, to extend the duties on imports, beyond comparison further, than would be practicable to the States separately, or to any partial confederacies: Hitherto I believe it may safely be asserted, that these duties have not upon an average exceeded in any States three per cent. In France they are estimated to be [21] about fifteen per cent and in Britain they exceed this proportion.[22] There seems to be nothing to hinder their being increased in this country, to at least treble their present amount. The single article of ardent spirits, under Fœderal regulation, might be made to furnish a considerable revenue. Upon a ratio to the [23] importation into this State, the whole quantity imported into the United States may [24] be estimated at four millions of Gallons; which at a shilling per gallon would produce two hundred thousand pounds. That article would well bear this rate of duty: and if it should tend to diminish the consumption of it, such an effect would be equally favorable to the agriculture, to the œconomy, to the morals and

20. "an adjoining" substituted for "a neighbouring" in Hopkins.
21. "at" substituted for "to be" in McLean and Hopkins.
22. "the proportion is still greater" substituted for "they exceed this proportion" in McLean and Hopkins.
In the newspaper the following note to this sentence was printed: "If my memory be right they amount to 20 per cent." It was omitted in McLean and Hopkins.
23. "According to the ratio of" substituted for "Upon a ratio to the" in Hopkins.
24. "at a low computation" inserted at this point in McLean and Hopkins.

to the health of the [25] society. There is perhaps nothing so much a subject of national extravagance, as these spirits.[26]

What will be the consequence, if we are not able to avail ourselves of the resource in question in its full extent? A nation cannot long exist without revenue. Destitute of this essential support, it must resign its independence and sink into the degraded condition of a province. This is an extremity to which no government will of choice accede. Revenue therefore must be had at all events. In this country, if the principal part be not drawn from commerce, it must fall with oppressive weight upon land. It has been already intimated, that excises in their true signification are too little in unison with the feelings of the people, to admit of great use being made of that mode of taxation, nor indeed, in the States where almost the sole employment is agriculture, are the objects, proper for excise sufficiently numerous to permit very ample collections in that way. Personal estate, (as has been [27] before remarked) from the difficulty of tracing it cannot be subjected to large contributions, by any other means, than by taxes on consumption. In populous cities, it may be enough the subject of conjecture, to occasion the oppression of individuals, without much aggregate benefit to the State; but beyond these circles it must in a great measure escape the eye and the hand of the tax-gatherer. As the necessities of the State, nevertheless, must be satisfied, in some mode or other,[28] the defect of other resources must throw the principal weight of the public burthens on the possessors of land. And as, on the other hand, the wants of the government can never obtain an adequate supply, unless all the sources of revenue are open to its demands, the finances of the community under such embarrassments, cannot be put into a situation consistent with its respectability, or its security. Thus we shall not even have the consolations of a full treasury to atone for the oppression of that valuable class of the [29] citizens, who are employed in the cultivation of the soil. But public and private distress will keep pace with each other in gloomy concert; and unite in deploring the infatuation of those councils, which led to disunion.

PUBLIUS.

25. "the" omitted in Hopkins.
26. "this very article" substituted for "these spirits" in McLean and Hopkins.
27. "has been" omitted in Hopkins.
28. "or other" omitted in Hopkins.
29. "the" omitted in Hopkins.

# The Federalist No. 13 [1]

[New York, November 28, 1787]

*To the People of the State of New-York.*

AS connected with the subject of revenue, we may with propriety consider that of œconomy. The money saved from one object may be usefully applied to another; and there will be so much the less to be drawn from the pockets of the people. If the States are united under one government, there will be but one national civil list to support; if they are divided into several confederacies, there will be as many different national civil lists to be provided for; and each of them, as to the principal departments coextensive with that which would be necessary for a government of the whole. The entire separation of the States into thirteen unconnected sovereignties is a project too extravagant and too replete with danger to have many advocates. The ideas of men who speculate upon the dismemberment of the empire, seem generally turned towards three confederacies; one consisting of the four northern, another of the four middle, and a third of the five southern States. There is little probability that there would be a greater [2] number. According to this distribution each confederacy would comprise an extent of territory larger than that of the kingdom of Great-Britain. No well informed man will suppose that the affairs of such a confederacy can be properly regulated by a government, less comprehensive in its organs or institutions, than that, which has been proposed by the Convention. When the dimensions of a State attain to a certain magnitude, it requires the same energy of government and the same terms of administration; which are requisite in one of much greater extent. This idea admits not of precise demonstration, because there is no rule by which we can measure the momentum of civil power, necessary to the government of any given number of individuals; but when we consider that the island of Britain, nearly commensurate

*The* [New York] *Independent Journal: or, the General Advertiser,* November 28, 1787. This essay appeared on November 29 in *The* [*New York*] *Daily Advertiser* and on November 30 in *The New-York Packet.*
    1. For background to this document, see "The Federalist. Introductory Note," October 27, 1787–May 28, 1788.
    2. "great" substituted for "greater" in Hopkins.

with each of the supposed confederacies, contains about eight millions of people, and when we reflect upon the degree of authority required to direct the passions of so large a society to the public good, we shall see no reason to doubt that the like portion of power would be sufficient to perform the same task in a society far more numerous. Civil power properly organised and exerted is capable of diffusing its force to a very great extent; and can in a manner reproduce itself in every part of a great empire by a judicious arrangement of subordinate institutions.

The supposition, that each confederacy into which the States would be likely to be divided, would require a government not less comprehensive, than the one proposed, will be strengthened by another supposition,[3] more probable than that which presents us with three confederacies as the alternative to a general union. If we attend carefully to geographical and commercial considerations, in conjunction with the habits and prejudices of the different States, we shall be led to conclude, that in case of disunion they will most naturally league themselves under two governments. The four eastern States, from all the causes that form the links of national sympathy and connection, may with certainty be expected to unite. New-York, situated as she is, would never be unwise enough to oppose a feeble and unsupported flank to the weight of that confederacy. There are obvious reasons, that would facilitate her accession to it. New-Jersey is too small a State to think of being a frontier, in opposition to this still more powerful combination; nor do there appear to be any obstacles to her admission into it. Even Pennsylvania would have strong inducements to join the northern league. An active foreign commerce on the basis of her own navigation is her true policy, and coincides with the opinions and dispositions of her citizens. The more southern States, from various circumstances, may not think themselves much interested in the encouragement of navigation. They may prefer a system, which would give unlimited scope to all nations, to be the carriers as well as the purchasers of their commodities. Pennsylvania may not choose to confound her interests in a connection so adverse to her policy. As she must at all events be a frontier, she may deem it most consistent with her safety to have her exposed side turned towards the weaker

3. "conjecture" substituted for "supposition" in Hopkins.

power of the southern, rather than towards the stronger power of the northern confederacy. This would give her the fairest chance to avoid being the FLANDERS of America. Whatever may be the determination of Pennsylvania, if the northern confederacy includes New-Jersey, there is no likelihood of more than one confederacy to the south of that State.

Nothing can be more evident than that the thirteen States will be able to support a national government, better than one half, or one third, or any number less than the whole. This reflection must have great weight in obviating that objection to the proposed plan, which is founded on the principle of expence; an objection however, which, when we come to take a nearer view of it, will appear in every light to stand on mistaken ground.

If in addition to the consideration of a plurality of civil lists, we take into view the number of persons who must necessarily be employed to guard the inland communication, between the different confederacies, against illicit trade, and who in time will infallibly spring up out of the necessities of revenue; and if we also take into view the military establishments, which it has been shewn would unavoidably result from the jealousies and conflicts of the several nations, into which the States would be divided, we shall clearly discover, that a separation would be not less injurious to the œconomy than to the tranquillity, commerce, revenue and liberty of every part.

PUBLIUS.

## Election as Manager of the St. Andrew's Society

*New York, November 30, 1787.* On this date at the annual assembly of the St. Andrew's Society of New York State, Hamilton and five other men were elected managers of the Society for 1788.

The [New York] *Independent Journal: or, the General Advertiser,* December 1, 1787.

# The Federalist No. 15 [1]

[New York, December 1, 1787]

*To the People of the State of New-York.*

IN the course of the preceding papers, I have endeavoured, my Fellow Citizens, to place before you in a clear and convincing light, the importance of Union to your political safety and happiness. I have unfolded to you a complication of dangers to which you would be exposed should you permit that sacred knot which binds the people of America together to be severed or dissolved by ambition or by avarice, by jealousy or by misrepresentation. In the sequel of the inquiry, through which I propose to accompany you, the truths intended to be inculcated will receive further confirmation from facts and arguments hitherto unnoticed. If the road, over which you will still have to pass, should in some places appear to you tedious or irksome, you will recollect, that you are in quest of information on a subject the most momentous which can engage the attention of a free people: that the field through which you have to travel is in itself spacious, and that the difficulties of the journey have been unnecessarily increased by the mazes [2] with which sophistry has beset the way. It will be my aim to remove the obstacles to your progress in as compendious a manner, as it can be done, without sacrificing utility to dispatch.

In pursuance of the plan, which I have laid down for the discussion of the subject, the point next in order to be examined is the "insufficiency of the present confederation to the preservation of the Union." It may perhaps be asked, what need is there of reasoning or proof to illustrate a position, which is not either [3] controverted or doubted; to which the understandings and feelings of all classes of men assent; and which in substance is admitted by the opponents

---

*The* [New York] *Independent Journal: or, the General Advertiser,* December 1, 1787. This essay appeared on December 4 in both *The New-York Packet* and *The* [New York] *Daily Advertiser.*

1. For background on this document, see "The Federalist. Introductory Note," October 27, 1787–May 28, 1788.

2. In the newspaper, "magic"; the substitution was made in McLean and Hopkins.

3. "neither" substituted for "not either" in McLean and Hopkins.

as well as by the friends of the New Constitution? It must in truth be acknowledged that however these may differ in other respects, they in general appear to harmonise in this sentiment at least,[4] that there are material imperfections in our national system, and that something is necessary to be done to rescue us from impending anarchy. The facts that support this opinion are no longer objects of speculation. They have forced themselves upon the sensibility of the people at large, and have at length extorted from those, whose mistaken policy has had the principal share in precipitating the extremity, at which we are arrived, a reluctant confession of the reality of [5] those defects in the scheme of our Fœderal Government, which have been long pointed out and regretted by the intelligent friends of the Union.

We may indeed with propriety be said to have reached almost the last stage of national humiliation. There is scarcely any thing that can wound the pride, or degrade the character of an independent nation,[6] which we do not experience. Are there engagements to the performance of which we are held by every tie respectable among men? These are the subjects of constant and unblushing violation. Do we owe debts to foreigners and to our own citizens contracted in a time of imminent peril, for the preservation of our political existence? These remain without any proper or satisfactory provision for their discharge. Have we valuable territories and important posts in the possession of a foreign power, which by express stipulations ought long since to have been surrendered? [7] These are still retained, to the prejudice of our interests not less than of our rights. Are we in a condition to resent, or to repel the aggression? We have neither troops nor treasury nor government.* Are we even

* I mean for the Union.

4. "the opinion" substituted for "this sentiment at least" in Hopkins.

5. "many of" inserted at this point in McLean and Hopkins.

6. "people" substituted for "nation" in Hopkins.

7. The treaty of peace of 1783 between Great Britain and the United States had established the independence of the United States, and settled certain differences between the two countries. Other provisions of the treaty, enjoining both parties to certain acts, had not been fulfilled. Just as the Americans had not abided by Articles IV, V, and VI of the treaty, the British had not abided by Article VII, which stipulated that "His Britannic Majesty shall with all convenient speed . . . withdraw all his armies, garrisons and fleets from the said United States, and from every post, place and Harbour within the same." The British maintained that the failure of the United States to abide by the treaty gave Britain the right to retain possession of several frontier posts on the American side of the boundary.

in a condition to remonstrate with dignity? The just imputations on our own faith, in respect to the same treaty, ought first to be removed. Are we entitled by nature and compact to a free participation in the navigation of the Mississippi? Spain excludes us from it. Is public credit an indispensable resource in time of public danger? We seem to have abandoned its cause as desperate and irretrievable. Is commerce of importance to national wealth? Ours is at the lowest point of declension. Is respectability in the eyes of foreign powers a safe guard against foreign encroachments? The imbecility of our Government even forbids them to treat with us: Our ambassadors abroad are the mere pageants of mimic sovereignty. Is a violent and unnatural decrease in the value of land a symptom of national distress? The price of improved land in most parts of the country is much lower than can be accounted for by the quantity of waste land at market, and can only be fully explained by that want of private and public confidence, which are so alarmingly prevalent among all ranks and which have a direct tendency to depreciate property of every kind. Is private credit the friend and patron of industry? That most useful kind which relates to borrowing and lending is reduced within the narrowest limits, and this still more from an opinion of insecurity than from the [8] scarcity of money. To shorten an enumeration of particulars which can afford neither pleasure nor instruction it may in general be demanded, what indication is there of national disorder, poverty and insignificance that could befal a community so peculiarly blessed with natural advantages as we are, which does not form a part of the dark catalogue of our public misfortunes?

This is the melancholy situation, to which we have been brought by those very maxims and councils, which would now deter us from adopting the proposed constitution; and which not content with having conducted us to the brink of a precipice, seem resolved to plunge us into the abyss, that awaits us below. Here, my Countrymen, impelled by every motive that ought to influence an enlightened people, let us make a firm stand for our safety, our tranquillity, our dignity, our reputation. Let us at last break the fatal charm which has too long seduced us from the paths of felicity and prosperity.

It is true, as has been before observed, that facts too stubborn

8. "a" substituted for "the" in McLean and Hopkins.

to be resisted have produced a species of general assent to the abstract proposition that there exist material defects in our national system; but the usefulness of the concession, on the part of the old adversaries of fœderal measures, is destroyed by a strenuous opposition to a remedy, upon the only principles, that can give it a chance of success. While they admit that the Government of the United States is destitute [9] of energy; they contend against conferring upon it those powers which are requisite to supply that energy: They seem still to aim at things repugnant and irreconcilable—at an augmentation of Fœderal authority without a diminution of State authority—at sovereignty in the Union and complete independence in the members. They still in fine seem to cherish with blind devotion the political monster of an *imperium in imperio*. This renders a full display of the principal defects of the confederation necessary, in order to shew, that the evils we experience do not proceed from minute or partial imperfections, but from fundamental errors in the structure of the building which cannot be amended otherwise than by an alteration in the first principles [10] and main pillars of the fabric.

The great and radical vice in the construction of the existing Confederation is in the principle of LEGISLATION for STATES or GOVERNMENTS, in their CORPORATE or COLLECTIVE CAPACITIES and as contradistinguished from the INDIVIDUALS of whom [11] they consist. Though this principle does not run through all the powers delegated to the Union; yet it pervades and governs those, on which the efficacy of the rest depends. Except as to the rule of apportionment, the United States have an indefinite discretion to make requisitions for men and money; but they have no authority to raise either by regulations extending to the individual citizens of America. The consequence of this is, that though in theory their resolutions concerning those objects are laws, constitutionally binding on the members of the Union, yet in practice they are mere recommendations, which the States observe or disregard at their option.

9. In the newspaper, "destituted"; the change was made in both McLean and Hopkins.
10. "in the very elements" substituted for "in the first principles" in Hopkins.
11. In the newspaper, "which"; the correction was made in McLean and Hopkins.

It is a singular instance of the capriciousness of the human mind, that after all the admonitions we have had from experience on this head, there should still be found men, who object to the New Constitution for deviating from a principle which has been found the bane of the old; and which is in itself evidently incompatible with the idea of [12] GOVERNMENT; a principle in short which if it is to be executed at all must substitute the violent and sanguinary agency of the sword to the mild influence of the Magistracy.

There is nothing absurd or impracticable in the idea of a league or alliance between independent nations, for certain defined purposes precisely stated in a treaty; regulating all the details of time, place, circumstance and quantity; leaving nothing to future discretion; and depending for its execution on the good faith of the parties. Compacts of this kind exist among all civilized nations subject to the usual vicissitudes of peace and war, of observance and non observance, as the interests or passions of the contracting powers dictate. In the early part of the present century, there was an epidemical rage in Europe for this species of compacts; from which the politicians of the times fondly hoped for benefits which were never realised. With a view to establishing the equilibrium of power and the peace of that part of the world, all the resources of negotiation were exhausted, and triple and quadruple alliances were formed; but they were scarcely formed before they were broken, giving an instructive but afflicting lesson to mankind how little dependence is to be placed on treaties which have no other sanction than the obligations of good faith; and which oppose general considerations of peace and justice to the impulse of any immediate interest and passion.

If the particular States in this country are disposed to stand in a similar relation to each other, and to drop the project of a general DISCRETIONARY SUPERINTENDENCE, the scheme would indeed be pernicious, and would entail upon us all the mischiefs that [13] have been enumerated under the first head; but it would have the merit of being at least consistent and practicable. Abandoning all views towards a confederate Government, this would bring us to a simple alliance offensive and defensive; and would place us in a

12. "a" inserted here in Hopkins.
13. "which" substituted for "that" in McLean and Hopkins.

situation to be alternately friends and enemies of each other as our mutual jealousies and rivalships nourished by the intrigues of foreign nations should prescribe to us.

But if we are unwilling to be placed in this perilous situation; if we will still adhere to the design of a national government, or which is the same thing of a superintending power under the direction of a common Council, we must resolve to incorporate into our plan those ingredients which may be considered as forming the characteristic difference between a league and a government; we must extend the authority of the union to the persons of the citizens,—the only proper objects of government.

Government implies the power of making laws. It is essential to the idea of a law, that it be attended with a sanction; or, in other words, a penalty or punishment for disobedience. If there be no penalty annexed to disobedience, the resolutions or commands which pretend to be laws will in fact amount to nothing more than advice or recommendation. This penalty, whatever it may be, can only be inflicted in two ways; by the agency of the Courts and Ministers of Justice, or by military force; by the COERTION of the magistracy, or by the COERTION of arms. The first kind can evidently apply only to men—the last kind must of necessity be employed against bodies politic, or communities or States. It is evident, that there is no process of a court by which their observance of the laws can in the last resort be enforced. Sentences may be denounced against them for violations of their duty; but these sentences can only be carried into execution by the sword. In an association where the general authority is confined to the collective bodies of the communities that compose it, every breach of the laws must involve a state of war, and military execution must become the only instrument of civil obedience. Such a state of things can certainly not deserve the name of government, nor would any prudent man choose to commit his happiness to it.

There was a time when we were told that breaches, by the States, of the regulations of the fœderal authority were not to be expected —that a sense of common interest would preside over the conduct of the respective members, and would beget a full compliance with all the constitutional requisitions of the Union. This language at the present day would appear as wild as a great part of what we now hear from the same quarter will be thought, when we shall have received further lessons from that best oracle of wisdom, experience. It at all times betrayed an ignorance of the true springs by which human conduct is actuated, and belied the original inducements to the establishment of civil power. Why has government been instituted at all? Because the passions of men will not conform to the dictates of reason and justice, without constraint. Has it been found that bodies of men act with more rectitude or greater disinterestedness than individuals? The contrary of this has been inferred by all accurate observers of the conduct of mankind; and the inference is founded upon obvious reasons. Regard to reputation has a less active influence, when the infamy of a bad action is to be divided among a number, than when it is to fall singly upon one. A spirit of faction which is apt to mingle its poison in the deliberations of all bodies of men, will often hurry [14] the persons of whom they are composed into improprieties and excesses, for which they would blush in a private capacity.

In addition to all this, there is in the nature of sovereign power an impatience of controul, that disposes those who are invested with the exercise of it, to look with an evil eye upon all external attempts to restrain or direct its operations. From this spirit it happens that in every political association which is formed upon the principle of uniting in a common interest a number of lesser sovereignties, there will be found a kind of excentric tendency in the subordinate or inferior orbs, by the operation of which there will be a perpetual effort in each to fly off from the common center. This tendency is not difficult to be accounted for. It has its origin in the love of power. Power controuled or abridged [15] is almost always the rival and enemy of that power by which it is controuled or abriged. This simple proposition will teach us how little reason there is to expect, that the persons, entrusted with the administration of the affairs of the particular members of a confederacy, will at all times be ready, with perfect good humour, and an unbiassed regard to the public weal, to execute the resolutions or decrees of the general authority. The reverse of this results from the constitution of human nature.[16]

14. In the newspaper, "harry"; the change appeared in McLean and Hopkins.
15. In the newspaper, "abused"; the substitution was made in McLean and Hopkins.
16. "man" substituted for "human nature" in McLean and Hopkins.

If therefore the measures of the confederacy cannot be executed, without the intervention of the particular administrations, there will be little prospect of their being executed at all. The rulers of the respective members, whether they have a constitutional right to do it or not, will undertake to judge of the propriety of the measures themselves. They will consider the conformity of the thing proposed or required to their immediate interests or aims, the momentary conveniences or inconveniences that would attend its adoption. All this will be done, and in a spirit of interested and suspicious scrutiny, without that knowledge of national circumstances and reasons of state,[17] which is essential to a right judgment, and with that strong predilection in favour of local objects, which can hardly fail to mislead the decision. The same process must be repeated in every member of which the body is constituted; and the execution of the plans, framed by the councils of the whole, will always fluctuate on the discretion of the ill-informed and prejudiced opinion of every part. Those who have been conversant in the proceedings of popular assemblies; who have seen how difficult it often is, when there is no exterior pressure of circumstances, to bring them to harmonious resolutions on important points, will readily conceive how impossible it must be to induce a number of such assemblies, deliberating at a distance from each other, at different times, and under different impressions, long to cooperate in the same views and pursuits.

In our case, the concurrence of thirteen distinct sovereign wills is requisite under the confederation to the complete execution of every important measure, that proceeds from the Union. It has happened as was to have been foreseen. The measures of the Union have not been executed; and [18] the delinquencies of the States have step by step matured themselves to an extreme; which has at length arrested all the wheels of the national government, and brought them to an awful stand. Congress at this time scarcely possess the means of keeping up the forms of administration; 'till the States can have time to agree upon a more substantial substitute for the present shadow of a fœderal government. Things did not come to this desperate extremity at once. The causes which have been specified

17. In the newspaper, "that"; the change was made in McLean and Hopkins.
18. "and" omitted in Hopkins.

produced at first only unequal and disproportionate degrees of compliance with the requisitions of the Union. The greater deficiencies of some States furnished the pretext of example and the temptation of interest to the complying, or to the [19] least delinquent States. Why should we do more in proportion than those who are embarked with us in the same political voyage? Why should we consent to bear more than our proper share of the common burthen? These were suggestions which human selfishness could not withstand, and which even speculative men, who looked forward to remote consequences, could not, without hesitation, combat. Each State yielding to the persuasive voice of immediate interest and [20] convenience has successively withdrawn its support, 'till the frail and tottering edifice seems ready to fall upon our heads and to crush us beneath its ruins.

PUBLIUS.

19. "at" substituted for "to the" in Hopkins.
20. "or" substituted for "and" in McLean and Hopkins.

## From Robert Troup

[*New York*] *December 3, 1787.* Requests Hamilton to make arrangements for the purchase of a house and lot which Troup wishes to buy.

ALS, Hamilton Papers, Library of Congress.

## The Federalist No. 16 [1]

[New York, December 4, 1787]

*To the People of the State of New-York.*

THE tendency of the principle of legislation for States, or communities, in their political capacities, as it has been exemplified by the experiment we have made of it, is equally attested by the events which have befallen all other governments of the confederate kind, of which we have any account, in exact proportion to its prevalence

*The New-York Packet,* December 4, 1787. This essay appeared on December 5 in *The* [New York] *Independent Journal: or, the General Advertiser,* and on December 6 in *The* [New York] *Daily Advertiser.*

1. For background on this document, see "The Federalist. Introductory Note," October 27, 1787–May 28, 1788.

in those systems. The confirmations of this fact will be worthy of a distinct and particular examination.[2] I shall content myself with barely observing here, that of all the confederacies of antiquity, which history has handed down to us, the Lycian and Achæan leagues, as far as there remain vestiges of them, appear to have been most free from the fetters of that mistaken principle, and were accordingly those which have best deserved, and have most liberally received the applauding suffrages of political writers.

This exceptionable principle may as truly as emphatically be stiled the parent of anarchy: It has been seen that delinquencies in the members of the Union are its natural and necessary offspring; and that whenever they happen, the only constitutional remedy is force, and the immediate effect of the use of it, civil war.

It remains to enquire how far so odious an engine of government, in its application to us, would even be capable of answering its end. If there should not be a large army, constantly at the disposal of the national government, it would either not be able to employ force at all, or when this could be done, it would amount to a war between different parts of the confederacy, concerning the infractions of a league; in which the strongest combination would be most likely to prevail, whether it consisted of those who supported, or of those who resisted the general authority. It would rarely happen that the delinquency to be redressed would be confined to a single member, and if there were more than one, who had neglected their duty, similarity of situation would induce them to unite for common defence. Independent of this motive of sympathy, if a large and influential State should happen to be the aggressing member, it would commonly have weight enough with its neighbours, to win over some of them as associates to its cause. Specious arguments of danger to the common[3] liberty could easily be contrived; plausible excuses for the deficiencies of the party, could, without difficulty be invented, to alarm the apprehensions, inflame the passions, and conciliate the good will even of those States which were not chargeable with any violation, or omission of duty. This would be the more likely to take place, as the delinquencies of the larger members might be expected sometimes to proceed from an ambitious

2. See essays 18, 19, and 20.
3. "general" substituted for "common" in McLean and Hopkins.

premeditation in their rulers, with a view to getting rid of all external controul upon their designs of personal aggrandizement; the better to effect which, it is presumable they would tamper before-hand with leading individuals in the adjacent States. If associates could not be found at home, recourse would be had to the aid of foreign powers, who would seldom be disinclined to encouraging the dissentions of a confederacy, from the firm Union of which they had so much to fear. When the sword is once drawn, the passions of men observe no bounds of moderation. The suggestions of wounded pride, the instigations of irritated resentment, would be apt to carry the States, against which the arms of the Union were exerted to any extremes necessary to revenge the affront, or to avoid the disgrace of submission. The first war of this kind would probably terminate in a dissolution of the Union.

This may be considered as the violent death of the confederacy. Its more natural death is what we now seem to be on the point of experiencing, if the fœderal system be not speedily renovated in a more substantial form. It is not probable, considering the genius of this country, that the complying States would often be inclined to support the authority of the Union by engaging in a war against the non-complying States. They would always be more ready to pursue the milder course of putting themselves upon an equal foot-ing with the delinquent members, by an imitation of their example. And the guilt of all would thus become the security of all. Our past experience has exhibited the operation of this spirit in its full light. There would in fact be an insuperable difficulty in ascertaining when force could with propriety be employed. In the article of pecuniary contribution, which would be the most usual source of delinquency, it would often be impossible to decide whether it has proceeded from disinclination, or inability. The pretence of the latter would always be at hand. And the case must be very flagrant in which its fallacy could be detected with sufficient certainty to justify the harsh ex-pedient of compulsion. It is easy to see that this problem alone, as often as it should occur, would open a wide field for the exercise of factious views, of partiality and of oppression, in the majority that happened to prevail in the national council.[4]

4. "to the majority that happened to prevail in the national council, for the exercise of factious views, of partiality, and of oppression" substituted for "for the exercise" through "council" in McLean and Hopkins.

It seems to require no pains to prove that the States ought not to prefer a national constitution, which could only be kept in motion by the instrumentality of a large army, continually on foot to execute the ordinary requisitions or decrees of the government. And yet this is the plain alternative involved by those who wish to deny it the power of extending its operations to individuals. Such a scheme, if practicable at all, would instantly degenerate into a military despotism; but it will be found in every light impracticable. The resources of the Union would not be equal to the maintenance of an army considerable enough to confine the larger States within the limits of their duty; nor would the means ever be furnished of forming such an army in the first instance. Whoever considers the populousness and strength of several of these States singly at the present juncture, and looks forward to what they will become, even at the distance of half a century, will at once dismiss as idle and visionary any scheme, which aims at regulating their movements by laws, to operate upon them in their collective capacities, and to be executed by a coertion applicable to them in the same capacities. A project of this kind is little less romantic than that [5] monster-taming spirit, which is [6] attributed to the fabulous heroes and demi-gods of antiquity.

Even in those confederacies, which have been composed of members smaller than many of our counties, the principle of legislation for sovereign States, supported by military coertion, has never been found effectual. It has rarely been attempted to be employed, but against the weaker members. And in most instances attempts to coerce the refractory and disobedient, have been the signals of bloody wars; in which one half of the confederacy has displayed its banners against the other half.[7]

The result of these observations to an intelligent mind must be clearly this, that if it be possible at any rate to construct a Fœderal Government capable of regulating the common concerns and preserving the general tranquility, it must be founded, as to the objects committed to its care, upon the reverse of the principle contended for by the opponents of the proposed constitution. It must carry its agency to the persons of the citizens. It must stand in need of no

5. "the" substituted for "that" in McLean and Hopkins.
6. "which is" omitted in McLean and Hopkins.
7. "half" omitted in Hopkins.

intermediate legislations; but must itself be empowered to employ the arm of the ordinary magistrate to execute its own resolutions. The majesty of the national authority must be manifested through the medium of the Courts of Justice. The government of the Union, like that of each State, must be able to address itself immediately to the hopes and fears of individuals; and to attract to its support, those passions, which have the strongest influence upon the human heart. It must in short, possess all the means and have a right to resort to all the methods of executing the powers, with which it is entrusted, that are possessed and exercised by the governments of the particular States.

To this reasoning it may perhaps be objected, that if any State should be disaffected to the authority of the Union, it could at any time obstruct the execution of its laws, and bring the matter to the same issue of force, with the necessity of which the opposite scheme is reproached.

The plausibility of this objection will vanish the moment we advert to the essential difference between a mere NON COMPLIANCE and a DIRECT and ACTIVE RESISTANCE. If the interposition of the State-Legislatures be necessary to give effect to a measure of the Union, they have only NOT TO ACT or TO ACT EVA-SIVELY, and the measure is defeated. This neglect of duty may be disguised under affected but unsubstantial provisions, so as not to appear, and of course not to excite any alarm in the people for the safety of the constitution. The State leaders may even make a merit of their surreptitious invasions of it, on the ground of some temporary convenience, exemption, or advantage.

But if the execution of the laws of the national government, should not require the intervention of the State Legislatures; if they were to pass into immediate operation upon the citizens themselves, the particular governments could not interrupt their progress without an open and violent exertion of an unconstitutional power. No omissions, nor evasions would answer the end. They would be obliged to act, and in such a manner, as would leave no doubt that they had encroached on the national rights. An experiment of this nature would always be hazardous—in the face of a constitution in any degree competent to its own defence, and of a people enlightened enough to distinguish between a legal exercise and an illegal usurpation of authority. The success of it would require not merely a factious majority in the Legislature, but the concurrence of the courts of justice, and of the body of the people. If the Judges were not embarked in a conspiracy with the Legislature they would pronounce the resolutions of such a majority to be contrary to the supreme law of the land, unconstitutional and void. If the people were not tainted with the spirit of their State representatives, they, as the natural guardians of the constitution, would throw their weight into the national scale, and give it a decided preponderancy in the contest. Attempts of this kind would not often be made with levity [8] or rashness; because they could seldom be made without danger to the authors; unless in cases of a [9] tyrannical exercise of the Fœderal authority.

If opposition to the national government should arise from the disorderly conduct of refractory, or seditious individuals, it could be overcome by the same means which are daily employed against the same evil, under the State governments. The Magistracy, being equally the Ministers of the law of the land, from whatever source it might emanate, would doubtless be as ready to guard the national as the local regulations from the inroads of private licentiousness. As to those partial commotions and insurrections which sometimes disquiet society, from the intrigues of an inconsiderable faction, or from sudden or occasional ill humours that do not infect the great body of the community, the general government could command more extensive resources for the suppression of disturbances of that kind, than would be in the power of any single member. And as to those mortal feuds, which in certain conjunctures spread a conflagration through a whole nation, or through a very large proportion of it, proceeding either from weighty causes of discontent given by the government, or from the contagion of some violent popular paroxysm, they do not fall within any ordinary rules of calculation. When they happen, they commonly amount to revolutions and dismemberments of empire. No form of government can always either avoid or controul them. It is in vain to hope to guard against

8. In the newspaper, "liberty"; the change was made in McLean and Hopkins.
9. "a" omitted in Hopkins.

events too mighty for human foresight or precaution, and it would be idle to object to a government because it could not perform impossibilities.

PUBLIUS.

## The Federalist No. 17 [1]

[New York, December 5, 1787]

*To the People of the State of New-York.*

AN objection of a nature different from that which has been stated and answered, in my last address, may perhaps be likewise urged against the principle of legislation for the individual citizens of America. It may be said, that it would tend to render the government of the Union too powerful, and to enable it to absorb in itself [2] those residuary authorities, which it might be judged proper to leave with the States for local purposes. Allowing the utmost latitude to the love of power, which any reasonable man can require, I confess I am at a loss to discover what temptation the persons entrusted with the administration of the general government could ever feel to divest the States of the authorities of that description. The regulation of the mere domestic police of a State appears to me to hold out slender allurements to ambition. Commerce, finance, negociation and war seem to comprehend all the objects, which have charms for minds governed by that passion; and all the powers necessary to these [3] objects ought in the first instance to be lodged in the national depository. The administration of private justice between the citizens of the same State, the supervision of agriculture

*The* [New York] *Independent Journal: or, the General Advertiser*, December 5, 1787. This essay appeared on December 7 in both *The New-York Packet* and *The* [New York] *Daily Advertiser*.

1. For background to this document, see "The Federalist. Introductory Note," October 27, 1787–May 28, 1788.

There has been some dispute over the authorship of this essay. It has been attributed to Madison by an article in the *City of Washington Gazette*, December 15, 1817; by Thomas Jefferson in a list of the authors of the essays which he made on the flyleaf of his copy of *The Federalist;* and by Paul Leicester Ford ("The Authorship of the Federalist," *The American Historical Review*, II [July, 1897], 672–82). There can be no doubt about its authorship, however, for Madison himself attributed it to H.

2. "in itself" omitted in Hopkins.

3. "those" substituted for "these" in McLean and Hopkins.

and of other concerns of a similar nature, all those things in short which are proper to be provided for by local legislation, can never be desirable cares of a general jurisdiction. It is therefore improbable that there should exist a disposition in the Fœderal councils to usurp the powers with which they are connected; because the attempt to exercise those powers[4] would be as troublesome as it would be nugatory; and the possession of them, for that reason, would contribute nothing to the dignity, to the importance, or to the splendour of the national government.

But let it be admitted for argument sake, that mere wantonness and lust of domination would be sufficient to beget that disposition, still it may be safely affirmed, that the sense of the constituent body of the national representatives, or in other words of the people of the several States would controul the indulgence of so extravagant an appetite. It will always be far more easy for the State governments to encroach upon the national authorities, than for the national government to encroach upon the State authorities. The proof of this proposition turns upon the greater degree of influence, which the State governments, if they administer their affairs with uprightness and prudence, will generally possess over the people; a circumstance which at the same time teaches us, that there is an inherent and intrinsic weakness in all Fœderal Constitutions; and that too much pains cannot be taken in their organization, to give them all the force which is compatible with the principles of liberty.

The superiority of influence in favour of the particular governments would result partly from the diffusive construction of the national government; but chiefly from the nature of the objects to which the attention of the State administrations would be directed.

It is a known fact in human nature that its affections are commonly weak in proportion to the distance or diffusiveness of the object. Upon the same principle that a man is[5] more attached to his family than to his neighbourhood, to his neighbourhood than to the community at large, the people of each State would be apt to feel a stronger byass towards their local governments than towards the government of the Union; unless the force of that principle should be destroyed by a much better administration of the latter.

4. "them" substituted for "those powers" in Hopkins.
5. In the newspaper, "is" was omitted; it was inserted in McLean and Hopkins.

This strong propensity of the human heart would find powerful auxiliaries in the objects of State regulation.

The variety of more minute interests, which will necessarily fall under the superintendence of the local administrations, and which will form so many rivulets of influence running through every part of the society, cannot be particularised without involving a detail too tedious and uninteresting to compensate for the instruction it might afford.

There is one transcendent advantage belonging to the province of the [6] State governments which alone suffices to place the matter in a clear and satisfactory light—I mean the ordinary administration of criminal and civil justice. This of all others is the most powerful, most universal and most attractive source of popular obedience and attachment. It is that,[7] which—being the immediate and visible guardian of life and property—having its benefits and its terrors in constant activity before the public eye—regulating all those personal interests and familiar concerns to which the sensibility of individuals is more immediately awake—contributes more than any other circumstance to impressing upon the minds of the people affection, esteem and reverence towards the government. This great cement of society which will diffuse itself almost wholly through the channels of the particular governments, independent of all other causes of influence, would ensure them so decided an empire over their respective citizens, as to render them at all times a complete counterpoise and not unfrequently dangerous rivals to the power of the Union.

The operations of the national government on the other hand falling less immediately under the observation of the mass of the citizens the benefits derived from it will chiefly be perceived and attended to by speculative men. Relating to more general interests, they will be less apt to come home to the feelings of the people; and, in proportion, less likely to inspire a habitual sense of obligation and an active sentiment of attachment.

The reasoning on this head has been abundantly exemplified by the experience of all Fœderal constitutions, with which we are ac-

6. "the" omitted in Hopkins.
7. "this" substituted for "that" in McLean and Hopkins.

quainted, and of all others, which have borne the least analogy to
them.

Though the ancient feudal[8] systems were not strictly speaking
confederacies, yet they partook of the nature of that species of
association. There was a common head, chieftain, or sovereign,
whose authority extended over the whole nation; and a number of
subordinate vassals; or feudatories, who had large portions of land
allotted to them and numerous trains of *inferior* vassals or retainers,
who occupied and cultivated that land upon the tenure of fealty or
obedience to the persons of whom they held it. Each principal
vassal was a kind of sovereign within his particular demesnes. The
consequences of this situation were a continual opposition to the
authority of the sovereign, and frequent wars between the great
barons, or chief feudatories themselves. The power of the head of
the nation was commonly too weak either to preserve the public
peace or to protect the people against the oppressions of their immediate lords. This period of European affairs is emphatically stiled
by historians the times of feudal anarchy.

When the sovereign happened to be a man of vigorous and warlike
temper and of superior abilities, he would acquire a personal weight
and influence, which answered for the time the purposes of a more
regular authority. But in general the power of the barons triumphed
over that of the prince; and in many instances his dominion was
entirely thrown off, and the great fiefs were erected into independent principalities or states. In those instances in which the monarch
finally prevailed over his vassals, his success was chiefly owing to
the tyranny of those vassals over their dependents. The barons,
or nobles equally the enemies of the sovereign and the oppressors
of the common people were dreaded and detested by both; till
mutual danger and mutual interest effected an union between them
fatal to the power of the aristocracy. Had the nobles, by a conduct
of clemency and justice, preserved the fidelity and devotion of their
retainers and followers, the contests between them and the prince
must almost always have ended in their favour and in the abrigement
or subversion of the royal authority.

8. In the newspaper, "Fœderal"; the correction was made in McLean and
Hopkins.

This is not an assertion founded merely in speculation or conjecture. Among other illustrations of its truth which might be cited Scotland will furnish a cogent example. The spirit of clanship which was at an early day introduced into that kingdom, uniting the nobles and their dependents by ties equivalent to those of kindred, rendered the aristocracy a constant overmatch for the power of the monarch; till the incorporation with England subdued its fierce and ungovernable spirit, and reduced it within those rules of subordination, which a more rational and a more energetic system of civil polity had previously established in the latter kingdom.

The separate governments in a confederacy may aptly be compared with the feudal baronies; with this advantage in their favour, that from the reasons already explained, they will generally possess the confidence and good will of the people; and with so important a support will be able effectually to oppose all incroachments of the national government. It will be well if they are not able to conteract its legitimate and necessary authority. The points of similitude consist in the rivalship of power, applicable to both, and in the CONCENTRATION of large portions of the strength of the community into particular depositories,[9] in one case at the disposal of individuals, in the other case at the disposal of political bodies.

A concise review of the events that have attended confederate governments will further illustrate this important doctrine; an inattention to which has been the great source of our political mistakes, and has given our jealousy a direction to the wrong side. This review shall form the subject of some ensuing papers.

PUBLIUS.

9. In the newspaper, "deposits"; "depositories" was substituted in McLean and Hopkins.

## To Angelica Church [1]

[New York, December 6, 1787]

I this morning wrote a short and hasty line to your other self [2] and did not then expect I should have been able to find a moment for the more agreeable purpose of dropping a line to you. Your husband has too much gallantry to be offended at this implication of preference. But I can not, however great my hurry, resist the strong desire I feel of thankg you for your invaluable letter by the last packet.[3] Imagine, *if you are able*, the pleasure it gave me. Notwithstanding the compliment you pay to my eloquence its resources could give you but a feeble image of what I should wish to convey.

This you will tell me is poetical enough. I seldom write to a lady without fancying the relation of lover and mistress. It has a very inspiring effect. And in your case the dullest materials could not help feeling that propensity.

I have a great opinion of your *discernment* and therefore I venture to rant. If you read this letter in a certain mood, you will easily divine that in which I write it.

You ask if your friend Kitty Livingston [4] is married? You recollect the proverb. She was ready, with as much eagerness as can be ascribed to the chaste wishes of a virgin heart, to sip the blissful cup, when alas! it slipped through her fingers—at least for a time, if not for ever. Her lover a buxom widower of five and forty braving summer heats and wintry ⟨blasts⟩ exerted himself with so much zeal in the service of his dulcinea that there is every appearance it will cost him his lungs. He is gone to the South of France, if possible, to preserve them. This method of speaking of the *misfortune of your friend* proceeds from pure levity not a particle of malice. I beg your pardon for it; and I hope you will be able to tell me in your next that you have not by the least propensity to a smile verified the maxim of that scurvy defamer of human nature—Rochefoucault.[5]

You ladies despise the pedantry of punctuation. There was a most critical *comma* in your last letter. It is my interest that it should have been designed; but I presume it was accidental. Unriddle this if you can. The proof that you do it rightly may be given by the omission or repetition of the same mistake in your next.

So Mr. Church resolves to be a parliament-man.[6] I had rather see him a member of our *new Congress;* but my fervent *wish* always is that much success may attend all his *wishes.* I am ⟨sincerely⟩ attached to him as well as to yourself.

We are all well here. Your father and mother are better than they have been for a long time past. Betsey sends her love. I do not choose to say *joins in mine.* Tis old fashioned.

Despairing of seeing you here my only hope is that the jumble of events will bring us together in Europe. I speak not from any immediate project of the sort but from a combination of possible circumstances.

Wherever I am believe always that there is no one can pay a more sincere or affectionate tribute to your deserts than I do—

Adieu ma chere, soeur                                          A Hamilton

New York
December 6th. 1787

Having sent Mr. Churchs letter to the office I cannot inclose this, I hope twill arrive safe notwithstanding.

Mrs. A Church

ALS, Massachusetts Historical Society, Boston.
    1. Angelica Schuyler Church, H's sister-in-law, had resided in England since 1782.
    2. H's letter to John B. Church has not been found.
    3. Angelica Church to H, October 2, 1787.
    4. Catharine Livingston, daughter of William Livingston, the governor of New Jersey. H was in error. Kitty Livingston had been married on April 14, 1787, to Matthew Ridley. Ridley "had come to America in 1770 and returned to England in '75. He had served on the Committee for the Relief of American Prisoners, gone to Nantes in the shipping business, revisited America and been sent back to France as agent for Maryland in November '81" (Howard Swiggett, *The Extraordinary Mr. Morris* [New York, 1952], 98).
    5. François, Duc de la Rochefoucauld, Prince de Marsillac, celebrated French marshal and courtier.
    6. John B. Church's wish to be a member of Parliament was fulfilled in 1790, when he was elected to the House of Commons from the borough of Wendover.

## To John B. Church

[*New York, December 6, 1787.* On December 6, 1787, Hamilton wrote to Angelica Church "I this morning wrote a short and hasty line to your other self." *Letter not found.*]

## Report of a Committee of the Trustees Columbia College

*New York, December 6, 1787.* As members of a committee of the trustees of Columbia College appointed "to settle the Accounts of Leonard Lispenard Esquire the late Treasurer of the Corporation," Hamilton, John Mason and Henry Brockholst Livingston on this date signed a report recommending a settlement of Lispenard's account.

DS, Columbia University Libraries.

## The Federalist No. 18 [1]

BY JAMES MADISON WITH THE ASSISTANCE OF
ALEXANDER HAMILTON

[New York, December 7, 1787]

*To the People of the State of New-York.*

AMONG the confederacies of antiquity, the most considerable was that of the Grecian republics associated under the Amphyctionic

*The New-York Packet,* December 7, 1787. This essay appeared on December 8 in *The* [New York] *Independent Journal: or, the General Advertiser* and was begun on December 7 and concluded on December 8 in *The* [New York] *Daily Advertiser.*

1. For background to this document, see "The Federalist. Introductory Note," October 27, 1787–May 28, 1788.

In most editions of *The Federalist* this essay has been attributed to H and Madison, an attribution based on the various claims of authorship that H allegedly made. In the Gideon edition of *The Federalist* the authorship is assigned to Madison. A note to essay 18 in that edition reads as follows:

"The subject of this and the two following numbers happened to be taken up by both Mr. H. and Mr. M. What had been prepared by Mr. H. who had entered more briefly into the subject, was left with Mr. M. on its appearing that the latter was engaged in it, with larger materials, and with a view to a more precise delineation; and from the pen of the latter, the several papers went to the Press. (The above note from the pen of Mr. Madison was written on the margin of the leaf, commencing with the present number, in the copy of the Federalist loaned by him to the publisher.)"

According to George Bancroft (*History of the Formation of the Constitution of the United States of America* [New York, 1882], II, 336–37), Madison made an even more emphatic claim to the sole authorship of essays 18, 19, and 20. Bancroft quotes the following "*Note in Mr. Madison's own hand*":

"No. 18 is attributed to Mr. Hamilton and Mr. Madison jointly. A. H. had drawn up something on the subjects of this (No. 18) and the two next Nos. (19 and 20). On finding that J. M. was engaged in them with larger materials, and with a view to a more precise delineation, he put what he had written into the hands of J. M. It is possible, though not recollected, that something in the draught may have been incorporated into the numbers as printed. But it was certainly not of a nature or amount to affect the impression left on the mind of J. M., from whose pen the papers went to the press, that they were of the class written by him. As the historical materials of A. H., as far as they went,

Council. From the best accounts transmitted [2] of this celebrated institution, it bore a very instructive analogy to the present confederation of the American States.

The members retained the character of independent and sovereign States, and had equal votes in the fœderal council. This council had a general authority to propose and resolve whatever it judged necessary for the common welfare of Greece—to declare and carry on war—to decide in the last resort all controversies between the members—to fine the aggressing party—to employ the whole force of the confederacy against the disobedient—to admit new members. The Amphyctions were the guardians of religion, and of the immense riches belonging to the Temple of Delphos, where they had the right of jurisdiction in controversies between the inhabitants and those who came to consult the oracle. As a further provision for the efficacy of the fœderal powers, they took on an oath mutually to defend and protect the united cities, to punish the violators of this oath, and to inflict vengeance on sacrilegious despoilers of the Temple.

In theory and upon paper, this apparatus of powers, seems amply sufficient for all general purposes. In several material instances, they exceed the powers enumerated in the articles of confederation. The

---

were doubtless similar, or the same with those provided by J. M., and as a like application of them probably occurred to both, an impression might be left on the mind of A. H. that the Nos. in question were written jointly. These remarks are made as well to account for a statement to that effect, if made by A. H., as in justice to J. M., who, always regarding them in a different light, had so stated them to an enquiring friend, long before it was known or supposed that a different impression existed any where.

(Signed) J. M."

As first pointed out by Edward G. Bourne ("The Authorship of the Federalist," *The American Historical Review*, II [April, 1897], 445), Madison's claim is substantiated by comparing the text of these essays with his "Notes of Ancient and Modern Confederacies, perparatory to the federal Convention of 1787" (Madison, *Letters*, I, 293-328). A comparison of essay 20, for example, with Madison's "Notes" reveals that seventeen out of twenty-four paragraphs were from that source. H's contribution, however, cannot be completely dismissed, for parts of the notes for his speech of June 18, 1787, to the Constitutional Convention are exactly the same as statements in essays 18, 19, and 20 of *The Federalist*. (See the notes to "Constitutional Convention. Speech on a Plan of Government," June 18, 1787). Although it is certain that Madison was the principal author of these essays, it is equally certain that H, however small his contribution, assisted him.

2. "best transmitted accounts" substituted for "best accounts transmitted" in Hopkins.

Amphyctions had in their hands the superstition of the times, one of the principal engines by which government was then maintained; they had [3] declared authority to use coertion [4] against refractory cities, and were bound by oath to exert this authority on the necessary occasions.

Very different nevertheless was the experiment from the theory. The powers, like those of the present Congress, were administered by deputies appointed wholly by the cities in their political capacities, and exercised over them in the same capacities. Hence the weakness, the disorders, and finally the destruction of the confederacy. The more powerful members instead of being kept in awe and subordination, tyrannized successively over all the rest. Athens, as we learn from Demosthenes, was the arbiter of Greece 73 years. The Lacedemonians next governed it 29 years; at a subsequent period, after the battle of Leuctra, the Thebans had their turn of domination.[5]

It happened but too often, according to Plutarch, that the deputies of the strongest cities, awed and corrupted those of the weaker,[6] and that judgment went in favor of the most powerful party.[7]

Even in the midst of defensive and dangerous wars with Persia and Macedon, the members never acted in concert, and were more or fewer of them, eternally the dupes, or the hirelings of the common enemy. The intervals of foreign war, were filled up by domestic vicissitudes, convulsions and carnage.

After the conclusion of the war with Xerxes, it appears that the

3. "a" inserted here in McLean and Hopkins.
4. In the newspaper, "exertion"; "coertion" was substituted in McLean and Hopkins.
5. This reference can be found in *The Three Orations of Demosthenes chief Orator among the Grecians, in favor of the Olynthians . . . with those his fower Orations titled expressly & by name against King Philip of Macedonie. . . . Englished out of the Greeke by Thomas Wylson. . . .* (Imprinted at London by Henrie Denham, 1570), 67–68.
6. "weakest" substituted for "weaker" in Hopkins.
7. Except for the addition of the phrase "according to Plutarch," this paragraph was copied from a paragraph in Madison's "Notes." Madison there gave as his source "Code de l'Hum." and added "See, also, Plutarch: Themistocles."
"Code de l'Hum." was Madison's short title for Fortuné Barthélemy de Felice, *Code de l'Humanité ou la Législation universelle, naturelle, civile et politique, avec l'histoire littéraire des plus grands hommes qui ont contribué à la perfection de ce Code. Composé par une société de Gens de Lettres. Le tout revu et mis en Ordre alphabétique par M. de F.* 13 tom. (Yverdon, 1778).

Lacedemonians, required that a number of the cities should be turned out of the confederacy for the unfaithful part they had acted. The Athenians finding that the Lacedemonians would lose fewer partizans by such a measure than themselves; and would become masters of the public deliberations, vigorously opposed and defeated the attempt. This piece of history proves at once the inefficiency of the union; the ambition and jealousy of its most powerful members, and the dependent and degraded condition of the rest. The smaller members, though entitled by the theory of their system, to revolve in equal pride and majesty around the common center, had become in fact,[8] satellites of the orbs of primary magnitude.

Had the Greeks, says the Abbe Milot,[9] been as wise as they were courageous, they would have been admonished by experience of the necessity of a closer Union, and would have availed themselves of the peace which followed their success against the Persian arms, to establish such a reformation. Instead of this obvious policy, Athens and Sparta, inflated with the victories and the glory they had acquired, became first rivals and then enemies; and did each other infinitely more mischief, than they had suffered from Xerxes. Their mutual jealousies, fears, hatreds and injuries ended in the celebrated Peloponnesian war; which itself ended in the ruin and slavery of the Athenians, who had begun it.

As a weak government, when not at war, is ever agitated by internal dissentions; so these never fail to bring on fresh calamities from abroad. The Phocians having ploughed up some consecrated ground belonging to the temple of Apollo; the Amphyctionic Council, according to the superstition of the age, imposed a fine on the sacrilegious offenders. The Phocians being abetted by Athens and Sparta, refused to submit to the decree. The Thebans, with others of the cities, undertook to maintain the authority of the Amphyctions, and to avenge the violated God. The latter being the weaker party, invited the assistance of Philip of Macedon, who had[10] se-

8. "had in fact become" substituted for "had become in fact" in Hopkins.
9. Charles Francois Xavier Millot, Élemens d'Histoire générale. (Continuée . . . par Delisle de Sales. 11 tom. [Paris, 1772–1811]). The quotation given can more readily be found in Elements of General History. Translated from the French of Abbé Millot (London, Printed for W. Strahan; and T. Cadell in the Strand, 1778), I, 205–06.
10. "had" omitted in Hopkins.

cretly fostered the contest. Philip gladly seized the opportunity of executing the designs he had long planned against the liberties of Greece. By his intrigues and bribes he won over to his interests the popular leaders of several cities; by their influence and votes, gained admission into the Amphyctionic council; and by his arts and his arms, made himself master of the confederacy.

Such were the consequences of the fallacious principle, on which this interesting establishment was founded. Had Greece, says a judicious observer on her fate, been united by a stricter confederation, and persevered in her Union, she would never have worn the chains of Macedon; and might have proved a barrier to the vast projects of Rome.[11]

The Achæan league, as it is called, was another society of Grecian republics, which supplies us with valuable instruction.

The Union here was far more intimate, and its organization much wiser, than in the preceding instance. It will accordingly appear, that though not exempt from a similar catastrophe, it by no means equally deserved it.

The cities composing this league, retained their municipal jurisdiction, appointed their own officers, and enjoyed a perfect equality. The Senate in which they were represented, had the sole and exclusive right of peace and war, of sending and receiving Ambassadors—of entering into treaties and alliances—of appointing a Chief Magistrate or Pretor, as he was called, who commanded their armies; and who with the advice and consent of ten of the Senators, not only administered the government in the recess of the Senate, but had a great share in its deliberations, when assembled. According to the primitive constitution, there were two Pretors associated in the administration; but on trial, a single one was preferred.

It appears that the cities had all the same laws and customs, the same weights and measures, and the same money. But how far this effect proceeded from the authority of the Fœderal Council, is left in uncertainty. It is said only, that the cities were in a manner compelled to receive the same laws and usages. When Lacedemon was brought into the League by Philopœmen, it was attended with an

11. This paragraph closely corresponds to a paragraph in Madison's "Notes." Madison there identifies the "judicious observer" as the author of *Code de l'Humanité*. See note 7.

abolition of the institutions and laws of Lycurgus, and an adoption of those of the Achæans. The Amphyctionic confederacies of which she had been a member, left her in the full exercise of her government and her legislation. This circumstance alone proves a very material difference in the genius of the two systems.

It is much to be regretted that such imperfect [12] monuments [13] remain of this curious political fabric.[14] Could its interior structure and regular operation be ascertained, it is probable that more light would be thrown by it on the science of fœderal government, than by any of the like experiments with which we are acquainted.

One important fact seems to be witnessed by all the historians who take notice of Achæan affairs. It is, that as well after the renovation of the league by Aratus, as before its dissolution by the arts of Macedon, there was infinitely more of moderation and justice in the administration of its government, and less of violence and sedition in the people, than were to be found in any of the cities exercising *singly* all the prerogatives of sovereignty. The Abbe Mably, in his observations on Greece, says that the popular government, which was so tempestuous elsewhere, caused no disorders in the members of the Achæan republic, *because it was there tempered by the general authority and laws of the confederacy.*[15]

We are not to conclude too hastily, however, that faction did not in a certain degree agitate the particular cities; much less, that a due subordination and harmony reigned in the general system. The contrary is sufficiently displayed in the vicissitudes and fate of the republic.

Whilst the Amphyctionic confederacy remained, that of the Achæans, which comprehended the less important cities only, made little figure on the theatre of Greece. When the former became a victim to Macedon, the latter was spared by the policy of Philip and Alexander. Under the successors of these Princes, however, a different policy prevailed. The arts of division were practised among the Achæans: Each city was seduced into a separate interest; the

12. "the" substituted for "such imperfect" in Hopkins.
13. "which" inserted here in Hopkins.
14. "are so imperfect" inserted here in Hopkins.
15. Gabriel Bonnot de Mably, *Observations sur les Grecs* (Genève, 1749). The information referred to may be found in *Observations on the Greeks. From the French of the Abbé de Mably* (2nd ed., Lynn, Printed by W. Whittingham, 1776), 224–27.

Union was dissolved. Some of the cities fell under the tyranny of Macedonian garrisons; others under that of usurpers springing out of their own confusions. Shame and oppressions 'ere long awakened their love of liberty. A few cities re-united. Their example was followed by others, as opportunities were found of cutting off their tyrants. The league soon embraced almost the whole Peleponnesus. Macedon saw its progress; but was hindered by internal dissentions from stopping it. All Greece caught the enthusiasm, and seemed ready to unite in one confederacy; when the jealousy and envy in Sparta and Athens, of the rising glory of the Achæans, threw a fatal damp on the enterprize. The dread of the Macedonian power induced the league to court the alliance of the Kings of Egypt and Syria; who, as successors of Alexander, were rivals of the King of Macedon. This policy was defeated by Cleomenes, King of Sparta, who was led by his ambition to make an unprovoked attack on his neighbours the Achæans; and who as an enemy to Macedon, had interest enough with the Egyptian and Syrian Princes, to effect a breach of their engagements with the league. The Achæans were now reduced to the dilemma of submitting to Cleomenes, or of supplicating the aid of Macedon, its former oppressor. The latter expedient was adopted. The contest of the Greeks always afforded a pleasing opportunity to that powerful neighbour, of intermeddling in their affairs. A Macedonian army quickly appeared: Cleomenes was vanquished. The Achæans soon experienced, as often happens, that a victorious and powerful ally, is but another name for a master. All that their most abject compliances could obtain from him, was a toleration of the exercise of their laws. Philip, who was now on the throne of Macedon, soon provoked, by his tyrannies, fresh combinations among the Greeks. The Achæans, though weakened by internal dissentions, and by the revolt of Messene one of its members, being joined by the Etolians and Athenians, erected the standard of opposition. Finding themselves, though thus supported, unequal to the undertaking, they once more had recourse to the dangerous expedient of introducing the succour of foreign arms. The Romans to whom the invitation was made, eagerly embraced it. Philip was conquered: Macedon subdued. A new crisis ensued to the league. Dissentions broke out among its members. These the Romans fostered. Callicrates and other popular leaders, became mercenary instruments for inveigling their countrymen. The more effectually to nourish discord and disorder, the Romans had, to the astonishment of those who confided in their sincerity, already proclaimed universal liberty * throughout Greece. With the same insidious views, they now seduced the members from the league, by representing to their pride, the violation it committed on their sovereignty. By these arts, this Union, the last hope of Greece, the last hope of antient liberty, was torne into pieces; and such imbecility and distraction introduced, that the arms of Rome found little difficulty in compleating the ruin which their arts had commenced. The Achæans were cut to pieces; and Achaia loaded with chains, under which it is groaning at this hour.

I have thought it not superfluous to give the outlines of this important portion of history; both because it teaches more than one lesson and because, as a supplement to the outlines of the Achæan constitution, it emphatically illustrates the tendency of fœderal bodies, rather to anarchy among the members, than to tyranny in the head.

PUBLIUS.

* This was but another name more specious for the independence of the members on the fœderal head.

## The Federalist No. 19 [1]

BY JAMES MADISON WITH THE ASSISTANCE OF
ALEXANDER HAMILTON

[New York, December 8, 1787]

*To the People of the State of New-York.*

THE examples of ancient confederacies, cited in my last paper, have not exhausted the source of experimental instruction on this subject. There are existing institutions, founded on a similar prin-

The [New York] *Independent Journal: or, the General Advertiser,* December 8, 1787. This essay appeared on December 10 in *The* [New York] *Daily Advertiser* and on December 11 in *The New-York Packet.*

1. For background to this document, see "The Federalist. Introductory Note," October 27, 1787–May 28, 1788. For a discussion of the authorship of this essay, see essay 18, note 1.

ciple, which merit particular consideration. The first which presents itself is the Germanic Body.

In the early ages of Christianity Germany was occupied by seven distinct nations, who had no common chief. The Franks, one of the number, having conquered the Gauls, established the kingdom which has taken its name from them. In the ninth century, Charlemagne, its warlike monarch, carried his victorious arms in every direction; and Germany became a part of his vast dominions. On the dismemberment, which took place under his sons, this part was erected into a seperate and independent empire. Charlemagne and his immediate descendants possessed the reality, as well as the ensigns and dignity of imperial power. But the principal vassals, whose fiefs had become hereditary, and who composed the national Diets which Charlemagne had not abolished, gradually threw off the yoke, and advanced to sovereign jurisdiction and independence. The force of imperial sovereignty was insufficient to restrain such powerful dependents; or to preserve the unity and tranquility of the empire. The most furious private wars, accompanied with every species of calamity, were carried on between the different Princes and States. The imperial authority, unable to maintain the public order, declined by degrees, till it was almost extinct in the anarchy, which agitated the long interval between the death of the last Emperor of the Suabian, and the accession of the first Emperor of the Austrian lines. In the eleventh century, the Emperors enjoyed full sovereignty: In the fifteenth they had little more than the symbols and decorations of power.

Out of this feudal system, which has itself many of the important features of a confederacy, has grown the federal system, which constitutes the Germanic empire. Its powers are vested in a Diet representing the component members of the confederacy; in the Emperor who is the executive magistrate, with a negative on the decrees of the Diet; and in the Imperial Chamber and Aulic Council, two judiciary tribunals having supreme jurisdiction in controversies which concern the empire, or which happen among its members.

The Diet possesses the general power of legislating for the empire —of making war and peace—contracting alliances—assessing quotas of troops and money—constructing fortresses—regulating coin— admitting new members, and subjecting disobedient members to the ban of the empire, by which the party is degraded from his sovereign rights, and his possessions forfeited. The members of the confederacy are expressly restricted from entering into compacts, prejudicial to the empire, from imposing tolls and duties on their mutual intercourse, without the consent of the Emperor and Diet; from altering the value of money; from doing injustice to one another; or from affording assistance or retreat to disturbers of the public peace. And the ban is denounced against such as shall violate any of these restrictions. The members of the Diet, as such, are subject in all cases to be judged by the Emperor and Diet, and in their private capacities, by the Aulic Council and Imperial Chamber.

The prerogatives of the Emperor are numerous. The most important of them are, his exclusive right to make propositions to the Diet—to negative its resolutions—to name ambassadors—to confer dignities and titles—to fill vacant electorates—to found universities—to grant privileges not injurious to the States of the empire—to receive and apply the public revenues—and generally to watch over the public safety. In certain cases, the electors form a council to him. In quality of Emperor he possesses no territory within the empire; nor receives any revenue for his support. But his revenue [2] and dominions, in other qualities, constitute him one of the most powerful princes in Europe.

From such a parade of constitutional powers, in the representatives and head of this confederacy, the natural supposition would be, that it must form an exception to the general character which belongs to its kindred systems. Nothing would be farther from the reality. The fundamental principle, on which it rests, that the empire is a community of sovereigns; that the Diet is a representation of sovereigns; and that the laws are addressed to sovereigns; render the empire a nerveless body; incapable of regulating its own members; insecure against external dangers; and agitated with unceasing fermentations in its own bowels.

The history of Germany is a history of wars between the Emperor and the Princes and States; of wars among the Princes and States themselves; of the licenciousness of the strong, and the oppresion of the weak; of foreign intrusions, and foreign intrigues; of requisitions of men and money, disregarded, or partially complied with;

2. "revenues" substituted for "revenue" in Hopkins.

of attempts to enforce them, altogether abortive, or attended with slaughter and desolation, involving the innocent with the guilty; of general imbecility, confusion and misery.

In the sixteenth century, the Emperor with one part of the empire on his side, was seen engaged against the other Princes and States. In one of the conflicts, the Emperor himself was put to flight, and very near being made prisoner by the Elector of Saxony. The late King of Prussia was more than once pitted against his Imperial Sovereign; and commonly proved an overmatch for him. Controversies and wars among the members themselves have been so common, that the German annals are crowded with the bloody pages which describe them. Previous to the peace of Westphalia, Germany was desolated by a war of thirty years, in which the Emperor, with one half of the empire was on one side; and Sweden with the other half on the opposite side. Peace was at length negociated and dictated by foreign powers; and the articles of it, to which foreign powers are parties, made a fundamental part of the Germanic constitution.

If the nation happens, on any emergency, to be more united by the necessity of self defence; its situation is still deplorable. Military preparations must be preceded by so many tedious discussions, arising from the jealousies, pride, separate views, and clashing pretensions, of sovereign bodies; that before the diet can settle the arrangements, the enemy are in the field; and before the fœderal troops are ready to take it, are retiring into winter quarters.

The small body of national troops which has been judged necessary in time of peace, is defectively kept up, badly paid, infected with local prejudices, and supported by irregular and disproportionate contributions to the treasury.

The impossibility of maintaining order, and dispensing justice among these sovereign subjects, produced the experiment of dividing the Empire into nine or ten circles or districts; of giving them an interior organization; and of charging them with the military execution of the laws against delinquent and contumacious members. This experiment has only served to demonstrate more fully, the radical vice of the constitution. Each circle is the miniature picture of the deformities of this political monster. They either fail to execute their commissions, or they do it with all the devastation and carnage of civil war. Sometimes whole circles are defaulters, and then they increase the mischief which they were instituted to remedy.

We may form some judgment of this scheme of military coertion, from a sample given by Thuanus.[3] In Donawerth, a free and imperial city, of the circle of Suabia, the Abbe de St. Croix enjoyed certain immunities which had been reserved to him. In the exercise of these, on some public occasion, outrages were committed on him, by the people of the city. The consequence was, that the city was put under the ban of the empire; and the Duke of Bavaria, though director of another circle, obtained an appointment to enforce it. He soon appeared before the city, with a corps of ten thousand troops and finding it a fit occasion, as he had secretely intended from the beginning, to revive an antiquated claim, on the pretext that his ancestors had suffered the place to be dismembered from his territory; * he took possession of it, in his own name; disarmed and punished the inhabitants, and re-annexed the city to his domains.

It may be asked perhaps what has so long kept this disjointed machine from falling entirely to pieces. The answer is obvious. The weakness of most of the members, who are unwilling to expose themselves to the mercy of foreign powers; the weakness of most of the principal members; compared with the formidable powers all around them; the vast weight and influence which the Emperor derives from his separate and hereditary dominions; and the interest he feels in preserving a system, with which his family pride is connected, and which constitutes him the first Prince in Europe;

* *Pfeffel, Nouvel abreg. chronol. de l'hist. &c. d'Allemagne, says the pretext was to indemnify himself for the expence of the expedition.*[4]

3. "Thuanus" was Jacques Auguste de Thou. The "sample" was from that author's famous sixteen-volume *Histoire Universelle,* the full title of which reads as follows: *Histoire universelle de Jacque-Auguste de Thou depuis 1543 jusqu'en 1607, traduite sur l'edition latine de Londres* [by A. F. Prévost d'Exiles, P. F. Guyot Desfontaines, J. B. Le Mascrier, J. Adam, C. Lebeau, N. Leduc, J. C. Fabre; with a preface by Georgeon and Notes by J. Dupuis]. (*Memoires de la vie de J. A. de Thou. Poésies latines. Suite de l'histoire* [1607–1610] . . . *par N. Rigault. Pièces Concernant la personne et les ouvrages de J. A. de Thou. Mémoires et instructions pour servir à justifier l'innocence de F. A. de Thou, de P. Du Puy. tom. xvi. Table des matières*). Londres, 1734. The passage to which the author is referring may be more readily found in *Histoire Universelle de Jacques-Auguste De Thou.* . . . (Basle, 1742), X, 195–97.
4. Christien Fredrich Pfeffel von Kriegelstein, *Nouvel Abrégé Cronologique de L'Histoire et du Droit Public d'Allemagne* (À Paris, 1776), II, 235–36.

these causes support a feeble and precarious union; whilst the re-
pellent quality, incident to the nature of sovereignty, and which
time continually strengthens, prevents any reform whatever, founded
on a proper consolidation. Nor is it to be imagined, if this obstacle
could be surmounted, that the neighbouring powers would suffer
a revolution to take place, which would give to the Empire the force
and pre-eminence to which it is entitled. Foreign nations have long
considered themselves as interested in the changes made by events
in this constitution; and have, on various occasions, betrayed their
policy of perpetuating its anarchy and weakness.

If more direct examples were wanting, Poland as a government
over local sovereigns, might not improperly be taken notice of. Nor
could any proof more striking, be given of the calamities flowing
from such institutions. Equally unfit for self-government, and self-
defence, it has long been at the mercy of its powerful neighbours;
who have lately had the mercy to disburden it of one third of its
people and territories.

The connection among the Swiss Cantons scarcely amounts to
a confederacy: Though it is sometimes cited as an instance of the
stability of such institutions.

They have no common treasury—no common troops even in war
—no common coin—no common judicatory, nor any other common
mark of sovereignty.

They are kept together by the peculiarity of their topographical
position, by their individual weakness and insignificancy; by the
fear of powerful neighbours, to one of which they were formerly
subject; by the few sources of contention among a people of such
simple and homogeneous manners; by their joint interest in their
dependent possessions; by the mutual aid they stand in need of, for
suppressing insurrections and rebellions; an aid expressly stipulated,
and often required and afforded; and by the necessity of some regular
and permanent provision for accommodating disputes among the
Cantons. The provision is, that the parties at variance shall each
choose four judges out of the neutral Cantons, who in case of disagreement, chuse an umpire. This tribunal, under an oath of impartiality, pronounces definitive sentence: which all the Cantons
are bound to enforce. The competency of this regulation may be
estimated, by a clause in their treaty of 1683, with Victor Amadæus

of Savoy; in which he obliges himself to enterpose as mediator in disputes between the Cantons; and to employ force, if necessary, against the contumacious party.

So far as the peculiarity of their case will admit of comparison with that of the United States, it serves to confirm the principle intended to be established. Whatever efficacy the Union may have had in ordinary cases, it appears that the moment a cause of difference sprang up, capable of trying its strength, it failed. The controversies on the subject of religion, which in three instances have kindled violent and bloody contests, may be said in fact to have severed the league. The Protestant and Catholic Cantons have since had their separate diets; where all the most important concerns are adjusted, and which have left the general diet little other business than to take care of the common bailages.

That separation had another consequence which merits attention. It produced opposite alliances with foreign powers; of Berne at [5] the head of the Protestant association, with the United Provinces; and of Luzerne, as the head of the Catholic association, with France.

PUBLIUS.

5. "as" substituted for "at" in McLean and Hopkins.

## The Federalist No. 20 [1]

BY JAMES MADISON WITH THE ASSISTANCE OF
ALEXANDER HAMILTON

[New York, December 11, 1787]

To the People of the State of New-York.

THE United Netherlands are a confederacy of republics, or rather of aristocracies, of a very remarkable texture; yet confirming all the lessons derived from those which we have already reviewed.

The New-York Packet, December 11, 1787. This essay also appeared on December 12 in The [New York] Independent Journal: or, the General Advertiser. It was begun on December 12 and concluded on December 13 in The [New York] Daily Advertiser.
   1. For background to this document, see "The Federalist. Introductory Note," October 27, 1787–May 28, 1788. For a discussion of the authorship of this essay, see essay 18, note 1.

The Union is composed of seven co-equal and sovereign States, and each State or province is a composition of equal and independent cities. In all important cases not only the provinces, but the cities must be unanimous.

The sovereignty of the Union is represented by the States General, consisting usually of about 50 deputies appointed by the provinces. They hold their seats, some for life, some for six, three and one years. From two provinces they continue in appointment during pleasure.

The States General have authority to enter into treaties and alliances—to make war and peace—to raise armies and equip fleets—to ascertain quotas and demand contributions. In all these cases however, unanimity and the sanction of their constituents are requisite. They have authority to appoint and receive Ambassadors—to execute treaties and alliances already formed—to provide for the collection of duties on imports and exports—to regulate the mint, with a saving to the provincial rights—to govern as sovereigns the dependent territories. The provinces are restrained, unless with the general consent, from entering into foreign treaties—from establishing imposts injurious to others, or charging their neighbours with higher duties than their own subjects. A Council of State, a chamber of accounts, with five colleges of admiralty, aid and fortify the fœderal administration.

The executive magistrate of the Union is the Stadtholder, who is now a hereditary Prince. His principal weight and influence in the republic are derived from his [2] independent title; from his great patrimonial estates; from his family connections with some of the chief potentates of Europe; and more than all, perhaps, from his being Stadtholder in the several provinces, as well as for the Union, in which provincial quality, he has the appointment of town magistrates under certain regulations, executes provincial decrees, presides when he pleases in the provincial tribunals; and has throughout the power of pardon.

As stadtholder of the Union, he has however considerable prerogatives.

In his political capacity he has authority to settle disputes between

2. In the newspaper, "this"; "his" was substituted in McLean and Hopkins.

the provinces, when other methods fail—to assist at the deliberations of the States General, and at their particular conferences—to give audiences [3] to foreign Ambassadors, and to keep agents for his particular affairs at foreign Courts.

In his military capacity, he commands the fœderal troops—provides for garrisons, and in general regulates military affairs—disposes of all appointments from Colonels to Ensigns, and of the governments and posts of fortified towns.

In his marine capacity, he is Admiral General, and superintends and directs every thing relative to naval forces, and other naval affairs —presides in the admiralties in person or by proxy—appoints Lieutenant Admirals and other officers—and establishes Councils of war, whose sentences are not executed till he approves them.

His revenue, exclusive of his private income, amounts to 300,000 florins. The standing army which he commands consists of about 40,000 men.

Such is the nature of the celebrated Belgic confederacy, as delineated on parchment. What are the characters which practice has stampt upon it? Imbecility in the government; discord among the provinces; foreign influence and indignities; a precarious existence in peace, and peculiar calamities from war.

It was long ago remarked by Grotius, that nothing but the hatred of his countrymen to the House of Austria, kept them from being ruined by the vices of their constitution.[4]

The Union of Utrecht, says another respectable writer, reposes an authority in the States General seemingly sufficient to secure harmony, but the jealousy in each province renders the practice very different from the theory.[5]

The same instrument says another, obliges each province to levy

3. "audience" substituted for "audiences" in Hopkins.
4. Madison took Grotius's statement from Gabriel Bonnot de Mably, *De L'Étude de L'Histoire*. The edition was probably that of 1778 (Nouvelle édition . . . corrigée [Mastreicht, 1778]). A more accessible source is *Collection Complète des Œuvres de L'Abbé de Mably*, (Paris, 1794–1795), XII, 204–05. According to Mably, "Grotius a dit que le haine de ses compatriotes contre la maison d'Austriche les avoit empêché d'être détruits par les vices de leur gouvernement."
5. In his "Notes" Madison identified the "respectable" writer as the author of *Code de l'Humanité*. For a full reference to that work, see essay 18, note 7.

certain contributions;[6] but this article never could and probably never will be executed; because the inland provinces who have little commerce cannot pay an equal quota.

In matters of contribution, it is the practice to wave the articles of the constitution. The danger of delay obliges the consenting provinces to furnish their quotas, without waiting for the others; and then to obtain reimbursement from the others, by deputations, which are frequent, or otherwise as they can. The great wealth and influence of the province of Holland, enable her to effect both these purposes.

It has more than once happened that the deficiencies have been ultimately to be collected at the point of the [7] bayonet; a thing practicable, though dreadful, in a confederacy, where one of the members, exceeds in force all the rest; and where several of them are too small to meditate resistance: but utterly impracticable in one composed of members, several of which are equal to each other in strength and resources, and equal singly to a vigorous and persevering defence.

Foreign Ministers, say Sir William Temple, who was himself a foreign Minister, elude matters taken ad referendum, by tampering with the provinces and cities.[8] In 1726, the treaty of Hanover was delayed by these means a whole year. Instances of a like nature are numerous and notorious.

In critical emergencies, the States General are often compelled to overleap their constitutional bounds. In 1688, they concluded a

6. Madison, in his "Notes," attributed this remark to "Burrish. Bat. illustrat." The complete title of that work is as follows: Onslow Burrish, *Batavia Illustrata: OR, a View of the Policy, and Commerce, of the United Provinces: Particularly of Holland, with an Enquiry into the Alliances of the States General, with the Emperor, France, Spain, and Great Britain* (London, 1728).

7. "the" was omitted in the newspaper; it was inserted in McLean and Hopkins.

8. The reference is to Sir William Temple's *Observations upon the United Provinces of the Netherlands* (London, 1673), 99–100. In discussing the formation of the treaty of 1668 between the United Provinces and England, Temple stated: "Upon this occasion I had the fortune to prevail with the States-General to conclude three Treaties, and upon them draw up and sign the several instruments, in the space of Five days; Without passing the essential forms of their Government by any recourse to the Provinces, which must likewise have had it to the several Cities; There, I knew, those Forreign Ministers whose Duty and Interest it was to oppose this Affair, expected to meet and to elude it, which could not have failed in case it had run that circle."

treaty of themselves at the risk of their heads. The treaty of Westphalia in 1648, by which their independence was formally and finally
recognized, was concluded without the consent of Zealand. Even as
recently as the last treaty of peace with Great Britain, the constitutional principle of unanimity was departed from. A weak constitution must necessarily terminate in dissolution, for want of proper
powers, or [9] the usurpation of powers requisite for the public safety.
Whether the usurpation, when once begun, will stop at the salutary
point, or go forward to the dangerous extreme, must depend on the
contingencies of the moment. Tyranny has perhaps oftener grown
out of the assumptions of power, called for, on pressing exigencies,
by a defective constitution, than by [10] the full exercise of the largest
constitutional authorities.

Notwithstanding the calamities produced by the Stadholdership,
it has been supposed, that without his influence in the individual
provinces, the causes of anarchy manifest in the confederacy, would
long ago have dissolved it. "Under such a government, says the
Abbé Mably, the Union could never have subsisted, if the provinces
had not a spring within themselves, capable of quickening their
tardiness, and compelling them to the same way of thinking. This
spring is the Stadtholder." [11] It is remarked by Sir William Temple,
"that in the intermission of the Stadtholdership, Holland by her riches
and her authority, which drew the others into a sort of dependence,
supplied the place." [12]

These are not the only circumstances which have controuled the
tendency to anarchy and dissolution. The surrounding powers impose an absolute necessity of Union to a certain degree, at the same
time, that they nourish by their intrigues, the constitutional vices,
which keep the republic in some degree [13] always at their mercy.

The true patriots have long bewailed the fatal tendency [14] of these

9. "from" inserted at this point in Hopkins.
10. "out of" substituted for "by" in McLean and Hopkins.
11. The statement was taken from Mably's *De L'Étude de l'Histoire*. See
note 4. The remark attributed to the Abbé de Mably was a paraphrase of the
following statement: ". . . on ne peut se déguiser que les vices de leur gouvernement et leur consternation n'eussent rendu leur perte inévitable" (*Collection Complète des Œuvres de L'Abbé de Mably*, XII, 204–05.)
12. Temple, *Observations upon the United Provinces of the Netherlands*,
119.
13. "measure" substituted for "degree" in Hopkins.
14. "operation" substituted for "tendency" in Hopkins.

vices, and have made no less than four regular experiments, by *extraordinary assemblies*, convened for the special purpose, to apply a remedy, as many times, has their laudable zeal found it impossible to *unite the public councils* in reforming the known, the acknowledged, the fatal evils of the existing constitution. Let us pause my fellow citizens, for one moment, over this melancholy and monitory lesson of history; and with the tear that drops for the calamities brought on mankind by their adverse opinions and selfish passions; let our gratitude mingle an ejaculation to Heaven, for the propitious concord which has distinguished the consultations for our political happiness.

A design was also conceived of establishing a general tax to be administered by the fœderal authority. This also had its adversaries and failed.

This unhappy people seem to be now suffering from popular convulsions, from dissentions among the States, and from the actual invasion of foreign arms, the crisis of their destiny. All nations have their eyes fixed on the awful spectacle. The first wish prompted by humanity is, that this severe trial may issue in such a revolution of their government, as will establish their Union, and render it the parent of tranquility, freedom and happiness: The next, that the asylum under which, we trust, the enjoyment of these blessings, will speedily be secured in this country, may receive and console them for the catastrophe of their own.

I make no apology for having dwelt so long on the contemplation of these fœderal precedents. Experience is the oracle of truth; and where its responses, are unequivocal, they ought to be conclusive and sacred. The important truth, which it unequivocally pronounces in the present case, is, that a sovereignty over sovereigns, a government over governments, a legislation for communities, as contradistinguished from individuals; as it is a solecism in theory; so in practice, it is subversive of the order and ends of civil polity, by substituting *violence* in [15] place of *law*, or the destructive *coertion* of the *sword*, in place of the mild and salutary *coertion* of the *magistracy*.

PUBLIUS.

15. "the" inserted at this point in Hopkins.

# The Federalist No. 21 [1]

[New York, December 12, 1787]

To the People of the State of New-York.

HAVING in the three last numbers taken a summary review of the principal circumstances and events, which have depicted [2] the genius and fate of other confederate governments; I shall now proceed in the enumeration of the most important of those defects, which have hitherto disappointed our hopes from the system established among ourselves. To form a safe and satisfactory judgment of the proper remedy, it is absolutely necessary that we should be well acquainted with the extent and malignity of the disease.

The next most palpable defect of the subsisting [3] confederation is the total want of a SANCTION to its laws. The United States as now composed, have no power to exact obedience, or punish disobedience to their resolutions, either by pecuniary mulcts by a suspension or divestiture of privileges, or in [4] any other constitutional mode. [5] There is no express delegation of authority to them to use force against delinquent members; and if such a right should be ascribed to the fœderal head, as resulting from the nature of the social compact between the States, it must be by inference and construction, in the face of that part of the second article, by which it is declared, [6] "each [7] State shall retain every power, jurisdiction and right, not *expressly* delegated to the United States in Congress assembled." There is doubtless, a striking absurdity in supposing that a right of this kind does not exist, [8] but we are reduced to the

The [New York] *Independent Journal: or, the General Advertiser,* December 12, 1787. This essay appeared on December 14 in both *The New-York Packet* and *The* [New York] *Daily Advertiser.*

   1. For background to this document, see "The Federalist. Introductory Note," October 27, 1787–May 28, 1788.

   2. "depict" substituted for "have depicted" in McLean and Hopkins.

   3. "existing" substituted for "subsisting" in McLean and Hopkins.

   4. "by" subsituted for "in" in McLean and Hopkins.

   5. "means" substituted for "mode" in McLean and Hopkins.

   6. In the newspaper, "that is" was inserted at this point; it was omitted in McLean and Hopkins.

   7. "that" inserted before the word "each" in Hopkins.

   8. "The want of such a right involves, no doubt, a striking absurdity;" substituted for "There is" through "not exist," in McLean and Hopkins.

dilemma either of embracing that supposition,[9] preposterous as it may seem, or of contravening or explaining away a provision, which has been of late a repeated theme of the eulogies of those, who oppose the new constitution; and the want [10] of which in that plan, has been the subject of much plausible animadversion and severe criticism. If we are unwilling to impair the force of this applauded provision, we shall be obliged to conclude, that the United States afford the extraordinary spectacle of a government, destitute even of the shadow of a constitutional power to enforce the execution of its own laws. It will appear from the specimens which have been cited,[11] that the American confederacy in this particular, stands discriminated from every other institution of a similar kind, and exhibits a new and unexampled phenomenon in the political world.

The want of a mutual guarantee of the State governments is another capital imperfection in the fœderal plan. There is nothing of this kind declared in the articles that compose it; and to imply a tacit guarantee from considerations of utility, would be a still more flagrant departure from the clause which has been mentioned, than to imply a tacit power of coertion, from the like considerations. The want of a guarantee, though it might in its consequences endanger the Union, does not so immediately attack its existence as the want of a constitutional sanction to its laws.

Without a guarantee, the assistance to be derived from the Union in repelling those domestic dangers, which may sometimes threaten the existence of the State constitutions, must be renounced. Usurpation may rear its crest in each State, and trample upon the liberties of the people; while the national government could legally do nothing more than behold its encroachments with indignation and regret. A successful faction may erect a tyranny on the ruins of order and law, while no succour could constitutionally be afforded by the Union to the friends and supporters of the government. The tempestuous situation, from which Massachusetts has scarcely emerged, evinces that dangers of this kind are not merely speculative.[12] Who can determine what might have been the issue of her late convul-

9. "supposing that deficiency" substituted for "embracing that supposition" in McLean and Hopkins.
10. "omission" substituted for "want" in McLean and Hopkins.
11. See essays 18, 19, and 20.
12. H is referring to Shays' Rebellion. See essay 6, note 15.

sions, if the mal-contents had been headed by a Caesar or by a Cromwell? Who can predict what effect a despostism established in Massachusetts, would have upon the liberties of New-Hampshire or Rhode-Island; of Connecticut or New-York?

The inordinate pride of State importance has suggested to some minds an objection to the principle of a guarantee in the fœderal Government; as involving an officious interference in the domestic concerns of the members. A scruple of this kind would deprive us of one of the principal advantages to be expected from Union; and can only flow from a misapprehension of the nature of the provision itself. It could be no impediment to reforms of the State Constitutions by a majority of the people in a legal and peaceable mode. This right would remain undiminished. The guarantee could only operate against changes to be effected by violence. Towards the prevention of calamities of this kind too many checks cannot be provided. The peace of society, and the stability of government, depend absolutely on the efficacy of the precautions adopted on this head. Where the whole power of the government is in the hands of the people, there is the less pretence for the use of violent remedies, in partial or occasional distempers of the State. The natural cure for an ill administration, in a popular or representative constitution, is a change of men. A guarantee by the national authority would be as much levelled [13] against the usurpations of rulers, as against the ferments and outrages of faction and sedition in the community.

The principle of regulating the contributions of the States to the common treasury by QUOTAS is another fundamental error in the confederation. Its repugnancy to an adequate supply of the national exigencies has been already pointed out,[14] and has sufficiently appeared from the trial which has been made of it. I speak of it now solely with a view to equality among the States. Those who have been accustomed to contemplate the circumstances, which produce and constitute natural [15] wealth, must be satisfied that there is no common standard, or barometer, by which the degrees of it can be ascertained. Neither the value of lands nor the numbers of the people, which have been successively proposed as the rule of State

13. "directed" substituted for "levelled" in McLean and Hopkins.
14. The subject was discussed in essay 15.
15. In the newspaper, "constitutional"; "and constitute natural" was substituted in McLean and Hopkins.

contributions, has any pretension to being a just representative. If we compare the wealth of the United Netherlands with that of Russia or Germany or even of France; and if we at that same time compare the total value of the lands, and the aggregate population of that constricted district,[16] with the total value of the lands, and the aggregate population of the immense regions of either of the three last mentioned countries,[17] we shall at once discover that there is no comparison between the proportion of either of these two objects and that of the relative wealth of those nations. If the like parallel were to be run between several of the American States; it would furnish a like result. Let Virginia be contrasted with North-Carolina, Pennsylvania with Connecticut, or Maryland with New-Jersey, and we shall be convinced that the respective abilities of those States, in relation to revenue, bear little or no analogy to their comparative stock in lands or to their comparative population. The position may be equally illustrated by a similar process between the counties of the same State. No man who is [18] acquainted with the State of New-York will doubt, that the active wealth of Kings County bears a much greater proportion to that of Montgomery, than it would appear to do,[19] if we should take either the total value of the lands or the total numbers of the people as a criterion!

The wealth of nations depends upon an infinite variety of causes. Situation, soil, climate, the nature of the productions, the nature of the government, the genius of the citizens—the degree of information they possess—the state of commerce, of arts, of industry—these circumstances and many much [20] too complex, minute, or adventitious, to admit of a particular specification, occasion differences hardly conceivable in the relative opulence and riches of different countries. The consequence clearly is, that there can be no common measure of national wealth; and of course, no general or stationary rule, by which the ability of a State to pay taxes can be determined. The attempt therefore to regulate the contributions

16. "the contracted territory of that republic" substituted for "that contracted district" in McLean and Hopkins.
17. "those kingdoms" substituted for "the three last mentioned countries" in McLean and Hopkins.
18. "who is" omitted in McLean and Hopkins.
19. In the newspaper, "be"; The substitution was made in McLean and Hopkins.
20. "more" substituted for "much" in McLean and Hopkins.

of the members of a confederacy, by any such rule, cannot fail to be productive of glaring inequality and extreme oppression.

This inequality would of itself be sufficient in America to work the eventual destruction of the Union, if any mode of inforcing a compliance with its requisitions could be devised. The suffering States would not long consent to remain associated upon a principle which distributed [21] the public burthens with so unequal a hand; and which was calculated to impoverish and oppress the citizens of some States, while those of others would scarcely be conscious of the small proportion of the weight they were required to sustain. This however is an evil inseparable from the principle of quotas and requisitions.

There is no method of steering clear of this inconvenience but by authorising the national government to raise its own revenues in its own way. Imposts, excises and in general all duties upon articles of consumption may be compared to a fluid, which will in time find its level with the means of paying them. The amount to be contributed by each citizen will in a degree be at his own option, and can be regulated by an attention to his resources. The rich may be extravagant, the poor can be frugal. And private oppression may always be avoided by a judicious selection of objects proper for such impositions. If inequalities should arise in some States from duties on particular objects, these will in all probability be counterballanced by proportional inequalities in other States from the duties on other objects. In the course of time and things, an equilibrium, as far as it is attainable, in so complicated a subject, will be established every where. Or if inequalities should still exist they would neither be so great in their degree, so uniform in their operation, nor so odious in their appearance, as those which would necessarily spring from quotas upon any scale, that can possibly be devised.

It is a signal advantage of taxes on articles of consumption, that they contain in their own nature a security against excess. They prescribe their own limit; which cannot be exceeded without defeating the end proposed—that is an extension of the revenue. When applied to this object, the saying is as just as it is witty, that "in political arithmetic, two and two do not always make four." If

21. In the newspaper, "distributes"; the change was made in McLean and Hopkins.

duties are too high they lessen the consumption—the collection is eluded; and the product to the treasury is not so great as when they are confined within proper and moderate bounds. This forms a complete barrier against any material oppression of the citizens, by taxes of this class, and is itself a natural limitation of the power of imposing them.

Impositions of this kind usually fall under the denomination of indirect taxes, and must always [22] constitute the chief part of the revenue raised in this country. Those of the direct kind, which principally relate to lands and buildings, may admit of a rule of apportionment. Either the value of land, or the number of the people may serve as a standard. The state of agriculture, and the populousness of a country, have been [23] considered as nearly connected [24] with each other. And as a rule for the purpose intended, numbers in the view of simplicity and certainty, are entitled to a preference. In every country it is an Herculean task to obtain a valuation of the land; in a country imperfectly settled and progressive in improvement, the difficulties are increased almost to impracticability. The expence of an accurate valuation is in all situations a formidable objection. In a branch of taxation where no limits to the discretion of the government are to be found in the nature of things,[25] the establishment of a fixed rule, not incompatible with the end, may be attended with fewer inconveniencies than to leave that discretion altogether at large.

PUBLIUS.

22. "for a long time" substituted for "always" in McLean and Hopkins.
23. "are" substituted for "have been" in McLean and Hopkins.
24. "having a near relation" substituted for "nearly connected" in McLean and Hopkins.
25. "the thing" substituted for "things" in McLean and Hopkins.

## The Federalist No. 22 [1]

[New York, December 14, 1787]

*To the People of the State of New-York.*

IN addition to the defects already enumerated in the existing Fœderal system,[2] there are others of not less importance, which concur in rendering it[3] altogether unfit for the administration of the affairs of the Union.

The want of a power to regulate commerce is by all parties allowed to be of the number. The utility of such a power has been anticipated under the first head of our inquiries;[4] and for this reason as well as from the universal conviction entertained upon the subject, little need be added in this place. It is indeed evident, on the most superficial view, that there is no object, either as it respects the interests of trade or finance that more strongly demands a Fœderal superintendence. The want of it has already operated as a bar to the formation of beneficial treaties with foreign powers; and has given occasions of dissatisfaction between the States. No nation acquainted with the nature of our political association would be unwise enough to enter into stipulations with the United States, by which they conceded[5] privileges of any[6] importance to them,[7] while they were apprised that the engagements on the part of the Union, might at any moment be violated by its members; and while they found from experience that they might enjoy every advantage they desired in our markets, without granting us any return, but such as their momentary convenience might suggest. It is not there-

*The New-York Packet,* December 14, 1787. This essay appeared on December 15 in *The* [NewYork] *Independent Journal: or, the General Advertiser.* It was begun on December 17 in *The* [New York] *Daily Advertiser* and concluded on December 18.

1. For background to this document, see "The Federalist. Introductory Note," October 27, 1787–May 28, 1788.

2. "of the existing federal system enumerated in the last number" substituted for "already enumerated in the existing Fœderal system" in Hopkins.

3. "that system" substituted for "it" in Hopkins.

4. See essay 11.

5. "conceding on their part" substituted for "by which they conceded" in McLean and Hopkins.

6. "any" omitted in McLean and Hopkins.

7. "to them" omitted in McLean and Hopkins.

fore to be wondered at, that Mr. Jenkinson in ushering into the House of Commons a bill for regulating the temporary intercourse between the two countries, should preface its introduction by a declaration that similar provisions in former bills had been found to answer every purpose to the commerce of Great Britain, & that it would be prudent to persist in the plan until it should appear whether the American government was likely or not to acquire greater consistency.*

Several States have endeavoured by separate prohibitions, restrictions and exclusions, to influence the conduct of that kingdom in this particular; but the want of concert, arising from the want of a general authority, and from clashing, and dissimilar views in the States, has hitherto frustrated every experiment of the kind; and will continue to do so as long as the same obstacles to an uniformity of measures continue to exist.

The interfering and unneighbourly regulations of some States, contrary to the true spirit of the Union, have in different instances given just cause of umbrage and complaint to others; and it is to be feared that examples of this nature, if not restrained by a national controul, would be multiplied and extended till they became not less serious sources of animosity and discord, than injurious impediments to the intercourse between the different parts of the confederacy. "The commerce of the German empire,† is in continual trammels from the multiplicity of the duties which the several Princes and States exact upon the merchandizes passing through their territories; by means of which the fine streams and navigable rivers with which Germany is so happily watered, are rendered almost useless." Though the genius of the people of this country might never permit this description to be strictly applicable to us,

* *This as nearly as I can recollect was the sense of his speech in introducing the last bill.*[8]
† *Encyclopedie* article *empire.*[9]

8. Presumably H's reference was to the parliamentary debate on the American Intercourse Bill which began in 1783. The published record of parliamentary debates, however, does not include the remarks attributed by H to Charles Jenkinson (created Lord Hawkesbury in 1786 and Earl of Liverpool in 1796). (See *The Parliamentary History of England* . . . [London, 1814], XXIII, 602.)

9. Denis Diderot and Jean Le Rond d'Alembert, *Encyclopédie, ou Dictionnaire Raisonné des Sciences, des Arts and des Métiers, par une Société de Gens de Lettres. Mis en ordre & publié par M. Diderot; & quant à la Partie Mathématique, par M. D'Alembert* (à Lausanne et à Berne, 1782), XII, 254.

yet we may reasonably expect, from the gradual conflicts of State regulations, that the citizens of each, would at length come to be considered and treated by the others in no better light than that of foreigners and aliens.

The power of raising armies, by the most obvious construction of the articles of the confederation, is merely a power of making requisitions upon the States for quotas of men. This practice, in the course of the late war, was found replete with obstructions to a vigorous and to an œconomical system of defence. It gave birth to a competition between the States, which created a kind of auction for men. In order to furnish the quotas required of them, they out-bid each other, till bounties grew to an enormous and insupportable size. The hope of a still further increase afforded an inducement to those who were disposed to serve to procrastinate their inlist-ment; and disinclined them to engaging for any considerable periods. Hence slow and scanty levies of men in the most critical emergencies of our affairs—short inlistments at an unparalleled expence—con-tinual fluctuations in the troops, ruinous to their discipline, and subjecting the public safety frequently to the perilous crisis of a disbanded army. Hence also those oppressive expedients for raising men which were upon several occasions practised, and which nothing but the enthusiasm of liberty would have induced the people to endure.

This method of raising troops is not more unfriendly to œconomy and vigor, than it is to an equal distribution of the burthen. The States near the seat of war, influenced by motives of self preserva-tion, made efforts to furnish their quotas, which even exceeded their abilities, while those at a distance from danger were for the most part as remiss as the others were diligent in their exertions. The immediate pressure of this inequality was not in this case, as in that of the contributions of money, alleviated by the hope of a final liquidation. The States which did not pay their proportions of money, might at least be charged with their deficiencies; but no account could be formed of the deficiencies in the supplies of men. We shall not, however, see much reason to regret the want of this, when we consider how little prospect there is, that the most delin-quent States will ever be able to make compensation for their pecuniary failures. The system of quotas and requisitions, whether it be applied to men or money, is in every view a system of imbecility in the union, and of inequality and injustice among the members.

The right of equal suffrage among the States is another exceptionable part of the confederation. Every idea of proportion, and every rule of fair representation conspire to condemn a principle, which gives to Rhode-Island an equal weight in the scale of power with Massachusetts, or Connecticut, or New-York; and to Delaware, an equal voice in the national deliberations with Pennsylvania or Virginia, or North-Carolina. Its operation contradicts that fundamental maxim of republican government, which requires that the sense of the majority should prevail. Sophistry may reply, that sovereigns are equal, and that a majority of the votes of the States will be a majority of confederated America. But this kind of logical legerdemain, will never counteract the plain suggestions of justice and common sense. It may happen that this majority of States is a small minority of the people of America; ‡ and two thirds of the people of America, could not long be persuaded, upon the credit of artificial distinctions and syllogistic subtleties, to submit their interests to the management and disposal of one third. The larger States would after a while revolt from the idea of receiving the law from the smaller. To acquiesce in such a privation of their due importance in the political scale, would be not merely to be insensible to the love of power, but even to sacrifice the desire of equality. It is neither rational to expect the first, nor just to require the last—the smaller States considering how peculiarly their safety and welfare depend on union,[10] ought readily to renounce a pretension; which, if not relinquished would prove fatal to its duration.

It may be objected to this, that not seven but nine States, or two thirds of the whole number must consent to the most important resolutions; and it may be thence inferred, that nine States would always comprehend a majority of the inhabitants of the Union. But

‡ *New-Hampshire, Rhode-Island, New-Jersey, Delaware, Georgia, South-Carolina and Maryland, are a majority of the whole number of the States, but they do not contain one third of the people.*

10. "Considering how peculiarly the safety and welfare of the smaller states depend on union, they" substituted for "the smaller" through "on union," in Hopkins.

this does not obviate the impropriety of an equal vote between States of the most unequal dimensions and populousness; nor is the inference accurate in point of fact; for we can enumerate nine States which contain less than a majority of the people; § and it is constitutionally possible, that these nine may give the vote. Besides there are matters of considerable moment determinable [11] by a bare majority; and there are others, concerning which doubts have been entertained, which if interpreted in favor of the sufficiency of a vote of seven States, would extend its operation to interests of the first magnitude. In addition to this, it is to be observed, that there is a probability of an increase in the number of States, and no provision for a proportional augmentation of the ratio of votes.

But this is not all; what at first sight may seem a remedy, is in reality a poison. To give a minority a negative upon the majority (which is always the case where more than a majority is requisite to a decision) is in its tendency to subject the sense of the greater number to that of the lesser number.[12] Congress from the non-attendance of a few States have been frequently in the situation of a Polish Diet, where a single veto [13] has been sufficient to put a stop to all their movements. A sixtieth part of the Union, which is about the proportion of Delaware and Rhode-Island, has several times been able to oppose an intire bar to its operations. This is one of those refinements which in practice has an effect, the reverse of what is expected from it in theory. The necessity of unanimity in public bodies, or of something approaching towards it, has been founded upon a supposition that it would contribute to security. But its real operation is to embarrass the administration, to destroy the energy of government, and to substitute the pleasure, caprice or artifices of an insignificant, turbulent or corrupt junto, to the regular deliberations and decisions of a respectable majority. In those emergencies of a nation, in which the goodness or badness, the weakness or strength of its government, is of the greatest importance, there is commonly a necessity for action. The public business must in some way or

§ *Add New-York and Connecticut, to the foregoing seven, and they will still be less than a majority.*

11. In the newspaper, "detainable"; "determinable" was substituted in McLean and Hopkins.

12. "number" omitted in Hopkins.

13. In the newspaper, "vote"; "veto" was substituted in McLean and Hopkins.

other go forward. If a pertinacious minority can controul the opinion of a majority respecting the best mode of conducting it; the majority in order that something may be done, must conform to the views of the minority; and thus the sense of the smaller number will over-rule that of the greater, and give a tone to the national proceedings. Hence tedious delays—continual negotiation and intrigue—contemptible compromises of the public good. And yet in such a system, it is even happy [14] when such compromises can take place: For upon some occasions things will not admit of accommodation; and then the measures of government must be injuriously suspended or fatally defeated. It is often, by the impracticability of obtaining the concurrence of the necessary number of votes, kept in a state of inaction. Its situation must always savour of weakness— sometimes border upon anarchy.

It is not difficult to discover that a principle of this kind gives greater scope to foreign corruption as well as to domestic faction, than that which permits the sense of the majority to decide; though the contrary of this has been presumed. The mistake has proceeded from not attending with due care to the mischiefs that may be occasioned by obstructing the progress of government at certain critical seasons. When the concurrence of a large number is required by the constitution to the doing of any national act, we are apt to rest satisfied that all is safe, because nothing improper will be likely *to be done;* but we forget how much good may be prevented, and how much ill may be produced, by the power of hindering the doing what may be necessary,[15] and of keeping affairs in the same unfavorable posture in which they may happen to stand at particular periods.

Suppose for instance we were engaged in a war, in conjunction with one foreign nation against another. Suppose the necessity of our situation demanded peace, and the interest or ambition of our ally led him to seek the prosecution of the war, with views that might justify us in making separate terms. In such a state of things, this ally of ours would evidently find it much easier by his bribes and intrigues to tie up the hands of government from making peace,

14. "fortunate" substituted for "happy" in Hopkins.
15. "that which is necessary for being done," substituted for "the doing what may be necessary," in McLean. In Hopkins "that which it is necessary to do" is substituted for the same words.

where two thirds of all the votes were requisite to that object, than where a simple majority would suffice. In the first case he would have to corrupt a smaller number;[16] in the last a greater number. Upon the same principle it would be much easier for a foreign power with which we were at war, to perplex our councils and embarrass our exertions. And in a commercial view we may be subjected to similar inconveniences. A nation, with which we might have a treaty of commerce, could with much greater facility prevent our forming a connection with her competitor in trade; tho' such a connection should be ever so beneficial to ourselves.

Evils of this description ought not to be regarded as imaginary. One of the weak sides of republics, among their numerous advantages, is that they afford too easy an inlet to foreign corruption. An hereditary monarch, though often disposed to sacrifice his subjects to his ambition, has so great a personal interest in the government, and in the external glory of the nation, that it is not easy for a foreign power to give him an equivalent for what he would sacrifice by treachery to the State. The world has accordingly been witness to few examples of this species of royal prostitution, though there have been abundant specimens of every other kind.

In republics, persons elevated from the mass of the community, by the suffrages of their fellow-citizens, to stations of great pre-eminence and power, may find compensations for betraying their trust, which to any but minds animated and guided[17] by superior virtue, may appear to exceed the proportion of interest they have in the common stock, and to over-balance the obligations of duty. Hence it is that history furnishes us with so many mortifying examples of the prevalency of foreign corruption in republican governments. How much this contributed to the ruin of the ancient commonwealths has been already delineated.[18] It is well known that the deputies of the United Provinces have, in various instances been purchased by the emissaries of the neighbouring kingdoms. The Earl of Chesterfield (if my memory serves me right) in a letter to his court, intimates that his success in an important negotiation, must depend on his obtaining a Major's commission for one of those

16. "number" omitted in Hopkins.
17. "actuated" substituted for "animated and guided" in McLean and Hopkins.
18. See essays 18, 19, and 20. "disclosed" substituted for "delineated" in McLean and Hopkins.

deputies. And in Sweden, the parties were alternately bought by France and England, in so barefaced and notorious a manner that it excited universal disgust in the nation; and was a principal cause that the most limited monarch in Europe, in a single day, without tumult, violence, or opposition, became one of the most absolute and uncontrouled.

A circumstance, which crowns the defects of the confederation, remains yet to be mentioned—the want of a judiciary power. Laws are a dead letter without courts to expound and define their true meaning and operation. The treaties of the United States to have any force at all, must be considered as part of the law of the land. Their true import as far as respects individuals, must, like all other laws, be ascertained by judicial determinations. To produce uniformity in these determinations, they ought to be submitted in the last resort, to one SUPREME TRIBUNAL. And this tribunal ought to be instituted under the same authority which forms the treaties themselves. These ingredients are both indispensable. If there is in each State, a court of final jurisdiction, there may be as many different final determinations on the same point, as there are courts. There are endless diversities in the opinions of men. We often see not only different courts, but the Judges of the same court differing from each other. To avoid the confusion which would unavoidably result from the contradictory decisions of a number of independent judicatories, all nations have found it necessary to establish one court [19] paramount to the rest—possessing a general superintendance, and authorised to settle and declare in the last resort, an uniform rule of civil justice.

This is the more necessary where the frame of the government is so compounded, that the laws of the whole are in danger of being contravened by the laws of the parts. In this case if the particular tribunals are invested with a right of ultimate jurisdiction,[20] besides the contradictions to be expected from difference of opinion, there will be much to fear from the bias of local views and prejudices, and from the interference of local regulations. As often as such an interference was to [21] happen, there would be reason to apprehend,

19. "tribunal" substituted for "court" in Hopkins.
20. "decision" substituted for "jurisdiction" in Hopkins.
21. "should" substituted for "was to" in Hopkins.

that the provisions of the particular laws might be preferred to those of the general laws; for nothing is more natural to men in office, than to look with peculiar deference towards [22] that authority to which they owe their official existence.

The treaties of the United States, under the present constitution, are liable to the infractions of thirteen different Legislatures, and as many different courts of final jurisdiction, acting under the authority of those Legislatures. The faith, the reputation, the peace of the whole union, are thus [23] continually at the mercy of the prejudices, the passions, and the interests of every member of which it is composed. Is it possible that foreign nations can either respect or confide in such a government? Is it possible that the People of America will longer consent to trust their honor, their happiness, their safety, on so precarious a foundation?

In this review of the Confederation, I have confined myself to the exhibition of its most material defects; passing over those imperfections in its details, by which even a great [24] part of the power intended to be conferred upon it has been in a great measure rendered abortive. It must be by this time evident to all men of reflection, who can divest themselves of the prepossessions of preconceived opinions,[25] that it is a system so radically vicious and unsound, as to admit not of amendment but by an entire change in its leading features and characters.

The organization of Congress, is itself utterly improper for the exercise of those powers which are necessary to be deposited in the Union. A single Assembly may be a proper receptacle of those slender, or rather fettered authorities, which have been heretofore delegated to the fœderal head; but it would be inconsistent with all the principles of good government, to intrust it with those additional powers which even the moderate and more rational adversaries of the proposed constitution admit ought to reside in the United States. If that plan should not be adopted; and if the necessity of union should be able to withstand the ambitious aims of those men, who

22. "from the deference with which men in office naturally look up to" substituted for "for nothing" through "towards" in McLean and Hopkins.

23. In the newspaper, "there"; change made in McLean and Hopkins.

24. "considerable" substituted for "great" in McLean and Hopkins.

25. "are either free from erroneous prepossessions, or can divest themselves of them" substituted for "can divest" through "opinions" in McLean and Hopkins.

may indulge magnificent schemes of personal aggrandizement from its dissolution; the probability would be, that we should run into the project of conferring supplementary powers upon Congress as they are now constituted; and either the machine, from the intrinsic feebleness of its structure, will moulder into pieces in spite of our ill-judged efforts to prop it; or by successive augmentations of its force and energy, as necessity might prompt, we shall finally accumulate in a single body, all the most important prerogatives of sovereignty; and thus entail upon our posterity, one of the most execrable forms of government that human infatuation ever contrived. Thus we should create in reality that very tyranny, which the adversaries of the new constitution either are, or affect to be solicitous to avert.

It has not a little contributed to the infirmities of the existing fœderal system, that it never had a ratification by the PEOPLE. Resting on no better foundation than the consent of the several Legislatures; it has been exposed to frequent and intricate questions concerning the validity of its powers; and has in some instances given birth to the enormous doctrine of a right of legislative repeal. Owing its ratification to the law of a State, it has been contended, that the same authority might repeal the law by which it was ratified. However gross a heresy it may be, to maintain that *a party* to *a compact* has a right to revoke that *compact*, the doctrine itself has had respectable advocates. The possibility of a question of this nature, proves the necessity of laying the foundations of our national government deeper than in the mere sanction of delegated authority. The fabric of American Empire ought to rest on the solid basis of THE CONSENT OF THE PEOPLE. The streams of national power ought to flow immediately from that pure original fountain of all legitimate authority.

PUBLIUS.

## The Federalist No. 23 [1]

[New York, December 18, 1787]

*To the People of the State of New-York.*

THE necessity of a Constitution, at least equally energetic with the one proposed, to the preservation of the Union, is the point, at the examination of which we are now arrived.

This enquiry will naturally divide itself into three branches—the objects to be provided for by a Fœderal Government—the quantity of power necessary to the accomplishment of those objects—the persons upon whom that power ought to operate. Its distribution and organization will more properly claim our attention under the succeeding head.

The principal purposes to be answered by Union are these—The common defence of the members—the preservation of the public peace as well against internal convulsions as external attacks—the regulation of commerce with other nations and between the States —the superintendence of our intercourse, political and commercial, with foreign countries.

The authorities essential to the care of the common defence are these—to raise armies—to build and equip fleets—to prescribe rules for the government of both—to direct their operations—to provide for their support. These powers ought to exist without limitation: *Because it is impossible to foresee or* [2] *define the extent and variety of national exigencies, or* [3] *the correspondent extent & variety of the means which may be necessary to satisfy them.* The circumstances that endanger the safety of nations are infinite; and for this reason no constitutional shackles can wisely be imposed on the power to which the care of it is committed. This power ought to be co-extensive with all the possible combinations of such circumstances; and

---

*The New-York Packet*, December 18, 1787. This essay appeared in *The New-York Journal, and Daily Patriotic Register* on the same day. On December 19 it appeared in both *The* [New York] *Independent Journal: or, the General Advertiser* and *The* [New York] *Daily Advertiser.*

1. For background to this document, see "The Federalist. Introductory Note," October 27, 1787–May 28, 1788.
2. "to" inserted in McLean and Hopkins.
3. "and" substituted for "or" in McLean and Hopkins.

ought to be under the direction of the same councils, which are appointed to preside over the common defence.

This is one of those truths, which to a correct and unprejudiced mind, carries its own evidence along with it; and may be obscured, but cannot be made plainer by argument or reasoning. It rests upon axioms as simple as they are universal. The *means* ought to be proportioned to the *end;* the persons, from whose agency the attainment of any *end* is expected, ought to possess the *means* by which it is to be attained.

Whether there ought to be a Fœderal Government intrusted with the care of the common defence, is a question in the first instance open to discussion; but the moment it is decided in the affirmative, it will follow, that that government ought to be cloathed with all the powers requisite to the complete execution of its trust. And unless it can be shewn, that the circumstances which may affect the public safety are reducible within certain determinate limits; unless the contrary of this position can be fairly and rationally disputed, it must be admitted, as a necessary consequence, that there can be no limitation of that authority, which is to provide for the defence and protection of the community, in any matter essential to its efficiency; that is, in any matter essential to the *formation, direction* or *support* of the NATIONAL FORCES.

Defective as the present Confederation has been proved to be, this principle appears to have been fully recognized by the framers of it; though they have not made proper or adequate provision for its exercise. Congress have an unlimited discretion to make requisitions of men and money—to govern the army and navy—to direct their operations. As their requisitions were [4] made constitutionally binding upon the States, who are in fact under the most solemn obligations to furnish the supplies required of them, the intention evidently was, that the United States should command whatever resources were by them judged requisite to "the common defence and general welfare." It was presumed that a sense of their true interests, and a regard to the dictates of good faith, would be found sufficient pledges for the punctual performance of the duty of the members to the Fœderal Head.

The experiment has, however demonstrated, that this expectation

4. "are" substituted for "were" in McLean and Hopkins.

was ill founded and illustory; and the observations made under the last head, will, I imagine, have sufficed to convince the impartial and discerning, that there is an absolute necessity for an entire change in the first principles of the system: That if we are in earnest about giving the Union energy and duration, we must abandon the vain project of legislating upon the States in their collective capacities: We must extend the laws of the Fœderal Government to the individual citizens of America: We must discard the fallacious scheme of quotas and requisitions, as equally impracticable and unjust. The result from all this is, that the Union ought to be invested with full power to levy troops; to build and equip fleets, and to raise the revenues, which will be required for the formation and support of an army and navy, in the customary and ordinary modes practiced in other governments.

If the circumstances of our country are such, as to demand a compound instead of a simple, a confederate instead of a sole government, the essential point which will remain to be adjusted, will be to discriminate the OBJECTS, as far as it can be done, which shall appertain to the different provinces or departments of power; allowing to each the most ample authority for fulfilling the objects [5] committed to its charge. Shall the Union be constituted the guardian of the common safety? Are fleets and armies and revenues necessary to this purpose? The government of the Union must be empowered to pass all laws, and to make all regulations which have relation to them. The same must be the case, in respect to commerce, and to every other matter to which its jurisdiction is permitted to extend. Is the administration of justice between the citizens of the same State, the proper department of the local governments? These must possess all the authorities which are connected with this object, and with every other that may be allotted to their particular cognizance and direction. Not to confer in each case a degree of power, commensurate to the end, would be to violate the most obvious rules of prudence and propriety, and improvidently to trust the great interests of the nation to hands, which are disabled from managing them with vigour and success.

Who so likely to make suitable provisions for the public defence, as that body to which the guardianship of the public safety is con-

5. "THOSE which may be" substituted for "the objects" in McLean and Hopkins.

fided—which, as the center of information, will best understand the extent and urgency of the dangers that threaten—as the representative of the WHOLE will feel itself most deeply interested in the preservation of every part—which, from the responsibility implied in the duty assigned to it, will be most sensibly impressed with the necessity of proper exertions—and which, by the extension of its authority throughout the States, can alone establish uniformity and concert in the plans and measures, by which the common safety is to be secured? Is there not a manifest inconsistency in devolving upon the Fœderal Government the care of the general defence, and leaving in the State governments the *effective* powers, by which it is to be provided for? Is not a want of co-operation the infallible consequence of such a system? And will not weakness, disorder, an undue distribution of the burthens and calamities of war, an unnecessary and intolerable increase of expence, be its natural and inevitable concomitants? Have we not had unequivocal experience of its effects in the course of the revolution, which we have just accomplished? [6]

Every view we may take of the subject, as candid enquirers after truth, will serve to convince us, that it is both unwise and dangerous to deny the Fœderal Government an unconfined authority, as [7] to all those objects which are intrusted to its management. It will indeed deserve the most vigilant and careful attention of the people, to see that it be modelled in such a manner, as to admit of its being safely vested with the requisite powers. If any plan which has been, or may be offered to our consideration, should not, upon a dispassionate inspection, be found to answer this description, it ought to be rejected. A government, the Constitution of which renders it unfit to be trusted [8] with all the powers, which a free people *ought to delegate to any government*, would be an unsafe and improper depository of the NATIONAL INTERESTS, wherever THESE can with propriety be confided, the co-incident powers may safely accompany them. This is the true result of all just reasoning upon the subject. And the adversaries of the plan, promulgated by the Convention, ought to have [9] confined themselves to showing that the internal structure of the proposed government, was such as to

6. "achieved" substituted for "accomplished" in McLean and Hopkins.
7. "in respect" substituted for "as" in McLean and Hopkins.
8. "intrusted" substituted for "trusted" in Hopkins.
9. "would have given a better impression of their candour, if they had" substituted for "ought to have" in McLean and Hopkins.

render it unworthy of the confidence of the people. They ought not to have wandered into inflammatory declamations, and unmeaning cavils about the extent of the powers. The POWERS are not too extensive for the OBJECTS of Fœderal administration, or in other words, for the management of our NATIONAL INTERESTS; nor can any satisfactory argument be framed to shew that they are chargeable with such an excess. If it be true, as has been insinuated by some of the writers on the other side, that the difficulty arises from the nature of the thing, and that the extent of the country will not permit us to form a government, in which such ample powers can safely be reposed, it would prove that we ought to contract our views, and resort to the expedient of separate Confederacies, which will move within more practicable spheres. For the absurdity must continually stare us in the face of confiding to a government, the direction of the most essential national interests,[10] without daring to trust it with the authorities which are indispensable to their proper and efficient management. Let us not attempt to reconcile contradictions, but firmly embrace a rational alternative.

I trust, however, that the impracticability of one general system cannot be shewn. I am greatly mistaken, if any thing of weight, has yet been advanced of this tendency; and I flatter myself, that the observations which have been made in the course of these papers, have sufficed [11] to place the reverse of that position in as clear a light as any matter still in the womb of time and experience can be [12] susceptible of. This at all events must be evident, that the very difficulty itself drawn from the extent of the country, is the strongest argument in favor of an energetic government; for any other can certainly never preserve the Union of so large an empire. If we embrace [13] the tenets of those, who oppose the adoption of the proposed Constitution, as the standard of our political creed,[14] we cannot fail to verify the gloomy doctrines, which predict the impracticability of a national system, pervading the entire limits of the present Confederacy.

PUBLIUS.

10. "concerns" substituted for "interests" in Hopkins.
11. "served" substituted for "sufficed" in McLean and Hopkins.
12. "is" substituted for "can be" in McLean and Hopkins.
13. "as the standard of our political creed" inserted at this point in Hopkins.
14. "as the standard of our political creed" omitted in Hopkins.

## *The Federalist No. 24* [1]

[New York, December 19, 1787]

*To the People of the State of New-York.*

TO the powers proposed to be conferred upon the Federal Government, in respect to the creation and direction of the national forces, I have met with but one specific objection, which, if I understand it rightly is this— [2] that proper provision has not been made against the existence of standing armies in time of peace; an objection which I shall now endeavor to shew, rests on weak and unsubstantial foundations.

It has indeed been brought forward in the most vague and general form, supported only by bold assertions—without the appearance of argument—without even the sanction of theoretical opinions, in contradiction to the practice of other free nations, and to the general sense of America, as expressed in most of the existing Constitutions. The propriety of this remark will appear the moment it is recollected, that the objection under consideration turns upon a supposed necessity of restraining the LEGISLATIVE authority of the nation, in the article of military establishments; a principle unheard of except in one or two of our State Constitutions, and rejected in all the rest.

A stranger to our politics, who was to read our news-papers, at the present juncture, without having previously inspected the plan reported by the Convention, would be naturally led to one of two conclusions: either that it contained a positive injunction that standing armies should be kept up in time of peace; or that it vested in the EXECUTIVE the whole power of levying troops, without subjecting his discretion in any shape, to the controul of the Legislature.

If he came afterwards to peruse the plan itself, he would be surprised to discover, that neither the one nor the other was the case;

*The* [New York] *Daily Advertiser*, December 19, 1787. This essay also appeared on the same day in both *The* [New York] *Independent Journal: or the General Advertiser* and *The New-York Journal, and Daily Patriotic Register.* On December 21 it appeared in *The New-York Packet.*

1. For background to this document, see "The Federalist. Introductory Note," October 27, 1787–May 28, 1788.

2. "is" substituted for "if I understand it rightly is this" in Hopkins.

that the whole power of raising armies was lodged in the *Legislature*, not in the *Executive;* that this Legislature was to be a popular body, consisting of the representatives of the people, periodically elected; and that, instead of the provision he had supposed in favor of standing armies, there was to be found, in respect to this object, an important qualification even of the Legislative discretion, in that clause which forbids the appropriation of money for the support of an army for any longer period than two years: a precaution, which, upon a nearer view of it, will appear to be a great and real security against the keeping up of troops,[3] without evident necessity.

Disappointed in his first surmise, the person I have supposed would be apt to pursue his conjectures a little further. He would naturally say to himself, it is impossible that all this vehement and pathetic declamation can be without some colorable pretext. It must needs be, that this people so jealous of their liberties, have in all the preceding models of the Constitutions, which they have established, inserted the most precise and rigid precautions on this point, the omission of which in the new plan has given birth to all this apprehension and clamour.

If under this impression he proceeded to pass in review the several State Constitutions, how great would be his disappointment to find that *two only* of them * contained an interdiction of standing armies

---

* This statement of the matter is taken from the printed collections of state constitutions—[4] Pennsylvania and North-Carolina are the two which contain the interdiction in these words—"as standing armies in time of peace are dangerous to liberty, *they ought not* to be kept up." This is in truth rather a *caution* than a *prohibition.* New-Hampshire, Massachusetts, Delaware, and Maryland, have in each of their bills of rights a clause to this effect—"standing armies are dangerous to liberty, and ought not to be raised or kept up *without the consent of the legislature;*" which is a formal admission of the authority of the legislature. New-York has no bill of her[5] rights and her Constitution says not a word about the matter. No bills of rights appear annexed to the constitutions of the other States, except the foregoing[6] and their constitutions are equally silent— I am told, however, that one or two states have bills of rights which do not appear in this collection, but that those also recognize the right of the legislative authority in this respect.

3. "military establishments" substituted for "the keeping up of troops" in Hopkins and McLean.

4. H presumably took his information from *The Constitutions of the Several Independent States of America; the Declaration of Independence; The Articles of Confederation Between the Said States; The Treaties Between His Most Christian Majesty and the United States of America.* Published by Order of Congress (Philadelphia: Printed by Francis Bailey . . . 1781).

5. "her" omitted in Hopkins.

6. "except the foregoing" omitted in Hopkins.

in time of peace; that the other eleven had either observed a profound silence on the subject, or had in express terms admitted the right of the legislature to authorise their existence.

Still however he would be persuaded that there must be some plausible foundation for the cry raised on this head. He would never be able to imagine, while any source of information remained unexplored, that it was nothing more than an experiment upon the public credulity, dictated either by a deliberate intention to deceive or by the overflowings of a zeal too intemperate to be ingenuous. It would probably occur to him that he would be likely to find the precautions he was in search of in the primitive compact between the States. Here, at length, he would expect to meet with a solution of the enigma. No doubt he would observe to himself the existing confederation must contain the most explicit provisions against military establishments in time of peace; and a departure from this model in a favourite point has occasioned the discontent which appears to influence these political champions.

If he should now apply himself to a careful and critical survey of the articles of Confederation, his astonishment would not only be encreased but would acquire a mixture of indignation at the unexpected discovery that these articles instead of containing the prohibition he looked for, and tho' they had with a jealous circumspection restricted the authority of the State Legislatures in this particular, had not imposed a single restraint on that of the United States. If he happened to be a man of quick sensibility or ardent temper, he could now no longer refrain from regarding [7] these clamours as [8] the dishonest artifices of a sinister and unprincipled opposition to a plan which ought at least to receive a fair and candid examination from all sincere lovers of their country. How else (he would say) could the authors of them have been tempted to vent such loud censures upon that plan, about a point, in which it seems to have conformed itself to the general sense of America, as declared in its different forms of Government; and in which it has even superadded a new and powerful guard unknown to any of them? If on the contrary he happened to be a man of calm and dispassionate feelings—he would indulge a sigh for the frailty of human nature; and would lament that in a matter so interesting to the happiness of

7. "pronouncing" substituted for "regarding" in McLean and Hopkins.
8. "to be" substituted for "as" in McLean and Hopkins.

millions the true merits of the question should be discolored and perplexed [9] by expedients so unfriendly to an impartial and right determination. Even such a man could hardly forbear remarking that a conduct of this kind has too much the appearance of an intention to mislead the people by alarming their passions rather than to convince them by arguments addressed to their understandings.

But however little this objection may be countenanced even by precedents among ourselves, it may be satisfactory to take a nearer view of its intrinsic merits. From a close examination it will appear that restraints upon the discretion of the Legislature in respect to military establishments in time of peace [10] would be improper to be imposed; and, if imposed, from the necessities of society, would be unlikely to be observed.

Though a wide ocean separates the United States from Europe; yet there are various considerations that warn us against an excess of confidence or security. On one side of us and stretching far into our rear are growing settlements subject to the dominion of Britain. On the other side and extending to meet the British settlements are colonies and establishments subject to the dominion of Spain. This situation and the vicinity of the West-India Islands belonging to these two powers create between them, in respect to their American possessions, and in relation to us, a common interest. The Savage tribes, on our western frontier, ought to be regarded as our natural enemies, their natural allies; because they have most to fear from us and most to hope from them. The improvements in the art of navigation have, as to the facility of communication, rendered distant nations in a great measure neighbours. Britain and Spain are among the principal maritime powers of Europe. A future concert of views between these nations ought not to be regarded as impracticable.[11] The increasing remoteness of consanguinity is every day diminishing the force of the family-compact between France and Spain. And politicians have ever with great reason estimated the ties of blood as feeble and precarious links of political connection. These circumstances combined admonish us not to be sanguine in considering ourselves as intirely out of the reach of danger.

9. "perplexed and obscured" substituted for "discolored and perplexed" in McLean and Hopkins.

10. "in time of peace" omitted in McLean and Hopkins.

11. "improbable" substituted for "impracticable" in McLean and Hopkins.

Previous to the revolution, and even since the peace, there has been a constant necessity for keeping small garrisons on our western frontier. No person can doubt that these will continue to be indispensible, if it should only be [12] against the ravages and depredations of the Indians. These garrisons must either be furnished by occasional detachments from the militia, or by permanent corps in the pay of the government. The first is impracticable; and if practicable, would be pernicious. The militia [13] would not long, if at all, submit to be dragged from their occupations and families to perform that most disagreeable duty in times of profound peace.[14] And if they could be prevailed upon, or compelled to do it, the increased expence of a frequent rotation of service and the loss of labor and disconcertion of the industrious pursuits of individuals, would form conclusive objections to the scheme. It would be as burthensome and injurious to the public, as ruinous to private citizens. The latter resource of permanent corps in the pay of Government amounts to a standing army in time of peace; a small one indeed, but not the less real for being small. Here is a simple view of the subject that shows us at once the impropriety of a constitutional interdiction of such establishments, and the necessity of leaving the matter to the discretion and prudence of the Legislature.

In proportion to our increase in strength, it is probable, nay it may be said certain, that Britain and Spain would augment their military establishments in our neighbourhood. If we should but [15] be willing to be exposed in a naked and defenceless condition to their insults or encroachments, we should find it expedient to encrease our frontier garrisons in some ratio to the force by which our western settlements might be annoyed. There are and will be particular posts the possession of which will include the command of large districts of territory and facilitate future invasions of the remainder. It may be added that some of those posts will be keys to the trade with the Indian nations. Can any men think it would be wise to leave such posts in a situation to be at any instant seized by one or the other of two neighbouring and formidable powers? To act this part would be to desert all the usual maxims of prudence and policy.

12. "to guard" inserted at this point in Hopkins.
13. "in times of profound peace" inserted at this point in Hopkins.
14. "in times of profound peace" omitted in Hopkins.
15. "not" substituted for "but" in McLean and Hopkins.

If we mean to be a commercial people or even to be secure on our Atlantic side, we must endeavour as soon as possible to have a navy. To this purpose there must be dock-yards and arsenals; and, for the defence of these, fortifications and probably garrisons. When a nation has become so powerful by sea, that it can protect its dock-yards by its fleets, this supersedes the necessity of garrisons for that purpose; but where naval establishments are in their infancy, moderate garrisons will, in all likelihood, be found an indispensible precaution [16] against descents for the destruction of the arsenals and dock-yards, and sometimes of the fleet itself.

PUBLIUS.

16. "security" substituted for "precaution" in McLean and Hopkins.

## The Federalist No. 25 [1]

[New York, December 21, 1787]

To the People of the State of New-York.

IT may perhaps be urged, that the objects enumerated in the preceding number ought to be provided for [2] by the State Governments, under the direction of the Union. But this would be in reality [3] an inversion of the primary principle of our political association; as it would in practice transfer the care of the common defence from the fœderal head to the individual members: A project oppressive to some States, dangerous to all, and baneful to the confederacy.

The territories of Britain, Spain and of the Indian nations in our neighbourhood, do not border on particular States; but incircle the Union from MAINE to GEORGIA. The danger, though in different degrees, is therefore common. And the means of guarding against it ought in like manner to be the objects of common councils and of a common treasury. It happens that some States, from local situa-

The New-York Packet, December 21, 1787. This essay appeared also on the same day in both The [New York] Daily Advertiser and The New-York Journal, and Daily Patriotic Register. On December 22 it appeared in The [New York] Independent Journal: or, the General Advertiser.

1. For background to this document, see "The Federalist. Introductory Note," October 27, 1787–May 28, 1788.
2. "for" omitted in Hopkins.
3. "in reality" omitted in McLean and Hopkins.

tion, are more directly exposed. NEW-YORK is of this class. Upon the plan of separate provisions, New-York would have to sustain the whole weight of the establishments requisite to her immediate safety, and to the mediate or ultimate protection of her neighbours. This would neither be equitable as it respected New-York, nor safe as it respected the other States. Various inconveniences would attend such a system. The States, to whose lot it might fall to support the necessary establishments, would be as little able as willing, for a considerable time to come, to bear the burthen of competent provisions. The security of all would thus be subjected to the parsimony, improvidence or inability of a part. If the resources of such part becoming more abundant and extensive,[4] its provisions should be proportionably enlarged, the other States would quickly take the alarm at seeing the whole military force of the Union in the hands of two or three of its members; and those probably amongst the most powerful. They would each choose to have some counterpoise; and pretences could easily be contrived. In this situation, military establishments, nourished by mutual jealousy, would be apt to swell beyond their natural or proper size; and being at the separate disposal of the members, they would be engines for the abridgment, or demolition of the national authority.

Reasons have been already given to induce a supposition, that the State Governments will too naturally be prone to a rivalship with that of the Union, the foundation of which will be the love of power; and that in any contest between the fœderal head and one of its members, the people will be most apt to unite with their local government: If in addition to this immense advantage, the ambition of the members should be stimulated by the separate and independent possession of military forces, it would afford too strong a temptation, and too great facility to them to make enterprises upon, and finally to subvert the constitutional authority of the Union. On the other hand, the liberty of the people would be less safe in this state of things, than in that which left the national forces in the hands of the national government. As far as an army may be considered as a dangerous weapon of power, it had better be in those hands, of which the people are most likely to be jealous, than in those of which they are least likely to be jealous.[5] For it is a truth which the experi-

4. "and extensive" omitted in McLean and Hopkins.
5. "so" substituted for "jealous" in Hopkins.

ence of all ages has attested, that the people are always [6] most in danger, when the means of injuring their rights are in the possession of those of whom they entertain the least suspicion.

The framers of the existing confederation, fully aware of the danger to the Union from the separate possession of military forces by the States, have in express terms, prohibited them from having either ships or troops, unless with the consent of Congress. The truth is, that the existence of a Fœderal Government and military establishments, under State authority, are not less at variance with each other, than a due supply of the fœderal treasury and the system of quotas and requisitions.

There are other lights [7] besides those already taken notice of, [8] in which the impropriety of restraints on the discretion of the national Legislature will be equally manifest. The design of the objection, which has been mentioned, is to preclude standing armies in time of peace; though we have never been informed how far it is desired [9] the prohibition should extend; whether to raising armies as well as to *keeping them up* in a season of tranquility or not. If it be confined to the latter, it will have no precise signification, and it will be ineffectual for the purpose intended. When armies are once raised, what shall be denominated "keeping them up," contrary to the sense of the constitution? What time shall be requisite to ascertain the violation? Shall it be a week, a month, or [10] a year? Or shall we say, they may be continued as long as the danger which occasioned their being raised continues? This would be to admit that they might be kept up *in time of peace* against threatening, or impending danger; which would be at once to deviate from the literal meaning of the prohibition, and to introduce an extensive latitude of construction. Who shall judge of the continuance of the danger? This must undoubtedly be submitted to the national government—and the matter would then be brought to this issue, that the national government, to provide against apprehended danger, might, in the first instance, raise troops, and might afterwards keep them on foot, as long as they

6. "commonly" substituted for "always" in McLean and Hopkins.
7. "views" substituted for "lights" in Hopkins.
8. "presented" substituted for "taken notice of" in McLean and Hopkins.
9. In the newspaper, "designed"; "desired" was substituted in McLean and Hopkins.
10. "or" omitted in Hopkins.

supposed the peace or safety of the community was in any degree of jeopardy. It is easy to perceive, that a discretion so latitudinary as this, would afford ample room for eluding the force of the provision.

The supposed [11] utility of a provision of this kind, must be founded upon a supposed probability, or [12] at least possibility, of a [13] combination between the executive and the [14] legislative [15] in some scheme of usurpation. Should this at any time happen, how easy would it be to fabricate pretences of approaching danger? Indian hostilities instigated by Spain or Britain, would always be at hand. Provocations to produce the desired appearances, might even be given to some foreign power, and appeased again by timely concessions. If we can reasonably presume such a combination to have been formed, and that the enterprize is warranted by a sufficient prospect of success; the army when once raised, from whatever cause, or on whatever pretext, may be applied to the execution of the project.

If to obviate this consequence, it should be resolved to extend the prohibition to the *raising* of armies in time of peace, the United States would then exhibit the most extraordinary spectacle, which the world has yet seen—that of a nation incapacitated by its constitution to prepare for defence, before it was actually invaded. As the ceremony of a formal denunciation of war has of late fallen into disuse, the presence of an enemy within our territories must be waited for as the legal warrant to the government to begin its levies of men for the protection of the State. We must receive the blow before we could even prepare to return it. All that kind of policy by which nations anticipate distant danger, and meet the gathering storm, must be abstained from, as contrary to the genuine maxims of a free government. We must expose our property and liberty to the mercy of foreign invaders, and invite them, by our weakness, to seize the naked and defenceless prey, because we are afraid that rulers, created by our choice—dependent on our will—might en-

---

11. "supposed" omitted in Hopkins.
12. "can only be vindicated on the hypothesis of a probability" substituted for "must be" through "probability, or" in Hopkins.
13. "a" omitted in Hopkins.
14. "the" omitted in McLean and Hopkins.
15. "legislature" substituted for "legislative" in Hopkins.

danger that liberty, by an abuse of the means necessary to its preservation.

Here I expect we shall be told, that the Militia of the country is its natural bulwark, and would be at all times [16] equal to the national defence. This doctrine in substance had like to have lost us our independence. It cost millions to the United States, that might have been saved. The facts, which from our own experience forbid a reliance of this kind, are too recent to permit us to be the dupes of such a suggestion. The steady operations of war against a regular and disciplined army, can only be successfully conducted by a force of the same kind. Considerations of œconomy, not less than of stability and vigor, confirm this position. The American Militia, in the course of the late war, have by their valour on numerous occasions, erected eternal monuments to their fame; but the bravest of them feel and know, that the liberty of their country could not have been established by their efforts alone, however great and valuable they were. War, like most other things, is a science to be acquired and perfected by diligence, by perseverance, by time, and by practice.

All violent policy, contrary to the natural and experienced course of human affairs, defeats itself. Pennsylvania at this instant affords an example of the truth of this remark. The bill of rights of that State declares, that standing armies are dangerous to liberty, and ought not to be kept up in time of peace. Pennsylvania, nevertheless, in a time of profound peace, from the existence of partial disorders in one or two of her counties, has resolved to raise a body of troops; and in all probability, will keep them up as long as there is an [17] appearance of danger to the public peace.[18] The conduct of Massachusetts affords a lesson on the same subject, though on different ground. That State (without waiting for the sanction of Congress as the articles of the confederation require) was compelled to raise troops to quell a domestic insurrection,[19] and still keeps a corps in pay to prevent a revival of the spirit of revolt. The particular constitution of Massachusetts opposed no obstacle to the measure; but the instance is still of use to instruct us, that cases are likely to occur

16. "would at all times be" substituted for "would be at all times" in Hopkins.
17. "any" substituted for "an" in McLean and Hopkins.
18. For information on the raising of troops in Pennsylvania, see essay 6, note 28.
19. H is referring, of course, to Shays' Rebellion. See essay 6, note 15.

under our governments, as well as under those of other nations, which will sometimes render a military force in time of peace essential to the security of the society; and that it is therefore improper, in this respect, to controul the legislative discretion. It also teaches us, in its application to the United States, how little the rights of a feeble government are likely to be respected, even by its own constituents. And it teaches us, in addition to the rest, how unequal parchment provisions are [20] to a struggle with public necessity.

It was a fundamental maxim of the Lacedemonian commonwealth, that the post of Admiral should not be conferred twice on the same person. The Pelopponesian confederates, having suffered a severe defeat at sea from the Athenians, demanded LYSANDER, who had before served with success in that capacity, to command the combined fleets. The Lacedemonians, to gratify their allies, and yet preserve the semblance of an adherence to their ancient institutions, had recourse to the flimsy subterfuge of investing LYSANDER with the real power of Admiral, under the nominal title of Vice-Admiral. This instance is selected from among a multitude that might be cited to confirm the truth already advanced and illustrated by domestic examples; which is, that nations pay little regard to rules and maxims calculated in their very nature to run counter to the necessities of society. Wise politicians will be cautious about fettering the government with restrictions, that cannot be observed; because they know that every breach of the fundamental laws, though dictated by necessity, impairs that sacred reverence, which ought to be maintained in the breasts of rulers towards the constitution of a country, and forms a precedent for other breaches, where the same plea of necessity does not exist at all, or is less urgent and palpable.

PUBLIUS.

20. "are parchment provisions" substituted for "parchment provisions are" in McLean and Hopkins.

## The Federalist No. 26 [1]

[New York, December 22, 1787]

*To the People of the State of New-York.*

IT was a thing hardly to be [2] expected, that in a popular revolution the minds of men should stop at that happy mean, which marks the salutary boundary between POWER and PRIVILEGE, and combines the energy of government with the security of private rights. A failure in this [3] delicate and important point is the great source of the inconveniences we experience; and if we are not cautious to avoid a repetition of the error, in our future attempts to rectify and ameliorate our system, we may travel from one chimerical project to another; we may try change after change; but we shall never be likely to make any material change for the better.

The idea of restraining the Legislative authority, in the means of [4] providing for the national defence, is one of those refinements, which owe their origin to a zeal for liberty more ardent than enlightened. We have seen however that it has not had thus far an extensive prevalency: [5] That even in this country, where it has [6] made its first appearance, Pennsylvania and North-Carolina are the only two States by which it has been in any degree patronised: And that all the others have refused to give it the least countenance; wisely judging [7] that confidence must be placed some where; that the necessity of doing it is implied in the very act of delegating power; and that it is better to hazard the abuse of that confidence, than to embarrass the government and endanger the public safety, by impolitic restrictions on the Legislative authority. The opponents of the proposed Constitution combat in this respect the general

*The* [New York] *Independent Journal: or, the General Advertiser,* December 22, 1787. This essay appeared on December 24 in *The* [New York] *Daily Advertiser.* On December 25 it appeared in *The New-York Packet* and *The New-York Journal, and Daily Patriotic Register.*

1. For background to this document, see "The Federalist. Introductory Note," October 27, 1787–May 28, 1788.
2. "have been" substituted for "be" in Hopkins.
3. In the newspaper, "the"; "this" was substituted in Hopkins and McLean.
4. "for" substituted for "of" in Hopkins.
5. See essay 24.
6. "has" omitted in Hopkins.
7. "they wisely judged" substituted for "wisely judging" in Hopkins.

decision of America; and instead of being taught by experience the propriety of correcting any extremes, into which we may have heretofore run, they appear disposed to conduct us into others still more dangerous and more extravagant. As if the tone of government had been found too high, or too rigid, the doctrines they teach are calculated to induce us to depress, or to relax it, by expedients which upon other occasions have been condemned or forborn. It may be affirmed without the imputation of invective, that if the principles they inculcate on various points could so far obtain as to become the popular creed, they would utterly unfit the people of this country for any species of government whatever. But a danger of this kind is not to be apprehended. The citizens of America have too much discernment to be argued into anarchy: And I am much mistaken if experience has not wrought a deep and solemn conviction in the public mind, that greater energy of government is essential to the welfare and prosperity of the community.

It may not be amiss in this place concisely to remark the origin and progress of the idea which aims at the exclusion of military establishments in time of peace. Though in speculative minds it may arise from a contemplation of the nature and tendency of such institutions fortified by the events that have happened in other ages and countries; yet as a national sentiment it must be traced to those habits of thinking, which we derive from the nation from whom [8] the inhabitants of these States have in general sprung.

In England for a long time after the Norman conquest the authority of the monarch was almost unlimited. Inroads were gradually made upon the prerogative, in favour of liberty, first by the Barons and afterwards by the people, 'till the greatest part of its most formidable pretensions became extinct. But it was not 'till the revolution in 1688, which elevated the Prince of Orange to the throne of Great Britain, that English liberty was completely triumphant. As incident to the undefined power of making war, an acknowleged prerogative of the crown, Charles IId. had by his own authority kept on foot in time of peace a body of 5,000 regular troops. And this number James IId. increased to 30,000; which [9] were paid out of his civil list. At the revolution, to abolish the exercise of so danger-

8. "which" substituted for "whom" in Hopkins.
9. "who" substituted for "which" in Hopkins.

ous an authority, it became an article of the bill of rights then framed, that "the [10] raising or keeping a standing army within the kingdom in time of peace, *unless with the consent of Parliament*, was against law."

In that kingdom, when the pulse of liberty was at its highest pitch, no security against the danger of standing armies was thought requisite, beyond a prohibition of their being raised or kept up by the mere authority of the executive magistrate. The patriots, who effected that memorable revolution, were too temperate and too well informed, to think of any restraint in the legislative discretion. They were aware that a certain number of troops for guards and garrisons were indispensable, that no precise bounds could be set to the national exigencies; that a power equal to every possible contingency must exist somewhere in the government; and that when they referred the exercise of that power to the judgement of the legislature, they had arrived at the ultimate point of precaution, which was reconciliable with the safety of the community.

From the same source, the people of America may be said to have derived a hereditary impression of danger to liberty from standing armies in time of peace. The circumstances of a revolution quickened the public sensibility on every point connected with the security of popular rights; and in some instances raised the warmth of our zeal beyond the degree which consisted with the due temperature of the body politic. The attempts of two of the states to restrict the authority of the legislature in the article of military establishments are of the number of these instances. The principles, which had taught us to be jealous of the power of an hereditary monarch, were by an injudicious excess extended to the representatives of the people in their popular assemblies. Even in some of the States, where this error was not adopted, we find unnecessary [11] declarations, that standing armies ought not to be kept up, in time of peace WITHOUT THE CONSENT OF THE LEGISLATURE —I call them unnecessary, because the reason, which had introduced a similar provision into the English bill of rights, is not applicable to any of the state constitutions. The power of raising

10. "the" omitted in McLean and Hopkins.
11. In the newspaper, "necessary"; "unnecessary" was substituted in McLean and Hopkins.

armies at all, under those constitutions, can by no construction be deemed to reside any where else, than in the legislatures themselves; and it was superfluous, if not absurd, to declare that a matter should not be done without the consent of a body, which alone had the power of doing it. Accordingly in some of those constitutions, and among others in [12] that of this [13] State of New-York; which has been justly celebrated both in Europe and in America as one of the best of the forms of government established in this country, there is a total silence upon the subject.

It is remarkable, that even in the two States,[14] which seem to have meditated an interdiction of military establishments in time of peace, the mode of expression made use of is rather cautionary [15] than prohibitory. It is not said, that standing armies *shall not be* kept up, but that they *ought not* to be kept up in time of peace. This ambiguity of terms appears to have been the result of a conflict between jealousy and conviction, between the desire of excluding such establishments at all events, and the persuasion that an absolute exclusion would be unwise and unsafe.

Can it be doubted that such a provision, whenever the situation of public affairs was understood to require a departure from it, would be interpreted by the Legislature into a mere admonition and would be made to yield to the necessities [16] or supposed necessities of the State? Let the fact already mentioned with respect to Pennsylvania decide.[17] What then (it may be asked) is the use of such a provision, if it cease to operate, the moment there is an inclination to disregard it?

Let us examine whether there be any comparison, in point of efficacy, between the provision alluded to and that which is contained in the New Constitution, for restraining the appropriations of money for military purposes to the period of two years. The former by aiming at too much is calculated to effect nothing; the latter, by steering clear of an imprudent extreme, and by being

12. In the newspaper, "is"; "in" was substituted in McLean and Hopkins.
13. "the" substituted for "this" in McLean and Hopkins.
14. Pennsylvania and North Carolina. See the preceding two essays for a discussion of the provisions of their constitutions which H is referring to here.
15. "monitory" substituted for "cautionary" in McLean and Hopkins.
16. "actual" substituted for "necessities" in Hopkins.
17. H is referring to the decision of the Pennsylvania legislature to raise troops in time of peace, which he had discussed in essays 6 and 25.

perfectly compatible with a proper provision for the exigencies of the nation, will have a salutary and powerful operation.

The Legislature of the United States will be *obliged* by this provision, once at least in every two years, to deliberate upon the propriety of keeping a military force on foot; to come to a new resolution on the point; and to declare their sense of the matter, by a formal vote in the face of their constituents. They are not *at liberty* to vest in the executive department permanent funds for the support of an army; if they were even incautious enough to be willing to repose in it so improper a confidence. As the spirit of party, in different degrees, must be expected to infect all political bodies, there will be no doubt persons in the national Legislature willing enough to arraign the measures and criminate the views of the majority. The provision for the support of a military force will always be a favourable topic for declamation. As often as the question comes forward, the public attention will be roused and attracted to the subject, by the party in opposition: And if the majority should be really disposed to exceed the proper limits the community will be warned of the danger and will have an opportunity of taking measures to guard against it. Independent of parties in the national Legislature itself, as often as the period of discussion arrived, the state Legislatures,[18] who will always be not only vigilant but suspicious and jealous guardians of the rights of the citizens, against incroachments from the Fœderal government, will constantly have their attention awake to the conduct of the national rulers and will be ready enough, if any thing improper appears, to sound the alarm to the people and not only to be the VOICE but if necessary the ARM of their discontent.

Schemes to subvert the liberties of a great community *require time to* mature them for execution. An army so large as seriously to menace those liberties could only be formed by progressive augmentations; which would suppose, not merely a temporary combination between the legislature and executive, but a continued conspiracy for a series of time. Is it probable that such a combination would exist at all? Is it probable that it would be persevered in and

18. In the newspaper, "legislature"; "legislatures" was substituted in McLean and Hopkins.

transmitted along,[19] through all the successive variations in the representative body, which biennial elections would naturally produce in both houses? Is it presumable, that every man, the instant he took his seat in the national senate, or house of representatives, would commence a traitor to his constituents and to his country? Can it be supposed, that there would not be found one man, discerning enough to detect so atrocious a conspiracy, or bold or honest enough to apprise his constituents of their danger? If such presumptions can fairly be made, there ought to be at once [20] an end of all delegated authority. The people should resolve to recall all the powers they have heretofore parted with out of their own hands; [21] and to divide themselves into as many states as there are counties, in order that they may be able to manage their own concerns in person.

If such suppositions could even be reasonably made, still the concealment of the design, for any duration, would be impracticable. It would be announced by the very circumstance of augmenting the army to so great an extent in time of profound peace. What colorable reason could be assigned in a country so situated, for such vast augmentations of the military force? It is impossible that the people could be long deceived; and the destruction of the project and of the projectors would quickly follow the discovery.

It has been said that the provision, which limits the appropriation of money for the support of an army to the period of two years would be unavailing; because the executive, when once possessed of a force large enough to awe the people into submission, would find resources in that very force sufficient to enable him to dispense with supplies from the acts [22] of the legislature. But the question again recurs: Upon what pretence could he be put into [23] possession of a force of that magnitude in time of peace? If we suppose it to have been erected,[24] in consequence of some domestic insurrection, or foreign war, then it becomes a case not within the principle of the objection; for this is levelled against the power of keeping up troops in time of peace. Few persons will be so visionary, as seriously

---

19. "along" omitted in Hopkins.
20. "at once to be" substituted for "to be at once" in Hopkins.
21. "out of their own hands" omitted in Hopkins.
22. "votes" substituted for "acts" in McLean and Hopkins.
23. "in" substituted for "into" in McLean and Hopkins.
24. "created" substituted for "erected" in McLean and Hopkins.

to contend, that military forces ought not to be raised to quell a rebellion, or resist an invasion; and if the defence of the community, under such circumstances, should make it necessary to have an army, so numerous as to hazard its liberty, this is one of those calamities for which there is neither preventative nor cure. It cannot be provided against by any possible form of government: It might even result from a simple league offensive and defensive; if it should ever [25] be necessary for the confederates or allies to form an army for common defence.

But it is an evil infinitely less likely to attend us in an united than in a disunited state; nay it may be safely asserted that it is an evil altogether unlikely to attend us in the better [26] situation. It is not easy to conceive a possibility, that dangers so formidable can assail the whole Union, as to demand a force considerable enough to place our liberties in the least jeopardy; especially if we take into our [27] view the aid to be derived from the militia, which ought always to be counted upon, as a valuable and powerful auxiliary. But in a state of disunion (as has been fully shewn in another place) [28] the contrary of this supposition would become not only probable but almost unavoidable.

PUBLIUS.

25. In the newspaper, "even"; "ever" was substituted in McLean and Hopkins.
26. "latter" was substituted for "better" in McLean and Hopkins.
27. "our" omitted in McLean and Hopkins.
28. See essay 8.

## The Federalist No. 27 [1]

[New York, December 25, 1787]

*To the People of the State of New-York.*

IT has been urged in different shapes that a constitution of the kind proposed by the Convention, cannot operate without the aid of a military force to execute its laws. This however, like most other things that have been alledged on that side, rests on mere general

*The New-York Packet,* December 25, 1787. This essay appeared on the same day in *The New-York Journal, and Daily Patriotic Register.* On December 26 it appeared in *The* [New York] *Independent Journal: or, the General Advertiser* and *The* [New York] *Daily Advertiser.*

1. For background to this document, see "The Federalist. Introductory Note," October 27, 1787–May 28, 1788.

assertion; unsupported by any precise or intelligible designation of the reasons upon which it is founded. As far as I have been able to divine the latent meaning of the objectors, it seems to originate in a pre-supposition that the people will be disinclined to the exercise of fœderal authority in any matter of an internal nature. Waving any exception that might be taken to the inaccuracy or inexplicitness of the distinction between internal and external, let us enquire what ground there is to pre-suppose that disinclination in the people? Unless we presume, at the same time, that the powers[2] of the General Government will be worse administered than those of the State governments, there seems to be no room for the presumption of ill-will, disaffection or opposition in the people. I believe it may be laid down as a general rule, that their confidence in and[3] obedience to a government, will commonly be proportioned to the goodness or badness of its administration. It must be admitted that there are exceptions to this rule; but these exceptions depend so entirely on accidental causes, that they cannot be considered as having any relation to the intrinsic merits or demerits of a constitution. These can only be judged of by general principles and maxims.

Various reasons have been suggested in the course of these papers, to induce a probability that the General Government will be better administered than the particular governments: The principal of which reasons[4] are that the extension of the spheres of election will present a greater option, or latitude of choice to the people, that through the medium of the State Legislatures, which[5] are select bodies of men, and who are to appoint the members of the national Senate,—there is reason to expect that this branch will generally be composed with peculiar care and judgment: That these circumstances promise greater knowledge and more extensive[6] information in the national councils: And that[7] they will be less apt to be tainted

2. In the newspaper, "power"; "powers" was substituted in McLean and Hopkins.
3. "their" inserted at this point in Hopkins.
4. "reasons" omitted in McLean and Hopkins.
5. "who" substituted for "which" in McLean and Hopkins.
6. "comprehensive" substituted for "extensive" in McLean and Hopkins.
7. In McLean at this point the following is inserted: "on account of the extent of the country from which those, to whose direction they will be committed, will be drawn." In Hopkins the insertion reads: "on account of the extent of the country from which will be drawn those to whose direction they will be committed."

by the spirit of faction, and more out of the reach of those occasional ill humors or temporary prejudices and propensities, which in smaller societies frequently contaminate the public councils,[8] beget injustice and oppression of [9] a part of the community, and engender schemes, which though they gratify a momentary inclination or desire, terminate in general distress, dissatisfaction and disgust. Several additional reasons of considerable force, to fortify that probability,[10] will occur [11] when we come to survey with a more critic[al] [12] eye, the interior structure of the edifice, which we are invited to erect. It will be sufficient here to remark, that until satisfactory reasons can be assigned to justify an opinion, that the fœderal government is likely to be administered in such a manner as to render it odious or contemptible to the people, there can be no reasonable foundation for the supposition, that the laws of the Union will meet with any greater obstruction from them, or will stand in need of any other methods to enforce their execution, than the laws of the particular members.

The hope of impunity is a strong incitement to sedition—the dread of punishment—a proportionately strong discouragement to it—will not the government of the Union, which, if possessed of a due degree of power, can [13] call to its aid the collective resources of the whole confederacy, be more likely to repress the *former* sentiment, and to inspire the *latter,* than that of a single State, which can only command the resources within itself? A turbulent faction in a State may easily suppose itself able to contend with the friends to the government in that State; but it can hardly be so infatuated as to imagine itself a match for [14] the combined efforts of the Union. If this reflection be just, there is less danger of resistance from irregular combinations of individuals, to the authority of the confederacy, than to that of a single member.

I will in this [15] place hazard an observation which will not be the

---

8. "deliberations" substituted for "councils" in McLean and Hopkins.

9. "towards" substituted for "of" in Hopkins.

10. "to fortify that probability" omitted in Hopkins.

11. "to fortify that probability" inserted at this point in Hopkins.

12. Only Hopkins made the change indicated by brackets in the text.

13. "can" was omitted in the newspaper; "can" was inserted in McLean and Hopkins.

14. "equal to" substituted for "a match for" in Hopkins.

15. "the first" substituted for "this" in Hopkins.

less just, because to some it may appear new; which is, that the more the operations of the national authority are intermingled in the ordinary exercise of government, the more the citizens are accustomed to meet with it in the common occurrences of their political life; the more it is familiarised to their sight and to their feelings; the further it enters into those objects which touch the most sensible cords, and put in motion the most active springs of the human heart; the greater will be the probability that it will conciliate the respect and attachment of the community. Man is very much a creature of habit. A thing that rarely strikes his senses will generally [16] have but little [17] influence upon his mind. A government continually at a distance and out of sight, can hardly be expected to interest the sensations of the people. The inference is, that the authority of the Union, and the affections of the citizens towards it, will be strengthened rather than weakened by its extension to what are called matters of internal concern; and [18] will have less occasion to recur to force in proportion to the familiarity and comprehensiveness of its agency. The more it circulates through those channels and currents, in which the passions of mankind naturally flow, the less will it require the aid of the violent and perilous expedients of compulsion.

One thing at all events, must be evident, that a government like the one [19] proposed, would bid much fairer to avoid the necessity of using force, than that [20] species of league contended for by most of its opponents; the authority of which should only operate upon the States in their political or collective capacities. It has been shewn,[21] that in such a confederacy, there can be no sanction for the laws but force; that frequent delinquencies in the members, are the natural offspring of the very frame of the government; and that as often as these happen they can only be redressed, if at all, by war and violence.

The plan reported by the Convention, by extending the authority of the fœderal head to the individual citizens of the several States, will enable the government to employ the ordinary magistracy of

16. "generally" omitted in Hopkins.
17. "a transient" substituted for "little" in McLean and Hopkins.
18. "that it" inserted at this point in McLean and Hopkins.
19. "that" substituted for "the one" in McLean.
20. "the" substituted for "that" in McLean and Hopkins.
21. See essays 15 and 16.

each in the execution of its laws. It is easy to perceive that this will tend to destroy, in the common apprehension, all distinction between the sources from which they might proceed; and will give the Fœderal Government the same advantage for securing a due obedience to its authority, which is enjoyed by the government of each State; in addition to the influence on public opinion, which will result from the important consideration of its having power to call to its assistance and support the resources of the whole Union. It merits particular attention in this place, that the laws of the confederacy, as to the *enumerated* and *legitimate* objects of its jurisdiction, will become the SUPREME LAW of the land; to the observance of which, all officers legislative, executive and judicial in each State, will be bound by the sanctity of an oath. Thus the Legislatures, Courts and Magistrates of the respective members will be incorporated into the operations of the national government, *as far as its just and constitutional authority extends;* and will be rendered auxiliary to the enforcement of its laws.* Any man, who will pursue by his own reflections the consequences of this situation, will perceive [23] that there is good ground to calculate upon a regular and peaceable execution of the laws of the Union; if its powers are administered with a common share of prudence.[24] If we will arbitrarily suppose the contrary, we may deduce any inferences we please from the supposition; for it is certainly possible, by an injudicious exercise of the authorities of the best government, that ever was or ever can be instituted, to provoke and precipitate the people into the wildest excesses. But though the adversaries of the proposed constitution should presume that the national rulers would be insensible to the motives of public good, or to the obligations of duty; I would still ask them, how the interests of ambition, or the views of encroachment, can be promoted by such a conduct?

PUBLIUS.

* *The sophistry which has been employed to show that this will tend to the distruction of the State Governments will, in its proper place, be fully detected.*[22]

22. See essays 31 and 44.
23. "if its powers are administered with a common share of prudence" inserted here in Hopkins.
24. "if its powers" through "prudence" omitted in Hopkins.

## The Federalist No. 28 [1]

[New York, December 26, 1787]

*To the People of the State of New-York.*

THAT there may happen cases, in which the national government may be necessitated to resort to force,[2] cannot be denied. Our own experience has corroborated the lessons taught by the examples of other nations; that emergencies of this sort will sometimes arise [3] in all societies, however constituted; that seditions and insurrections are unhappily maladies as inseparable from the body politic, as tumours and eruptions from the natural body; that the idea of governing at all times by the simple force of law (which we have been told is the only admissible principle of republican government) has no place but in the reveries [4] of those political doctors, whose sagacity disdains the admonitions of experimental instruction.

Should such emergencies at any time happen under the national government, there could be no remedy but force. The means to be employed must be proportioned to the extent of the mischief. If it should be a slight commotion in a small part of a State, the militia of the residue would be adequate to its suppression: and the natural presumption is, that they would be ready to do their duty. An insurrection, whatever may be its immediate cause, eventually endangers all government: Regard to the public peace, if not to the rights of the Union, would engage the citizens, to whom the contagion had not communicated itself, to oppose the insurgents: And if the general government should be found in practice conducive to the prosperity and felicity of the people, it were irrational to believe that they would be disinclined to its support.

If on the contrary the insurrection should pervade a whole State,

The [New York] *Independent Journal: or, the General Advertiser*, December 26, 1787. This essay appeared on December 28 in both *The New-York Packet* and *The* [New York] *Daily Advertiser.* On January 2, 1788, it appeared in *The New-York Journal, and Daily Patriotic Register.*

1. For background to this document, see "The Federalist. Introductory Note," October 27, 1787–May 28, 1788.
2. "under the necessity of resorting to force" substituted for "necessitated to restore to force" in Hopkins.
3. "exist" substituted for "arise" in McLean and Hopkins.
4. "reverie" substituted for "reveries" in Hopkins.

or a principal part of it, the employment of a different kind of force might become unavoidable. It appears that Massachusetts found it necessary to raise troops for repressing [5] the disorders within that State; [6] that Pennsylvania, from the mere apprehension of commotions among a part of her citizens, has thought proper to have recourse to the same measure.[7] Suppose the State of New-York had been inclined to re-establish her lost jurisdiction over the inhabitants of Vermont; [8] could she have hoped for success in such an enterprise from the efforts of the militia alone? Would she not have been compelled to raise and to maintain a more regular force for the execution of her design? If it must then be admitted that the necessity of recurring to a force different from the militia in cases of this extraordinary nature, is applicable to the State governments themselves, why should the possibility that the national government might be under a like necessity in similar extremities, be made an objection to its existence? Is it not surprising that men, who declare an attachment to the union in the abstract, should urge, as an objection to the proposed constitution, what applies with tenfold weight to the plan for which they contend; and what as far as it has any foundation in truth is an inevitable consequence of civil society upon an enlarged scale? Who would not prefer that possibility to the unceasing agitations and frequent revolutions which are the continual scourges of petty republics?

Let us pursue this examination in another light. Suppose, in lieu of one general system, two or three or even four confederacies were to be formed, would not the same difficulty oppose itself to the operations of either of these confederacies? Would not each of them be exposed to the same casualties; and, when these happened, be obliged to have recourse to the same expedients for upholding its authority, which are objected to a government for all the States? Would the militia in this supposition be more ready or more able to support the federal authority than in the case of a general union? All candid and intelligent men must upon due consideration acknowledge that the principle of the objection is equally applicable to either of the two cases; and that whether we have one government

5. "suppressing" substituted for "repressing" in McLean and Hopkins.
6. See essay 6, note 15.
7. See essay 6, note 28.
8. See essay 7, note 9.

for all the States, or different governments for different parcels of them, or even if there should be an intire separation of the States,[9] there might sometimes be a necessity to make use of a force constituted differently from the militia to preserve the peace of the community, and to maintain the just authority of the laws against those violent invasions of them which amount to insurrections and rebellions.

Independent of all other reasonings upon the subject, it is a full answer to those who require a more peremptory provision against military establishments in time of peace,[10] that the whole power of the proposed government is to be in the hands of the representatives of the people. This is the essential, and after all the only efficacious security for the rights and privileges of the people which is attainable in civil society.*

If the representatives of the people betray their constituents, there is then no resource [12] left but in the exertion of that original right of self-defence, which is paramount to all positive forms of government; and which, against the usurpations [13] of the national rulers, may be exerted with infinitely better prospect of success, than against those of the rulers of an individual State. In a single State, if the persons entrusted with supreme power became usurpers, the different parcels, subdivisions or districts, of which it consists, having no distinct government in each, can take no regular measures for defence. The citizens must rush tumultuously to arms, without concert, without system, without resource; except in their courage and despair. The usurpers, cloathed with the forms of legal authority, can too often crush the opposition in embryo. The smaller the extent of territory, the more difficult will it be for the people to form a regular or systematic plan of opposition; and the more easy will it be to defeat their early efforts. Intelligence can be more speedily

* *Its full efficacy will be examined hereafter.*[11]

9. "or as many unconnected governments as there are states" substituted for "or even" through "states" in McLean and Hopkins.

10. "to say" inserted at this point in McLean and Hopkins.

11. *The Federalist* essays were, of course, predicated on the assumption that the ultimate security of the rights of the people lay in the fact that power was in the hands of their representatives. See, for example, essay 17.

12. In the newspaper, "source"; "resource" was substituted in McLean and Hopkins.

13. "usurpation" substituted for "usurpations" in Hopkins.

obtained of their preparations and movements; and the military force
in the possession of the usurpers, can be more rapidly directed
against the part where the opposition has begun. In this situation,
there must be a peculiar coincidence of circumstances to ensure
success to the popular resistance.

The obstacles to usurpation and the facilities of resistance increase
with the increased extent of the state; provided the citizens understand their rights and are disposed to defend them. The natural
strength of the people in a large community, in proportion to the
artificial strength of the government, is greater than in a small; and
of course more competent to a struggle with the attempts of the
government to establish a tyranny. But in a confederacy the people,
without exaggeration, may be said to be entirely the masters of
their own fate. Power being almost always the rival of power; the
General Government will at all times stand ready to check the
usurpations of the state governments; and these will have the same
disposition towards the General Government. The people, by throw-
ing themselves into either scale, will infallibly make it preponderate.
If their rights are invaded by either, they can make use of the other,
as the instrument of redress. How wise will it be in them by cherish-
ing the Union to preserve to themselves an advantage which can
never be too highly prised!

It may safely be received as an axiom in our political system, that
the state governments will in all possible contingencies afford complete security against invasions of the public liberty by the national
authority. Projects of usurpation cannot be masked under pretences
so likely to escape the penetration of select bodies of men as of the
people at large. The Legislatures will have better means of information. They can discover the danger at a distance; and possessing all
the organs of civil power and the confidence of the people, they can
at once adopt a regular plan of opposition, in which they can combine all the resources of the community. They can readily communicate with each other in the different states; and unite their
common forces for the protection of their common liberty.

The great extent of the country is a further security. We have already experienced its utility against the attacks of a foreign power.[14]
And it would have precisely the same effect against the enterprises

14. "enemy" substituted for "power" in Hopkins.

of ambitious rulers in the national councils. If the fœderal army should be able to quell the resistance of one state, the distant states would be able [15] to make head with fresh forces. The advantages obtained in one place must be abandoned to subdue the opposition in others; and the moment the part which had been reduced to submission was left to itself its efforts would be renewed and its resistance revive.

We should recollect that the extent of the military force must at all events be regulated by the resources of the country. For a long time to come, it will not be possible to maintain a large army: and as the means of doing this increase, the population and natural strength of the community will proportionably increase. When will the time arrive, that the fœderal Government can raise and maintain an army capable of erecting a despotism over the great body of the people of an immense empire; who are in a situation, through the medium of their state governments, to take measures for their own defence with all the celerity, regularity and system of independent nations? The apprehension may be considered as a disease, for which there can be found no cure in the resources of argument and reasoning.

PUBLIUS.

15. "have it in their power" substituted for "be able" in Hopkins.

## The Federalist No. 29 [1]

[New York, January 9, 1788]

*To the People of the State of New-York.*

THE power of regulating the militia and of commanding its services in times of insurrection and invasion are natural incidents to the duties of superintending the common defence, and of watching over the internal peace of the confederacy.

It requires no skill in the science of war to discern that uniformity

*The* [New York] *Independent Journal: or, the General Advertiser,* January 9, 1788. This essay appeared on January 10 in *The* [New York] *Daily Advertiser,* on January 11 in *The New-York Packet,* and on January 12 in *The New-York Journal, and Daily Patriotic Register.* In the McLean edition this essay is numbered 29, and in the newspapers it is numbered 35.
    1. For background to this document, see "The Federalist. Introductory Note," October 27, 1787–May 28, 1788.

in the organization and discipline of the militia would be attended with the most beneficial effects, whenever they were called into service for the public defence. It would enable them to discharge the duties of the camp and of the field with mutual intelligence and concert; an advantage of peculiar moment in the operations of an army; And it would fit them much sooner to acquire the degree of proficiency in military functions, which would be essential to their usefulness. This desirable uniformity can only be accomplished by confiding the regulation of the militia to the direction of the national authority. It is therefore with the most evident propriety that the plan of the Convention proposes to empower the union "to provide for organizing, arming and disciplining the militia, and for governing such part of them as may be employed in the service of the United States, *reserving to the states respectively the appointment of the officers and the authority of training the militia according to the discipline prescribed by Congress.*"

Of the different grounds which have been taken in opposition to the [2] plan of the Convention,[3] there is none that was so little to have been expected, or is so untenable in itself, as the one from which [4] this particular provision has been attacked. If a well regulated militia be the most natural defence of a free country, it ought certainly to be under the regulation and at the disposal of that body which is constituted the guardian of the national security. If standing armies are dangerous to liberty, an efficacious power over the militia, in the [5] body to whose care the protection of the State is committed,[6] ought as far as possible to take away the inducement and the pretext to such unfriendly institutions. If the fœderal government can command the aid of the militia in those emergencies which call for the military arm in support of the civil magistrate, it can the better dispense with the employment of a different kind of force. If it cannot avail itself of the former, it will be obliged to recur to the latter. To render an army unnecessary will be a more certain method of preventing its existence than a thousand prohibitions upon paper.

2. "this" substituted for "the" in McLean and Hopkins.
3. "of the Convention" omitted in McLean and Hopkins.
4. In the newspaper, "which from"; "from which" was substituted in McLean and Hopkins.
5. "same" inserted at this point in McLean and Hopkins.
6. "to whose" through "committed" omitted in McLean and Hopkins.

In order to cast an odium upon the power of calling forth the militia to execute the Laws of the Union, it has been remarked that there is no where any provision in the proposed Constitution for calling out [7] the POSSE COMITATUS to assist the magistrate in the execution of his duty; whence it has been inferred that military force was intended to be his only auxiliary. There is a striking incoherence in the objections which have appeared, and sometimes even from the same quarter, not much calculated to inspire a very favourable opinion of the sincerity or fair dealing of their authors. The same persons who tell us in one breath that the powers of the federal government will be despotic and unlimited, inform us in the next that it has not authority sufficient even to call out the POSSE COMITATUS. The latter fortunately is as much short of the truth as the former exceeds it. It would be as absurd to doubt that a right to pass all laws *necessary* and *proper* to execute its declared powers would include that of requiring the assistance of the citizens to the officers who may be entrusted with the execution of those laws; as it would be to believe that a right to enact laws necessary and proper for the imposition and collection of taxes would involve that of varying the rules of descent and [8] alienation of landed property or of abolishing the trial by jury in cases relating to it. It being therefore evident that the supposition of a want of power to require the aid of the POSSE COMITATUS is entirely destitute of colour, it will follow that the conclusion which has been drawn from it, in its application to the authority of the federal government over the militia is as uncandid as it is illogical. What reason could there be to infer that force was intended to be the sole instrument of authority merely because there is a power to make use of it when necessary? What shall we think of the motives which could induce men of sense to reason in this [9] manner? How shall we prevent a conflict between charity and judgment? [10]

By a curious refinement upon the spirit of republican jealousy, we are even taught to apprehend danger from the militia itself in the hands of the federal government. It is observed that select corps may

7. "requiring the aid of" substituted for "calling out" in McLean and Hopkins.
8. "of the" inserted at this point in McLean and Hopkins.
9. "extraordinary" inserted at this point in McLean and Hopkins.
10. "conviction" substituted for "judgment" in McLean and Hopkins.

be formed, composed of the young and [11] ardent, who may be rendered subservient to the views of arbitrary power. What plan for the regulation of the militia may be pursued by the national government is impossible to be foreseen. But so far from viewing the matter in the same light with those who object to select corps as dangerous, were the Constitution ratified, and were I to deliver my sentiments to a member of the federal legislature from this State [12] on the subject of a militia establishment, I should hold to him in substance the following discourse:

"The project of disciplining all the militia of the United States is as futile as it would be injurious, if it were capable of being carried into execution. A tolerable expertness in military movements is a business that requires time and practice. It is not a day or even [13] a week [14] that will suffice for the attainment of it. To oblige the great body of the yeomanry and of the other classes of the citizens to be under arms for the purpose of going through military exercises and evolutions as often as might be necessary, to acquire the degree of perfection which would intitle them to the character of a well regulated militia, would be a real grievance to the people, and a serious public inconvenience and loss. It would form an annual deduction from the productive labour of the country to an amount which, calculating upon the present numbers of the people, would not fall far short of the whole expence of the civil establishments of all the States.[15] To attempt a thing which would abridge the mass of labour and industry to so considerable an extent would be unwise; and the experiment, if made, could not succeed, because it would not long be endured. Little more can reasonably be aimed at with respect to the people at large than to have them properly armed and equipped; and in order to see that this be not neglected, it will be necessary to assemble them once or twice in the course of a year.

"But though the scheme of disciplining the whole nation must be abandoned as mischievous or impracticable; yet it is a matter of the

11. "the" inserted at this point in McLean and Hopkins.
12. "from this State" omitted in McLean and Hopkins.
13. "nor" substituted for "or even" in McLean and Hopkins.
14. "nor even a month" inserted at this point in McLean and Hopkins.
15. "a million of pounds" substituted for "the whole" through "the States" in McLean and Hopkins.

utmost importance that a well digested plan should as soon as possible be adopted for the proper establishment of the militia. The attention of the government ought particularly to be directed to the formation of a select corps of moderate size [16] upon such principles as will really fit it [17] for service in case of need. By thus circumscribing the plan it will be possible to have an excellent body of well trained militia ready to take the field whenever the defence of the State shall require it. This will not only lessen the call for military establishments; but if circumstances should at any time oblige the government to form an army of any magnitude, that army can never be formidable to the liberties of the people, while there is a large body of citizens little if at all inferior to them in discipline and the use of arms, who stand ready to defend their own rights and those of their fellow citizens. This appears to me the only substitute that can be devised for a standing army; [18] the best possible security against it, if it should exist."

Thus differently from the adversaries of the proposed constitution should I reason on the same subject; deducing arguments of safety from the very sources which they represent as fraught with danger and perdition. But how the national Legislature may reason on the point is a thing which neither they nor I can foresee.

There is something so far fetched and so extravagant in the idea of danger to liberty from the militia, that one is at a loss whether to treat it with gravity or with raillery; whether to consider it as a mere trial of skill, like the paradoxes of rhetoricians, as a disingenuous artifice to instill prejudices at any price or as the serious offspring of political fanaticism. Where in the name of common sense are our fears to end if we may not trust our sons, our brothers, our neighbours, our fellow-citizens? What shadow of danger can there be from men who are daily mingling with the rest of their countrymen; and who participate with them in the same feelings, sentiments, habits and interests? What reasonable cause of apprehension can be inferred from a power in the Union to prescribe regulations for the militia and to command its services when necessary; while the particular States are to have the *sole and exclusive*

16. In the newspaper, "extent"; "size" substituted in McLean and Hopkins.
17. In the newspaper, "them"; "it" substituted in McLean and Hopkins.
18. "and" inserted at this point in McLean and Hopkins.

*appointment of the officers?* If it were possible seriously to indulge a jealousy of the militia upon any conceivable establishment under the Fœderal Government, the circumstance of the officers being in the appointment of the States ought at once to extinguish it. There can be no doubt that this circumstance will always secure to them a preponderating influence over the militia.

In reading many of the publications against the Constitution, a man is apt to imagine that he is perusing some ill written tale or romance; which instead of natural and agreeable images exhibits to the mind nothing but frightful and distorted shapes—Gorgons Hydras and Chimeras dire—discoloring and disfiguring whatever it represents and transforming every thing it touches into a monster.

A sample of this is to be observed in the exaggerated and improbable suggestions which have taken place respecting the power of calling for the services of the militia. That of New-Hampshire is to be marched to Georgia, of Georgia to New Hampshire, of New-York to Kentuke and of Kentuke to Lake Champlain. Nay the debts due to the French and Dutch are to be paid in Militia-men instead of Louis d'ors and ducats. At one moment there is to be a large army to lay prostrate the liberties of the people; at another moment the militia of Virginia are to be dragged from their homes five or six hundred miles to tame the republican contumacy of Massachusetts; and that of Massachusetts is to be transported an equal distance to subdue the refractory haughtiness of the aristocratic Virginians. Do the persons, who rave at this rate, imagine, that their art or their eloquence can impose any conceits [19] or absurdities upon the people of America for infallible truths?

If there should be an army to be made use of as the engine of despotism what need of the militia? If there should be no army, whither would the militia, irritated by being called upon [20] to undertake a distant and hopeless [21] expedition for the purpose of rivetting the chains of slavery upon a part of their countrymen direct their course, but to the seat of the tyrants, who had meditated so foolish as well as so wicked a project; to crush them in

19. In the newspaper, "concerts"; "conceits" was substituted in McLean and Hopkins.

20. "at being required" substituted for "by being called upon" in McLean and Hopkins.

21. "distressing" substituted for "hopeless" in McLean and Hopkins.

their imagined intrenchments of power and to [22] make them an example of the just vengeance of an abused and incensed people? Is this the way in which usurpers stride to dominion over a numerous and enlightened nation? Do they begin by exciting the detestation of the very instruments of their intended usurpations? Do they usually commence their career by wanton and disgustful acts of power calculated to answer no end, but to draw upon themselves universal hatred and execration? Are suppositions of this sort the sober admonitions of discerning patriots to a discerning people? Or are they the inflammatory ravings of chagrined incendiaries or distempered enthusiasts? If we were even to suppose the national rulers actuated by the most ungovernable ambition, it is impossible to believe that they would employ such preposterous means to accomplish their designs.

In times of insurrection or invasion it would be natural and proper that the militia of a neighbouring state should be marched into another to resist a common enemy or to guard the republic against the violences of faction or sedition. This was frequently the case in respect to the first object in the course of the late war; and this mutual succour is indeed a principal end of our political association. If the power of affording it be placed under the direction of the union, there will be no danger of a supine and listless inattention to the dangers of a neighbour, till its near approach had superadded the incitements of self preservation to the too feeble impulses of duty and sympathy.[23]

PUBLIUS.

22. "to" omitted in Hopkins.
23. In the newspaper there was an additional paragraph which reads as follows:
"I have now gone through the examination of such of the powers proposed to be vested in the United States, which may be considered as having an immediate relation to the energy of the government; and have endeavoured to answer the principal objections which have been made to them. I have passed over in silence those minor authorities which are either too inconsiderable to have been thought worthy of the hostilities of the opponents of the Constitution, or of too manifest propriety to admit of controversy. The mass of judiciary power however might have claimed an investigation under this head, had it not been for the consideration that its organization and its extent may be more advantageously considered in connection. This has determined me to refer it to the branch of our enquiries, upon which we shall next enter."

## The Federalist No. 30 [1]

[New York, December 28, 1787]

*To the People of the State of New-York.*

IT has been already observed, that the Fœderal Government ought to possess the power of providing for the support of the national forces; in which proposition was intended to be included the expence of raising troops, of building and equiping fleets, and all other expences in any wise connected with military arrangements and operations. But these are not the only objects to which the jurisdiction of the Union, in respect to revenue, must necessarily be empowered to extend—It must embrace a provision for the support of the national civil list—for the payment of the national debts contracted, or that may be contracted—and in general for all those matters which will call for disbursements out of the national treasury. The conclusion is, that there must be interwoven in the frame of the government, a general power of taxation in one shape or another.

Money is with propriety considered as the vital principle of the body politic; as that which sustains its life and motion, and enables it to perform its most essential functions. A complete power therefore to procure a regular and adequate supply of it,[2] as far as the resources of the community will permit, may be regarded as an indispensable ingredient in every constitution. From a deficiency in this particular, one of two evils must ensue; either the people must be subjected to continual plunder as a substitute for a more eligible mode of supplying the public wants, or the government must sink into a fatal atrophy, and in a short course of time perish.

In the Ottoman or Turkish empire, the sovereign, though in other respects absolute master of the lives and fortunes of his subjects,

*The New-York Packet,* December 28, 1787. This essay appeared on December 29 in *The* [New York] *Independent Journal: or, the General Advertiser* and *The* [New York] *Daily Advertiser.* In *The New-York Journal, and Daily Patriotic Register* it was begun on January 2 and concluded on January 4. In the McLean edition this essay is numbered 30, and in the newspapers it is numbered 29.

1. For background to this document, see "The Federalist. Introductory Note," October 28, 1787–May 28, 1788.
2. "revenue" substituted for "it" in McLean and Hopkins.

has no right to impose a new tax. The consequence is, that he permits the Bashaws or Governors of provinces to pillage the people without mercy;[3] and in turn squeezes out of them the sums of which he stands in need to satisfy his own exigencies and those of the State. In America, from a like cause, the government of the Union has gradually dwindled into a state of decay, approaching nearly to annihilation. Who can doubt that the happiness of the people in both countries would be promoted by competent authorities in the proper hands, to provide the revenues which the necessities of the public might require?

The present confederation, feeble as it is, intended to repose in the United States, an unlimited power of providing for the pecuniary wants of the Union. But proceeding upon an erroneous principle, it has been done in such a manner as entirely to have frustrated the intention. Congress by the articles which compose that compact (as has been already stated) are authorised to ascertain and call for any sums of money necessary, in their judgment, to the service of the United States; and their requisitions, if conformable to the rule of apportionment, are in every constitutional sense obligatory upon the States. These have no right to question the propriety of the demand—no discretion beyond that of devising the ways and means of furnishing the sums demanded. But though this be strictly and truly the case; though the assumption of such a right[4] be an infringement of the articles of Union; though it may seldom or never have been avowedly claimed; yet in practice it has been constantly exercised; and would continue to be so, as long as the revenues of the confederacy should remain dependent on the intermediate agency of its members. What the consequences of this system have been, is within the knowledge of every man, the least conversant in our public affairs, and has been amply[5] unfolded in different parts of these inquiries. It is this which has chiefly contributed to reduce us to a situation which[6] affords ample cause, both[7] of mortification to ourselves, and of triumph to our enemies.

What remedy can there be for this situation but, in a change of

3. "at discretion" substituted for "without mercy" in McLean and Hopkins.
4. "would" inserted at this point in McLean and Hopkins.
5. "abundantly" substituted for "amply" in McLean and Hopkins.
6. "that" substituted for "which" in Hopkins.
7. "both" omitted in McLean and Hopkins.

the system, which has produced it? In a change of the fallacious and delusive system of quotas and requisitions? What substitute can there be imagined for this *ignis fatuus* in finance, but that of permitting the national government to raise its own revenues by the ordinary methods of taxation, authorised in every well ordered constitution of civil government? Ingenious men may declaim with plausibility on any subject; but no human ingenuity can point out any other expedient to rescue us from the inconveniences and embarrassments, naturally resulting from defective supplies of the public treasury.

The more intelligent adversaries of the new constitution admit the force of this reasoning; but they qualify their admission by a distinction between what they call *internal* and *external* taxation.[8] The former they would reserve to the State governments; the latter, which they explain into commercial imposts, or rather duties on imported articles, they declare themselves willing to concede to the Fœderal Head. This distinction, however, would violate that fundamental maxim of good sense and sound policy, which dictates that every POWER ought to be proportionate to its OBJECT; and would still leave the General Government in a kind of tutelage to the State governments, inconsistent with every idea of vigor or efficiency. Who can pretend that commercial imposts are or would be alone equal to the present and future exigencies of the Union? Taking into the account the existing debt, foreign and domestic, upon any plan of extinguishment, which a man moderately impressed with the importance of public justice and public credit could approve, in addition to the establishments, which all parties will acknowledge to be necessary, we could not reasonably flatter ourselves, that this resource alone, upon the most improved scale, would even suffice for its present necessities. Its future necessities admit not of calculation or limitation; and upon the principle, more than once adverted to, the power of making provision for them as they arise, ought to be equally unconfined. I believe it may be regarded as a position, warranted by the history of mankind, that *in the usual progress of things, the necessities of a nation in every stage of its existence will be found at least equal to its resources.*

To say that deficiencies may be provided for by requisitions upon

8. "taxations" substituted for "taxation" in Hopkins.

the States, is on the one hand, to acknowledge that this system cannot be depended upon; and on the other hand, to depend upon it for every thing beyond a certain limit. Those who have carefully attended to its vices and deformities as they have been exhibited by experience, or delineated in the course of these papers, must feel an invincible repugnancy to trusting the national interests, in any degree, to its operation. Its inevitable tendency, whenever it is brought into activity,[9] must be to enfeeble the Union and sow the seeds of discord and contention between the Fœderal Head and its members, and between the members themselves. Can it be expected that the deficiencies would be better supplied in this mode, than the total wants of the Union have heretofore been supplied, in the same mode? It ought to be recollected, that if less will be required from the States, they will have proportionably less means to answer the demand. If the opinions of those who contend for the distinction which has been mentioned, were to be received as evidence of truth, one would be led to conclude that there was some known point in the œconomy of national affairs, at which it would be safe to stop, and [10] say, thus far the ends of public happiness will be promoted by supplying the wants of government, and all beyond this is unworthy of our care or anxiety. How is it possible that a government half supplied and always necessitous, can fulfil the purposes of its institution—can provide for the security of—advance the prosperity —or support the reputation of the commonwealth? How can it ever possess either energy or stability, dignity or credit, confidence at home or respectability abroad? How can its administration be any thing else than a succession of expedients temporising, impotent, disgraceful? How will it be able to avoid a frequent sacrifice of its engagements to immediate necessity? How can it undertake or execute any liberal or enlarged plans of public good?

Let us attend to what would be the effects of this situation in the very first war in which we should happen to be engaged. We will presume for argument sake, that the revenue arising from the impost-[11] duties answer the purposes of a provision for the public debt, and of a peace establishment for the Union. Thus circum-

9. "Whenever it is brought into activity, its inevitable tendency" substituted for "Its inevitable" through "activity" in Hopkins.
10. "to" inserted at this point in McLean and Hopkins.
11. "import" substituted for "impost" in McLean and Hopkins.

stanced, a war breaks out. What would be the probable conduct of the government in such an emergency? Taught by experience that proper dependence could not be placed on the success of requisitions: unable by its own authority to lay hold of fresh resources, and urged by considerations of national danger, would it not be driven to the expedient of diverting the funds already appropriated from their proper objects to the defence of the State? It is not easy to see how a step of this kind could be avoided; and if it should be taken, it is evident that it would prove the destruction of public credit at the very moment that it was become essential to the public safety. To imagine that at such a crisis credit might be dispensed with, would be the extreme of infatuation. In the modern system of war, nations the most wealthy are obliged to have recourse to large loans. A country so little opulent as ours, must feel this necessity in a much stronger degree. But who would lend to a government that prefaced its overtures for borrowing, by an act which demonstrated that no reliance could be placed on the steadiness of its measures for paying? The loans it might be able to procure, would be as limited in their extent as burthensome in their conditions. They would be made upon the same principles that usurers commonly lend to bankrupt and fraudulent debtors; with a sparing hand, and at enormous premiums.

It may perhaps be imagined, that from the scantiness of the resources of the country, the necessity of diverting the established funds in the case supposed, would exist; though the national government should possess an unrestrained power of taxation. But two considerations will serve to quiet all apprehension on this head; one is, that we are sure the resources of the community in their full extent, will be brought into activity for the benefit of the Union; the other is, that whatever deficiencies there may be, can without difficulty be supplied by loans.

The power of creating new funds upon new objects of taxation by its own authority,[12] would enable the national government to borrow, as far as its necessities might require. Foreigners as well as the citizens of America, could then reasonably repose confidence in its engagements; but to depend upon a government, that must itself

12. "by its own authority, new funds from new objects of taxation" substituted for "new funds" through "authority" in Hopkins.

depend upon thirteen other governments for the means of fulfilling its contracts, when once its situation is clearly understood, would require a degree of credulity, not often to be met with in the pecuniary transactions of mankind, and little reconcileable with the usual sharp-sightedness of avarice.

Reflections of this kind, may have trifling weight with men, who hope to see realized in America, the halcyon scenes of the poetic or fabulous age; [13] but to those who believe we are likely to experience a common portion of the vicissitudes and calamities, which have fallen to the lot of other nations, they must appear entitled to serious attention. Such men must behold the actual situation of their country with painful solicitude, and deprecate the evils which ambition or revenge might, with too much facility, inflict upon it.

PUBLIUS.

13. "the halcyon scenes of the poetic or fabulous age realized in America;" substituted for "realized" through "fabulous age;" in Hopkins.

# 1788

## The Federalist No. 31 [1]

[New York, January 1, 1788]

*To the People of the State of New-York.*

IN disquisitions of every kind there are certain primary truths or first principles upon which all subsequent reasonings must depend. These contain an internal evidence, which antecedent to all reflection or combination commands the assent of the mind. Where it produces not this effect, it must proceed either from some defect or [2] disorder in the organs of perception, or from the influence of some strong interest, or passion, or prejudice. Of this nature are the maxims in geometry, that "The whole is greater than its part; that things equal to the same are equal to one another; that two straight lines cannot inclose a space; and that all right angles are equal to each other." Of the same nature are these other maxims in ethics and politics, that there cannot be an effect without a cause; that the means ought to be proportioned to the end; that every power ought to be commensurate with its object; that there ought to be no limitation of a power destined to effect a purpose, which is itself incapable of limitation. And there are other truths in the two latter sciences, which if they cannot pretend to rank in the class of axioms, are yet [3] such direct inferences from them, and so obvious in themselves, and so agreeable to the natural and unsophisticated dictates of common sense, that they challenge the assent of a sound and unbiassed mind, with a degree of force and conviction almost equally irresistable.

*The New-York Packet,* January 1, 1788. This essay appeared on January 2 in *The* [New York] *Independent Journal: or, the General Advertiser* and *The* [New York] *Daily Advertiser,* and on January 5 in *The New-York Journal, and Daily Patriotic Register.* In the McLean edition this essay is numbered 31, and in the newspapers, it is numbered 30.

1. For background to this document, see "The Federalist. Introductory Note," October 27, 1787–May 28, 1788.
2. "defect or" omitted in McLean and Hopkins.
3. "yet" omitted in Hopkins.

The objects of geometrical enquiry are so intirely abstracted from those pursuits which stir up and put in motion the unruly passions of the human heart, that mankind without difficulty adopt not only the more simple theorems of the science, but even those abstruse paradoxes, which however they may appear susceptible of demonstration, are at variance with the natural conceptions which the mind, without the aid of philosophy, would be led to entertain upon the subject. The INFINITE DIVISIBILITY of matter, or in other words, the INFINITE divisibility of a FINITE thing, extending even to the minutest atom, is a point agreed among geometricians; though not less incomprehensible to common sense, than any of those mysteries in religion, against which the batteries of infidelity have been so industriously levelled.

But in the sciences of morals and politics men are found far less tractable. To a certain degree it is right and useful, that this should be the case. Caution and investigation are a necessary armour against error and imposition. But this untractableness may be carried too far, and may degenerate into obstinacy, perverseness or disingenuity. Though it cannot be pretended that the principles of moral and political knowledge have in general the same degree of certainty with those of the mathematics; yet they have much better claims in this respect, than to judge from the conduct of men in particular situations, we should be disposed to allow them. The obscurity is much oftener in the passions and prejudices of the reasoner than in the subject. Men upon too many occasions do not give their own understandings fair play; but yielding to some untoward bias they entangle themselves in words and confound themselves in subtleties.

How else could it happen (if we admit the objectors to be sincere in their opposition) that positions so clear as those which manifest the necessity of a general power of taxation in the government of the union, should have to encounter any adversaries among men of discernment? Though these positions have been elsewhere fully stated,[4] they will perhaps not be improperly recapitulated in this place, as introductory to an examination of what may have been offered by way of objection to them. They are in substance as follow:

A government ought to contain in itself every power requisite to

4. See essay 30.

the full accomplishment of the objects committed to its care, and to the complete execution of the trusts for which it is responsible; free from every other control, but a regard to the public good and to the sense of the people.

As the duties of superintending the national defence and of securing the public peace against foreign or domestic violence, involve a provision for casualties and dangers, to which no possible limits can be assigned, the power of making that provision ought to know no other bounds than the exigencies of the nation and the resources of the community.

As revenue is the essential engine by which the means of answering the national exigencies must be procured, the power of procuring that article in its full extent, must necessarily be comprehended in that of providing for those exigencies.

As theory and practice conspire to prove that the power of procuring revenue is unavailing, when exercised over the States in their collective capacities, the Federal government must of necessity be invested with an unqualified power of taxation in the ordinary modes.

Did not experience evince the contrary, it would be natural to conclude that the propriety of a general power of taxation in the national government might safely be permitted to rest on the evidence of these propositions, unassisted by any additional arguments or illustrations. But we find in fact, that the antagonists of the proposed constitution, so far from acquiescing in their justness or truth, seem to make their principal and most zealous effort against this part of the plan. It may therefore be satisfactory to analize the arguments with which they combat it.

Those of them, which have been most labored with that view, seem in substance to amount to this: "It is not true, because the exigencies of the Union may not be susceptible of limitation, that its power of laying taxes ought to be unconfined. Revenue is as requisite to the purposes of the local administrations as to those of the Union; and the former are at least of equal importance with the latter to the happiness of the people. It is therefore as necessary, that the State Governments should be able to command the means of supplying their wants, as, that the National Government should possess the like faculty, in respect to the wants of the Union. But an indefinite power of taxation in the *latter* might, and probably would in time deprive the former of the means of providing for their own necessities; and would subject them entirely to the mercy of the national Legislature. As the laws of the Union are to become the supreme law of the land; as it is to have power to pass all laws that may be NECESSARY for carrying into execution, the authorities with which it is proposed to vest it; the national government might at any time abolish the taxes imposed for State objects, upon the pretence of an interference with its own. It might alledge a necessity of doing this, in order to give efficacy to the national revenues: And thus all the resources of taxation might by degrees, become the subjects of fœderal monopoly, to the intire exclusion and destruction of the State Governments."

This mode of reasoning appears some times to turn upon the supposition of usurpation in the national government; at other times it seems to be designed only as a deduction from the constitutional operation of its intended powers. It is only in the latter light, that it can be admitted to have any pretensions to fairness. The moment we launch into conjectures about the usurpations of the fœderal Government, we get into an unfathomable abyss, and fairly put ourselves out of the reach of all reasoning. Imagination may range at pleasure till it gets bewildered amidst the labyrinths of an enchanted castle, and knows not on which side to turn to extricate itself from the perplexities into which it has so rashly adventured.[5] Whatever may be the limits or modifications of the powers of the Union, it is easy to imagine an endless train of possible dangers; and by indulging an excess of jealousy and timidity, we may bring ourselves to a state of absolute scepticism and irresolution. I repeat here what I have observed in substance in another place [6] that all observations founded upon the danger of usurpation, ought to be referred to the composition and structure of the government, not to the nature or [7] extent of its powers. The State governments, by their original constitutions, are invested with complete sovereignty. In what does our security consist against usurpations from that quarter? Doubtless in the manner of their formation, and in a due

5. "escape from the apparitions which itself has raised" substituted for "extricate" through "adventured" in McLean and Hopkins.

6. A similar observation was made by Hamilton in the concluding paragraphs of essay 23.

7. "and" substituted for "or" in Hopkins.

dependence of those who are to administer them upon the people. If the proposed construction of the Fœderal Government, be found upon an impartial examination of it, to be such as to afford, to a proper extent, the same species of security, all apprehensions on the score of usurpation ought to be discarded.

It should not be forgotten, that a disposition in the State governments to encroach upon the rights of the Union, is quite as probable, as a disposition in the Union to encroach upon the rights of the State Governments. What side would be likely to prevail in such a conflict, must depend on the means which the contending parties could employ towards ensuring success. As in republics, strength is always on the side of the people; and as there are weighty reasons to induce a belief, that the State governments will commonly possess most influence over them, the natural conclusion is, that such contests will be most apt to end to the disadvantage of the Union; and that there is greater probability of encroachments by the members upon the Fœderal Head, than by the Fœderal Head upon the members. But it is evident, that all conjectures of this kind, must be extremely vague and fallible, and that it is by far the safest course to lay them altogether aside; and to confine our attention wholly to the nature and extent of the powers as they are delineated in the constitution. Every thing beyond this, must be left to the prudence and firmness of the people; who, as they will hold the scales in their own hands, it is to be hoped, will always take care to preserve the constitutional equilibrium between the General and the State Governments. Upon this ground, which is evidently the true one, it will not be difficult to obviate the objections, which have been made to an indefinite power of taxation in the United States.

PUBLIUS.[8]

8. In the newspaper a postscript to this essay reads as follows: "We are obliged to omit the subsequent part of this No. until our next, for want of room." The note was in error, for the essay was completed in this issue of *The New-York Packet*, January 1, 1788.

## The Federalist No. 32 [1]

[New York, January 2, 1788]

*To the People of the State of New-York.*

ALTHOUGH I am of opinion that there would be no real danger of the consequences, which seem to be apprehended [2] to the State Governments, from a power in the Union to controul them in the levies of money; because I am persuaded that the sense of the people, the extreme hazard of provoking the resentments of the State Governments, and a conviction of the utility and necessity of local administrations, for local purposes, would be a complete barrier against the oppressive use of such a power: Yet I am willing here to allow in its full extent the justness of the reasoning, which requires that the individual States should possess an independent and uncontrolable authority to raise their own revenues for the supply of their own wants. And making this concession I affirm that (with the sole exception of duties on imports and exports) they would under the plan of the Convention retain that authority in the most absolute and unqualified sense; and that an attempt on the part of the national Government to abrige them in the exercise of it would be a violent assumption of power unwarranted by any article or clause of its Constitution.

An intire consolidation of the States into one complete national sovereignty would imply an intire subordination of the parts; and whatever powers might remain in them would be altogether dependent on the general will. But as the plan of the Convention aims only at a partial Union or consolidation, the State Governments would clearly retain all the rights of sovereignty which they before had and which were not by that act *exclusively* delegated to the United States. This exclusive delegation or rather this alienation of

The [New York] *Independent Journal: or the General Advertiser*, January 2, 1788. This essay appeared on January 3 in The [New York] *Daily Advertiser*, on January 4 in *The New-York Packet*, and on January 8 in *The New-York Journal, and Daily Patriotic Register*. It was printed in the newspapers as essay 31. In the McLean edition it was divided and the resulting two essays numbered 32 and 33.

1. For background to this document, see "The Federalist. Introductory Note," October 27, 1787–May 28, 1788.
2. "which seem to be apprehended" omitted in Hopkins.

State sovereignty would only exist in three cases; where the Constitution in express terms granted an exclusive authority to the Union; where it granted in one instance an authority to the Union; and in another prohibited the States from exercising the like authority; and where it granted an authority to the Union, to which a similar authority in the States would be absolutely and totally *contradictory* and *repugnant*. I use these terms to distinguish this last case from another which might appear to resemble it; but which would in fact be essentially different; I mean where the exercise of a concurrent jurisdiction might be productive of occasional interferences in the *policy* of any branch of administration, but would not imply any direct contradiction or repugnancy in point of constitutional authority. These three cases of exclusive jurisdiction in the Fœderal Government may be exemplified by the following instances: The last clause but one in the 8th section of the 1st. article provides expressly that Congress shall exercise "*exclusive legislation*" over the district to be appropriated as the seat of government. This answers to the first case. The first clause of the same section impowers Congress "*to lay and collect taxes, duties, imposts or excises*" and the 2d. clause of the 10th. section of the same article declares that "*no State shall* without the consent of Congress, *lay any imposts or duties on imports or exports* except for the purpose of executing its inspection laws." Hence would result an exclusive power in the Union to lay duties on imports and exports with the particular exception mentioned; but this power is abriged by another clause which declares that no tax or duty shall be laid on articles exported from any State; in consequence of which qualification it now only extends to the *duties on imports*, This answers to the second case. The third will be found in that clause, which declares that Congress shall have power "to establish an UNIFORM RULE of naturalization throughout the United States." This must necessarily be exclusive; because if each State had power to prescribe a DISTINCT RULE there could [3] be no UNIFORM RULE.

A case which may perhaps be thought to resemble the latter, but which is in fact widely different, affects the question immediately under consideration. I mean the power of imposing taxes on all

3. At this point "not" was inserted in the newspapers; "not" omitted in McLean and Hopkins.

articles other than exports and imports. This, I contend, is manifestly a concurrent and coequal authority in the United States and in the individual States. There is plainly no expression in the granting clause which makes that power *exclusive* in the Union. There is no independent clause or sentence which prohibits the States from exercising it. So far is this from being the case, that a plain and conclusive argument to the contrary is to be deduced [4] from the restraint laid upon the States in relation to duties on imports and exports. This restriction implies an admission, that if it were not inserted the States would possess the power it excludes, and it implies a further admission, that as to all other taxes the authority of the States remains undiminished. In any other view it would be both unnecessary and dangerous; it would be unnecessary because if the grant to the Union of the power of laying such duties implied the exclusion of the States, or even their subordination in this particular there could be no need of such a restriction; it would be dangerous because the introduction of it leads directly to the conclusion which has been mentioned and which if the reasoning of the objectors [5] be just, could not have been intended; I mean that the States in all cases to which the restriction did not apply would have a concurrent power of taxation with the Union. The restriction in question amounts to what lawyers call a NEGATIVE PREGNANT; that is a *negation* of one thing and an *affirmance* of another; a negation of the authority of the States to impose taxes on imports and exports, and an affirmance of their authority to impose them on all other articles. It would be mere sophistry to argue that it was meant to exclude them *absolutely* from the imposition of taxes of the former kind, and to leave them at liberty to lay others *subject to the controul* of the national Legislature. The restraining or prohibitory clause only says, that they shall not *without the consent of Congress* lay such duties; and if we are to understand this in the sense last mentioned, the Constitution would then be made to introduce a formal provision for the sake of a very absurd conclusion; which is that the States *with the consent* of the national Legislature might tax imports and exports; and that they might tax every other

4. "deducible" substituted for "to be deduced" in McLean and Hopkins.
5. In the newspapers, "objections"; "objectors" was substituted in McLean and Hopkins.

article *unless controuled* by the same body. If this was the intention why not leave [6] it in the first instance to what is alleged to be the natural operation of the original clause conferring a general power of taxation upon the Union? It is evident that this could not have been the intention and that it will not bear a construction of the kind.

As to a supposition of repugnancy between the power of taxation in the States and in the Union, it cannot be supported in that sense which would be requisite to work an exclusion of the States. It is indeed possible that a tax might be laid on a particular article by a State which might render it *inexpedient* and that thus [7] a further tax should be laid on the same article by the Union; but it would not imply a constitutional inability to impose a further tax. The quantity of the imposition, the expediency or inexpediency of an increase on either side, would be mutually questions of prudence; but there would be involved no direct contradiction of power. The particular policy of the national and the State systems of finance might now and then not exactly coincide, and might require reciprocal forbearances. It is not however a mere possibility of inconvenience in the exercise of powers, but an immediate constitutional repugnancy, that can by implication alienate and extinguish a pre-existing right of sovereignty.

The necessity of a concurrent jurisdiction in certain cases results from the division of the sovereign power; and the rule that all authorities of which the States are not explicitly divested in favour of the Union remain with them in full vigour, is not only a theoretical consequence of that division, but is clearly admitted by the whole tenor of the instrument which contains the articles of the proposed constitution. We there find that notwithstanding the affirmative grants of general authorities, there has been the most pointed care in those cases where it was deemed improper that the like authorities should reside in the States, to insert negative clauses prohibiting the exercise of them by the States. The tenth section of the first article consists altogether of such provisions. This circumstance is a clear indication of the sense of the Convention, and furnishes a rule of interpretation out of the body of the act which justifies the

6. "was it not left" substituted for "not leave it" in McLean and Hopkins.
7. "thus" omitted in McLean and Hopkins.

position I have advanced, and refutes every hypothesis to the contrary.

PUBLIUS

## The Federalist No. 33 [1]

[New York, January 2, 1788]

*To the People of the State of New-York.*

The residue of the argument against the provisions in [2] the constitution, in respect to taxation, is ingrafted upon the following clauses; [3] the last clause of the eighth section of the first article of the plan under consideration, [4] authorises the national legislature "to make all laws which shall be *necessary* and *proper,* for carrying into execution *the powers* by that Constitution vested in the government of the United States, or any department or officer thereof;" and the second clause of the sixth article declares, that "the Constitution and the Laws of the United States made *in pursuance thereof,* and the treaties made by their authority shall be the *supreme law* of the land; any thing in the constitution or laws of any State to the contrary notwithstanding."

These two clauses have been the sources of much virulent invective and petulant declamation against the proposed constitution, they have been held up to the people, in all the exaggerated colours of misrepresentation, as the pernicious engines by which their local governments were to be destroyed and their liberties exterminated —as the hideous monster whose devouring jaws would spare neither sex nor age, nor high nor low, nor sacred nor profane; and yet strange as it may appear, after all this clamour, to those who may

The [New York] *Independent Journal: or, the General Advertiser,* January 2, 1788. This essay appeared on January 3 in The [New York] *Daily Advertiser,* on January 4 in *The New-York Packet,* and on January 8 in *The New-York Journal, and Daily Patriotic Register.* In the newspapers this essay is published as the concluding part of essay 31. See "The Federalist No. 32," note 1. In the McLean edition it was numbered 33.

1. For background to this document, see "The Federalist. Introductory Note," October 27, 1787–May 28, 1788.
2. "of" substituted for "in" in Hopkins.
3. This sentence appeared in McLean and Hopkins but not in the newspapers.
4. "of the plan under consideration" omitted in Hopkins.

not have [5] happened to contemplate them in the same light, it may be affirmed with perfect confidence, that the constitutional operation of the intended government would be precisely the same, if these clauses were entirely obliterated, as if they were repeated in every article. They are only declaratory of a truth, which would have resulted by necessary and unavoidable implication from the very act of constituting a Fœderal Government, and vesting it with certain specified powers. This is so clear a proposition, that moderation itself can scarcely listen to the railings which have been so copiously vented against this part of the plan, without emotions that disturb its equanimity.

What is a power, but the ability or faculty of doing a thing? What is the ability to do a thing but the power of employing the *means* necessary to its execution? What is a LEGISLATIVE power but a power of making LAWS? What are the *means* to execute a LEGISLATIVE power but LAWS? What is the power of laying and collecting taxes but a *legislative power*, or a power of *making laws*, to lay and collect taxes? What are the proper means of executing such a power but *necessary* and *proper* laws?

This simple train of enquiry furnishes us at once with a test by which to judge [6] of the true nature of the clause complained of. It conducts us to this palpable truth, that a power to lay and collect taxes must be a power to pass all laws *necessary* and *proper* for the execution of that power; and what does the unfortunate and calumniated provision in question do more than declare the same truth; to wit, that the national legislature to whom the power of laying and collecting taxes had been previously given, might in the execution of that power pass all laws *necessary* and *proper* to carry it into effect? I have applied these observations thus particularly to the power of taxation, because it is the immediate subject under consideration, and because it is the most important of the authorities proposed to be conferred upon the Union. But the same process will lead to the same result in relation to all other powers declared in the constitution. And it is *expressly* to execute these powers, that the sweeping clause, as it has been affectedly called, authorises the

5. "have" was omitted in the newspapers; "have" inserted at this point in McLean and Hopkins.
6. "by which to judge" omitted in McLean and Hopkins.

national legislature to pass all *necessary* and *proper* laws. If there is [7] any thing exceptionable, it must be sought for in the specific powers, upon which this general declaration is predicated. The declaration itself, though it may be chargeable with tautology or redundancy, is at least perfectly harmless.

But SUSPICION may ask why then was it [8] introduced? The answer is, that it could only have been done for greater caution, and to guard against all cavilling refinements in those who might hereafter feel a disposition to curtail and evade the legitimate authorities of the Union. The Convention probably foresaw what [9] it has been a principal aim of these papers to inculcate that the danger which most threatens our political welfare, is, that the State Governments will finally sap the foundations of the Union; and might therefore think it necessary, in so cardinal a point, to leave nothing to construction. Whatever may have been the inducement to it, the wisdom of the precaution is evident from the cry which has been raised against it; as that very cry betrays a disposition to question the great and essential truth which it is manifestly the object of that provision to declare.

But it may be again asked, who is to judge of the *necessity* and *propriety* of the laws to be passed for executing the powers of the Union? I answer first that this question arises as well and as fully upon the simple grant of those powers, as upon the declaratory clause: And I answer in the second place, that the national government, like every other, must judge in the first instance of the proper exercise of its powers; and its constituents in the last. If the Fœderal Government should overpass the just bounds of its authority, and make a tyrannical use of its powers; the people whose creature it is must appeal to the standard they have formed, and take such measures to redress the injury done to the constitution, as the exigency may suggest and prudence justify. The propriety of a law in a constitutional light, must always be determined by the nature of the powers upon which it is founded. Suppose by some forced constructions of its authority (which indeed cannot easily be imagined) the Fœderal Legislature should attempt to vary the law

7. "be" substituted for "is" in McLean and Hopkins.
8. "it" omitted in the newspapers; "it" inserted at this point in McLean and Hopkins.
9. In the newspapers "that"; "what" was substituted in McLean and Hopkins.

of descent in any State; would it not be evident that in making such an attempt it had exceeded its jurisdiction and infringed upon that of the State? Suppose again that upon the pretence of an inter-ference with its revenues, it should undertake to abrogate a land tax imposed by the authority of a State, would it not be equally evident that this was an invasion of that concurrent jurisdiction in respect to this species of tax which its [10] constitution plainly sup-poses to exist in the State governments? If there ever should be a doubt on this head the credit of it will be intirely due to those reasoners, who, in the imprudent zeal of their animosity to the plan of the Convention, have laboured to invelope it in a cloud calculated to obscure the plainest and simplest truths.

But it is said, that the laws of the Union are to be the *supreme law* of the land. But [11] what inference can be drawn from this or what would they amount to, if they were not to be supreme? It is evident they would amount to nothing. A LAW by the very meaning of the term includes supremacy. It is a rule which those to whom it is prescribed are bound to observe. This results from every political association. If individuals enter into a state of society the laws of that society must be the supreme regulator of their conduct. If a number of political societies enter into a larger politi-cal society, the laws which the latter may enact, pursuant to the powers entrusted to it by its constitution, must necessarily be su-preme over those societies, and the individuals of whom they are composed. It would otherwise be a mere treaty, dependent on the good faith of the parties, and not a government; which is only another word for POLITICAL POWER AND SUPREMACY. But it will not follow from this doctrine that acts of the larger society which are *not pursuant* to its constitutional powers but which are invasions of the residuary authorities of the smaller so-cieties will become the supreme law of the land. These will be merely acts of usurpation and will deserve to be treated as such. Hence we perceive that the clause which declares the supremacy of the laws of the Union, like the one we have just before con-sidered, only declares a truth, which flows immediately and neces-sarily from the institution of a Fœderal Government. It will not,

10. "the" substituted for "its" in Hopkins.
11. "But" omitted in McLean and Hopkins.

I presume, have escaped observation that it *expressly* confines this supremacy to laws made *pursuant to the Constitution;* which I mention merely as an instance of caution in the Convention; since that limitation would have been to be understood though it had not been expressed.

Though a law therefore for [12] laying a tax for the use of the United States would be supreme in its nature, and could not legally be opposed or controuled; yet a law for [13] abrogating or preventing the collection of a tax laid by the authority of a State (unless upon imports and exports) would not be the supreme law of the land, but an usurpation of [14] power not granted by the constitution. As far as an improper accumulation of taxes on the same object might tend to render the collection difficult or precarious, this would be a mutual inconvenience not arising from a superiority or defect of power on either side, but from an injudicious exercise of power by one or the other, in a manner equally disadvantageous to both. It is to be hoped and presumed however that mutual interest would dictate a concert in this respect which would avoid any material inconvenience. The inference from the whole is—that the individual States would, under the proposed constitution, retain an independent and uncontroulable authority to raise revenue to any extent of which they may stand in need by every kind of taxation except duties on imports and exports. It will be shewn in the next paper that this CONCURRENT JURISDICTION in the article of taxation was the only admissible substitute for an intire subordination, in respect to this branch of power, of the [15] State authority to that of the Union.

PUBLIUS.

12. "for" omitted in Hopkins.
13. "for" omitted in Hopkins.
14. "a" inserted at this point in Hopkins.
15. "the" omitted in McLean and Hopkins.

# *The Federalist No. 34* [1]

[New York, January 5, 1788]

*To the People of the State of New-York.*

I FLATTER myself it has been clearly shewn in my last number, that the particular States, under the proposed Constitution, would have CO-EQUAL authority with the Union in the article of revenue, except as to duties on imports. As this leaves open to the States far the greatest part of the resources of the community, there can be no color for the assertion, that they would not possess means, as abundant as could be desired, for the supply of their own wants, independent of all external control. That the field is sufficiently wide, will more fully appear, when we come to advert to [2] the inconsiderable share of the public expences, for which, it will fall to the lot of the State Governments to provide.

To argue upon abstract principles, that this co-ordinate authority cannot exist, is to [3] set up supposition and theory,[4] against fact and reality. However proper such reasonings might be, to show that a thing *ought not to exist,* they are wholly to be rejected, when they are made use of to prove that it does not exist, contrary to the evidence of the fact itself. It is well known, that in the Roman Republic, the Legislative authority in the last resort, resided for ages in two different political bodies; not as branches of the same Legislature, but as distinct and independent Legislatures, in each of which an opposite interest prevailed; in one, the Patrician—in the other, the Plebeian. Many arguments might have been adduced to prove the unfitness of two such seemingly contradictory authorities, each having power to *annul* or *repeal* the acts of the other. But a man

*The* [New York] *Daily Advertiser,* January 5, 1788. On the same day this essay also appeared in *The New-York Packet* and *The* [New York] *Independent Journal: or, the General Advertiser,* and on January 8 was printed in *The New-York Journal, and Daily Patriotic Register.* In the McLean edition this essay is numbered 34, and in the newspapers it is numbered 32.

1. For background to this document, see "The Federalist. Introductory Note," October 27, 1787–May 28, 1788.

2. "develope" substituted for "advert to" in McLean and Hopkins.

3. "would be to" substituted for "is to" in McLean and Hopkins.

4. "theory and supposition" substituted for "supposition and theory" in McLean and Hopkins.

would have been regarded as frantic, who should have attempted at Rome, to disprove their existence. It will readily be understood, that I allude to the COMITIA CENTURIATA, and COMITIA TRIBUTA.[5] The former, in which the people voted by Centuries, was so arranged as to give a superiority to the Patrician interest: in the latter, in which numbers prevailed, the Plebeian interest had an entire predominancy. And yet these two Legislatures co-existed for ages, and the Roman Republic attained to the utmost height[6] of human greatness.

In the case particularly under consideration, there is no such contradiction as appears in the example cited, there is no power on either side to annul the acts of the other. And in practice, there is little reason to apprehend any inconvenience; because, in a short course of time, the wants of the States will naturally reduce themselves within *a very narrow compass;* and in the interim, the United States will, in all probability, find it convenient to abstain wholly from those objects, to which the particular States would be inclined to resort.

To form a more precise judgment of the true merits of this question, it will be well to advert to the proportion between the objects that will require a Federal provision in respect to revenue; and those which will require a State provision. We shall discover that the former are altogether unlimited; and, that the latter are circumscribed within very moderate bounds. In pursuing this enquiry, we must bear in mind, that we are not to confine our view to the present period, but to look forward to remote futurity. Constitutions of civil Government are not to be framed upon a calculation of existing exigencies; but upon a combination of these, with the probable exigencies of ages, according to the natural and tried

5. In *The New-York Packet* on January 8, 1788, a list of *"ERRATA in the FEDERALIST,* No. 32" was printed. It was stated that *"These errors happened partly by the hurry of the Writer, and partly by that of the Printer."* The corrections read:

*"IN the second paragraph for* COMITIA TRIBUTA *and* COMITIA CENTURIATA *read* COMITIA CENTURIATA *and* COMITIA TRIBUTA.

*"For* tribes *in the same paragraph read* Centuries.

*"For* 100,000 *wherever it occurs read* 200,000.

*"At the end of these words in the fourth paragraph 'The support of a navy' add 'and of naval wars must baffle all the efforts of political arithmetic.' "*

These changes have been incorporated in the text without notes.

6. "pinacle" substituted for "utmost height" in McLean and Hopkins.

course of human affairs. Nothing therefore can be more fallacious, than to infer the extent of any power, proper to be lodged in the National Government, from an estimate of its immediate necessities. There ought to be a CAPACITY to provide for future contingencies, as they may happen; and, as these are illimitable in their nature,[7] it is impossible safely to limit that capacity. It is true, perhaps, that a computation might be made, with sufficient accuracy to answer the purpose [8] of the quantity of revenue, requisite to discharge the subsisting engagements of the Union, and to maintain those establishments, which for some time to come, would suffice in time of peace. But would it be wise, or would it not rather be the extreme of folly, to stop at this point, and to leave the Government entrusted with the care of the National defence, in a state of absolute incapacity to provide for the protection of the community, against future invasions of the public peace, by foreign war, or domestic convulsions? If, on the contrary, we ought [9] to exceed this point, where can we stop, short of an indefinite power of providing for emergencies as they might [10] arise? Though it is [11] easy to assert, in general terms, the possibility of forming a rational judgment of a due provision against probable dangers; yet we may safely challenge those who make the assertion, to bring forward their data, and may affirm, that they would be found as vague and uncertain, as any that could be produced to establish the probable duration of the world. Observations, confined to the mere prospects of internal attacks, can deserve no weight, though even these will admit of no satisfactory calculation: But if we mean to be a commercial people, it must form a part of our policy, to be able one day to defend that commerce. The support of a navy, and of naval wars [12] must baffle all the efforts of political arithmetic admitting that we ought to try the novel and absurd experiment in politics, of tying up the hands of Government from offensive war,

7. "so" inserted here in McLean and Hopkins.
8. In the newspaper, "purposes"; "purpose" substituted in McLean and Hopkins.
9. "we must be obliged" substituted for "on the contrary, we ought" in McLean and Hopkins.
10. "may" substituted for "might" in McLean and Hopkins.
11. "be" substituted for "is" in McLean and Hopkins.
12. "would involve contingencies that" inserted at this point in McLean and Hopkins.

founded upon reasons of state: Yet, certainly we ought not to disable it from guarding the community against the ambition or enmity of other Nations. A cloud has been for some time hanging over the European world. If it should break forth into a storm, who can insure us, that in its progress, a part of its fury would not be spent upon us? No reasonable man would hastily pronounce that we are entirely out of its reach. Or if the combustible materials that now seem to be collecting, should be dissipated without coming to maturity; or, if a flame should be kindled, without extending to us, what security can we have, that our tranquility will long remain undisturbed from some other cause, or from some other quarter? Let us recollect, that peace or war, will not always be left to our option; that however moderate or unambitious we may be, we cannot count upon the moderation, or hope to extinguish the ambition of others. Who could have imagined, at the conclusion of the last war, that France and Britain, wearied and exhausted as they both were, would so soon [13] have looked with so hostile an aspect upon each other? To judge from the history of mankind, we shall be compelled to conclude, that the fiery and destructive passions of war, reign in the human breast, with much more powerful sway, than the mild and beneficent sentiments of peace; and, that to model our political systems upon speculations of lasting tranquility, is [14] to calculate on the weaker springs of the human character.

What are the chief sources of expence in every Government? What has occasioned that enormous accumulation of debts with which several of the European Nations are oppressed? The answer, plainly is, wars and rebellions—the support of those institutions which are necessary to guard the body politic, against these two most mortal diseases of society. The expences arising from those institutions, which are relative [15] to the mere domestic police of a State—to the support of its Legislative, Executive and Judicial [16] departments, with their different appendages, and to the internal [17] encouragement of agriculture and manufactures, (which will com-

13. "already" substituted for "so soon" in Hopkins.
14. "would be" substituted for "is" in McLean and Hopkins.
15. "relate" substituted for "are relative" in Hopkins.
16. "judiciary" substituted for "Judicial" in McLean and Hopkins.
17. "internal" omitted in McLean and Hopkins.

prehend almost all the objects of State expenditure) are insignificant, in comparison with those which relate to the National defence.

In the kingdom of Great-Britain, where all the ostentatious apparatus of Monarchy is to be provided for, not above a fifteenth part of the annual income of the nation is appropriated to the class of expences last mentioned; the other fourteen fifteenths are absorbed in the payment of the interest of debts, contracted for carrying on the wars in which that country has been engaged, and in the maintenance of fleets and armies. If on the one hand it should be observed, that the expences incurred in the prosecution of the ambitious enterprizes and vain-glorious pursuits of a Monarchy, are not a proper standard by which to judge of those which might be necessary in a republic; it ought on the other hand to be remarked, that there should be as great a disproportion, between the profusion and extravagance of a wealthy kingdom in its domestic administration, and the frugality and œconomy, which, in that particular, become the modest simplicity of republican Government. If we balance a proper deduction from one side against that which it is supposed ought to be made from the other, the proportion may still be considered as holding good.

But let us advert to [18] the large debt which we have ourselves contracted in a single war, and let us only calculate on a common share of the events which disturb the peace of nations, and we shall instantly perceive without the aid of any elaborate illustration, that there must always be an immense disproportion between the objects of Federal and State expenditures.[19] It is true that several of the States separately are incumbered with considerable debts, which are an excrescence of the late war.[20] But [21] when these [22] are discharged, the only call for revenue of any consequence, which the State Governments will continue to experience, will be for the mere support of their respective civil lists; to which, if we add all contingencies, the total amount in every State, ought not to exceed two hundred thousand pounds.[23]

18. "take a view of" substituted for "advert to" in McLean and Hopkins.
19. "expenditure" substituted for "expenditures" in McLean and Hopkins.
20. "But this cannot happen again if the proposed system be adopted" inserted at this point in McLean and Hopkins.
21. "and" substituted for "but" in McLean and Hopkins.
22. "debts" inserted at this point in McLean and Hopkins.
23. "to fall considerably short of a million of dollars" substituted for "not to exceed" through "pounds" in Hopkins.

In framing a Government for posterity as well as ourselves,[24] we ought in those provisions which are designed to be permanent, to calculate not on temporary, but on permanent causes of expence. If this principle be a just one,[25] our attention would be directed to a provision in favor of the State Governments for an annual sum of about 200,000 pounds;[26] while the exigencies of the Union could be susceptible of no limits, even in imagination. In this view of the subject by what logic can it be maintained, that the local Governments ought to command in perpetuity, an EXCLUSIVE source of revenue for any sum beyond the extent of 200,000 pounds?[27] To extend its power further, in *exclusion* of the authority of the Union, would be to take the resources of the community out of those hands which stood in need of them for the public welfare, in order to put them in[28] other hands, which could have no just or proper occasion for them.

Suppose then the Convention had been inclined to proceed upon the principle of a repartition of the objects of revenue between the Union and its members, in *proportion* to their comparative necessities; what particular fund could have been selected for the use of the States, that would not either have been too much or too little; too little for their present, and[29] too much for their[30] future wants. As to the line of separation between external and internal taxes, this would leave to the States at a rough computation, the command of two thirds of the resources of the community, to defray from a tenth to a twentieth part[31] of its expences, and to the Union, one third of the resources of the community, to defray from nine tenths to nineteen twentieths of its expences. If we desert this boundary, and content ourselves with leaving to the States an exclusive power of taxing houses and lands, there would still be a great disproportion between the *means* and the *end;* the possession of one third of the resources of the community, to supply at most one tenth of its wants.

24. "If it cannot be denied to be a just principle, that in framing a constitution of government for a nation" substituted for "In framing" through "ourselves" in McLean and Hopkins.
25. "If this principle be a just one" omitted in McLean and Hopkins.
26. "1,000,000 of dollars" substituted in Hopkins.
27. Hopkins substituted "that which has been stated" for "the extent of 200,000 pounds."
28. "into" substituted for "in" in McLean and Hopkins.
29. "and" omitted in McLean and Hopkins.
30. In the newspaper, "the"; "their" substituted in McLean and Hopkins.
31. "part" omitted in McLean and Hopkins.

If any fund could have been selected and appropriated equal to and not greater than the object, it would have been inadequate to the discharge of the existing debts of the particular States, and would have left them dependent on the Union for a provision for this purpose.

The preceeding train of observations will justify the position which has been elsewhere laid down,[32] that, "A CONCURRENT JURISDICTION in the article of taxation, was the only admissible substitute for an entire subordination, in respect to this branch of power, of the [33] State authority to that of the Union." Any separation of the objects of revenue, that could have been fallen upon, would have amounted to a sacrifice of the great INTERESTS of the Union to the POWER of the individual States. The Convention thought the concurrent jurisdiction preferable to that subordination; and it is evident that it has at least the merit of reconciling an indefinite constitutional power of taxation in the Federal Government, with an adequate and independent power in the States to provide for their own necessities. There remain a few other lights, in which this important subject of taxation will claim a further consideration.

PUBLIUS.

32. See essay 33.
33. "the" omitted in McLean and Hopkins.

## The Federalist No. 35 [1]

[New York, January 5, 1788]

*To the People of the State of New-York.*

BEFORE we proceed to examine any other objections to an indefinite power of taxation in the Union, I shall make one general remark; which is, that if the jurisdiction of the national government in the article of revenue should be restricted to particular objects,

*The* [New York] *Independent Journal: or, the General Advertiser,* January 5, 1788. This essay appeared on January 7 in *The* [New York] *Daily Advertiser,* on January 8 in *The New-York Packet,* and on January 9 in *The New-York Journal, and Daily Patriotic Register.* In the McLean edition this essay is numbered 35, and in the newspapers it is numbered 33.
    1. For background to this document, see "The Federalist. Introductory Note," October 27, 1787–May 28, 1788.

it would [2] naturally occasion an undue proportion of the public burthens to fall upon those objects. Two evils would spring from this source, the oppression of particular branches of industry, and an unequal distribution of the taxes, as well among the several States as among the citizens of the same State.

Suppose, as has been contended for, the fœderal power of taxation were to be confined to duties on imports, it is evident that the government, for want of being able to command other resources, would frequently be tempted to extend these duties to an injurious excess. There are persons who imagine that this [3] can never be carried to too great a length; [4] since the higher they are, the more it is alleged they will tend to discourage an extravagant consumption, to produce a favourable balance of trade, and to promote domestic manufactures. But all extremes are pernicious in various ways. Exorbitant duties on imported articles would [5] beget a general spirit of smuggling; which is always prejudicial to the fair trader, and eventually to the revenue itself: They tend to render other classes of the community tributary in an improper degree to the manufacturing classes to whom they give a premature monopoly of the markets: They sometimes force industry out of its more natural channels into others in which it flows with less advantage. And in the last place they oppress the merchant, who is often obliged to pay them himself without any retribution from the consumer. When the demand is equal to the quantity of goods at market, the consumer generally pays the duty; but when the markets happen to be overstocked, a great proportion falls upon the merchant, and sometimes not only exhausts his profits, but breaks in upon his capital. I am apt to think that a division of the duty between the seller and the buyer more often happens than is commonly imagined. It is not always possible to raise the price of a commodity, in exact proportion to every additional imposition laid upon it. The merchant especially, in a country of small commercial capital, is often under a necessity of keeping prices down, in order to a more expeditious sale.

2. In the newspaper "will"; "would" was substituted in McLean and Hopkins.
3. In the newspaper, "they"; "this" was substituted in McLean and Hopkins.
4. "the case" substituted for "carried to too great a length" in McLean and Hopkins.
5. "serve to" inserted at this point in McLean and Hopkins.

The maxim that the consumer is the payer, is so much oftener true than the reverse of the proposition, that it is far more equitable [6] the duties on imports should go into a common stock, than that they should redound to the exclusive benefit of the importing States. But it is not so generally true as to render it equitable that those duties should form the only national fund. When they are paid by the merchant, they operate as an additional tax upon the importing State; whose citizens pay their proportion of them in the character of consumers. In this view they are productive of inequality among the States; which inequality would be encreased with the encreased extent of the duties. The confinement of the national revenues to this species of imposts, would be attended with inequality, from a different cause between the manufacturing and the non-manufacturing States. The States which can go furthest towards the supply of their own wants, by their own manufactures, will not, according to their numbers of wealth, consume so great a proportion of imported articles, as those States which are not in the same favourable situation; they would not therefore in this mode alone contribute to the public treasury in a ratio to their abilities. To make them do this, it is necessary that recourse be had to excises; the proper objects of which are particular kinds of manufactures. New-York is more deeply interested in these considerations than such of her citizens as contend for limiting the power of the Union to external taxation can be aware of—New-York is an importing State, and is not likely speedily to be to any great extent a manufacturing State.[7] She would of course suffer in a double light from restraining the jurisdiction of the Union to commercial imposts.

So far as these observations tend to inculcate a danger of the import duties being extended to an injurious extreme it may be observed, conformably to a remark made in another part of these papers,[8] that the interest of the revenue itself would be a sufficient guard against such an extreme. I readily admit that this would be the case as long as other resources were open; but if the avenues to

6. "that" inserted at this point in Hopkins.
7. "and from a greater disproportion between her population and territory, is less likely, than some other states, speedily to become in any considerable degree a manufacturing state" substituted for "and is not" through "State" in McLean and Hopkins.
8. See essay 21.

them were closed HOPE stimulated by necessity would [9] beget experiments fortified by rigorous precautions and additional penalties; which for a time would [10] have the intended effect, till there had been leisure to contrive expedients to elude these new precautions. The first success would be apt to inspire false opinions; which it might require a long course of subsequent experience to correct. Necessity, especially in politics, often occasions false hopes, false reasonings and a system of measures, correspondently erroneous. But even if this supposed excess should not be a consequence of the limitation of the fœderal power of taxation the inequalities spoken of would still ensue, though not in the same degree, from the other causes that have been noticed. Let us now return to the examination of objections—

One, which if we may judge from the frequency of its repetition seems most to be relied on, is that the house of representatives is not sufficiently numerous for the reception of all the different classes of citizens; in order to combine the interests and feelings of every part of the community, and to produce a due [11] sympathy between the representative body and its constituents. This argument presents itself under a very specious and seducing form; and is well calculated to lay hold of the prejudices to those to whom it is addressed. But when we come to dissect it with attention it will appear to be made up of nothing but fair sounding words. The object it seems to aim at is in the first place impracticable, and in the sense in which it is contended for is unnecessary. I reserve for another place the discussion of the question which relates to the sufficiency of the representative body in respect to numbers; [12] and shall content myself with examining here the particular use which has been made of a contrary supposition in reference to the immediate subject of our inquiries.

The idea of an actual representation of all classes of the people by persons of each class is altogether visionary. Unless it were expressly provided in the Constitution that each different occupation should send one or more members the thing would never take place in

9. "might" substituted for "would" in McLean and Hopkins.
10. "might" substituted for "would" in McLean and Hopkins.
11. "true" substituted for "due" in McLean.
12. See essay 54.

practice. Mechanics and manufacturers will always be inclined with few exceptions to give their votes to merchants in preference to persons of their own professions or trades. Those discerning citizens are well aware that the mechanic and manufacturing arts furnish the materials of mercantile enterprise and industry. Many of them indeed are immediately connected with the operations of commerce. They know that the merchant is their natural patron and friend; and they are aware that however great the confidence they may justly feel in their own good sense, their interests can be more effectually promoted by the merchant than by themselves. They are sensible that their habits in life have not been such as to give them those acquired endowments, without which in a deliberative assembly the greatest natural abilities are for the most part useless; and that the influence and weight and superior acquirements of the merchants render them more equal to a contest with any spirit which might happen to infuse itself into the public councils unfriendly to the manufacturing and trading interests. These considerations and many others that might be mentioned prove, and experience confirms it, that artisans and manufacturers will commonly be disposed to bestow their votes upon merchants and those whom they recommend. We must therefore consider merchants as the natural representatives of all these classes of the community.

With regard to the learned professions, little need be observed; they truly form no distinct interest in society; and according to their situation and talents will be indiscriminately the objects of the confidence and choice of each other and of other parts of the community.

Nothing remains but the landed interest; and this in a political view and particularly in relation to taxes I take to be perfectly united from the wealthiest landlord to the poorest tenant. No tax can be laid on land which will not affect the proprietor of millions [13] of acres as well as the proprietor of a single acre. Every land-holder will therefore have a common interest to keep the taxes on land as low as possible; and common interest may always be reckoned upon as the surest bond of sympathy. But if we even could suppose a distinction of interest between the opulent land-holder and the middling farmer, what reason is there to conclude that the first would

13. "thousands" substituted for "millions" in Hopkins.

stand a better chance of being deputed to the national legislature than the last? If we take fact as our guide and look into our own senate and assembly we shall find that moderate proprietors of land prevail in both; nor is this less the case in the senate which consists of a smaller number than in the Assembly, which is composed of a greater number. Where the qualifications of the electors are the same, whether they have to choose a small or a large number their votes will fall upon those in whom they have most confidence; whether these happen to be men of large fortunes or of moderate property or of no property at all.

It is said to be necessary that all classes of citizens should have some of their own number in the representative body, in order that their feelings and interests may be the better understood and attended to. But we have seen that this will never happen under any arrangement that leaves the votes of the people free. Where this is the case, the representative body, with too few exceptions to have any influence on the spirit of the government, will be composed of land-holders, merchants, and men of the learned professions. But where is the danger that the interests and feelings of the different classes of citizens will not be understood or attended to by these three descriptions of men? Will not the land-holder know and feel whatever will promote or injure the interests of landed property? and will he not from his own interest in that species of property be sufficiently prone to resist every attempt to prejudice or incumber it? Will not the merchant understand and be disposed to cultivate as far as may be proper the interests of the mechanic and manufacturing arts to which his commerce is so nearly allied? Will not the man of the learned profession, who will feel a neutrality to the rivalships between [14] the different branches of industry, be likely to prove an impartial arbiter between them, ready to promote either, so far as it shall appear to him conducive to the general interests of the society? [15]

If we take into the account the momentary humors or dispositions which may happen to prevail in particular parts of the society, and to which a wise administration will never be inattentive, is the man whose situation leads to extensive inquiry and information less likely

14. "among" substituted for "between" in Hopkins.
15. "community" substituted for "society" in Hopkins.

to be a competent judge of their nature, extent and foundation than one whose observation does not travel beyond the circle of his neighbours and acquaintances? Is it not natural that a man who is a candidate for the favour of the people and who is dependent on the suffrages of his fellow-citizens for the continuance of his public honors should take care to inform himself of their dispositions and inclinations and should be willing to allow them their proper degree of influence upon his conduct. This dependence, and the necessity of being bound himself and his posterity by the laws to which he gives his assent are the true, and they are the [16] strong chords of sympathy between the representatives and the constituent.

There is no part of the administration of government that requires extensive information and a thorough knowledge of the principles of political economy so much as the business of taxation. The man who understands those principles best will be least likely to resort to oppressive expedients, or to sacrifice any particular class of citizens to the procurement of revenue. It might be demonstrated that the most productive system of finance will always be the least burthensome. There can be no doubt that in order to a judicious exercise of the power of taxation it is necessary that the person in whose hands it is should be acquainted with the general genius, habits and modes of thinking of the people at large and with the resources of the country. And this is all that can be reasonably meant by a knowledge of the interests and feelings of the people. In any other sense the proposition has either no meaning, or an absurd one. And in that sense let every considerate citizen judge for himself where the requisite qualification is most likely to be found.

PUBLIUS.

16. "the" omitted in the newspaper; it was inserted in McLean and Hopkins.

## *The Federalist No. 36* [1]

[New York, January 8, 1788]

*To the People of the State of New-York.*

WE have seen that the result of the observations, to which the foregoing number has been principally devoted, is that from the natural operation of the different interests and views of the various classes of the community, whether the representation of the people be more or less numerous, it will consist almost entirely of proprietors of land, of merchants and [2] members of the learned professions, who will truly represent all those different interests and views. If it should be objected that we have seen other descriptions of men in the local Legislatures; I answer, that it is admitted there are exceptions to the rule, but not in sufficient number to influence the general complexion or character of the government. There are strong minds in every walk of life that will rise superior to the disadvantages of situation, and will command the tribute due to their merit, not only from the classes to which they particularly belong, but from the society in general. The door ought to be equally open to all; and I trust, for the credit of human nature, that we shall see examples of such vigorous plants flourishing in the soil of Fœderal, as well as of State Legislation; but occasional instances of this sort, will not render the reasoning founded upon the general course of things less conclusive.

The subject might be placed in several other lights that would lead all to the same result; and in particular it might be asked, what greater affinity or relation of interest can be conceived between the carpenter and [3] blacksmith, and the linen manufacturer or stocking weaver, than between the merchant and either of them? It is notori-

*The New-York Packet*, January 8, 1788. This essay appeared on January 9 in *The* [New York] *Independent Journal: or, the General Advertiser*, and on January 10 in *The* [New York] *Daily Advertiser*. It was begun on January 11 in *The New-York Journal, and Daily Patriotic Register* and concluded on January 12. In the McLean edition this essay is numbered 36, and in the newspapers it is numbered 34.

1. For background to this document, see "The Federalist. Introductory Note," October 27, 1787–May 28, 1788.
2. "of" inserted at this point in McLean and Hopkins.
3. In the newspaper "or"; "and" substituted in McLean and Hopkins.

ous, that there are often as great rivalships between different branches of the mechanic or manufacturing arts, as there are between any of the departments of labor and industry; so that unless the representative body were to be far more numerous than would be consistent with any idea of regularity or wisdom in its deliberations,[4] it is impossible that what seems to be the spirit of the objection we have been considering, should ever be realised in practice. But I forbear to dwell any [5] longer on a matter, which has hitherto worn too loose a garb to admit even of an accurate inspection of its real shape or tendency.

There is another objection of a somewhat more precise nature that [6] claims our attention. It has been asserted that a power of internal taxation in the national Legislature could never be exercised with advantage, as well from the want of a sufficient knowledge of local circumstances as from an interference between the revenue laws of the Union and of the particular States. The supposition of a want of proper knowledge, seems to be entirely destitute of foundation. If any question is depending in a State Legislature respecting one of the counties which demands a knowledge of local details, how is it acquired? No doubt from the information of the members of the county. Cannot the like knowledge be obtained in the national Legislature from the representatives of each State? And is it not to be presumed that the men who will generally be sent there, will be possessed of the necessary degree of intelligence, to be able to communicate that information? Is the knowledge of local circumstances, as applied to taxation, a minute topographical acquaintance with all the mountains, rivers, streams, high-ways and bye-paths in each State, or is it a general acquaintance with its situation and resources—with the state of its agriculture, commerce, manufactures—with the nature of its products and consumptions— with the different degrees and kinds of its wealth, property and industry?

Nations in general, even under governments of the more popular kind, usually commit the administration of their finances to single men or to boards composed of a few individuals, who digest and

4. "deliberation" substituted for "deliberations" in Hopkins.
5. "any" omitted in McLean and Hopkins.
6. "which" substituted for "that" in McLean and Hopkins.

prepare, in the first instance, the plans of taxation, which are afterwards passed into laws [7] by the authority of the sovereign or Legislature.

Inquisitive and enlightened Statesmen are deemed every where [8] best qualified to make a judicious selection of the objects proper for revenue; which is a clear indication, as far as the sense of mankind can have weight in the question, of the species of knowledge of local circumstances requisite to the purposes of taxation.

The taxes intended to be comprised under the general denomination of internal taxes, may be subdivided into those of the *direct* and those of the *indirect* kind. Though the objection be made to both, yet the reasoning upon it seems to be confined to the former branch. And indeed, as to the latter, by which must be understood duties and excises on articles of consumption, one is at a loss to conceive what can be the nature of the difficulties apprehended. The knowledge relating to them, must evidently be of a kind that will either be suggested by the nature of the article itself, or can easily be procured from any well informed man, especially of the mercantile class. The circumstances that may distinguish its situation in one State from its situation in another must be few, simple, and easy to be comprehended. The principal thing to be attended to would be to avoid those articles which had been previously appropriated to the use of a particular State; and there could be no difficulty in ascertaining the revenue system of each. This could always be known from the respective codes of laws, as well as from the information of the members of the several States.

The objection when applied to real property, or to houses and lands, appears to have, at first sight, more foundation; but even in this view, it will not bear a close examination. Land taxes are commonly laid in one or two modes, either by *actual* valuations permanent or periodical, or by occasional assessments, at the discretion or according to the best judgment of certain officers, whose duty it is to make them. In either case the EXECUTION of the business, which alone requires the knowledge of local details, must be devolved upon [9] discreet persons in the character of commissioners

7. "law" substituted for "laws" in McLean and Hopkins.
8. "every where deemed" substituted for "deemed every where" in McLean and Hopkins.
9. "confided to" substituted for "devolved upon" in Hopkins.

or assessors, elected by the people or appointed by the government for the purpose. All that the law can do must be to name the persons or to prescribe the manner of their election or appointment, to fix their numbers and qualifications; and to draw the general outlines of their powers and duties. And what is there in all this, that cannot as well be performed by the national Legislature as by a State Legislature? The attention of either can only reach to general principles; local details, as already observed, must be referred to those who are to execute the plan.

But there is a simple point of view in which this matter may be placed, that must be altogether satisfactory. The national Legislature can make use of the *system of each State within that State*. The method of laying and collecting this species of taxes in each State, can, in all its parts, be adopted and employed by the Fœderal Government.

Let it be recollected, that the proportion of these taxes is not to be left to the discretion of the national Legislature: but is to be determined by the numbers of each State as described in the second section of the first article. An actual census or enumeration of the people must furnish the rule; a circumstance which effectually shuts the door to partiality or oppression. The abuse of this power of taxation seems to have been provided against with guarded circumspection. In addition to the precaution just mentioned, there is a provision that "all duties, imposts and excises, shall be UNIFORM throughout the United States."

It has been very properly observed by different speakers and writers on the side of the Constitution, that if the exercise of the power of internal taxation by the Union,[10] should be discovered on experiment, to be really inconvenient, the Fœderal Government may then [11] forbear the use of it and have recourse to requisitions in its stead. By way of answer to this, it has been triumphantly asked, why not in the first instance omit that ambiguous power and rely upon the latter resource? Two solid answers may be given; the first is, that the [12] exercise of that power, if convenient, will be preferable,

10. "should be judged beforehand upon mature consideration, or" inserted here in McLean and Hopkins.
11. "then" omitted in McLean and Hopkins.
12. "actual" inserted at this point in McLean and Hopkins.

because it will be more effectual; and [13] it is impossible to prove in theory or otherwise than by the experiment that it cannot be advantageously exercised. The contrary indeed appears most probable. The second answer is, that the existence of such a power in the Constitution, will have a strong influence in giving efficacy to requisitions. When the States know that the Union can supply itself without their agency, it will be a powerful motive for exertion on their part.

As to the interference of the revenue laws of the Union, and of its members; we have already seen that there can be no clashing or repugnancy of authority. The laws cannot therefore in a legal sense, interfere with each other; and it is far from impossible to avoid an interference even in the policy of their different systems. An effectual expedient for this purpose will be mutually to abstain from those objects, which either side may have first had recourse to. As neither can *controul* the other, each will have an obvious and sensible interest in this reciprocal forbearance. And where there is an *immediate* common interest, we may safely count upon its operation. When the particular debts of the States are done away, and their expences come to be limited within their natural compass, the possibility almost of interference will vanish. A small land tax will answer the purposes [14] of the States, and will be their most simple and most fit resource.

Many spectres have been raised out of this power of internal taxation to excite the apprehensions of the people—double sets of revenue officers—a duplication of their burthens by double taxations, and the frightful forms of odious and oppressive poll taxes, have been played off with all the ingenious dexterity of political legerdemain.

As to the first point, there are two cases, in which there can be no room for double sets of officers; one where the right of imposing the tax is exclusively vested in the Union, which applies to the duties on imports; and [15] the other, where the object has not fallen under any State regulation or provision, which may be applicable to a variety of objects. In other cases, the probability is, that the United

13. "the power may be found both *convenient* and *necessary;* for" substituted for "that power" through "effectual; and" in McLean and Hopkins.
14. "purpose" substituted for "purposes" in Hopkins.
15. "and" omitted in McLean and Hopkins.

States will either wholly abstain from the objects pre-occupied for local purposes, or will make use of the State officers and State regulations, for collecting the additional imposition. This will best answer the views of revenue, because it will save expence in the collection, and will best avoid any occasion of disgust to the State governments and to the people. At all events, here is a practicable expedient for avoiding such an inconvenience; and nothing more can be required than to show that evils predicted do not necessarily result from the plan.

As to any argument derived from a supposed system of influence, it is a sufficient answer to say, that it ought not to be presumed; but the supposition is susceptible of a more precise answer. If such a spirit should infest the councils of the Union, the most certain road to the accomplishment of its aim would be to employ the State officers as much as possible, and to attach them to the Union by an accumulation of their emoluments. This would serve to turn the tide of State influence into the channels of the national government, instead of making fœderal influence flow in an opposite and adverse current. But all suppositions of this kind are invidious, and ought to be banished from the consideration of the great question before the people. They can answer no other end than to cast a mist over the truth.

As to the suggestion of double taxation, the answer is plain. The wants of the Union are to be supplied in one way or another; if to be done [16] by the authority of the Fœderal Government,[17] it will not be [18] to be done by that of the State governments.[19] The quantity of taxes to be paid by the community, must be the same in either case; with this advantage, if the provision is to be made by the Union, that the capital resource of commercial imposts, which is the most convenient branch of revenue, can be prudently improved to a much greater extent under fœderal than under State regulation, and of course will render it less necessary to recur to more inconvenient methods; and with this further advantage, that as far as there may be any real difficulty in the exercise of the power of internal taxa-

16. "to be done" omitted in Hopkins.
17. "then" inserted at this point in Hopkins.
18. "remain" substituted for "be" in Hopkins.
19. In the newspaper, "government"; "governments" substituted in McLean and Hopkins.

tion, it will impose a disposition to greater care in the choice and arrangement of the means; and must naturally tend to make it a fixed point of policy in the national administration to go as far as may be practicable in making the luxury of the rich tributary to the public treasury, in order to diminish the necessity of those impositions, which might create dissatisfaction in the poorer and most numerous classes of the society. Happy it is when the interest which the government has in the preservation of its own power, coincides with a proper distribution of the public burthens, and tends to guard the least wealthy part of the community from oppression!

As to poll taxes, I, without scruple, confess my disapprobation of them; and though they have prevailed from an early period in those States * which have uniformly been the most tenacious of their rights, I should lament to see them introduced into practice under the national government. But does it follow because there is a power to lay them, that they will actually be laid? Every State in the Union has power to impose taxes of this kind; and yet in several of them they are unknown in practice. Are the State governments to be stigmatised as tyrannies because they possess this power? If they are not, with what propriety can the like power justify such a charge against the national government, or even be urged as an obstacle to its adoption? As little friendly as I am to the species of imposition, I still feel a thorough conviction, that the power of having recourse to it ought to exist in the Fœderal Government. There are certain emergencies of nations, in which expedients that in the ordinary state of things ought to be foreborn, become essential to the public weal. And the government from the possibility of such emergencies ought ever to have the option of making use of them. The real scarcity of objects in this country; which may be considered as productive sources of revenue, is a reason peculiar to itself, for not abridging the discretion of the national councils in this respect. There may exist certain critical and tempestuous conjunctures of the State, in which a poll tax may become an inestimable resource. And as I know nothing to exempt this portion of the globe from the common calamities that have befallen other parts of it, I acknowledge my aversion to every project that is calculated to disarm the government of a single weapon, which in any possible

* *The New-England States.*

contingency might be usefully employed for the general defence and security.

I have now gone through the examination of those powers proposed to be conferred upon the federal government; which relate more peculiarly to its energy, and to its efficiency for answering the great and primary objects of union. There are others, which though omitted here, will in order to render the view of the subject more complete, be taken notice of under the next head of our enquiries. I flatter myself the progress already made will have sufficed to satisfy the candid and judicious part of the community, that some of the objections which have been most strenuously urged against the constitution, and which were most formidable in their first appearance, are not only destitute of substance, but if they had operated in the formation of the plan, would have rendered it incompetent to the great ends of public happiness and national prosperity. I equally flatter myself that a further and more critical investigation of the system will serve to recommend it still more to every sincere and disinterested advocate for good government; and will leave no doubt with men of this character of the propriety and expediency of adopting it. Happy will it be for ourselves, and most honorable for human nature, if we have wisdom and virtue enough, to set so glorious an example to mankind! [20]

PUBLIUS.

20. This paragraph appears in McLean and Hopkins but does not appear in the newspapers.

## From John Fitch [1]

New York 29 January 1788

Honoured Sir

Having exausted considerable sums of money in forming a Boat to be propelled by the force of steam a considerable part of which has been expended in experiments in learning to make a Steam Engine that being so useful a Machine for most great works, I humbly flatter myself it is deserving the notice of Congress and that it will in time superceed the greatest part of Water works as well as all other Boats on our Western Waters. This is Sir to inform

you that I am about to present a petition to Congress for some assistance and so far as you shall judge the honour and interest of
our Empire requires the notice of my petition the subscriber humbly
begs your Patronage and would not forget the obligation.[2] He
flatters himself and believes he can make it appear very evident
that he has carried his Boat sufficiently fast to merit that reward
held up by Congress on the petition of Mr. Ramsey.[3] But should
there be doubts on that head the testimonials accompyning his
petition will undoubtedly justify Congress in granting something to
enable him to pursue it a little further on the same principles that
Mr. Harrison received a premium for a partial improvement for
his Time-pece.[4] And further the information and certificates that I
shall put on the files of your House will undoubtedly raise the Lands
in our Western Territory in a greater or less degree more than if
the scheem was returned into the Chaos of Night at it was before I
suggested the Idea which appears to me but just that I should have
some compensation for and be it ever so small I never shall need
it so much as at the present time. And as I have exhibited to the
World what was never seen before I am of opinion it ought to be
noticed if it promised no success as it may lay the foundation for
future improvements. But where there is every prospect of Success
not only for Vessels of all Sizes but in all great Works he thinks
that the propriety of his prayer is very obvious and humbly begs
leave to submit to your Consideration his representation of the matter
to the President of Congress

    Which will Oblige your most Devoted Humble Servant

John Fitch

The Honoble. Alexander Hambleton Esqr.

ALS, John Fitch Papers, Library of Congress.
    1. Fitch was an inventor and metal craftsman. In 1785, after a varied career
he settled in Bucks County, Pennsylvania, and devoted his efforts to the invention of a steamboat. In August, 1787, he launched a steam-powered boat
on the Delaware River. He was, however, in constant financial difficulties, and
repeatedly sought to obtain subsidies from various state legislatures and the
Continental Congress.
    2. Fitch's letter "praying Congress to grant him a premium for his invention
of a *steam boat*" was dated January 24, 1788, and was referred to a committee
on February 5, 1788. The committee reported on March 5, and Congress in
accordance with its recommendations instructed the Board of Treasury to
grant Fitch an unspecified number of acres of the land belonging to the United
States (*JCC*, XXXIV, 26, 80).

3. In 1785, James Rumsey, like Fitch, had begun experimenting with the use of steam power for a boat. In December, 1787, Rumsey demonstrated his boat on the Potomac River. If, as Fitch states, Rumsey drew up a petition to the Continental Congress, he did not submit it, for the *Journals* of the Continental Congress mention no petition from Rumsey.

4. John Harrison, an English horologist, who was awarded £10,000 by Parliament in 1773 for his invention of a "time piece" to measure longitude. Harrison died in 1776.

## Draft of an Act to Incorporate the Freeholders and Inhabitants of Marbletown

[*New York, January–February, 1788.*] In 1788, Hamilton drafted an "Act to incorporate the Freeholders and Inhabitants of Marbletown." [1]

ADf, Hamilton Papers, Library of Congress.

1. The draft was presumably submitted to the New York legislature. If so, the legislature refused to act on it, for the town of Marbletown was incorporated by a general act of incorporation dated March 7, 1788 (see "An Act for dividing the counties of this State into towns," *Laws of the State of New York,* II, 755).

## Appointment as Delegate to the Continental Congress

[Poughkeepsie, New York, February 2, 1788]

*State of New York*

THE PEOPLE of the State of New york by
the Grace of GOD free and Independent
To ALL to whom these presents shall come send
Greeting.

*Whereas* our Senate and Assembly on the Twenty second day of January last nominated and appointed the Honorable Ezra L'Hommedieu, Egbert Benson, Alexander Hamilton, Abraham Yates, Junior and Leonard Gansevort Esquires DELEGATES to represent our said State in the United States in Congress Assembled from the said day of their appointment until the first Monday of November Next, [1] and thence forward until Ten days after the first Subsequent meeting of the Legislature. PROVIDED nevertheless that the Delegates so nominated and appointed shall not on any account hold their Seats in Congress longer than one year to be computed from the day of their appointment as aforesaid. NOW THEREFORE KNOW YE that in pursuance of the said Nomination and appointment We have by these presents Commissioned the said Ezra L'Hommedieu Egbert Benson, Alexander Hamilton, Abraham Yates, Junior and Leonard Gansevort with full power and authority to them the said Ezra L'Hommedieu, Egbert Benson, Alexander Hamilton, Abraham Yates Junior and Leonard Gansevort to represent our said State in the said Congress accordingly: IN TESTIMONY whereof we have caused these our Letters to be made patent, and the great Seal of our said State to be hereunto affixed WITNESS our Trusty and well beloved GEORGE CLINTON Esquire Governor of our said State General and Commander in Chief of all the Militia and Admiral of the Navy of the same, At Poughkeepsie in our County of Dutchess the Second day of February in the year of our Lord One Thousand seven hundred and Eighty Eight and in the Twelfth year of our INDEPENDENCE.[2]

Geo Clinton

Passed the Secretary's office
the 2d February 1788.

Lewis A. Scott, Secretary

D, Papers of the Continental Congress, National Archives.
1. On January 22, 1788, the New York legislature elected delegates to represent the state in 1788 in the Continental Congress. The Assembly nominated H, Abraham Yates, Jr., Egbert Benson, Ezra L'Hommedieu, and Leonard Gansevoort. The Senate also nominated the first four men, but it selected William Floyd instead of Gansevoort. A joint ballot of both Senate and House was taken and the list selected by the Assembly was chosen (New York Senate *Journal,* 1788, 11–12).
2. H attended the Continental Congress on February 25, 1788. An entry of that date in the Papers of the Continental Congress reads as follows: "Mr. Alexander Hamilton and Mr. Leonard Gansevoort Delegates for New York attended and produced Credentials of their appointment which were read" (*JCC,* XXXIV, 56).

## [*The Federalist No. 49*] [1]

[New York, February 2, 1788]

*The* [New York] *Independent Journal: or, the General Advertiser,* February 2, 1788. This essay appeared on February 5, 1788, in *The New-York Packet,* and on February 6, 1788, in *The* [New York] *Daily Advertiser.* In the McLean edition this essay is mistakenly numbered 69, in the newspapers it is numbered 48.
1. The authorship of this essay has been disputed. However, because H himself attributed it to James Madison, it has not been included in these volumes. For a discussion of the dispute over its authorship, see "The Federalist. Introductory Note," October 27, 1787–May 28, 1788.

## The Federalist No. 50 [1]

By JAMES MADISON or ALEXANDER HAMILTON

[New York, February 5, 1788]

*To the People of the State of New-York.*

IT may be contended perhaps, that instead of *occasional* appeals to the people, which are liable to the objections urged against them, *periodical* appeals are the proper and adequate means *of preventing and correcting infractions of the Constitution.*

It will be attended to, that in the examination of these expedients, I confine myself to their aptitude for *enforcing* the Constitution by keeping the several departments of power within their due bounds, without particularly considering them, as provisions for *altering* the Constitution itself. In the first view, appeals to the people at fixed periods, appear to be nearly as ineligible, as appeals in particular occasions as they emerge. If the periods be separated by short intervals, the measures to be reviewed and rectified, will have been of recent date, and will be connected with all the circumstances which tend to viciate and pervert the result of occasional revisions. If the periods be distant from each other, the same remark will be applicable to all recent measures, and in proportion as the remoteness of the others may favor a dispassionate review of them, this advantage is inseparable from inconveniencies which seem to counterbalance

*The New-York Packet,* February 5, 1788. This essay appeared on February 6 in *The* [New York] *Independent Journal: or, the General Advertiser,* and on February 9 in *The* [New York] *Daily Advertiser.* In the McLean edition this essay is numbered 50, in the newspapers it is numbered 49.

1. For background to this document, see "The Federalist. Introductory Note," October 27, 1788–May 28, 1788.

Both H and Madison claimed the authorship of this essay. Edward G. Bourne ("The Authorship of the Federalist," *The American Historical Review,* II [April, 1897], 449–51), and J. C. Hamilton (*The Federalist,* I, cxiii), the most able advocates for the claim of Madison and H respectively, have attempted to resolve the problem of authorship by reference to internal evidence. The proof which J. C. Hamilton offers for H's authorship is weak; and although the proof Bourne offers for Madison's authorship is not conclusive, it indicates that Madison's claim is more plausible than H's. The lists in which H and Madison made their claims to the authorship, as shown in "The Federalist. Introductory Note," October 27, 1787–May 28, 1788, also indicate (but do not prove) that Madison was the author.

it. In the first place, a distant prospect of public censure would be a very feeble restraint on power from those excesses, to which it might be urged by the force of present motives. Is it to be imagined, that a legislative assembly, consisting of a hundred or two hundred members, eagerly bent on some favorite object, and breaking through the restraints of the Constitution in pursuit of it, would be arrested in their career, by considerations drawn from a censorial revision of their conduct at the future distance of ten, fifteen or twenty years? In the next place, the abuses would often have compleated their mischievous effects, before the remedial provision would be applied. And in the last place, where this might not be the case, they would be of long standing, would have taken deep root, and would not easily be extirpated.

The scheme of revising the Constitution in order to correct recent breaches of it, as well as for other purposes, has been actually tried in one of the States. One of the objects of the council of censors, which met in Pennsylvania, in 1783 and 1784, was, as we have seen,[2] to enquire "whether the Constitution had been violated, and whether the legislative and executive departments had encroached on each other." This important and novel experiment in politics, merits in several points of view, very particular attention. In some of them it may perhaps, as a single experiment, made under circumstances somewhat peculiar, be thought to be not absolutely conclusive. But as applied to the case under consideration, it involves some facts which I venture to remark, as a compleat and satisfactory illustration of the reasoning which I have employed.

First. It appears from the names of the gentlemen, who composed the council, that some at least of its most active and leading members, had also been active and leading characters in the parties which pre-existed in the State.

Secondly. It appears that the same active and leading members of the council, had been active and influential members of the legislative and executive branches, within the period to be reviewed; and even patrons or opponents of the very measures to be thus brought to the test of the Constitution. Two of the members had been Vice-Presidents of the State, and several others, members of the executive

2. See essay 48.

council, within the seven preceding years. One of them had been Speaker, and a number of others distinguished members of the legislative assembly, within the same period.

Thirdly. Every page of their proceedings witnesses the effect of all these circumstances on the temper of their deliberations. Throughout the continuance of the council, it was split into two fixed and violent parties. The fact is acknowledged and lamented by themselves. Had this not been the case, the face of their proceedings exhibit a proof equally satisfactory. In all questions, however unimportant in themselves, or unconnected with each other, the same names, stand invariably contrasted on the opposite columns. Every unbiassed observer, may infer without danger of mistake, and at the same time, without meaning to reflect on either party, or any individuals of either party, that unfortunately *passion*, not *reason*, must have presided over their decisions. When men exercise their reason coolly and freely, on a variety of distinct questions, they inevitably fall into different opinions, on some of them. When they are governed by a common passion, their opinions if they are so to be called, will be the same.

Fourthly. It is at least problematical, whether the decisions of this body, do not, in several instances, misconstrue the limits prescribed for the legislative and executive departments, instead of reducing and limiting them within their constitutional places.

Fifthly. I have never understood that the decisions of the council on constitutional questions, whether rightly or erroneously formed, have had any effect in varying the practice founded on legislative constructions. It even appears, if I mistake not, that in one instance, the cotemporary Legislature denied the constructions of the council, and actually prevailed in the contest.

This censorial body therefore, proves at the same time, by its researches, the existence of the disease; and by its example, the inefficacy of the remedy.

This conclusion cannot be invalidated by alledging that the State in which the experiment was made, was at that crisis, and had been for a long time before, violently heated and distracted by the rage of party. Is it to be presumed, that at any future septennial epoch, the same state will be free from parties? Is it to be presumed that any other State, at the same or any other given period, will be exempt from them? Such an event ought to be neither presumed nor desired; because an extinction of parties necessarily implies either a universal alarm for the public safety, or an absolute extinction of liberty.

Were the precaution taken of excluding from the assemblies elected by the people to revise the preceding administration of the government, all persons who should have been concerned in the government within the given period, the difficulties would not be obviated. The important task would probably devolve on men, who with inferior capacities, would in other respects, be little better qualified. Although they might not have been personally concerned in the administration, and therefore not immediately agents in the measures to be examined; they would probably have been involved in the parties connected with these measures, and have been elected under their auspices.

PUBLIUS.

## The Federalist No. 51 [1]

By JAMES MADISON *or* ALEXANDER HAMILTON

[New York, February 6, 1788]

*To the People of the State of New-York.*

TO what expedient then shall we finally resort for maintaining in practice the necessary partition of power among the several departments, as laid down in the constitution? The only answer that can be given is, that as all these exterior provisions are found to be inadequate, the defect must be supplied, by so contriving the interior

*The* [New York] *Independent Journal: or, the General Advertiser*, February 6, 1788. This essay appeared on February 8 in *The New-York Packet* and on February 11 in *The* [New York] *Daily Advertiser*. In the McLean edition this essay is numbered 51, in the newspapers it is numbered 50.

1. For background to this document, see "The Federalist. Introductory Note," October 27, 1787–May 28, 1788.

Essay 51, like essay 50, was claimed by H and Madison. The internal evidence presented by Edward G. Bourne ("The Authorship of the Federalist," *The American Historical Review*, II [April, 1897], 449–51), strongly indicates Madison's authorship. Bourne printed in parallel columns sentences from essay 51 which correspond very closely, sometimes exactly, to earlier writings by Madison. For other reasons why Madison's claim to the authorship of this essay outweighs (but does not necessarily obviate) that of H, see "The Federalist. Introductory Note," October 27, 1787–May 28, 1788.

structure of the government, as that its several constituent parts may, by their mutual relations, be the means of keeping each other in their proper places. Without presuming to undertake a full development of this important idea, I will hazard a few general observations, which may perhaps place it in a clearer light, and enable us to form a more correct judgment of the principles and structure of the government planned by the convention.

In order to lay a due foundation for that separate and distinct exercise of the different powers of government, which to a certain extent, is admitted on all hands to be essential to the preservation of liberty, it is evident that each department should have a will of its own; and consequently should be so constituted, that the members of each should have as little agency as possible in the appointment of the members of the others. Were this principle rigorously adhered to, it would require that all the appointments for the supreme executive, legislative, and judiciary magistracies, should be drawn from the same fountain of authority, the people, through channels, having no communication whatever with one another. Perhaps such a plan of constructing the several departments would be less difficult in practice than it may in contemplation appear. Some difficulties however, and some additional expence, would attend the execution of it. Some deviations therefore from the principle must be admitted. In the constitution of the judiciary department in particular, it might be inexpedient to insist rigorously on the principle; first, because peculiar qualifications being essential in the members, the primary consideration ought to be to select that mode of choice, which best secures these qualifications; secondly, because the permanent tenure by which the appointments are held in that department, must soon destroy all sense of dependence on the authority conferring them.

It is equally evident that the members of each department should be as little dependent as possible on those of the others, for the emoluments annexed to their offices. Were the executive magistrate, or the judges, not independent of the legislature in this particular, their independence in every other would be merely nominal.

But the great security against a gradual concentration of the several powers in the same department, consists in giving to those who administer each department, the necessary constitutional means, and personal motives, to resist encroachments of the others. The provision for defence must in this, as in all other cases, be made commensurate to the danger of attack. Ambition must be made to counteract ambition. The interest of the man must be connected with the constitutional rights of the place. It may be a reflection on human nature, that such devices should be necessary to controul the abuses of government. But what is government itself but the greatest of all reflections on human nature? If men were angels, no government would be necessary. If angels were to govern men, neither external nor internal controuls on government would be necessary. In framing a government which is to be administered by men over men, the great difficulty lies in this: You must first enable the government to controul the governed; and in the next place, oblige it to controul itself. A dependence on the people is no doubt the primary controul on the government; but experience has taught mankind the necessity of auxiliary precautions.

This policy of supplying by opposite and rival interests, the defect of better motives, might be traced through the whole system of human affairs, private as well as public. We see it particularly displayed in all the subordinate distributions of power; where the constant aim is to divide and arrange the several offices in such a manner as that each may be a check on the other; that the private interest of every individual, may be a centinel over the public rights. These inventions of prudence cannot be less requisite in the distribution of the supreme powers of the state.

But it is not possible to give to each department an equal power of self defence. In republican government the legislative authority, necessarily, predominates. The remedy for this inconveniency is, to divide the legislature into different branches; and to render them by different modes of election, and different principles of action, as little connected with each other, as the nature of their common functions, and their common dependence on the society, will admit. It may even be necessary to guard against dangerous encroachments by still further precautions. As the weight of the legislative authority requires that it should be thus divided, the weakness of the executive may require, on the other hand, that it should be fortified. An absolute negative, on the legislature, appears at first view to be the natural defence with which the executive magistrate should be armed. But perhaps it would be neither altogether safe, nor alone sufficient. On ordinary occasions, it might not be exerted with the requisite firmness; and on extraordinary occasions, it might be perfidiously abused. May not this defect of an absolute negative be supplied, by some qualified connection between this weaker department, and the weaker branch of the stronger department, by which the latter may be led to support the constitutional rights of the former, without being too much detached from the rights of its own departmen[t]?

If the principles on which these observations are founded be just, as I persuade myself they are, and they be applied as a criterion, to the several state constitutions, and to the federal constitution, it will be found, that if the latter does not perfectly correspond with them, the former are infinitely less able to bear such a test.

There are moreover two considerations particularly applicable to the federal system of America, which place that system[2] in a very interesting point of view.

*First.* In a single republic, all the power surrendered by the people, is submitted to the administration of a single government; and[3] usurpations are guarded against by a division of the government into distinct and separate departments. In the compound republic of America, the power surrendered by the people, is first divided between two distinct governments, and then the portion allotted to each, subdivided among distinct and separate departments. Hence a double security arises to the rights of the people. The different governments will controul each other; at the same time that each will be controuled by itself.

*Second.* It is of great importance in a republic, not only to guard the society against the oppression of its rulers; but to guard one part of the society against the injustice of the other part. Different interests necessarily exist in different classes of citizens. If a majority be united by a common interest, the rights of the minority will be insecure. There are but two methods of providing against this evil: The one by creating a will in the community independent of the majority, that is, of the society itself; the other by comprehending in the society so many separate descriptions of citizens, as

2. "it" substituted for "that system" in Hopkins.
3. "the" inserted at this point in Hopkins.

will render an unjust combination of a majority of the whole, very improbable, if not impracticable. The first method prevails in all governments possessing an hereditary or self appointed authority. This at best is but a precarious security; because a power independent of the society may as well espouse the unjust views of the major, as the rightful interests, of the minor party, and may possibly be turned against both parties. The second method will be exemplified in the federal republic of the United States. Whilst all authority in it will be derived from and dependent on the society, the society itself will be broken into so many parts, interests and classes of citizens, that the rights of individuals or of the minority, will be in little danger from interested combinations of the majority. In a free government, the security for civil rights must be the same as for religious rights. It consists in the one case in the multiplicity of interests, and in the other, in the multiplicity of sects. The degree of security in both cases will depend on the number of interests and sects; and this may be presumed to depend on the extent of country and number of people comprehended under the same government. This view of the subject must particularly recommend a proper federal system to all the sincere and considerate friends of republican government: Since it shews that in exact proportion as the territory of the union may be formed into more circumscribed confederacies or states, oppressive combinations of a majority will be facilitated, the best security under the republican form, for the rights of every class of citizens, will be diminished; and consequently, the stability and independence of some member of the government, the only other security, must be proportionally increased. Justice is the end of government. It is the end of civil society. It ever has been, and ever will be pursued, until it be obtained, or until liberty be lost in the pursuit. In a society under the forms of which the stronger faction can readily unite and oppress the weaker, anarchy may as truly be said to reign, as in a state of nature where the weaker individual is not secured against the violence of the stronger: And as in the latter state even the stronger individuals are prompted by the uncertainty of their condition, to submit to a government which may protect the weak as well as themselves: So in the former state, will the more powerful factions or parties [4] be

4. "or parties" omitted in Hopkins.

gradually induced by a like motive, to wish for a government which will protect all parties, the weaker as well as the more powerful. It can be little doubted, that if the state of Rhode Island was separated from the confederacy, and left to itself, the insecurity of rights under the popular form of government within such narrow limits, would be displayed by such reiterated oppressions of factious majorities, that some power altogether independent of the people would soon be called for by the voice of the very factions whose misrule had proved the necessity of it. In the extended republic of the United States, and among the great variety of interests, parties and sects which it embraces, a coalition of a majority of the whole society could seldom take place on[5] any other principles than those of justice and the general good; and[6] there being thus less danger to a minor from the will of the major party, there must be less pretext also, to provide for the security of the former, by introducing into the government a will not dependent on the latter; or in other words, a will independent of the society itself. It is no less certain than it is important, notwithstanding the contrary opinions which have been entertained, that the larger the society, provided it lie within a practicable sphere, the more duly capable it will be of self government. And happily for the *republican cause*, the practicable sphere may be carried to a very great extent, by a judicious modification and mixture of the *federal principle*.

PUBLIUS.

5. "upon" substituted for "on" in McLean and Hopkins.
6. "Whilst" substituted for "and" in McLean and Hopkins.

## *The Federalist No. 52* [1]

By JAMES MADISON *or* ALEXANDER HAMILTON

[New York, February 8, 1788]

*To the People of the State of New-York.*

FROM the more general enquiries pursued in the four last papers,

*The New-York Packet*, February 8, 1788. This essay was printed in *The* [New York] *Independent Journal: or, the General Advertiser* on February 9. In the McLean edition this essay is numbered 52, in the newspapers it is numbered 51.

1. For the background to this document, see "The Federalist. Introductory Note," October 27, 1787–May 28, 1788.

Essay 52 was claimed by Madison and H in their several lists. No student

I pass on to a more particular examination of the several parts of the government. I shall begin with the House of Representatives.

The first view to be taken of this part of the government, relates to the qualifications of the electors and the elected. Those of the former are to be the same with those of the electors of the most numerous branch of the State Legislatures. The definition of the right of suffrage is very justly regarded as a fundamental article of republican government. It was incumbent on the Convention therefore to define and establish this right, in the Constitution. To have left it open for the occasional regulation of the Congress, would have been improper for the reason just mentioned. To have submitted it to the legislative discretion of the States, would have been improper for the same reason; and for the additional reason, that it would have rendered too dependent on the State Governments, that branch of the Fœderal Government, which ought to be dependent on the people alone. To have reduced the different qualifications in the different States, to one uniform rule, would probably have been as dissatisfactory to some of the States, as it would have been difficult to the Convention. The provision made by the Convention appears therefore, to be the best that lay within their option. It must be satisfactory to every State; because it is conformable to the standard already established, or which may be established by the State itself. It will be safe to the United States; because, being fixed by the State Constitutions, it is not alterable by the State Government, and it cannot be feared that the people of the States will alter this part of their Constitutions, in such a manner as to abridge the rights secured to them by the Fœderal Constitution.

The qualifications of the elected being less carefully and properly defined by the State Constitutions, and being at the same time more susceptible of uniformity, have been very properly considered and regulated by the Convention. A representative of the United States must be of the age of twenty-five years; must have been seven

---

of *The Federalist* has been able to prove by internal evidence that either of the two men wrote this essay; E. G. Bourne, for example ("The Authorship of the Federalist," *The American Historical Review*, II [April, 1897], 451), presents only one similarity between essay 52 and Madison's other writings, and J. C. Hamilton (*The Federalist*, I, cxv) gives no convincing parallels between it and other writings by H.

For the reasons why Madison's claim to authorship of this essay outweighs (but does not obviate) that of H, see "The Federalist. Introductory Note," October 27, 1787–May 28, 1788.

years a citizen of the United States, must at the time of his election, be an inhabitant of the State he is to represent, and during the time of his service must be in no office under the United States. Under these reasonable limitations, the door of this part of the Fœderal Government, is open to merit of every description, whether native or adoptive, whether young or old, and without regard to poverty or wealth, or to any particular profession of religious faith.

The term for which the Representatives are to be elected, falls under a second view which may be taken of this branch. In order to decide on the propriety of this article, two questions must be considered; first, whether biennial elections will, in this case, be safe; secondly, whether they be necessary or useful.

First. As it is essential to liberty that the government in general, should have a common interest with the people; so it is particularly essential that the branch of it under consideration, should have an immediate dependence on, & an intimate sympathy with the people. Frequent elections are unquestionably the only policy by which this dependence and sympathy can be effectually secured. But what particular degree of frequency may be absolutely necessary for the purpose, does not appear to be susceptible of any precise calculation; and must depend on a variety of circumstances with which it may be connected. Let us consult experience, the guide that ought always to be followed, whenever it can be found.

The scheme of representation, as a substitute for a meeting of the citizens in person, being at most but very imperfectly known[2] to ancient polity; it is in more modern times only, that we are to expect instructive examples. And even here, in order to avoid a research too vague and diffusive, it will be proper to confine ourselves to the few examples which are best known, and which bear the greatest analogy to our particular case. The first to which this character ought to be applied, is the House of Commons in Great Britain. The history of this branch of the English Constitution, anterior to the date of Magna Charta, is too obscure to yield instruction. The very existence of it has been made a question among political antiquaries. The earliest records of subsequent date prove, that Parliaments were to *sit* only, every year; not that they were to be *elected*

2. "being but imperfectly known" substituted for "being at most but very imperfectly known" in Hopkins.

every year. And even these annual sessions were left so much at the discretion of the monarch, that under various pretexts, very long and dangerous intermissions, were often contrived by royal ambition. To remedy this grievance, it was provided by a statute in the reign of Charles the second, that the intermissions should not be protracted beyond a period of three years. On the accession of Wil. III. when a revolution took place in the government, the subject was still more seriously resumed, and it was declared to be among the fundamental rights of the people, that Parliaments ought to be held *frequently*. By another statute which passed a few years later in the same reign, the term "frequently" which had alluded to the triennial period settled in the time of Charles II. is reduced to a precise meaning, it being expressly enacted that a new parliament shall be called within three years after the determination of the former. The last change from three to seven years is well known to have been introduced pretty early in the present century, under an alarm for the Hanoverian succession. From these facts it appears, that the greatest frequency of elections which has been deemed necessary in that kingdom, for binding the representatives to their constituents, does not exceed a triennial return of them. And if we may argue from the degree of liberty retained even under septennial elections, and all the other vicious ingredients in the parliamentary constitution, we cannot doubt that a reduction of the period from seven to three years, with the [3] other necessary reforms, would so far extend the influence of the people over their representatives, as to satisfy us, that biennial elections under the fœderal system, cannot possibly be dangerous to the requisite dependence of the house of representatives on their constituents.

Elections in Ireland till of late were regulated entirely by the discretion of the crown, and were seldom repeated except on the accession of a new Prince, or some other contingent event. The parliament which commenced with George II. was continued throughout his whole reign, a period of about thirty-five years. The only dependence of the representatives on the people consisted, in the right of the latter to supply occasional vacancies, by the election of new members, and in the chance of some event which might produce a general new election. The ability also of the Irish parliament, to

3. "some" substituted for "the" in Hopkins.

maintain the rights of their constituents, so far as the disposition might exist, was extremely shackled by the controul of the crown over the subjects of their deliberation. Of late these shackles, if I mistake not, have been broken; and octennial parliaments have besides been established. What effect may be produced by this partial reform, must be left to further experience. The example of Ireland, from this view of it, can throw but little light on the subject. As far as we can draw any conclusion from it, it must be, that if the people of that country have been able, under all these disadvantages, to retain any liberty whatever, the advantage of biennial elections would secure to them every degree of liberty which might depend on a due connection between their representatives and themselves.

Let us bring our enquiries nearer home. The example of these States when British colonies claims particular attention; at the same time that it is so well known, as to require little to be said on it. The principle of representation, in one branch of the Legislature at least, was established in all of them. But the periods of election were different. They varied from one to seven years. Have we any reason to infer from the spirit and conduct of the representatives of the people, prior to the revolution, that biennial elections would have been dangerous to the public liberties? The spirit which every where displayed itself at the commencement of the struggle; and which vanquished the obstacles to independence, is the best of proofs [4] that a sufficient portion of liberty had been every where enjoyed to inspire both a sense of its worth, and a zeal for its proper enlargement. This remark holds good as well with regard to the then colonies, whose elections were least frequent, as to those whose elections were most frequent. Virginia was the colony which stood first in resisting the parliamentary usurpations of Great-Britain: it was the first also in espousing by public act, the resolution of independence. In Virginia nevertheless, if I have not been misinformed, elections under the former government were septennial. This particular example is brought into view, not as a proof of any peculiar merit, for the priority in those instances, was probably accidental; and still less of any advantage in *septennial* elections, for when compared with a greater frequency they are inadmissible:

4. "proof" substituted for "proofs" in Hopkins.

but merely as a proof, and I conceive it to be a very substantial proof, that the liberties of the people can be in no danger from *biennial* elections.

The conclusion resulting from these examples will be not a little strengthened by recollecting three circumstances. The first is that the Fœderal Legislature will possess a part only of that supreme legislative authority which is vested completely in the British parliament, and which with a few exceptions was exercised by the colonial Assemblies and the Irish Legislature. It is a received and well founded maxim, that, where no other circumstances affect the case, the greater the power is, the shorter ought to be its duration; and, conversely, the smaller the power, the more safely may its duration be protracted. In the second place, it has, on another occasion, been shewn [5] that the Fœderal Legislature will not only be restrained by its dependence on the people as other legislative bodies are; but that it will be moreover watched and controuled by the several collateral Legislatures, which other legislative bodies are not. And in the third place, no comparison can be made between the means that will be possessed by the more permanent branches of the Fœderal Government for seducing, if they should be disposed to seduce, the House of Representatives from their duty to the people; and the means of influence over the popular branch, possessed by the other branches of the governments above cited. With less power therefore to abuse, the Fœderal Representatives, can be less tempted on one side, and will be doubly watched on the other.

PUBLIUS.

5. See essay 46.

## *To Philip Schuyler* [1]

[New York, February 9, 1788]

My Dear Sir

An application will be made to the Council of appointment [2] by Mr. Nicholas Carmer [3] of this city; an ancient and respectable inhabitant; for the appointment of an Inspector of Mahogany and other lumber for this City. I recommend him, *on every account*, to your patronage.

The mail of this Evening I am informed brings the most favourable accounts from Massachusettes.[4] I am inclined to consider the favourable issue of things there as reduced to a certainty.

I remain Most Affecty   D Sir   Yr. Obed ser        Alx Hamilton

Saturday Feby 9th.

ALS, Mr. George T. Bowdoin, New York City.
   1. The name of the addressee does not appear on this letter. The first line suggests that it was sent to a member of the New York Council of Appointment. Schuyler, H's father-in-law, was a member of the council and the letter presumably was addressed to him.
   2. The Council of Appointment consisted of four senators, one from each district in the state, and the governor *ex officio* as its presiding officer. The council had full powers of appointment. In 1788, it consisted of John Vanderbilt, Anthony Hoffman, David Hopkins, and Schuyler.
   3. Carmer was active in the politics of New York City. He later became assistant alderman of the third and fourth wards.
   4. H is referring to the Massachusetts Ratifying Convention which, on February 6, had accepted the Constitution by a vote of 187 to 168.


# [*The Federalist No. 53*] [1]

[New York, February 9, 1788]

*The* [New York] *Independent Journal: or, the General Advertiser,* February 9, 1788. This essay was printed on February 12 in *The New-York Packet*. In the McLean edition this essay is numbered 53, in the newspapers it is numbered 52.
   1. Although this essay has on occasion been attributed to H, he did not claim it on the Kent list. Under the circumstances, there can be no doubt that it was written by James Madison. See "The Federalist. Introductory Note," October 27, 1787–May 28, 1788.


# *The Federalist No. 54* [1]

By JAMES MADISON *or* ALEXANDER HAMILTON

[New York, February 12, 1788]

*To the People of the State of New-York.*
   THE next view which I shall take of the House of Representatives,

*The New-York Packet,* February 12, 1788. This essay was printed in *The* [New York] *Independent Journal: or, the General Advertiser* on February 13. In the McLean edition this essay is numbered 54, in the newspapers it is numbered 53.
   1. For background to this document, see "The Federalist. Introductory Note," October 27, 1787–May 28, 1788.
   No internal evidence discovered by any student of *The Federalist* has proved

relates to the apportionment of its members to [2] the several States, which is to be determined by the same rule with that of direct taxes.

It is not contended that the number of people in each State ought not to be the standard for regulating the proportion of those who are to represent the people of each State. The establishment of the same rule for the apportionment of taxes, will probably be as little contested; though the rule itself in this case, is by no means founded on the same principle. In the former case, the rule is understood to refer to the personal rights of the people, with which it has a natural and universal connection. In the latter, it has reference to the proportion of wealth, of which it is in no case a precise measure, and in ordinary cases a very unfit one. But notwithstanding the imperfection of the rule as applied to the relative wealth and contributions of the States, it is evidently the least exceptionable among the practicable rules; [3] and had too recently obtained the general sanction of America, not to have found a ready preference with the Convention.

---

that this essay was written by either H or Madison. It is logical—however much it must be remembered that the rules of logic are a rather treacherous method for establishing the authorship of these disputed essays—to assume that Madison would have written on the clause in the Constitution relative to the counting of slaves in the apportionment of representatives for the Federal legislature. It also is reasonable to assume that he would have been the more likely person to present the southern point of view. One piece of internal evidence, overlooked by other students of *The Federalist*, suggests Madison's authorship. In writing on the question of representation of property as well as of persons in the national legislature, the author of essay 54 wrote: "Upon this principle it is, that in several of the States, and particularly in the State of New-York, one branch of the government is intended more especially to be the guardian of property, and is accordingly elected by that part of the society which is most interested in this object of government." In essay 35 of *The Federalist*, undoubtedly written by H, there is a different assessment of the New York Senate. "If we take fact as our guide," H wrote, "and look into our own senate and assembly, we shall find that moderate proprietors of land prevail in both; nor is this less the case in the Senate, which consists of a small number, than in the assembly. Where the qualifications of the electors are the same . . . their votes will fall upon those in whom they have most confidence; whether these happen to be men of large fortunes or of moderate property, or of no property at all." Unless H changed his interpretation of a fact to prove whatever point he happened to be making in a given essay, he could not have written both essay 35 and essay 54.

For other reasons why Madison's claim to the authorship of this essay outweighs (but does not necessarily obviate) that of H, see "The Federalist. Introductory Note," October 27, 1787–May 28, 1788.

2. "among" substituted for "to" in Hopkins.

3. "those that are practicable" substituted for "the practicable rules" in Hopkins.

All this is admitted, it will perhaps be said: But does it follow from an admission of numbers for the measure of representation, or of slaves combined with free citizens, as a ratio of taxation, that slaves ought to be included in the numerical rule of representation? Slaves are considered as property, not as persons. They ought therefore to be comprehended in estimates of taxation which are founded on property, and to be excluded from representation which is regulated by a census of persons. This is the objection, as I understand it, stated in its full force. I shall be equally candid in stating the reasoning which may be offered on the opposite side.

We subscribe to the doctrine, might one of our southern brethren observe, that representation relates more immediately to persons, and taxation more immediately to property, and we join in the application of this distinction to the case of our slaves. But we must deny the fact that slaves are considered merely as property, and in no respect whatever as persons. The true state of the case is, that they partake of both these qualities; being considered by our laws, in some respects, as persons, and in other respects, as property. In being compelled to labor not for himself, but for a master; in being vendible by one master to another master; and in being subject at all times to be restrained in his liberty, and chastised in his body, by the capricious will of another,[4] the slave may appear to be degraded from the human rank, and classed with those irrational animals, which fall under the legal denomination of property. In being protected on the other hand in his life & in his limbs, against the violence of all others, even the master of his labor and his liberty; and in being punishable himself for all violence committed against others; the slave is no less evidently regarded by the law as a member of the society; not as a part of the irrational creation; as a moral person, not as a mere article of property. The Fœderal Constitution therefore, decides with great propriety on the case of our slaves, when it views them in the mixt character of persons and of property. This is in fact their true character. It is the character bestowed on them by the laws under which they live; and it will not be denied[5] that these are the proper criterion; because it is only under the pretext that the laws have transformed the

4. "his owner" substituted for "another" in Hopkins.
5. "disputed" substituted for "denied" in Hopkins.

negroes into subjects of property, that a place is disputed them [6] in the computation of numbers; and it is admitted that if the laws were to restore the rights which have been taken away, the negroes could no longer be refused an equal share of representation with the other inhabitants.

This question may be placed in another light. It is agreed on all sides, that numbers are the best scale of wealth and taxation, as they are the only proper scale of representation. Would the Convention have been impartial or consistent, if they had rejected the slaves from the list of inhabitants when the shares of representation were to be calculated; and inserted them on the lists when the tariff of contributions was to be adjusted? Could it be reasonably expected that the southern States would concur in a system which considered their slaves in some degree as men, when burdens were to be imposed, but refused to consider them in the same light when advantages were to be conferred? Might not some surprize also be expressed that those who reproach the southern States with the barbarous policy of considering as property a part of their human brethren, should themselves contend that the government to which all the States are to be parties, ought to consider this unfortunate race more compleately in the unnatural light of property, than the very laws of which they complain!

It may be replied perhaps [7] that slaves are not included in the estimate of representatives in any of the States possessing them. They neither vote themselves, nor increase the votes of their masters. Upon what principle then ought they to be taken into the fœderal estimate of representation? In rejecting them altogether, the Constitution would in this respect have followed the very laws which have been appealed to, as the proper guide.

This objection is repelled by a single observation. It is a fundamental principle of the proposed Constitution, that as the aggregate number of representatives allotted to the several States, is to be determined by a fœderal rule founded on the aggregate number of inhabitants, so the right of choosing this allotted number in each State is to be exercised by such part of the inhabitants, as the State itself may designate. The qualifications on which the right

6. "denied to them" substituted for "disputed them" in Hopkins.
7. "perhaps replied" substituted for "replied perhaps" in Hopkins.

of suffrage depend, are not perhaps the same in any two States. In some of the States the difference is very material. In every State, a certain proportion of inhabitants are deprived of this right by the Constitution of the State, who will be included in the census by which the Fœderal Constitution apportions the representatives. In this point of view, the southern States might retort the complaint, by insisting, that the principle laid down by the Convention required that no regard should be had to the policy of particular States towards their own inhabitants; and consequently, that the slaves as inhabitants should have been admitted into the census according to their full number, in like manner with other inhabitants, who by the policy of other States, are not admitted to all the rights of citizens. A rigorous adherence however to this principle is waved by those who would be gainers by it. All that they ask is, that equal moderation be shewn on the other side. Let the case of the slaves be considered as it is in truth a peculiar one. Let the compromising expedient of the Constitution be mutually adopted, which regards them as inhabitants, but as debased by servitude below the equal level of free inhabitants, which regards the *slave* as divested of two fifths of the *man*.

After all may not another ground be taken on which this article of the Constitution, will admit of a still more ready defence. We have hitherto proceeded on the idea that representation related to persons only, and not at all to property. But is it a just idea? Government is instituted no less for protection of the property, than of the persons of individuals. The one as well as the other, therefore may be considered as represented by those who are charged with the government. Upon this principle it is, that in several of the States, and particularly in the State of New-York, one branch of the government is intended more especially to be the guardian of property, and is accordingly elected by that part of the society which is most interested in this object of government.[8] In the Fœderal Constitution, this policy does not prevail. The rights of property are committed into the same hands with the personal rights. Some attention ought therefore to be paid to property in the choice of those hands.

8. New York State senators were chosen by freeholders who were actual residents and who possessed freeholds of the value of £ 100 over and above all debts charged thereon.

For another reason the votes allowed in the Fœderal Legislature to the people of each State, ought to bear some proportion to the comparative wealth of the States. States have not like individuals, an influence over each other arising from superior advantages of fortune. If the law allows an opulent citizen but a single vote in the choice of his representative, the respect and consequence which he derives from his fortunate situation, very frequently guide the votes of others to the objects of his choice; and through this imperceptible channel the rights of property are conveyed into the public representation. A State possesses no such influence over other States. It is not probable that the richest State in the confederacy will ever influence the choice of a single representative in any other State. Nor will the representatives of the larger and richer States possess any other advantage in the Fœderal Legislature over the representatives of other States, than what may result from their superior number alone; as far therefore as their superior wealth and weight may justly entitle them to any advantage, it ought to be secured to them by a superior share of representation. The new Constitution is in this respect materially different from the existing confederation, as well as from that of the United Netherlands, and other similar confederacies. In each of the latter the efficacy of the fœderal resolutions depends on the subsequent and voluntary resolutions of the States composing the Union. Hence the States, though possessing an equal vote in the public councils, have an unequal influence, corresponding with the unequal importance of these subsequent and voluntary resolutions. Under the proposed Constitution, the fœderal acts will take effect without the necessary intervention of the individual States. They will depend merely on the majority of votes in the Fœderal Legislature, and consequently each vote whether proceeding from a larger or a smaller State, or a State more or less wealthy or powerful, will have an equal weight and efficacy; in the same manner as the votes individually given in a State Legislature, by the representatives of unequal counties or other districts, have each a precise equality of value and effect; or if there be any difference in the case, it proceeds from the difference in the personal character of the individual representative, rather than from any regard to the extent of the district from which he comes.

Such is the reasoning which an advocate for the southern interests might employ on this subject: And although it may appear to be a little strained in some points, yet on the whole, I must confess, that it fully reconciles me to the scale of representation, which the Convention have established.

In one respect the establishment of a common measure for representation and taxation will have a very salutary effect. As the accuracy of the census to be obtained by the Congress, will necessarily depend in a considerable degree on the disposition, if not the co-operation of the States, it is of great importance that the States should feel as little bias as possible to swell or to reduce the amount of their numbers. Were their share of representation alone to be governed by this rule they would have an interest in exaggerating their inhabitants. Were the rule to decide their share of taxation alone, a contrary temptation would prevail. By extending the rule to both objects, the States will have opposite interests, which will controul and ballance each other; and produce the requisite impartiality.

PUBLIUS.

## The Federalist No. 55 [1]

By JAMES MADISON or ALEXANDER HAMILTON

[New York, February 13, 1788]

*To the People of the State of New-York.*

THE number of which the House of Representatives is to consist, forms another, and a very interesting point of view under which this branch of the federal legislature may be contemplated. Scarce

*The* [New York] *Independent Journal: or, the General Advertiser,* February 13, 1788. On February 15, this essay appeared in *The New-York Packet.* In the McLean edition this essay is numbered 55, in the newspapers it is numbered 54.

1. For background to this document, see "The Federalist. Introductory Note," October 27, 1787–May 28, 1788.

This essay was claimed by both H and Madison, but no scholar has been able to find convincing parallels between essay 55 and the earlier writings of either Madison or Hamilton. The most careful student of Madison's contribution to *The Federalist,* Edward G. Bourne ("The Authorship of the Federalist," *The American Historical Review,* II [April, 1897], 443–60) fails even to discuss the Virginian's authorship. J. C. Hamilton (*The Federalist,* I, cxxvii) points out several statements in essay 55 that are exactly similar to passages in H's notes for

any article indeed in the whole constitution seems to be rendered more worthy of attention, by the weight of character and the apparent force of argument, with which it has been assailed. The charges exhibited against it are, first, that so small a number of representatives will be an unsafe depositary of the public interests; secondly, that they will not possess a proper knowledge of the local circumstances of their numerous constituents; thirdly, that they will be taken from that class of citizens which will sympathize least with the feelings of the mass of the people, and be most likely to aim at a permanent elevation of the few on the depression of the many; fourthly, that defective as the number will be in the first instance, it will be more and more disproportionate, by the increase of the people, and the obstacles which will prevent a correspondent increase of the representatives.

In general it may be remarked on this subject, that no political problem is less susceptible of a precise solution, than that which relates to the number most convenient for a representative legislature: Nor is there any point on which the policy of the several states is more at variance; whether we compare their legislative assemblies directly with each other, or consider the proportions which they respectively bear to the number of their constituents. Passing over the difference between the smallest and largest states, as Delaware, whose most numerous branch consists of twenty-one representatives,

---

a speech before the New York Ratifying Convention on June 20, 1788. Since similarities between the later writings of either H or Madison and *The Federalist* prove little, as both men presumably read *all* the essays, J. C. Hamilton's evidence is unconvincing.

The only parallel between essay 55 and H's earlier writings which has been found is as follows:

| Essay 55 | H's Answer to Madison's Speech of June 6, 1787, before the Constitutional Convention |
|---|---|
| In all very numerous assemblies, of whatever characters composed, passion never fails to wrest the sceptre from reason. Had every Athenian been a Socrates; every Athenian assembly would still have been a mob. | The Assembly when chosen will meet in one room, if they are drawn from half the globe, & will be liable to all the passions of popular assemblies ("Constitutional Convention. Notes Taken in the Federal Convention," June 1–26, 1787). |

For the reasons why Madison's claim to the authorship of this essay outweighs (but does not necessarily obviate) that of H, see "The Federalist. Introductory Note," October 27, 1787–May 28, 1788.

and Massachusetts, where it amounts to between three and four hundred; a very considerable difference is observable among states nearly equal in population. The number of representatives in Pennsylvania is not more than one-fifth of that in the state last mentioned. New-York, whose population is to that of South-Carolina as six to five, has little more than one third of the number of representatives. As great a disparity prevails between the states of Georgia and Delaware, or Rhode-Island. In Pennsylvania the representatives do not bear a greater proportion to their constituents than of one for every four or five thousand. In Rhode-Island, they bear a proportion of at least one for every thousand. And according to the constitution of Georgia, the proportion may be carried to one for every ten electors; and must unavoidably far exceed the proportion in any of the other States.

Another general remark to be made is, that the ratio between the representatives and the people, ought not to be the same where the latter are very numerous, as where they are very few. Were the representatives in Virginia to be regulated by the standard in Rhode-Island, they would at this time amount to between four and five hundred; and twenty or thirty years hence, to a thousand. On the other hand, the ratio of Pennsylvania, if applied to the state of Delaware, would reduce the Representative assembly of the latter to seven or eight members. Nothing can be more fallacious than to found our political calculations on arithmetical principles. Sixty or seventy men, may be more properly trusted with a given degree of power than six or seven. But it does not follow, that six or seven hundred would be proportionally a better depositary. And if we carry on the supposition to six or seven thousand, the whole reasoning ought to be reversed. The truth is, that in all cases a certain number at least seems to be necessary to secure the benefits of free consultation and discussion, and to guard against too easy a combination for improper purposes: As on the other hand, the number ought at most to be kept within a certain limit, in order to avoid the confusion and intemperance of a multitude. In all very numerous assemblies, of whatever characters composed, passion never fails to wrest the sceptre from reason. Had every Athenian citizen been a Socrates; every Athenian assembly would still have been a mob.

It is necessary also to recollect here the observations which were applied to the case of biennial elections.[2] For the same reason that the limited powers of the Congress and the controul of the state legislatures, justify less frequent elections than the public safety might otherwise require; the members of the Congress need be less numerous than if they possessed the whole power of legislation, and were under no other than the ordinary restraints of other legislative bodies.

With these general ideas in our minds, let us weigh the objections which have been stated against the number of members proposed for the House of Representatives. It is said in the first place, that so small a number cannot be safely trusted with so much power.

The number of which this branch of the legislature is to consist at the outset of the government, will be sixty five. Within three years a census is to be taken, when the number may be augmented to one for every thirty thousand inhabitants; and within every successive period of ten years, the census is to be renewed, and augmentations may continue to be made under the above limitation. It will not be thought an extravagant conjecture, that the first census, will, at the rate of one for every thirty thousand raise the number of representatives to at least one hundred. Estimating the negroes in the proportion of three fifths, it can scarcely be doubted that the population of the United States will by that time, if it does not already, amount to three millions. At the expiration of twenty five years, according to the computed rate of increase, the number of representatives will amount to two hundred; and of fifty years to four hundred. This is a number which I presume will put an end to all fears arising from the smallness of the body. I take for granted here what I shall in answering the fourth objection hereafter shew, that the number of representatives will be augmented from time to time in the manner provided by the constitution. On a contrary supposition, I should admit the objection to have very great weight indeed.

The true question to be decided then is whether the smallness of the number, as a temporary regulation, be dangerous to the public liberty: Whether sixty five members for a few years, and a hundred or two hundred for a few more, be a safe depositary for a limited and well guarded power of legislating for the United States? I must own that I could not give a negative answer to this question, without

2. See essay 52.

first obliterating every impression which I have received with regard to the present genius of the people of America, the spirit, which actuates the state legislatures, and the principles which are incorporated with the political character of every class of citizens. I am unable to conceive that the people of America in their present temper, or under any circumstances which can speedily happen, will chuse, and every second year repeat the choice of sixty five or an hundred men, who would be disposed to form and pursue a scheme of tyranny or treachery. I am unable to conceive that the state legislatures which must feel so many motives to watch, and which possess so many means of counteracting the federal legislature, would fail either to detect or to defeat a conspiracy of the latter against the liberties of their common constituents. I am equally unable to conceive that there are at this time, or can be in any short time, in the United States any sixty five or an hundred men capable of recommending themselves to the choice of the people at large, who would either desire or dare within the short space of two years, to betray the solemn trust committed to them. What change of circumstances time and a fuller population of our country may produce, requires a prophetic spirit to declare, which makes no part of my pretensions. But judging from the circumstances now before us, and from the probable state of them within a moderate period of time, I must pronounce that the liberties of America can not be unsafe in the number of hands proposed by the federal constitution.

From what quarter can the danger proceed? Are we afraid of foreign gold? If foreign gold could so easily corrupt our federal rulers, and enable them to ensnare and betray their constituents, how has it happened that we are at this time a free and independent nation? The Congress which conducted us through the revolution were a less numerous body than their successors will be; they were not chosen by nor responsible to their fellow citizens at large; though appointed from year to year, and recallable at pleasure, they were generally continued for three years; and prior to the ratification of the federal articles, for a still longer term; they held their consultations always under the veil of secrecy; they had the sole transaction of our affairs with foreign nations; through the whole course of the war, they had the fate of their country more in their hands, than it is to be hoped will ever be the case with our future representatives; and from the greatness of the prize at stake and the eagerness of the party which lost it, it may well be supposed, that the use of other means than force would not have been scrupled; yet we know by happy experience that the public trust was not betrayed; nor has the purity of our public councils in this particular ever suffered even from the whispers of calumny.

Is the danger apprehended from the other branches of the federal government? But where are the means to be found by the President or the Senate, or both? Their emoluments of office it is to be presumed will not, and without a previous corruption of the house of representatives cannot, more than suffice for very different purposes: Their private fortunes, as they must all be American citizens, cannot possibly be sources of danger. The only means then which they can possess, will be in the dispensation of appointments. Is it here that suspicion rests her charge? Sometimes we are told that this fund of corruption is to be exhausted by the President in subduing the virtue of the Senate. Now the fidelity of the other house is to be the victim. The improbability of such a mercenary and perfidious combination of the several members of government standing on as different foundations as republican principles will well admit, and at the same time accountable to the society over which they are placed, ought alone to quiet this apprehension. But fortunately the constitution has provided a still further safeguard. The members of the Congress are rendered ineligible to any civil offices that may be created or of which the emoluments may be increased, during the term of their election. No offices therefore can be dealt out to the existing members, but such as may become vacant by ordinary casualties; and to suppose that these would be sufficient to purchase the guardians of the people, selected by the people themselves, is to renounce every rule by which events ought to be calculated, and to substitute an indiscriminate and unbounded jealousy, with which all reasoning must be vain. The sincere friends of liberty who give themselves up to the extravagancies of this passion are not aware of the injury they do their own cause. As there is a degree of depravity in mankind which requires a certain degree of circumspection and distrust: So there are other qualities in human nature, which justify a certain portion of esteem and confidence. Republican government presupposes the existence of these qualities in a higher degree than any other form. Were the pictures which have been drawn by the political jealousy of some among us, faithful likenesses of the human character, the inference would be that there is not sufficient virtue among men for self government; and that nothing less than the chains of despotism can restrain them from destroying and devouring one another.

PUBLIUS.

## The Federalist No. 56 [1]

### By JAMES MADISON or ALEXANDER HAMILTON

[New York, February 16, 1788]

*To the People of the State of New-York.*

THE *second* charge against the House of Representatives is, that it will be too small to possess a due knowledge of the interests of its constituents.

As this objection evidently proceeds from a comparison of the proposed number of representatives, with the great extent of the United States, the number of their inhabitants, and the diversity of their interests, without taking into view at the same time the circumstances which will distinguish the Congress from other legislative bodies, the best answer that can be given to it, will be a brief explanation of these peculiarities.

It is a sound and important principle that the representative ought to be acquainted with the interests and circumstances of his constituents. But this principle can extend no farther than to those circumstances and interests, to which the authority and care of the representative relate. An ignorance of a variety of minute and particular objects, which do not lie within the compass of legislation, is consistent with every attribute necessary to a due performance of the legislative trust. In determining the extent of information required in the exercise of a particular authority, recourse then must be had to the objects within the purview of that authority.

What are to be the objects of federal legislation? Those which are of most importance, and which seem most to require local knowledge, are commerce, taxation, and the militia.

A proper regulation of commerce requires much information, as has been elsewhere remarked; [2] but as far as this information relates to the laws and local situation of each individual state, a very few representatives would be very [3] sufficient vehicles of it to the federal councils.

Taxation will consist, in great measure, of duties which will be involved in the regulation of commerce. So far the preceding remark is applicable to this object. As far as it may consist of internal collections, a more diffusive knowledge of the circumstances of the state may be necessary. But will not this also be possessed in sufficient degree by a very few intelligent men diffusively elected within the state. Divide the largest state into ten or twelve districts, and it will be found that there will be no peculiar local interest in either, which will not be within the knowledge of the representative of the district. Besides this source of information, the laws of the state framed by representatives from every part of it, will be almost of themselves a sufficient guide. In every state there have been made, and must continue to be made, regulations on this subject, which will in many cases leave little more to be done by the federal legislature, than to review the different laws, and reduce them into one general act. A skilful individual in his closet, with all the local codes before him, might compile a law on some subjects of taxation for the whole union, without any aid from oral information; and it may be expected, that whenever internal taxes may be necessary, and particularly in cases requiring uniformity throughout the states, the more simple objects will be preferred. To be fully sensible of the facility which will be given to this branch of federal legislation, by the assistance of the state codes, we need only suppose for a moment, that this or any other state were divided into a number of parts, each having and exercising within itself a power of local legislation. Is it not evident that a degree of local information and preparatory labour would be found in the several volumes of their proceedings, which would very much shorten the labours of the general legislature, and render a much smaller number of members sufficient for it? The federal councils will derive great advantage from another circumstance. The representatives of each state will not only bring with them a considerable knowledge of its laws, and a local knowledge of their respective districts; but will probably in all cases have been members, and may even at the very time be members of the state legislature, where all the local information and interests of the state are assembled, and from whence they may easily be conveyed by a very few hands into the legislature of the United States.

The observations made on the subject of taxation apply with greater force to the case of the militia. For however different the rules of discipline may be in different states; They are the same throughout each particular state; and depend on circumstances which can differ but little in different parts of the same state.[4]

The attentive reader will discern that the reasoning here used to prove the sufficiency of a moderate number of representatives, does not in any respect contradict what was urged on another occasion with regard to the extensive information which the representatives ought to possess, and the time that might be necessary for acquiring it.[5] This information, so far as it may relate to local objects, is rendered necessary and difficult, not by a difference of laws and local circumstances within a single state; but of those among different states. Taking each state by itself, its laws are the same, and its interests but little diversified. A few men therefore will possess all the knowledge requisite for a proper representation of them. Were the interests and affairs of each individual state, perfectly simple and uniform, a knowledge of them in one part would involve a knowledge of them in every other, and the whole state might be competently represented, by a single member taken from any part of it. On a comparison of the different states together, we find a great dissimilarity in their laws, and in many other circumstances connected with the objects of federal legislation, with all of which the federal representatives ought to have some acquaintance. Whilst a few representatives therefore from each state may bring with them a due knowledge of their own state, every representative will have much information to acquire concerning all the other states. The changes of time, as was formerly remarked,[6] on the comparative situation of the different states, will have an assimilating effect.[7] The effect of time on the internal affairs of the states taken singly, will be just the contrary. At present some of the states are little more than a society of husbandmen. Few of them have made much progress in those branches of industry, which give a variety and complexity to the affairs of a nation. These however will in all of them be the fruits of a more advanced population; and will require on the part of each state a fuller representation. The foresight of the Convention has accordingly taken care that the progress of population may be accompanied with a proper increase of the representative branch of the government.

The experience of Great Britain which presents to mankind so many political lessons, both of the monitory and exemplary kind, and which has been frequently consulted in the course of these enquiries, corroborates the result of the reflections which we have just made. The number of inhabitants in the two kingdoms of England and Scotland, cannot be stated at less than eight millions. The representatives of these eight millions in the House of Commons, amount to five hundred fifty eight. Of this number one ninth are elected by three hundred and sixty four persons, and one half by five thousand seven hundred and twenty three persons.* It cannot be supposed that the half thus elected, and who do not even reside among the people at large, can add any thing either to the security of the people against the government; or to the knowledge of their circumstances and interests, in the legislative councils. On the contrary it is notorious that they are more frequently the representatives and instruments of the executive magistrate, than the guardians and advocates of the popular rights. They might therefore with great propriety be considered as something more than a mere deduction from the real representatives of the nation. We will however consider them, in this light alone, and will not extend the deduction, to a considerable number of others, who do not reside among their constituents, are very faintly connected with them, and have very little particular knowledge of their affairs. With all these concessions two hundred and seventy nine persons only will be the depository of the safety, interest and happiness of eight millions; that is to say: There will be one representative only to maintain the rights and explain the situation *of twenty eight thousand six hundred and seventy* constituents, in an assembly exposed to the whole force of executive influence, and extending its authority to every object of legislation within a nation whose affairs are in the highest degree

* Burgh's polit. disquis.[8]

diversified and complicated. Yet it is very certain not only that a valuable portion of freedom has been preserved under all these circumstances, but that the defects in the British code are chargeable in a very small proportion, on the ignorance of the legislature concerning the circumstances of the people. Allowing to this case the weight which is due to it: And comparing it with that of the House of Representatives as above explained, it seems to give the fullest assurance that a representative for every *thirty thousand inhabitants* will render the latter both a safe and competent guardian of the interests which will be confided to it.

PUBLIUS.

*The* [New York] *Independent Journal: or, the General Advertiser,* February 16, 1788. This essay appeared in *The New-York Packet* on February 19. In the McLean edition this essay is numbered 56, in the newspapers it is numbered 55.

1. For background to this document, see "The Federalist. Introductory Note," October 27, 1787–May 28, 1788.

Essay 56 is one of those disputed essays the authorship of which cannot be assigned on the basis of internal evidence to either Madison or H. Edward G. Bourne ("The Authorship of the Federalist," *The American Historical Review,* II [April, 1897], 453) gives the following example to demonstrate Madison's authorship:

| Essay 56 | Madison |
|---|---|
| Divide the largest state into ten or twelve districts, and it will be found that there will be no peculiar local interest in either, which will not be within the knowledge of the representative of the district. | [In the Virginia Convention, Madison said:] Could not ten intelligent men chosen from ten districts from this State lay direct taxes on a few objects in the most judicious manner? Can any one divide this state into ten districts so as not to contain men of sufficient information? |

Bourne argues that because the Constitution assigned Virginia ten representatives and New York six, Madison would be more likely than H to use the figure ten as an example. He further states that some months later in the New York Ratifying Convention H in illustrating the adequacy of the representation provided by the Constitution spoke of a state as being divided into six districts. The argument is not convincing because the author of essay 56 spoke of "ten or twelve districts" which might mean, using the same kind of logic employed by Bourne, that H, unlike Madison, did not remember the exact number of districts into which Virginia was divided; also, in the same paragraph in essay 56 it is stated, "suppose . . . that this or any other state were divided into a number of parts . . . ," a statement which suggests that the author arbitrarily had selected his figures. Bourne also adduces as evidence of Madison's authorship the fact that in the closing paragraph of this essay the word "monitory . . . almost a favorite word with Madison," is used. For an example of H's use of the same word, see note 36 to "The Federalist. Introductory Note," October 27, 1787–May 28, 1788.

J. C. Hamilton (*The Federalist*, I, cxxviii), also using internal evidence, gives the following example to prove that essay 56 was written by H:

| Essay 56 | Hamilton |
|---|---|
| What are to be the objects of federal legislation? Those which are of most importance, and which seem most to require local knowledge, are *commerce, taxation*, and *the militia* . . . the representatives of each State will not only bring with them, a considerable knowledge of its laws, and a *local knowledge* of their respective districts. | *Knowledge of local circumstances*— Objects to be considered: These— *Commerce-Taxation*. As to *taxation*— *State Systems* ("New York Ratifying Convention. Notes for a Speech," June 20, 1788). |

One might give as further evidence of H's authorship the fact that in revising the essays for publication by McLean he deleted paragraph seven and substituted another paragraph for it. Although in the McLean edition H occasionally altered or changed a word in Madison's essays, in no other instance did he make a major change. Had he not believed that he was the author of the essay, one might argue, it is unlikely he would have made the substitution.

As suggested by the research of Bourne and J. C. Hamilton, however, the evidence is contradictory. One could, for example, indicate passages that are remarkably similar to statements made by H in essay 36; one could, on the other hand, point out statements which are almost the same as statements made by Madison in essay 53. An example of these similarities follows:

| Essay 56 | Essay 36 [Hamilton] |
|---|---|
| As far as it may consist of internal collections, a more diffusive knowledge of the circumstances of the state may be necessary. But will not this also be possessed in sufficient degree by a very few intelligent men diffusively elected within the state. Divide the largest state into ten or twelve districts, and it will be found that there will be no peculiar local interest in either, which will not be within the knowledge of the representative of the district. | It has been asserted that a power of internal taxation in the national Legislature, could never be exercised with advantage, as well from the want of a sufficient knowledge of local circumstances, as from an interference between the revenue laws of the Union, and of the particular States. The supposition of a want of proper knowledge, seems to be entirely destitute of foundation. If any question is depending in a State Legislature, respecting one of the counties, which demands a knowledge of local details, how is it acquired? No doubt from the information of the members of the county. Cannot the like knowledge be obtained in the national Legislature, from the representatives of each State? |
| To be fully sensible of the facility which will be given to this branch of federal legislation, by the assistance of the state codes. . . . | there could be no difficulty in ascertaining the revenue system of each. This could always be known from the respective codes of laws. |

Essay 56 | Essay 53 [Madison]

Were the interests and affairs of each individual state, perfectly simple and uniform, a knowledge of them in one part would involve a knowledge of them in every other, and the whole state might be competently represented, by a single member taken from any part of it. On a comparison of the different states together, we find a great dissimilarity in their laws, and in many other circumstances connected with the objects of federal legislation, with all of which the federal representatives ought to have some acquaintance. Whilst a few representatives therefore from each state may bring with them a due knowledge of their own state, every representative will have much information to acquire concerning all the other states.

In a single state the requisite knowledge, relates to the existing laws which are uniform throughout the state, and with which all the citizens are more or less conversant; and to the general affairs of the state, which lie within a small compass, are not very diversified, and occupy much of the attention and conversation of every class of people. The great theatre of the United States presents a very different scene. The laws are so far from being uniform, that they vary in every state; whilst the public affairs of the union are spread throughout a very extensive region, and are extremely diversified by the local affairs connected with them, and can with difficulty be correctly learnt in any other place, than in the central councils, to which a knowledge of them will be brought by the representatives of every part of the empire.

[Speaking of knowledge requisite for enactment of national taxes:] A skilful individual in his closet, with all the local codes before him. . . .

[Speaking of knowledge requisite for legislation on foreign affairs:] Some portion of this knowledge may, no doubt, be acquired in a man's closet.

The changes of time, as was formerly remarked, on the comparative situation of the different states, will have an assimilating effect.

It is true that all these difficulties will, by degrees, be very much diminished.

Examples might be multiplied, but they would all lead to the same question: Did Madison borrow from essay 36, or did H borrow from essay 53? The question, it seems, is not susceptible of an answer. Both Bourne and Douglass Adair ("The Authorship of the Disputed Federalist Papers," Part II, *The William and Mary Quarterly*, I [July, 1944], 260) give as evidence for Madison's authorship a reference to James Burgh's *Political Disquisitions*. They argue that because the Virginian took notes from Burgh in his "Additional Memorandum for the Convention of Virginia" (Madison, *Letters*, I, 393, note), and because no reference to Burgh can be found in the writings of H, Madison must have written essay 56. The argument is based on the erroneous assumption that because H did not again refer to Burgh in other writings he could not have read him. In the first place, there is no positive evidence that H had not read Burgh and, in the second place, H referred in *The Federalist* to many authors who are not mentioned in his other writings. For example, in essay 71, definitely written by H, there is a reference to "the celebrated Junius," the famous English letter writer of the eighteenth century. So far as can be determined, H made no other reference to Junius.

Since one can demonstrate the authorship of either man by carefully looking for parallels in his other writings, it is obvious that internal evidence cannot decide the problem of authorship. For the reasons why Madison's claim to the

authorship of this essay outweighs (but does not necessarily obviate) that of H, see "The Federalist. Introductory Note," October 27, 1787–May 28, 1788.
2. See essay 53.
3. "very" omitted in Hopkins.
4. The following was substituted in McLean and Hopkins for this paragraph: "With regard to the regulation of the militia, there are scarcely any circumstances in reference to which local knowledge can be said to be necessary. The general face of the country, whether mountainous or level, most fit for the operations of infantry or cavalry, is almost the only consideration of this nature that can occur. The art of war teaches general principles of organization, movement, and discipline, which apply universally."
5. See essay 53.
6. See essay 53.
7. "tendency" substituted for "effect" in Hopkins.
8. The reference is to James Burgh, *Political Disquisitions: Or, an Enquiry into public Errors, Defects, and Abuses* . . . (London, 1774), I, 45, 48.

# *The Federalist No. 57* [1]

## By JAMES MADISON *or* ALEXANDER HAMILTON

[New York, February 19, 1788]

*To the People of the State of New-York.*

THE *third* charge against the House of Representatives is, that it will be taken from that class of citizens which will have least sympathy with the mass of the people, and be most likely to aim at an ambitious sacrifice of the many to the aggrandizement of the few.

*The New-York Packet*, February 19, 1788. This essay appeared in *The* [New York] *Independent Journal: or, the General Advertiser* on February 20. In the McLean edition this essay is numbered 57, in the newspapers it is numbered 56.
1. For background to this document see "The Federalist. Introductory Note." October 27, 1787–May 28, 1788.
Essay 57 was claimed by H and Madison. No Madison scholar has presented internal evidence to demonstrate his authorship; J. C. Hamilton (*The Federalist,* I, cxxviii, cxxix) found several statements in essay 57 that are similar to statements in H's notes for his speech before the New York Ratifying Convention on June 20, 1788. They are as follows:

| Essay 57 | Hamilton |
|---|---|
| Let me now ask, what there is in the Constitution of the House of Representatives, that violates the principles of republican government, or favors the elevation of the few on the ruins of the many? . . . Who are to be the electors? . . . Not the rich more than the poor. . . . No qualification of wealth, of birth. | Elevation of few. First—No qualifications either for electors or elected. |

Of all the objections which have been framed against the Fœderal Constitution, this is perhaps the most extraordinary. Whilst the objection itself is levelled against a pretended oligarchy, the principle of it strikes at the very root of republican government.

The aim of every political Constitution is or ought to be first to obtain for rulers, men who possess most wisdom to discern, and most virtue to pursue the common good of the society; and in the next place, to take the most effectual precautions for keeping them virtuous, whilst they continue to hold their public trust. The elective mode of obtaining rulers is the characteristic policy of republican government. The means relied on in this form of government for preventing their degeneracy are numerous and various. The most effectual one is such a limitation of the term of appointments, as will maintain a proper responsibility to the people.

Let me now ask what circumstance [2] there is in the Constitution of the House of Representatives, that violates the principles of republican government; or favors the elevation of the few on the ruins of the many? Let me ask whether every circumstance is not, on the contrary, strictly conformable to these principles; and scrupulously impartial to the rights and pretensions of every class and description of citizens?

| | |
|---|---|
| This cannot be said without maintaining that five or six thousand citizens are less capable of chusing a fit representative, or more liable to be corrupted by an unfit one, than five or six hundred. | Five Thousand no less fit to choose than five hundred—not so easily corrupted. |

However striking the similarity, the evidence is subject to the important qualification that H's remarks at the New York Ratifying Convention were made four months after essay 57 was written. Whether he borrowed from Madison or remembered what he had written earlier is an open question.

J. C. Hamilton also gives as evidence of Hamilton's authorship the following statement from essay 57: "The members of Assembly, for the *cities* and *counties* of New York and Albany, are *elected* by very nearly as many *voters* as will be entitled to a representative in Congress, calculating on the number of sixty five representatives only." He argues that H would have been more likely to have had this information and to have used it as an illustration than would Madison.

Internal evidence thus suggests H's authorship; but because the evidence is weak and because parallels between statements in essay 57 and Madison's writings might be found by an assiduous search, it should not be relied on. In addition, external evidence—the lists made or allegedly made by the two men—supports (but does not conclusively demonstrate) Madison's claim.

2. "circumstance" omitted in Hopkins.

Who are to be the electors of the Fœderal Representatives? Not the rich more than the poor; not the learned more than the ignorant; not the haughty heirs of distinguished names, more than the humble sons of obscure and unpropitious fortune. The electors are to be the great body of the people of the United States. They are to be the same who exercise the right in every State of electing the correspondent branch of the Legislature of the State.

Who are to be the objects of popular choice? Every citizen whose merit may recommend him to the esteem and confidence of his country. No qualification of wealth, of birth, of religious faith, or of civil profession, is permitted to fetter the judgment or disappoint the inclination of the people.

If we consider the situation of the men on whom the free suffrages of their fellow citizens may confer the representative trust, we shall find it involving every security which can be devised or desired for their fidelity to their constituents.

In the first place, as they will have been distinguished by the preference of their fellow citizens, we are to presume, that in general, they will be somewhat distinguished also, by those qualities which entitle them to it, and which promise a sincere and scrupulous regard to the nature of their engagements.

In the second place, they will enter into the public service under circumstances which cannot fail to produce a temporary affection at least to their constituents. There is in every breast a sensibility to marks of honor, of favor, of esteem, and of confidence, which, apart from all considerations of interest, is some pledge for grateful and benevolent returns. Ingratitude is a common topic of declamation against human nature; and it must be confessed, that instances of it are but too frequent and flagrant both in public and in private life. But the universal and extreme indignation which it inspires, is itself a proof of the energy and prevalence of the contrary sentiment.

In the third place, these [3] ties which bind the representative to his constituents are strengthened by motives of a more selfish nature. His pride and vanity attach him to a form of government which favors his pretensions, and gives him a share in its honors and distinctions. Whatever hopes or projects might be entertained by a

3. "those" substituted for "these" in McLean and Hopkins.

few aspiring characters, it must generally happen that a great proportion of the men deriving their advancement from their influence with the people, would have more to hope from a preservation of the [4] favor, than from innovations in the government subversive of the authority of the people.

All these securities however would be found very insufficient without the restraint of frequent elections. Hence, in the fourth place, the House of Representatives is so constituted as to support in the members an habitual recollection of their dependence on the people. Before the sentiments impressed on their minds by the mode of their elevation, can be effaced by the exercise of power, they will be compelled to anticipate the moment when their power is to cease, when their exercise of it is to be reviewed, and when they must descend to the level from which they were raised; there for ever to remain, unless a faithful discharge of their trust shall have established their title to a renewal of it.

I will add as a fifth circumstance in the situation of the House of Representatives, restraining them from oppressive measures, that they can make no law which will not have its full operation on themselves and their friends, as well as on the great mass of the society. This has always been deemed one of the strongest bonds by which human policy can connect the rulers and the people together. It creates between them that communion of interests and sympathy of sentiments of which few governments have furnished examples; but without which every government degenerates into tyranny. If it be asked what is to restrain the House of Representatives from making legal discriminations in favor of themselves and a particular class of the society? I answer, the genius of the whole system, the nature of just and constitutional laws, and above all the vigilant and manly spirit which actuates the people of America, a spirit which nourishes freedom, and in return is nourished by it.

If this spirit shall ever be so far debased as to tolerate a law not obligatory on the Legislature as well as on the people, the people will be prepared to tolerate anything but liberty.

Such will be the relation between the House of Representatives and their constituents. Duty, gratitude, interest, ambition itself, are the chords by which they will be bound to fidelity and sympathy

4. "their" substituted for "the" in Hopkins.

with the great mass of the people. It is possible that these may all be insufficient to controul the caprice and wickedness of man. But are they not all that government will admit, and that human prudence can devise? Are they not the genuine and the characteristic means by which Republican Government provides for the liberty and happiness of the people? Are they not the identical means on which every State Government in the Union, relies for the attainment of these important ends? What then are we to understand by the objection which this paper has combatted? What are we to say to the men who profess the most flaming zeal for Republican Government, yet boldly impeach the fundamental principle of it; who pretend to be champions for the right and the capacity of the people to chuse their own rulers, yet maintain that they will prefer those only who will immediately and infallibly betray the trust committed to them?

Were the objection to be read by one who had not seen the mode prescribed by the Constitution for the choice of representatives, he could suppose nothing less than that some unreasonable qualification of property was annexed to the right of suffrage; or that the right of eligibility was limited to persons of particular families or fortunes; or at least that the mode prescribed by the State Constitutions was in some respect or other very grossly departed from. We have seen how far such a supposition would err as to the two first points. Nor would it in fact be less erroneous as to the last. The only difference discoverable between the two cases, is, that each representative of the United States will be elected by five or six thousand citizens; whilst in the individual States the election of a representative is left to about as many hundred. Will it be pretended that this difference is sufficient to justify an attachment to the State Governments and an abhorrence to the Fœderal Government? If this be the point on which the objection turns, it deserves to be examined.

Is it supported by *reason?* This cannot be said, without maintaining that five or six thousand citizens are less capable of chusing a fit representative, or more liable to be corrupted by an unfit one, than five or six hundred. Reason, on the contrary assures us, that as in so great a number, a fit representative would be most likely to be found, so the choice would be less likely to be diverted from him, by the intrigues of the ambitious, or the bribes of the rich.

Is the *consequence* from this doctrine admissible? If we say that

five or six hundred citizens are as many as can jointly exercise
their right of suffrage, must we not deprive the people of the immediate choice of their public servants in every instance where the
administration of the government does not require as many of them
as will amount to one for that number of citizens?

Is the doctrine warranted by *facts?* It was shewn in the last
paper, that the real representation in the British House of Commons
very little exceeds the proportion of one for every thirty thousand
inhabitants. Besides a variety of powerful causes, not existing here,
and which favor in that country, the pretensions of rank and wealth,
no person is eligible as a representative of a county, unless he possess
real estate of the clear value of six hundred pounds sterling per year;
nor of a city or borough, unless he possess a like estate of half that
annual value. To this qualification on the part of the county representatives, is added another on the part of the county electors,
which restrains the right of suffrage to persons having a freehold
estate of the annual value of more than twenty pounds sterling according to the present rate of money. Notwithstanding these unfavorable circumstances, and notwithstanding some very unequal
laws in the British code, it cannot be said that the representatives
of the nation have elevated the few on the ruins of the many.

But we need not resort to foreign experience on this subject. Our
own is explicit and decisive. The districts in New-Hampshire in
which the Senators are chosen immediately by the people are nearly
as large as will be necessary for her representatives in the Congress.
Those of Massachusetts are larger, than will be necessary for that
purpose. And those of New-York still more so. In the last State
the members of Assembly, for the cities and counties of New-York
and Albany, are elected by very nearly as many voters, as will be
entitled to a representative in the Congress, calculating on the number of sixty-five representatives only. It makes no difference that in
these senatorial districts and counties, a number of representatives
are voted for by each elector at the same time. If the same electors,
at the same time are capable of choosing four or five representatives,
they cannot be incapable of choosing one. Pennsylvania is an additional example. Some of her counties which elect her State representatives, are almost as large as her districts will be by which her
Fœderal Representatives will be elected. The city of Philadelphia

is supposed to contain between fifty and sixty thousand souls. It will therefore form nearly two districts for the choice of Fœderal Representatives. It forms however but one county, in which every elector votes for each of its representatives in the State Legislature. And what may appear to be still more directly to our purpose, the whole city actually elects a *single member* for the executive council. This is the case in all the other counties of the State.

Are not these facts the most satisfactory proofs of the fallacy which has been employed against the branch of the Fœderal Government under consideration? Has it appeared on trial that the Senators of New-Hampshire, Massachusetts, and New-York; or the Executive Council of Pennsylvania; or the members of the Assembly in the two last States, have betrayed any peculiar disposition to sacrifice the many to the few; or are in any respect less worthy of their places than the representatives and magistrates appointed in other States, by very small divisions of the people?

But there are cases of a stronger complexion than any which I have yet quoted. One branch of the Legislature of Connecticut is so constituted that each member of it is elected by the whole State. So is the Governor of that State, of Massachusetts, and of this State, and the President of New-Hampshire. I leave every man to decide whether the result of any one of these experiments can be said to countenance a suspicion that a diffusive mode of chusing representatives of the people tends to elevate traitors, and to undermine the public liberty.

PUBLIUS.

## The Federalist No. 58 [1]

By JAMES MADISON *or* ALEXANDER HAMILTON

[New York, February 20, 1788]

*To the People of the State of New-York.*

THE remaining charge against the House of Representatives which I am to examine, is grounded on a supposition that the number of members will not be augmented from time to time, as the progress of population may demand.

It has been admitted that this objection, if well supported, would have great weight. The following observations will shew that like most other objections against the constitution, it can only proceed from a partial view of the subject; or from a jealousy which discolours and disfigures every object which is beheld.[2]

1. Those who urge the objection seem not to have recollected that the federal constitution will not suffer by a comparison with the state constitutions, in the security provided for a gradual augmentation of the number of representatives. The number which is to prevail in the first instance is declared to be temporary. Its duration is limited to the short term of three years.

Within every successive term of ten years, a census of inhabitants is to be repeated. The unequivocal objects of these regulations are, first, to readjust from time to time the apportionment of representatives to the number of inhabitants; under the single exception that each state shall have one representative at least; Secondly, to augment the number of representatives at the same periods; under the sole

The [New York] Independent Journal: or, the General Advertiser, February 20, 1788. This essay appeared on February 22 in The New-York Packet. In the McLean edition this essay is numbered 58, in the newspapers it is numbered 57.

1. For background to this document, see "The Federalist. Introductory Note," October 27, 1787–May 28, 1788.

The authorship of essay 58, like that of the preceding seven essays, has been disputed for a century and a half. No student of The Federalist has found internal evidence pointing to the authorship of either man. Bourne ("The Authorship of the Federalist," The American Historical Review, II [April, 1897], 443–60) gives no evidence to prove Madison's authorship, and J. C. Hamilton (The Federalist, I, cxxix) gives only one piece of evidence which points up similarities between essay 58 and the notes that H made for his speech before the New York Ratifying Convention, June 20, 1788. The author of essay 58 answers a supposition "that the number of members of the House of Representatives, will not be augmented from time to time, as the progress of population may demand" and infers "that the larger States will be strenuous advocates for increasing the number and weight of that part of the legislature in which their influence predominates." In notes prepared for his use for his speech before the New York Ratifying Convention, H wrote: "Numbers will not be augmented. Large States to increase influence will be for increasing representatives." (See "New York Ratifying Convention. Notes for a Speech," June 20, 1788.) The evidence is unconvincing, because any man of the time, not only H, might have made the statement which J. C. Hamilton quotes from essay 58, and because H's notes were made four months after the essay was written.

For the reasons why Madison's claim to the authorship of this essay outweighs (but does not necessarily obviate) that of H, see "The Federalist. Introductory Note," October 27, 1787–May 28, 1788.

2. "it beholds" substituted for "is beheld" in Hopkins.

limitation, that the whole number shall not exceed one for every thirty thousand inhabitants. If we review the constitutions of the several states, we shall find that some of them contain no determinate regulations on this subject; that others correspond pretty much on this point with the federal constitution; and that the most effectual security in any of them is resolvable into a mere directory provision.

2. As far as experience has taken place on this subject, a gradual increase of representatives under the state constitutions, has at least kept pace with that of the constituents; and it appears that the former have been as ready to concur in such measures, as the latter have been to call for them.

3. There is a peculiarity in the federal constitution which ensures a watchful attention in a majority both of the people and of their representatives, to a constitutional augmentation of the latter. The peculiarity lies in this, that one branch of the legislature is a representation of citizens; the other of the states: in the former consequently the larger states will have most weight; in the latter, the advantage will be in favour of the smaller states. From this circumstance it may with certainty be inferred, that the larger states will be strenuous advocates for increasing the number and weight of that part of the legislature in which their influence predominates. And it so happens that four only of the largest, will have a majority of the whole votes in the house of representatives. Should the representatives or people therefore of the smaller states oppose at any time a reasonable addition of members, a coalition of a very few states will be sufficient to overrule the opposition; a coalition, which notwithstanding the rivalship and local prejudices which might prevent it on ordinary occasions, would not fail to take place, when not merely prompted [3] by common interest, but justified by equity and the principles of the constitution.

It may be alledged, perhaps, that the senate would be prompted by like motives to an adverse coalition; and as their concurrence would be indispensable, the just and constitutional views of the other branch might be defeated. This is the difficulty which has probably created the most serious apprehensions in the jealous friends of a numerous

3. "upon" inserted here in the newspaper; it was omitted in McLean and Hopkins.

representation. Fortunately it is among the difficulties which, existing only in appearance, vanish on a close and accurate inspection. The following reflections will, if I mistake not, be admitted to be conclusive and satisfactory on this point.

Notwithstanding the equal authority which will subsist between the two houses on all legislative subjects, except the originating of money bills, it cannot be doubted that the house composed of the greater number of members,[4] when supported by the more powerful states, and speaking the known and determined sense of a majority of the people, will have no small advantage in a question depending on the comparative firmness of the two houses.

This advantage must be increased by the consciousness felt by the same side, of being supported in its demands, by right, by reason, and by the constitution; and the consciousness on the opposite side, of contending against the force of all these solemn considerations.

It is farther to be considered that in the gradation between the smallest and largest states, there are several which, though most likely in general to arrange themselves among the former, are too little removed in extent and population from the latter, to second an opposition to their just and legitimate pretensions. Hence it is by no means certain that a majority of votes, even in the senate, would be unfriendly to proper augmentations in the number of representatives.

It will not be looking too far to add, that the senators from all the new states may be gained over to the just views of the house of representatives, by an expedient too obvious to be overlooked. As these states will for a great length of time advance in population with peculiar rapidity, they will be interested in frequent reapportionments of the representatives to the number of inhabitants. The large states therefore, who will prevail in the house of representatives, will have nothing to do, but to make reapportionments and augmentations mutually conditions of each other; and the senators from all the most growing states will be bound to contend for the latter, by the interest which their states will feel in the former.

These considerations seem to afford ample security on this subject, and ought alone to satisfy all the doubts and fears which have been indulged with regard to it. Admitting however that, they should all be insufficient to subdue the unjust policy of the smaller states, or

4. "numbers" substituted for "number of members" in Hopkins.

their predominant influence in the councils of the senate; a constitutional and infallible resource, still remains with the larger states,
by which they will be able at all times to accomplish their just
purposes. The house of representatives can not only refuse, but they
alone can propose the supplies requisite for the support of government. They in a word hold the purse; that powerful instrument by
which we behold in the history of the British constitution, an infant
and humble representation of the people, gradually enlarging the
sphere of its activity and importance, and finally reducing, as far
as it seems to have wished, all the overgrown prerogatives of the
other branches of the government. This power over the purse, may
in fact be regarded as the most compleat and effectual weapon with
which any constitution can arm the immediate representatives of
the people, for obtaining a redress of every grievance, and for
carrying into effect every just and salutary measure.

But will not the house of representatives be as much interested
as the senate in maintaining the government in its proper functions,
and will they not therefore be unwilling to stake its existence or [5]
its reputation on the pliancy of the senate? Or if such a trial of
firmness between the two branches were hazarded, would not the
one be as likely first to yield as the other? These questions will create
no difficulty with those who reflect, that in all cases the smaller the
number and the more permanent and conspicuous the station of
men in power, the stronger must be the interest which they will
individually feel in whatever concerns the government. Those who
represent the dignity of their country in the eyes of other nations,
will be particularly sensible to every prospect of public danger, or
of a dishonorable stagnation in public affairs. To those causes we
are to ascribe the continual triumph of the British house of commons
over the other branches of the government, whenever the engine
of a money bill has been employed. An absolute inflexibility on the
side of the latter, although it could not have failed to involve every
department of the state in the general confusion, has neither been
apprehended nor experienced. The utmost degree of firmness that
can be displayed by the federal senate or president will not be more
than equal to a resistance in which they will be supported by constitutional and patriotic principles.

5. "for" substituted for "or" in McLean.

In this review of the constitution of the house of representatives, I have passed over the circumstance of economy which in the present state of affairs might have had some effect in lessening the temporary number of representatives; and a disregard of which would probably have been as rich a theme of declamation against the constitution as has been furnished by the smallness of the number proposed. I omit also any remarks on the difficulty which might be found, under present circumstances, in engaging in the federal service, a large number of such characters as the people will probably elect. One observation however I must be permitted, to add, on this subject, as claiming in my judgment a very serious attention. It is, that in all legislative assemblies, the greater the number composing them may be, the fewer will be the men who will in fact direct their proceedings. In the first place, the more numerous any assembly may be, of whatever characters composed, the greater is known to be the ascendancy of passion over reason. In the next place, the larger the number, the greater will be the proportion of members of limited information and of weak capacities. Now it is precisely on characters of this description that the eloquence and address of the few are known to act with all their force. In the antient republics, where the whole body of the people assembled in person, a single orator, or an artful statesman, was generally seen to rule with as compleat a sway, as if a sceptre had been placed in his single hands. On the same principle the more multitudinous a representative assembly may be rendered, the more it will partake of the infirmities incident to collective meetings of the people. Ignorance will be the dupe of cunning; and passion the slave of sophistry and declamation. The people can never err more than in supposing that by multiplying their representatives, beyond a certain limit, they strengthen the barrier against the government of a few. Experience will forever admonish them that on the contrary, *after securing a sufficient number for the purposes of safety, of local information, and of diffusive sympathy with the whole society*, they will counteract their own views by every addition to their representatives. The countenance of the government may become more democratic; but the soul that animates it will be more oligarchic. The machine will be enlarged, but the fewer and often, the more secret will be the springs by which its motions are directed.

As connected with the objection against the number of representatives, may properly be here noticed, that which has been suggested against the number made competent for legislative business.
It has been said that more than a majority ought to have been required for a quorum, and in particular cases, if not in all, more than
a majority of a quorum for a decision. That some advantages might
have resulted from such a precaution, cannot be denied. It might
have been an additional shield to some particular interests, and
another obstacle generally to hasty and partial measures. But these
considerations are outweighed by the inconveniencies in the opposite scale. In all cases where justice or the general good might require new laws to be passed, or active measures to be pursued, the
fundamental principle of free government would be reversed. It
would be no longer the majority that would rule; the power would
be transferred to the minority. Were the defensive privilege limited
to particular cases, an interested minority might take advantage of
it to screen themselves from equitable sacrifices to the general weal,
or in particular emergencies to extort unreasonable indulgences.
Lastly, it would facilitate and foster the baneful practice of seces-
sions; a practice which has shewn itself even in states where a majority
only is required; a practice subversive of all the principles of order
and regular government; a practice which leads more directly to
public convulsions, and the ruin of popular governments, than any
other which has yet been displayed among us.

PUBLIUS.

## Account with James Robinson

*New York, February 22, 1788–October 19, 1790.* An account of
carpentry work done by Robinson for Hamilton. The bill totals
£51.4.1.

D, Hamilton Papers, Library of Congress.

## The Federalist No. 59 [1]

[New York, February 22, 1788]

*To the People of the State of New-York.*

THE natural order of the subject leads us to consider in this place, that provision of the Constitution which authorises the national Legislature to regulate in the last resort the election of its own members. It is in these words—"The *times, places* and *manner* of holding elections for Senators and Representatives, shall be prescribed in each State by the Legislature thereof; but the Congress may at any time by law, make or alter *such regulations* except as to [2] *places* of choosing senators." * This provision has not only been declaimed against by those who condemn the Constitution in the gross; but it has been censured by those, who have objected with less latitude and greater moderation; and in one instance, it has been thought exceptionable by a gentleman who has declared himself the advocate of every other part of the system.

I am greatly mistaken, notwithstanding, if there be any article in the whole plan more completely defensible than this. Its propriety rests upon the evidence of this plain proposition, that *every government ought to contain in itself the means of its own preservation.* Every just reasoner will at first sight, approve an adherence to this rule, in the work of the Convention; and will disapprove every deviation from it, which may not appear to have been dictated by the necessity of incorporating into the work some particular ingredient, with which a rigid conformity to the rule was incompatible. Even in this case, though he may acquiesce in the necessity; yet he will not cease to regard [3] a departure from so fundamental a principle, as a portion of imperfection in the system which may prove the seed of future weakness and perhaps anarchy.

It will not be alledged that an election law could have been framed and inserted into [4] the Constitution, which would have been always [5] applicable to every probable change in the situation of the country; and it will therefore not be denied that a discretionary power over

* I Clause, 4 Sect. of the Ist Art.

*The New-York Packet*, February 22, 1788. This essay was printed in *The* [New York] *Independent Journal: or, the General Advertiser* on February 23. In the McLean edition this essay is numbered 59, and in the newspapers it is numbered 58.

    1. For background to this document, see "The Federalist. Introductory Note," October 27, 1787–May 28, 1788.

    2. "the" inserted in the newspapers; it was omitted in McLean and Hopkins.

    3. "and to regret" inserted at this point in the newspaper; it was omitted in McLean and Hopkins.

    4. "in" substituted for "into" in Hopkins.

    5. "always" omitted in McLean and Hopkins.

elections ought to exist somewhere. It will, I presume, be as readily conceded, that there were only three ways, in which this power could have been reasonably modified and disposed,[6] that it must either have been lodged wholly in the National Legislature, or wholly in the State Legislatures, or primarily in the latter, and ultimately in the former. The last mode has with reason been preferred by the Convention. They have submitted the regulation of elections for the Fœderal Government in the first instance to the local administrations; which in ordinary cases, and when no improper views prevail, may be both more convenient and more satisfactory; but they have reserved to the national authority a right to interpose, whenever extraordinary circumstances might render that interposition necessary to its safety.

Nothing can be more evident, than that an exclusive power of regulating elections for the National Government, in the hands of the State Legislatures, would leave the existence of the Union entirely at their mercy. They could at any moment annihilate it, by neglecting to provide for the choice of persons to administer its affairs. It is to little purpose to say that a neglect or omission of this kind, would not be likely to take place. The constitutional possibility of the thing, without an equivalent for the risk, is an unanswerable objection. Nor has any satisfactory reason been yet assigned for incurring that risk. The extravagant surmises of a distempered jealousy can never be dignified with that character. If we are in a humour to presume abuses of power, it is as fair to presume them on the part of the State Governments, as on the part of the General Government. And as it is more consonant to the rules of a just theory to intrust the Union with the care of its own existence, than to transfer that care to any other hands; if abuses of power are to be hazarded, on the one side, or on the other, it is more rational to hazard them where the power would naturally be placed, than where it would unnaturally be placed.

Suppose an article had been introduced into the Constitution, empowering the United States to regulate the elections for the particular States, would any man have hesitated to condemn it, both as an unwarrantable transposition of power, and as a premeditated engine for the destruction of the State governments? The violation

6. "organized" substituted for "modified and disposed" in Hopkins.

of principle in this case would have required no comment; and to an unbiassed observer, it will not be less apparent in the project of subjecting the existence of the National Government, in a similar respect to the pleasure of the State governments. An impartial view of the matter cannot fail to result in a conviction, that each, as far as possible, ought to depend on itself for its own preservation.

As an objection to this position, it may be remarked, that the Constitution of the national Senate, would involve in its full extent the danger which it is suggested might flow from an exclusive power in the State Legislatures to regulate the fœderal elections. It may be alledged, that by declining the appointment of Senators they might at any time give a fatal blow to the Union; and from this, it may be inferred, that as its existence would be thus rendered dependent upon them in so essential a point, there can be no objection to entrusting them with it, in the particular case under consideration. The interest of each State, it may be added, to maintain its representation in the national councils, would be a complete security against an abuse of the trust.

This argument though specious, will not upon examination be found solid. It is certainly true, that the State Legislatures, by forbearing the appointment of Senators, may destroy the National Government. But it will not follow, that because they have the power to do this in one instance, they ought to have it in every other. There are cases in which the pernicious tendency of such a power may be far more decisive, without any motive,[7] equally cogent with that which must have regulated the conduct of the Convention, in respect to the construction of the Senate, to recommend their admission into the system.[8] So far as that construction [9] may expose the Union to the possibility of injury from the State Legislatures, it is an evil; but it is an evil, which could not have been avoided without excluding the States, in their political capacities, wholly from a place in the organization of the National Government. If this had been done, it would doubtless have been interpreted into an entire dereliction of the fœderal principle; and would certainly have deprived the State governments of that absolute safe-guard, which

7. "to recommend their admission into the system" inserted here in Hopkins.
8. "to recommend their admission into the system" omitted in Hopkins.
9. "mode of formation" substituted for "construction" in Hopkins.

they will enjoy under this provision. But however wise it may have been, to have submitted in this instance to an inconvenience, for the attainment of a necessary advantage, or a greater good, no inference can be drawn from thence to favor an accumulation of the evil, where no necessity urges, nor any greater good invites.

It may easily be discerned also,[10] that the National Government would run a much greater risk from a power in the State Legislatures over the elections of its House of Representatives, than from their power of appointing the members of its Senate. The Senators are to be chosen for the period of six years; there is to be a rotation, by which the seats of a third part of them are to be vacated, and replenished every two years; and no State is to be entitled to more than two Senators: A quorum of the body is to consist of sixteen members. The joint result of these circumstances would be, that a temporary combination of a few States, to intermit the appointment of Senators, could neither annul the existence nor impair the activity of the body: And it is not from a general or permanent combination of the States, that we can have any thing to fear. The first might proceed from sinister designs in the leading members of a few of the State Legislatures; the last would suppose a fixed and rooted disaffection in the great body of the people; which will either never exist at all, or will in all probability proceed from an experience of the inaptitude of the General Government to the advancement of their happiness; in which event no good citizen could desire its continuance.

But with regard to the Fœderal House of Representatives, there is intended to be a general election of members once in two years. If the State Legislatures were to be invested with an exclusive power of regulating these elections, every period of making them would be a delicate crisis in the national situation; which might issue in a dissolution of the Union, if the leaders of a few of the most important States should have entered into a previous conspiracy to prevent an election.

I shall not deny that there is a degree of weight in the observation, that the interest of each State to be represented in the fœderal councils will be a security against the abuse of a power over its

10. "It may also be easily discerned," substituted for "It may easily be discerned, also" in Hopkins.

elections in the hands of the State Legislatures. But the security will not be considered as complete, by those who attend to the force of an obvious distinction between the interest of the people in the public felicity, and the interest of their local rulers in the power and consequence of their offices. The people of America may be warmly attached to the government of the Union at times, when the particular rulers of particular States, stimulated by the natural rivalship of power and by the hopes of personal aggrandisement, and supported by a strong faction in each of those States, may be in a very opposite temper. This diversity of sentiment, between a majority of the people and the individuals who have the greatest credit in their councils, is exemplified in some of the States, at the present moment, on the present question. The scheme of separate confederacies, which will always multiply the chances of ambition, will be a never failing bait to all such influential characters in the State administrations as are capable of preferring their own emolument and advancement to the public weal; with so effectual a weapon in their hands as the exclusive power of regulating elections for the National Government a combination of a few such men, in a few of the most considerable States, where the temptation will always be the strongest, might accomplish the destruction of the Union, by seizing the opportunity of some casual dissatisfaction among the people (and which perhaps they may themselves have excited) to discontinue the choice of members for the Fœderal House of Representatives. It ought never to be forgotten, that a firm Union of this country, under an efficient government, will probably be an encreasing object of jealousy to more than one nation of Europe; and that enterprises to subvert it will sometimes originate in the intrigues of foreign powers, and will seldom fail to be patronised and abetted by some of them. Its preservation therefore ought in no case, that can be avoided, to be committed to the guardianship of any but those, whose situation will uniformly beget an immediate interest in the faithful and vigilant performance of the trust.

PUBLIUS.

## The Federalist No. 60 [1]

[New York, February 23, 1788]

*To the People of the State of New-York.*

WE have seen that an incontroulable power over the elections for the federal government could not without hazard be committed to the state legislatures. Let us now see what would be [2] the dangers on the other side; that is, from confiding the ultimate right of regulating its own elections to the union itself. It is not pretended, that this right would ever be used for the exclusion of any state from its share in the representation. The interest of all would in this respect at least be the security of all. But it is alledged that it might be employed in such a manner as to promote the election of some favourite class of men in exclusion of others; by confining the places of election to particular districts, and rendering it impracticable to the citizens at large to partake in the choice. Of all chimerical suppositions, this seems to be the most chimerical. On the one hand no rational calculation of probabilities would lead us to imagine, that the disposition, which a conduct so violent and extraordinary would imply, could ever find its way into the national councils; and on the other,[3] it may be concluded with certainty, that if so improper a spirit should ever gain admittance into them, it would display itself in a form altogether different and far more decisive.

The improbability of the attempt may be satisfactorily inferred from this single reflection, that it could never be made without causing an immediate revolt of the great body of the people,— headed and directed by the state governments. It is not difficult to conceive that this characteristic right of freedom may, in certain turbulent and factious seasons, be violated in respect to a particular

---

The [New York] *Independent Journal: or, the General Advertiser*, February 23, 1788. This essay was printed on February 26 in *The New-York Packet*. In the McLean edition this essay is numbered 60, in the newspapers it is numbered 59.

1. For background to this document, see "The Federalist. Introductory Note," October 27, 1787–May 28, 1788.
2. "are" substituted for "would be" in Hopkins.
3. "hand" inserted at this point in Hopkins.

class of citizens by a victorious and overbearing [4] majority; but that so fundamental a privilege, in a country so [5] situated and so [6] enlightened, should be invaded to the prejudice of the great mass of the people, by the deliberate policy of the government; without occasioning a popular revolution, is altogether inconceivable and incredible.

In addition to this general reflection, there are considerations of a more precise nature, which forbid all apprehension on the subject. The dissimilarity in the ingredients, which will compose the national government; and still more in the manner in which they will be brought into action in its various branches must form a powerful obstacle to a concert of views, in any partial scheme of elections. There is sufficient diversity in the state of property, in the genius, manners, and habits of the people of the different parts of the union to occasion a material diversity of disposition in their representatives towards the different ranks and conditions in society. And though an intimate intercourse under the same government will promote a gradual assimilation, in temper and sentiment,[7] yet there are causes as well physical as moral, which may in a greater or less degree permanently nourish different propensities and inclinations in this particular.[8] But the circumstance, which will be likely to have the greatest influence in the matter, will be the dissimilar modes of constituting the several component parts of the government. The house of representatives being to be elected immediately by the people; the senate by the state legislatures; the president by electors chosen for that purpose by the people; there would be little probability of a common interest to cement these different branches in a predilection for any particular class of electors.

As to the senate it is impossible that any regulation of "time and manner," which is all that is proposed to be submitted to the national government in respect to that body, can affect the spirit which will

4. "and overbearing" omitted in McLean and Hopkins.
5. "so" omitted in McLean and Hopkins.
6. "so" omitted in McLean and Hopkins.
7. Instead of "in temper and sentiment" the newspaper reads: "in some of these respects"; in Hopkins the same phrase reads, "of temper and sentiment"; in McLean "of temper and sentiments."
8. In the newspaper, "respect"; "particular" was substituted in McLean and Hopkins.

direct the choice of its members. The collective sense of the state legislatures can never be influenced by extraneous circumstances of that sort: A consideration, which alone ought to satisfy us that the discrimination apprehended would never be attempted. For what inducement could the senate have to concur in a preference, in which itself would not be included? Or to what purpose would it be established in reference to one branch of the legislature; if it could not be extended to the other? The composition of the one would in this case counteract that of the other. And we can never suppose that it would embrace the appointments to the senate, unless we can at the same time suppose the voluntary co-operation of the state legislatures. If we make the latter supposition, it then becomes immaterial where the power in question is placed; whether in their hands or in those of the union.

But what is to be the object of this capricious partiality in the national councils? Is it to be exercised in a discrimination between the different departments of industry, or between the different kinds of property, or between the different degrees of property? Will it lean in favor of the landed interest, or the monied interest, or the mercantile interest, or the manufacturing interest? Or to speak in the fashionable language of the adversaries of the Constitution; will it court the elevation of the "wealthy and the well born" to the exclusion and debasement of all the rest of the society?

If this partiality is to be exerted in favor of those who are concerned in any particular description of industry or property, I presume it will readily be admitted that the competition for it will lie between landed men and merchants. And I scruple not to affirm, that it is infinitely less likely, that either of them should gain an ascendant in the national councils, than that the one or the other of them should predominate in all the local councils. The inference will be, that a conduct tending to give an undue preference to either is much less to be dreaded from the former than from the latter.

The several states are in various degrees addicted to agriculture and commerce. In most, if not all of them, agriculture [9] is predominant. In a few of them, however, commerce [10] nearly divides its empire, and in most of them has a considerable share of influence.

9. "the first" substituted for "agriculture" in Hopkins.
10. "the latter" substituted for "commerce" in Hopkins.

In proportion as either prevails, it will be conveyed into the national representation, and for the very reason that this will be an emanation from a greater variety of interests, and in much more various proportions, than are to be found in any single state, it will be much less apt to espouse either of them, with a decided partiality, than the representation of any single state.

In a country consisting chiefly of the cultivators of land where the rules of an equal representation obtain the landed interest must upon the whole preponderate in the government. As long as this interest prevails in most of the state legislatures, so long it must maintain a correspondent superiority in the national senate, which will generally be a faithful copy of the majorities of those assemblies. It cannot therefore be presumed that a sacrifice of the landed to the mercantile class will ever be a favorite object of this branch of the federal legislature. In applying thus particularly to the senate a general observation suggested by the situation of the country, I am governed by the consideration, that the credulous votaries of state power, cannot upon their own principles suspect that the state legislatures would be warped from their duty by any external influence. But as in reality the same situation must have the same effect in the primitive composition at least of the federal house of representatives; an improper byass towards the mercantile class is as little to be expected from this quarter or from the other.

In order perhaps to give countenance to the objection at any rate, it may be asked, is there not danger of an opposite byass in the national government, which may dispose it to [11] endeavour to secure a monopoly of the federal administration to the landed class? As there is little likelihood that the supposition of such a byass will have any terrors for those who would be immediately injured by it, a laboured answer to this question will be dispensed with. It will be sufficient to remark, first, that for the reasons elsewhere assigned,[12] it is less likely that any decided partiality should prevail in the councils of the union than in those of any of its members. Secondly that there would be no temptation to violate the constitution in favor of the landed class, because that class would in the natural course of things enjoy as great a preponderancy as itself could desire. And thirdly that men accustomed to investigate the sources of public

11. "produce an" substituted for "dispose it to" in Hopkins.
12. See essay 35.

prosperity, upon a large scale, must be too well convinced of the utility of commerce, to be inclined to inflict upon it so deep a wound as would result from [13] the entire exclusion of those who would best understand its interest from a share in the management of them. The importance of commerce in the view of revenue alone must effectually guard it against the enmity of a body which would be continually importuned in its favour by the urgent calls of public necessity.

I the rather consult brevity in discussing the probability of a preference founded upon a discrimination between the different kinds of industry and property; because, as far as I understand the meaning of the objectors, they contemplate a discrimination of another kind. They appear to have in view, as the objects of the preference with which they endeavour to alarm us, those whom they designate by the description of the "wealthy and the well born." These, it seems, are to be exalted to an odious pre-eminence over the rest of their fellow citizens. At one time however their elevation is to be a necessary consequence of the smallness of the representative body; at another time it is to be effected by depriving the people at large of the opportunity of exercising their right of suffrage in the choice of that body.

But upon what principle is the discrimination of the places of election to be made in order to answer the purpose of the meditated preference? Are the wealthy and the well born, as they are called, confined to particular spots in the several states? Have they by some miraculous instinct or foresight set apart in each of them a common place of residence? Are they only to be met with in the towns or [14] cities? Or are they, on the contrary, scattered over the face of the country as avarice or chance may have happened to cast their own lot, or that of their predecessors? If the latter is the case, (as every intelligent man knows it to be) * is it not evident that the policy of confining the places of elections to particular districts would be as subversive of its own aim as it would be exceptionable on every other account? The truth is that there is no method of securing to the rich the preference apprehended, but by prescribing qualifications of property either for those who may elect, or

* *Particularly in the Southern States and in this State.*

13. "be occasioned by" substituted for "result from" in McLean and Hopkins.
14. "and the" substituted for "or" in Hopkins.

be elected. But this forms no part of the power to be conferred upon the national government. Its authority would be expressly restricted to the regulation of the *times*, the *places*, and the *manner* of elections. The qualifications of the persons who may choose or be chosen, as has been remarked upon another occasion,[15] are defined and fixed in the constitution; and are unalterable by the legislature.

Let it however be admitted, for argument sake, that the expedient suggested might be successful; and let it at the same time be equally taken for granted that all the scruples which a sense of duty or an apprehension of the danger of the experiment might inspire, were overcome in the breasts of the national rulers; still, I imagine, it will hardly be pretended, that they could ever hope to carry such an enterprise into execution, without the aid of a military force sufficient to subdue, the resistance of the great body of the people. The improbability of the existence of a force equal to that object, has been discussed and demonstrated in different parts of these papers;[16] but that the futility of the objection under consideration may appear in the strongest light, it shall be conceded for a moment that such a force might exist; and the national government shall be supposed to be in the actual possession of it. What will be the conclusion? With a disposition to invade the essential rights of the community, and with the means of gratifying that disposition, is it presumable that the persons who were actuated by it would amuse themselves in the ridiculous task of fabricating election laws for securing a preference to a favourite class of men? Would they not be likely to prefer a conduct better adapted to their own immediate aggrandisement? Would they not rather boldly resolve to perpetuate themselves in office by one decisive act of usurpation, than to trust to precarious expedients, which in spite of all the precautions that might accompany them, might terminate in the dismission, disgrace and ruin of their authors? Would they not fear that citizens not less tenacious than conscious of their rights would flock from the remotest extremes of their respective states to the places of election, to overthrow their tyrants, and to substitute men who would be disposed to avenge the violated majesty of the people?

PUBLIUS.

15. See essay 59.
16. See essays 24–29.

## *The Federalist No. 61* [1]

[New York, February 26, 1788]

*To the People of the State of New-York.*

THE more candid opposers of the provision respecting elections contained in the plan of the Convention, when pressed in argument, will sometimes concede the propriety of that provision; with this qualification however that it ought to have been accompanied with a declaration that all elections should be had [2] in the counties where the electors resided. This say they, was a necessary precaution against an abuse of the power. A declaration of this nature, would certainly have been harmless: So far as it would have had the effect of quieting apprehensions, it might not have been undesirable. But it would in fact have afforded little or no additional security against the danger apprehended; and the want of it will never be considered by an impartial and judicious examiner as a serious, still less, as an insuperable objection to the plan. The different views taken of the subject in the two preceding papers must be sufficient to satisfy all dispassionate and discerning men, that if the public liberty should ever be the victim of the ambition of the national rulers, the power under examination at least will be guiltless of the sacrifice.

If those who are inclined to consult their jealousy only would exercise it in a careful inspection of the several State Constitutions, they would find little less room for disquietude and alarm from the latitude which most of them allow in respect to elections, than from the latitude [3] which is proposed to be allowed to the National Government in the same respect. A review of their situation, in this particular, would tend greatly to remove any ill impressions which may remain in regard to this matter. But as that review would lead into lengthy [4] and tedious details, I shall content myself with the

*The New-York Packet*, February 26, 1788. This essay appeared on February 27 in *The* [New York] *Independent Journal: or, the General Advertiser*. In the McLean edition this essay is numbered 61, in the newspapers it is numbered 60.

1. For background to this document, see "The Federalist. Introductory Note," October 27, 1787–May 28, 1788.
2. "held" substituted for "had" in Hopkins.
3. "that" substituted for "the latitude" in Hopkins.
4. "long" substituted for "lengthy" in Hopkins.

single example of the State in which I write. The Constitution of New-York makes no other provision for *locality* of elections, than that the members of the Assembly shall be elected in the *counties*, those of the Senate in the great districts into which the State is or may be divided; these at present are four in number, and comprehend each from two to six counties. It may readily be perceived that it would not be more difficult to the Legislature of New-York to defeat the suffrages of the citizens of New-York by confining elections to particular places, than to [5] the Legislature of the United States to defeat the suffrages of the citizens of the Union, by the like expedient. Suppose for instance, the city of Albany was to be appointed the sole place of election for the county and district of which it is a part, would not the inhabitants of that city speedily become the only electors of the members both of the Senate and Assembly, for that county and district? Can we imagine that the electors who reside in the remote subdivisions of the county of Albany, Saratoga, Cambridge, &c. or in any part of the county of Montgomery, would take the trouble to come to the city of Albany to give their votes for members of the Assembly or Senate, sooner than they would repair to the city of New-York to participate in the choice of the members of the Fœderal House of Representatives? The alarming indifference discoverable in the exercise of so invaluable a privilege under the existing laws, which afford every facility to it, furnishes a ready answer to this question. And, abstracted from any experience on the subject, we can be at no loss to determine that when the place of election is at an *inconvenient distance* from the elector, the effect upon his conduct will be the same whether that distance be twenty miles or twenty thousand miles. Hence it must appear that objections to the particular modification of the fœderal power of regulating elections will in substance apply with equal force to the modification of the like power in the Constitution of this State; and for this reason it will be impossible to acquit the one and to condemn the other. A similar comparison would lead to the same conclusion in respect to the Constitutions of most of the other States.

If it should be said that defects in the State Constitutions furnish no apology for those which are to be found in the plan proposed;

5. "for" substituted for "to" in Hopkins.

I answer, that as the former have never been thought chargeable with inattention to the security of liberty, where the imputations thrown on the latter can be shown to be applicable to them also, the presumption is that they are rather the cavilling refinements of a predetermined opposition, than the well founded inferences of a candid research after truth. To those who are disposed to consider, as innocent ommissions in the State Constitutions, what they regard as unpardonable blemishes in the plan of the Convention, nothing can be said; or at most they can only be asked to assign some substantial reason why the representatives of the people in a single State should be more impregnable to the lust of power or other sinister motives, than the representatives of the people of the United States? If they cannot do this, they ought at least to prove to us, that it is easier to subvert the liberties of three millions of people, with the advantage of local governments to head their opposition, than of two hundred thousand people, who are destitute of that advantage. And in relation to the point immediately under consideration, they ought to convince us that it is less probable a predominant faction in a single State, should, in order to maintain its superiority, incline to a preference of a particular class of electors, than that a similar spirit should take possession of the representatives of thirteen States spread over a vast region, and in several respects distinguishable from each other by a diversity of local circumstances, prejudices and interests.

Hitherto my observations have only aimed at a vindication of the provision in question, on the ground of theoretic propriety, on that of the danger of placing the power elsewhere, and on that of the safety of placing it in the manner proposed. But there remains to be mentioned a positive advantage which will result [6] from this disposition, and which could not as well have been obtained from any other: I allude to the circumstance of uniformity in the time of elections for the Fœderal House of Representatives. It is more than possible, that this uniformity may be found by experience to be of great importance to the public welfare; both as a security against the perpetuation of the same spirit in the body; and as a cure for the diseases of faction. If each State may choose its own time of election, it is possible there may be at least as many different periods

6. "accrue" substituted for "result" in McLean and Hopkins.

as there are months in the year. The times of election in the several States as they are now established for local purposes, vary between extremes as wide as March and November. The consequence of this diversity would be, that there could never happen a total dissolution or renovation of the body at one time. If an improper spirit of any kind should happen to prevail in it, that spirit would be apt to infuse itself into the new members as they come forward in succession. The mass would be likely to remain nearly the same; assimilating constantly to itself its gradual accretions. There is a contagion in example which few men have sufficient force of mind to resist. I am inclined to think that treble the duration in office, with the condition of a total dissolution of the body at the same time, might be less formidable to liberty, than one third of that duration, subject to gradual and successive alterations.

Uniformity in the time of elections seems not less requisite for executing the idea of a regular rotation in the Senate; and for conveniently assembling the Legislature at a stated period in each year.

It may be asked, why then could not a time have been fixed in the Constitution? As the most zealous adversaries of the plan of the Convention in this State, are in general not less zealous admirers of the Constitution of the State, the question may be retorted, and it may be asked, why was not a time for the like purpose fixed in the Constitution of this State? No better answer can be given, than that it was a matter which might safely be entrusted to legislative discretion, and that if a time had been appointed, it might upon experiment have been found less convenient that some other time. The same answer may be given to the question put on the other side. And it may be added, that the supposed danger of a gradual change being merely speculative, it would have been hardly adviseable upon that speculation to establish, as a fundamental point, what would deprive several States of the convenience of having the elections for their own governments, and for the National Government, at the same epoch.[7]

PUBLIUS.

7. In the newspaper, "epochs"; "epoch" was substituted in McLean and Hopkins.

## The Federalist No. 62 [1]

By JAMES MADISON or ALEXANDER HAMILTON

[New York, February 27, 1788]

*To the People of the State of New-York.*

HAVING examined the constitution of the house of representatives, and answered such of the objections against it as seemed to merit notice, I enter next on the examination of the senate. The heads into which this member of the government may be considered, are—I. the qualifications of senators—II. the appointment of them by the state legislatures—III. the equality of representation in the senate—IV. the number of senators, and the term for which they are to be elected—V. the powers vested in the senate.

I. The qualifications proposed for senators, as distinguished from those of representatives, consist in a more advanced age, and a longer period of citizenship. A senator must be thirty years of age at least; as a representative, must be twenty-five. And the former must have been a citizen nine years; as seven years are required for the latter. The propriety of these distinctions is explained by the nature of the senatorial trust; which requiring greater extent of information and stability of character, requires at the same time that the senator should have reached a period of life most likely to supply these advantages; and which participating immediately in transactions with foreign nations, ought to be exercised by none who are not thoroughly weaned from the prepossessions and habits incident to foreign birth and education. The term of nine years

The [New York] *Independent Journal: or, the General Advertiser*, February 27, 1788. This essay appeared in *The New-York Packet* on February 29. In the McLean edition this essay is numbered 62, in the newspapers it is numbered 61.

1. For background to this document, see "The Federalist. Introductory Note," October 27, 1787–May 28, 1788.

Although claimed by both H and Madison, essay 62 probably was written by Madison. The case presented for his authorship by Edward G. Bourne ("The Authorship of the Federalist," *The American Historical Review*, II [April, 1897], 454–59) is as convincing as internal evidence can be. It is very difficult to make out a case for H's authorship. For reasons why the external evidence also indicates that Madison's claim to authorship outweighs (but does not necessarily obviate) that of H, see "The Federalist. Introductory Note," October 27, 1787–May 28, 1788.

appears to be a prudent mediocrity between a total exclusion of adopted citizens, whose merit and talents may claim a share in the public confidence; and an indiscriminate and hasty admission of them, which might create a channel for foreign influence on the national councils.

II. It is equally unnecessary to dilate on the appointment of senators by the state legislatures. Among the various modes which might have been devised for constituting this branch of the government, that which has been proposed by the convention is probably the most congenial with the public opinion. It is recommended by the double advantage of favouring a select appointment, and of giving to the state governments such an agency in the formation of the federal government, as must secure the authority of the former; and may form a convenient link between the two systems.

III. The equality of representation in the senate is another point, which, being evidently the result of compromise between the opposite pretensions of the large and the small states, does not call for much discussion. If indeed it be right that among a people thoroughly incorporated into one nation, every district ought to have a *proportional* share in the government; and that among independent and sovereign states bound together by a [2] simple league, the parties however unequal in size, ought to have an *equal* share in the common councils, it does not appear to be without some reason, that in a compound republic partaking both of the national and federal character, the government ought to be founded on a mixture of the principles of proportional and equal representation. But it is superfluous to try by the standards of theory, a part of the constitution which is allowed on all hands to be the result not of theory, but "of a spirit of amity, and that mutual deference and concession which the peculiarity of our political situation rendered indispensable." A common government with powers equal to its objects, is called for by the voice, and still more loudly by the political situation of America. A government founded on principles more consonant to the wishes of the larger states, is not likely to be obtained from the smaller states. The only option then for the former lies between the proposed government and a government still more objectionable. Under this alternative the advice of prudence must

2. "a" omitted in the newspaper. It was inserted in McLean and Hopkins.

be, to embrace the lesser evil; and instead of indulging a fruitless anticipation of the possible mischiefs which may ensue, to contemplate rather the advantageous consequences which may qualify the sacrifice.

In this spirit it may be remarked, that the equal vote allowed to each state, is at once a constitutional recognition of the portion of sovereignty remaining in the individual states, and an instrument for preserving that residuary sovereignty. So far the equality ought to be no less acceptable to the large than to the small states; since they are not less solicitous to guard by every possible expedient against an improper consolidation of the states into one simple republic.

Another advantage accruing from this ingredient in the constitution of the senate, is the additional impediment it must prove against improper acts of legislation. No law or resolution can now be passed without the concurrence first of a majority of the people, and then of a majority of the states. It must be acknowledged that this complicated check on legislation may in some instances be injurious as well as beneficial; and that the peculiar defence which it involves in favour of the smaller states would be more rational, if any interests common to them, and distinct from those of the other states, would otherwise be exposed to peculiar danger. But as the larger states will always be able by their power over the supplies to defeat unreasonable exertions of this prerogative of the lesser states; and as the facility and excess of law-making seem to be the diseases to which our governments are most liable, it is not impossible that this part of the constitution may be more convenient in practice than it appears to many in contemplation.

IV. The number of senators and the duration of their appointment come next to be considered. In order to form an accurate judgment on both these points, it will be proper to enquire into the purposes which are to be answered by a senate; and in order to ascertain these it will be necessary to review the inconveniencies which a republic must suffer from the want of such an institution.

*First.* It is a misfortune incident to republican government, though in a less degree than to other governments, that those who administer it, may forget their obligations to their constituents, and prove unfaithful to their important trust. In this point of view, a senate, as a second branch of the legislative assembly, distinct from, and dividing the power with, a first, must be in all cases a salutary check on the government. It doubles the security to the people, by requiring the concurrence of two distinct bodies in schemes of usurpation or perfidy, where the ambition or corruption of one, would otherwise be sufficient. This is a precaution founded on such clear principles, and now so well understood in the United States, that it would be more than superfluous to enlarge on it. I will barely remark that as the improbability of sinister combinations will be in proportion to the dissimilarity in the genius of the two bodies; it must be politic to distinguish them from each other by every circumstance which will consist with a due harmony in all proper measures, and with the genuine principles of republican government.

*Secondly.* The necessity of a senate is not less indicated by the propensity of all single and numerous assemblies, to yield to the impulse of sudden and violent passions, and to be seduced by factious leaders, into intemperate and pernicious resolutions. Examples on this subject might be cited without number; and from proceedings within the United States, as well as from the history of other nations. But a position that will not be contradicted need not be proved. All that need be remarked is that a body which is to correct this infirmity ought itself [3] be free from it, and consequently ought to be less numerous. It ought moreover to possess great firmness, and consequently ought to hold its authority by a tenure of considerable duration.

*Thirdly.* Another defect to be supplied by a senate lies in a want of due acquaintance with the objects and principles of legislation. It is not possible that an assembly of men called for the most part from the pursuits of a private nature, continued in appointment for a short time, and led by no permanent motive to devote the intervals of public occupation to a study of the laws, the affairs and the comprehensive interests of their country, should, if left wholly to themselves, escape a variety of important errors in the exercise of their legislative trust. It may be affirmed, on the best grounds, that no small share of the present embarrassments of America is to be charged on the blunders of our governments; and that these have proceeded from the heads rather than the hearts

3. "to" inserted in Hopkins.

of most of the authors of them. What indeed are all the repealing, explaining and amending laws, which fill and disgrace our voluminous codes, but so many monuments of deficient wisdom; so many impeachments exhibited by each succeeding, against each preceding session; so many admonitions to the people of the value of those aids which may be expected from a well constituted senate?

A good government implies two things; first, fidelity to the object of government, which is the happiness of the people; secondly, a knowledge of the means by which that object can be best attained. Some governments are deficient in both these qualities: Most governments are deficient in the first. I scruple not to assert that in the American governments, too little attention has been paid to the last. The federal constitution avoids this error; and what merits particular notice, it provides for the last in a mode which increases the security for the first.

*Fourthly*. The mutability in the public councils, arising from a rapid succession of new members, however qualified they may be, points out in the strongest manner, the necessity of some stable institution in the government. Every new election in the states, is found to change one half of the representatives. From this change of men must proceed a change of opinions; and from a change of opinions, a change of measures. But a continual change even of good measures is inconsistent with every rule of prudence, and every prospect of success. The remark is verified in private life, and becomes more just as well as more important, in national transactions.

To trace the mischievous effects of a mutable government would fill a volume. I will hint a few only, each of which will be perceived to be a source of innumerable others.

In the first place it forfeits the respect and confidence of other nations, and all the advantages connected with national character. An individual who is observed to be inconstant to his plans, or perhaps to carry on his affairs without any plan at all, is marked at once by all prudent people as a speedy victim to his own unsteadiness and folly. His more friendly neighbours may pity him; but all will decline to connect their fortunes with his; and not a few will seize the opportunity of making their fortunes out of his. One nation is to another what one individual is to another; with this melancholy distinction perhaps, that the former with fewer of the benevolent emotions than the latter, are under fewer restraints also from taking undue advantage of the indiscretions of each other. Every nation consequently whose affairs betray a want of wisdom and stability, may calculate on every loss which can be sustained from the more systematic policy of its wiser neighbours. But the best instruction on this subject is unhappily conveyed to America by the example of her own situation. She finds that she is held in no respect by her friends; that she is the derision of her enemies; and that she is a prey to every nation which has an interest in speculating on her fluctuating councils and embarrassed affairs.

The internal effects of a mutable policy are still more calamitous. It poisons the blessings of liberty itself. It will be of little avail to the people that the laws are made by men of their own choice, if the laws be so voluminous that they cannot be read, or so incoherent that they cannot be understood; if they be repealed or revised before they are promulged, or undergo such incessant changes that no man who knows what the law is to day can guess what it will be to morrow. Law is defined to be a rule of action; but how can that be a rule, which is little known and less fixed?

Another effect of public instability is the unreasonable advantage it gives to the sagacious, the enterprising and the moneyed few, over the industrious and uninformed mass of the people. Every new regulation concerning commerce or revenue; or in any manner affecting the value of the different species of property, presents a new harvest to those who watch the change, and can trace its consequences; a harvest reared not by themselves but by the toils and cares of the great body of their fellow citizens. This is a state of things in which it may be said with some truth that laws are made for the *few* not for the *many*.

In another point of view great injury results from an unstable government. The want of confidence in the public councils damps every useful undertaking; the success and profit of which may depend on a continuance of existing arrangements. What prudent merchant will hazard his fortunes in any new branch of commerce, when he knows not but that his plans may be rendered unlawful before they can be executed? What farmer or manufacturer will lay himself out for the encouragement given to any particular cultivation or establishment, when he can have no assurance that his preparatory labors and advances will not render him a victim to an inconstant government? In a word no great improvement or laudable enterprise, can go forward, which requires the auspices of a steady system of national policy.

But the most deplorable effect of all is that diminution of attachment and reverence which steals into the hearts of the people, towards a political system which betrays so many marks of infirmity, and disappoints so many of their flattering hopes. No government any more than an individual will long be respected, without being truly respectable, nor be truly respectable without possessing a certain portion of order and stability.

PUBLIUS.

## The Federalist No. 63 [1]

By JAMES MADISON *or* ALEXANDER HAMILTON

[New York, March 1, 1788]

*To the People of the State of New-York.*

A FIFTH desideratum illustrating the utility of a senate, is the want of a due sense of national character. Without a select and stable member of the government, the esteem of foreign powers will not only be forfeited by an unenlightened and variable policy, proceeding from the causes already mentioned; but the national councils will not possess that sensibility to the opinion of the world, which is perhaps not less necessary in order to merit, than it is to obtain, its respect and confidence.

An attention to the judgment of other nations is important to every government for two reasons: The one is, that independently of the merits of any particular plan or measure, it is desireable on various accounts, that it should appear to other nations as the offspring of a wise and honorable policy: The second is, that in doubt-

*The* [New York] *Independent Journal: or, the General Advertiser,* March 1, 1788. This essay appeared in *The New-York Packet* on March 4. In the McLean edition this essay is numbered 63, in the newspapers it is numbered 62.

1. For background to this document, see "The Federalist. Introductory Note," October 27, 1787–May 28, 1788.

For the reasons why Madison's claim to the authorship of this essay is superior to that of H, see essay 62, note 1.

ful cases, particularly where the national councils may be warped by some strong passion, or momentary interest, the presumed or known opinion of the impartial world, may be the best guide that can be followed. What has not America lost by her want of character with foreign nations? [2] And how many errors and follies would she not have avoided, if the justice and propriety of her measures had in every instance been previously tried by the light in which they would probably appear to the unbiassed part of mankind.

Yet however requisite a sense of national character may be, it is evident that it can never be sufficiently possessed by a numerous and changeable body. It can only be found in a number so small, that a sensible degree of the praise and blame of public measures may be the portion of each individual; or in an assembly so durably invested with public trust, that the pride and consequence of its members may be sensibly incorporated with the reputation and prosperity of the community. The half-yearly representatives of Rhode-Island, would probably have been little affected in their deliberations on the iniquitous measures of that state, by arguments drawn from the light in which such measures would be viewed by foreign nations, or even by the sister states; whilst it can scarcely be doubted, that if the concurrence of a select and stable body had been necessary, a regard to national character alone, would have prevented the calamities under which that misguided people is now labouring.

I add as a *sixth* defect, the want in some important cases of a due responsibility in the government to the people, arising from that frequency of elections, which in other cases produces this responsibility. This [3] remark will perhaps appear not only new but paradoxical. It must nevertheless be acknowledged when explained, to be as undeniable as it is important.

Responsibility in order to be reasonable must be limited to objects within the power of the responsible party; and in order to be effectual, must relate to operations of that power, of which a ready and proper judgment can be formed by the constituents. The objects of government may be divided into two general classes; the one

2. "with foreign nations by her want of character" substituted for "by her want of character with foreign nations" in Hopkins.
3. "The" substituted for "This" in McLean and Hopkins.

depending on measures which have singly an immediate and sensible operation; the other depending on a succession of well chosen and well connected measures, which have a gradual and perhaps unobserved operation. The importance of the latter description to the collective and permanent welfare of every country needs no explanation. And yet it is evident, that an assembly elected for so short a term as to be unable to provide more than one or two links in a chain of measures, on which the general welfare may essentially depend, ought not to be answerable for the final result, any more than a steward or tenant, engaged for one year, could be justly made to answer for places or improvements, which could not be accomplished in less than half a dozen years. Nor is it possible for the people to estimate the *share* of influence which their annual assemblies may respectively have on events resulting from the mixed transactions of several years. It is sufficiently difficult at any rate [4] to preserve a personal responsibility in the members of a *numerous* body, for such acts of the body as have an immediate, detached and palpable operation on its constituents.

The proper remedy for this defect must be an additional body in the legislative department, which, having sufficient permanency to provide for such objects as require a continued attention, and a train of measures, may be justly and effectually answerable for the attainment of those objects.

Thus far I have considered the circumstances which point out the necessity of a well constructed senate, only as they relate to the representatives of the people. To a people as little blinded by prejudice, or corrupted by flattery, as those whom I address, I shall not scruple to add, that such an institution may be sometimes necessary, as a defence to the people against their own temporary errors and delusions. As the cool and deliberate sense of the community ought in all governments, and actually will in all free governments ultimately prevail over the views of its rulers; so there are particular moments in public affairs, when the people stimulated by some irregular passion, or some illicit advantage, or misled by the artful misrepresentations of interested men, may call for measures which they themselves will afterwards be the most ready to lament and

4. "at any rate" omitted in the newspaper; it was inserted at this point in McLean and Hopkins.

condemn. In these critical moments, how salutary will be the interference of some temperate and respectable body of citizens, in order
to check the misguided career, and to suspend the blow meditated
by the people against themselves, until reason, justice and truth, can
regain their authority over the public mind? What bitter anguish
would not the people of Athens have often escaped,[5] if their government had contained so provident a safeguard against the tyranny
of their own passions? Popular liberty might then have escaped the
indelible reproach of decreeing to the same citizens, the hemlock
on the one day, and statues on the next.

It may be suggested that a people spread over an extensive region,
cannot like the crouded inhabitants of a small district, be subject
to the infection of violent passions; or to the danger of combining
in the [6] pursuit of unjust measures. I am far from denying that this
is a distinction of peculiar importance. I have on the contrary endeavoured in a former paper, to shew that it is one of the principal
recommendations of a confederated republic.[7] At the same time this
advantage ought not to be considered as superseding the use of
auxiliary precautions. It may even be remarked that the same extended situation which will exempt the people of America from
some of the dangers incident to lesser republics, will expose them
to the inconveniency of remaining for a longer time, under the influence of those misrepresentations which the combined industry
of interested men may succeed in distributing among them.

It adds no small weight to all these considerations, to recollect,
that history informs us of no long lived republic which had not a
senate. Sparta, Rome and Carthage are in fact the only states to
whom that character can be applied. In each of the two first there
was a senate for life. The constitution of the senate in the last, is
less known. Circumstantial evidence makes it probable that it was
not different in this particular from the two others. It is at least
certain that it had some quality or other which rendered it an anchor
against popular fluctuations; and that a smaller council drawn out
of the senate was appointed not only for life; but filled up vacancies
itself. These examples, though as unfit for the imitation, as they are

5. "avoided" substituted for "escaped" in Hopkins.
6. "the" omitted in the newspaper; it was inserted at this point in McLean
and Hopkins.
7. See essays 10 and 14.

repugnant to the genius of America, are notwithstanding, when compared with the fugitive and turbulent existence of other antient republics, very instructive proofs of the necessity of some institution that will blend stability with liberty. I am not unaware of the circumstances which distinguish the American from other popular governments, as well antient as modern; and which render extreme circumspection necessary in reasoning from the one case to the other. But after allowing due weight to this consideration, it may still be maintained that there are many points of similitude which render these examples not unworthy of our attention. Many of the defects as we have seen, which can only be supplied by a senatorial institution, are common to a numerous assembly frequently elected by the people, and to the people themselves. There are others peculiar to the former, which require the controul of such an institution. The people can never wilfully betray their own interests: But they may possibly be betrayed by the representatives of the people; [8] and the danger will be evidently greater where the whole legislative trust is lodged in the hands of one body of men, than where the concurrence of separate and dissimilar bodies is required in every public act.

The difference most relied on between the American and other republics, consists in the principle of representation, which is the pivot on which the former move, and which is supposed to have been unknown to the latter, or at least to the antient part of them. The use which has been made of this difference, in reasonings contained in former papers, will have shewn that I am disposed neither to deny its existence nor to undervalue its importance.[9] I feel the less restraint therefore in observing that the position concerning the ignorance of the antient government on the subject of representation is by no means precisely true in the latitude commonly given to it. Without entering into a disquisition which here would be [10] misplaced, I will refer to a few known facts in support of what I advance.

In the most pure democracies of Greece, many of the executive functions were performed not by the people themselves, but by of-

8. "their representatives" substituted for "the representatives of the people" in Hopkins.
9. See essay 14.
10. "would here be" substituted for "here would be" in Hopkins.

ficers elected by the people and *representing* the people [11] in their *executive* capacity.

Prior to the reform of Solon, Athens was governed by nine Archons, annually *elected by the people at large.* The degree of power delegated to them seems to be left in great obscurity. Subsequent to that period, we find an assembly first of four and afterwards of six hundred members, annually *elected by the people;* and *partially* representing them in their *legislative* capacity; since they were not only associated with the people in the function of making laws; but had the exclusive right of originating legislative propositions to the people. The senate of Carthage also, whatever might be its power or the duration of its appointment, appears to have been *elective* by the suffrages of the people. Similar instances might be traced in most if not all the popular governments of antiquity.

Lastly in Sparta, we meet with the Ephori, and in Rome with the Tribunes; two bodies, small indeed in number, but annually *elected by the whole body of the people,* and considered as the *representatives* of the people, almost in their *plenipotentiary* capacity. The Cosmi of Crete were also annually *elected by the people;* and have been considered by some authors as an institution analogous to those of Sparta and Rome; with this difference only that in the election of that representative body, the right of suffrage was communicated to a part only of the people.

From these facts, to which many others might be added, it is clear that the principle of representation was neither unknown to the antients, nor wholly overlooked in their political constitutions. The true distinction between these and the American Governments lies *in the total exclusion of the people in their collective capacity* from any share in the *latter,* and not in the *total exclusion of representatives of the people,* from the administration of the *former.* The distinction however thus qualified must be admitted to leave a most advantageous superiority in favor of the United States. But to ensure to this advantage its full effect, we must be careful not to separate it from the other advantage, of an extensive territory. For it cannot be believed that any form of representative government, could have succeeded within the narrow limits occupied by the democracies of Greece.

11. "them" substituted for "the people" in Hopkins.

In answer to all these arguments, suggested by reason, illustrated by [12] examples, and enforced by our own experience, the jealous adversary of the constitution will probably content himself with repeating, that a senate appointed not immediately by the people, and for the term of six years, must gradually acquire a dangerous preeminence in the government, and finally transform it into a tyrannical aristocracy.

To this general answer the general reply ought to be sufficient; that liberty may be endangered by the abuses of liberty, as well as by the abuses of power; that there are numerous instances of the former as well as of the latter; and that the former rather than the latter is apparently most to be apprehended by the United States. But a more particular reply may be given.

Before such a revolution can be effected, the senate, it is to be observed, must in the first place corrupt itself; must next corrupt the state legislature, must then corrupt the house of representatives, and must finally corrupt the people at large. It is evident that the senate must be the first corrupted, before it can attempt an establishment of tyranny. Without corrupting the state legislatures, it cannot prosecute the attempt, because the periodical change of members would otherwise regenerate the whole body. Without exerting the means of corruption with equal succession the house of representatives, the opposition of that co-equal branch of the government would inevitably defeat the attempt; and without corrupting the people themselves, a succession of new representatives would speedily restore all things to their pristine order. Is there any man who can seriously persuade himself, that the proposed senate can, by any possible means within the compass of human address, arrive at the object of a lawless ambition, through all these obstructions?

If reason condemns the suspicion, the same sentence is pronounced by experience. The constitution of Maryland furnishes the most apposite example. The senate of that state is elected, as the federal senate will be, indirectly by the people; and for a term less by one year only, than the federal senate. It is distinguished also by the remarkable prerogative of filling up its own vacancies within the term of its appointment: and at the same time, is not under the con-

12. "other" inserted here in the newspaper; it was omitted in McLean and Hopkins.

troul of any such rotation, as is provided for the federal senate. There are some other lesser distinctions, which would expose the former to colorable objections [13] that do not lie against the latter. If the federal senate therefore really contained the danger which has been so loudly proclaimed, some symptoms at least of a like danger ought by this time to have been betrayed by the senate of Maryland; but no such symptoms have appeared. On the contrary the jealousies at first entertained by men of the same description with those who view with terror the correspondent part of the federal constitution, have been gradually extinguished by the progress of the experiment; and the Maryland constitution is daily deriving from the salutary operations [14] of this part of it, a reputation in which it will probably not be rivalled by that of any state in the union.

But if any thing could silence the jealousies on this subject, it ought to be the British example. The senate there, instead of being elected for a term of six years, and of being unconfined to particular families or fortunes, is an hereditary assembly of opulent nobles. The house of representatives, instead of being elected for two years and by the whole body of the people, is elected for seven years; and in very great proportion, by a very small proportion of the people. Here unquestionably ought to be seen in full display, the aristocratic usurpations and tyranny, which are at some future period to be exemplified in the United States. Unfortunately however for the antifederal argument [15] the British history informs us, that this hereditary assembly has not even been able to defend itself against the continual encroachments of the house of representatives; and that it no sooner lost the support of the monarch, than it was actually crushed by the weight of the popular branch.

As far as antiquity can instruct us on this subject, its examples support the reasoning which we have employed. In Sparta the Ephori, the annual representatives of the people, were found an overmatch for the senate for life, continually gained on its authority, and finally drew all power into their own hands. The tribunes of Rome, who were the representatives of the people, prevailed, it is well known, in almost every contest with the senate for life, and

13. "subjections" substituted for "objections" in McLean.
14. "operation" substituted for "operations" in McLean and Hopkins.
15. "in" inserted here in the newspapers; it was omitted in McLean and Hopkins.

in the end gained the most complete triumph over it. This fact is the more remarkable, an unanimity was required in every act of the tribunes, even after their number was augmented to ten. It proves the irresistable force possessed by that branch of a free government, which has the people on its side. To these examples might be added that of Carthage, whose senate, according to the testimony of Polybius, instead of drawing all power into its vortex, had at the commencement of the second punic war, lost almost the whole of its original portion.

Besides the conclusive evidence resulting from this assemblage of facts, that the federal senate will never be able to transform itself, by gradual usurpations, into an independent and aristocratic body; we are warranted in believing that if such a revolution should ever happen from causes which the foresight of man cannot guard against, the house of representatives with the people on their side will at all times be able to bring back the constitution to its primitive form and principles. Against the force of the immediate representatives of the people, nothing will be able to maintain even the constitutional authority of the senate, but such a display of enlightened policy, and attachment to the public good, as will divide with that branch of the legislature, the affections and support of the entire body of the people themselves.

PUBLIUS.

## Report of a Committee of the Trustees of Columbia College

*New York, March 2, 1788.* As members of a committee of the trustees of Columbia College, Hamilton and Brockholst Livingston reported on a "letter of the Reverend Mr. Benjamin Moore [1] of the 13th Decembr. Ulto: respecting a demand made on him by Mr. Leonard Lispenard [2] for the rent of a house occupied by Mr. Moore during part of the late war." Hamilton and Livingston reported "that there exists no just claim upon this Corporation for the rent of the said house while in the occupation of Mr. Moore."

D, signed by H and Brockholst Livingston, Columbia University Libraries.
1. The Reverend Dr. Benjamin Moore—after the flight, in 1775, of Myles

Cooper the Loyalist president of King's College—was made president *pro tempore* and retained the title until 1784.

2. Lispenard, prominent New York merchant and landholder, had been treasurer of King's College during the American Revolution.

## The Federalist No. 65 [1]

[New York, March 7, 1788]

*To the People of the State of New-York.*

THE remaining powers, which the plan of the Convention allots to the Senate, in a distinct capacity, are comprised in their participation with the Executive in the appointment to offices, and in their judicial character as a court for the trial of impeachments. As in the business of appointments the Executive will be the principal agent, the provisions relating to it will most properly be discussed in the examination of that department.[2] We will therefore conclude this head with a view of the judicial character of the Senate.

A well constituted court for the trial of impeachments, is an object not more to be desired than difficult to be obtained in a government wholly elective. The subjects of its jurisdiction are those offenses which proceed from the misconduct of public men, or in other words from the abuse or violation of some public trust. They are of a nature which may with peculiar propriety be denominated POLITICAL, as they relate chiefly to injuries done immediately to the society itself. The prosecution of them, for this reason, will seldom fail to agitate the passions of the whole community, and to divide it into parties, more or less friendly or inimical, to the accused. In many cases, it will connect itself with the pre-existing factions, and will inlist all their animosities, partialities, influence and interest on one side, or on the other; and in such cases there will always be the greatest danger, that the decision will be regulated more by

*The New-York Packet*, March 7, 1788. This essay appeared in *The* [New York] *Independent Journal: or, the General Advertiser* on March 8. In the McLean edition this essay is numbered 65, in the newspapers it is numbered 64.

1. For background to this document, see "The Federalist. Introductory Note," October 27, 1787–May 28, 1788.

2. See essays 67–77.

the comparitive strength of parties than by the real demonstrations of innocence or guilt.

The delicacy and magnitude of a trust, which so deeply concerns the political reputation and existence of every man engaged in the administration of public affairs, speak for themselves. The difficulty of placing it rightly in a government resting entirely on the basis of periodical elections will as readily be perceived, when it is considered that the most conspicuous characters in it will, from that circumstance, be too often the leaders, or the tools of the most cunning or the most numerous faction; and on this account can hardly be expected to possess the requisite neutrality towards those, whose conduct may be the subject of scrutiny.

The Convention, it appears, thought the Senate the most fit depositary of this important trust. Those who can best discern the intrinsic difficulty of the thing will be least hasty in condemning that opinion; and will be most inclined to allow due weight to the arguments which may be supposed to have produced it.

What it may be asked is the true spirit of the institution itself? Is it not designed as a method of NATIONAL INQUEST into the conduct of public men? If this be the design of it, who can so properly be the inquisitors for the nation, as the representatives of the nation themselves? It is not disputed that the power of originating the inquiry, or in other words of preferring the impeachment ought to be lodged in the hands of one branch of the legislative body; will not the reasons which indicate the propriety of this arrangement, strongly plead for an admission of the other branch of that body to a share in the inquiry? The model, from which the idea of this institution has been borrowed, pointed out that course to the Convention: In Great Britain, it is the province of the house of commons to prefer the impeachment; and of the house of lords to decide upon it. Several of the State constitutions have followed the example. As well the latter as the former seem to have regarded the practice of impeachments, as a bridle in the hands of the legislative body upon the executive servants of the government. Is not this the true light in which it ought to be regarded?

Where else, than in the Senate could have been found a tribunal sufficiently dignified, or sufficiently independent? What other body would be likely to feel *confidence enough in its own situation,* to

preserve unawed and uninfluenced the necessary impartiality between an *individual* accused, and the *representatives of the people,
his accusers?*

Could the Supreme Court have been relied upon as answering this
description? It is much to be doubted whether the members of that
tribunal would, at all times, be endowed with so eminent a portion
of fortitude, as would be called for in the execution of so difficult
a task; & it is still more to be doubted, whether they would possess
the degree of credit and authority, which might, on certain occasions, be indispensable, towards reconciling the people to a decision,
that should happen to clash with an accusation brought by their
immediate representatives. A deficiency in the first would be fatal
to the accused; in the last, dangerous to the public tranquillity. The
hazard in both these respects could only be avoided, if at all, by
rendering that tribunal more numerous than would consist with
a reasonable attention to œconomy. The necessity of a numerous
court for the trial of impeachments is equally dictated by the nature
of the proceeding. This can never be tied down by such strict rules,
either in the delineation of the offence by the prosecutors, or in
the construction of it by the judges, as in common cases serve to
limit the discretion of courts in favor of personal security. There
will be no jury to stand between the Judges, who are to pronounce
the sentence of the law and the party who is to receive or suffer
it. The awful discretion, which a court of impeachments must necessarily have, to doom to honor or to infamy the most confidential
and the most distinguished characters of the community, forbids
the commitment of the trust to a small number of persons.

These considerations seem alone sufficient to authorise a conclusion, that the Supreme Court would have been an improper substitute for the Senate, as a court of impeachments. There remains
a further consideration which will not a little strengthen this conclusion. It is this—The punishment, which may be the consequence
of conviction upon impeachment, is not to terminate the chastise-
ment of the offender. After having been sentenced to a perpetual
ostracism from the esteem and confidence, and [3] honors and emoluments of his country; he will still be liable to prosecution and punishment in the ordinary course of law. Would it be proper that the

3. In the newspaper, "the"; "and" was substituted in McLean and Hopkins.

persons, who had disposed of his fame and his most valuable rights as a citizen in one trial, should in another trial, for the same offence, be also the disposers of his life and his fortune? Would there not be the greatest reason to apprehend, that error in the first sentence would be the parent of error in the second sentence? That the strong bias of one decision would be apt to overrule the influence of any new lights, which might be brought to vary the complexion of another decision? Those, who know any thing of human nature, will not hesitate to answer these questions in the affirmative; and will be at no loss to perceive, that by making the same persons Judges in both cases, those who might happen to be the objects of prosecution would in a great measure be deprived of the double security, intended them by a double trial. The loss of life and estate would often be virtually included in a sentence, which, in its terms, imported nothing more than dismission from a present, and disqualification for a future office. It may be said, that the intervention of a jury, in the second instance, would obviate the danger. But juries are frequently influenced by the opinions of Judges. They are sometimes induced to find special verdicts which refer the main question to the decision of the court. Who would be willing to stake his life and his estate upon the verdict of a jury, acting under the auspices of Judges, who had predetermined his guilt?

Would it have been an improvement of the plan, to have united the Supreme Court with the Senate, in the formation of the court of impeachments? This Union would certainly have been attended with several advantages; but would they not have been overballanced by the signal disadvantages, already stated, arising from the agency of the same Judges in the double prosecution to which the offender would be liable? To a certain extent, the benefits of that Union will be obtained from making the Chief Justice of the Supreme Court the President of the court of impeachments, as is proposed to be done in the plan of the Convention; while the inconveniencies of an intire incorporation of the former into the latter will be substantially avoided. This was perhaps the prudent mean. I forbear to remark upon the additional pretext for clamour, against the Judiciary, which so considerable an augmentation of its authority would have afforded.

Would it have been desirable to have composed the court for the trial of impeachments of persons wholly distinct from the other departments of the government? There are weighty arguments, as well against, as in favor of such a plan. To some minds, it will not appear a trivial objection, that it would [4] tend to increase the complexity of the political machine; and to add a new spring to the government, the utility of which would at best be questionable. But an objection, which will not be thought by any unworthy of attention, is this—A court formed upon such a plan would either be attended with [5] heavy expence, or might in practice be subject to a variety of casualties and inconveniencies. It must either consist of permanent officers stationary at the seat of government, and of course entitled to fixed and regular stipends, or of certain officers of the State governments, to be called upon whenever an impeachment was actually depending. It will not be easy to imagine any third mode materially different, which could rationally be proposed. As the court, for reasons already given, ought to be numerous; the first scheme will be reprobated by every man, who can compare the extent of the public wants, with the means of supplying them; the second will be espoused with caution by those, who will seriously consider the difficulty of collecting men dispersed over the whole union; the injury to the innocent, from the procrastinated determination of the charges which might be brought against them; the advantage to the guilty, from the opportunities which delay would afford to [6] intrigue and corruption; and in some cases the detriment to the State, from the prolonged inaction of men, whose firm and faithful execution of their duty might have exposed them to the persecution of an intemperate or designing majority in the House of Representatives. Though this latter supposition may seem harsh, and might not be likely often to be verified; yet it ought not to be forgotten, that the demon of faction will at certain seasons extend his sceptre over all numerous bodies of men.

But though one or the other of the substitutes which have been examined, or some other that might be devised, should be thought

4. In the newspaper, "could"; "would" was substituted in McLean and Hopkins.

5. "a" inserted at this point in the newspaper; it was omitted in McLean and Hopkins.

6. "for" substituted for "to" in Hopkins.

preferable to the plan, in this respect,[7] reported by the Convention, it will not follow, that the Constitution ought for this reason to be rejected. If mankind were to resolve to agree in no institution of government, until every part of it had been adjusted to the most exact standard of perfection, society would soon become a general scene of anarchy, and the world a desert. Where is the standard of perfection to be found? Who will undertake to unite the discordant opinions of a whole community, in the same judgment of it; and to prevail upon one conceited projector to renounce his *infallible* criterion, for the *fallible* criterion of his more *conceited neighbor?* To answer the purpose of the adversaries of the Constitution, they ought to prove, not merely, that particular provisions in it are not the best, which might have been imagined; but that the plan upon the whole is bad and pernicious.

PUBLIUS.

7. "should, in this respect, be thought preferable to the plan" substituted for "should be thought preferable to the plan, in this respect" in Hopkins.

## The Federalist No. 66 [1]

[New York, March 8, 1788]

*To the People of the State of New-York.*

A review of the principal objections that have appeared against the proposed court for the trial of impeachments, will not improbably eradicate the remains of any unfavourable impressions, which may still exist, in regard to this matter.

The *first* of these objections is, that the provision in question confounds legislative and judiciary authorities in the same body; in violation of that important and well established maxim, which requires a separation between the different departments of power. The true meaning of this maxim has been discussed and ascertained in another place, and has been shewn to be entirely compatible with

*The* [New York] *Independent Journal: or, the General Advertiser,* March 8, 1788. This essay was printed in *The New-York Packet* on March 11. In the McLean edition this essay is numbered 66, in the newspapers it is numbered 65.
    1. For background to this document, see "The Federalist. Introductory Note," October 27, 1787–May 28, 1788.

a partial intermixture of those departments for special purposes, preserving them in the main distinct and unconnected.[2] This partial intermixture is even in some cases not only proper, but necessary to the mutual defence of the several members of the government, against each other. An absolute or qualified negative in the executive, upon the acts of the legislative body, is admitted by the ablest adepts in political science, to be an indefensible barrier against the encroachments of the latter upon the former. And it may perhaps with not less reason be contended that the powers relating to impeachments are as before intimated, an essential check in the hands of that body upon the encroachments of the executive. The division of them between the two branches of the legislature; assigning to one the right of accusing, to the other the right of judging; avoids the inconvenience of making the same persons both accusers and judges; and guards against the danger of persecution from the prevalency of a factious spirit in either of those branches. As the concurrence of two-thirds of the senate will be requisite to a condemnation, the security to innocence, from this additional circumstance, will be as complete as itself can desire.

It is curious to observe with what vehemence this part of the plan is assailed, on the principle here taken notice of, by men who profess to admire without exception the constitution of this state; while that [3] constitution makes the senate, together with the chancellor and judges of the supreme court, not only a court of impeachments, but the highest judicatory in the state in all causes, civil and criminal. The proportion, in point of numbers, of the chancellor and judges to the senators, is so inconsiderable, that the judiciary authority of New-York in the last resort may, with truth, be said to reside in its senate. If the plan of the convention be in this respect chargeable with a departure from the celebrated maxim which has been so often mentioned, and seems to be so little understood, how much more culpable must be the constitution of New-York? *

A *second* objection to the senate, as a court of impeachments, is,

---

* In that of New-Jersey also the final judiciary authority is in a branch of the legislature. In New-Hampshire, Massachusetts, Pennsylvania, and South-Carolina, one branch of the legislature is the court for the trial of impeachments.

2. The principle of a "separation between the different departments of power" was discussed in essays 47–52.
3. "very" inserted at this point in Hopkins.

that it contributes to an undue accumulation of power in that body, tending to give to the government a countenance too aristocratic. The senate, it is observed, is to have concurrent authority with the executive in the formation of treaties, and in the appointment to offices: If, say the objectors, to these prerogatives is added that of deciding [4] in all cases of impeachment, it will give a decided predominancy to senatorial influence. To an objection so little precise in itself, it is not easy to find a very precise answer. Where is the measure or criterion to which we can appeal, for determining [5] what will give the senate too much, too little, or barely the proper degree of influence? Will it not be more safe, as well as more simple, to dismiss such vague and uncertain calculations, to examine each power by itself, and to decide on general principles where it may be deposited with most advantage and least inconvenience?

If we take this course it will lead to a more intelligible, if not to a more certain result. The disposition of the power of making treaties, which has obtained in the plan of the convention, will then, if I mistake not, appear to be fully justified by the considerations stated in a former number,[6] and by others which will occur under the next head of our enquiries.[7] The expediency of the junction of the senate with the executive [8] will, I trust, be placed in a light not less satisfactory, in the disquisitions under the same head. And I flatter myself the observations in my last paper must have gone no inconsiderable way towards proving that it was not easy, if practicable, to find a more fit receptacle for the power of determining impeachments, than that which has been chosen. If this be truly the case, the hypothetical danger [9] of the too great weight of the senate ought to be discarded from our reasonings.

But this hypothesis, such as it is has already been refuted in the remarks applied to the duration in [10] office prescribed for the senators.[11] It was by them shewn, as well on the credit of historical ex-

4. "determining" substituted for "deciding" in McLean and Hopkins.
5. "estimating" substituted for "determining" in McLean and Hopkins.
6. H's reference was to essay 64, written by John Jay.
7. See essays 68 and 75.
8. "in the power of appointing to offices" inserted here in McLean and Hopkins.
9. In the newspaper, "dread"; "danger" was substituted in McLean and Hopkins.
10. "of" substituted for "in" in Hopkins.
11. See essay 63.

amples, as from the reason of the thing, that the most *popular* branch of every government, partaking of the republican genius, by being generally the favorite of the people, will be as generally a full match, if not an overmatch, for every other member of the government.[12]

But independent of this most active and operative principle; to secure the equilibrium of the national house of representatives, the plan of the convention has provided in its favor, several important counterpoises to the additional authorities, to be conferred upon the senate. The exclusive privilege of originating money bills will belong to the house of representatives. The same house will possess the sole right of instituting impeachments: Is not this a complete counterballance to that of determining them? The same house will be the umpire in all elections of the president, which do not unite the suffrages of a majority of the whole number of electors; a case which it cannot be doubted will sometimes, if not frequently, happen. The constant possibility of the thing must be a fruitful source of influence to that body. The more it is contemplated, the more important will appear this ultimate, though contingent power of deciding the competitions of the most illustrious citizens of the union, for the first office in it. It would not perhaps be rash to predict, that as a mean of influence it will be found to outweigh all the peculiar attributes of the senate.

A third objection to the senate as a court of impeachments is drawn from the agency they are to have in the appointments to office. It is imagined that they would be too indulgent judges of the conduct of men, in whose official creation they had participated. The principle of this objection would condemn a practice, which is to be seen in all the state governments, if not in all the governments with which we are acquainted: I mean that of rendering those, who hold offices during pleasure, dependent on the pleasure of those, who appoint them. With equal plausibility might it be alledged in this case that the favoritism of the latter would always be an asylum for the misbehavior of the former. But that practice, in contradiction to this principle, proceeds upon the presumption, that the responsibility of those who appoint, for the fitness and competency of the persons, on whom they bestow their choice, and the interest

12. See essay 63.

they will [13] have in the respectable and prosperous administration of affairs, will inspire a sufficient disposition, to dismiss from a share in it, all such, who, by their conduct, shall [14] have proved themselves unworthy of the confidence reposed in them. Though facts may not always correspond with this presumption, yet if it be in the main just, it must destroy the supposition, that the senate, who will merely sanction the choice of the executive, should feel a byass towards the objects of that choice, strong enough to blind them to the evidences of guilt so extraordinary as to have induced the representatives of the nation to become its accusers.

If any further argument were necessary to evince the improbability of such a byass, it might be found in the nature of the agency of the senate, in the business of appointments. It will be the office of the president to *nominate,* and with the advice and consent of the senate to *appoint.* There will of course be no exertion of *choice* on the part of the senate. They may defeat one choice of the executive, and oblige him to make another; but they cannot themselves *choose*—they can only ratify or reject the choice, of the president.[15] They might even entertain a preference to some other person, at the very moment they were assenting to the one proposed; because there might be no positive ground of opposition to him; and they could not be sure, if they withheld their assent, that the subsequent nomination would fall upon their own favorite, or upon any other person in their estimation more meritorious than the one rejected. Thus it could hardly happen that the majority of the senate would feel any other complacency towards the object of an appointment, than such, as the appearances of merit, might inspire, and the proofs of the want of it, destroy.

A fourth objection to the senate, in the capacity of a court of impeachments, is derived from their union with the executive in the power of making treaties. This, it has been said, would constitute the senators their own judges, in every case of a corrupt or perfidious execution of that trust. After having combined with the executive in betraying the interests of the nation in a ruinous treaty, what

13. "will" omitted in McLean and Hopkins.
14. "may" substituted for "shall" in McLean and Hopkins.
15. "he may have made" substituted for "of the president" in McLean and Hopkins.

prospect, it is asked, would there be of their being made to suffer the punishment, they would deserve, when they were themselves to decide upon the accusation brought against them for the treachery of which they had been guilty?

This objection has been circulated [16] with more earnestness and with [17] greater show of reason, than any other which has appeared against this part of the plan; and yet I am deceived if it does not rest upon an erroneous foundation.

The security essentially intended by the constitution against corruption and treachery in the formation of treaties, is to be sought for in the numbers and characters of those who are to make them. The JOINT AGENCY of the chief magistrate of the union, and of two-thirds of the members of a body selected by the collective wisdom of the legislatures of the several states, is designed to be the pledge for the fidelity of the national councils in this particular. The convention might with propriety have meditated the punishment of the executive, for a deviation from the instructions of the senate, or a want of integrity in the conduct of the negociations committed to him: They might also have had in view the punishment of a few leading individuals in the senate, who should have prostituted their influence in that body, as the mercenary instruments of foreign corruption: But they could not with more or with equal propriety have contemplated the impeachment and punishment of two-thirds of the senate, consenting to an improper treaty, than of a majority of that or of the other branch of the national legislature, consenting to a pernicious or unconstitutional law: a principle which I believe has never been admitted into any government. How in fact could a majority of the house of representatives impeach themselves? Not better, it is evident, than two-thirds of the senate might try themselves. And yet what reason is there, that a majority of the house of representatives, sacrificing the interests of the society, by an unjust and tyrannical act of legislation, should escape with impunity more than two-thirds of the senate, sacrificing the same interests in an injurious treaty with a foreign power? The truth is, that in all such cases it is essential to the free-

16. In the newspaper, "calculated"; "circulated" was substituted in McLean and Hopkins.
17. "a" inserted at this point in Hopkins.

dom and to the necessary independence of the deliberations of the body, that the members of it should be exempt from punishment for acts done in a collective capacity; and the security to the society must depend on the care which is taken to confide the trust to proper hands, to make it their interest to execute it with fidelity, and to make it as difficult as possible for them to combine in any interest opposite to that of the public good.

So far as might concern the misbehaviour of the executive in perverting the instructions, or contravening the views of the senate, we need not be apprehensive of the want of a disposition in that body to punish the abuse of their confidence, or to vindicate their own authority. We may thus far count upon their pride, if not upon their virtue. And so far even as might concern the corruption of leading members, by whose arts and influence the majority may have been inveigled into measures odious to the community; if the proofs of that corruption should be satisfactory, the usual propensity of human nature will warrant us in concluding, that there would be commonly no defect of inclination in the body, to divert the public resentment from themselves, by a ready sacrifice of the authors of their mismanagement and disgrace.

PUBLIUS.

## The Federalist No. 67 [1]

[New York, March 11, 1788]

*To the People of the State of New-York.*

THE Constitution of the executive department of the proposed government claims next [2] our attention.

There is hardly any part of the system which could have been attended with greater [3] difficulty in the arrangement of it than this; and there is perhaps none, which has been inveighed against with less candor, or criticised with less judgment.

*The New-York Packet,* March 11, 1788. This essay appeared in *The* [New York] *Independent Journal: or, the General Advertiser* on March 12. In the McLean edition this essay is numbered 67, in the newspapers it is numbered 66.
  1. For background to this document, see "The Federalist. Introductory Note," October 27, 1787–May 28, 1788.
  2. "next claims" substituted for "claims next" in Hopkins.
  3. In the newspaper, "great"; "greater" substituted in McLean and Hopkins.

Here the writers against the Constitution seem to have taken pains to signalize their talent of misrepresentation, calculating upon the aversion of the people to monarchy, they have endeavoured to inlist all their jealousies and apprehensions in opposition to the intended President of the United States; not merely as the embryo but as the full grown progeny of that detested parent. To establish the pretended affinity they have not scrupled to draw resources even from the regions of fiction. The authorities of a magistrate, in few instances greater, and in some instances less, than those of a Governor of New-York, have been magnified into more than royal prerogatives. He has been decorated with attributes superior in dignity and splendor to those of a King of Great-Britain. He has been shown to us with the diadem sparkling on his brow, and the imperial purple flowing in his train. He has been seated on a throne surrounded with minions and mistresses; giving audience to the envoys of foreign potentates, in all the supercilious pomp of majesty. The images of Asiatic despotism and voluptuousness have scarcely been wanting to crown the exaggerated scene. We have been almost [4] taught to tremble at the terrific visages of murdering janizaries; and to blush at the unveiled mysteries of a future seraglio.

Attempts so [5] extravagant as these to disfigure, or it might rather be said,[6] to metamorphose the object, render it necessary to take an accurate view of its real nature and form; in order as well [7] to ascertain its true aspect and genuine appearance, as [8] to unmask the disingenuity and [9] expose the fallacy of the counterfeit resemblances which have been so insidiously as well as industriously propagated.

In the execution of this task there is no man, who would not find it an arduous effort, either to behold the moderation or to treat with seriousness the devices, not less weak than wicked, which have been contrived to pervert the public opinion in relation to the subject. They so far exceed the usual, though unjustifiable, licenses of party-artifice, that even in a disposition the most candid and tolerant they must force the sentiments which favor an indulgent construction of

4. "almost" omitted in Hopkins.
5. "so" omitted in Hopkins.
6. "or rather" substituted for "or it might rather be said" in Hopkins.
7. "as well" omitted in Hopkins.
8. "as" omitted in Hopkins.
9. "to" inserted at this point in Hopkins.

the conduct of political adversaries to give place to a voluntary and unreserved indignation. It is impossible not to bestow the imputation of deliberate imposture and deception upon the gross pretence of a similitude between a King of Great-Britain and a magistrate of the character marked out for that of the President of the United States. It is still more impossible to withhold that imputation from the rash and barefaced expedients which have been employed to give success to the attempted imposition.

In one instance, which I cite as a sample of the general spirit, the temerity has proceeded so far as to ascribe to the President of the United States a power, which by the instrument reported is *expressly* allotted to the executives of the individual States. I mean the power of filling casual vacancies in the Senate.

This bold experiment upon the discernment of his countrymen, has been hazarded by a writer who (whatever may be his real merit) has had no inconsiderable share in the applauses of his party; * and who upon this [11] false and unfounded suggestion, has built a series of observations equally false and unfounded. Let him now be confronted with the evidence of the fact; and let him, if he be able, justify or extenuate the shameful outrage he has offered to the dictates of truth and to the rules of fair dealing.

The second clause of the second section of the second article empowers the President of the United States "to nominate, and by and with the advice and consent of the Senate to appoint ambassadors, other public ministers and consuls, judges of the Supreme Court, and all other *officers* of the United States, whose appointments are *not* in the Constitution *otherwise provided for,* and *which shall be established by law.*" Immediately after this clause follows another in these words—"The President shall have power to fill up all *vacancies* that may happen *during the recess of the Senate,* by granting commissions which shall *expire at the end of their next session.*" It is from this last provision that the pretended power of the President to fill vacancies in the Senate has been deduced. A slight attention to

---

* See Cato No. 5.[10]

10. A series of newspaper articles signed "Cato," presumably written by George Clinton, had appeared in the New York press in the fall of 1787. The fifth essay appeared in *The New-York Journal, and Daily Patriotic Register* on November 22. It is reprinted in Ford, *Essays on the Constitution,* 265–69.
11. "his" substituted for "this" in McLean.

the connection of the clauses and to the obvious meaning of the terms will satisfy us that the deduction is not even colorable.

The first of these two clauses it is clear only provides a mode for appointing such officers, "whose appointments are *not otherwise provided for* in the Constitution, and which *shall be established by law;*" of course it cannot extend to the appointment of senators; whose appointments are *otherwise provided for* in the Constitution,† and who are *established by the Constitution,* and will not require a future establishment by law. This position will hardly be contested.

The last of these two clauses, it is equally clear, cannot be understood to comprehend the power of filling vacancies in the Senate, for the following reasons—*First.* The relation in which that clause stands to the other, which declares the general mode of appointing officers of the United States, denotes it to be nothing more than a supplement to the other; for the purpose of establishing an auxiliary method of appointment in cases, to which the general method was inadequate. The ordinary power of appointment is confided to the President and Senate *jointly,* and can therefore only be exercised during the session of the Senate; but as it would have been improper to oblige this body to be continually in session for the appointment of officers; and as vacancies might happen *in their recess,* which it might be necessary for the public service to fill without delay, the succeeding clause is evidently intended to authorise the President *singly* to make temporary appointments "during the recess of the Senate, by granting commissions which should expire at the end of their next session." *Secondly.* If this clause is to be considered as supplementary to the one which precedes, the *vacancies* of which it speaks must be construed to relate to the "officers" described in the preceding one; and this we have seen excludes from its description the members of the Senate. *Thirdly.* The time within which the power is to operate "during the recess of the Senate" and the duration of the appointments "to the end of the next session" of that body, conspire to elucidate the sense of the provision; which if it had been intended to comprehend Senators would naturally have referred the temporary power of filling vacancies to the recess of the State Legislatures, who are to make the permanent appointments, and not to the recess of the national Senate, who are to have no

† Article I. § 3. Clause I.

concern in those appointments; and would have extended the duration in office of the temporary Senators to the next session of the Legislature of the State, in whose representation the vacancies had happened, instead of making it to expire at the end of the ensuing session of the national Senate. The circumstances of the body authorised to make the permanent appointments, would of course have governed the modification of a power which related to the temporary appointments; and as the national Senate is the body whose situation is alone contemplated in the clause upon which the suggestion under examination has been founded, the vacancies to which it alludes can only be deemed to respect those officers, in whose appointment that body has a concurrent agency with the President. But, *lastly*, the first and second clauses of the third section of the first article, not only obviate the possibility of doubt, but destroy the pretext of misconception.[12] The former provides that "the Senate of the United States shall be composed of two Senators from each State, chosen *by the Legislature thereof* for six years," and the latter directs that "if vacancies in that body should happen by resignation or otherwise *during the recess of the Legislature of* ANY STATE, the Executive THEREOF may make temporary appointments until the *next meeting of the Legislature*, which shall then fill such vacancies." Here is an express power given, in clear and unambiguous terms, to the State executives to fill the casual vacancies in the Senate by temporary appointments; which not only invalidates the supposition, that the clause before considered could have been intended to confer that power upon the President of the United States; but proves that this supposition, destitute as it is even of the merit of plausibility, must have originated in an intention to deceive the people, too palpable to be obscured by sophistry, and [13] too atrocious to be palliated by hypocrisy.

I have taken the pains to select this instance of misrepresentation, and to place it in a clear and strong light, as an unequivocal proof of the unwarrantable arts which are practised to prevent a fair and impartial judgment of the real merits of the constitution [14] submitted to the consideration of the people. Nor have I scrupled in so flagrant

12. "obviate all possibility of doubt" substituted for "not only" through "misconception" in Hopkins.
13. "and" omitted in Hopkins.
14. "plan" substituted for "constitution" in Hopkins.

a case to allow myself in a severity of animadversion little congenial with the general spirit of these papers. I hesitate not to submit it to the decision of any candid and honest adversary of the proposed government, whether language can furnish epithets of too much asperity for so shameless and so prostitute an attempt to impose on the citizens of America.

PUBLIUS.

## The Federalist No. 68 [1]

[New York, March 12, 1788]

To the People of the State of New-York.

THE mode of appointment of the chief magistrate of the United States is almost the only part of the system, of any consequence, which has escaped without severe censure, or which has received the slightest mark of approbation from its opponents. The most plausible of these, who has appeared in print, has even deigned to admit, that the election of the president is pretty well guarded.* I venture somewhat further; and hesitate not to affirm, that if the manner of it be not perfect, it is at least excellent. It unites in an eminent degree all the advantages; the union of which was to be desired.[3]

It was desireable, that the sense of the people should operate in the choice of the person to whom so important a trust was to be confided. This end will be answered by committing the right of making it, not to any pre-established body, but to men, chosen by the people for the special purpose, and at the particular conjuncture. It was equally desirable, that the immediate election should be made

* Vide Federal Farmer.[2]

The [New York] Independent Journal: or, the General Advertiser, March 12, 1788. This essay was printed on March 14 in The New-York Packet. In the McLean edition it is numbered 68, and in the newspapers it is numbered 67.

1. For background to this document, see "The Federalist. Introductory Note," October 27, 1787–May 28, 1788.

2. H is referring to Richard Henry Lee, Observations Leading to a Fair Examination of the System of Government, Proposed by the Late Convention; and to Several Essential and Necessary Alterations in it. In a Number of Letters from the Federal Farmer to the Republican (N. P., 1787). H's specific reference is to Letter III. Lee was one of Virginia's ablest opponents of the proposed Constitution.

3. "wished for" substituted for "desired" in Hopkins.

by men most capable of analizing the qualities adapted to the station, and acting under circumstances favourable to deliberation and to a judicious combination of all the reasons and inducements, which [4] were proper to govern their choice. A small number of persons, selected by their fellow citizens from the general mass, will be most likely to possess the information and discernment requisite to so complicated an investigation.[5]

It was also peculiarly desirable, to afford as little opportunity as possible to tumult and disorder. This evil was not least to be dreaded in the election of a magistrate, who was to have so important an agency in the administration of the government, as the president of the United States.[6] But the precautions which have been so happily concerted in the system under consideration, promise an effectual security against this mischief. The choice of *several* to form an intermediate body of electors, will be much less apt to convulse the community, with any extraordinary or violent movements, than the choice of *one* who was himself to be the final object of the public wishes. And as the electors, chosen in each state, are to assemble and vote in the state, in which they are chosen, this detached and divided situation will expose them much less to heats and ferments, which [7] might be communicated from them to the people, than if they were all to be convened at one time, in one place.

Nothing was more to be desired, than that every practicable obstacle should be opposed to cabal, intrigue and corruption. These most deadly adversaries of republican government might naturally have been expected to make their aproaches from more than one quarter, but chiefly from the desire in foreign powers to gain an improper ascendant in our councils. How could they better gratify this, than by raising a creature of their own to the chief magistracy of the union? But the convention have guarded against all danger of this sort with the most provident and judicious attention. They have not made the appointment of the president to depend on any [8] pre-existing bodies of men who might be tampered with before hand to prostitute their votes; but they have referred it in the first instance

4. "that" substituted for "which" in Hopkins.
5. In the newspaper, "such complicated investigations"; "so complicated an investigation" was substituted in McLean and Hopkins.
6. "as the president of the United States" omitted in Hopkins.
7. "that" substituted for "which" in Hopkins.
8. "any" omitted in Hopkins.

to an immediate act of the people of America, to be exerted in the choice of persons for the temporary and sole purpose of making the appointment. And they have excluded from eligibility to this trust, all those who from situation might be suspected of too great devotion to the president in office. No senator, representative, or other person holding a place of trust or profit under the United States, can be of the number of the electors. Thus, without corrupting the body of the people, the immediate agents in the election will at least enter upon the task, free from any sinister byass. Their transient existence, and their detached situation, already taken notice of, afford [9] a satisfactory prospect of their continuing so, to the conclusion of it. The business of corruption, when it is to embrace so considerable a number of men, requires time, as well as means. Nor would it be found easy suddenly to embark them, dispersed as they would be over thirteen states, in any combinations, founded upon motives, which though they could not properly be denominated corrupt, might yet be of a nature to mislead them from their duty.

Another and no less important desideratum was, that the executive should be independent for his continuance in office on all, but the people themselves. He might otherwise be tempted to sacrifice his duty to his complaisance for those whose favor was necessary to the duration of his official consequence. This advantage will also be secured, by making his re-election to depend on a special body of representatives, deputed by the society for the single purpose of making the important choice.

All these advantages will be happily combined in the plan devised by the convention; which is, that the people of [10] each state shall choose a number of persons as electors, equal to the number of senators and representatives of such state in the national government, who shall assemble within the state and vote for some fit person as president. Their votes, thus given, are to be transmitted to the seat of the national government, and the person who may happen to have a majority of the whole number of votes will be the president. But as a majority of the votes might not always happen to centre on [11] one man and as it might be unsafe to permit less than a majority

9. "afforded" substituted for "afford" in McLean.
10. "the people of" omitted in Hopkins.
11. "in" substituted for "on" in Hopkins.

to be conclusive, it is provided, that in such a contingency, the house of representatives shall select out of the candidates, who shall have the five highest numbers of votes, the man who in their opinion may be best qualified for the office.

This process of election affords a moral certainty, that the office of president, will seldom [12] fall to the lot of any man, who is not in an eminent degree endowed with the requisite qualifications. Talents for low intrigue and the little arts of popularity may alone suffice to elevate a man to the first honors in a single state; but it will require other talents and a different kind of merit to establish him in the esteem and confidence of the whole union, or of so considerable a portion of it as would be necessary to make him a successful candidate for the distinguished office of president of the United States. It will not be too strong to say, that there will be a constant probability of seeing the station filled by characters preeminent for ability and virtue. And this will be thought no inconsiderable recommendation of the constitution, by those, who are able to estimate the share, which the executive in every government must necessarily have in its good or ill administration. Though we cannot acquiesce in the political heresy of the poet who says—

"For forms of government let fools [13] contest—
"That which is best administered is best."

—yet we may safely pronounce, that the true test of a good government is its aptitude and tendency to produce a good administration.

The vice-president is to be chosen in the same manner with the president; with this difference, that the senate is to do, in respect to the former, what is to be done by the house of representatives, in respect to the latter.

The appointment of an extraordinary person, as vice president, has been objected to as superfluous, if not mischievous. It has been alledged, that it would have been preferable to have authorised the senate to elect out of their own body an officer, answering [14] that description. But two considerations seem to justify the ideas of the convention in this respect. One is, that to secure at all times the possibility of a definitive resolution of the body, it is necessary that

12. In the newspaper, "never"; "seldom" was substituted in Hopkins.
13. In the newspaper, "facts"; "fools" was substituted in McLean and Hopkins.
14. "to" inserted at this point in McLean and Hopkins.

the president should have only a casting vote. And to take the senator of any state from his seat as senator, to place him in that of president of the senate, would be to exchange, in regard to the state from which he came, a constant for a contingent vote. The other consideration is, that as the vice-president may occasionally become a substitute for the president, in the supreme executive magistracy, all the reasons, which recommend the mode of election prescribed for the one, apply with great, if not with equal, force to the manner of appointing the other. It is remarkable, that in this as in most other instances, the objection, which is made, would be [15] against the constitution of this state. We have a Lieutenant Governor chosen by the people at large, who presides in the senate, and is the constitutional substitute for the Governor in casualties similar to those, which would authorise the vice-president to exercise the authorities and discharge the duties of the president.

PUBLIUS.

15. "lie" substituted for "be" in McLean and Hopkins.

## Report of a Committee of the Trustees of Columbia College

*New York, March 13, 1788.* On this date Hamilton and Morgan Lewis,[1] members of a committee to whom was referred an "Application of Messrs. Van Zandt and Kettlelas," [2] reported that the two men had offered to pay in 1776 the full amount of principal and interest due on their bond to the college in continental currency and that the treasurer of the college had refused the payment.

D, signed by H and Morgan Lewis, Columbia University Libraries.
1. Lewis was chief justice of the State of New York.
2. Winant (Wynant) Van Zandt and Peter Kettlelas, prominent New York merchants.

## The Federalist No. 69 [1]

[New York, March 14, 1788]

*To the People of the State of New-York.*

I PROCEED now to trace the real characters of the proposed executive as they are marked out in the plan of the Convention. This will serve to place in a strong light the unfairness of the representations which have been made in regard to it.

The first thing which strikes our attention is that the executive authority, with few exceptions, is to be vested in a single magistrate. This will scarcely however be considered as a point upon which any comparison can be grounded; for if in this particular there be a resemblance to the King of Great-Britain, there is not less a resemblance to the Grand Signior, to the Khan of Tartary, to the man of the seven mountains, or to the Governor of New-York.

That magistrate is to be elected for *four* years; and is to be re-eligible as often as the People of the United States shall think him worthy of their confidence. In these circumstances, there is a total dissimilitude between *him* and a King of Great-Britain; who is an *hereditary* monarch, possessing the crown as a patrimony descendible to his heirs forever; but there is a close analogy between *him* and a Governor of New-York, who is elected for *three* years, and is re-eligible without limitation or intermission. If we consider how much less time would be requisite for establishing a dangerous influence in a single State, than for establishing a like influence throughout the United States, we must conclude that a duration of *four* years for the Chief Magistrate of the Union, is a degree of permanency far less to be dreaded in that office, than a duration of *three* years for a correspondent office in a single State.

The President of the United States would be liable to be impeached, tried, and upon conviction of treason, bribery, or other high crime or misdemeanors, removed from office; and would afterwards

*The New-York Packet*, March 14, 1788. This essay appeared in *The* [New York] *Independent Journal: or, the General Advertiser* on March 15. In the McLean edition this essay is numbered 69, in the newspapers it is numbered 68.
    1. For background to this document, see "The Federalist. Introductory Note," October 27, 1787–May 28, 1788.

be liable to prosecution and punishment in the ordinary course of law. The person of the King of Great-Britain is sacred and inviolable: There is no constitutional tribunal to which he is amenable; no punishment to which he can be subjected without involving the crisis of a national revolution. In this delicate and important circumstance or personal responsibility, the President of confederated America would stand upon no better ground than a Governor of New-York and upon worse ground than the Governors of Virginia [2] and Delaware.

The President of the United States is to have power to return a bill, which shall have passed the two branches of the Legislature, for re-consideration; but the bill so returned is [3] to become a law, if [4] upon that re-consideration it be approved by two thirds of both houses. The King of Great Britain, on his part, has an absolute negative upon the acts of the two houses of Parliament. The disuse of that power for a considerable time past, does not affect the reality of its existence; and is to be ascribed wholly to the crown's having found the means of substituting influence to authority, or the art of gaining a majority in one or the other of the two houses, to the necessity of exerting a prerogative which could seldom be exerted without hazarding some degree of national agitation. The qualified negative of the President differs widely from this absolute negative of the British sovereign; and tallies exactly with the revisionary authority of the Council of revision of this State, of which the Governor is a constituent part. In this respect, the power of the President would exceed that of the Governor of New-York; because the former would possess singly what the latter shares with the Chancellor and Judges: But it would be precisely the same with that of the Governor of Massachusetts, whose constitution, as to this article, seems to have been the original from which the Convention have copied.

The President is to be the "Commander in Chief of the army and navy of the United States, and of the militia of the several States, when called to the actual service of the United States. He is to have power to grant reprieves and pardons for offences against the United States, *except in cases of impeachment;* to recommend to the con-

2. In the newspaper "Maryland." The substitution was made in McLean and Hopkins.
3. "not" inserted at this point in McLean and Hopkins.
4. "unless" substituted for "if" in McLean and Hopkins.

sideration of Congress such measures as he shall judge necessary and expedient; to convene on extraordinary occasions both houses of the Legislature, or either of them, and in case of disagreement between them *with respect to the time of adjournment,* to adjourn them to such time as he shall think proper; to take care that the laws be faithfully executed; and to commission all officers of the United States." In most of these particulars the power of the President will resemble equally that of the King of Great-Britain and of the Governor of New-York. The most material points of difference are these—First; the President will have only the occasional command of such part of the militia of the nation, as by legislative provision may be called into the actual service of the Union. The King of Great Britain and the Governor of New-York have at all times the entire command of all the militia within their several jurisdictions. In this article therefore the power of the President would be inferior to that of either the Monarch or the Governor. Secondly; the President is to be Commander in Chief of the army and navy of the United States. In this respect his authority would be nominally the same with that of the King of Great-Britain, but in substance much inferior to it. It would amount to nothing more than the supreme command and direction of the military and naval forces, as first General and Admiral of the confederacy; while that of the British King extends to the *declaring* of war and to the *raising* and *regulating* of fleets and armies; all which by the Constitution under consideration would appertain to the Legislature.* The Governor

* *A writer in a Pennsylvania paper, under the signature of* Tamony *has asserted that the King of Great-Britain owes his prerogatives as Commander in Chief to an annual mutiny bill.*[5] *The truth is on the contrary that his prerogative in this respect is immemorial, and was only disputed "contrary to all reason and precedent," as Blackstone, vol. 1, p. 262,*[6] *expresses it, by the long parliament of Charles the first, but by the statute the 13, of Charles second, ch. 6, it was declared to be in the King alone, for that the sole supreme government and command of the militia within his Majesty's realms and dominions, and of all forces by sea and land, and of all forts and places of strength,* ever was and is *the undoubted right of his Majesty and his royal predecessors Kings and Queens of England, and that both or either House of Parliament cannot nor ought to pretend to the same.*

5. The letter signed "Tamony" was dated December 20, 1787, and printed in *The Virginia Independent Chronicle,* January 9, 1788. It was reprinted in *The* [Philadelphia] *Independent Gazetteer,* February 1, 1788. "Tamony" had written:

"The office of president is treated with levity and intimated to be a machine calculated for state pageantry. Suffer me to view the commander of the fleets and armies of America, with a reverential awe, inspired by the contemplation

of New-York on the other hand, is by the Constitution of the State vested only with the command of its militia and navy. But the Constitutions of several of the States, expressly declare their Governors to be the [7] Commanders in Chief as well of the army as navy; and it may well be a question whether those of New-Hampshire and Massachusetts, in particular, do not in this instance confer larger powers upon their respective governors, than could be claimed by a President of the United States. Thirdly; the power of the President in respect to pardons would extend to all cases, *except those of impeachment.* The Governor of New-York may pardon in all cases, even in those of impeachment, except for treason and murder. Is not the power of the Governor in this article, on a calculation of political consequences, greater than that of the President? All conspiracies and plots against the government, which have not been matured into actual treason, may be screened from punishment of every kind, by the interposition of the prerogative of pardoning. If a Governor of New-York therefore should be at the head of any such conspiracy, until the design had been ripened into actual hostility, he could ensure his accomplices and adherents an entire impunity. A President of the Union on the other hand, though he may even pardon treason, when prosecuted in the ordinary course of law, could shelter no offender in any degree from the effects of impeachment & conviction. Would not the prospect of a total indemnity for all the preliminary steps be a greater temptation to undertake and persevere in an enterprise against the public liberty than the mere prospect of an exemption from death and confiscation, if the final execution of the design, upon an actual appeal to arms, should miscarry? Would this last expectation have any influence at all, when the probability was computed that the person who was to afford that exemption might himself be involved in the consequences of the measure; and might be incapacitated by his agency

---

of his great prerogatives, though not dignified with the magic name of King, he will possess more supreme power, than Great Britain allows her hereditary monarchs, who derive ability to support an army from annual supplies, and owe the command of one to an annual mutiny law. The American president may be granted supplies for two years, and his command of a standing army is unrestrained by law or limitation."

6. The reference is to one of the many editions of Sir William Blackstone's *Commentaries on the Laws of England.*

7. "the" omitted in McLean and Hopkins.

in it, from affording the desired impunity? The better to judge of this matter, it will be necessary to recollect that by the proposed Constitution the offence of treason is limited "to levying war upon the United States, and adhering to their enemies, giving them aid and comfort," and that by the laws of New-York it is confined within similar bounds. Fourthly; the President can only adjourn the national Legislature in the single case of disagreement about the time of adjournment. The British monarch may prorogue or even dissolve the Parliament. The Governor of New-York may also prorogue the Legislature of this State for a limited time; a power [8] which in certain situations may be employed to very important purposes.

The President is to have power with the advice and consent of the Senate to make treaties; provided two thirds of the Senators present concur. The King of Great-Britain is the sole and absolute representative of the nation in all foreign transactions. He can of his own accord make treaties of peace, commerce, alliance, and of every other description. It has been insinuated, that his authority in this respect is not conclusive, and that his conventions with foreign powers are subject to the revision, and stand in need of the ratification of Parliament. But I believe this doctrine was never heard of 'till it was broached upon the present occasion. Every jurist † of that kingdom, and every other man acquainted with its constitution knows, as an established fact, that the prerogative of making treaties exists in the crown in its utmost plenitude; and that the compacts entered into by the royal authority have the most complete legal validity and perfection, independent of any other sanction. The Parliament, it is true, is sometimes seen employing itself in altering the existing laws to conform them to the stipulations in a new treaty; and this may have possibly given birth to the imagination that its co-operation was necessary to the obligatory efficacy of the treaty. But this parliamentary interposition proceeds from a different cause; from the necessity of adjusting a most artificial and intricate system of revenue and commercial laws to the changes made in them by the operation of the treaty; and of adapting new provisions and precautions to the new state of things, to keep the machine from running

† *Vide Blackstone's Commentaries, vol. 1,[9] page 257.*

8. "prerogative" substituted for "power" in Hopkins.
9. "vol. 1" omitted in the newspaper; inserted in McLean and Hopkins.

into disorder. In this respect therefore, there is no comparison between the intended power of the President, and the actual power of the British sovereign. The one can perform alone, what the other can only do with the concurrence of a branch of the Legislature. It must be admitted that in this instance the power of the fœderal executive would exceed that of any State executive. But this arises naturally from the exclusive possession by the Union of that part of the sovereign power, which relates to treaties. If the confederacy were to be dissolved, it would become a question, whether the executives of the several States were not solely invested with that delicate and important prerogative.

The President is also to be authorised to receive Ambassadors and other public Ministers. This, though it has been a rich theme of declamation, is more a matter of dignity than of authority. It is a circumstance, which will be without consequence in the administration of the government; and it was far more convenient that it should be arranged in this manner, than that there should be a necessity of convening the Legislature, or one of its branches, upon every arrival of a foreign minister; though it were merely to take the place of a departed predecessor.

The President is to nominate and *with the advice and consent of the Senate* to appoint Ambassadors and other public Ministers, Judges of the Supreme Court, and in general all officers of the United States established by law and whose appointments are not otherwise provided for by the Constitution. The King of Great-Britain is emphatically and truly stiled the fountain of honor. He not only appoints to all offices, but can create offices. He can confer titles of nobility at pleasure; and has the disposal of an immense number of church preferments. There is evidently a great inferiority, in the power of the President in this particular, to that of the British King; nor is it equal to that of the Governor of New-York, if we are to interpret the meaning of the constitution of the State by the practice which has obtained under it. The power of appointment is with us lodged in a Council composed of the Governor and four members of the Senate chosen by the Assembly. The Governor *claims* and has frequently *exercised* the right of nomination, and is *entitled* to a casting vote in the appointment. If he really has the right of nominating, his authority is in this respect equal to that of the President, and exceeds it in the article of the casting vote. In the national government, if the Senate should be divided, no appointment could be made: In the government of New-York, if the Council should be divided the Governor can turn the scale and confirm his own nomination.†† If we compare the publicity which must necessarily attend the mode of appointment by the President and an entire branch of the national Legislature, with the privacy in the mode of appointment by the Governor of New-York, closeted in a [11] secret apartment with at most four, and frequently with only two persons; and if we at the same time consider how much more easy it must be to influence the small number of which a Council of Appointment consists than the considerable number of which the national Senate would consist, we cannot hesitate to pronounce, that the power of the Chief Magistrate of this State in the disposition of offices must in practice be greatly superior to that of the Chief Magistrate of the Union.

Hence it appears, that except as to the concurrent authority of the President in the article of treaties, it would be difficult to determine whether that Magistrate would in the aggregate, possess more or less power than the Governor of New-York. And it appears yet more unequivocally that there is no pretence for the parallel which has been attempted between him and the King of Great-Britain. But to render the contrast, in this respect, still more striking, it may be of use to throw the principal circumstances of dissimilitude into a closer groupe.

The President of the United States would be an officer elected by the people for *four* years. The King of Great-Britain is a perpetual and *hereditary* prince. The one would be amenable to personal punishment and disgrace: The person of the other is sacred and inviolable. The one would have a qualified negative upon the acts of the legislative body: The other has an *absolute* negative. The

‡ *Candor however demands an acknowledgement; that I do not think the claim of the Governor to a right of nomination well founded. Yet it is always justifiable to reason from the practice of a government till its propriety has been constitutionally questioned. And independent of this claim, when we take into view the other considerations [10] and pursue them through all their consequences, we shall be inclined to draw much the same conclusion.*

10. In the newspaper, "consideration"; "considerations" substituted in Mc-Lean and Hopkins.

11. "a" omitted in McLean.

one would have a right to command the military and naval forces of the nation: The other in addition to this right, possesses that of *declaring* war, and of *raising* and *regulating* fleets and armies by his own authority. The one would have a concurrent power with a branch of the Legislature in the formation of treaties: The other is the *sole possessor* of the power of making treaties. The one would have a like concurrent authority in appointing to offices: The other is the sole author of all appointments. The one can infer no privileges whatever: The other can make denizens of aliens, noblemen of commoners, can erect corporations with all the rights incident to corporate bodies. The one can prescribe no rules concerning the commerce or currency of the nation: The other is in several respects the arbiter of commerce, and in this capacity can establish markets and fairs, can regulate weights and measures, can lay embargoes for a limited time, can coin money, can authorise or prohibit the circulation of foreign coin. The one has no particle of spiritual jurisdiction: The other is the supreme head and Governor of the national church! What answer shall we give to those who would persuade us that things so unlike resemble each other? The same that ought to be given to those who tell us, that a government, the whole power of which would be in the hands of the elective and periodical servants of the people, is an aristocracy, a monarchy, and a despotism.

PUBLIUS.

## The Federalist No. 70 [1]

[New York, March 15, 1788]

*To the People of the State of New-York.*

THERE is an idea, which is not without its advocates, that a vigorous executive is inconsistent with the genius of republican government. The enlightened well wishers to this species of government must at least hope that the supposition is destitute of foundation; since they can never admit its truth, without at the same time

*The* [New York] *Independent Journal: or, the General Advertiser,* March 15, 1788. This essay appeared in *The New-York Packet* on March 18. In the McLean edition this essay is numbered 70, in the newspapers it is numbered 69.

1. For background to this document, see "The Federalist. Introductory Note," October 27, 1787–May 28, 1788.

admitting the condemnation of their own principles. Energy in the executive is a leading character in the definition of good government. It is essential to the protection of the community against foreign attacks: It is not less essential to the steady administration of the laws, to the protection of property against those irregular and high handed combinations, which sometimes interrupt the ordinary course of justice to the security of liberty against the enterprises and assaults of ambition, of faction and of anarchy. Every man the least conversant in Roman story knows how often that republic was obliged to take refuge in the absolute power of a single man, under the formidable title of dictator, as well against the intrigues of ambitious individuals, who aspired to the tyranny, and the seditions of whole classes of the community, whose conduct threatened the existence of all government, as against the invasions of external enemies, who menaced the conquest and destruction of Rome.

There can be no need however to multiply arguments or examples on this head. A feeble executive implies a feeble execution of the government. A feeble execution is but another phrase for a bad execution: And a government ill executed, whatever it may be in theory, must be in practice a bad government.

Taking it for granted, therefore, that all men of sense will agree in the necessity of an energetic executive; it will only remain to inquire, what are the ingredients which constitute this energy—how far can they be combined with those other ingredients which constitute safety in the republican sense? And how far does this combination characterise the plan, which has been reported by the convention?

The ingredients, which constitute energy in the executive, are first unity, secondly duration, thirdly an adequate provision for its support, fourthly competent powers.[2]

The circumstances[3] which constitute safety in the republican sense are, Ist. a due dependence on the people, secondly[4] a due responsibility.

Those politicians and statesmen, who have been the most cele-

2. The words "first," "secondly," "thirdly," and "fourthly," omitted in McLean and Hopkins.
3. "ingredients" substituted for "circumstances" in McLean and Hopkins.
4. The words "Ist" and "secondly" omitted in McLean and Hopkins.

brated for the soundness of their principles, and for the justness of
their views, have declared in favor of a single executive and a
numerous legislature. They have with great propriety considered
energy as the most necessary qualification of the former, and have
regarded this as most applicable to power in a single hand; while
they have with equal propriety considered the latter as best adapted
to deliberation and wisdom, and best calculated to conciliate the
confidence of the people and to secure their privileges and interests.

That unity is conducive to energy will not be disputed. Decision,
activity, secrecy, and [5] dispatch will generally characterise the proceedings [6] of one man, in a much more eminent degree, than the
proceedings of any greater number; and in proportion as the number is increased, these qualities will be diminished.

This unity may be destroyed in two ways; either by vesting the
power in two or more magistrates of equal dignity and authority;
or by vesting it ostensibly in one man, subject in whole or in part
to the controul and co-operation of others, in the capacity of
counsellors to him. Of the first the two consuls of Rome may serve
as an example; of the last we shall find examples in the constitutions
of several of the states. New-York and New-Jersey, if I recollect
right, are the only states, which have entrusted the executive authority wholly to single men.* Both these methods of destroying the
unity of the executive have their partisans; but the votaries of an
executive council are the most numerous. They are both liable, if
not to equal, to similar objections; and may in most lights be examined in conjunction.

The experience of other nations will afford little instruction on
this head. As far however as it teaches any thing, it teaches us not
to be inamoured of plurality in the executive. We have seen that
the Achæans on an experiment of two Prætors, were induced to
abolish one.[7] The Roman history records many instances of mischiefs
to the republic from the dissentions between the consuls, and be-

---

* *New-York has no council except for the single purpose of appointing
to offices; New-Jersey has a council, whom the governor may consult. But
I think from the terms of the constitution their resolutions do not bind him.*

5. "and" omitted in the newspaper; inserted in McLean and Hopkins.
6. In the newspaper, "proceeding"; "proceedings" was substituted in McLean
and Hopkins.
7. See essay 18.

tween the military tribunes, who were at times substituted to the consuls. But it gives us no specimens of any peculiar advantages derived to the state, from the circumstance of the [8] plurality of those magistrates. That the dissentions between them were not more frequent, or more fatal, is matter of astonishment; until we advert to the singular position in which the republic was almost continually placed and to the prudent policy pointed out by the circumstances of the state, and pursued by the consuls, of making a division of the government between them. The Patricians engaged in a perpetual struggle with the Plebeians for the preservation of their antient authorities and dignities; the consuls, who were generally chosen out of the former body, were commonly united by the personal interest they had in the defence of the privileges of their order. In addition to this motive of union, after the arms of the republic had considerably expanded the bounds of its empire, it became an established custom with the consuls to divide the administration between themselves by lot; one of them remaining at Rome to govern the city and its environs; the other taking the command in the more distant provinces. This expedient must no doubt have had great influence in preventing those collisions and rivalships, which might otherwise have embroiled the peace of [9] the republic.

But quitting the dim light of historical research, and attaching ourselves purely to the dictates of reason and good sense, we shall discover much greater cause to reject than to approve the idea of plurality in the executive, under any modification whatever.

Wherever two or more persons are engaged in any common enterprize or pursuit, there is always danger of difference of opinion. If it be a public trust or office in which they are cloathed with equal dignity and authority, there is peculiar danger of personal emulation and even animosity. From either and especially from all these causes, the most bitter dissentions are apt to spring. Whenever these happen, they lessen the respectability, weaken the authority, and distract the plans and operations of those whom they divide. If they should unfortunately assail the supreme executive magistracy of a country, consisting of a plurality of persons, they might impede or frustrate the most important measures of the government, in the

8. "circumstances of the" omitted in McLean and Hopkins.
9. "peace of" omitted in McLean and Hopkins.

most critical emergencies of the state. And what is still worse, they might split the community into the most [10] violent and irreconcilable factions, adhering differently to the different individuals who composed the magistracy.

Men often oppose a thing merely because they have had no agency in planning it, or because it may have been planned by those whom they dislike. But if they have been consulted and have happened to disapprove, opposition then becomes in their estimation an indispensable duty of self love. They seem to think themselves bound in honor, and by all the motives of personal infallibility to defeat the success of what has been resolved upon, contrary to their sentiments. Men of upright, benevolent tempers have too many opportunities of remarking with horror, to what desperate lengths this disposition is sometimes carried, and how often the great interests of society are sacrificed to the vanity, to the conceit and to the obstinacy of individuals, who have credit enough to make their passions and their caprices interesting to mankind. Perhaps the question now before the public may in its consequences afford melancholy proofs of the effects of this despicable frailty, or rather detestable vice in the human character.

Upon the principles of a free government, inconveniencies from the source just mentioned must necessarily be submitted to in the formation of the legislature; but it is unnecessary and therefore unwise to introduce them into the constitution of the executive. It is here too that they may be most pernicious. In the legislature, promptitude of decision is oftener an evil than a benefit. The differences of opinion, and the jarrings of parties in that department of the government, though they may sometimes obstruct salutary plans, yet often promote deliberations and circumspection; and serve to check excesses in the majority. When a resolution too is once taken, the opposition must be at an end. That resolution is a law, and resistance to it punishable. But no favourable circumstances palliate or atone for the disadvantages of dissention in the executive department. Here they are pure and unmixed. There is no point at which they cease to operate. They serve to embarrass and weaken the execution of the plan or measure, to which they relate, from the first step to the final conclusion of it. They constantly counteract those

10. "most" omitted in McLean and Hopkins.

qualities in the executive, which are the most necessary ingredients in its composition, vigour and expedition, and this without any counterballancing good. In the conduct of war, in which the energy of the executive is the bulwark of the national security, every thing would be to be apprehended from its plurality.

It must be confessed that these observations apply with principal weight to the first [11] case supposed, that is to a plurality of magistrates of equal dignity and authority; a scheme the advocates for which are not likely to form a numerous sect: But they apply, though not with equal, yet with considerable weight, to the project of a council, whose concurrence is made constitutionally necessary to the operations of the ostensible executive. An artful cabal in that council would be able to distract and to enervate the whole system of administration. If no such cabal should exist, the mere diversity of views and opinions would alone be sufficient to tincture the exercise of the executive authority with a spirit of habitual feebleness and delatoriness.

But one of the weightiest objections to a plurality in the executive, and which lies as much against the last as the first plan, is that it tends to conceal faults, and destroy responsibility. Responsibility is of two kinds, to censure and to punishment. The first is the most important of the two; especially in an elective office. Man,[12] in public trust, will much oftener act in such a manner as to render him [13] unworthy of being any longer trusted, than in such a manner as to make him [14] obnoxious to legal punishment. But the multiplication of the executive adds to the difficulty of detection in either case. It often becomes impossible, amidst mutual accusations, to determine on whom the blame or the punishment of a pernicious measure, or series of pernicious measures ought really to fall. It is shifted from one to another with so much dexterity, and under such plausible appearances, that the public opinion is left in suspense about the real author. The circumstances which may have led to any national miscarriage or misfortune are sometimes so complicated, that where there are a number of actors who may have had different degrees and kinds of agency, though we may clearly see upon the whole that

11. In the newspaper, "full"; "first" was substituted in McLean and Hopkins.
12. "Men" substituted for "Man" in McLean and Hopkins.
13. "them" substituted for "him" in McLean and Hopkins.
14. "them" substituted for "him" in McLean and Hopkins.

there has been mismanagement, yet it may be impracticable to pronounce to whose account the evil which may have been incurred is truly chargeable.

"I was overruled by my council. The council were so divided in their opinions, that it was impossible to obtain any better resolution on the point." These and similar pretexts are constantly at hand, whether true or false. And who is there that will either take the trouble or incur the odium of a strict scrutiny into the secret springs of the transaction? Should there be found a citizen zealous enough to undertake the unpromising task, if there happen to be a collusion between the parties concerned, how easy is it to cloath the circumstances with so much ambiguity, as to render it uncertain what was the precise conduct of any of those parties?

In the single instance in which the governor of this state is coupled with a council, that is in the appointment to offices, we have seen the mischiefs of it in the view now under consideration.[15] Scandalous appointments to important offices have been made. Some cases indeed have been so flagrant, that ALL PARTIES have agreed in the impropriety of the thing. When enquiry has been made, the blame has been laid by the governor on the members of the council; who on their part have charged it upon his nomination: While the people remain altogether at a loss to determine by whose influence their interests have been committed to hands so unqualified, and [16] so manifestly improper. In tenderness to individuals, I forbear to descend to particulars.

It is evident from these considerations, that the plurality of the executive tends to deprive the people of the two greatest securities they can have for the faithful exercise of any delegated power; first, the restraints of public opinion, which lose their efficacy as well on account of the division of the censure attendant on bad measures among a number, as on account of the uncertainty on whom it ought to fall; and secondly, the opportunity of discovering with facility and clearness the misconduct of the persons they trust, in order either to their removal from office, or to their actual punishment, in cases which admit of it.

In England the king is a perpetual magistrate; and it is a maxim,

15. See essay 69.
16. "so unqualified, and" omitted in Hopkins.

which has obtained for the sake of the public peace, that he is un-accountable for his administration, and his person sacred. Nothing therefore can be wiser in that kingdom than to annex to the king a constitutional council, who may be responsible to the nation for the advice they give. Without this there would be no responsibility whatever in the executive department; an idea inadmissible in a free government. But even there the king is not bound by the resolutions of his council, though they are answerable for the advice they give. He is the absolute master of his own conduct, in the exercise of his office; and may observe or disregard the council given to him at his sole discretion.

But in a republic, where every magistrate ought to be personally responsible for his behaviour in office, the reason which in the British constitution dictates the propriety of a council not only ceases to apply, but turns against the institution. In the monarchy of Great-Britain, it furnishes a substitute for the prohibited responsibility of the chief magistrate; which serves in some degree as a hostage to the national justice for his good behaviour. In the American republic it would serve to destroy, or would greatly diminish the intended and necessary responsibility of the chief magistrate himself.

The idea of a council to the executive, which has so generally obtained in the state constitutions, has been derived from that maxim of republican jealousy, which considers power as safer in the hands of a number of men than of a single man. If the maxim should be admitted to be applicable to the case, I should contend that the advantage on that side would not counterballance the numerous disadvantages on the opposite side. But I do not think the rule at all applicable to the executive power. I clearly concur in opinion in this particular with a writer whom the celebrated Junius [17] pronounces to be "deep, solid and ingenious," that, "the executive power is more easily confined when it is one:" * [18] That it is far more safe

* De Lome. [19]

17. *Junius. Stat. Nominis Umbra* (London: Printed for Henry Sampson Woodfull . . . 1772), I, xxxi.

18. Junius referred to Jean Louis de Lolme, *The Constitution of England, or An Account of the English Government; In which it is compared with the Republican Form of Government, and occasionally with the other Monarchies in Europe* (3rd ed., London, 1781), 215.

19. In the newspapers, "De Lostme"; "De Lome" substituted in McLean and Hopkins.

there should be a single object for the jealousy and watchfulness of the people; and [20] in a word that all multiplication of the executive is rather dangerous than friendly to liberty.

A little consideration will satisfy us, that the species of security sought for in the multiplication of the executive is unattainable. Numbers must be so great as to render combination difficult; or they are rather a source of danger than of security. The united credit and influence of several individuals must be more formidable to liberty than the credit and influence of either of them separately. When power therefore is placed in the hands of so small a number of men, as to admit of their interests and views being easily combined in a common enterprise, by an artful leader, it becomes more liable to abuse and more dangerous when abused, than if it be lodged in the hands of one man; who from the very circumstance of his being alone will be more narrowly watched and more readily suspected, and who cannot unite so great a mass of influence as when he is associated with others. The Decemvirs of Rome, whose name denotes their number,† were more to be dreaded in their usurpation than any ONE of them would have been. No person would think of proposing an executive much more numerous than that body, from six to a dozen have been suggested for the number of the council. The extreme of these numbers is not too great for an easy combination; and from such a combination America would have more to fear, than from the ambition of any single individual. A council to a magistrate, who is himself responsible for what he does, are generally nothing better than a clog upon his good intentions; are often the instruments and accomplices of his bad, and are almost always a cloak to his faults.

I forbear to dwell upon the subject of expence; though it be evident that if the council should be numerous enough to answer the principal end, aimed at by the institution, the salaries of the members, who must be drawn from their homes to reside at the seat of government, would form an item in the catalogue of public expenditures, too serious to be incurred for an object of equivocal utility.

I will only add, that prior to the appearance of the constitution,

† *Ten.*

20. "and" omitted in Hopkins.

I rarely met with an intelligent man from any of the states, who did not admit as the result of experience, that the UNITY of the Executive of this state was one of the best of the distinguishing features of our constitution.

PUBLIUS.

## The Federalist No. 71 [1]

[New York, March 18, 1788]

*To the People of the State of New-York.*

DURATION in office has been mentioned as the second requisite to the energy of the executive authority. This has relation to two objects: To the personal firmness of the Executive [2] Magistrate in the employment of his constitutional powers; and to the stability of the system of administration which may have been adopted under his auspices. With regard to the first, it must be evident, that the longer the duration in office, the greater will be the probability of obtaining so important an advantage. It is a general principle of human nature, that a man will be interested in whatever he possesses, in proportion to the firmness or precariousness of the tenure, by which he holds it; will be less attached to what he holds by a momentary or uncertain title, than to what he enjoys by a durable or certain title; [3] and of course will be willing to risk more for the sake of the one, than for the sake [4] of the other. This remark is not less applicable to a political privilege, or honor, or trust, than to any article of ordinary property. The inference from it is, that a man acting in the capacity of Chief Magistrate, under a consciousness, that in a very short time he *must* lay down his office, will be apt to feel himself too little interested in it, to hazard any material censure or perplexity, from the independent exertion of his powers, or from

*The New-York Packet*, March 18, 1788. This was printed in *The* [New York] *Independent Journal: or, the General Advertiser* on March 19. In the McLean edition this essay is numbered 71, in the newspapers it is numbered 70.
    1. For background to this document, see "The Federalist. Introductory Note," October 27, 1787–May 28, 1788.
    2. "chief" substituted for "Executive" in Hopkins.
    3. "by a title durable or certain" substituted for "by a durable or certain title" in Hopkins.
    4. "for the sake" omitted in Hopkins.

encountering the ill-humors, however transient, which may happen to prevail either in a considerable part of the society itself, or even in a predominant faction in the legislative body. If the case should only be, that he *might* lay it down, unless continued by a new choice; and if he should be desirous of being continued, his wishes conspiring with his fears would tend still more powerfully to corrupt his integrity, or debase his fortitude. In either case feebleness and irresolution must be the characteristics of the station.

There are some, who would be inclined to regard the servile pliancy of the executive to a prevailing current, either in the community, or in the Legislature, as its best recommendation. But such men entertain very crude notions, as well of the purposes for which government was instituted, as of the true means by which the public happiness may be promoted. The republican principle demands, that the deliberate sense of the community should govern the conduct of those to whom they entrust the management of their affairs; but it does not require an unqualified complaisance to every sudden breese of passion, or to every transient impulse which the people may receive from the arts of men, who flatter their prejudices to betray their interests. It is a just observation, that the people commonly *intend* the PUBLIC GOOD. This often applies to their very errors. But their good sense would despise the adulator, who should pretend that they always *reason right* about the *means* of promoting it. They know from experience, that they sometimes err; and the wonder is, that they so seldom err as they do; beset as they continually are by the wiles of parasites and sycophants, by the snares of the ambitious, the avaricious, the desperate; by the artifices of men, who possess their confidence more than they deserve it, and of those who seek to possess, rather than to deserve it. When occasions present themselves in which the interests of the people are at variance with their inclinations, it is the duty of the persons whom they have appointed to be the guardians of those interests, to withstand the temporary delusion, in order to give them time and opportunity for more cool and sedate reflection. Instances might be cited, in which a conduct of this kind has saved the people from very fatal consequences of their own mistakes, and has procured lasting monuments of their gratitude to the men, who had courage and magnanimity enough to serve them at the peril of their displeasure.

But however inclined we might be to insist upon an unbounded complaisance in the executive to the inclinations of the people, we can with no propriety contend for a like complaisance to the humors of the Legislature. The latter may sometimes stand in opposition to the former; and at other times the people may be entirely neutral. In either supposition, it is certainly desirable that the executive should be in a situation to dare to act his own opinion with vigor and decision.

The same rule, which teaches the propriety of a partition between the various branches of power, teaches us [5] likewise that this partition ought to be so contrived as to render the one independent of the other. To what purpose separate the executive, or the judiciary, from the legislative, if both the executive and the judiciary are so constituted as to be at the absolute devotion of the legislative? Such a separation must be merely nominal and incapable of producing the ends for which it was established. It is one thing to be subordinate to the laws, and [6] another to be dependent on the legislative body. The first comports with, the last violates, the fundamental principles of good government; and whatever may be the forms of the Constitution, unites all power in the same hands. The tendency of the legislative authority to absorb every other, has been fully displayed and illustrated by examples, in some preceding numbers.[7] In governments purely republican, this tendency is almost irresistable. The representatives of the people, in a popular assembly, seem sometimes to fancy that they are the people themselves; and betray strong symptoms of impatience and disgust at the least sign of opposition from any other quarter; as if the exercise of its rights by either the executive or judiciary, were a breach of their privilege and an outrage to their dignity. They often appear disposed to exert an imperious controul over the other departments; and as they commonly have the people on their side, they always act with such momentum as to make it very difficult for the other members of the government to maintain the balance of the Constitution.

It may perhaps be asked how the shortness of the duration in office can affect the independence of the executive on the legislature,

5. "us" omitted in McLean and Hopkins.
6. "and" omitted in Hopkins.
7. The subject was discussed at length in essays 48 and 49.

unless the one were possessed of the power of appointing or displacing the other? One answer to this enquiry may be drawn from the principle already remarked,[8] that is from the slender interest a man is apt to take in a short lived advantage, and the little inducement it affords him to expose himself on account of it to any considerable inconvenience or hazard. Another answer, perhaps more obvious, though not more conclusive, will result from the consideration [9] of the influence of the legislative body over the people, which might be employed to prevent the re-election of a man, who by an upright resistance to any sinister project of that body, should have made himself obnoxious to its resentment.

It may be asked also whether a duration of four years would answer the end proposed, and if it would not, whether a less period which would at least be recommended by greater security against ambitious designs, would not for that reason be preferable to a longer period, which was at the same time too short for the purpose of inspiring the desired firmness and independence of the magistrate?

It cannot be affirmed, that a duration of four years or any other limited duration would completely answer the end proposed; but it would contribute towards it in a degree which would have a material influence upon the spirit and character of the government. Between the commencement and termination of such a period there would always be a considerable interval, in which the prospect of annihilation would be sufficiently remote not to have an improper effect upon the conduct of a man endued with a tolerable portion of fortitude; and in which he might reasonably promise himself, that there would be time enough, before it arrived, to make the community sensible of the propriety of the measures he might incline to pursue. Though it be probable, that as he approached the moment when the public were by a new election to signify their sense of his conduct, his confidence and with it, his firmness would decline; yet both the one and the other would derive support from the opportunities, which his previous continuance in the station had afforded him of establishing himself in the esteem and good will of his constituents. He might then hazard with safety,[10] in proportion

8. "mentioned" substituted for "remarked" in Hopkins.
9. "circumstance" substituted for "consideration" in Hopkins.
10. "with prudence, hazard the incurring of reproach" substituted for "hazard with safety" in Hopkins.

to the proofs he had given of his wisdom and integrity, and to the title he had acquired to the respect and attachment of his fellow citizens. As on the one hand, a duration of four years will contribute to the firmness of the executive in a sufficient degree to render it a very valuable ingredient in the composition; so on the other, it is not long enough to justify any alarm for the public liberty. If a British House of Commons, from the most feeble beginnings, *from the mere power of assenting or disagreeing to the imposition of a new tax,* have by rapid strides, reduced the prerogatives of the crown and the privileges of the nobility within the limits they conceived to be compatible with the principles of a free government; while they raised themselves to the rank and consequence of a coequal branch of the Legislature; if they have been able in one instance to abolish both the royalty and the aristocracy, and to overturn all the ancient establishments as well in the church as State; if they have been able on a recent occasion to make the monarch tremble at the prospect of an innovation * attempted by them; what would be to be feared from an elective magistrate of four years duration, with the confined authorities of a President of the United States? What but that he might be unequal to the task which the Constitution assigns him? I shall only add that if his duration be such as to leave a doubt of his firmness, that doubt is inconsistent with a jealousy of his encroachments.

PUBLIUS.

* *This was the case with respect to Mr. Fox's India bill which was carried in the House of Commons, and rejected in the House of Lords, to the entire satisfaction, as it is said, of the people.*[11]

11. In 1783, Charles James Fox introduced in the House of Commons a bill providing for the reorganization of the government of India. When the Commons, by a vote of two to one, passed it, George III sent word to the House of Lords that he would regard as a personal enemy anyone who voted for it. It was defeated by thirteen votes.

# The Federalist No. 72 [1]

[New York, March 19, 1788]

*To the People of the State of New-York.*

THE ADMINISTRATION of government, in its largest sense, comprehends all the operations of the body politic, whether legislative, executive or judiciary, but in its most usual and perhaps in its most precise signification, it is limited to executive details, and falls peculiarly within the province of the executive department. The actual conduct of foreign negotiations, the preparatory plans of finance, the application and disbursement of the public monies, in conformity to the general appropriations of the legislature, the arrangement of the army and navy, the direction of the operations of war; these and other matters of a like nature constitute what seems to be most properly understood by the administration of government. The persons therefore, to whose immediate management these different matters are committed, ought to be considered as the assistants or deputies of the chief magistrate; and, on this account, they ought to derive their offices from his appointment, at least from his nomination, and ought [2] to be subject to his superintendence. This view of the subject [3] will at once suggest to us the intimate connection between the duration of the executive magistrate in office, and the stability of the system of administration. To reverse and [4] undo what has been done by a predecessor is very often considered by a successor, as the best proof he can give of his own capacity and desert; and, in addition to this propensity, where the alteration has been the result of public choice, the person substituted is warranted in supposing, that the dismission of his predecessor has proceeded from a dislike to his measures, and that the less he resembles him the more he will recommend himself to the favor of his constituents.

*The* [New York] *Independent Journal: or, the General Advertiser,* March 19, 1788. On March 21 this essay was printed in *The New-York Packet.* In the McLean edition this essay is numbered 72, in the newspapers it is numbered 71.

1. For background to this document, see "The Federalist. Introductory Note," October 27, 1787–May 28, 1788.
2. "ought" omitted in Hopkins.
3. "thing" substituted for "subject" in Hopkins.
4. "reverse and" omitted in Hopkins.

These considerations, and the influence of personal confidences and attachments, would be likely to induce every new president to promote a change of men to fill the subordinate stations; and these causes together could not fail to occasion a disgraceful and ruinous mutability in the administration of the government.

With a positive duration of considerable extent, I connect the circumstance of re-eligibility. The first is necessary to give to [5] the officer himself the inclination and the resolution to act his part well, and to the community time and leisure to observe the tendency of his measures, and thence to form an experimental estimate of their merits. The last is necessary to enable the people, when they see reason to approve of his conduct, to continue him in the station, in order to prolong the utility of his talents and virtues, and to secure to the government, the advantage of permanency in a wise system of administration.

Nothing appears more plausible at first sight, nor more ill founded upon close inspection, than a scheme, which in relation to the present point has had some respectable advocates—I mean that of continuing the chief magistrate in office for a certain time, and then excluding him from it, either for a limited period, or for ever after. This exclusion whether temporary or perpetual would have nearly the same effects; and these effects would be for the most part rather pernicious than salutary.

One ill effect of the exclusion would be a diminution of the inducements to good behaviour. There are few men who would not feel much less zeal in the discharge of a duty, when they were conscious that the advantages [6] of the station, with which it was connected, must be relinquished at a determinate period, than when they were permitted to entertain a hope of *obtaining* by *meriting* a continuance of them. This position will not be disputed, so long as it is admitted that the desire of reward is one of the strongest incentives of human conduct, or that the best security for the fidelity of mankind is to make their interest coincide with their duty. Even the love of fame, the ruling passion of the noblest minds, which would prompt a man to plan and undertake extensive and arduous enterprises for the public benefit, requiring considerable time to mature

5. "to" omitted in McLean and Hopkins.
6. "advantage" substituted for "advantages" in McLean and Hopkins.

and perfect them, if he could flatter himself with the prospect of being allowed to finish what he had begun, would on the contrary deter him from the undertaking, when he foresaw that he must quit the scene, before he could accomplish the work, and must commit that, together with his own reputation, to hands which might be unequal or unfriendly to the task. The most to be expected from the generality of men, in such a situation, is the negative merit of not doing harm instead of the positive merit of doing good.

Another ill effect of the exclusion would be the temptation to sordid [7] views, to peculation, and in some instances, the usurpation. An avaricious man, who might happen to fill the offices, looking forward to a time when he must at all events yield up the emoluments [8] he enjoyed, would feel a propensity, not easy to be resisted by such a man, to make the best use of the opportunity he enjoyed,[9] while it [10] lasted; and might not scruple to have recourse to the most corrupt expedients to make the harvest as abundant as it was transitory; [11] though the same man [12] probably, with a different prospect before him, might content himself with the regular perquisites [13] of his station,[14] and might even be unwilling to risk the consequences of an abuse of his opportunities. His avarice might be a guard upon his avarice. Add to this, that the same man might be vain or ambitious as well as avaricious. And if he could expect to prolong his honors, by his good conduct, he might hesitate to sacrifice his appetite for them to his appetite for gain. But with the prospect before him of approaching and inevitable annihilation, his avarice would be likely to get the victory over his caution, his vanity or his ambition.

An ambitious man too, when he found [15] himself seated on the summit of his country's honors, when he looked [16] forward to the

7. In the newspaper, "sacred"; "sordid" was substituted in McLean and Hopkins.
8. "advantages" substituted for "emoluments" in McLean and Hopkins.
9. "his opportunities" substituted for "the opportunity he enjoyed" in McLean and Hopkins.
10. "they" substituted for "it" in McLean and Hopkins.
11. In the newspaper, "transient"; "transitory" was substituted in McLean and Hopkins.
12. "person" substituted for "man" in Hopkins.
13. "emoluments" substituted for "perquisites" in Hopkins.
14. In the newspaper, "situation"; "station" was substituted in McLean and Hopkins.
15. "finding" substituted for "when he found" in McLean and Hopkins.
16. "looking" substituted for "when he looked" in McLean and Hopkins.

time at which he must descend from the exalted eminence forever; and reflected [17] that no exertion of merit on his part could save him from the unwelcome reverse: Such a man, in such a situation,[18] would be much more violently tempted to embrace a favorable conjuncture for attempting the prolongation of his power, at every personal hazard, than if he had the probability of answering the same end by doing his duty.

Would it promote the peace of the community, or the stability of the government, to have half a dozen men who had had credit enough to be raised [19] to the seat of the supreme magistracy, wandering among the people like discontented ghosts, and sighing for a place which they were destined [20] never more to possess?

A third ill effect of the exclusion would be the depriving the community of the advantage of the experience gained by the chief magistrate in the exercise of his office. That experience is the parent of wisdom is an adage, the truth of which is recognized by the wisest as well as the simplest of mankind. What more desirable or more essential than this quality in the governors of nations? Where more desirable or more essential than in the first magistrate of a nation? Can it be wise to put this desirable and essential quality under the ban of the constitution; and to declare that the moment it is acquired, its possessor shall be compelled to abandon the station in which it was acquired, and to which it is adapted? This nevertheless is the precise import of all those regulations, which exclude men from serving their country, by the choice of their fellow citizens, after they have, by a course of service fitted themselves for doing it with a greater degree of utility.

A fourth ill effect of the exclusion would be the banishing men from stations, in which in certain emergencies of the state their presence might be of the greatest moment to the public interest or safety. There is no nation which has not at one period or another experienced an absolute necessity of the services of particular men, in particular situations, perhaps it would not be too strong to say,

17. "reflecting" substituted for "reflected" in McLean and Hopkins.
18. "Such a man, in such a situation," omitted in McLean and Hopkins.
19. "to raise themselves" substituted for "to be raised" in McLean and Hopkins.
20. In the newspaper, "descried"; "destined" was substituted in McLean and Hopkins.

to the preservation of its political existence. How unwise therefore must be every such self-denying ordinance, as serves to prohibit a nation from making use of its own citizens, in the manner best suited to its exigences and circumstances! Without supposing the personal essentiality of the man, it is evident that a change of the chief magistrate, at the breaking out of a war, or at [21] any similar crisis, for another even of equal merit, would at all times be detrimental to the community; inasmuch as it would substitute inexperience to experience, and would tend to unhinge and set afloat the already settled train of the administration.

A fifth ill effect of the exclusion would be, that it would operate as a constitutional interdiction of stability in the administration. *By necessitating* [22] a change of men, in the first office in the nation, it would necessitate a mutability of measures. It is not generally to be expected, that men will vary; and measures remain uniform. The contrary is the usual course of things. And we need not be apprehensive there will be too much stability, while there is even the option of changing; nor need we desire to prohibit the people from continuing their confidence, where they think it may be safely placed, and where by constancy on their part, they may obviate the fatal inconveniences of fluctuating councils and a variable policy.

These are some of the disadvantages, which would flow from the principle of exclusion. They apply most forcibly to the scheme of a perpetual exclusion; but when we consider that even a partial exclusion [23] would always render the re-admission of the person a remote and precarious object, the observations which have been made will apply nearly as fully to one case as to the other.

What are the advantages promised to counterballance these disadvantages? [24] They are represented to be Ist. Greater independence in the magistrate: 2dly. Greater security to the people. Unless the exclusion be perpetual there will be no pretence to infer the first advantage. But even in that case, may he have no object beyond his present station to which he may sacrifice his independence? May

21. "at" omitted in McLean and Hopkins.
22. "By inducing the necessity of" substituted for "*By necessitating*" in Hopkins.
23. "one" substituted for "exclusion" in McLean and Hopkins.
24. In the newspaper, "these advantages"; "these disadvantages" was substituted in McLean; "the evils" was substituted in Hopkins.

he have no connections, no friends, for whom he may sacrifice it? May he not be less willing, by a firm conduct, to make personal enemies, when he acts under the impression, that a time is fast approaching, on the arrival of which he not only MAY, but MUST be exposed to their resentments, upon an equal, perhaps upon an inferior footing? It is not an easy point to determine whether his independence would be most promoted or impaired by such an arrangement.

As to the second supposed advantage, there is still greater reason to entertain doubts concerning it.[25] If the exclusion were to be perpetual,[26] a man of irregular ambition, of whom alone there could be reason in any case to entertain apprehensions, would with infinite reluctance yield to the necessity of taking his leave forever of a post, in which his passion for power and pre-eminence had acquired the force of habit. And if he had been fortunate or adroit enough to conciliate the good will of people he might induce them to consider as a very odious and unjustifiable restraint upon themselves, a provision which was calculated to debar them of the right of giving a fresh proof of their attachment to a favorite. There may be conceived circumstances, in which this disgust of the people, seconding the thwarted ambition of such a favourite, might occasion greater danger to liberty, than could ever reasonably be dreaded from the possibility of a perpetuation in office, by the voluntary suffrages of the community, exercising a constitutional privilege.

There is an excess of refinement in the idea of disabling the people to continue in office men, who had entitled themselves, in their opinion, to approbation and confidence; the advantages of which are at best speculative and equivocal; and are over-balanced by disadvantages far more certain and decisive.

PUBLIUS.

25. "especially" inserted at this point in McLean and Hopkins.
26. At this point in Hopkins the comma is changed to a period, and "In this case as already intimated" is inserted.

## The Federalist No. 73 [1]

[New York, March 21, 1788]

*To the People of the State of New-York.*

THE third ingredient towards constituting the vigor of the executive authority is an adequate provision for its support. It is evident that without proper attention to this article, the separation of the executive from the legislative department would be merely nominal and nugatory. The Legislature, with a discretionary power over the salary and emoluments of the Chief Magistrate, could render him as obsequious to their will, as they might think proper to make him. They might in most cases either reduce him by famine, or tempt him by largesses, to surrender at discretion his judgment to their inclinations. These expressions taken in all the latitude of the terms would no doubt convey more than is intended. There are men who could neither be distressed nor won into a sacrifice of their duty; but this stern virtue is the growth of few soils: And in the main it will be found, that a power over a man's support is a power over his will. If it were necessary to confirm so plain a truth by facts, examples would not be wanting, even in this country, of the intimidation or seduction of the executive by the terrors, or allurements, of the pecuniary arrangements of the legislative body.

It is not easy therefore to commend too highly the judicious attention which has been paid to this subject in the proposed Constitution. It is there provided that "The President of the United States shall, at stated times, receive for his services a compensation, *which shall neither be increased nor diminished, during the period for which he shall have been elected,* and he shall *not receive within that period any other emolument* from the United States or any of them." It is impossible to imagine any provision which would have been more eligible than this. The Legislature on the appointment of a President is once for all to declare what shall be the compensation for his services during the time for which he shall have

*The New-York Packet,* March 21, 1788. This essay appeared in *The* [New York] *Independent Journal: or, the General Advertiser* on March 22. In the McLean edition this essay is numbered 73, in the newspapers it is numbered 72.

1. For background to this document, see "The Federalist. Introductory Note," October 27, 1787–May 28, 1788.

been elected. This done, they will have no power to alter it either by increase or diminution, till a new period of service by a new election commences. They can neither weaken his fortitude by operating upon his necessities; nor corrupt his integrity, by appealing to his avarice. Neither the Union nor any of its members will be at liberty to give, nor will he be at liberty to receive any other emolument, than that which may have been determined by the first act. He can of course have no pecuniary inducement to renounce or desert the independence intended for him by the Constitution.

The last of the requisites to energy which have been enumerated are competent powers. Let us proceed to consider those which are proposed to be vested in the President of the United States.

The first thing that offers itself to our observation, is the qualified negative of the President upon the acts or resolutions of the two Houses of the Legislature; or in other words his power of returning all bills with objections; to [2] have the effect of preventing their becoming laws, unless they should afterwards be ratified by two thirds of each of the component members of the legislative body.

The propensity of the legislative department to intrude upon the rights and to absorb the powers of the other departments, has been already [3] suggested and repeated; [4] the insufficiency of a mere parchment delineation of the boundaries of each, has also been remarked upon; and the necessity of furnishing each with constitutional arms for its own defence, has been inferred and proved.[5] From these clear and indubitable principles results the propriety of a negative, either absolute or qualified, in the executive, upon the acts of the legislative branches. Without the one or the other the former would be absolutely unable to defend himself against the depredations of the latter. He might gradually be stripped of his authorities by successive resolutions, or annihilated by a single vote. And in the one mode or the other, the legislative and executive powers might speedily come to be blended in the same hands. If even no propensity had ever discovered itself in the legislative body, to invade the rights of the executive, the rules of just reasoning and theoretic propriety would of themselves teach us, that the one ought not to be left at

2. "which will" substituted for "to" in Hopkins.
3. "more than once" inserted at this point in McLean and Hopkins.
4. "and repeated" omitted in McLean and Hopkins.
5. See essays 48 and 49. H had also discussed the subject in essays 69 and 71.

the mercy of the other, but ought to possess a constitutional and effectual power of self defence.

But the power in question has a further use. It not only serves as a shield to the executive, but it furnishes an additional security against the enaction of improper laws. It establishes a salutary check upon the legislative body calculated to guard the community against the effects of faction, precipitancy, or of any impulse unfriendly to the public good, which may happen to influence a majority of that body.

The propriety of a negative, has upon some occasions been combated by an observation, that it was not to be presumed a single man would possess more virtue or wisdom, than a number of men; and that unless this presumption should be entertained, it would be improper to give the executive magistrate any species of controul over the legislative body.

But this observation when examined will appear rather specious than solid. The propriety of the thing does not turn upon the supposition of superior wisdom or virtue in the executive: But upon the supposition that the legislative will not be infallible: That the love of power may sometimes betray it into a disposition to encroach upon the rights of the other members of the government; that a spirit of faction may sometimes pervert its deliberations; that impressions of the moment may sometimes hurry it into measures which itself on maturer reflection would condemn. The primary inducement to conferring the power in question upon the executive, is to enable him to defend himself; the secondary one [6] is to encrease the chances in favor of the community, against the passing of bad laws, through haste, inadvertence, or design. The oftener a measure is brought under examination, the greater the diversity in the situations of those who are to examine it, the less must be the danger of those errors which flow from want of due deliberation, or of those missteps which proceed from the contagion of some common passion or interest. It is far less probable, that culpable views of any kind should infect all the parts of the government, at the same moment and in relation to the same object, than that they should by turns govern and mislead every one of them.

It may perhaps be said, that the power of preventing bad laws

6. "one" omitted in Hopkins.

includes that of preventing good ones; and may be used to the one purpose as well as to the other. But this objection will have little weight with those who can properly estimate the mischiefs of that inconstancy and mutability in the laws, which form [7] the greatest blemish in the character and genius of our governments. They will consider every institution calculated to restrain the excess of law-making, and to keep things in the same state, in which they may happen to be at any given period, as much more likely to do good than harm; because it is favorable to greater stability in the system of legislation. The injury which may possibly be done by defeating a few good laws will be amply compensated by the advantage of preventing a number of bad ones.

Nor is this all. The superior weight and influence of the legislative body in a free government, and the hazard to the executive in a trial of strength with that body, afford a satisfactory security, that the negative would generally be employed with great caution, and that [8] there would oftener be room for a charge of timidity than of rashness, in the exercise of it.[9] A King of Great-Britain, with all his train of sovereign attributes, and with all the influence he draws from a thousand sources, would at this day hesitate to put a negative upon the joint resolutions of the two houses of Parliament. He would not fail to exert the utmost resources of that influence to strangle a measure disagreeable to him, in its progress to the throne, to avoid being reduced to the dilemma of permitting it to take effect, or of risking the displeasure of the nation, by an opposition to the sense of the legislative body. Nor is it probable that he would ultimately venture to exert his prerogative,[10] but in a case of manifest propriety, or extreme necessity. All well informed men in that kingdom will accede to the justness of this remark. A very considerable period has elapsed since the negative of the crown has been exercised.

If a magistrate, so powerful and so well fortified as a British monarch, would have scruples about the exercise of the power under

7. In the newspaper, "forms"; "form" was substituted in McLean and Hopkins.
8. "in its exercise" inserted at this point in Hopkins.
9. "in the exercise of it" omitted in Hopkins.
10. In the newspaper, "prerogatives"; "prerogative" was substituted in McLean and Hopkins.

consideration, how much greater caution may be reasonably expected in a President of the United States, cloathed for the short period of four years with the executive authority of a government wholly and purely republican?

It is evident that there would be greater danger of his not using his power when necessary, than of his using it too often, or too much. An argument indeed against its expediency has been drawn from this very source. It has been represented on this account as a power odious in appearance; useless in practice. But it will not follow, that because it might be [11] rarely exercised,[12] it would never be exercised. In the case for which it is chiefly designed, that of an immediate attack upon the constitutional rights of the executive, or in a case in which the public good was evidently and palpably sacrificed, a man of tolerable firmness would avail himself of his constitutional means of defence, and would listen to the admonitions of duty and responsibility. In the former supposition, his fortitude would be stimulated by his immediate interest in the power of his office; in the latter by the probability of the sanction of his constituents; who though they would naturally incline to the legislative body in a doubtful case, would hardly suffer their partiality to delude them in a very plain case.[13] I speak now with an eye to a magistrate possessing only a common share of firmness. There are men, who under any circumstances will have the courage to do their duty at every hazard.

But the Convention have pursued a mean in this business; which will both facilitate the exercise of the power vested in this respect in the executive magistrate, and make its efficacy to depend on the sense of a considerable part of the legislative body. Instead of an absolute negative,[14] it is proposed to give the executive the qualified negative already described. This is a power, which would be much more readily exercised than the other. A man who might be afraid to defeat a law by his single VETO, might not scruple to return it for re-consideration; subject to being finally rejected only in the event of more than one third of each house concurring in the sufficiency of his objections. He would be encouraged by the reflec-

11. "be" omitted in Hopkins.
12. "exercised" omitted in Hopkins.
13. "one" substituted for "case" in Hopkins.
14. "negative" omitted in Hopkins.

tion, that if his opposition should prevail, it would embark in it a very respectable proportion of the legislative body, whose influence would be united with his in supporting the propriety of his conduct, in the public opinion. A direct and categorical negative has something in the appearance of it more harsh, and more apt to irritate, than the mere suggestion of argumentative objections to be approved or disapproved, by those to whom they are addressed. In proportion as it would be less apt to offend, it would be more apt to be exercised; and for this very reason it may in practice be found more effectual. It is to be hoped that it will not often happen, that improper views will govern so large a proportion as two-thirds of both branches of the Legislature at the same time; and this too in defiance [15] of the counterpoising weight of the executive. It is at any rate far less probable, that this should be the case, than that such views should taint the resolutions and conduct of a bare majority. A power of this nature, in the executive, will often have a silent and unperceived though forcible operation. When men engaged in unjustifiable pursuits are aware, that obstructions may come from a quarter which they cannot controul, they will often be restrained, by the bare apprehension of opposition, from doing what they would with eagerness rush into, if no such external impediments were to be feared.

This qualified negative, as has been elsewhere remarked, is in this State vested in a council, consisting of the Governor, with the Chancellor and Judges of the Supreme Court, or any two of them.[16] It has been freely employed upon a variety of occasions, and frequently with success. And its utility has become so apparent, that persons who in compiling the Constitution were violent opposers of it, have from experience become its declared admirers.*

I have in another place remarked, that the Convention in the for-

* Mr. Abraham Yates, a warm opponent of the plan of the Convention, is of this number.[17]

15. In the newspaper, "spite"; "defiance" was substituted in McLean and Hopkins.
16. See essay 69.
17. Abraham Yates, Jr., of Albany was a prominent and influential New York politician and an Antifederalist. Throughout the seventeen-eighties he wrote and spoke eloquently against any aggrandizement of the powers of the Continental Congress, and in 1788 he was a leader of the opposition to the Constitution.

mation of this part of their plan, had departed from the model of the Constitution of this State, in favor of that of Massachusetts [18] —two strong reasons may be imagined for this preference. One is [19] that the Judges, who are to be the interpreters of the law, might receive an improper bias from having given a previous opinion in their revisionary capacities. The other is [20] that by being often associated with the executive they might be induced to embark too far in the political views of that magistrate, and thus a dangerous combination might by degrees be cemented between the executive and judiciary departments. It is impossible to keep the Judges too distinct from every other avocation than that of expounding the laws. It is peculiarly dangerous to place them in a situation to be either corrupted or influenced by the executive.

PUBLIUS.

18. See essay 69.
19. "is" omitted in Hopkins.
20. "is" omitted in Hopkins.

## To Jeremiah Wadsworth

[New York, March 23, 1788]

Dear Sir

I have reflected on the subject of our conversation respecting the property belonging to Mr. Church and yourself now in the City of Philadelphia and agree in opinion with you that it will be altogether adviseable to remove it from that place to this City or Connecticut or both, so as to have it more immediately under your eye.[1] I would therefore by all means advise the step.

I remain   Yr. Affet & Obed                                A Hamilton

New York March 23d. 1788
Jeremiah Wadsworth Esqr

ALS, Connecticut Historical Society, Hartford.
    1. During the American Revolution John B. Church and Wadsworth had formed a business partnership which had been dissolved in 1785. From the time of his retirement from the Army in 1782, H had managed the American business affairs of Church, who at the war's end had returned to Europe. The property in Philadelphia owned by Wadsworth and Church was handled by John Chaloner, a Philadelphia merchant. When Church returned to the

United States for a visit in 1785, he concluded that Chaloner had been inept in the management of his affairs. It was probably for this reason that Wadsworth and H decided to remove the property still belonging to Wadsworth and Church from Philadelphia.

## The Federalist No. 74 [1]

[New York, March 25, 1788]

*To the People of the State of New-York.*

THE President of the United States is to be "Commander in Chief of the army and navy of the United States, and of the militia of the several States *when called into the actual service* of the United States." The propriety of this provision is so evident in itself; [2] and it is at the same time so consonant to the precedents of the State constitutions in general, that little need be said to explain or enforce it. Even those of them, which have in other respects coupled the Chief Magistrate with a Council, have for the most part concentrated [3] the military authority in him alone. Of all the cares or concerns of government, the direction of war most peculiarly demands those qualities which distinguish the exercise of power by a single hand. The direction of war implies the direction of the common strength; and the power of directing and employing the common strength, forms an usual and essential part in the definition of the executive authority.

"The President may require the opinion in writing of the principal officer in each of the executive departments upon any subject relating to the duties of their respective offices." This I consider as a mere redundancy in the plan; as the right for which it provides would result of itself from the office.

He is also to be [4] authorised "to grant reprieves and pardons for offences against the United States *except in cases of impeachment.*" Humanity and good policy conspire to dictate, that the benign

*The New-York Packet*, March 25, 1788. This essay appeared in *The* [New York] *Independent Journal: or, the General Advertiser* on March 26. In the McLean edition this essay is numbered 74, in the newspapers it is numbered 73.
 1. For background to this document, see "The Federalist. Introductory Note," October 27, 1787–May 28, 1788.
 2. "in itself" omitted in Hopkins.
 3. "concentrated" substituted for "concentred" in Hopkins.
 4. "to be" omitted in Hopkins.

prerogative for pardoning should be as little as possible fettered or embarrassed. The criminal code of every country partakes so much of necessary severity, that without an easy access to exceptions in favor of unfortunate guilt, justice would wear a countenance too sanguinary and cruel. As the sense of responsibility is always strongest in proportion as it is undivided, it may be inferred that a single man would be most ready to attend to the force of those motives, which might plead for a mitigation of the rigor of the law, and least apt to yield to considerations, which were calculated to shelter a fit object of its vengeance. The reflection, that the fate of a fellow creature depended on his *sole fiat,* would naturally inspire scrupulousness and caution: The dread of being accused of weakness or connivance would beget equal circumspection, though of a different kind. On the other hand, as men generally derive confidence from their numbers,[5] they might often encourage each other in an act of obduracy, and might be less sensible to the apprehension of suspicion or [6] censure for an injudicious or affected clemency. On these accounts, one man appears to be a more eligible dispenser of the mercy of the government than a body of men.

The expediency of vesting the power of pardoning in the President has, if I mistake not, been only contested in relation to the crime of treason. This, it has been urged, ought to have depended upon the assent of one or both of the branches of the legislative body. I shall not deny that there are strong reasons to be assigned for requiring in this particular the concurrence of that body or of a part of it. As treason is a crime levelled at the immediate being of the society, when the laws have once ascertained the guilt of the offender, there seems a fitness in refering the expediency of an act of mercy towards him to the judgment of the Legislature. And this ought the rather to be the case, as the supposition of the connivance of the Chief Magistrate ought not to be entirely excluded. But there are also strong objections to such a plan. It is not to be doubted that a single man of prudence and good sense, is better fitted, in delicate conjunctures, to balance the motives, which may plead for and against the remission of the punishment, than any numerous body whatever. It deserves particular attention, that treason will

5. "number" substituted for "numbers" in Hopkins.
6. "suspicion or" omitted in Hopkins.

often be connected with seditions, which embrace a large proportion of the community; as lately happened in Massachusetts.[7] In every such case, we might expect to see the representation of the people tainted with the same spirit, which had given birth to the offense. And when parties were pretty equally matched,[8] the secret sympathy of the friends and favorers of the condemned person,[9] availing itself of the good nature and weakness of others, might frequently bestow impunity where the terror of an example was necessary. On the other hand, when the sedition had proceeded from causes which had inflamed the resentments of the major party, they might often be found obstinate and inexorable, when policy demanded a conduct of forbearance and clemency. But the principal argument for reposing the power of pardoning in this case in the Chief Magistrate is this—In seasons of insurrection or rebellion, there are often critical moments, when a well timed offer of pardon to the insurgents or rebels may restore the tranquility of the commonwealth; and which, if suffered to pass unimproved, it may never be possible afterwards to recall. The dilatory process of convening the Legislature, or one of its branches, for the purpose of obtaining its sanction to the measure, would frequently be the occasion of letting slip the golden opportunity. The loss of a week, a day, an hour, may sometimes be fatal. If it should be observed that a discretionary power with a view to such contingencies might be occasionally conferred upon the President; it may be answered in the first place, that it is questionable whether, in a limited constitution, that power could be delegated by law; and in the second place, that it would generally be impolitic before-hand to take any step which might hold out the prospect of impunity. A proceeding of this kind, out of the usual course, would be likely to be construed into an argument of timidity or of weakness, and would have a tendency to embolden guilt.

PUBLIUS.

7. H is referring, of course, to Shays' Rebellion. See essay 6, note 15.
8. "poised" substituted for "matched" in Hopkins.
9. "person" omitted in Hopkins and McLean.

## The Federalist No. 75 [1]

[New York, March 26, 1788]

*To the People of the State of New-York.*

THE president is to have power "by and with the advice and consent of the senate, to make treaties, provided two-thirds of the senators present concur." Though this provision has been assailed on different grounds, with no small degree of vehemence, I scruple not to declare my firm persuasion, that it is one of the best digested and most unexceptionable parts of the plan. One ground of objection is, the trite topic of the intermixture of powers; some contending that the president ought alone to possess the power [2] of making treaties; and [3] others, that it ought to have been exclusively deposited in the senate. Another source of objection is derived from the small number of persons by whom a treaty may be made: Of those who espouse this objection, a part are of opinion that the house of representatives ought to have been associated in the business, while another part seem to think that nothing more was necessary than to have substituted two-thirds of *all* the members of the senate to two-thirds of the members *present.* As I flatter myself the observations made in a preceding number, upon this part of the plan, must have sufficed to place it to a discerning eye in a very favourable light,[4] I shall here content myself with offering only some supplementary remarks, principally with a view to the objections which have been just stated.

With regard to the intermixture of powers, I shall rely upon the explanations already [5] given, in other places [6] of the true sense of the rule,[7] upon which that objection is founded; and shall take it for

The [New York] *Independent Journal: or, the General Advertiser,* March 26, 1788. This essay appeared in *The New-York Packet* on March 28. In the McLean edition this essay is numbered 75, and in the newspapers it is numbered 74.

1. For background to this document, see "The Federalist. Introductory Note," October 27, 1787–May 28, 1788.
2. "prerogative" substituted for "power" in Hopkins.
3. "and" omitted in Hopkins.
4. The subject had been discussed by John Jay in essay 64.
5. "heretofore" substituted for "already" in Hopkins.
6. "in other places" omitted in Hopkins.
7. See essays 47 and 48.

granted, as an inference from them, that the union of the executive with the senate, in the article of treaties, is no infringement of that rule. I venture to add that the particular nature of the power of making treaties indicates a peculiar propriety in that union. Though several writers on the subject of government place that power in the class of executive authorities, yet this is evidently an arbitrary disposition: For if we attend carefully to its operation, it will be found to partake more of the legislative than of the executive character, though it does not seem strictly to fall within the definition of either of them.[8] The essence of the legislative authority is to enact laws, or in other words to prescribe rules for the regulation of the society, while the execution of the laws and the employment of the common strength, either for this purpose or for the common defence, seem to comprise all the functions of the executive magistrate. The power of making treaties is plainly neither the one nor the other. It relates neither to the execution of the subsisting laws, nor to the enaction of new ones, and still less to an exertion of the common strength. Its objects are CONTRACTS with foreign nations, which have the force of law, but derive it from the obligations of good faith. They are not rules prescribed by the sovereign to the subject, but agreements between sovereign and sovereign. The power in question seems therefore to form a distinct department, and to belong properly neither to the legislative nor to the executive. The qualities elsewhere detailed, as indispensable in the management of foreign negotiations,[9] point out the executive as the most fit agent in those transactions; while the vast importance of the trust, and the operation of treaties as laws, plead strongly for the participation of the whole or a part [10] of the legislative body in the office [11] of making them.

However proper or safe it may in governments where the executive magistrate is an hereditary monarch, to commit to him the entire power of making treaties, it would be utterly unsafe and improper to entrust that power to an elective magistrate for four years duration. It has been remarked upon another occasion, and the remark is unquestionably just, that an hereditary monarch, though often

8. "of them" omitted in Hopkins.
9. See essays 53 and 64.
10. "portion" substituted for "part" in McLean and Hopkins.
11. In the newspaper, "effect"; "office" substituted in McLean and Hopkins.

the oppressor of his people, has personally too much at stake in the government to be in any material danger of being corrupted by foreign powers.[12] But a man raised from the station of a private citizen to the rank of chief magistrate, possessed of but a moderate or slender fortune, and looking forward to a period not very remote, when he may probably be obliged to return to the station from which he was taken, might sometimes be under temptations to sacrifice his duty to his [13] interest, which it would require superlative virtue to withstand. An avaricious man might be tempted to betray the interests of the state to [14] the acquisition of wealth. An ambitious man might make his own aggrandizement, by the aid of a foreign power, the price of his treachery to his constituents. The history of human conduct does not warrant that exalted opinion of human virtue which would make it wise in a nation to commit interests of so delicate and momentous a kind as those which concern its intercourse with the rest of the world to the sole disposal of a magistrate, created and circumstanced, as would be a president of the United States.

To have entrusted the power of making treaties to the senate alone, would have been to relinquish the benefits of the constitutional agency of the president, in the conduct of foreign negotiations. It is true, that the senate would in that case have the option of employing him in this capacity; but they would also have the option of letting it alone; and pique or cabal might induce the latter rather than the former. Besides this, the ministerial servant of the senate could not be expected to enjoy the confidence and respect of foreign powers in the same degree with the constitutional representative of the nation; and of course would not be able to act with an equal degree of weight or efficacy. While the union would from this cause lose a considerable advantage in the management of its external concerns, the people would lose the additional security, which would result from the co-operation of the executive. Though it would be imprudent to confide in him solely so important a trust; yet it cannot be doubted, that his participation in it [15] would materially add to the safety of the society. It must indeed be clear to

12. See essay 22.
13. "his" omitted in Hopkins.
14. "for" substituted for "to" in Hopkins.
15. "in it" omitted in Hopkins.

a demonstration, that the joint possession of the power in question by the president and senate would afford a greater prospect of security, than the separate possession of it by either of them. And whoever has maturely weighed the circumstances, which must concur in the appointment of a president will be satisfied, that the office will always bid fair to be filled by men of such characters as to render their concurrence in the formation of treaties peculiarly desirable, as well on the score of wisdom as on that of integrity.

The remarks made in a former number, which has been alluded to in an other part of this paper,[16] will apply with conclusive force against the admission of the house of representatives to a share in the formation of treaties.[17] The fluctuating and taking its future increase into the account, the multitudinous composition of that body, forbid us to expect in it those qualities which are essential to the proper execution of such a trust. Accurate and comprehensive knowledge of foreign politics; a steady and systematic adherence to the same views; a nice and uniform sensibility to national character, decision, *secrecy* and dispatch; are incompatible with the genius of a body so variable and so numerous. The very complication of the business by introducing a necessity of the concurrence of so many different bodies, would of itself afford a solid objection. The greater frequency of the calls upon the house of representatives, and the greater length of time which it would often be necessary to keep them together when convened, to obtain their sanction in the progressive stages of a treaty, would be source of so great inconvenience and expence, as alone ought to condemn the project.

The only objection which remains to be canvassed is that which would substitute the proportion of two thirds of all the members composing the senatorial body to that of two thirds of the [18] members *present*. It has been shewn under the second head of our inquiries that all provisions which require more than the majority of any body to its resolutions have a direct tendency to embarrass the operations of the government and an indirect one to subject the sense of the majority to that of the minority. This consideration seems sufficient to determine our opinion, that the convention have

16. "which" through "paper" omitted in Hopkins.
17. See essay 64.
18. "thirds of the" omitted in the newspaper and inserted in McLean and Hopkins.

gone as far in the endeavour to secure the advantage of numbers in the formation of treaties as could have been [19] reconciled either with the activity of the public councils or with a reasonable regard to the major sense of the community. If two thirds of the whole number of members had been required, it would in many cases from the non attendance of a part amount in practice to a necessity of unanimity. And the history of every political establishment in which this principle has prevailed is a history of impotence, perplexity and disorder. Proofs of this position might be adduced from the examples of the Roman tribuneship, the Polish diet and the states general of the Netherlands; did not an example at home render foreign precedents unnecessary.

To require a fixed proportion of the whole body would not in all probability contribute to the advantages of a numerous agency, better than merely to require a proportion of the attending members. The former by making a determinate number at all times requisite to a resolution [20] diminishes the motives to punctual attendance. The latter by making the capacity of the body to depend on a *proportion* which may be varied by the absence or presence of a single member, has the contrary effect. And as, by promoting punctuality, it tends to keep the body complete, there is great likelihood that its resolutions would generally be dictated by as great a number in this case as in the other; while there would be much fewer occasions of delay. It ought not to be forgotten that under the existing confederation two members *may* and usually *do* represent a state; whence it happens that Congress, who now are solely invested with *all the powers* of the union, rarely consists of a greater number of persons than would compose the intended senate. If we add to this, that as the members vote by states, and that where there is only a single member present from a state, his vote is lost, it will justify a supposition that the active voices in the senate, where the members are to vote individually, would rarely fall short in number of the active voices in the existing Congress. When in addition to these considerations we take into view the co-operation of the president, we shall not hesitate to infer that the people of America would have

19. "been" omitted in the newspaper and inserted in McLean and Hopkins.
20. "by increasing the difficulty of resolutions disagreeable to the minority" substituted for "by making" through "resolution" in McLean and Hopkins.

greater security against an improper use of the power of making treaties, under the new constitution, than they now enjoy under the confederation. And when we proceed still one step further, and look forward to the probable augmentation of the senate, by the erection of new states, we shall not only perceive ample ground of confidence in the sufficiency of the numbers,[21] to whose agency that power will be entrusted; but we shall probably be led to conclude that a body more numerous than the senate would be[22] likely to become, would be very little fit for the proper discharge of the trust.

PUBLIUS.

21. In the newspaper, "members"; "numbers" substituted in McLean and Hopkins.
22. "is" substituted for "would be" in Hopkins.

## The Federalist No. 76 [1]

[New York, April 1, 1788]

*To the People of the State of New-York.*

THE President is "to *nominate* and by and with the advice and consent of the Senate to appoint Ambassadors, other public Ministers and Consuls, Judges of the Supreme Court, and all other officers of the United States, whose appointments are not otherwise provided for in the Constitution. But the Congress may by law vest the appointment of such inferior officers as they think proper in the President alone, or in the Courts of law, or in the heads of departments. The President shall have power to fill up *all vacancies* which may happen *during the recess of the Senate*, by granting commissions which shall *expire* at the end of their next session."

It has been observed in a former paper, "that the true test of a good government is its aptitude and tendency to produce a good administration."[2] If the justness of this observation be admitted, the mode of appointing the officers of the United States contained in the foregoing clauses, must when examined be allowed to be entitled

*The New-York Packet,* April 1, 1788. This essay was printed on April 2 in *The* [New York] *Independent Journal: or, the General Advertiser.* In the McLean edition this essay is numbered 76, in the newspapers it is numbered 75.
1. For background to this document, see "The Federalist. Introductory Note," October 27, 1787–May 28, 1788.
2. The quotation is from essay 68.

to particular commendation. It is not easy to conceive a plan better calculated than this,[3] to produce[4] a judicious choice of men for filling the offices of the Union; and it will not need proof, that on this point must essentially depend the character of its administration.

It will be agreed on all hands, that the power of appointment in ordinary cases ought to be[5] modified[6] in one of three ways. It ought either to be vested in a single man—or in a *select* assembly of a moderate number—or in a single man with the concurrence of such an assembly. The exercise of it by the people at large, will be readily admitted to be impracticable; as,[7] waving every other consideration it would leave them little time to do any thing else. When therefore mention is made in the subsequent reasonings of an assembly or body of men, what is said must be understood to relate to a select body or assembly of the description already given. The people collectively from their number and from their dispersed situation cannot be regulated in their movements by that systematic spirit of cabal and intrigue, which will be urged as the chief objections to reposing the power in question in a body of men.

Those who have themselves reflected upon the subject, or who have attended to the observations made in other parts of these papers, in relation to the appointment of the President, will I presume agree to the position that there would always be great probability of having the place supplied by a man of abilities, at least respectable. Premising this, I proceed to lay it down as a rule, that one man of discernment is better fitted to analise and estimate the peculiar qualities adapted to particular offices, than a body of men of equal, or perhaps even of superior discernment.

The sole and undivided responsibility of one man will naturally beget a livelier sense of duty and a more exact regard to reputation. He will on this account feel himself under stronger obligations, and more interested to investigate with care the qualities requisite to the stations to be filled, and to prefer with impartiality the persons who may have the fairest pretentions to them. He will have *fewer* personal attachments to gratify than a body of men, who may each

3. "than this" omitted in Hopkins.
4. "to promote" substituted for "to produce" in McLean and Hopkins.
5. "can be properly" substituted for "ought to be" in McLean and Hopkins.
6. "only" inserted at this point in McLean and Hopkins.
7. "since" substituted for "as" in Hopkins.

be supposed to have an equal number, and will be so much the less liable to be misled by the sentiments of friendship and of affection. A single well directed man by a single understanding, cannot be distracted and warped by that diversity of views, feelings and interests, which frequently distract and warp the resolutions of a collective body.[8] There is nothing so apt to agitate the passions of mankind as personal considerations, whether they relate to ourselves or to others, who are to be the objects of our choice or preference. Hence, in every exercise of the power of appointing to offices by an assembly of men, we must expect to see a full display of all the private and party likings and dislikes, partialities and antipathies, attachments and animosities, which are felt by those who compose the assembly. The choice which may at any time happen to be made under such circumstances will of course be the result either of a victory gained by one party over the other, or of a compromise between the parties. In either case, the intrinsic merit of the candidate will be too often out of sight. In the first, the qualifications best adapted to uniting the suffrages of the party will be more considered than [9] those which fit the person for the station. In the last the coalition will commonly turn upon some interested equivalent—"Give us the man we wish for this office, and you shall have the one you wish for that." This will be the usual condition of the bargain. And it will rarely happen that the advancement of the public service will be the primary object either of party victories or of party negociations.

The truth of the principles here advanced seems to have been felt by the most intelligent of those who have found fault with the provision made in this respect by the Convention. They contend that the President ought solely to have been authorized to make the appointments under the Fœderal Government. But it is easy to shew that every advantage to be expected from such an arrangement would in substance be derived from the power of *nomination*, which is proposed to be conferred upon him; while several disadvantages which might attend the absolute power of appointment in the hands of that officer, would be avoided. In the act of nomination his judgment alone would be exercised; and as it would be his sole duty to point out the man, who with the approbation of the Senate should

8. This sentence omitted in McLean and Hopkins.
9. "than" omitted in the newspaper and inserted in McLean and Hopkins.

fill an office, his responsibility would be as complete as if he were to make the final appointment. There can in this view be no difference between nominating and appointing. The same motives which would influence a proper discharge of his duty in one case would exist in the other. And as no man could be appointed, but upon his previous nomination, every man who might be appointed would be in fact his choice.

But might not his nomination be overruled? I grant it might, yet this could [10] only be to make place for another nomination by himself. The person ultimately appointed must be the object of his preference, though perhaps not in the first degree. It is also not very [11] probable that his nomination would often be overruled. The Senate could not be tempted by the preference they might feel to another to reject the one proposed; because they could not assure themselves that the person they might wish would be brought forward by a second or by any subsequent nomination. They could not even be certain that a future nomination would present a candidate in any degree more acceptable to them: And as their dissent might cast a kind of stigma upon the individual rejected; and might have the appearance of a reflection upon the judgment of the chief magistrate; it is not likely that their sanction would often be refused, where there were not special and strong reasons for the refusal.

To what purpose then require the co-operation of the Senate? I answer that the necessity of their concurrence would have a powerful, though in general a silent operation. It would be an excellent check upon a spirit of favoritism in the President, and would tend greatly to preventing the appointment of unfit characters from State prejudice, from family connection, from personal attachment, or from a view to popularity. And,[12] in addition to this, it would be an efficacious source of stability in the administration.

It will readily be comprehended, that a man, who had himself the sole disposition of offices, would be governed much more by his private inclinations and interests, than when he was bound to submit the propriety of his choice to the discussion and determination of a different and independent body; and that body an entire branch of

10. "But his nomination may be overruled: This it certainly may, yet it can" substituted for "But might" through "this could" in McLean and Hopkins.
11. "very" omitted in Hopkins.
12. "And" omitted in Hopkins.

the Legislature. The possibility of rejection would be a strong motive to care in proposing. The danger to his own reputation, and, in the case of an elective magistrate, to his political existence, from betraying a spirit of favoritism, or an unbecoming pursuit of popularity, to the observation of a body, whose opinion would have great weight in forming that of the public, could not fail to operate as a barrier to the one and to the other. He would be both ashamed and afraid to bring forward for the most distinguished or lucrative stations, candidates who had no other merit, than that of coming from the same State to which he particularly belonged, or of being in some way or other personally allied to him, or of possessing the necessary insignificance and pliancy to render them the obsequious instruments of his pleasure.

To this reasoning, it has been objected, that the President by the influence of the power of nomination may secure the compliance of the Senate to his views. The supposition of universal venality in human nature is little less an error in political reasoning than the supposition [13] of universal rectitude. The institution of delegated power implies that there is a portion of virtue and honor among mankind, which may be a reasonable foundation of confidence. And experience justifies the theory: It has been found to exist in the most corrupt periods of the most corrupt governments. The venality of the British House of Commons has been long a topic of accusation against that body, in the country to which they belong, as well as in this; and it cannot be doubted that the charge is to a considerable extent well founded. But it is as little to be doubted that there is always a large proportion of the body, which consists of independent and public spirited men, who have an influential weight in the councils of the nation. Hence it is (the present reign not excepted) that the sense of that body is often seen to controul the inclinations of the monarch, both with regard to men and to measures. Though it might therefore be allowable to suppose, that the executive might occasionally influence some individuals in the Senate; yet the supposition that he could in general purchase the integrity of the whole body would be forced and improbable. A man disposed to view human nature as it is, without either flattering its virtues or exaggerating its vices, will see sufficient ground of confidence in the

13. "that" substituted for "the supposition" in Hopkins.

probity of the Senate, to rest satisfied not only that it will be impracticable to the Executive to corrupt or seduce a majority of its members; but that the necessity of its co-operation in the business of appointments will be a considerable and salutary restraint upon the conduct of that magistrate. Nor is the integrity of the Senate the only reliance. The constitution has provided some important guards against the danger of executive influence upon the legislative body: It declares that "No Senator, or representative shall, during the time *for which he was elected*, be appointed to any civil office under the United States, which shall have been created, or the emoluments whereof shall have been encreased during such time; and no person holding any office under the United States shall be a member of either house during his continuance in office."

PUBLIUS.

## *The Federalist No. 77* [1]

[New York, April 2, 1788]

*To the People of the State of New-York.*

IT has been mentioned as one of the advantages to be expected from the co-operation of the senate, in the business of appointments, that it would contribute to the stability of the administration.[2] The consent of that body would be necessary to displace as well as to appoint.[3] A change of the chief magistrate therefore would not occasion so violent or so general a revolution in the officers of the government, as might be expected if he were the sole disposer of offices. Where a man in any station had given satisfactory evidence of his fitness for it, a new president would be restrained from at-

The [New York] *Independent Journal: or, the General Advertiser*, April 2, 1788. This essay was printed on April 4 in *The New-York Packet*. In the McLean edition this essay is numbered 77, in the newspapers it is numbered 76.

1. For background to this document, see "The Federalist. Introductory Note," October 27, 1787–May 28, 1788.

2. See essay 76.

3. "This construction has since been rejected by the legislature; and it is now settled in practice, that the power of displacing belongs exclusively to the president." This sentence is inserted as a footnote in Hopkins at this point. This is one of the two interpolations in the Hopkins edition which related statements in *The Federalist* to events after 1787–1788. For the other see essay 8, note 27.

tempting a change, in favour of a person more agreeable to him, by the apprehension that the discountenance of the senate might frustrate the attempt, and bring some degree of discredit upon himself. Those who can best estimate the value of a steady administration will be most disposed to prize a provision, which connects the official existence of public men with the approbation or disapprobation of that body, which from the greater permanency of its own composition, will in all probability be less subject to inconstancy, than any other member of the government.

To this union of the senate with the president, in the article of appointments, it has in some cases been objected,[4] that it would serve to give the president an undue influence over the senate; and in others, that it would have an opposite tendency; a strong proof that neither suggestion is true.

To state the first in its proper form is to refute it. It amounts to this—The president would have an improper *influence over* the senate; because the senate would have the power of *restraining* him. This is an absurdity in terms. It cannot admit of a doubt that the intire power of appointment would enable him much more effectually to establish a dangerous empire over that body, than a mere power of nomination subject to their controul.

Let us take a view of the converse of the proposition—"The senate would influence the executive." As I have had occasion to remark in several other instances,[5] the indistinctness of the objection forbids a precise answer. In what manner is this influence to be exerted? In relation to what objects? The power of influencing a person, in the sense in which it is here used, must imply a power of conferring a benefit upon him. How could the senate confer a benefit upon the president by the manner of employing their right of negative upon his nominations? If it be said they might sometimes gratify him [6] by an acquiesence in a favorite choice, when public motives might dictate a different conduct; I answer that the instances in which the president could be personally interested in the

4. In the newspaper, "suggested"; "objected" substituted in McLean and Hopkins.

5. The possibility of the Senate influencing the executive is considered in several of the discussions of the office of the executive, which is the subject of essays 67–79.

6. "him" omitted in the newspaper and inserted in McLean and Hopkins.

result, would be too few to admit of his being materially affected by the compliances of the senate.[7] The POWER which can *originate* the disposition of honors and emoluments, is more likely to attract than to be attracted by the POWER which can merely obstruct their course. If by influencing the president be meant *restraining* him, this is precisely what must have been intended. And it has been shewn that the restraint would be salutary, at the same time that it would not be such as to destroy a single advantage to be looked for from the uncontrouled agency of that magistrate. The right of nomination would produce all the good of that of appointment, and would in a great measure avoid its ills.[8]

Upon a comparison of the plan for the appointment of the officers of the proposed government with that which is established by the constitution of this state a decided preference must be given to the former. In that plan the power of nomination is unequivocally vested in the executive. And as there would be a necessity for submitting each nomination to the judgment of an entire branch of the legislature, the circumstances attending an appointment, from the mode of conducting it, would naturally become matters of notoriety; and the public would [9] be at no loss to determine what part had been performed by the different actors. The blame of a bad nomination would fall upon the president singly and absolutely. The censure of rejecting a good one would lie entirely at the door of the senate; aggravated by the consideration of their having counteracted the good intentions of the executive. If an ill appointment should be made the executive for nominating and the senate for approving would participate though in different degrees in the opprobrium and disgrace.

The reverse of all this characterises the manner of appointment in this state. The council of appointment consists of from three to five persons, of whom the governor is always one. This small body, shut up in a private apartment, impenetrable to the public eye, proceed to the execution of the trust committed to them. It is known that the governor claims the right of nomination, upon the strength

7. "Besides this, it is evident that" inserted at this point in McLean and Hopkins.
8. "without the ill" substituted for "of that" through "its ills" in McLean and Hopkins.
9. "could" substituted for "would" in McLean and Hopkins.

of some ambiguous expressions in the constitution; but it is not known to what extent, or in what manner he exercises it; nor upon what occasions he is contradicted or opposed. The censure of a bad appointment, on account of the uncertainty of its author, and for want of a determinate object, has neither poignancy nor duration. And while an unbounded field for cabal and intrigue lies open, all idea of responsibility is lost. The most that the public can know is, that the governor claims the right of nomination: That *two* out of the considerable number of *four* men can too [10] often be managed without much difficulty: That if some of the members of a particular council should happen to be of an uncomplying character, it is frequently not impossible to get rid of their opposition, by regulating the times of meeting in such a manner as to render their attendance inconvenient: And that, from whatever cause it may proceed, a great number of very improper appointments are from time to time made. Whether a governor of this state avails himself of the ascendant he must necessarily have, in this delicate and important part of the administration, to prefer to offices men who are best qualified for them: Or whether he prostitutes that advantage to the advancement of persons, whose chief merit is their implicit devotion to his will, and to the support of a despicable and dangerous system of personal influence, are questions which unfortunately for the community can only be the subjects of speculation and conjecture.

Every mere council of appointment, however constituted, will be a conclave, in which cabal and intrigue will have their full scope. Their number, without an unwarrantable increase of expence, cannot be large enough to preclude a facility of combination. And as each member will have his friends and connections to provide for, the desire of mutual gratification will beget a scandalous bartering of votes and bargaining for places. The private attachments of one man might easily be satisfied; but to satisfy the private attachments of a dozen, or of twenty men, would occasion a monopoly of all the principal employments of the government, in a few families, and would lead more directly to an aristocracy or an oligarchy, than any measure that could be contrived. If to avoid an accumulation of offices, there was to be a frequent change in the persons, who were to compose the council, this would involve the mischiefs of a mutable

10. "too" omitted in Hopkins.

administration in their full extent. Such a council would also be more liable to executive influence than the senate, because they would be fewer in number, and would act less immediately under the public inspection. Such a council in fine as a substitute for the plan of the convention, would be productive of an increase of expence, a multiplication of the evils which spring from favouritism and intrigue in the distribution of the [11] public honors, a decrease of stability in the administration of the government, and a diminution of the security against an undue influence of the executive. And yet such a council has been warmly contended for as an essential amendment in the proposed constitution.

I could not with propriety conclude my observations on the subject of appointments, without taking notice of a scheme, for which there has appeared some, though but a [12] few advocates; I mean that of uniting the house of representatives in the power of making them. I shall however do little more than mention it, as I cannot imagine that it is likely to gain the countenance of any considerable part of the community. A body so fluctuating, and at the same time so numerous, can never be deemed proper for the exercise of that power. Its unfitness will appear manifest to all, when it is recollected that in half a century it may consist of three or four hundred persons. All the advantages of the stability, both of the executive and of the senate, would be defeated by this union; and infinite delays and embarrassments would be occasioned. The example of most of the states in their local constitutions, encourages us to reprobate the idea.

The only remaining powers of the executive, are comprehended in giving information to congress of the state of the union; in recommending to their consideration such measures as he shall judge expedient; in convening them, or either branch, upon extraordinary occasions; in adjourning them when they cannot themselves agree upon the time of adjournment; in receiving ambassadors and other public ministers; in faithfully executing the laws; and in commissioning all the officers of the United States.

Except some cavils about the power of convening *either* house of the legislature and that of receiving ambassadors, no objection has been made to this class of authorities; nor could they possibly admit

11. "the" omitted in Hopkins.
12. "a" omitted in Hopkins.

of any. It required indeed an insatiable avidity for censure to invent exceptions to the parts which have been excepted to.[13] In regard to the power of convening either house of the legislature, I shall barely remark, that in respect to the senate at least, we can readily discover a good reason for it. As this body has a concurrent power with the executive in the article of treaties, it might often be necessary to call it together with a view to this object, when it would be unnecessary and improper to convene the house of representatives. As to the reception of ambassadors, what I have said in a former paper will furnish a sufficient answer.

We have now compleated a survey of the structure and powers of the executive department, which, I have endeavoured to show, combines, as far as republican principles would admit, all the requisites to energy. The remaining enquiry is; does it also combine the requisites to safety in the republican sense—a due dependence on the people—a due responsibility? The answer to this question has been anticipated in the investigation of its other characteristics, and is satisfactorily deducible from these circumstances, from [14] the election of the president once in four years by persons immediately chosen by the people for that purpose; and from [15] his being at all times liable [16] to impeachment, trial, dismission from office, incapacity to serve in any other; and to the forfeiture of life and estate by subsequent prosecution in the common course of law. But these precautions, great as they are, are not the only ones, which the plan of the convention has provided in favor of the public security. In the only instances in which the abuse of the executive authority was materially to be feared, the chief magistrate of the United States would by that plan be subjected to the controul of a branch of the legislative body. What more could be desired by an enlightened and reasonable people? [17]

PUBLIUS.

13. "assailed" substituted for "excepted to" in Hopkins.
14. "from" omitted in McLean and Hopkins.
15. "from" omitted in McLean.
16. "his liability, at all times," substituted for "and from his being at all times liable" in Hopkins.
17. "What more can an enlightened and reasonable people desire?" substituted for this sentence in McLean and Hopkins.

## To James Madison

[New York, April 3, 1788]

I have been very delinquent My Dear Sir in not thanking you sooner for your letter from Philadelphia.[1] The remarks you make on a certain subject are important and will be attended to. There is truly much embarrassment in the case.

I think however the principles we have talked of, in respect to the legislative authorities, are not only just but will apply to the other departments.[2] Nor will the consequences appear so disagreeable, as they may seem at first sight, when we attend to the true import of the rule established.[3] The states *retain* all the authorities they were *before* possessed of, not alienated in the three modes pointed out; [4] but this does not include cases which are the *creatures* of the New Constitution. For instance, the crime of treason against the United States *immediately*, is a crime known only to the New Constitution. There of course *was* no power in the state constitutions to pardon that crime. There will therefore be none under the new &c. This or something like it seems to me to afford the best solution of the difficulty.

I send you the Fœderalist from the beginning to the conclusion of the commentary on the Executive branch.[5] If our suspicions of the author be right, he must be too much engaged to make a rapid progress in what remains. The Court of Chancery & a Circuit Court are now setting.

We are told that your election has succeeded; [6] with which we all felicitate ourselves. I will thank you for an account of the result generally.

In this state our prospects are much as you left them—a moot point which side will prevail. Our friends to the Northward are active.

I remain Yr. affectionate & obedt serv      A Hamilton

April 3d.

ALS, James Madison Papers, Library of Congress.
  1. Letter not found. Madison, who had left New York on March 5, 1788, presumably wrote to H from Philadelphia en route to Virginia to attend the Virginia Ratifying Convention.

2. H is presumably referring to *The Federalist* essays 52–66 in which the House of Representatives and the Senate are discussed.

3. In this paragraph H is presumably answering questions contained in the letter Madison had written him from Philadelphia.

4. The "three modes pointed out" are discussed in *The Federalist* essay 62. H stated in that essay that the sovereignty of the Federal authorities was limited in the following three ways: 1. "where the Constitution in express terms granted an exclusive authority to the Union"; 2. "where it granted in one instance an authority to the Union and in another prohibited the States from exercising the like authority"; and 3. "where it granted an authority to the Union, to which a similar authority in the States would be absolutely and totally *contradictory* and *repugnant*."

5. The discussion of the executive was concluded in essay 77. The first volume of *The Federalist*, which contained the first thirty-six essays, was published on March 22, 1788, by J. and A. McLean. H probably sent Madison a copy of this book and newspaper copies of the remaining forty-one essays.

6. Elections to the Virginia Ratifying Convention had been held during the second week in March, 1788. Madison had been elected one of the delegates to the Convention.

## Campaign Broadside [1]

NEW-YORK, *12th of April*, 1788.

Friends and Countrymen

FROM a sincere Attachment to yourselves, and a Regard to our mutual Interest, we are induced to apprize you of our Opinions on a Subject, which we view as of the most essential Consequence to both.

YOUR Countrymen in New-York, in Union of Sentiment with the true Friends of America, have long lamented the want of a FIRM, NATIONAL GOVERNMENT; without which they consider Property as insecure, and Liberty without a substantial Basis.

IN Order to avert the Calamities incident to such a Situation, and to rescue us from one so truly Dangerous, a respectable Body of the most tried Patriots of America have digested, and *submitted* to the PEOPLE, a PLAN OF GOVERNMENT, which we have good reason to believe, if accepted, will *deliver* this Country from the Misfortunes with which it is now threatened.

FROM the fullest Persuasion, that it will be ADVISEABLE for the People of the State of New-York to join in supporting a Federal Government for the United States—and from the most entire Conviction that the new Constitution is well calculated to PRESERVE all the Rights and Privileges which FREEMEN hold dear, we cannot refrain from recommending it to your most serious Consideration—we had almost said to your hearty support. We conceive it more especially our Duty to do so, at this Time, because we have the best Authority to believe, that the Influence of some Characters, whose political conduct we do not approve, is employed to engage your Suffrages at the ensuing Election, in supporting a Cause which we believe to be hostile to the Happiness of this Country: We have Reason to suspect also, that our Sentiments on this Subject have been industriously misrepresented to you; a Circumstance which first suggested the Propriety of the present Address. We assure you, Friends and Countrymen, that the SCOTSMEN of this City, with very few Exceptions, are friendly to the New Plan of Government.

WE beg you to believe that whilst we are thus anxious to communicate to you our Sentiments on this important subject, we by no means aim at any improper Influence over your Opinions—we know and feel that we are addressing Freemen—we therefore intreat you, maturely to reflect before you give your Votes, where your Confidence may most sagely be reposed: whether in men who it is to be feared may have an Interest in artfully misrepresenting Facts, or in such whose political Conduct is directed to the Public Good.

WE trust that before the ensuing Election, you will weigh very seriously, the Counsel which we now offer to you: be persuaded, that it has proceeded from the best Intentions, and flows from the best Judgement, of

Your affectionate Countrymen,[2]

Printed document, New-York Historical Society, New York City.

1. This broadside was an appeal to the "Scotsmen" of New York City to elect Federalists to the state's Ratifying Convention.

2. At the end of this document are printed the names of fifty-five New York City residents, including that of H. Although most of the names indicate that the sponsors of this broadside were of Scottish origin, the list includes two Van Cortlandts.

Following the names of New York City residents is the following statement:

"We, the Subscribers, of the City of Albany, having with Pleasure, perused the above Address, signed by a worthy and respectable Number of our Countrymen of the City of New York . . . , we do fully agree with them in Sentiment, and as such would wish to recommend the same to all our Friends and Countrymen, who may attend the ensuing Election. Albany, 21st April, 1788."

This statement is followed by the names of fifteen residents of Albany.

## Account with William Backhouse and Company [1]

New York, April 18, 1788. Backhouse on this date made the last entry in an account which he had kept with Hamilton who was acting as agent and legal representative for John B. Church. The account deals with bills of exchange which Backhouse discounted for Church. The first entry is February 18, 1788, the last April 18, 1788.

D, Hamilton Papers, Library of Congress.
1. William Backhouse was a NewYork City merchant whose place of business was on Mill Street.

## Appointment as Delegate to the General Meeting of the Society of the Cincinnati

New York, May 3, 1788. Baron von Steuben, president of the Society of the Cincinnati of the State of New York, signed a certification that Hamilton and six other men [1] had been appointed delegates to represent New York in the "General Meeting of the society of ye. Cincinnati to be holden in the City of Philadelphia on Monday the fifth day of May 1788."

DS, Papers of the Society of the Cincinnati, Library of Congress.
1. The other delegates were von Steuben, Robert R. Livingston, William Duer, James Miles Hughes, Morgan Lewis, and Benjamin Walker.

## To James Madison

[New York, May 11,[1] 1788]

My Dr Sir

I believe I am in your debt a letter or two, which is owing to my occupations in relation to the elections &c.[2]

These are now over in this state, but the result is not known. All depends upon Albany where both sides claim the victory.[3] Our doubts will not be removed till the latter end of the month. I hope your expectations of Virginia have not diminished.[4]

Respecting the first volume of Publius [5] I have executed your commands.[6] The books have been sent addressed to the care of Governor Randall.[7] The second we are informed will be out in the course of a week, & an equal number shall be forwarded.[8]

Inclosed is a letter committed to my care by a Mr. Van der Kemp which I forward with pleasure [9]

Believe me with great attachment    Yrs.        A Hamilton

ALS, James Madison Papers, Library of Congress.

1. In *JCHW*, I, 451, and *HCLW*, IX, 428, this letter is incorrectly dated May 4, 1788. The envelope is stamped "New York, May 11."

2. The New York legislature had voted on February 1, 1788, to call a convention to decide on the Constitution. Elections were held on the last Tuesday in April.

3. Albany returned Antifederalist delegates to the New York Ratifying Convention. Despite H's optimism, the Antifederalists won forty-six seats and nine counties; the Federalists won only four counties and elected only nineteen delegates.

4. The Virginia Ratifying Convention, scheduled to meet on June 1, 1788, had been elected early in March. Madison, presumably, had written H expressing confidence that the Convention would adopt the Constitution.

5. The first volume of *The Federalist*, containing the first thirty-six essays, was published on March 22, 1788, by J. and A. McLean and Company.

6. Madison probably had asked H to send him volume one of *The Federalist*.

7. H was mistaken. Edmund Randolph was the governor of Virginia and it was, presumably, to him that Madison wished the "Publius" essays sent. See H to Madison, May 19, 1788.

8. The second volume of *The Federalist* was published on May 28, 1788, by J. and A. McLean and Company.

9. Letter not found. Presumably Francis A. Vanderkemp, a Mennonite minister from Holland, who immigrated to the United States as a political refugee in 1788. He was befriended by H. See Vanderkemp to H, September 15, 1800.

## From John Jay

Office for foreign Affairs [New York] 15th May 1788

Dr. Sir

Mr. Richard Laurence of Staten Island has complained to Congress, and to the King of Great Britain, that Judgments have been obtained and executed against him in certain Actions of Trespass, which he says were commenced and prosecuted in Violation of the Treaty of Peace. In these Actions I understand you was concerned for him, and as it is important that the Facts which concern the Merits of his Complaint be ascertained with Precision, I take the

Liberty of requesting the Favor of you to furnish me with a State of them as soon as you conveniently can.

With great Esteem and Regard I am, Dr. Sir,   Your most obt. and hble Servt                            John Jay

The Honorable A. Hamilton Esqr.

LS, Hamilton Papers, Library of Congress; LC, Papers of the Continental Congress, National Archives.

## To James Madison

[New York, May 19, 1788]

Some days since I wrote to you, My Dear Sir, inclosing a letter from a Mr. V Der Kemp &c.[1]

I then mentioned to you that the question of a majority for or against the constitution would depend upon the County of Albany. By the latter accounts from that quarter I fear much that the issue there has been against us.[2]

As Clinton is truly the leader of his party, and is inflexibly obstinate I count little on overcoming opposition by reason. Our only chances will be the previous ratification by nine states,[3] which may shake the firmness of his followers; and a change in the sentiments of the people which have been for some time travelling towards the constitution, though the first impressions made by every species of influence and artifice were too strong to be eradicated in time to give a decisive turn to the elections. We shall leave nothing undone to cultivate a favourable disposition in the citizens at large.

The language of the Antifœderalists is that if all the other states adopt, New York ought still to hold out. I have the most direct intelligence, but in a manner, which forbids a public use being made of it, that Clinton has in several conversations declared his opinion of the *inutility* of the UNION. Tis an unhappy reflection, that the friends to it should by quarrelling for straws among themselves promote the designs of its adversaries.

We think here that the situation of your state is critical.[4] Let me know what you now think of it. I believe you meet nearly at the time we do. It will be of vast importance that an exact communication should be kept up between us at that period; and the moment *any decisive* question is taken, if favourable, I request you to dispatch an express to me with pointed orders to make all possible diligence, by changing horses &c. All expences shall be thankfully and liberally paid.

I executed your commands respecting the first vol of the Fœderalist.[5] I sent 40 of the common copies & twelve of the finer ones addressed to the care of Governor Randolph.[6] The Printer announces the second vol in a day or two,[7] when an equal number of the two kinds shall also be forwarded. He informs that the Judicial department trial by jury bill of rights &c. is discussed in some additional papers which have not yet appeared in the Gazettes.[8]

I remain with great sincerity & attachment

New York May 19. 1788
Mr. Maddison

AL[S], James Madison Papers, Library of Congress.
  1. See H to Madison, May 11, 1788.
  2. H's fears were justified, for Albany County elected an Antifederalist delegation to the Ratifying Convention.
  3. When this letter was written, only eight states had ratified the Constitution.
  4. The Virginia Ratifying Convention was scheduled to meet on June 1.
  5. See H to Madison, May 11, 1788.
  6. Edmund Randolph, the governor of Virginia.
  7. Volume two of *The Federalist* was published on May 28, 1788.
  8. The second volume of *The Federalist* included eight essays, numbers 78–85, which had not appeared previously in the newspapers.

## To Gouverneur Morris

[New York, May 19, 1788]

My Dear Sir

I acknowlege my delinquency in not thanking you before for your obliging letter from Richmond.[1] But the truth is that I have been so overwhelmed in avocations of one kind or another that I have scarcely had a moment to spare to a friend. You I trust will be the less disposed to be inexorable, as I hope you believe there is no one for whom I have more *inclination* than yourself—I mean of the *male* kind.

Your account of the situation of Virginia was interesting,[2] and the present appearances as represented here justify your conjectures. It does not however appear that the adoption of the constitution can be considered as out of doubt in that state. Its conduct upon the occasion will certainly be of critical importance.

In this state, as far as we can judge, the elections have gone wrong.[3] The event however will not certainly be known till the end of the month. Violence rather than moderation is to be looked for from the opposite party. Obstinacy seems the prevailing trait in the character of its leader.[4] The language is, that if all the other states adopt, this is to persist in refusing the constitution. It is reduced to a certainty that Clinton has in several conversations declared the UNION unnecessary; though I have the information through channels which do not permit a public use to be made of it.

We have, notwithstanding the unfavourable complexion of things, two sources of hope—one the chance of a ratification by nine states before we decide and the influence of this upon the firmness of the *followers,* the other the probability of a change of sentiment in the people, auspicious to the constitution. The current has been for some time running towards it; though the whole flood of official influence accelerated by a torrent of falsehood, early gave the public opinion so violent a direction in a wrong channel that it was not possible suddenly to alter its course. This is a mighty stiff simile; but you know what I mean; and after having started it, I did not choose to give up the chace.

Adieu Yrs. Sincerely                                   A Hamilton
New York May 19. 1788

The members of the Convention in this City, by a Majority of nine or ten to one, will be[5]   John Jay
                                          Robert R. Livingston
                                          Richard Morris
                                          John Sloss Hobart
                                          James Duane
                                          Isaac Rosevelt
                                          Richard Harrison
                                          Nicholas Lowe
                                          Alexander Hamilton

G Morris Esqr

ALS, Hamilton Papers, Library of Congress.

1. Letter not found. Morris, an influential member of the Constitutional Convention, had gone to Virginia in the fall of 1787 to settle some of the business affairs of Robert Morris, in which he too was involved.

2. Morris presumably had written to H about the chances of the adoption of the Constitution by the Virginia Ratifying Convention which was scheduled to meet on June 1.

3. The New York elections had been held during the last week in April, 1788. They resulted in the election of a majority of Antifederalists.

4. H is referring, of course, to Governor George Clinton.

5. The results of the New York City election were announced on May 31, 1788, in The [New York] Independent Journal: or, the General Advertiser as follows:

| | |
|---|---|
| John Jay, | 2735 |
| Richard Morris, | 2716 |
| John S. Hobart, | 2713 |
| Alexander Hamilton, | 2713 |
| Robert R. Livingston, | 2712 |
| Isaac Rosevelt, | 2701 |
| James Duane, | 2680 |
| Richard Harrison, | 2677 |
| Nicholas Low, | 2651 |

## Account with New York State

[New York, May 21, 1788. On this date Hamilton submitted a bill to New York State. Document not found].

ADS, sold by Samuel Freeman, November 18, 1924, lot 167.

## From Marquis de Lafayette

Paris May the 24th 1788

My dear Hamilton

It is a Hard thing for me to Be separated from the friends I love the Best, and to think that our daily Conversations are Reduced to a few letters, the Arrival of Which is ever lengthy and sometimes Uncertain. I Hope, However, My dear friend, you don't question My Continual and Affectionate Remembrance of the Happy days I Have Past With You. I Hope You often think of me, and of the pleasure I'd Have to Embrace You Again. When that Happiness is to Be Expected I don't Know. But When I took the penn to write to You, I Was so Painfully struck With the difference Between this, and our former Hourly Correspondence, that it Has damped

My Spirits, and Better fitted me for tender Effusions than political Accounts. I Must However Speack to You of the Revolution Now Going on in this Country.[1] Every Publications Have Been Sent to Mr Jay;[2] and I Hope they Will Be printed. You Will find a difference Between our Assertions and those of the King Which Must Convince You that Such a Contestation Could not long Subsist; and that despotism or liberty (*monarchical liberty* I mean) must Conquer. Government Have lately Struck a Great Blow, and as the people Could Not Be Roused, I Have for a few days thought We Were Gone. But a passive discontent, Non obedience, and a Kind of Quacker Resistance Will, I Hope, suffice to Undo the fatal scheme, and I Now expect that a National Assembly Will Be the only Means for Government to Get Rid of the things that Have Been laid in their Way.[3] The Parliaments, our Courts of justice, Have Been the Medium for the friends of liberty to set forth their claims, and they Have Behaved Nobly—after all, the french Constitution, supposing it to Become as Good or Better than that of England, Will Bear No Comparison With the Worst Constitution that May Be pointed out within the United States,—it Must Be poisoned With abuses which it is impossible, and Perhaps improper for the present to Eradicate. This letter Will Be delivered By Mr de Warville, who altho He Has writen Against chattelux's[4] journal,[5] is a writer in favor of America and liberty, and wishes to write on American Affairs. He Has a Military fellow traveller and I Beg leave to Introduce Both. He Will explain to You What Has Been done in this Country Respecting the Negroe trade, and slavery. I don't Know wether You Had me Enlisted in the Societies at Newyork and Elsewhere;[6] if Not, I Beg You Will do it—I am Making an Experiment at Cayenne on a plantation I Have purchased on purpose. Adieu, My Dear Hamilton, my most Affectionate Respects wait on Mrs. Hamilton, Doctor Cochran,[7] His Lady, all friends.

Most affectionately   Yours                              Lafayette

I will tell you *Between us* that I Had a letter from M. de Moustier[8] wherein I perceive that He Must Be put in Good Humour With Congressional people. I wish Him to Be pleased, in order that His Representations Be favourable.

ALS, Hamilton Papers, Library of Congress.

1. For Lafayette's earlier accounts of "the Revolution Now Going on in this Country," see his letters to H of April 12, 1787, and October 15, 1787.

2. John Jay was Secretary for Foreign Affairs.

3. In the preceding three sentences, Lafayette is presumably referring to the attempt of Louis XVI to reduce the power of the parlements. On May 8, 1788, in a speech from the throne, Louis XVI denounced the parlements as obstacles to good government and ordered them to register a series of decrees by which the entire judiciary was to be reformed and a new high court, the *Cour Plénière*, established. However desirable the reforms may have been, the opponents of the King considered them an attempt to re-establish arbitrary government.

4. Jean Pierre Brissot de Warville described his visit in his *Nouveau Voyage dans les États-Unis de l'Amérique Septentrionale, fait en 1788*, published in Paris in 1791. Warville returned to France in 1789.

5. François-Jean, Marquis de Chastellux, who had come to America in 1780 with the army of Rochambeau, published his observations on the Americans in *Voyages dans l'Amérique Septentrionale dans les années 1780, 81 et 82*. (Paris, 1786.)

6. Lafayette is presumably referring to membership in the various manumission societies.

7. Dr. John Cochran, who had served as chief physician and surgeon during the American Revolution, had married Gertrude Schuyler, Elizabeth Hamilton's aunt.

8. Eleanor François Elie, Comte de Moustier, was French Minister to the United States.


# Continental Congress. Amendment to Supplement to Land Ordinance [1]

[New York, May 28, 1788]

That the persons intitled to lands by virtue of such warrants [2] shall be at liberty to locate them on any part of the two tracts or districts of land reserved and set apart for the purpose of satisfying the military bounties due to the late army provided that each location be made either in contact with some point or part of the external boundary of the said tracts respectively or of some prior location therein. Locations to be made by causing a survey of the tracts located— [3]

AD, Papers of the Continental Congress, National Archives.

1. According to the editor of the *Journals* of the Continental Congress, this report was "in the writing of Abraham Baldwin (?)," delegate from Georgia (*JCC*, XXXIV, 185, note 2). It is in the writing of H.

Although H presented his credentials as a New York delegate to the Continental Congress on February 25, 1788, he did not attend until the date of this report.

2. On March 19, 1788, a committee of the Congress had reported an amendment to the Land Ordinance of May 20, 1785. It concerned the location of the land bounties granted by Congress to the officers and soldiers of the Con-

tinental Army. The amendment offered on May 28 was an addition to that paragraph of the March 19 amendment which reads, in part, as follows: "That the Secretary of War issue Warrants for bounties of Land to each of the Officers and Soldiers of the late continental Army who may be entitled to such bounties . . . [with] *Compensation for their expences in locating the same.*" (*JCC*, XXXIV, 97.)

3. According to the endorsement, this amendment was agreed to on May 28 and 29, 1788.

## The Federalist No. 78 [1]

[New York, May 28, 1788]

*To the People of the State of New-York.*

WE proceed now to an examination of the judiciary department of the proposed government.

In unfolding the defects of the existing confederation, the utility and necessity of a federal judicature have been clearly pointed out.[2] It is the less necessary to recapitulate the considerations there urged; as the propriety of the institution in the abstract is not disputed: The only questions which have been raised being relative to the manner of constituting it, and to its extent. To these points therefore our observations shall be confined.

The manner of constituting it seems to embrace these several objects— 1st. The mode of appointing the judges— 2d. The tenure by which they are to hold their places— 3d. The partition of the judiciary authority between different courts, and their relations to each other.

*First.* As to the mode of appointing the judges: This is the same with that of appointing the officers of the union in general, and has been so fully discussed in the two last numbers, that nothing can be said here which would not be useless repetition.

*Second.* As to the tenure by which the judges are to hold their places: This chiefly concerns their duration in office; the provisions for their support; and[3] the precautions for their responsibility.

J. and A. McLean, *The Federalist*, II, 290–99, published May 28, 1788, numbered 78. This essay appeared on June 14 in *The* [New York] *Independent Journal: or, the General Advertiser* and is numbered 77. In *The New-York Packet* it was begun on June 17 and concluded on June 20 and is numbered 78.

1. For background to this document, see "The Federalist. Introductory Note," October 27, 1787–May 28, 1788.
2. See essay 22.
3. "and" omitted in Hopkins.

According to the plan of the convention, all the judges who may be appointed by the United States are to hold their offices *during good behaviour,* which is conformable to the most approved of the state constitutions; and [4] among the rest, to that of this state. Its propriety having been drawn into question by the adversaries of that plan, is no light symptom of the rage for objection which disorders their imaginations and judgments. The standard of good behaviour for the continuance in office of the judicial magistracy is certainly one of the most valuable of the modern improvements in the practice of government. In a monarchy it is an excellent barrier to the despotism of the prince: In a republic it is a no less excellent barrier to the encroachments and oppressions of the representative body. And it is the best expedient which can be devised in any government, to secure a steady, upright and impartial administration of the laws.

Whoever attentively considers the different departments of power must perceive, that in a government in which they are separated from each other, the judiciary, from the nature of its functions, will always be the least dangerous to the political rights of the constitution; because it will be least in a capacity to annoy or injure them. The executive not only dispenses the honors, but holds the sword of the community. The legislature not only commands the purse, but prescribes the rules by which the duties and rights of every citizen are to be regulated. The judiciary on the contrary has no influence over either the sword or the purse, no direction either of the strength or of the wealth of the society, and can take no active resolution whatever. It may truly be said to have neither FORCE nor WILL, but merely judgment; and must ultimately depend upon the aid of the executive arm even [5] for the efficacy of its judgments.[6]

This simple view of the matter suggests several important consequences. It proves incontestibly that the judiciary is beyond comparison the weakest of the three departments of power; * that it

* The celebrated [7] Montesquieu speaking of them says, "of the three powers above mentioned, the JUDICIARY is next to nothing." Spirit of Laws, vol. I, page 186.[8]

4. "and" omitted in Hopkins.
5. "even" omitted in Hopkins.
6. "efficacious exercise even of this faculty" substituted for "efficacy of its judgments" in Hopkins.
7. "The celebrated" omitted in Hopkins.
8. H's reference is to Montesquieu, *The Spirit of Laws,* Book XI, Ch. 6.

can never attack with success either of the other two; and that all possible care is requisite to enable it to defend itself against their attacks. It equally proves, that though individual oppression may now and then proceed from the courts of justice, the general liberty of the people can never be endangered from that quarter; I mean, so long as the judiciary remains truly distinct from both the legislative and executive. For I agree that "there is no liberty, if the power of judging be not separated from the legislative and executive powers." † And [9] it proves, in the last place, that as liberty can have nothing to fear from the judiciary alone, but would have every thing to fear from its union with either of the other departments; that as all the effects of such an union must ensue from a dependence of the former on the latter, notwithstanding a nominal and apparent separation; that as from the natural feebleness of the judiciary, it is in continual jeopardy of being overpowered, awed or influenced by its coordinate branches; and [11] that as nothing can contribute so much to its firmness and independence, as permanency in office, this quality may therefore be justly regarded as an indispensable ingredient in its constitution; and in a great measure as the citadel of the public justice and the public security.

The complete independence of the courts of justice is peculiarly essential in a limited constitution. By a limited constitution I understand one which contains certain specified exceptions to the legislative authority; such for instance as that it shall pass no bills of attainder, no *ex post facto* laws, and the like. Limitations of this kind can be preserved in practice no other way than through the medium of the courts of justice; whose duty it must be to declare all acts contrary to the manifest tenor of the constitution void. Without this, all the reservations of particular rights or privileges would amount to nothing.

Some perplexity respecting the right of the courts to pronounce legislative acts void, because contrary to the constitution, has arisen from an imagination that the doctrine would imply a superiority of the judiciary to the legislative power. It is urged that the authority which can declare the acts of another void, must necessarily be

† Idem. page 181.[10]

9. "And" omitted in Hopkins.
10. The reference is to Montesquieu, *The Spirit of Laws*, Book XI, Ch. 6.
11. "and" omitted in Hopkins.

superior to the one whose acts may be declared void. As this doctrine is of great importance in all the American constitutions, a brief
discussion of the grounds on which it rests cannot be unacceptable.

There is no position which depends on clearer principles, than
that every act of a delegated authority, contrary to the tenor of the
commission under which it is exercised, is void. No legislative act
therefore contrary to the constitution can be valid. To deny this
would be to affirm that the deputy is greater than his principal; that
the servant is above his master; that the representatives of the people
are superior to the people themselves; that men acting by virtue
of powers may do not only what their powers do not authorise, but
what they forbid.

If it be said that the legislative body are themselves the constitutional judges of their own powers, and that the construction they
put upon them is conclusive upon the other departments, it may
be answered, that this cannot be the natural presumption, where it
is not to be collected [12] from any particular provision in the constitution. It is not otherwise to be supposed that the constitution
could intend to enable the representatives of the people to substitute their *will* to that of their constituents. It is far more rational
to suppose that the courts were designed to be an intermediate body
between the people and the legislature, in order, among other things,
to keep the latter within the limits assigned to their authority. The
interpretation of the laws is the proper and peculiar province of the
courts. A constitution is in fact, and must be, regarded by the judges
as a fundamental law. It therefore belongs [13] to them to ascertain
its meaning as well as the meaning of any particular act proceeding
from the legislative body. If there should happen to be an irrecon-
cileable variance between the two, that which has the superior
obligation and validity ought of course to be preferred; or [14] in
other words, the constitution ought to be preferred to the statute,
the intention of the people to the intention of their agents.

Nor does this [15] conclusion by any means suppose a superiority
of the judicial to the legislative power. It only supposes that the
power of the people is superior to both; and that where the will of

12. "recollected" substituted for "collected" in Hopkins.
13. "must therefore belong" substituted for "therefore belongs" in Hopkins.
14. "or" omitted in Hopkins.
15. "the" substituted for "this" in Hopkins.

the legislature declared in its statutes, stands in opposition to that of the people declared in the constitution, the judges ought to be governed by the latter, rather than the former. They ought to regulate their decisions by the fundamental laws, rather than by those which are not fundamental.

This exercise of judicial discretion in determining between two contradictory laws, is exemplified in a familiar instance. It not uncommonly happens, that there are two statutes existing at one time, clashing in whole or in part with each other, and neither of them containing any repealing clause or expression. In such a case, it is the province of the courts to liquidate and fix their meaning and operation: So far as they can by any fair construction be reconciled to each other; reason and law conspire to dictate that this should be done: Where this is impracticable, it becomes a matter of necessity to give effect to one, in exclusion of the other. The rule which has obtained in the courts for determining their relative validity is that the last in order of time shall be preferred to the first. But this is mere rule of construction, not derived from any positive law, but from the nature and reason of the thing. It is a rule not enjoined upon the courts by legislative provision, but adopted by themselves, as consonant to truth and propriety, for the direction of their conduct as interpreters of the law. They thought it reasonable, that between the interfering acts of an *equal* authority, that which was the last indication of its will, should have the preference.

But in regard to the interfering acts of a superior and subordinate authority, of an original and derivative power, the nature and reason of the thing indicate the converse of that rule as proper to be followed. They teach us that the prior act of a superior ought to be prefered to the subsequent act of an inferior and subordinate authority; and that, accordingly, whenever a particular statute contravenes the constitution, it will be the duty of the judicial tribunals to adhere to the latter, and disregard the former.

It can be of no weight to say, that the courts on the pretence of a repugnancy, may substitute their own pleasure to the constitutional intentions of the legislature. This might as well happen in the case of two contradictory statutes; or it might as well happen in every adjudication upon any single statute. The courts must declare the sense of the law; and if they should be disposed to exercise *will* instead of *judgment*, the consequence would equally be the substitution of their pleasure to that of the legislative body. The observation, if it proved any thing, would prove that there ought to be no judges distinct from that body.

If then the courts of justice are to be considered as the bulwarks of a limited constitution against legislative encroachments, this consideration will afford a strong argument for the permanent tenure of judicial offices, since nothing will contribute so much as this to that independent spirit in the judges, which must be essential to the faithful performance of so arduous a duty.

This independence of the judges is equally requisite to guard the constitution and the rights of individuals from the effects of those ill humours which the arts of designing men, or the influence of particular conjunctures, sometimes disseminate among the people themselves, and which, though they speedily give place to better information and more deliberate reflection, have a tendency in the mean time to occasion dangerous innovations in the government, and serious oppressions of the minor party in the community. Though I trust the friends of the proposed constitution will never concur with its enemies * in questioning that fundamental principle of republican government, which admits the right of the people to alter or abolish the established constitution whenever they find it inconsistent with their happiness; yet it is not to be inferred from this principle, that the representatives of the people, whenever a momentary inclination happens to lay hold of a majority of their constituents incompatible with the provisions in the existing constitution, would on that account be justifiable in a violation of those provisions; or that the courts would be under a greater obligation to connive at infractions in this shape, than when they had proceeded wholly from the cabals of the representative body. Until

---

* Vide Protest of the minority of the convention of Pennsylvania, Martin's speech, &c.[16]

16. H is referring to "The Address and Reasons of Dissent of the Minority of the Convention of the State of Pennsylvania to their Constituents." Signed by twenty-one members of the Pennsylvania Ratifying Convention, the address appeared in *The Pennsylvania Packet and Daily Advertiser* on December 18, 1787, six days after Pennsylvania had ratified the Constitution.

"Martin's speech" presumably refers to an address by Luther Martin, a member of the Constitutional Convention and bitter foe of the proposed Constitution, before the Maryland House of Delegates on January 27, 1788.

the people have by some solemn and authoritative act annulled or changed the established form, it is binding upon themselves collectively, as well as individually; and no presumption, or even knowledge of their sentiments, can warrant their representatives in a departure from it, prior to such an act. But it is easy to see that it would require an uncommon portion of fortitude in the judges to do their duty as faithful guardians of the constitution, where legislative invasions of it had been instigated by the major voice of the community.

But it is not with a view to infractions of the constitution only that the independence of the judges may be an essential safeguard against the effects of occasional ill humours in the society. These sometimes extend no farther than to the injury of the private rights of particular classes of citizens, by unjust and partial laws. Here also the firmness of the judicial magistracy is of vast importance in mitigating the severity, and confining the operation of such laws. It not only serves to moderate the immediate mischiefs of those which may have been passed, but it operates as a check upon the legislative body in passing them; who, perceiving that obstacles to the success of an iniquitous intention are to be expected from the scruples of the courts, are in a manner compelled by the very motives of the injustice they meditate, to qualify their attempts. This is a circumstance calculated to have more influence upon the character of our governments, than but few may be aware of.[17] The benefits of the integrity and moderation of the judiciary have already been felt in more states than one; and though they may have displeased those whose sinister expectations they may have disappointed, they must have commanded the esteem and applause of all the virtuous and disinterested. Considerate men of every description ought to prize whatever will tend to beget or fortify that temper in the courts; as no man can be sure that he may not be to-morrow the victim of a spirit of injustice, by which he may be a gainer to-day. And every man must now feel that the inevitable tendency of such a spirit is to sap the foundations of public and private confidence, and to introduce in its stead, universal distrust and distress.

That inflexible and uniform adherence to the rights of the con-

17. "imagine" substituted for "be aware of" in Hopkins.

stitution and of individuals, which we perceive to be indispensable in the courts of justice, can certainly not be expected from judges who hold their offices by a temporary commission. Periodical appointments, however regulated, or by whomsoever made, would in some way or other be fatal to their necessary independence. If the power of making them was committed either to the executive or legislature, there would be danger of an improper complaisance to the branch which possessed it; if to both, there would be an unwillingness to hazard the displeasure of either; if to the people, or to persons chosen by them for the special purpose, there would be too great a disposition to consult popularity, to justify a reliance that nothing would be consulted but the constitution and the laws.

There is yet a further and a weighty reason for the permanency of the [18] judicial offices; which is deducible from the nature of the qualifications they require. It has been frequently remarked with great propriety, that a voluminous code of laws is one of the inconveniences necessarily connected with the advantages of a free government. To avoid an arbitrary discretion in the courts, it is indispensable that they should be bound down by strict rules and precedents, which serve to define and point out their duty in every particular case that comes before them; and it will readily be conceived from the variety of controversies which grow out of the folly and wickedness of mankind, that the records of those precedents must unavoidably swell to a very considerable bulk, and must demand long and laborious study to acquire a competent knowledge of them. Hence it is that there can be but few men in the society, who will have sufficient skill in the laws to qualify them for the stations of judges. And making the proper deductions for the ordinary depravity of human nature, the number must be still smaller of those who unite the requisite integrity with the requisite knowledge. These considerations apprise us, that the government can have no great option between fit characters; and that a temporary duration in office, which would naturally discourage such characters from quitting a lucrative line of practice to accept a seat on the bench, would have a tendency to throw the administration of justice into hands less able, and less well qualified to conduct it with utility and dignity. In the present circumstances of this country,

18. "the" omitted in Hopkins.

and in those in which it is likely to be for a long time to come, the disadvantages on this score would be greater than they may at first sight appear; but it must be confessed that they are far inferior to those which present themselves under the other aspects of the subject.

Upon the whole there can be no room to doubt that the convention acted wisely in copying from the models of those constitutions which have established *good behaviour* as the tenure of their [19] judicial offices in point of duration; and that so far from being blameable on this account, their plan would have been inexcuseably defective if it had wanted this important feature of good government. The experience of Great Britain affords an illustrious comment on the excellence of the institution.

PUBLIUS.

19. "their" omitted in Hopkins.

## The Federalist No. 79 [1]

[New York, May 28, 1788]

*To the People of the State of New-York.*

NEXT to permanency in office, nothing can contribute more to the independence of the judges than a fixed provision for their support. The remark made in relation to the president, is equally applicable here.[2] In the general course of human nature, *a power over a man's subsistence amounts to a power over his will*. And we can never hope to see realised in practice the complete separation of the judicial from the legislative power, in any system, which leaves the former dependent for pecuniary resources [3] on the occasional grants of the latter. The enlightened friends to good government, in every state, have seen cause to lament the want of precise and explicit precautions in the state constitutions on this head. Some of these indeed

J. and A. McLean, *The Federalist*, II, 299–303, published May 28, 1788, numbered 79. This essay appeared on June 18 in *The* [New York] *Independent Journal: or, the General Advertiser* and is numbered 78. In *The New-York Packet* it appeared on June 24 and it is numbered 79.

1. For background to this document, see "The Federalist. Introductory Note," October 27, 1787–May 28, 1788.
2. See essay 73.
3. "resource" substituted for "resources" in Hopkins.

have declared that *permanent* * salaries should be established for the judges; but the experiment has in some instances shewn that such expressions are not sufficiently definite to preclude legislative evasions. Something still more positive and unequivocal has been evinced to be requisite. The plan of the convention accordingly has provided, that the judges of the United States "shall at *stated times* receive for their services a compensation, which shall not be *diminished* during their continuance in office."

This, all circumstances considered, is the most eligible provision that could have been devised. It will readily be understood, that the fluctuations in the value of money, and in the state of society, rendered a fixed rate of compensation in the constitution inadmissible. What might be extravagant to day, might in half a century become penurious and inadequate. It was therefore necessary to leave it to the discretion of the legislature to vary its provisions in conformity to the variations in circumstances; yet under such restrictions as to put it out of the power of that body to change the condition of the individual for the worse. A man may then be sure of the ground upon which he stands, and can never be deterred from his duty by the apprehension of being placed in a less eligible situation. The clause which has been quoted combines both advantages. The salaries of judicial offices may from time to time be altered, as occasion shall require, yet so as never to lessen the allowance with which any particular judge comes into office, in respect to him. It will be observed that a difference has been made by the convention between the compensation of the president and of the judges. That of the former can neither be increased nor diminished. That of the latter can only not be diminished. This probably arose from the difference in the duration of the respective offices. As the president is to be elected for no more than four years, it can rarely happen that an adequate salary, fixed at the commencement of that period, will not continue to be such to the end of it. But with regard to the judges, who, if they behave properly, will be secured in their places for life, it may well happen, especially in the early stages of the government, that a stipend, which would be very sufficient at their first appointment, would become too small in the progress of their service.

* Vide Constitution of Massachusetts, Chap. 2, Sect. 1. Art. 13.

This provision for the support of the judges bears every mark of prudence and efficacy; and it may be safely affirmed that, together with the permanent tenure of their offices, it affords a better prospect of their independence than is discoverable in the constitutions of any of the states, in regard to their own judges.

The precautions for their responsibility are comprised in the article respecting impeachments. They are liable to be impeached for malconduct by the house of representatives, and tried by the senate, and if convicted, may be dismissed from office and disqualified for holding any other. This is the only provision on the point, which is consistent with the necessary independence of the judicial character, and is the only one which we find in our own constitution in respect to our own judges.

The want of a provision for removing the judges on account of inability, has been a subject of complaint. But all considerate men will be sensible that such a provision would either not be practiced upon, or would be more liable to abuse than calculated to answer any good purpose. The mensuration of the faculties of the mind has, I believe, no place in the catalogue of known arts. An attempt to fix the boundary between the regions of ability and inability, would much oftener give scope to personal and party attachments and enmities, than advance the interests of justice, or the public good. The result, except in the case of insanity, must for the most part be arbitrary; and insanity without any formal or express provision, may be safely pronounced to be a virtual disqualification.

The constitution of New-York, to avoid investigations that must forever be vague and dangerous, has taken a particular age as the criterion of inability. No man can be a judge beyond sixty. I believe there are few at present, who do not disapprove of this provision. There is no station in relation to which it is less proper than to that of a judge. The deliberating and comparing faculties generally preserve their strength much beyond that period, in men who survive it; and when in addition to this circumstance, we consider how few there are who outlive the season of intellectual vigour, and how improbable it is that any considerable proportion of the bench, whether more or less numerous, should be in such a situation at the same time, we shall be ready to conclude that limitations of this sort have little to recommend them. In a republic, where fortunes are

not affluent, and pensions not expedient, the dismission of men from
stations in which they have served their country long and usefully,
on which they depend for subsistence, and from which it will be
too late to resort to any other occupation for a livelihood, ought to
have some better apology to humanity, than is to be found in the
imaginary danger of a superannuated bench.

                                                              PUBLIUS.


## The Federalist No. 80 [1]

[New York, May 28, 1788]

*To the People of the State of New-York.*

TO judge with accuracy of the proper [2] extent of the federal
judicature, it will be necessary to consider in the first place what
are its proper objects.

It seems scarcely to admit of controversy that the judiciary authority of the union ought to extend to these several descriptions of
causes.[3] 1st. To all those which arise out of the laws of the United
States, passed in pursuance of their just and constitutional powers
of legislation; 2d. to all those which concern the execution of the
provisions expressly contained in the articles of union; 3d. to all
those in which the United States are a party; 4th to all those which
involve the PEACE of the CONFEDERACY, whether they relate
to the intercourse between the United States and foreign nations,
or to that between the States themselves; 5th. to all those which
originate on the high seas, and are of admiralty or maritime jurisdiction; and lastly, to all those in which the state tribunals cannot be
supposed to be impartial and unbiassed.

The first point depends upon this obvious consideration that there
ought always to be a constitutional method of giving efficacy to constitutional provisions. What for instance would avail restrictions on

J. and A. McLean, *The Federalist*, II, 303–10, published May 28, 1788, numbered 80. This essay appeared on June 21 in *The* [New York] *Independent
Journal: or, the General Advertiser* and is numbered 79. In *The New-York
Packet* it was begun on June 27 and concluded on July 1 and is numbered 80.
   1. For background to this document, see "The Federalist. Introductory
Note," October 27, 1787–May 28, 1788.
   2. "due" substituted for "proper" in Hopkins.
   3. "cases" substituted for "causes" in Hopkins.

the authority of the state legislatures, without some constitutional mode of enforcing the observance of them? The states, by the plan of the convention are prohibited from doing a variety of things; some of which are incompatible with the interests of the union, and others with the principles of good government. The imposition of duties on imported articles, and the emission of paper money, are specimens of each kind. No man of sense will believe that such prohibitions would be scrupulously regarded, without some effectual power in the government to restrain or correct the infractions of them. This power must either be a direct negative on the state laws, or an authority in the federal courts, to over-rule such as might be in manifest contravention of the articles of union. There is no third course that I can imagine. The latter appears to have been thought by the convention preferable to the former, and I presume will be most agreeable to the states.

As to the second point, it is impossible by any argument or comment to make it clearer than it is in itself. If there are such things as political axioms, the propriety of the judicial power of a government being co-extensive with its legislative, may be ranked among the number. The mere necessity of uniformity in the interpretation of the national laws, decides the question. Thirteen independent courts of final jurisdiction over the same causes, arising upon the same laws, is a hydra in government, from which nothing but contradiction and confusion can proceed.

Still less need be said in regard to the third point. Controversies between the nation and its members or citizens, can only be properly referred to the national tribunals. Any other plan would be contrary to reason, to precedent, and to decorum.

The fourth point rests on this plain proposition, that the peace of the WHOLE ought not to be left at the disposal of a PART. The union will undoubtedly be answerable to foreign powers for the conduct of its members. And the responsibility for an injury ought ever to be accompanied with the faculty of preventing it. As the denial or perversion of justice by the sentences of courts, as well as in any other manner,[4] is with reason classed among the just causes of war, it will follow that the federal judiciary ought to have cognizance of all causes in which the citizens of other countries are concerned.

4. "as well as in any other manner" omitted in Hopkins.

This is not less essential to the preservation of the public faith, than to the security of the public tranquility. A distinction may perhaps be imagined between cases arising upon treaties and the laws of nations, and those which may stand merely on the footing of the municipal law. The former kind may be supposed proper for the federal jurisdiction, the latter for that of the states. But it is at least problematical whether an unjust sentence against a foreigner, where the subject of controversy was wholly relative to the *lex loci*, would not, if unredressed, be an aggression upon his sovereign, as well as one which violated the stipulations in a treaty or the general laws [5] of nations. And a still greater objection to the distinction would result from the immense difficulty, if not impossibility, of a practical discrimination between the cases of one complection and those of the other. So great a proportion of the cases [6] in which foreigners are parties involve national questions, that it is by far most safe and most expedient to refer all those in which they are concerned to the national tribunals.

The power of determining causes between two states, between one state and the citizens of another, and between the citizens of different states, is perhaps not less essential to the peace of the union than that which has been just examined. History gives us a horrid picture of the dissentions and private wars which distracted and desolated Germany prior to the institution of the IMPERIAL CHAMBER by Maximilian, towards the close of the fifteenth century; and informs us at the same time of the vast influence of that institution in appeasing the disorders and establishing the tranquility of the empire. This was a court invested with authority to decide finally all differences between [7] the members of the Germanic body.

A method of terminating territorial disputes between the states, under the authority of the federal head, was not unattended to, even in the imperfect system by which they have been hitherto held together. But there are many [8] other sources, besides interfering claims of boundary, from which bickerings and animosities may spring up among the members of the union. To some of these we have been witnesses in the course of our past experience. It will readily be

5. "law" substituted for "laws" in Hopkins.
6. "controversies" substituted for "cases" in Hopkins.
7. "among" substituted for "between" in Hopkins.
8. "many" omitted in Hopkins.

conjectured that I allude to the fradulent laws which have been passed in too many of the states. And though the proposed constitution establishes particular guards against the repetition of those instances which have heretofore made their appearance, yet it is warrantable to apprehend that the spirit which produced them will assume new shapes that could not be foreseen, nor specifically provided against. Whatever practices may have a tendency to disturb the harmony between [9] the states, are proper objects of federal superintendence and control.

It may be esteemed the basis of the union, that "the citizens of each state shall be entitled to all the privileges and immunities of citizens of the several states." And if it be a just principle that every government *ought to possess the means of executing its own provisions by its own authority,* it will follow, that in order to the inviolable maintenance of that equality of privileges and immunities to which the citizens of the union will be entitled, the national judiciary ought to preside in all cases in which one state or its citizens are opposed to another state or its citizens. To secure the full effect of so fundamental a provision against all evasion and subterfuge, it is necessary that its construction should be committed to that tribunal, which, having no local attachments, will be likely to be impartial between the different states and their citizens, and which, owing its official existence to the union, will never be likely to feel any bias inauspicious to the principles on which it is founded.

The fifth point will demand little animadversion. The most bigotted idolizers of state authority have not thus far shewn a disposition to deny the national judiciary the cognizance of maritime causes. These so generally depend on the laws of nations, and so commonly affect the rights of foreigners, that they fall within the considerations which are relative to the public peace. The most important part of them are by the present confederation submitted to federal jurisdiction.

The reasonableness of the agency of the national courts in cases in which the state tribunals cannot be supposed to be impartial, speaks for itself. No man ought certainly to be a judge in his own cause, or in any cause in respect to which he has the least interest or bias. This principle has no inconsiderable weight in designating the fed-

9. "of" substituted for "between" in Hopkins.

eral courts as the proper tribunals for the determination of controversies between different states and their citizens. And it ought to have the same operation in regard to some cases between the citizens of the same state. Claims to land under grants of different states, founded upon adverse pretensions of boundary, are of this description. The courts of neither of the granting states could be expected to be unbiassed. The laws may have even prejudged the question, and tied the courts down to decisions in favour of the grants of the state to which they belonged. And even [10] where this had not been done, it would be natural that the judges, as men, should feel a strong predilection to the claims of their own government.

Having thus laid down and discussed the principles which ought to regulate the constitution of the federal judiciary, we will proceed to test, by these principles, the particular powers of which, according to the plan of the convention, it is to be composed. It is to comprehend, "all cases in law and equity arising under the constitution, the laws of the United States, and treaties made, or which shall be made under their authority; to all cases affecting ambassadors, other public ministers and consuls; to all cases of admiralty and maritime jurisdiction; to controversies to which the United States shall be a party; to controversies between two or more states, between a state and citizens of another state, between citizens of different states, between citizens of the same state claiming lands under grants of different states, and between a state or the citizens thereof, and foreign states, citizens and subjects." This constitutes the entire mass of the judicial authority of the union. Let us now review it in detail. It is then to extend,

*First.* To all cases in law and equity *arising under the constitution* and *the laws of the United States.* This corresponds to the two first classes of causes which have been enumerated as proper for the jurisdiction of the United States. It has been asked what is meant by "cases arising under the constitution," in contradistinction from those "arising under the laws of the United States." The difference has been already explained. All the restrictions upon the authority of the state legislatures, furnish examples of it.[11] They

10. "even" omitted in Hopkins.
11. "of it" omitted in Hopkins.

are not, for instance, to emit paper money; but the interdiction results from the constitution, and will have no connection with any law of the United States. Should paper money, notwithstanding, be emitted, the controversies concerning it would be cases arising upon [12] the constitution, and not upon [13] the laws of the United States, in the ordinary signification of the terms. This may serve as a sample of the whole.

It has also been asked, what need of the word "equity"? What equitable causes can grow out of the constitution and laws of the United States? There is hardly a subject of litigation between individuals, which may not involve those ingredients of *fraud, accident, trust* or *hardship,* which would render the matter an object of equitable, rather than of legal jurisdiction, as the distinction is known and established in several of the states. It is the peculiar province, for instance, of a court of equity to relieve against what are called hard bargains: These are contracts, in which, though there may have been no direct fraud or deceit, sufficient to invalidate them in a court of law; yet there may have been some undue and unconscionable advantage taken of the necessities or misfortunes of one of the parties, which a court of equity would not tolerate. In such cases, where foreigners were concerned on either side, it would be impossible for the federal judicatories to do justice without an equitable, as well as a legal jurisdiction. Agreements to convey lands claimed under the grants of different states, may afford another example of the necessity of an equitable jurisdiction in the federal courts. This reasoning may not be so palpable in those states where the formal and technical distinction between LAW and EQUITY is not maintained as in this state, where it is exemplified by every day's practice.

The judiciary authority of the union is to extend—

*Second.* To treaties made, or which shall be made under the authority of the United States, and to all cases affecting ambassadors, other public ministers and consuls. These belong to the fourth class of the enumerated cases, as they have an evident connection with the preservation of the national peace.

12. "under" substituted for "upon" in Hopkins.
13. "under" substituted for "upon" in Hopkins.

*Third.* To cases of admiralty and maritime jurisdiction. These form altogether the fifth of the enumerated classes of causes proper for the cognizance of the national courts.

*Fourth.* To controversies to which the United States shall be a party. These constitute the third of those classes.

*Fifth.* To controversies between two or more states, between a state and citizens of another state, between citizens of different states. These belong to the fourth of those classes, and partake in some measure of the nature of the last.

*Sixth.* To cases between the citizens of the same state, *claiming lands under grants of different states.* These fall within the last class, and *are the only instance* [14] *in which the proposed constitution directly contemplates the cognizance of disputes between the citizens of the same state.*

*Seventh.* To cases between a state and the citizens thereof, and foreign states, citizens, or subjects. These have been already explained to belong to the fourth of the enumerated classes, and have been shewn to be in a peculiar manner the proper subjects of the national judicature.

From this review of the particular powers of the federal judiciary, as marked out in the constitution, it appears, that they are all conformable to the principles which ought to have governed the structure of that department, and which were necessary to the perfection of the system. If some partial inconveniencies should appear to be connected with the incorporation of any of them into the plan, it ought to be recollected that the national legislature will have ample authority to make such *exceptions* and to prescribe such regulations as will be calculated to obviate or remove these inconveniencies. The possibility of particular mischiefs can never be viewed by a well-informed mind as a solid objection to a general [15] principle, which is calculated to avoid general mischiefs, and to obtain general advantages.

PUBLIUS.

14. "instances" substituted for "instance" in Hopkins.
15. "general" omitted in Hopkins.

## *The Federalist No. 81* [1]

[New York, May 28, 1788]

*To the People of the State of New-York.*

LET us now return to the partition of the judiciary authority between different courts, and their relations to each other.

"The judicial power of the United States is (by the plan of the convention) [2] to be vested in one supreme court, and in such inferior courts as the congress may from time to time ordain and establish." *

That there ought to be one court of supreme and final jurisdiction is a proposition which has not been, and [3] is not likely to be contested. The reasons for it have been assigned in another place,[4] and are too obvious to need repetition. The only question that seems to have been raised concerning it, is whether it ought to be a distinct body, or a branch of the legislature. The same contradiction is observable in regard to this matter, which has been remarked in several other cases. The very men who object to the senate as a court of impeachments, on the ground of an improper intermixture of powers, advocate,[5] by implication at least,[6] the propriety of vesting the ultimate decision of all causes in the whole, or in a part of the legislative body.

The arguments or rather suggestions, upon which this charge is founded, are to this effect: "The authority of the proposed [7] supreme court of the United States, which is to be a separate and independent body, will be superior to that of the legislature. The power of construing the laws, according to the *spirit* of the con-

---

* Article 3. Sec. 1.

J. and A. McLean, *The Federalist*, II, 310–22, published May 28, 1788, numbered 81. This essay was begun on June 25 and concluded on June 28 in *The* [New York] *Independent Journal: or, the General Advertiser* and is numbered 80. In *The New-York Packet* it was begun on July 4 and concluded on July 8 and is numbered 81.

1. For background to this document, see "The Federalist. Introductory Note," October 27, 1787–May 28, 1788.
2. "(by the plan of the convention)" omitted in Hopkins.
3. "has not been, and" omitted in Hopkins.
4. See essay 22.
5. "are advocates" substituted for "advocate" in Hopkins.
6. "for" inserted at this point in Hopkins.
7. "proposed" omitted in Hopkins.

stitution, will enable that court to mould them into whatever shape it may think proper; especially as its decisions will not be in any manner subject to the revision or correction of the legislative body. This is as unprecedented as it is dangerous. In Britain, the judicial power in the last resort, resides in the house of lords, which is a branch of the legislature; and this part of the British government has been imitated in the state constitutions in general. The parliament of Great-Britain, and the legislatures of the several states, can at any time rectify by law, the exceptionable decisions of their respective courts. But the errors and usurpations of the supreme court of the United States will be uncontrolable and remediless." This, upon examination, will be found to be altogether made of false reasoning upon misconceived fact.

In the first place, there is not a syllable in the plan under consideration,[8] which *directly* empowers the national courts to construe the laws according to the spirit of the constitution, or which gives them any greater latitude in this respect, than may be claimed by the courts of every state. I admit however, that the constitution ought to be the standard of construction for the laws, and that wherever there is an evident opposition, the laws ought to give place to the constitution. But this doctrine is not deducible from any circumstance peculiar to the plan of the convention; but from the general theory of a limited constitution; and as far as it is true, is equally applicable to most, if not to all the state governments. There can be no objection therefore, on this account, to the federal judicature, which will not lie against the local judicatures in general, and which will not serve to condemn every constitution that attempts to set bounds to the [9] legislative discretion.

But perhaps the force of the objection may be thought to consist in the particular organization of the proposed [10] supreme court; in its being composed of a distinct body of magistrates, instead of being one of the branches of the legislature, as in the government of Great-Britain and in that of this state. To insist upon this point, the authors of the objection must renounce the meaning they have laboured to annex to the celebrated maxim requiring a separation

8. "under consideration" omitted in Hopkins.
9. "the" omitted in Hopkins.
10. "proposed" omitted in Hopkins.

of the departments of power. It shall nevertheless be conceded to them, agreeably to the interpretation given to that maxim in the course of these papers, that it is not violated by vesting the ultimate power of judging in a *part* of the legislative body. But though this be not an absolute violation of that excellent rule; yet it verges so nearly upon it, as on this account alone to be less eligible than the mode preferred by the convention. From a body which had had even a partial agency in passing bad laws, we could rarely expect a disposition to temper and moderate them in the application. The same spirit, which had operated in making them would be too apt to operate in interpreting them: [11] Still less could it be expected, that men who had infringed the constitution, in the character of legislators, would be disposed to repair the breach, in the character [12] of judges. Nor is this all: Every reason, which recommends the tenure of good behaviour for judicial offices, militates against placing the judiciary power in the last resort in a body composed of men chosen for a limited period. There is an absurdity in referring the determination of causes in the first instance to judges of permanent standing, and in the last to those of a temporary and mutable constitution. And there is a still greater absurdity in subjecting the decisions of men selected for their knowledge of the laws, acquired by long and laborious study, to the revision and control of men, who for want of the same advantage cannot but be deficient in that knowledge. The members of the legislature will rarely be chosen with a view to those qualifications which fit men for the stations of judges; and as on this account there will be great reason to apprehend all the ill consequences of defective information; so on account of the natural propensity of such bodies to party divisions, there will be no less reason to fear, that the pestilential breath of faction may poison the fountains of justice. The habit of being continually marshalled on opposite sides, will be too apt to stifle the voice both of law and of equity.

These considerations teach us to applaud the wisdom of those states, who have committed the judicial power in the last resort, not to a part of the legislature, but to distinct and independent bodies

11. "influence their construction" substituted for "operate in interpreting them" in Hopkins.
12. "that" substituted for "the character" in Hopkins.

of men. Contrary to the supposition of those, who have represented the plan of the convention in this respect as novel and unprecedented, it is but a copy of the constitutions of New-Hampshire, Massachusetts, Pennsylvania, Delaware, Maryland, Virginia, North-Carolina, South-Carolina and Georgia; and the preference which has been given to these models is highly to be commended.

It is not true, in the second place, that the parliament of Great Britain, or the legislatures of the particular states, can rectify the exceptionable decisions of their respective courts, in any other sense than might be done by a future legislature of the United States. The theory neither of the British, nor the state constitutions, authorises the revisal of a judicial sentence, by a legislative act. Nor is there anything in the proposed constitution more than in either of them, by which it is forbidden. In the former as well [13] as in the latter, the impropriety of the thing, on the general principles of law and reason, is the sole obstacle. A legislature without exceeding its province cannot reverse a determination once made, in a particular case; though it may prescribe a new rule for future cases. This is the principle, and it applies in all its consequences, exactly in the same manner and extent, to the state governments, as to the national government, now under consideration. Not the least difference can be pointed out in any view of the subject.

It may in the last place be observed that the supposed danger of judiciary encroachments on the legislative authority, which has been upon many occasions reiterated, is in reality a phantom. Particular misconstructions and contraventions of the will of the legislature may now and then happen; but they can never be so extensive as to amount to an inconvenience, or in any sensible degree to affect the order of the political system. This may be inferred with certainty from the general nature of the judicial power; from the objects to which it relates; from the manner in which it is exercised; from its comparative weakness, and from its total incapacity to support its usurpations by force. And the inference is greatly fortified by the consideration of the important constitutional check, which the power of instituting impeachments, in one part of the legislative body, and of determining upon them in the other, would give to that body upon the members of the judicial department. This is

13. "as well" omitted in Hopkins.

alone a complete security. There never can be danger that the judges, by a series of deliberate usurpations on the authority of the legislature, would hazard the united resentment of the body entrusted with it, while this body was possessed of the means of punishing their presumption by degrading them from their stations. While this ought to remove all apprehensions on the subject, it affords at the same time a cogent argument for constituting the senate a court for the trial of impeachments.

Having now examined, and I trust removed the objections to the distinct and independent organization of the supreme court, I proceed to consider the propriety of the power of constituting inferior courts,* and the relations which will subsist between these and the former.

The power of constituting inferior courts is evidently calculated to obviate the necessity of having recourse to the supreme court, in every case of federal cognizance. It is intended to enable the national government to institute or *authorise* in each state or district of the United States, a tribunal competent to the determination of matters of national jurisdiction within its limits.

But why, it is asked, might not the same purpose have been accomplished by the instrumentality of the state courts? This admits of different answers. Though the fitness and competency of those [14] courts should be allowed in the utmost latitude; yet the substance of the power in question, may still be regarded as a necessary part of the plan, if it were only to empower [15] the national legislature to commit to them the cognizance of causes arising out of the national constitution. To confer the power of determining such causes upon the existing courts of the several states,[16] would perhaps be as much "to constitute tribunals," as to create new courts with the

---

* This power has been absurdly represented as intended to abolish all the county courts in the several states, which are commonly called inferior courts. But the expressions of the constitution are to constitute "tribunals INFERIOR TO THE SUPREME COURT," and the evident design of the provision is to enable the institution of local courts subordinate to the supreme, either in states or larger districts. It is ridiculous to imagine that county courts were in contemplation.

14. "these" substituted for "those" in Hopkins.
15. "authorize" substituted for "empower" in Hopkins.
16. "To confer upon the existing courts of the several states the power of determining such causes," substituted for "To confer" through "several states" in Hopkins.

like power. But ought not a more direct and explicit provision to have been made in favour of the state courts? There are, in my opinion, substantial reasons against such a provision: The most discerning cannot foresee how far the prevalency of a local spirit may be found to disqualify the local tribunals for the jurisdiction of national causes; whilst every man may discover that courts constituted like those of some of the states, would be improper channels of the judicial authority of the union. State judges, holding their offices during pleasure, or from year to year, will be too little independent to be relied upon for an inflexible execution of the national laws. And if there was a necessity for confiding [17] the original cognizance of causes arising under those laws to them,[18] there would be a correspondent necessity for leaving the door of appeal as wide as possible. In proportion to the grounds of confidence in, or diffidence [19] of the subordinate tribunals, ought to be the facility or difficulty of appeals. And well satisfied as I am of the propriety of the appellate jurisdiction in the several classes of causes to which it is extended by the plan of the convention, I should consider every thing calculated to give in practice, an *unrestrained course* to appeals as a source of public and private inconvenience.

I am not sure but that it will be found highly expedient and useful to divide the United States into four or five, or half a dozen districts; and to institute a federal court in each district, in lieu of one in every state. The judges of these courts, with the aid of the state judges,[20] may hold circuits for the trial of causes in the several parts of the respective districts. Justice through them may be administered with ease and dispatch; and appeals may be safely circumscribed within a very narrow compass. This plan appears to me at present the most eligible of any that could be adopted, and in order to it, it is necessary that the power of constituting inferior courts should exist in the full extent in which it is to be found [21] in the proposed constitution.

These reasons seem sufficient to satisfy a candid mind, that the want of such a power would have been a great defect in the plan.

17. "to them" inserted here in Hopkins.
18. "to them" omitted in Hopkins.
19. "distrust" substituted for "diffidence" in Hopkins.
20. "with the aid of the state judges" omitted in Hopkins.
21. "seen" substituted for "to be found" in Hopkins.

Let us now examine in what manner the judicial authority is to be distributed between the supreme and the inferior courts of the union.

The supreme court is to be invested with original jurisdiction, only "in cases affecting ambassadors, other public ministers and consuls, and those in which A STATE shall be a party." Public ministers of every class, are the immediate representatives of their sovereigns. All questions in which they are concerned, are so directly connected with the public peace, that as well for the preservation of this, as out of respect to the sovereignties they represent, it is both expedient and proper, that such questions should be submitted in the first instance to the highest judicatory of the nation. Though consuls have not in strictness a diplomatic character, yet as they are the public agents of the nations to which they belong, the same observation is in a great measure applicable to them. In cases in which a state might happen to be a party, it would ill suit its dignity to be turned over to an inferior tribunal. Though it may rather be a digression from the immediate subject of this paper, I shall take occasion to mention here, a supposition which has excited some alarm upon very mistaken grounds: It has been suggested that an assignment of the public securities of one state to the citizens of another, would enable them to prosecute that state in the federal courts for the amount of those securities. A suggestion which the following considerations prove to be without foundation.

It is inherent in the nature of sovereignty, not to be amenable to the suit of an individual *without its consent*. This is the general sense and the general practice of mankind; and the exemption, as one of the attributes of sovereignty, is now enjoyed by the government of every state in the union. Unless therefore, there is a surrender of this immunity in the plan of the convention, it will remain with the states, and the danger intimated must be merely ideal. The circumstances which are necessary to produce an alienation of state sovereignty, were discussed in considering the article of taxation, and need not be repeated here.[22] A recurrence to the principles there established will satisfy us, that there is no colour to pretend that the state governments, would by the adoption of that plan, be divested of the privilege of paying their own debts in their own way, free from every constraint but that which flows from the obliga-

22. See essay 32.

tions of good faith. The contracts between a nation and individuals are only binding on the conscience of the sovereign, and have no pretensions to a compulsive force. They confer no right of action independent of the sovereign will. To what purpose would it be to authorise suits against states, for the debts they owe? How could recoveries be enforced? It is evident that it could not be done without waging war against the contracting state; and to ascribe to the federal courts, by mere implication, and in destruction of a pre-existing right of the state governments, a power which would involve such a consequence, would be altogether forced and unwarrantable.

Let us resume the train of our observations; we have seen that the original jurisdiction of the supreme court would be confined to two classes of causes, and those of a nature rarely to occur. In all other causes [23] of federal cognizance, the original jurisdiction would appertain to the inferior tribunals, and the supreme court would have nothing more than an appellate jurisdiction, "with such *exceptions*, and under such *regulations* as the congress shall make."

The propriety of this appellate jurisdiction has been scarcely called in question in regard to matters of law; but the clamours have been loud against it as applied to matters of fact. Some well intentioned men in this state, deriving their notions from the language and forms which obtain in our courts, have been induced to consider it as an implied supersedure of the trial by jury, in favour of the civil law mode of trial, which prevails in our courts of admiralty, probates and chancery. A technical sense has been affixed to the term "appellate", which in our law parlance is commonly used in reference to appeals in the course of the civil law. But if I am not misinformed, the same meaning would not be given to it in any part of New-England. There an appeal from one jury to another is familiar both in language and practice, and is even a matter of course, until there have been two verdicts on one side. The word "appellate" therefore will not be understood in the same sense in New-England as in New-York, which shews the impropriety of a technical interpretation derived from the jurisprudence of any [24] particular state. The expression taken in the abstract, denotes nothing more than the power

23. "cases" substituted for "causes" in Hopkins.
24. "a" substituted for "any" in Hopkins.

of one tribunal to review the proceedings of another, either as to the law or fact, or both. The mode of doing it may depend on ancient custom or legislative provision, (in a new government it must depend on the latter) and may be with or without the aid of a jury, as may be judged adviseable. If therefore the re-examination of a fact once determined by a jury, should in any case be admitted under the proposed constitution, it may be so regulated as to be done by a second jury, either by remanding the cause to the court below for a second trial of the fact, or by directing an issue immediately out of the supreme court.

But it does not follow that the re-examination of a fact once ascertained by a jury, will be permitted in the supreme court. Why may it not be said, with the strictest propriety, when a writ of error is brought from an inferior to a superior court of law in this state, that the latter has jurisdiction of the fact, as well as the law? It is true it cannot institute a new enquiry concerning the fact, but it takes cognizance of it as it appears upon the record, and pronounces the law arising upon it.* This is jurisdiction of both fact and law, nor is it even possible to separate them. Though the common law courts of this state ascertain disputed facts by a jury, yet they unquestionably have jurisdiction of both fact and law; and accordingly, when the former is agreed in the pleadings, they have no recourse to a jury, but proceed at once to judgment. I contend therefore on this ground, that the expressions, "appellate jurisdiction, both as to law and fact," do not necessarily imply a re-examination in the supreme court of facts decided by juries in the inferior courts.

The following train of ideas may well be imagined to have influenced the convention in relation to this particular provision. The appellate jurisdiction of the supreme court (may it have been argued) [25] will extend to causes determinable in different modes, some in the course of the COMMON LAW, and [26] others in the course of the CIVIL LAW. In the former, the revision of the law only, will be, generally speaking, the proper province of the supreme court; in the latter, the re-examination of the fact is agreeable to

* This word is a compound of JUS and DICTIO, juris, dictio, or a speaking or pronouncing of the law.

25. "it may have been argued" substituted for "(may it have been argued)" in Hopkins.
26. "and" omitted in Hopkins.

usage, and in some cases, of which prize causes are an example, might be essential to the preservation of the public peace. It is therefore necessary, that the appellate jurisdiction should, in certain cases, extend in the broadest sense to matters of fact. It will not answer to make an express exception of cases, which shall have been originally tried by a jury, because in the courts of some of the states, *all causes* are tried in this mode; † and such an exception would preclude the revision of matters of fact, as well where it might be proper, as where it might be improper. To avoid all inconveniencies, it will be safest to declare generally, that the supreme court shall possess appellate jurisdiction, both as to law and *fact*, and that this jurisdiction shall be subject to such *exceptions* and regulations as the national legislature may prescribe. This will enable the government to modify it in such a manner as will best answer the ends of public justice and security.

This view of the matter, at any rate puts it out of all doubt that the supposed *abolition* of the trial by jury, by the operation of this provision, is fallacious and untrue. The legislature of the United States would certainly have full power to provide that in appeals to the supreme court there should be no re-examination of facts where they had been tried in the original causes by juries. This would certainly be an authorised exception; but if for the reason already intimated it should be thought too extensive, it might be qualified with a limitation to such causes only as are determinable at common law in that mode of trial.

The amount of the observations hitherto made on the authority of the judicial department is this—that it has been carefully restricted to those causes which are manifestly proper for the cognizance of the national judicature, that in the partition of this authority a very small portion of original jurisdiction has been reserved to the supreme court, and the rest consigned to the subordinate tribunals— that the supreme court will possess an appellate jurisdiction both as to law and fact in all the cases referred to them, but subject to any *exceptions* and *regulations* which may be thought adviseable; that this appellate jurisdiction does in no case *abolish* the trial by jury,

† I hold that the states will have concurrent jurisdiction with the subordinate federal judicatories, in many cases of federal cognizance, as will be explained in my next paper.

and that an ordinary degree of prudence and integrity in the national councils will insure us solid advantages from the establishment of the proposed judiciary, without exposing us to any of the inconveniencies which have been predicted from that source.

PUBLIUS.

## The Federalist No. 82 [1]

[New York, May 28, 1788]

*To the People of the State of New-York.*

THE erection of a new government, whatever care or wisdom may distinguish the work, cannot fail to originate questions of intricacy and nicety; and these may in a particular manner be expected to flow from the establishment of a constitution founded upon the total or partial incorporation of a number of distinct sovereignties. 'Tis [2] time only that can mature and perfect so compound a system, can [3] liquidate the meaning of all the parts, and can [4] adjust them to each other in a harmonious and consistent WHOLE.

Such questions accordingly have arisen upon the plan proposed by the convention, and particularly concerning the judiciary department. The principal of these respect the situation of the state courts in regard to those causes, which are to be submitted to federal jurisdiction. Is this to be exclusive, or are those courts to possess a concurrent jurisdiction? If the latter, in what relation will they stand to the national tribunals? These are inquiries which we meet with in the mouths of men of sense, and which are certainly intitled to attention.

The principles established in a former paper * teach us, that the

---

* Vol. I,[5] No. XXXII.

J. and A. McLean, *The Federalist*, II, 322–27, published May 28, 1788, numbered 82. This essay appeared on July 2 in *The* [New York] *Independent Journal: or, the General Advertiser* and is numbered 81. In *The New-York Packet* it appeared on July 11 and is numbered 82.
  1. For background to this document, see "The Federalist. Introductory Note," October 27, 1787–May 28, 1788.
  2. "'Tis" omitted in Hopkins.
  3. "can" omitted in Hopkins.
  4. "can" omitted in Hopkins.
  5. "Vol. I" omitted in Hopkins.

states will retain all *pre-existing* authorities, which may not be exclusively delegated to the federal head; and that this exclusive delegation can only exist in one of three cases; where an exclusive authority is in express terms granted to the union; or where a particular authority is granted to the union, and the exercise of a like authority is prohibited to the states, or where an authority is granted to the union with which a similar authority in the states would be utterly incompatible. Though these principles may not apply with the same force to the judiciary as to the legislative power; yet I am inclined to think that they are in the main just with respect to the former as well as the latter. And under this impression I shall lay it down as a rule that the state courts will *retain* the jurisdiction they now have, unless it appears to be taken away in one of the enumerated modes.

The only thing in the proposed constitution, which wears the appearance of confining the causes of federal cognizance to the federal courts is contained in this passage—"The JUDICIAL POWER of the United States *shall be vested* in one supreme court, and in *such* inferior courts as the congress shall from time to time ordain and establish." This might either be construed to signify, that the supreme and subordinate courts of the union should alone have the power of deciding those causes, to which their authority is to extend; or simply to denote that the organs of the national judiciary should be one supreme court and as many subordinate courts as congress should think proper to appoint, or in other words, that the United States should exercise the judicial power with which they are to be invested through one supreme tribunal and a certain number of inferior ones to be instituted by them. The first excludes, the last admits the concurrent jurisdiction of the state tribunals: And as the first would amount to an alienation of state power by implication, the last appears to me the most natural and [6] the most defensible construction.

But this doctrine of concurrent jurisdiction is only clearly applicable to those descriptions of causes of which the state courts have previous cognizance. It is not equally evident in relation to cases which may grow out of, and be *peculiar* to the constitution to be established: For not to allow the state courts a right of juris-

6. "the most natural and" omitted in Hopkins.

diction in such cases can hardly be considered as the abridgement of a pre-existing authority. I mean not therefore to contend that the United States in the course of legislation upon the objects entrusted to their direction may not commit the decision of causes arising upon a particular regulation to the federal courts solely, if such a measure should be deemed expedient; but I hold that the state courts will be divested of no part of their primitive jurisdiction, further than may relate to an appeal; and I am even of opinion, that in every case in which they were not expressly excluded by the future acts of the national legislature, they will of course take cognizance of the causes to which those acts may give birth. This I infer from the nature of judiciary power, and from the general 'genius of the system. The judiciary power of every government looks beyond its own local or municipal laws, and in civil cases lays hold of all subjects of litigation between parties within its jurisdiction though the causes of dispute are relative to the laws of the most distant part of the globe. Those of Japan not less than of New-York may furnish the objects of legal discussion to our courts. When in addition to this, we consider the state governments and the national governments as they truly are, in the light of kindred systems and as parts of ONE WHOLE, the inference seems to be conclusive that the state courts would have a concurrent jurisdiction in all cases arising under the laws of the union, where it was not expressly prohibited.

Here another question occurs—what relation would subsist between the national and state courts in these instances of concurrent jurisdiction? I answer that an appeal would certainly lie from the latter to the supreme court of the United States. The constitution in direct terms, gives an appellate jurisdiction to the supreme court in all the enumerated cases of federal cognizance, in which it is not to have an original one; without a single expression to confine its operation to the inferior federal courts. The objects of appeal, not the tribunals from which it is to be made, are alone contemplated. From this circumstance and from the reason of the thing it ought to be construed to extend to the state tribunals. Either this must be the case, or the local courts must be excluded from a concurrent jurisdiction in matters of national concern, else the judiciary authority of the union may be eluded at the pleasure of every plantiff or prosecutor. Neither of these consequences ought without evident necessity to be involved; the latter would be intirely inadmissible, as it would defeat some of the most important and avowed purposes of the proposed government, and would essentially embarrass its measures. Nor do I perceive any foundation for such a supposition. Agreeably to the remark already made, the national and state systems are to be regarded as ONE WHOLE. The courts of the latter will of course be natural auxiliaries to the execution of the laws of the union, and an appearl from them will as naturally lie to that tribunal, which is destined to unite and assimilate the principles of national justice and the rules of national decisions. The evident aim of the plan of the convention is that all the causes of the specified classes, shall for weighty public reasons receive their original or' final determination in the courts of the union. To confine therefore the general expressions giving [7] appellate jurisdiction to the supreme court to appeals from the subordinate federal courts, instead of allowing their extension to the state courts, would be to abridge the latitude of the terms, in subversion of the intent, contrary to every sound rule of interpretation.

But could an appeal be made to lie from the state courts to the subordinate federal judicatories? This is another of the questions which have been raised, and of greater difficulty than the former. The following considerations countenance the affirmative. The plan of the convention in the first place authorises the national legislature "to constitute tribunals inferior to the supreme court" *. It declares in the next place that, "the JUDICIAL POWER of the United States *shall be vested* in one supreme court and in such inferior courts as congress shall ordain and establish;" and it then proceeds to enumerate the cases to which this judicial power shall extend. It afterwards divides the jurisdiction of the supreme court into original and appelate, but gives no definition of that of the subordinate courts. The only outlines described for them are that they shall be "inferior to the supreme court" and that they shall not exceed the specified limits of the federal judiciary. Whether their authority shall be original or appellate or both is not declared. All this seems to be left to the discretion of the legislature. And this being the case, I

* Section 8th, Article 1st.
7. "which give" substituted for "giving" in Hopkins.

perceive at present no impediment to the establishment of an appeal from the state courts to the subordinate national tribunals; and many advantages attending the power of doing it may be imagined. It would diminish the motives to the multiplication of federal courts, and would admit of arrangements calculated to contract the appellate jurisdiction of the supreme court. The state tribunals may then be left with a more entire charge of federal causes; and appeals in most cases in which they may be deemed proper instead of being carried to the supreme court, may be made to lie from the state courts to district courts of the union.

PUBLIUS.

## The Federalist No. 83 [1]

[New York, May 28, 1788]

*To the People of the State of New-York.*

THE objection to the plan of the convention, which has met with most success in this state, and perhaps in several of the other states,[2] is *that* [3] relative to *the want of a constitutional provision* for the trial by jury in civil cases. The disingenuous form in which this objection is usually stated, has been repeatedly adverted to and exposed; but continues to be pursued in all the conversations and writings of the opponents of the plan. The mere silence of the constitution in regard to *civil causes*, is represented as an abolition of the trial by jury; and the declamations to which it has afforded a pretext, are artfully calculated to induce a persuasion that this pretended abolition is complete and universal; extending not only to every species of civil, but even to *criminal causes*. To argue with respect to the latter, would, however,[4] be as vain and fruitless, as to attempt the

J. and A. McLean, *The Federalist*, II, 327–44, published May 28, 1788, numbered 83. In *The* [New York] *Independent Journal: or, the General Advertiser* this essay was begun on July 5, continued on July 9, concluded on July 12, and is numbered 82. In *The New-York Packet* it was begun on July 15, continued on July 18, concluded on July 22, and is numbered 83.

1. For background to this document, see "The Federalist. Introductory Note," October 27, 1787–May 28, 1788.
2. "and perhaps in several of the other states" omitted in Hopkins.
3. "that" omitted in Hopkins.
4. "however" omitted in Hopkins.

serious proof of the *existence* of *matter,* or [5] to demonstrate any of those propositions which by their own internal evidence force conviction, when expressed in language adapted to convey their meaning.

With regard to civil causes, subtleties almost too contemptible for refutation, have been adopted to countenance the surmise that a thing, which is only *not provided for,* is entirely *abolished.* Every man of discernment must at once perceive the wide difference between *silence* and *abolition.* But as the inventors of this fallacy have attempted to support it by certain *legal maxims* of interpretation, which they have perverted from their true meaning, it may not be wholly useless to explore the ground they have taken.

The maxims on which they rely are of this nature, "a specification of particulars is an exclusion of generals;" or, "the expression of one thing is the exclusion of another." Hence, say they, as the constitution has established the trial by jury in criminal cases, and is silent in respect to civil, this silence is an implied prohibition of trial by jury in regard to the latter.

The rules of legal interpretation are rules of *common sense,* adopted by the courts in the construction of the laws. The true test therefore, of a just application of them, is its conformity to the source from which they are derived. This being the case, let me ask if it is consistent with reason or [6] common sense to suppose, that a provision obliging the legislative power to commit the trial of criminal causes to juries, is a privation of its right to authorise or permit that mode of trial in other cases? Is it natural to suppose, that a command to do one thing, is a prohibition to the doing of another, which there was a previous power to do, and which is not incompatible with the thing commanded to be done? If such a supposition would be unnatural and unreasonable, it cannot be rational to maintain that an injunction of the trial by jury in certain cases is an interdiction of it in others.

A power to constitute courts, is a power to prescribe the mode of trial; and consequently, if nothing was said in the constitution on the subject of juries, the legislature would be at liberty either to adopt that institution, or to let it alone. This discretion in regard to

5. "the serious proof of the existence of matter, or" omitted in Hopkins.
6. "reason or" omitted in Hopkins.

criminal causes is abridged by the [7] express injunction of trial by jury in all such cases; but it is of course left at large in relation to civil causes, there being a total silence on this head. The specification of an obligation to try all criminal causes in a particular mode, excludes indeed the obligation or necessity [8] of employing the same mode in civil causes, but does not abridge *the power* of the legislature to exercise [9] that mode if it should be thought proper. The pretence therefore, that the national legislature would not be at full [10] liberty to submit all the civil causes of federal cognizance to the determination of juries, is a pretence destitute of all just [11] foundation.

From these observations, this conclusion results, that the trial by jury in civil cases would not be abolished, and that the use attempted to be made of the maxims which have been quoted, is contrary to reason and common sense,[12] and therefore not admissible.[13] Even if these maxims had a precise technical sense, corresponding with the ideas of those who employ them upon the present occasion, which, however, is not the case, they would still be inapplicable to a constitution of government. In relation to such a subject, the natural and obvious sense of its provisions, apart from any technical rules, is the true criterion of construction.

Having now seen that the maxims relied upon will not bear the use made of them, let us endeavour to ascertain their proper use and true meaning.[14] This will be best done by examples. The plan of the convention declares that the power of congress or in other words of the *national legislature,* shall extend to certain enumerated cases. This specification of particulars evidently excludes all pretension to a general legislative authority; because an affirmative grant of special powers would be absurd as well as useless, if a general authority was intended.

In like manner, the judicial [15] authority of the federal judicatures,

---

7. "an" substituted for "the" in Hopkins.
8. "or necessity" omitted in Hopkins.
9. "appoint" substituted for "exercise" in Hopkins.
10. "full" omitted in Hopkins.
11. "just" omitted in Hopkins.
12. "and common sense" omitted in Hopkins.
13. "inadmissible" substituted for "not admissible" in Hopkins.
14. "application" substituted for "use and true meaning" in Hopkins.
15. "judicial" omitted in Hopkins.

is declared by the constitution to comprehend certain cases particularly specified. The expression of those cases marks the precise limits beyond which the federal courts cannot extend their jurisdiction; because the objects of their cognizance being enumerated, the specification would be nugatory if it did not exclude all ideas of more extensive authority.

These examples might be [16] sufficient to elucidate the maxims which have been mentioned, and [17] designate the manner in which they should be used. But that there may be no possibility of misapprehension upon this subject I shall add one case more, to demonstrate the proper use of these maxims, and the abuse which has been made of them.[18]

Let us suppose that by the laws of this state, a married woman was incapable of conveying her estate, and that the legislature, considering this as an evil, should enact that she might dispose of her property by deed executed in the presence of a magistrate. In such a case there can be no doubt but the specification would amount to an exclusion of any other mode of conveyance; because the woman having no previous power to alienate her property, the specification determines the particular mode which she is, for that purpose, to avail herself of. But let us further suppose that in a subsequent part of the same act it should be declared that no woman should dispose of any estate of a determinate value without the consent of three of her nearest relations, signified by their signing the deed; could it be inferred from this regulation that a married woman might not procure the approbation of her relations to a deed for conveying property of inferior value? The position is too absurd to merit a refutation, and yet this is precisely the position which those must establish who contend that the trial by juries, in civil cases, is abolished, because it is expressly provided for in cases of a criminal nature.[19]

From these observations [20] it must appear unquestionably true that trial by jury is in no case abolished by the proposed constitution, and it is equally true that in those controversies between individuals

16. "are" substituted for "might be" in Hopkins.
17. "to" inserted at this point in Hopkins.
18. This sentence omitted in Hopkins.
19. This paragraph omitted in Hopkins.
20. "what has been said" substituted for "these observations" in Hopkins.

in which the great body of the people are likely to be interested, that institution will remain precisely in the same situation in which it is placed by the state constitutions, and will be in no degree altered or influenced by the adoption of the plan under consideration.[21] The foundation of this assertion is that the national judiciary will have no cognizance of them, and of course they will remain determinable as heretofore by the state courts only, and in the manner which the state constitutions and laws prescribe. All land causes, except where claims under the grants of different states come into question, and all other controversies between the citizens of the same state, unless where they depend upon positive violations of the articles of union by acts of the state legislatures, will belong exclusively to the jurisdiction of the state tribunals. Add to this that admiralty causes, and almost all those which are of equity jurisdiction are determinable under our own government without the intervention of a jury, and the inference from the whole will be that this institution, as it exists with us at present, cannot possibly be affected to any great extent by the proposed alteration in our system of government.

The friends and adversaries of the plan of the convention, if they agree in nothing else, concur at least in the value they set upon the trial by jury: Or if there is any difference between them, it consists in this; the former regard it as a valuable safeguard to liberty, the latter represent it as the very palladium of free government. For my own part, the more the operation of the institution has fallen under my observation, the more reason I have discovered for holding it in high estimation; and it would be altogether superfluous to examine to what extent it deserves to be esteemed useful or essential in a representative republic, or how much more merit it may be entitled to as a defence against the oppressions of an hereditary monarch, than as a barrier to the tyranny of popular magistrates in a popular government. Discussions of this kind would be more curious than beneficial, as all are satisfied of the utility of the institution, and of its friendly aspect to liberty. But I must acknowledge that I cannot readily discern the inseparable connection between the existence of liberty and the trial by jury in civil cases. Arbitrary impeachments,

21. "and will be in no degree altered or influenced by the adoption of the plan under consideration" omitted in Hopkins.

arbitrary methods of prosecuting pretended offences, and arbitrary punishments upon arbitrary convictions have ever appeared to me to be [22] the great engines of judicial despotism; and these have all [23] relation to criminal proceedings. The trial by jury in criminal cases, aided by the *habeas corpus* act, seems therefore to be alone concerned in the question. And both of these are provided for in the most ample manner in the plan of the convention.

It has been observed, that trial by jury is a safeguard against an oppressive exercise of the power of taxation. This observation deserves to be canvassed.

It is evident that it can have no influence upon the legislature, in regard to the *amount* of the taxes to be laid, to the *objects* upon which they are to be imposed, or to the *rule* by which they are to be apportioned. If it can have any influence therefore, it must be upon the mode of collection, and the conduct of the officers entrusted with the execution of the revenue laws.

As to the mode of collection in this state, under our own constitution, the trial by jury is in most cases out of use. The taxes are usually levied by the more summary proceeding of distress and sale, as in cases of rent. And it is acknowledged on all hands, that this is essential to the efficacy of the revenue laws. The dilatory course of a trial at law to recover the taxes imposed on individuals, would neither suit the exigencies of the public, nor promote the convenience of the citizens. It would often occasion an accumulation of costs, more burthensome than the original sum of the tax to be levied.

And as to the conduct of the officers of the revenue, the provision in favor of trial by jury in criminal cases, will afford the [24] security aimed at.[25] Wilful abuses of a public authority, to the oppression of the subject, and every species of official extortion, are offences against the government; for which, the persons who commit them, may be indicted and punished according to the circumstances of the case.

The excellence of the trial by jury in civil cases, appears to depend on circumstances foreign to the preservation of liberty. The strong-

22. "to be" omitted in Hopkins.
23. "all these have" substituted for "these have all" in Hopkins.
24. "desired" inserted at this point in Hopkins.
25. "aimed at" omitted in Hopkins.

est argument in its favour is, that it is a security against corruption. As there is always more time and better opportunity to tamper with a standing body of magistrates than with a jury summoned for the occasion, there is room to suppose, that a corrupt influence would more easily find its way to the former than to the latter. The force of this consideration, is however, diminished by others. The sheriff who is the summoner of ordinary juries, and the clerks of courts who have the nomination of special juries, are themselves standing officers, and acting individually, may be supposed more accessible to the touch of corruption than the judges, who are a collective body. It is not difficult to see that it would be in the power of those officers to select jurors who would serve the purpose of the party as well as a corrupted bench. In the next place, it may fairly be supposed that there would be less difficulty in gaining some of the jurors promiscuously taken from the public mass, than in gaining men who had been chosen by the government for their probity and good character. But making every deduction for these considerations the trial by jury must still be a valuable check upon corruption. It greatly multiplies the impediments to its success. As matters now stand, it would be necessary to corrupt both court and jury; for where the jury have gone evidently wrong, the court will generally grant a new trial, and it would be in most cases of little use to practice upon the jury, unless the court could be likewise gained. Here then is a doubt security; and it will readily be perceived that this complicated agency tends to preserve the purity of both institutions. By increasing the obstacles to success it discourages attempts to seduce the integrity of either. The temptations to prostitution, which the judges might have to surmount, must certainly be much fewer while the co-operation of a jury is necessary, than they might be if they had themselves the exclusive determination of all causes.

Nothwithstanding therefore the doubts I have expressed as to the essentiality of trial by jury, in civil cases, to liberty, I admit that it is in most cases, under proper regulations, an excellent method of determining questions of property; and that on this account alone it would be entitled to a constitutional provision in its favour, if it were possible to fix [26] the limits within which it ought to be compre-

26. "with accuracy" inserted at this point in Hopkins.

hended. There is however, in all cases, great difficulty in this; [27] and men not blinded by enthusiasm, must be sensible that in a federal government which is a composition of societies whose ideas and institutions in relation to the matter materially vary from each other, that difficulty must be not a little augmented. For my own part, at every new view I take of the subject, I become more convinced of the reality of the obstacles, which we are authoritatively informed, prevented the insertion of a provision on this head in the plan of the convention.

The great difference between the limits of the jury trial in different states is not generally understood. And as it must have considerable influence on the sentence we ought to pass upon the omission complained of, in regard to this point, an explanation of it is necessary. In this state our judicial establishments resemble more nearly, than in any other, those of Great-Britain. We have courts of common law, courts of probates (analogous in certain matters to the spiritual courts in England) a court of admiralty, and a court of chancery. In the courts of common law only the trial by jury prevails, and this with some exceptions. In all the others a single judge presides and proceeds in general either according to the course of the cannon or civil law, without the aid of a jury.* In New-Jersey there is a court of chancery which proceeds like ours, but neither courts of admiralty, nor of probates, in the sense in which these last are established with us. In that state the courts of common law have the cognizance of those causes, which with us are determinable in the courts of admiralty and of probates, and of course the jury trial is more extensive in New-Jersey than in New-York. In Pennsylvania this is perhaps still more the case, for there is no court of chancery in that state, and its common law courts have equity jurisdiction. It has a court of admiralty, but none of probates, at least on the plan of ours. Delaware has in these respects imitated Pennsylvania. Maryland approaches more nearly to New-York, as does also Virginia, except that the latter has a plurality of chancellors. North-Carolina

* It has been erroneously insinuated, with regard to the court of chancery, that this court generally tries disputed facts by a jury. The truth is, that references to a jury in that court rarely happen, and are in no case necessary, but where the validity of a devise of land comes into question.

27. "This, however, is in its own nature an affair of much difficulty" substituted for "There is however, in all cases, great difficulty in this" in Hopkins.

bears most affinity to Pennsylvania; South-Carolina to Virginia. I believe however that in some of those states which have distinct courts of admiralty, the causes depending in them are triable by juries. In Georgia there are none but common law courts, and an appeal of course lies from the verdict of one jury to another, which is called a special jury, and for which a particular mode of appointment is marked out. In Connecticut they have no distinct courts, either of chancery or of admiralty, and their courts of probates have no jurisdiction of causes. Their common law courts have admiralty, and to a certain extent, equity jurisdiction. In cases of importance their general assembly is the only court of chancery. In Connecticut therefore the trial by jury extends in *practice* further than in any other state yet mentioned. Rhode Island is I believe in this particular pretty much in the situation of Connecticut. Massachusetts and New-Hampshire, in regard to the blending of law, equity and admiralty, jurisdictions are in a similiar predicament. In the four eastern states the trial by jury not only stands upon a broader foundation than in the other states, but it is attended with a peculiarity unknown in its full extent to any of them. There is an appeal *of course* from one jury to another till there have been two verdicts out of three on one side.

From this sketch it appears, that there is a material diversity as well in the modification as in the extent of the institution of trial by jury in civil cases in the several states; and from this fact, these obvious reflections flow. First, that no general rule could have been fixed upon by the convention which would have corresponded with the circumstances of all the states; and secondly, that more, or at least as much might have been hazarded, by taking the system of any one state for a standard, as by omitting a provision altogether, and leaving the matter as it has been left,[28] to legislative regulation.

The propositions which have been made for supplying the omission, have rather served to illustrate than to obviate the difficulty of the thing. The minority of Pennsylvania have proposed this mode of expression for the purpose—"trial by jury shall be as heretofore"[29]—and this I maintain would be absolutely senseless and

28. "done" substituted for "left" in Hopkins.
29. The Pennsylvania Ratifying Convention had assembled in November, 1787. Despite the opposition of some members of the Convention, the adoption

nugatory.[30] The United States, in their united or [31] collective capacity, are the OBJECT to which all general provisions in the constitution must necessarily be construed [32] to refer. Now it is evident, that though trial by jury with various limitations is known in each state individually, yet in the United States *as such*, it is at this time altogether [33] unknown, because the present federal government has no judiciary power whatever; and consequently there is no proper [34] antecedent or previous [35] establishment to which the term *heretofore* could [36] relate. It would therefore be destitute of a [37] precise meaning, and inoperative from its uncertainty.

As on the one hand, the form of the provision would not fulfil the intent of its proposers; so on the other, if I apprehend that intent rightly, it would be in itself inexpedient. I presume it to be, that causes in the federal courts should be tried by jury, if in the state where the courts sat, that mode of trial would obtain in a similiar case in the state courts—that is to say admiralty causes should be tried in Connecticut by a jury, and in New-York without one. The capricious operation of so dissimilar a method of trial in the same cases, under the same government, is of itself sufficient to indispose every well regulated judgment towards it. Whether the cause should be tried with or without a jury, would depend in a great number of cases, on the accidental situation of the court and parties.

But this is not in my estimation the greatest objection. I feel a deep and deliberate conviction, that there are many cases in which the trial by jury is an ineligible one. I think it so particularly in cases [38] which concern the public peace with foreign nations; that is in most cases where the question turns wholly on the laws of

---

of the Constitution was secured on December 15, 1787, by a vote of 46 to 23. The opponents of the Constitution argued during the Convention that they would approve it if certain safeguards were adopted. A series of fifteen amendments were recommended. Among them was the amendment covering trial by jury discussed in this number of *The Federalist* by H.

30. "inapplicable and indeterminate" substituted for "absolutely senseless and nugatory" in Hopkins.

31. "united or" omitted in Hopkins.

32. "be understood" substituted for "necessarily be construed" in Hopkins.

33. "strictly speaking" substituted for "at this time altogether" in Hopkins.

34. "proper" omitted in Hopkins.

35. "or previous" omitted in Hopkins.

36. "properly" inserted at this point in Hopkins.

37. "a" omitted in Hopkins.

38. "suits" substituted for "cases" in Hopkins.

nations. Of this nature among others are all prize causes. Juries cannot be supposed competent to investigations, that require a thorough knowledge of the laws and usages of nations, and they will sometimes be under the influence of impressions which will not suffer them to pay sufficient regard to those considerations of public policy which ought to guide their enquiries. There would of course be always danger that the rights of other nations might be infringed by their decisions, so as to afford occasions of reprisal and war. Though the proper [39] province of juries be to determine matters of fact, yet in most cases legal consequences are complicated with fact in such a manner as to render a separation impracticable.

It will add great weight to this remark in relation to prize causes to mention that the method of determining them has been thought worthy of particular regulation in various treaties between different powers of Europe, and that pursuant to such treaties they are determinable in Great-Britain in the last resort before the king himself in his privy council, where the fact as well as the law undergoes a re-examination. This alone demonstrates the impolicy of inserting a fundamental provision in the constitution which would make the state systems a standard for the national government in the article under consideration, and the danger of incumbering the government with any constitutional provisions, the propriety of which is not indisputable.

My convictions are equally strong that great advantages result from the separation of the equity from the law jurisdiction; and that the causes which belong to the former would be improperly committed to juries. The great and primary use of a court of equity is to give relief *in extraordinary cases*, which are *exceptions* * to general rules. To unite the jurisdiction of such cases with the ordinary jurisdiction must have a tendency to unsettle the general rules and to subject every case that arises to a *special* determination. While the separation of the one from the other [40] has the contrary effect of rendering one a sentinel over the other, and of keeping

---

* It is true that the principles by which that relief is governed are now reduced to a regular system, but it is not the less true that they are in the main, applicable to SPECIAL circumstances which form exceptions to general rules.

39. "true" substituted for "proper" in Hopkins.
40. "a separation between the jurisdictions" substituted for "the separation of the one from the other" in Hopkins.

each within the expedient limits. Besides this the circumstances that constitute cases proper for courts of equity, are in many instances so nice and intricate, that they are incompatible with the genius of trials by jury. They require often such long, deliberate [41] and critical investigation as would be impracticable to men called [42] from their occupations and obliged to decide before they were permitted to return to them. The simplicity and expedition which form the distinguishing characters of this mode of trial require that the matter to be decided should be reduced to some single and obvious point; while the litigations usual in chancery frequently comprehend a long train of minute and independent particulars.

It is true that the separation of the equity from the legal jurisdiction is peculiar to the English system of jurisprudence; which is the model that [43] has been followed in several of the states. But it is equally true, that the trial by jury has been unknown in every case [44] in which they have been united. And the separation is essential to the preservation of that institution in its pristine purity. The nature of a court of equity will readily permit the extension of its jurisdiction to matters of law, but it is not a little to be suspected, that the attempt to extend the jurisdiction of the courts of law to matters of equity will not only be unproductive of the advantages which may be derived from courts of chancery, on the plan upon which they are established in this state, but will tend gradually to change the nature of the courts of law, and to undermine the trial by jury, by introducing questions too complicated for a decision in that mode.

These appear to be conclusive reasons against incorporating the systems of all the states in the formation of the national judiciary; according to what may be conjectured to have been the intent of the Pennsylvania minority. Let us now examine how far the proposition of Massachusetts is calculated to remedy the supposed defect.

It is in this form— "In civil actions between citizens of different states, every issue of fact, arising in *actions at common law*, may be tried by a jury, if the parties, or either of them, request it." [45]

41. "deliberate" omitted in Hopkins.
42. "occasionally" inserted in Hopkins.
43. "the model which" substituted for "which is the model that" in Hopkins.
44. "instance" substituted for "case" in Hopkins.
45. Massachusetts had accompanied its ratification of the Constitution with

This at best is a proposition confined to one description of causes; and the inference is fair either that the Massachusetts convention considered that as the only class of federal causes, in which the trial by jury would be proper; or that if desirous of a more extensive provision, they found it impracticable to devise one which would properly answer the end. If the first, the omission of a regulation respecting so partial an object, can never be considered as a material imperfection in the system. If the last, it affords a strong corroboration of the extreme difficulty of the thing.

But this is not all: If we advert to the observations already made respecting the courts that subsist in the several states of the union, and the different powers exercised by them, it will appear, that there are no expressions more vague and indeterminate than those which have been employed to characterise *that* species of causes which it is intended shall be entitled to a trial by jury. In this state the boundaries between actions at common law and actions of equitable jurisdiction are ascertained in conformity to the rules which prevail in England upon that subject. In many of the other states, the boundaries are less precise. In some of them, every cause is to be tried in a court of common law, and upon that foundation every action may be considered as an action at common law to be determined by a jury, if the parties or either of them chuse it. Hence the same irregularity and confusion would be introduced by a compliance with this proposition, that I have already noticed as resulting from the regulation proposed by the Pennsylvania minority. In one state a cause would receive its determination from a jury, if the parties or either of them requested it; but in another state a cause exactly similar to the other must be decided without the intervention of a jury, because the state judicatories [46] varied as to common law jurisdiction.

It is obvious therefore that the Massachusetts proposition, upon this subject,[47] cannot operate as a general regulation until some uniform plan, with respect to the limits of common law and equitable jurisdictions shall be adopted by the different states. To devise a

---

nine proposed amendments. Among them was the amendment discussed by H.
46. "tribunals" substituted for "judicatories" in Hopkins.
47. "upon this subject" omitted in Hopkins.

plan of that kind is a task arduous in itself, and which it would require much time and reflection to mature. It would be extremely
difficult, if not impossible, to suggest any general regulation that
would be acceptable to all the states in the union, or that would
perfectly quadrate with the several state institutions.

It may be asked, why could not a reference have been made to the
constitution of this state, taking that, which is allowed by me to be
a good one, as a standard for the United States? I answer that it is
not very probable the other states should entertain the same opinion
of our institutions which we do ourselves. It is natural to suppose
that they are hitherto [48] more attached to their own, and that each
would struggle for the preference. If the plan of taking one state
as a model for the whole had been thought of in the convention,
it is to be presumed that the adoption of it in that body, would have
been rendered difficult by the predilection of each representation
in favour of its own government; and it must be uncertain which of
the states would have been taken as the model. It has been shewn
that many of them would be improper ones. And I leave it to conjecture whether, under all circumstances, it is most likely that
New-York or some other state would have been preferred. But
admit that a judicious selection could have been effected in the
convention, still there would have been great danger of jealousy and
disgust in the other states, at the partiality which had been shewn
to the institutions of one. The enemies of the plan would have been
furnished with a fine pretext for raising a host of local prejudices
against it, which perhaps might have hazarded in no inconsiderable
degree, its final establishment.

To avoid the embarrassments of a definition of the cases which
the trial by jury ought to embrace, it is some times suggested by
men of enthusiastic tempers, that a provision might have been inserted for establishing it in all cases whatsoever. For this I believe
no precedent is to be found in any member of the union; and the
considerations which have been stated in discussing the proposition
of the minority of Pennsylvania, must satisfy every sober mind that
the establishment of the trial by jury in *all* cases, would have been
an unpardonable error in the plan.

In short, the more it is considered, the more arduous will appear

48. "hitherto" omitted in Hopkins.

the task of fashioning a provision in such a form, as not to express too little to answer the purpose, or too much to be adviseable; or which might not have opened other sources of opposition to the great and essential object of introducing a firm national government.

I cannot but persuade myself on the other hand, that the different lights in which the subject has been placed in the course of these observations, will go far towards removing in candid minds, the apprehensions they may have entertained on the point. They have tended to shew that the security of liberty is materially concerned only in the trial by jury in criminal cases, which is provided for in the most ample manner in the plan of the convention; that even in far the greatest proportion of civil cases, and those in which the great body of the community is interested, that mode of trial will remain in its full force, as established in the state constitutions, untouched and unaffected by the plan of the convention: That it is in [49] no case abolished * by that plan; and that there are great if not insurmountable difficulties in the way of making any precise and proper provision for it in a constitution for the United States.

The best judges of the matter will be the least anxious for a constitutional establishment of the trial by jury in civil cases, and will be the most ready to admit that the changes which are continually happening in the affairs of society, may render a different mode of determining questions of property, preferable in many cases, in which that mode of trial now prevails. For my own part, I acknowledge myself to be convinced that even in this state, it might be advantageously extended to some cases to which it does not at present apply, and might as advantageously be abridged in others. It is conceded by all reasonable men, that it ought not to obtain in all cases. The examples of innovations which contract its ancient limits, as well in these states as in Great-Britain, afford a strong presumption that its former extent has been found inconvenient; and give room to suppose that future experience may discover the propriety and utility of other exceptions. I suspect it to be impossible in the nature of the thing, to fix the salutary point at which the

* Vide No. LXXXI, in which the supposition of its being abolished by the appellate jurisdiction in matters of fact being vested in the supreme court is examined and refuted.

49. "in" omitted in McLean and inserted at this point in Hopkins.

operation of the institution ought to stop; and this is with me a strong argument for leaving the matter to the discretion of the legislature.

This is now clearly understood to be the case in Great-Britain, and it is equally so in the state of Connecticut; and yet it may be safely affirmed, that more numerous encroachments have been made upon the trial by jury in this state since the revolution, though provided for by a positive article of our constitution, than has happened in the same time either in Connecticut or Great-Britain. It may be added that these encroachments have generally originated with the men who endeavour to persuade the people they are the warmest defenders of popular liberty, but who have rarely suffered constitutional obstacles to arrest them in a favourite career. The truth is that the general GENIUS of a government is all that can be substantially relied upon for permanent effects. Particular provisions, though not altogether useless, have far less virtue and efficacy than are commonly ascribed to them; and the want of them will never be with men of sound discernment a decisive objection to any plan which exhibits the leading characters of a good government.

It certainly sounds not a little harsh and extraordinary to affirm that there is no security for liberty in a constitution which expressly establishes the trial by jury in criminal cases, because it does not do it in civil also; while it is a notorious fact that Connecticut, which has been always regarded as the most popular state in the union, can boast of no constitutional provision for either.

PUBLIUS.

## The Federalist No. 84 [1]

[New York, May 28, 1788]

*To the People of the State of New-York.*

IN the course of the foregoing review of the constitution I have

J. and A. McLean, *The Federalist*, II, 344–57, published on May 28, 1788, numbered 84. In *The* [New York] *Independent Journal: or, the General Advertiser* this essay was begun on July 16, continued on July 26, concluded on August 9, and is numbered 83. In *The New-York Packet* it was begun on July 29, continued on August 8, concluded on August 12, and is numbered 84.

1. For background to this document, see "The Federalist. Introductory Note," October 27, 1787–May 28, 1788.

taken notice of, and [2] endeavoured to answer, most of the objections which have appeared against it. There however remain a few which either did not fall naturally under any particular head, or were forgotten in their proper places. These shall now be discussed; but as the subject has been drawn into great length, I shall so far consult brevity as to comprise all my observations on these miscellaneous points in a single paper.

The most considerable of these remaining objections is, that the plan of the convention contains no bill of rights. Among other answers given to this, it has been upon different occasions remarked, that the constitutions of several of the states are in a similar predicament. I add, that New-York is of this [3] number. And yet the opposers of the new system in this state,[4] who [5] profess an unlimited admiration for its [6] constitution, are among the most intemperate partizans of a bill of rights. To justify their zeal in this matter, they alledge two things; one is, that though the constitution of New-York has no bill of rights prefixed to it, yet it contains in the body of it various provisions in favour of particular privileges and rights, which in substance amount to the same thing; the other is, that the constitution adopts in their full extent the common and statute law of Great-Britain, by which many other rights not expressed in it [7] are equally secured.

To the first I answer, that the constitution proposed [8] by the convention contains, as well as the constitution of this state, a number of such provisions.

Independent of those, which relate to the structure of the government, we find the following: Article I. section 3. clause 7. "Judgment in cases of impeachment shall not extend further than to removal from office, and disqualification to hold and enjoy any office of honour, trust or profit under the United States; but the party convicted shall nevertheless be liable and subject to indictment, trial, judgment and punishment, according to law." Section 9. of the same article, clause 2. "The privilege of the writ of *habeas corpus*

2. "taken notice of and" omitted in Hopkins.
3. "the" substituted for "this" in Hopkins.
4. "persons who in this state oppose the new system" substituted for "opposers of the new system in this state" in Hopkins.
5. "while they" substituted for "who" in Hopkins.
6. "our particular" substituted for "its" in Hopkins.
7. "in it" omitted in Hopkins.
8. "offered" substituted for "proposed" in Hopkins.

shall not be suspended, unless when in cases of rebellion or invasion the public safety may require it." Clause 3. "No bill of attainder or *ex post facto* law shall be passed." Clause 7. "No title of nobility shall be granted by the United States: And no person holding any office of profit or trust under them, shall, without the consent of congress, accept of any present, emolument, office or title, of any kind whatever, from any king, prince or foreign state." Article III. section 2. clause 3. "The trial of all crimes, except in cases of impeachment, shall be by jury; and such trial shall be held in the state where the said crimes shall have been committed; but when not committed within any state, the trial shall be at such place or places as the congress may by law have directed." Section 3, of the same article, "Treason against the United States shall consist only in levying war against them, or in adhering to their enemies, giving them aid and comfort. No person shall be convicted of treason unless on the testimony of two witness to the same overt act, or on confession in open court." And clause 3, of the same section. "The congress shall have power to declare the punishment of treason, but no attainder of treason shall work corruption of blood, or forfeiture, except during the life of the person attainted."

It may well be a question whether these are not upon the whole, of equal importance with any which are to be found in the constitution of this state. The establishment of the writ of *habeas corpus,* the prohibition of *ex post facto* laws, and of TITLES OF NOBILITY, *to which we have no corresponding provisions in our constitution,* are perhaps greater securities to liberty and republicanism [9] than any it contains. The creation of crimes after the commission of the fact, or in other words, the subjecting of men to punishment for things which, when they were done, were breaches of no law, and the practice of arbitrary imprisonments have been in all ages the favourite and most formidable instruments of tyranny. The observations of the judicious Blackstone * in reference to the latter, are well worthy of recital. "To bereave a man of life (says he) or by violence to confiscate his estate, without accusation or trial,

* Vide Blackstone's Commentaries, vol. I, page 136.[10]

9. "and republicanism" omitted in Hopkins.
10. The reference is to Sir William Blackstone's *Commentaries on the Laws of England,* ten editions of which had appeared by 1787.

would be so gross and notorious an act of despotism, as must at
once convey the alarm of tyranny throughout the whole nation;
but confinement of the person by secretly hurrying to goal, where
his sufferings are unknown or forgotten, is a less public, a less striking, and therefore *a more dangerous engine* of arbitrary government." And as a remedy for this fatal evil, he is every where peculiarly emphatical in his encomiums on the *habeas corpus* act, which
in one place he calls "the BULWARK of the British constitution." †

Nothing need be said to illustrate the importance of the prohibition
of titles of nobility. This may truly be denominated the corner stone
of republican government; for so long as they are excluded, there
can never be serious danger that the government will be any other
than that of the people.

To the second, that is, to the pretended establishment of the
common and statute law by the constitution, I answer, that they are
expressly made subject "to such alterations and provisions as the
legislature shall from time to time make concerning the same." They
are therefore at any moment liable to repeal by the ordinary legislative power, and of course have no constitutional sanction. The only
use of the declaration was to recognize the ancient law, and to remove doubts which might have been occasioned by the revolution.
This consequently can be considered as no part of a declaration of
rights, which under our constitutions must be intended as limitations
of [12] the power of the government itself.

It has been several times truly remarked, that bills of rights are
in their origin, stipulations between kings and their subjects, abridg-
ments of prerogative in favor of privilege, reservations of rights
not surrendered to the prince. Such was MAGNA CHARTA, obtained by the Barons, sword in hand, from king John. Such were
the subsequent confirmations of that charter by subsequent [13] princes.
Such was the *petition of right* assented to by Charles the First, in
the beginning of his reign. Such also was the declaration of right
presented by the lords and commons to the prince of Orange in
1688, and afterwards thrown into the form of an act of parliament,

† Idem, vol. 4, page 438.[11]

11. *Ibid.* The correct page reference is "421" instead of "438."
12. "to limit" substituted for "as limitations of" in Hopkins.
13. "succeeding" substituted for "subsequent" in Hopkins.

called the bill of rights. It is evident, therefore, that according to their primitive signification, they have no application to constitutions professedly founded upon the power of the people, and executed by their immediate representatives and servants. Here, in strictness, the people surrender nothing, and as they retain every thing, they have no need of particular reservations. "WE THE PEOPLE of the United States, to secure the blessings of liberty to ourselves and our posterity, do *ordain* and *establish* this constitution for the United States of America." Here [14] is a better recognition of popular rights than volumes of those aphorisms which make the principal figure in several of our state bills of rights, and which would sound much better in a treatise of ethics than in a constitution of government.

But a minute detail of particular rights is certainly far less applicable to a constitution like that under consideration, which is merely intended to regulate the general political interests of the nation, than to a constitution [15] which has the regulation of every species of personal and private concerns. If therefore the loud clamours against the plan of the convention on this score, are well founded, no epithets of reprobation will be too strong for the constitution of this state. But the truth is, that both of them contain all, which in relation to their objects, is reasonably to be desired.

I go further, and affirm that bills of rights, in the sense and in the extent in which [16] they are contended for, are not only unnecessary in the proposed constitution, but would even be dangerous. They would contain various exceptions to powers which are not granted; and on this very account, would afford a colourable pretext to claim more than were granted. For why declare that things shall not be done which there is no power to do? Why for instance, should it be said, that the liberty of the press shall not be restrained, when no power is given by which restrictions may be imposed? I will not contend that such a provision would confer a regulating power; but it is evident that it would furnish, to men disposed to usurp, a plausible pretence for claiming that power. They might urge with a semblance of reason, that the constitution ought not to

14. "This" substituted for "Here" in Hopkins.
15. "one" substituted for "a constitution" in Hopkins.
16. "to the extent" substituted for "in the extent in which" in Hopkins.

be charged with the absurdity of providing against the abuse of an authority, which was not given, and that the provision against restraining the liberty of the press afforded a clear implication, that a power to prescribe proper regulations concerning it, was intended to be vested in the national government. This may serve as a specimen of the numerous handles which would be given to the doctrine of constructive powers, by the indulgence of an injudicious zeal for bills of rights.

On the subject of the liberty of the press, as much has been said, I cannot forbear adding a remark or two: In the first place, I observe that there is not a syllable concerning it in the constitution of this state, and [17] in the next, I contend that whatever has been said about it in that of any other state, amounts to nothing. What signifies a declaration that "the liberty of the press shall be inviolably preserved?" What is the liberty of the press? Who can give it any definition which would not leave the utmost latitude for evasion? I hold it to be impracticable; and from this, I infer, that its security, whatever fine declarations may be inserted in any constitution respecting it, must altogether depend on public opinion, and on the general spirit of the people and of the government.* And here, after all, as intimated upon another occasion, must we seek for the only solid basis of all our rights.

There remains but one other view of this matter to conclude the

* To show that there is a power in the constitution by which the liberty of the press may be affected, recourse has been had to the power of taxation. It is said that duties may be laid upon publications so high as to amount to a prohibition. I know not by what logic it could be maintained that the declarations in the state constitutions, in favour of the freedom of the press, would be a constitutional impediment to the imposition of duties upon publications by the state legislatures. It cannot certainly be pretended that any degree of duties, however low, would be an abrigement of the liberty of the press. We know that newspapers are taxed in Great-Britain, and yet it is notorious that the press no where enjoys greater liberty than in that country. And if duties of any kind may be laid without a violation of that liberty, it is evident that the extent must depend on legislative discretion, regulated by public opinion; so that after all, general declarations respecting the liberty of the press will give it no greater security than it will have without them. The same invasions of it may be effected under the state constitutions which contain those declarations through the means of taxation, as under the proposed constitution which has nothing of the kind. It would be quite as significant to declare that government ought to be free, that taxes ought not to be excessive, &c., as that the liberty of the press ought not to be restrained.

17. "and" omitted in Hopkins.

point. The truth is, after all the declamation we have heard, that the constitution is itself in every rational sense, and to every useful purpose, A BILL OF RIGHTS. The several bills of rights, in Great-Britain, form its constitution, and conversely the constitution of each state is its bill of rights. And the proposed constitution, if adopted, will be the bill of rights of the union. Is it one object of a bill of rights to declare and specify the political privileges of the citizens in the structure and administration of the government? This is done in the most ample and precise manner in the plan of the convention, comprehending various precautions for the public security, which are not to be found in any of the state constitutions. Is another object of a bill of rights to define certain immunities and modes of proceeding, which are relative to personal and private concerns? This we have seen has also been attended to, in a variety of cases, in the same plan. Adverting therefore to the substantial meaning of a bill of rights, it as absurd to allege that it is not to be found in the work of the convention. It may be said that it does not go far enough, though it will not be easy to make this appear; but it can with no propriety be contended that there is no such thing. It certainly must be immaterial what mode is observed as to the order of declaring the rights of the citizens, if they are to be found [18] in any part of the instrument which establishes the government. And hence it must be apparent that much of what has been said on this subject rests merely on verbal and nominal distinctions, which are [19] entirely foreign from the substance of the thing.

Another objection, which has been made, and [20] which from the frequency of its repetition it is to [21] be presumed is relied on, is of this nature: It is improper (say the objectors) to confer such large powers, as are proposed, upon the national government; because the seat of that government must of necessity be too remote from many of the states to admit of a proper knowledge on the part of the constituent, of the conduct of the representative body. This argument, if it proves any thing, proves that there ought to be no general government whatever. For the powers which it seems to be agreed on all hands, ought to be vested in the union, cannot be safely intrusted

18. "provided for" substituted for "to be found" in Hopkins.
19. "which are" omitted in Hopkins.
20. "which has been made and" omitted in Hopkins.
21. "may" substituted for "it is to" in Hopkins.

to a body which is not under every requisite controul. But there are satisfactory reasons to shew that the objection is in reality not well founded. There is in most of the arguments which relate to distance a palpable illusion of the imagination. What are the sources of information by which the people in Montgomery [22] county must regulate their judgment of the conduct of their representatives in the state legislature? Of personal observation they can have no benefit. This is confined to the citizens on the spot. They must therefore depend on the information of intelligent men, in whom they confide —and how must these men obtain their information? Evidently from the complection of public measures, from the public prints, from correspondences with their representatives, and with other persons who reside at the place of their deliberation.[23] This does not apply to Montgomery county only, but to all the counties, at any considerable distance from the seat of government.[24]

It is equally evident that the same [25] sources of information would be open to the people, in relation to the conduct of their representatives in the general government; and the impediments to a prompt communication which distance may be supposed to create, will be overballanced by the effects of the vigilance of the state governments. The executive and legislative bodies of each state will be so many centinels over the persons employed in every department of the national administration; and as it will be in their power to adopt and pursue a regular and effectual system of intelligence, they can never be at a loss to know the behaviour of those who represent their constituents in the national councils, and can readily communicate the same knowledge to the people. Their disposition to apprise the community of whatever may prejudice its interests from another quarter, may be relied upon, if it were only from the rivalship of power. And we may conclude with the fullest assurance, that the people, through that channel, will be better informed of the conduct of their national representatives, than they can be by any means they now possess of that of their state representatives.

It ought also to be remembered, that the citizens who inhabit the

22. "any distant" substituted for "Montgomery" in Hopkins. Montgomery was New York's largest and westernmost county in 1788.
23. "deliberations" substituted for "deliberation" in Hopkins.
24. This sentence omitted in Hopkins.
25. "like" substituted for "same" in Hopkins.

country at and near the seat of government, will in all questions that affect the general liberty and prosperity, have the same interest with those who are at a distance; and that they will stand ready to sound the alarm when necessary, and to point out the actors in any pernicious project. The public papers will be expeditious messengers of intelligence to the most remote inhabitants of the union.

Among the many extraordinary [26] objections which have appeared against the proposed constitution, the most extraordinary and the least colourable one,[27] is derived from the want of some provision respecting the debts due *to* the United States. This has been represented as a tacit relinquishment of those debts, and as a wicked contrivance to screen public defaulters. The newspapers have teemed with the most inflammatory railings on this head; and [28] yet there is nothing clearer than that the suggestion is entirely void of foundation, and is [29] the offspring of extreme ignorance or extreme dishonesty. In addition to the remarks I have made upon the subject in another place,[30] I shall only observe, that as it is a plain dictate of common sense, so it is also an established doctrine of political law, that *"States neither lose any of their rights, nor are discharged from any of their obligations by a change in the form of their civil government.*\*

The last objection of any consequence which I [33] at present recollect,[34] turns upon the article of expence. If it were even true

\* Vide Rutherford's Institutes, vol. 2. book 11. chap. x. sec. xiv, and xv.[31]— Vide also Grotius, book II, chap. ix, sect. viii, and ix.[32]

26. "curious" substituted for "extraordinary" in Hopkins.
27. "one" omitted in Hopkins.
28. "and" omitted in Hopkins.
29. "and is" omitted in Hopkins.
30. See essay 43.
31. Thomas Rutherforth (Rutherford), *Institutes of Natural Law: Being the Substance of a Course of Lectures on Grotius de Jure Belli et Pacis . . .* 2 Vols. (Cambridge, 1754-1756).
32. The reference is to Grotius, *Law of Nature and Nations.* The complete title, as taken from the edition of 1646, reads: *Hugo Grotius on the Law of War and Peace. Three Books. Wherein are set forth the law of nature and of nations. Also the principles of public law . . .* (Amsterdam, Johan Blaeu, 1646).
Book II, Ch. IX, Section viii is entitled "such rights [i.e., the rights of the people] are not extinguished by a change of government; and herein also the question of what is due to a new king or to a liberated people is treated." Section ix is entitled "What becomes of such rights if people are joined together."
33. "which I" omitted in Hopkins.
34. "recollected" substituted for "recollect" in Hopkins.

that the adoption of the proposed government would occasion a considerable increase of expence, it would be an objection that ought to have no weight against the plan. The great bulk of the citizens of America, are with reason convinced that union is the basis of their political happiness. Men of sense of all parties now, with few exceptions, agree that it cannot be preserved under the present system, nor without radical alterations; that new and extensive powers ought to be granted to the national head, and that these require a different organization of the federal government, a single body being an unsafe depository of such ample authorities. In conceding all this, the question of expence must be [35] given up, for it is impossible, with any degree of safety, to narrow the foundation upon which the system is to stand. The two branches of the legislature are in the first instance, to consist of only sixty-five persons, which is [36] the same number of which congress, under the existing confederation, may be composed. It is true that this number is intended to be increased; but this is to keep pace with the increase [37] of the population and resources of the country. It is evident, that a less number would, even in the first instance, have been unsafe; and that a continuance of the present number would, in a more advanced stage of population, be a very inadequate representation of the people.

Whence is the dreaded augmentation of expence to spring? One source pointed out,[38] is the multiplication of offices under the new government. Let us examine this a little.

It is evident that the principal departments of the administration under the present government, are the same which will be required under the new. There are now a secretary at war, a secretary for foreign affairs, a secretary for domestic affairs, a board of treasury consisting of three persons, a treasurer, assistants, clerks, &c. These offices are indispensable under any system, and will suffice under the new as well as under [39] the old. As to ambassadors and other ministers and agents in foreign countries, the proposed constitution can make no other difference, than to render their characters,

35. "is" substituted for "must be" in Hopkins.
36. "which is" omitted in Hopkins.
37. "progress" substituted for "increase" in Hopkins.
38. "indicated" substituted for "pointed out" in Hopkins.
39. "under" omitted in Hopkins.

where they reside, more respectable, and their services more useful. As to persons to be employed in the collection of the revenues, it is unquestionably true that these will form a very considerable addition to the number of federal officers; but it will not follow, that this will occasion an increase of public expence. It will be in most cases nothing more than an exchange of state officers [40] for national officers. In the collection of all duties, for instance, the persons employed will be wholly of the latter description. The states individually will stand in no need of any for this purpose. What difference can it make in point of expence, to pay officers of the customs appointed by the state, or those appointed [41] by the United States? There is no good reason to suppose, that either the number or the salaries of the latter, will be greater than those of the former.[42]

Where then are we to seek for those additional articles of expence which are to swell the account to the enormous size that has been represented to us? [43] The chief item which occurs to me, respects the support of the judges of the United States. I do not add the president, because there is now a president of congress, whose expences may not be far, if any thing, short of those which will be incurred on account of the president of the United States. The support of the judges will clearly be an extra expence, but to what extent will depend on the particular plan which may be adopted in practice in regard to this matter. But it can upon no reasonable plan amount to a sum which will be an object of material consequence.

Let us now see what there is to counterballance any extra expences [44] that may attend the establishment of the proposed government. The first thing that [45] presents itself is, that a great part of the business, which now keeps congress sitting through the year, will be transacted by the president. Even the management of foreign negociations will naturally devolve upon him according to general principles concerted with the senate, and subject to their final concurrence. Hence it is evident, that a portion of the year will suffice for the session of both the senate and the house of representatives:

40. "officers" omitted in Hopkins.
41. "those appointed" omitted in Hopkins.
42. This sentence omitted in Hopkins.
43. "to us" omitted in Hopkins.
44. "expense" substituted for "expences" in Hopkins.
45. "which" substituted for "that" in Hopkins.

We may suppose about a fourth for the latter, and a third or perhaps a half for the former. The extra business of treaties and appointments may give this extra occupation to the senate. From this circumstance we may infer, that until the house of representatives shall be increased greatly beyond its present number, there will be a considerable saving of expence from the difference between the constant session of the present, and the temporary session of the future congress.

But there is another circumstance, of great importance in the view of the economy. The business of the United States has hitherto occupied the state legislatures as well as congress. The latter has made requisitions which the former have had to provide for. Hence it has [46] happened that the sessions of the state legislatures have been protracted greatly beyond what was necessary for the execution of the mere local business of the states.[47] More than half their time has been frequently employed in matters which related to the United States. Now the members who compose the legislatures of the several states amount to two thousand and upwards; which number has hitherto performed what under the new system will be done in the first instance by sixty-five persons, and probably at no future period by above a fourth or a fifth of that number. The congress under the proposed government will do all the business of the United States themselves, without the intervention of the state legislatures, who thenceforth will have only to attend to the affairs of their particular states, and will not have to sit in any proportion as long as they have heretofore done. This difference, in the time of the sessions of the state legislatures, will be all [48] clear gain, and will alone form an article of saving, which may be regarded as an equivalent for any additional objects of expence that may be occasioned by the adoption of the new system.

The result from these observations is, that the sources of additional expence from the establishment of the proposed constitution are much fewer than may have been imagined, that they are counterbalanced by considerable objects of saving, and that while it is questionable on which side the scale will preponderate, it is certain

46. "It has thence" substituted for "thence it has" in Hopkins.
47. "Of the states" omitted in Hopkins.
48. "all" omitted in Hopkins.

that a government less expensive would be incompetent to the purposes of the union.

PUBLIUS.

## The Federalist No. 85 [1]

[New York, May 28, 1788]

*To the People of the State of New-York.*

ACCORDING to the formal division of the subject of these papers, announced in my first number, there would appear still to remain for discussion, two points, "the analogy of the proposed government to your own state constitution," and "the additional security, which its adoption will afford to republican government, to liberty and to property." But these heads have been so fully anticipated and [2] exhausted in the progress of the work, that it would now scarcely be possible to do any thing more than repeat, in a more dilated form, what has been heretofore said; which the advanced stage of the question, and the time already spent upon it conspire to forbid.

It is remarkable, that the resemblance of the plan of the convention to the act which organizes the government of this state holds, not less with regard to many of the supposed defects, than to the real excellencies of the former. Among the pretended defects, are the re-eligibility of the executive, the want of a council, the omission of a formal bill of rights, the omission of a provision respecting the liberty of the press: These and several others, which have been noted in the course of our inquiries, are as much chargeable on the existing constitution of this state, as on the one proposed for the Union. And a man must have slender pretensions to consistency, who can rail at the latter for imperfections which he finds no difficulty in excusing in the former. Nor indeed can there be a better

J. and A. McLean, *The Federalist*, II, 357–65, published May 28, 1788, numbered 85. In *The* [New York] *Independent Journal: or, the General Advertiser* this essay was begun on August 13 and concluded on August 16 and is numbered 84. In the *New-York Packet* it appeared on August 14 and is numbered 85.

1. For background to this document, see "The Federalist. Introductory Note," October 27, 1787–May 28, 1788.
2. "so completely" inserted at this point in Hopkins.

proof of the insincerity and affectation of some of the zealous adversaries of the plan of the convention among us,[3] who profess to be the [4] devoted admirers of the government under which they live,[5] than the fury with which they have attacked that plan, for matters in regard to which our own constitution is equally, or perhaps more vulnerable.

The additional securities to republican government, to liberty and to property, to be derived from the adoption of the plan under consideration,[6] consist chiefly in the restraints which the preservation of the union will impose on [7] local factions and insurrections, and on [8] the ambition of powerful individuals in single states, who might acquire credit and influence enough, from leaders and favorites, to become the despots of the people; in the diminution of the opportunities to foreign intrigue, which the dissolution of the confederacy would invite and facilitate; in the prevention of extensive military establishments, which could not fail to grow out of wars between the states in a disunited situation; in the express guarantee of a republican form of government to each; in the absolute and universal exclusion of titles of nobility; and in the precautions against the repetition of those practices on the part of the state governments, which have undermined the foundations of property and credit, have planted mutual distrust in the breasts of all classes of citizens, and have occasioned an almost universal prostration of morals.

Thus have I, my [9] fellow citizens, executed the task I had assigned to myself; with what success, your conduct must determine. I trust at least you will admit, that I have not failed in the assurance I gave you respecting the spirit with which my endeavours should be conducted. I have addressed myself purely to your judgments, and have studiously avoided those asperities which are too apt to disgrace political disputants of all parties, and which have been not a little provoked by the language and conduct of the opponents of the constitution. The charge of a conspiracy against the liberties of the people, which has been indiscriminately brought against the

3. "among us" omitted in Hopkins.
4. "the" omitted in Hopkins.
5. "of this state" substituted for "under which we live" in Hopkins.
6. "under consideration" omitted in Hopkins.
7. "upon" substituted for "on" in Hopkins.
8. "upon" substituted for "on" in Hopkins.
9. "my" omitted in Hopkins.

advocates of the plan, has something in it too wanton and too malignant not to excite the indignation of every man who feels in his own
bosom a refutation of the calumny. The perpetual changes which
have been rung upon the wealthy, the well-born and the great, have
been [10] such as to inspire the disgust of all sensible men. And the
unwarrantable concealments and misrepresentations which have been
in various ways practiced to keep the truth from the public eye,
have been [11] of a nature to demand the reprobation of all honest
men. It is not impossible [12] that these circumstance may have occasionally betrayed me into intemperances of expression which I
did not intend: It is certain that I have frequently felt a struggle
between sensibility and moderation, and if the former has in some
instances prevailed, it must be my excuse that it has been neither
often nor much.

Let us now pause and ask ourselves whether, in the course of
these papers, the proposed constitution has not been satisfactorily
vindicated from the aspersions thrown upon it, and whether it has
not been shewn to be worthy of the public approbation, and necessary to the public safety and prosperity. Every man is bound to
answer these questions to himself, according to the best of his conscience and understanding, and to act agreeably to the genuine and
sober dictates of his judgment. This is a duty, from which nothing
can give him a dispensation. 'Tis one that he is called upon, nay,
constrained by all the obligations that form the bands of society, to
discharge sincerely and honestly. No partial motive, no particular
interest, no pride of opinion, no temporary passion or prejudice,
will justify to himself, to his country or [13] to his posterity, an improper election of the part he is to act. Let him beware of an obstinate adherence to party. Let him reflect that the object upon
which he is to decide is not a particular interest of the community,
but the very existence of the nation. And let him remember that a
majority of America has already given its sanction to the plan, which
he is to approve or reject.

I shall not dissemble, that I feel an intire confidence in the argu-

10. "are" substituted for "have been" in Hopkins.
11. "are" substituted for "have been" in Hopkins.
12. "possible" substituted for "not impossible" in Hopkins.
13. "or" omitted in Hopkins.

ments, which recommend the proposed system to your adoption; and that I am unable to discern any real force in those by which it has been opposed.[14] I am persuaded, that it is the best which our political situation, habits and opinions will admit, and superior to any the revolution has produced.

Concessions on the part of the friends of the plan, that it has not a claim to absolute perfection, have afforded matter of no small triumph to its enemies. Why, say they, should we adopt an imperfect thing? Why not amend it, and make it perfect before it is irrevocably established? This may be plausible enough,[15] but it is only plausible.[16] In the first place I remark, that the extent of these concessions has been greatly exaggerated. They have been stated as amounting to an admission, that the plan is radically defective; and that, without material alterations, the rights and the interests of the community cannot be safely confided to it. This, as far as I have understood the meaning of those who make the concessions, is an intire perversion of their sense. No advocate of the measure can be found who will not declare as his sentiment, that the system, though it may not be perfect in every part, is upon the whole a good one, is the best that the present views and circumstances of the country will permit, and is such an one as promises every species of security which a reasonable people can desire.

I answer in the next place, that I should esteem it the extreme of imprudence to prolong the precarious state of our national affairs, and to expose the union to the jeopardy of successive experiments, in the chimerical pursuit of a perfect plan. I never expect to see a perfect work from imperfect man. The result of the deliberations of all collective bodies must necessarily be a compound as well of the errors and prejudices, as of the good sense and wisdom of the individuals of whom they are composed. The compacts which are to embrace thirteen distinct states, in a common bond of amity and union, must as necessarily be a compromise of as many dissimilar interests and inclinations. How can perfection spring from such materials?

The reasons assigned in an excellent little pamphlet lately published

14. "assailed" substituted for "opposed" in Hopkins.
15. "enough" omitted in Hopkins.
16. "it is plausible only" substituted for "it is only plausible" in Hopkins.

in this city * are unanswerable to [17] shew the utter improbability of assembling a new convention, under circumstances in any degree so favourable to a happy issue, as those in which the late convention met, deliberated and concluded. I will not repeat the arguments there used, as I presume the production itself has had an extensive circulation. It is certainly well worthy the perusal of every friend to his country. There is however one point of light in which the subject of amendments still remains to be considered; and in which it has not yet been exhibited to public view.[19] I cannot resolve to conclude, without first taking a survey of it in this aspect.

It appears to me susceptible of absolute [20] demonstration, that it will be far more easy to obtain subsequent than previous amendments to the constitution. The moment an alteration is made in the present plan, it becomes, to the purpose of adoption, a new one, and must undergo a new decision of each state. To its complete establishment throughout the union, it will therefore require the concurrence of thirteen states. If, on the contrary, the constitution proposed [21] should once be ratified by all the states as it stands, alterations in it may at any time be affected by nine states. Here then [22] the chances are as thirteen to nine * † in favour of subsequent amendments, rather than of the original adoption of an intire system.

This is not all. Every constitution for the United States must inevitably consist of a great variety of particulars, in which thirteen independent states are to be accommodated in their interests or opinions of interest. We may of course expect to see, in any body of men charged with its original formation, very different combinations of the parts upon different points. Many of those who form the majority on one question may become the minority on a second, and an association dissimilar to either may constitute the ma-

* Intitled "An Address to the people of the state of New-York." [18]

* † It may rather be said TEN for though two-thirds may set on foot the measure, three-fourths must ratify.

17. "unanswerably" substituted for "are unanswerable to" in Hopkins.
18. *An Address to the People of the State of New-York*, written by John Jay, was first published in April. It was reprinted in *The American Museum*, June, 1788.
19. "to public view" omitted in Hopkins.
20. "complete" substituted for "absolute" in Hopkins.
21. "proposed" omitted in Hopkins.
22. "In this view alone" substituted for "Here then" in Hopkins.

jority on a third. Hence the necessity of moulding and arranging all the particulars which are to compose the whole in such a manner as to satisfy all the parties to the compact; and hence also an immense multiplication of difficulties and casualties in obtaining the collective assent to a final act. The degree of that multiplication must evidently be in a ratio to the number of particulars and the number of parties.

But every amendment to the constitution, if once established, would be a single proposition, and might be brought forward singly. There would then be no necessity for management or compromise, in relation to any other point, no giving nor taking. The will of the requisite number would at once bring the matter to a decisive issue. And consequently whenever nine † [23] or rather ten states, were united in the desire of a particular amendment, that amendment must infallibly take place.[24] There can therefore be no comparison between the facility of effecting an amendment, and that of establishing in the first instance a complete constitution.

In opposition to the probability of subsequent amendments it has been urged, that the persons delegated to the administration of the national government, will always be disinclined to yield up any portion of the authority of which they were once possessed. For my own part I acknowledge a thorough conviction that any amendments which may, upon mature consideration, be thought useful, will be applicable to the organization of the government, not to the mass of its powers; and on this account alone, I think there is no weight in the observation just stated. I also think there is little weight [25] in it on another account. The intrinsic difficulty of governing THIRTEEN STATES at any rate,[26] independent of calculations upon an ordinary degree of public spirit and integrity, will, in my opinion, constantly *impose* on the national rulers the *necessity* of a spirit of accommodation to the reasonable expectations of their constituents. But there is yet a further consideration, which proves beyond the possibility of doubt, that the observation is futile. It is this, that the national rulers, whenever nine states concur, will have

23. The dagger refers to H's preceding note.
24. "prevail" substituted for "take place" in Hopkins.
25. "force" substituted for "weight" in Hopkins.
26. "at any rate" omitted in Hopkins.

no option upon the subject. By the fifth article of the plan the congress will be *obliged*, "on the application of the legislatures of two-thirds of the states, (which at present amounts [27] to nine) to call a convention for proposing amendments, which *shall be valid* to all intents and purposes, as part of the constitution, when ratified by the legislatures of three-fourths of the states, or by conventions in three-fourths thereof." The words of this article are peremptory. The Congress "*shall* call a convention." Nothing in this particular is left to the [28] discretion of that body.[29] And [30] of consequence all the declamation about their disinclination to a change, vanishes in air. Nor however difficult it may be supposed to unite two-thirds or three-fourths of the state legislatures, in amendments which may affect local interest, can there be any room to apprehend any such difficulty in a union on points which are merely relative to the general liberty or security of the people. We may safely rely on the disposition of the state legislatures to erect barriers against the encroachments of the national authority.

If the foregoing argument is [31] a fallacy, certain it is that I am myself deceived by it; for it is, in my conception, one of those rare instances in which a political truth can be brought to the test of mathematical demonstration. Those who see the matter in the same light with me,[32] however zealous they may be for amendments, must agree in the propriety of a previous adoption, as the most direct road to their own object.

The zeal for attempts to amend, prior to the establishment of the constitution, must abate in every man, who, is ready to accede to the truth of the following observations of a writer, equally solid and ingenious: "To balance a large state or society (says he) whether monarchical or republican, on general laws, is a work of so great difficulty, that no human genius, however comprehensive, is able by the mere dint of reason and reflection, to effect it. The judgments of many must unite in the work: EXPERIENCE must guide their labour: Time must bring it to perfection: And the FEELING

27. "amount" substituted for "amounts" in Hopkins.
28. "the" omitted in Hopkins.
29. "of that body" omitted in Hopkins.
30. "And" omitted in Hopkins.
31. "be" substituted for "is" in Hopkins.
32. "with me" omitted in Hopkins.

of inconveniences must correct the mistakes which they *inevitably* fall into, in their first trials and experiments." * These judicious reflections contain a lesson of moderation to all the sincere lovers of the union, and ought to put them upon their guard against hazarding anarchy, civil war, a perpetual alienation of the states from each other, and perhaps the military despotism of a victorious demagogue, in the pursuit of what they are not likely to obtain, but from TIME and EXPERIENCE. It may be in me a defect of political fortitude, but I acknowledge, that I cannot entertain an equal tranquillity with those who affect to treat the dangers of a longer continuance in our present situation as imaginary. A NATION without a NATIONAL GOVERNMENT is, in my view,[34] an awful spectacle. The establishment of a constitution, in time of profound peace, by the voluntary consent of a whole people, is a PRODIGY, to the completion of which I look forward with trembling anxiety.[35] I can reconcile it to no rules of prudence to let go the hold we now have, in so arduous an enterprise,[36] upon seven out of the thirteen states; and after having passed over so considerable a part of the ground to recommence the course. I dread the more the consequences of new attempts, because I KNOW that POWERFUL INDIVIDUALS, in this and in other states, are enemies to a general national government, in every possible shape.

PUBLIUS.

* Hume's Essays, vol. I, page 128.—The rise of arts and sciences.[33]

33. H is referring to the following edition of David Hume's writings: *Essays and Treatises on Several Subjects* (4th ed., London, Printed for A. Millar, in the Strand, and A. Kincaid and A. Donaldson, in Edinburgh, 1753). The quotation was taken from "Of the Rise of Progress of the Arts and Sciences," I, 175–76.

34. "in my view" omitted in Hopkins.

35. "In so arduous an enterprise" inserted at this point in Hopkins.

36. "in so arduous an enterprise" omitted in Hopkins.

# INDEX

## COMPILED BY JEAN G. COOKE